9781487803902

W0028369

AN IDEOLOGICAL HISTORY
OF THE
COMMUNIST PARTY OF CHINA

(Volume 1)

www.royalcollins.com

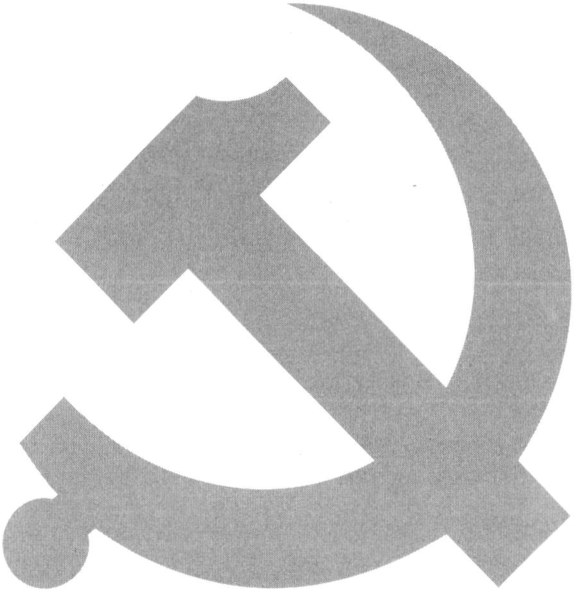

An Ideological History of the Communist Party of China

(Volume 1)

Huang Yibing

Zheng Qian (Chief Editor)
Translated by Shelly Bryant and Sun Li

Books Beyond Boundaries
ROYAL COLLINS

An Ideological History of the Communist Party of China, Volume 1

Huang Yibing
Translated by Shelly Bryant and Sun Li

First English Edition 2020
By Royal Collins Publishing Group Inc.
BKM ROYALCOLLINS PUBLISHERS PRIVATE LIMITED
www.royalcollins.com

Original Edition © Guangdong Education Publishing House, China
All rights reserved.

No part of this publication may be reproduced, stored in a retrieval system, or transmitted, in any form or by any means, electronic, mechanical, photocopying or otherwise, without the written permission from the publisher.

Copyright © Royal Collins Publishing Group Inc.
Groupe Publication Royal Collins Inc.
BKM ROYALCOLLINS PUBLISHERS PRIVATE LIMITED

Headquarters: 550-555 boul. René-Lévesque O Montréal (Québec) H2Z1B1 Canada
India office: 805 Hemkunt House, 8th Floor, Rajendra Place, New Delhi 110 008

ISBN: 978-1-4878-0390-2

We are grateful for the financial assistance of B&R Book Program in the publication of this book.

Contents

Chapter 1: The Spread of Marxism and the Source of the Party's Guiding Ideology — 3

   I. The Early Days of Marxism in China — 3

   II. Establishing the Communist Party of China on the Guiding Principles of Marxism — 14

Chapter 2: The New Democratic Revolution Period: Proposing the Basic Question of a Guiding Ideology — 23

   I. The Communist Party's Early Exploration of the Fundamental Questions of the Chinese Revolution — 23

   II. Various Twists in the Process of Exploring the Basic Issues of the Agrarian Revolutionary War in the Early Stages of the Chinese Revolution — 43

Chapter 3: The Elucidation of the New Democracy Theory — 65

   I. The Initial Formation of the New Democratic Theoretical System — 65

   II. Further Development of the New Democratic Theory — 82

Chapter 4: The Basic Principles of the New Democratic Revolution — 91

    I. The Party's Understanding of Modern China's National Situation — 91

    II. The "Two Stages" of the Chinese Revolution — 99

    III. The Nature and Basic Characteristics of the New Democratic Revolution — 107

Chapter 5: The General Direction of the New Democratic Revolution — 119

    I. The Formation of the Party's Analytical View of China's Social Class Structure — 119

    II. General Direction of the New Democratic Revolution — 129

Chapter 6: China's Revolutionary Path Theory — 149

    I. The Impact of the City-centered Theory on the Communist Party of China — 149

    II. The Establishment of the Concept of an "Armed Division of Workers and Peasants" — 164

    III. The Theory of Encircling the City — 177

    IV. The Theory of Constructing Revolutionary Base Areas — 189

Chapter 7: Thoughts on the United Front — 213

    I. Ideas Concerning the Establishment of the United Front — 213

    II. Ideas and Strategic Policies for Establishing the Anti-Japanese National United Front — 228

    III. Thoughts and Policies on the People's Democratic United Front — 244

Chapter 8: The Theory of Armed Struggle — 273

    I. Armed Struggle as the Main Form of Struggle in the Chinese Revolution — 273

II. The CPC's Theory of Military Dialectics	288
III. Thoughts on the Construction of the People's Army	299
IV. The Theory of the People's War	326
V. Strategies and Tactics in the People's War	339

Chapter 9: *The Theory of Party-Building* — **357**

I. Party-Building: A Great Project	357
II. The Party's Ideological Construction	373
III. The Party's Organizational Construction	394
IV. Building the Party's Work Style	428
V. Thoughts on Party Leadership	466

Chapter 10: *The Establishment of Mao Zedong Thought as the Guideline for the Party* — **481**

I. The Party's Recognition and Acceptance of Mao Zedong Thought	481
II. The Strategy of Transferring from Rural to Urban Areas	494
III. Efforts to Adhere to the Concept of a New Democratic Society	507

Notes — *551*

Index — *573*

AN IDEOLOGICAL HISTORY
OF THE
COMMUNIST PARTY OF CHINA

(Volume 1)

CHAPTER 1

The Spread of Marxism and the Source of the Party's Guiding Ideology

The Early Days of Marxism in China

1. Chinese Ideology and Cultural Awakening

The 20th century was a period of great change in modern Chinese society. The people in the capital, Beijing, entered the 20th century under the shadow of the national humiliation inflicted by the Eight-Nation Alliance. At the time, it seemed that only the prospect of bleak destruction lay before the Chinese people.

Foreign capitalism had invaded China since the Second Opium War in 1840, leading to great changes in Chinese society and gradually reducing it to a semi-colonial, semi-feudal society. With the aim of enslaving and destroying China, the foreign powers invaded through military, political, economic, and cultural means. As China's feudal rulers sought to maintain their own rule of power, they sought refuge through imperialism, thereby becoming agents of Western powers. Led by Sun Yat-sen, the 1911 Xinhai Revolution overthrew the old monarchical system of imperial China, creating a relatively complete modern national democratic revolution, which opened the gates of progress, but failed to change the traditional social structures and improve the plight of the people. After Yuan Shikai seized power in the Republic of China, the political situation began to deteriorate. He completely wiped out the fledgling democracy that had been initiated with the Xinhai Revolution and openly returned to a despicable restoration of the monarchy. After Yuan's fall, China plunged into a period of disputes between warlord separatists. Manipulated by imperial powers, the warlords used the slogan "Reunification of Force," and many minor warlords used "the security of the people" as an excuse to wage their own battles for power and oppress the people. Continuous fighting between the warlords over a period of several years brought great destruction and infinite hardship to Chinese society and its people. In the years leading up to 1915 and after, several major famines occurred in China, compounding the suffering of the people.

Imperialist aggression also forced China to eventually adopt a capitalist mode of production. From the beginning of the 1860s, China had its own national industry. After the First Sino-Japanese War, China's national economy saw greater development. From 1895–1913, a total of 548 factories were set up nationwide, with a capital of 120.279 million yuan. The total capital of 463 of those factories was 90.821 million yuan. With the development of China's national economy, the Chinese proletariat grew and flourished. In 1894, China had about 100,000 industrial workers. By 1914, on the eve of World War I, the number of industrial workers had increased to 1 million. This indicates that, though China had hit on a windfall, it had also created a revolutionary force. The dual development of the rise and fall of national oppression and a newly forged modern industry constituted the major trends of the entire movement toward an overall modern Chinese society. Imperialism and feudal forces combined to push China into a dark abyss, but the emergence of national industry and new social forces had brought some light to China's prospects. In the course of 110 years of semi-colonialism and semi-feudalism in China, the early years of the 20th century (1901–1915) can be called the country's lowest point.

The First World War accelerated the evolution of Chinese society, triggering an unprecedented cultural awakening of the mind. During the war, on September 15, 1915, Chen Duxiu founded *Youth Magazine* (renamed *New Youth* from Volume 2, Issue 1) in Shanghai, and it promptly evolved into a weapon to be launched against Confucianism, ushering in a new cultural movement that opposed old traditions. Those fighting for this new culture were very radical, not recognizing traditional authority and dogma, while advocating a break of the spiritual yoke through the application of "rational" criticism and a reexamination of all things. People called this cultural movement "ideological enlightenment."

Like Enlightenment Thought in the West in the 15th century, in essence and content, this movement was a criticism of feudal ideology and culture that opened the way for the development of capitalism. However, there were some differences in the timing of the two. The Western Enlightenment anticipated the outbreak of Europe's bourgeois revolution, while the Chinese New Culture Movement was an idea born of the bourgeois revolution. It broke out in the context of imperialist wars around the world and fighting among domestic warlords. For this reason, it was bound to reinforce the resistance of imperialists and feudalists to a certain extent, providing new historical material for Marxism's later spread in China and the outbreak of the patriotic May Fourth Movement, which laid the necessary ideological groundwork and establishing the necessary conditions.

World War I also exposed the shortcoming of Western civilization, breaking down that particular idol in the minds of the Chinese people. It was a brutal war, costing not only more than ten thousand lives on the battlefield, but also are than twenty thousand nonfatal casualties, leaving many disabled, and almost completely destroying the accumulation of material civilization in a matter of just a few years. Liang Qichao traveled to Europe at the end of the war, visiting England, France, Belgium, and other countries. In his article *Touring Europe*, he described the beginning of the destruction of production in Europe, a crisis of faith, and scenes of social chaos and poverty, lamenting the situation there in which "the entire society was caught in fear and angst, like a boat that had lost its direction in wind and fog, and did not know where to go."[1] This could not help but shock those in China who had long been obsessed with learning from the West.

It was also at this time that many advanced thinkers started to realize that Chinese society had to change, but that it had to move in a different direction from Western capitalism. After traveling in Europe, Liang concluded that social revolution – unfortunately the major feature of the 20th century – was something no country could avoid, but that each nation must go through it sooner or later. In his later analysis of the evils of capitalism, Zheng Zhenduo pointed out that "there is no room for societies dominated by capitalism."[2] China's progressive intellectuals began to undergo profound changes, moving from a longing for Western parliamentary democracy to a feeling of disappointment in it, and from a pursuit of capitalism to a negative view of it. At that time, the journal *Min Xing* recorded, "Republicanism is not our end. A worldwide revolution is inevitable."[3]

The idol in the minds of the people collapsed, but the road carried on. There were great political changes happening around the world, partly ushered in by World War I and the October Revolution in Russia, so that a group of scholars concerned about the future of the motherland and the destiny of the Chinese people began to reconsider the transformation of social programs. At this time, Marxism captured the attention of progressives in China, creating a boom in the promotion of socialism.

Hundreds of publications advocating "social transformation" sprouted up, most of them favorably disposed toward, or even longing for, socialism. In many publications, practically every issue had at least one article introducing or promoting socialism, and often several of such articles. In the articles written by some young people, socialism was lauded as a "a blessing for humanity," and it was believed that in China, "there must be construction to progress, and that construction must be in accordance with the principles of socialism."[4] Socialism was seen as "the ideal for the present and future of humanity."[5]

Though socialism had become exceedingly popular, it must be noted that the concept of "socialism" as discussed during this period was quite complex. In addition to Marx's scientific socialism, it also included various schools popularly referred to as "socialism," including Stirner's "non-political individualism," Proudhon's "social anarchism," Bakunin's "collective anarchy," Kropotkin's "mutualism," and Saneatsu Mushakoji's "the new village doctrine," among others.

What is certain is that the spread of Chinese socialist ideology after the war was greatly influenced by the crisis Western capitalism was then facing. In 1920, when the journal *The Communist Party* was founded in Shanghai, it pointed out that "the transformation of the economy naturally accounts for the transformation of humankind, for the most part. Aside from the capitalist and socialist approach to the means of production, there is no other alternative. Capitalism in Europe and America has developed, and it has collapsed… It will be replaced by socialist production methods."[6]

A good socialist society was desirable, but what did such a society look like, and how could it be achieved? At that time, news of the October Revolution in Russia came to China. Lenin had led the revolution to victory, so socialism was moving out of the theory books to become a living reality, and Marxism was the ideological weapon used to effect this transformation. After the October Revolution, having survived civil war and foreign intervention, Russia now stepped firmly onto the world stage, presenting a stark contrast to the declining Western capitalism. As a result, Chinese intellectuals started to turn their attention to the Soviet Union, and to Marxism.

2. The Spread of Marxism in China

The Chinese people came into contact with Marx and his theory quite early. From September 1902 through 1906, Liang Qichao published a number of articles introducing Marx and his teaching in *Xinmin Congbao*. In November 1905, the bourgeoisie democratic revolutionary Zhu Zhixin published an article entitled "A Short Review of the German Revolution" in the second issue of the *People's Daily*, in which he introduced the life and teachings of Marx and Engels. Sun Yat-sen, Song Jiaoren, Liao Zhongkai, and others likewise mentioned Marx's teaching. Some anarchist writers also mentioned Marx and Engels by name in their journals and translated extracts of their works. However, these introductions were quite piecemeal, and some even misrepresented things, and many did not believe in Marxism, but were instead quite critical. Such articles could not have much of an impact on the revolution in China at that time. It was not until the May Fourth period, amid propaganda and agitation among China's intellectuals, that Marxism became an irresistible ideological trend.

Of those who were spreading Marxist thought during the May Fourth period, the most influential were Li Dazhao and Chen Duxiu. They influenced a whole generation of Chinese people, both ideologically and politically.

Li Dazhao was the first person to spread Marxist thought in China, and he played a leading role in early propaganda work. From July to November 1918, he published "A Comparative Analysis of the French and Russian Revolutions," "The Victory of the Common People," "The Victory of Bolshevism," and other similar articles. Through his in-depth historical view, he helped promote the value and significance of the October Revolution. After the May Fourth Movement, he compiled all the articles he had edited for *New Youth* and published them in Volume 5 of the six-volume *Marxist Studies*, and published the text *My View of Marxism*,[7] marking the first time Marxist economic theory, historical materialism, and the theory of socialism were fully elaborated in China. Li fully affirmed the

Marxist historical position, calling it an "original theory for world reform." He said that Marxist socialist theory could be divided into three parts: 1) the theory of the past, or the theory of history, 2) the theory of the present, or economic theory, also referred to as the economic theory of capitalism, and 3) the theory of the future, or political theory, also termed the socialist movement theory or social democracy. It was noted that "his teaching is a self-contained organic, systematic organization." This teaching included Marx's theory of history, which revealed the social development of material and class relations, elucidating the theory of productive forces and relations of production, economic foundations, and superstructures, and his theories of class and class struggle. Marx's economic theory clarified, "The theory of residual labor and value" exposes "the secrets of modern capitalism" and "the way in which the capitalists plundered labor," a fundamental concept in Marx's economic theory. Marx observed modern society's economic situation through the lens of the concepts of historical materialism and surplus value, and in analyzing and studying the capitalist economic system, he foresaw the need to replace it with a socialist system. He then asserted that "the final obstacle to realizing a socialist system is class competition." Li Dazhao emphasized that Marx's "three theories are inextricably linked, and class competition is like a golden thread running through them, forming a fundamental link between the three principles." After that, Li published "The Marxist Philosophy of History" and other articles to promote historical materialism. He also set up courses in historical materialism, socialism, and the socialist movement at Peking University and the Peking Girl's High School. In the course on the Marxist system of thought, he focused on historical materialism propaganda, reflecting his urgent enthusiasm for seeking out theoretical guidance in addressing the Chinese problem.

Unlike Li Dazhao, Chen Duxiu was formerly a radical democratic who became a Marxist, coming onto the scene later than Li. However, as long-time editor of *New Youth*, Chen had a certain reputation in the New Cultural Movement, and so soon became the most influential promoter of Marxism in China. In March 1920, he came into contact with Marxism via the article "Malthusian Population Theory and the Chinese Population Problem." From there, he began making some criticisms of the Malthusian theory, while holding onto some reservations about Marxism. In the subsequent speech "Worker's Consciousness," Chen expressed the Marxist views that "labor has created the world" and that "workers are the most useful and valuable class." He emphasized that the ancients had said that

"Those who govern use their minds; those who are governed, their bodies." He said that it was correct to reverse the statement to read, "Those who use their bodies govern, while those who use their minds are governed."[8]

Of course, the real change Chen's thought underwent, going from review, approval, then on to advocacy, and finally to promoting socialism, began with the September 1920 article "On Politics." In the revolutionary article, Chen criticized anarchy's opposition to politics, to the law, to power, and to the views of the state, pointing out that the root of all the world's inequalities lay in the existence of the bourgeoisie. "The removal of this injustice, this bitter suffering, can only be achieved when the oppressed working class is given new strength and gains national status. When the bourgeoisie is completely overthrown through political, legal, and other means, then we can expect to remove the private ownership of property, along with the labor wage and other systems, thereby removing inequality in the economic situation." In saying this, he offered support for Marxist thought and positions, showing that he was clearly in favor of Marxism and its use of the "revolutionary hand to build nations for the working class (i.e. the productive class), and to build up political or legal systems to prohibit all internal and external plundering as the top priority for a modern society."[9]

Chen had a sense of historic mission and an ideal of opposing warlord politics and pursuing the well-being of the people. As a revolutionary with a strong sense of action, he had an affinity for the Marxist theory of social revolution. He founded publications, organized groups, and wrote articles to expose the evils of the capitalist system and disseminate socialist ideology, becoming a driving force behind the spread of Marxism in China.

Comparing Li and Chen, Li's most important achievement was establishing a firm historical materialism, believing in the usefulness of mobilizing the masses in the historical process and recognizing the power of social development lying in the inherent nature of the people rather than any external force.[10] It was because of this fundamental understanding that Li emphasized both theory and practice and actively participated with the masses.

Besides Li and Chen, many students who had also studied in Japan, such as Li Da, Yang Anan, and Li Hanjun, had come into contact with Marxism, which they in turn promoted in China through numerous translations and publications. Li Da translated *Historical Materialism*, *Marxist Economic Theory*, and *An Overview of Social Issues*, which he sent back to be published in China. *Marxist Economic*

Theory was included in the Marxist research bibliography established by Li Dazhao at Peking University. Having returned to China, Yang published several articles in the Guangdong publication *China News*, including "Socialism" and "Marxism: Scientific Socialism," from October to December 1919. The former praised Marx's *Das Kapital*, calling it a "socialist classic." The latter systematically introduced Marxist historical materialism and the theories of class struggle and surplus value. In 1919, Li Hanjun worked for two years before the Communist Party was established on translating and writing over 60 articles about Marxism. Shao Piaoping, another progressive news reporter, also contributed to the spread of Marxism.

3. Disputes and Decisions During the Spread of Marxism in China

During the May Fourth period, among those who introduced and studied Marxist thought, some did not believe it to be true, or to be a tool that would bring about transformation in China, while others saw it as a type of Western thinking and did not link it to what was happening in China. Still others sought to prevent China from pursuing a Marxist path and began to search for ways to block it. In terms of class attributes, Marxism was a theory committed to liberating the working classes, so it was naturally not accepted by representatives of other classes. For this reason, the spread of Marxism in China, especially in the early days, when Marxist scholars sought to connect the theory to the fate of China, could not be done without dispute. Marxism could only progress through struggle.

The first dispute arose over the cultural choices for China, that is, the question of whether China's issues should be solved under the guidance of Marxism. In July 1919, Hu Shih, one of the advocates of the May Fourth New Cultural Movement, published an article entitled "More Study of the Issues and Less Talk about Ideology," triggering a heated debate in scholarly circles from July through September of that year. Armed with his theory based on empiricism, Hu believed that "the greatest danger to public opinion is the ideologies on paper, which do not look deeply into the real issues in China today." He went on to say, "The first duty of one who wants to understand public opinion is to carefully examine the true social situation. All theory and all ideology are only for the purpose of this study." He was very disgusted with what he saw as the popular "empty talk" of his day.

After the publication of Hu's article, Li Dazhao and Lan Gongwu wrote a rebuttal. From their perspective, all the issues were intertwined with an all-encompassing social structure, and the problem-solving ideological propositions needed only to be tested through social experimentation. People needed to apply ideology when evaluating situations and problems, and as tools for solving such inter-connected problems. Li agreed with Hu's view that actual problems needed to be studied seriously and that vague talk about ideology was to be avoided, but he saw no basic conflict between problem studies and ideological discussions. He pointed out that "solving a social problem requires the collective action of the majority of the people," and went on to say that, "to turn a social issue into a public concern of the majority of the people," it was necessary to "first have an ideal and ideology moving toward a common direction," and finally, "On the one hand, our social movement must study actual problems, and on the other, must promote ideal doctrines. These are interconnected, and they are parallel." At the same time, he pointed out that the study of the issues must be based on theory, and that before any problems could be studied, it was necessary to study many ideologies.[11]

In fact, the "issue vs. ideology" dispute helped advance the thinking of intellectuals of that time, particularly in the areas of the development of ideology and the fate of modern Chinese history. Hu Shih tried to persuade people to spend less time talking about theory, arguing instead that China did not need to undergo a profound revolution to address the problems he had pointed to. Li Dazhao pointed out that the popularity of Bolshevism was a great change in global culture, particularly noting the significance of the theory of class struggle as a key component of historical materialism. If one did not attach significance to class struggle, failing to apply theory as a tool to guide the workers to come together in an actual movement, then economic revolution would never be achieved. Through this argument, Li and the young Marxists around the country demonstrated Marxist thought suitable to China's needs, according to the level of knowledge at that time. This had a positive effect on the spread of Marxism.

The "issue vs. ideology" debate further aroused ideological thought for China's future in scholarly circles. In September 1920, Zhang Dongsun published his article "A Lesson from Traveling in the Mainland" in Shanghai, in which he states that there was only one way forward for China, and that was to increase wealth through the development of industry. He later added that the quickest way to develop industry was through capitalism. Early Marxists criticized this argument severely, forming the "question of socialism" controversy to be addressed as Marxism continued to spread. In May 1921, Li Da pointed out in *New Youth* that China was the world's market, that capitalist countries had already founded deep-rooted, unbreakable economic ties in China, and that faced with an era of immature industry and with heavy political and economic pressure from other countries, the development of capitalism and war with other capitalist countries would have been quite disastrous.[12]

In the debate with Zhang Dongsun and others, the early Marxists drew contrasts between socialism and capitalism and, in demonstrating the advantages and disadvantages of each system, showed that only socialism was capable of developing China's productive forces. Li Dazhao wrote, "In China today, the development of industry will have to be achieved through a government organized by pure producers to eradicate the domestic classes that plunder others, to resist capitalism in this world, and to proceed according to a socialist organization of commerce."[13] Chen Duxiu likewise emphasized that he wanted "*all* Chinese to have a life, and that if capitalist means of production are not abolished, socialist means of production cannot be established."[14] He added, "At this time, we in China can talk not just about the possibility of socialism, but must discuss its necessity as well."[15] This indicated that the path to socialism was the common preference among early Communists in their debates, and that the preference of this system pointed to the need to develop China's advanced production forces.

The third dispute was with the anarchists. In the early days of the May Fourth Movement, anarchism spread widely among young intellectuals, which had a positive effect on opposing the autocratic monarchy and enlightening people's ideological consciousness. However, this came from an extreme form of individualism, advocating the absolute freedom of the individual and opposing any organization or discipline, as well as all power, authority, and nations, advocating anarchy and absolute egalitarianism. They opposed Marxist national doctrine and the proletarian dictatorship, thus becoming a major obstacle to the spread of Marxism. In this way, before the debate concerning socialism with Zhang Dongsun and the others had finished, another debate – this over anarchism – began with Huang Lingshuang and other anarchists. In this debate, *New Youth*, *The Communist Party*, and other journals published special articles criticizing anarchism. In January 1922, *Pioneer*, a journal published among China's socialist youth movement, published a special issue focused on criticism of anarchism.

Marxist criticism of anarchism revolved around the form of revolution, the nature of the state, and the necessity of the rule of the proletariat. On the one hand, they pointed out that the Chinese proletariat had endured much under the long plunder of imperialism and capitalism, and that this unbearable suffering led to a strong need for the seizing of state power through violent revolution. On the other hand, it was pointed out that only by the dictatorship of the proletariat could the interests of the workers be protected. Therefore, the feudal aristocratic or bourgeois state must be completely overturned and the state power of the proletariat must be consolidated and strengthened, which was the correct path from capitalism to communism. The Marxists further criticized the anarchists' egalitarianism over the issue of distribution, focusing on refuting their fallacy of "absolute freedom." They pointed out that, in human society, freedom is always relative, and that "absolute freedom" simply does not exist. The scope of the struggle against anarchy was quite great.

The confrontation between Marxism and competing schools of thought was the first one in the spread of Marxism, and it had a far-reaching influence on Chinese thought. In the course of this debate, with unwavering faith, the early Marxists courageously took up the theoretical weapon of Marxism and used it to criticize various improper thoughts embraced by the bourgeoisie and petty bourgeoisie. In hopes of saving their country and its people, they were determined to transform the progress of Chinese society and enter a new age. After this confrontation, during which the scientific and truthful nature of Marxism was first demonstrated, it was widely acknowledged that only scientific socialism could achieve national salvation, fundamentally transforming the goals of Chinese society. In the process of establishing their own beliefs and choices about what sort of ideology would transform China, and in finally settling on scientific socialism, they became Marxists and quickly began spreading Marxist thought, bringing together masses of workers to create the early organization of the Communist Party of China.

II

Establishing the Communist Party of China on the Guiding Principles of Marxism

1. The Struggle of China's Early Marxists

Once the progressive elements in China had accepted Marxism, they immediately applied it to their studies of the situation and problems in China. This sort of orientation toward practical values reflected the ideological situation of Chinese intellectuals at the time. After the May Fourth Movement, a trend toward social transformation was on the rise. The Work and Mutual Aid Group, established in 1919, was sponsored by Chen Duxiu, Li Dazhao, Cai Yuanpei, and other well-known figures. This trend of encouraging young people to step up in society served to promote a greater social consciousness in China. At the same time, the disputes with non-Marxist schools of thought helped to push early Marxists to study actual issues in China. Not long after Hu Shih promoted his idea that "more research be dedicated to the issues," many socialists and their followers turned their attention to the workers and peasants, studying their living conditions. By contrast, Hu and his followers were rarely engaged in such social surveys and labor movements.

Li Dazhao made outstanding contributions to the development of the orientation toward practical value. Even before the May Fourth Movement, he had published many articles on the subject, encouraging young people to work in cooperation with the masses to dive into the social situation in China. Under Li's influence, in March 1919, Deng Zhongxia and other young students organized a series of educational lectures at Peking University, aimed at educating and mobilizing the population. After the May Fourth Movement, Li went with a group of revolutionaries in Beijing to investigate the living conditions of rickshaw workers. At the same time, he organized a group that included Deng Zhongxia and Zhang Guotao to go to the Changxindian Railway to do publicity, establish remedial labor schools and workers' clubs, and organize the labor force.

In March 1920, the Peking University Civilians Lecture Group not only gave speeches in the city, but also went to factories in Lugouqiao, Changxindian, Tongxian, and other rural places to deliver lectures, conduct surveys, and try to gain some understanding of the people from the lower classes. They used their school holidays to travel to factories and rural villages to deliver lectures on "What is Civil Education," "The Republican Spirit," and similar topics. Through these lectures, these young intellectuals got a taste of the hardships the workers and peasants faced, saw how backward their education was, and sought ways to make their message more easily understood by the peasants so that they could instill new ideas in the rural people. Deng Zhongxia gained great experience through the lectures at Changxindian, which served as a foundation for him to later become a labor leader in the workers' movement.

Another way the Marxists came to grips with the reality of their situation was to set up supplemental schools, night schools, and literacy classes for workers, as well as numerous workers' clubs. In this way, they could instill scientific socialist thought in the minds of the workers, cultivating a backbone upon which their later work would stand, and organize large groups of workers to form a foundation for the struggle that would allow them to establish trade unions and lead the workers. At the same time, these activities were conducive to establishing close connections between the Marxists and the lower classes, encouraging greater participation in the struggle among the working classes. This method of educating the masses was used often by the Party's workers' movements.

On May 1, 1920, the International Labor Day Commemorative Event marked an important beginning in the Chinese Marxist Workers' Movement. They took this opportunity to promote the value of labor among the workers, the great role of the working class, and the evil of the capitalist system, and called on the working class to fight together. In Shanghai, Chen Duxiu personally participated in and guided a joint meeting between the Chinese Industry Association, the Chinese Federation of Trade Unions, and five other industry groups, co-sponsored with the preparations for the Labor Day Commemorative Event. At the event, the speaker talked of the sanctity of labor, arousing the people's passion. The resolutions included 1) require an eight hour work day, 2) organize real work unions for the people, and 3) foster cooperation among the masses. After the meeting, these seven groups published *A Reply to the Russian Labor Groups*, in which was stated, "We must strive to create a new, beautiful world with permanent peace among all humankind, and we have decided to take up the responsibility to cooperate with you."

A similar commemorative event was simultaneously held in Beijing. On May 1, classes were not convened at Peking University, allowing more than five hundred workers and students to hold the commemorative event on campus that day. Li Dazhao delivered a speech at the meeting. Work and study groups went together in cars to hold parades in the eastern and western parts of the city. Fluttering banners went before the cars, with slogans such as "The Sanctity of Labor" and "Long Live May 1" written on them in red characters, with red flags erected behind the cars to manifest a revolutionary spirit. Chanting the slogan "Long Live Labor," they distributed printed brochures of *The May First Labor Declaration in Beijing* from either side of the cars.

Alongside workers and students in Shanghai and Beijing, those from other areas, such as Tangshan, Harbin, Jiujiang, Guangzhou, Shantou, and Zhangzhou, likewise held commemorative events. This was the first time Marxism was integrated into China's Labor Movement activities. In this regard, Cai Hesen commented, "China's first May Day was widely publicized, with 10,000 copies of *New Youth* issued, so the event had a great, universal impact."[16]

Mao Zedong was a model of early Marxism in practice. As early as the autumn of 1919, he organized a seminar in Changsha. This seminar was conducted for the purpose of studying politics, economics, social issues, education, labor, international affairs, and other issues, as well as to explore ways to unite the people, the feasibility of socialism, and issues concerning Confucianism. There were more than 140 topics in all. Mao was often deeply involved with the railway workers, masonry workers, porters, and other manual laborers. He made friends with them as he set up night schools and established trade unions. In order to draw nearer to the workers, Mao often removed his gown and wore a short tunic as he went among them. He learned the language of the workers, came to understand their demands, and became familiar with their lives.

The practical publicity of the Marxist intellectuals involved in-depth promotion among the workers and farmers as they organized the workers and sought to promote ways of integrating Marxism into the Chinese Workers' Movement. At the same time, their own thoughts and feelings also underwent a change, gradually transforming them into pioneer warriors who had attained a communist mindset. Workers and farmers started to pick up Marxist thought, from which a number of progressives with communist ideals emerged. The conditions in China were ripe for the establishment of the Communist Party.

2. Creation of the Party and Establishment of the Marxist Revolution in China

With the spread of Marxism, the decision to gradually integrate it into the Chinese Workers' Movement, and the emergence of progressives with communist ideals, it was natural that the next issue on the agenda was the organization of the working class into Party organs. Li Dazhao said, "Even though it is not currently possible to say for sure what the strength of China's working class is, if the friends of the C group can establish a strong, sophisticated organization, giving attention to the training of the members in their groups, then China may be ready for complete reform."[17] While attending the Montargis Conference of the New Citizen Study Society, Cai Hesen said that no matter what it cost, the proletarian revolution "must build a party first, that is, the Communist Party." This was because the Party was "the promoter of the revolutionary movement, its advocate, vanguard, and army." With the Party, revolutionary and labor movements would have a nerve center.[18] This showed that China's progressive elements had placed their confidence in the Communist Party.

Under the leadership of Li Dazhao, the Marxist Research Society of Peking University was established in March 1920. This was the earliest institute in China set up specifically for the purpose of studying Marxism. Its membership was comprised mainly of students from Peking University, the leading members among them being Deng Zhongxia, Guo Junyu, Huang Rikui, Fan Hongjie, He Mengxiong, Li Jun, Zhu Wushan, Zhang Guotao, Liu Renjing, Luo Zhanglong, and others. This was a faction that believed in the inevitability of Marxism, and their goal was to establish the Communist Party. It was at this time that the Communist Party International representative Grigori Voitinsky came to China. His task was to understand the Chinese situation, to make contact with progressive forces in China, and to investigate whether it was possible to establish the Communist International East Asia Secretariat in Shanghai.[19] In his numerous discussions with Li Dazhao and others, he said he wanted their support and assistance in establishing the work of the Communist Party. Through Li's introduction, Voitinsky traveled to Shanghai to meet Chen Duxiu. Based on his observation and survey in Beijing and Shanghai, Voitinsky felt the work for the establishment of the Party had matured and suggested that Chen organize the Communist Party of China. This was completely in accord with Chen's own thinking. Chen introduced Voitinsky to Li Hanjun, who was busy promoting socialism in *The Weekly Review*, along with other editors. After numerous discussions, they decided to set up an underground group until the Party was ready to be formally established. In May that year, Shanghai's Marxist research institute was established, led by Chen Duxiu, and with Li Hanjun, Shen Xuanlu, Shao Lizi, Chen Wangdao, Shi Cuntong, Yu Xiusong, Shen Yanbing, Yang Mingzhai, and others as members.

The Comintern representative remained at this time to offer guidance in the work of establishing the Communist Party for East Asian countries, preparing to set up the East Asian Secretariat in Shanghai, with sections responsible for the work in China, Korea, and Japan. With Voitinsky's efforts, "the work in the Chinese section went smoothly. Because of the workers' and students' organizations in Beijing, Shanghai, Tianjin, Guangzhou, Hankou, Nanjing, and other cities, the foundations for the communist organizations have been laid."[20] In August 1920, Chen Duxiu, Li Hanjun, Shen Xuanlu, Chen Wangdao, Yu Xiusong, Shi Cuntong (in Japan), Yang Mingzhai, Li Da, and others initiated the formal establishment of the Shanghai Communist Party. As soon as this organization was set up, it took on the task of building the national Party. Shortly after the establishment of the Shanghai Party Organization, a lecturer from Beijing Normal University, Zhang Shenfu, invited the British philosopher Bertrand Russell to Shanghai to deliver lectures. In Chen's home, the two held many broad discussions on the establishment of the Party. They thought that, since they were able to draw people into the Party, it was best to absorb those people, and that Li Dazhao should establish a Communist Organization in Beijing. In late September, Zhang Shenfu brought Chen's views to Beijing to discuss party building matters with Li, and it was agreed that they should immediately start developing Party members. At the beginning of October, Zhang Guotao returned to Beijing to participate in discussions on party building and to tell Li about Chen's suggestions for establishing the Party in Beijing. So the trio of Li Dazhao, Zheng Shenfu, and Zhang Guotao formally established the Beijing Communist Party Organization in Li's office. The Communist Party of Beijing was the main base for propagating Marxism in Northern China and cultivating revolutionary personnel.

The Party organizations in various areas were driven by the establishment of the Shanghai and Beijing branches to pursue the establishment of the Party

Organization on their own soil. From late 1920 through the first half of 1921, Dong Biwu, Chen Tanqiu, and others in Wuhan, Chen Gongbo, Tan Pingshan, and others in Guangzhou, Mao Zedong, He Shuheng, and others in Changsha, Wang Jinmei, Deng Enming, and others in Jinan, Shi Cuntong, Zhou Fuhai, and others in Japan, and Zhang Shenfu, Zhao Shiyan, Chen Gongpei, Zhou Enlai, and others in France all established branches of the Communist Party in their respective locations. The names of these early organizations were not uniform. The Shanghai organization was originally called the Communist Party of China, while the Beijing organization was called the Communist Party of China, Beijing Branch. They were local branches of the subsequent Communist Party of China, though later, people developed the habit of calling them the "Communism Group." Most of the members of these organizations were progressives who had developed their knowledge during the May Fourth Movement. In their understanding of Marxism and their observation of the actual issues in China, they had gone deeper into these matters than other people of their generation. The above branches of the Communist Party had been formed in many places, setting the stage to officially initiate the Communist Party of China.

The local organizations moved from a decentralized focus to concentrate on the establishment of a unified national level Communist Party organization, remaining under the guidance of the Comintern. In June 1921, the Comintern Communist sent Malyn and Nikolsky from the Secretariat in Irkutsk to Shanghai, where they proposed the immediate convening of the National General Assembly for the purpose of formally establishing the Communist Party of China. Subsequently, Li Da gave notice to the local Party organizations, asking each to send two representatives to the meeting. On July 23, the First National Congress of the Communist Party of China was officially convened in Shanghai. Those in attendance included Li Da, Li Hanjun, Zhang Guotao, Liu Renjing, Mao Zedong, He Shuheng, Dong Biwu, Chen Tanqiu, Wang Jingmei, Deng Enming, Chen Gongbo, Zhou Fuhai, and Bao Huiceng, representing more than fifty members around the country. Malyn and Nikolsky attended the meeting, though Li Dazhao was unable to attend the meeting. Chen Duxiu was unable to attend the meeting, either, but he commissioned Bao Huiceng to raise the ideas that "the entire party should be democratic, should believe in communism, and should be committed to achieving the rule of the proletariat and the implementation of communism" as issues for the General Assembly to discuss.

The First Program of the Communist Party of China, adopted by the General Assembly, stipulated that "the Party is to be named the Communist Party of China" and that "the Party's objective is to overthrow the power of the capitalist class" and "recognize the inalienable right to rule of the proletariat," to "eradicate capitalism and private ownership of property" and "join the Comintern." The essence of the Party program lay in the implementation of socialist revolution and replacing capitalism with communism.

After the establishment of the Party, there was a heated debate about the allocation of work. Li Hanjun and others believed that the Chinese proletariat was too naive and did not understand Marxist thought, so they advocated the unity of progressive intellectuals who would engage in Marxist studies and publicity.[21] Most delegates disagreed with this opinion, believing the Party must concentrate on socialist struggle and engage in practical work. The CPC decided at the first session to make the workers' movement the focus of its efforts and to make specific arrangements for Party work. This was reflected in the First Resolution of the Communist Party of China (hereafter referred to as the Resolution). The Resolution provided that the basic task of the Party was the establishment of industrial unions, and "where there is more than one industrial sector, they should be organized into trade unions." Further, "the Party will instill the spirit of class struggle." It emphasized the need to set up workers' schools to raise workers' consciousness in order to guide the workers' movement. In view of the small number of Party members and the imperfect local organizations, the Party's General Assembly, for the purpose of guiding and driving the workers' movement, would not set up the Central Committee, but instead, the Central Bureau to lead the work of the entire Party. The General Assembly elected three members to the Central Bureau, Chen Duxiu, Li Da, and Zhang Guotao. Chen served as Secretary, Li as Head of the Publicity Committee, and Zhang as Head of Party Organization.

The establishment of the Communist Party of China marked the beginning of a new epoch in Chinese history. It was a new party for the working class in China, with the goal of ushering in communism through struggle and with Marxist thought as the unified guiding principle for the action of the Party. Though the Party was still quite weak, it actually represented progressive forces that met the requirements for the development of the nation, representing the direction Chinese culture must take in order to advance so that the Chinese people could develop trust in the leadership and its strong core.

Despite its lack of an understanding of the particularity of Chinese society and the revolution and generally following the proletarian party's program from capitalist countries, in essence, the program stipulated by the CPC at the first National Congress still brought the principle of Marxist proletarian revolution in as the foundation of the Party. Marxist theory had yet to be integrated into the actual situation in China, a fact the early Marxist thinkers in China were keenly aware of. As mentioned earlier, in August 1919, Li Dazhao had mentioned in a chapter of *Another Look at Issues and Ideology* that "if a socialist is to give his theory some impact, he must consider how it may be put into practice." Liu Renjing wrote in a letter to Yun Daiying in December 1920, "We are always seeking a communism that fits our nation."[22] Though the idea is clear, to really combine "issues" and "ideology" and to "find a policy that integrates communism into the national situation" was a huge task for the Communist Party of China, which was unattainable within a period as short as the first CPC National Congress. It had to come about through a long period of struggle, with many victories and many defeats. Only through this long process of struggle could communism be realized.

CHAPTER 2

The New Democratic Revolution Period: Proposing the Basic Question of a Guiding Ideology

I

The Communist Party's Early Exploration of the Fundamental Questions of the Chinese Revolution

1. **Proposing Revolutionary Practice and the Program of Democratic Revolution**

After a year-long process of founding the Communist Party of China, through the study and mastery of Marxism and the practice of revolutionary struggle, some basic understanding was beginning to form with regard to fundamental issues such as the domestic and foreign situation, China's social condition, and the question of the Chinese revolution.

During this period, the international and domestic situation were characterized by imperialist countries' renewed efforts to reestablish their position, their aggression constituting a clear attempt to wreak further havoc on China. Domestically, conflicts and power plays among various warlords were further agitated. Under these circumstances, the political forces of various parties offered different proposals and advocated different means for China to find a way out. The ruling class, made up of warlords controlling the central government at a given time, advocated "the unification of armed forces," while each provincial warlord demanded "autonomy" or the "self-government of the Federation." In essence, these two opposing claims aimed to safeguard the interests of the various warlords themselves, rather than solving the problems faced by China. Among the bourgeoisie, some reformists, represented by Hu Shih, advocated the establishment of "good government" in the hope that "good governors" would save the country without needing to oppose imperialism or overthrow warlord rule. When asked how the "good governors" would come to power and how they would rule in practice once they came to power, these advocates had no answer. Although Sun Yat-sen held to the position of the democratic revolution, he did not go so far as to put forward the program of mobilizing the masses to fight in the revolution. In November 1920, when the Guangdong army expelled Gui warlord forces from Guangdong, Sun returned from Shanghai to Guangzhou to re-establish the "protection of the law." In April 1921, he was elected as a member of parliament through a special election held in Guangdong, becoming the first president of the Republic of China. He planned to rely on the forces of Chen Jiongming to launch the Northern Expedition, using Guangdong as a base. Though Chen, a member of the Kuomintang, ostensibly supported Sun's cause, even promoting the pursuit of socialism, he secretly accepted imperialist measures and covertly colluded with the warlords. In June 1922, the armed rebellion showed itself openly, finally exposing Chen's reactionary act as an imperialist tool. Sun was forced to leave Guangzhou, his enforcement campaign a complete failure.

Where was China to go? What was the way forward for the Chinese people? Many patriots spread false ideas in answer to these questions, creating confusion and turmoil. It was in this milieu that the CPC applied the basic principles of Marxist-Leninist thought to their actual situation and first proposed a program of democratic revolution in China.

When the Communist Party of China grasped the notion of using socialism to overthrow the dark rule of reactionaries through class struggle, they probed more deeply into the actual struggle in their own context and discovered that the semi-colonial, semi-feudal conditions under which they were living meant that the most urgent need for the Chinese people was not to immediately initiate a socialist revolution. Because foreign capital controlled most of China's modern industry, whether in Shanghai, Changsha, Hong Kong, or any other city, a strike or workers' movement would inevitably lead to a clash with the imperialists, and the degree of opposition to imperialism differed from place to place. Even if workers were simply to demand better living conditions, such economic struggles could easily turn into political struggles against imperialism and opposition to the warlord government. The imperialist forces constantly colluded with the feudal warlords, doing everything possible to undermine and even suppress the forces of mass struggle. The Communist Party of China realized that the actual struggle in which the Chinese revolution should first engage had to be against imperial aggression and feudal warlordism, if the state were to be free and the people liberated, not to mention achieving the ideals of socialism and communism. For this reason, some goals were shared by the CPC and Chinese bourgeois democrats for the revolutionary struggle in China. This fact furthered the understanding of the basic issues concerning the Chinese revolution, leading to the practice and promotion of the CPC's socialist ideals and determining the objectives of the struggle and corresponding strategies for carrying it out.

During the process of exploring and formulating a revolutionary program suited to national conditions in China, the CPC obtained help and guidance from Lenin and the Comintern (or Communist International). This played an important role in setting the Party's direction and helping it correctly grasp the progress of China's revolution.

During this period, on the one hand, the Party explored the basic issues of the Chinese revolution through revolutionary practice. On the other, it accepted Lenin's theory of ethnic and colonial issues. As it began to combine these two views, a revolutionary program generally suited to China's national conditions percolated and gradually took form.

The Party first put together propaganda aimed at organizing trade unions and youth league organizations to promote anti-imperialist, anti-feudal political ideas. In May 1922, the First National Labor Conference and the First Congress of the Chinese Socialist Youth League were held, and the CPC put forward the political slogans, "overthrow imperialism" and "overthrow the warlords."

On June 15, 1922, the Central Committee of the CPC issued *The Communist Party of China's Position on the Current Situation*. The focus of this pamphlet was an analysis of the 1911 Revolution, the collusion between foreign imperialists and Chinese feudal warlords, and the Chinese people's history of oppression and their current situation. It pointed to imperialist aggression and warlord politics as China's internal concerns, noting that foreign invasion was the root cause of all the suffering the people were then enduring. The document criticized feudal armies for the current situation and responded to the reactionary arguments spread by the bourgeois reformists by pointing out that in solving the current issues, the key was to overthrow imperialism and the feudal warlords through revolutionary means so that a democratic political system could be established. The document went on to state that in order to achieve the most urgent task faced by the proletariat at that time, the CPC advocated setting up a united democratic front that included the CPC, the Kuomintang, and other revolutionary parties and groups, whereby they could confront the common enemy and free the Chinese people from the dark oppression of imperialism and the feudal warlords.

This was the first time the CPC had made a major public announcement regarding the democratic revolution in China, stating its own political views and explaining their roots in the combination of Marxism-Leninism and the analysis of the current situation in China. It marked a new beginning for the revolutionary question in China and a completion of the formulation of the Party's democratic revolution. It also set the political agenda and laid a foundation for the Second National Congress of the Communist Party of China.

The CPC held its Second National Congress in Shanghai on July 16–23, 1922. The Declaration of the Second National Congress of the Communist Party of China, passed by the Congress, was a significant historical document. Its analysis of the history of capitalism and imperialist aggression against China and the Chinese community evolving into a semi-colonial and semi-feudal society emphasized that "all sorts of facts have proven that the greatest suffering of the Chinese people, whether bourgeois workers or peasants, is capitalist imperialism and the feudal forces of warlord bureaucrats. For this reason, the democratic revolutionary movement opposing those two forces is extremely significant. It is through the success of the democratic revolution that independence and relative freedom can be obtained." On the basis of its analysis of the international and domestic situations and the nature of Chinese society, the declaration proposed that given the historical conditions of that time, the Party's goals were to eliminate strife and overthrow the warlords so that domestic peace could be established, to overthrow the foreign imperialists' unjust oppression so that the complete independence of the Chinese nation could be achieved, and to unify

China as a true democratic republic. In fact, the formulation of the program for democratic revolution was the minimum requirement for the Party's anti-imperialist, anti-feudalist agenda at that time. The declaration further pointed out that the Party's goal was to "organize the proletariat and employ class struggle as a means for establishing the dictatorship of the proletariat, eradicating the system of private ownership of property, and gradually attaining a communist society." This indicated that The Declaration of the Second National Congress of the Communist Party of China adhered to the ultimate goals of the Party as stipulated in the First National Congress, maintaining this as its main agenda.

The Declaration of the Second National Congress of the Communist Party of China tentatively clarified the nature, objectives, motives, and policies of the Chinese revolution at that stage, offering a brief summary of the missions and goals and indicating a future direction for the revolution. This summary indicated that the nature of the movement was a democratic revolution, its object was the overthrow of imperialism and the feudal warlords, its impetus was the workers, peasants, petty bourgeoisie, and national bourgeoisie who would form one of the revolutionary forces, its strategy was to be forming a united front at various levels, its task was the overthrow of the warlords and foreign imperialists so that the independence and reunification of the Chinese nation could be realized, and its future was to be a transformation into a socialist revolution.

The Second National Congress of the Communist Party of China marked the first time the goal of carrying out a democratic revolution and establishing socialism in the future was stated not merely as a means of opposing imperialism and the feudal warlords, but as a combined objective with that endeavor, noting that democratic revolution was a step in the process of creating the conditions in which socialism and communism could be established. This indicated a profound understanding of China's national conditions and the issue of Chinese revolution on the part of the CPC. The integration of the basic tenets of Marxism with China's national condition was one of the Party's important achievements, in that it indicated the correct path for the Chinese revolution to attain independence and liberation for a nation mired in suffering. The determination directly made by the First Congress was that it would first engage in a democratic revolution then shift from there to a socialist revolution, marking a major shift in the Party's strategic policy.

The Second National Congress of the CPC made a preliminary distinction between the concrete links between the democratic and socialist revolutions. The Declaration of the Second National Congress of the Communist Party of China states, "The democratic revolution has succeeded, but the proletariat has not been able to win some freedom and rights, nor has complete liberation been achieved. But with the success of the democratic revolution, the naive bourgeoisie will develop rapidly and come to a position of confrontation with the proletariat. For this reason, the proletariat must operate at the level of the bourgeoisie and carry out the second step of 'the dictatorship of the proletariat combined with poor peasants.' If this succeeds, the second step in the democratic revolution, class struggle, will be an instant success." The CPC estimated two possible outcomes for the future of the democratic revolution. The first was that if the power of the proletariat showed great development through the process of revolution, victory in the democratic revolution would be sufficient to enable the immediate implementation of the dictatorship of the proletariat. The other possibility was that with the victory of the democratic revolution, the bourgeoisie would "seize power from feudalism," requiring the proletariat to go through a long period to make itself strong, after which it could carry out the second phase of revolution. At that time, the young Communist Party members made initial preparations to organize a workers' movement, but they lacked revolutionary experience. Some were influenced by the historical experience of bourgeois revolutions in Europe and the US, and so gave more thought to the second possibility as a direction for China's democratic revolution. Others, more influenced by Russian history from the February Revolution to the October Revolution, considered it preferable to move quickly from the democratic revolution to the socialist revolution. However, China was a semi-colonial, semi-feudal country with a complex national situation, so there was no clear answer to the question of which path would lead to the best future, making it impossible to know with any certainty.

A political party's policy is its banner. The revolutionary program proposed by the Second National Congress was the first statement of a persistent pursuit of the high ideals of the proletarian party in its struggle to establish a communist society, clearly putting forward the CPC's current course of action and its revolutionary task, which was to engage in anti-imperialist, anti-feudal democratic revolution. Just a year after its founding, the Communist Party of China was able to identify China's national conditions and establish the relationship between minor objectives and the overall objective. This demonstrated that it was only through the guidance of Marxism and an understanding of the real national condition in China that the Party could scientifically analyze the social situation in China and accurately reflect the aspirations and demands of the Chinese people, thereby indicating the correct direction for the Chinese revolution so that the Party could shoulder the burden and take up the historical responsibility for leading the Chinese revolution.

In order to lead the Party's program of democratic revolution, the Second National Congress passed nine resolutions. The Resolutions on the Democratic United Front called for workers and peasants all over the country to unite under the banner of the Communist Party. At the same time, it proposed that all revolutionary parties and joint bourgeoisie level democrats organize as a united front for democracy and invited revolutionary parties such as the Kuomintang to hold joint meetings to discuss specific ways to cooperate. This was a change from the policy in the Declaration of the First National Congress of the Communist Party of China that prohibited contact with other parties. As the CPC's earliest proposal for a united front, it was of great importance for the development of the Chinese revolution.

2. The Initial Formation of the Basic Ideas of the Chinese Revolution

In 1925, the May 30th Movement marked the height of the Great Revolution. The political attitude of all classes of Chinese society was more fully demonstrated in the internal leadership of the Revolutionary United Front, but the conflicts likewise grew increasingly evident. The rich, lively revolutionary practice provided many new lessons for Party members, and the complex revolutionary struggle brought to light many new issues that lacked readily available solutions. For instance, what was the nature of and development model for the Chinese revolution? What approach should the proletariat take to managing relationships among its various allies, such as the ethnic bourgeoisie, the urban petty bourgeoisie, and peasants? And without production, how could a class establish its own leadership in the midst of revolution? Both before and after the May 30th Movement, Party leaders such as Chen Duxiu, Li Dazhao, Qu Qiubai, Mao Zedong, Cai Hesen, Deng Zhongxia, Zhou Enlai, and Yun Daiying acted on the basis of a summary of their practical experience in revolution to employ many aspects of revolutionary thought to probe into these issues and make a wide range of expositions in an effort to elevate the Party's understanding of the basic issues related to the Chinese revolution, bringing it to a new level.

The Party's understanding of the nature and the future of the Chinese revolution underwent a gradual deepening process. The Second National Congress made it clear that the nature of the Chinese revolution was that of a bourgeoisie-democratic revolution against imperialism and feudal warlords, and that the future was socialism. In May 1923, Cai Hesen said, "The nature of the Chinese revolutionary movement is that of a democratic revolution, which is different from the bourgeoisie revolution in America."[1]

After the May 30th Movement, the Communist Party held further discussions regarding the nature of the revolution. Mao Zedong pointed out that the revolution in Europe, the US, Japan, and other places was "a bourgeoisie revolution" that was "meant to build a state in which the nation is dominated by the bourgeoisie," while China's national revolution aimed "to reform the petty bourgeoisie, the semi-proletariat, and the proletariat," and its purpose was "to build a nation under the cooperation and rule of the revolutionary people."[2] Qu Qiubai believed that in the age of imperialism – that is, the beginning of the social revolution – the weak nations in colonies "must contain the seeds of the proletarian revolution." But because "in the international arena, this revolution is nothing but a part of the worldwide proletarian revolution. Within the framework of a single country, even if it is only a bourgeoisie revolution, the bulk of the revolutionary force uses the proletariat as its main force."

Although Party members had not yet come up with the new concept of democratic revolution at that time, they had already begun to address the fundamental issues of their day, the revolutionary leadership and the goals of the struggle. In this, it was different from previous democratic revolutions. It was precisely for this reason that the Party's new theory of the democratic revolution could address those specific ideological conditions.

Regarding the future of the Chinese revolution, and particularly the issue of the relationship between the democratic revolution and the socialist revolution, the Fourth National Congress of the Communist Party of China believed that after the October Revolution, the "Chinese national revolutionary movement" was "a part of a larger worldwide revolution" that was "connected with all communist movements to overthrow capitalism." After the May 30th Movement, Qu Qiubai pointed out that "the revolution may be a bourgeoisie revolution, but the victory will not be a bourgeoisie victory,"[3] for if the bourgeoisie was victorious in the revolution, it would soon compromise with the enemy. He also pointed out that his time was the era of imperialism and the dawn of socialist revolution, so that "weaker, smaller private capitalism in the colonies will see no further development among the people,"[4] making it possible for workers within those countries to systematically develop their economy in such a way as to gradually evolve toward socialism. He frequently pointed out that the democratic revolution in China was "the first step toward communism."[5] Qu was correct to emphasize the importance of the proletariat's role in leading the Chinese revolution and the non-capitalist nature of that revolution, but there were two misunderstandings in his thinking. First, he rejected the idea that the Chinese revolution would happen in two steps, and thus confused the boundaries between the democratic and socialist revolutions. His second misunderstanding lay in his view of the notion that a non-capitalist future required the immediate elimination of the private capitalist economy, leading him to propose an anti-bourgeoisie platform in the stage of the democratic revolution.

In the democratic revolution, determining how to understand and treat the bourgeoisie was a complicated issue. Party members' understanding of this issue was gradually deepened and enhanced. The First National Congress believed that the bourgeoisie was the object of the revolution, while the Second National Congress determined that the democrats and bourgeoisie could join forces. The Third National Congress came to the recognition that, to a certain extent, the bourgeoisie in China had two sides. By the Fourth National Congress, it was asserted more confidently that the bourgeoisie in China was divided into the counter-revolutionary "big business comprador class" and the "emerging national industry bourgeoisie." During the May 30th Movement, the national bourgeoisie initially actively participated in the struggle against imperialism, even playing an important role, but later it wavered and compromised, demonstrating its political fickleness. This ultimately provided objective conditions for the Party to conduct a more in-depth analysis of the characteristics of this class.

On December 1, 1925, Mao Zedong published "An Analysis of All Classes of Chinese Society," in which he offered an excellent discussion on this issue. He wrote that the middle class held "a contradictory attitude" toward the revolution and "in receiving foreign investment, the warlords feel the pain of oppression, so they need a revolution, causing them to favor an anti-imperialist, anti-feudal revolutionary movement." However, when the revolution "has the courageous participation of its own proletariat, along with assistance from the international proletariat, their desire to achieve the status of big bourgeoisie makes them feel threatened, and they begin to doubt the revolution."[6] The right wing of the Party intensified its struggle in the revolution, rushing to the aid of the imperialists and warlords, like any good comprador class. The left wing was quite revolutionary in some points, but because it compromised too easily, the revolution was not sustainable. For this reason, they could be taken as allies, but "we must be on our guard at all times, so that they will not disrupt our front."[7]

Gaining such recognition was very important. With the Kuomintang and the CPC uniting in their revolutionary efforts, it was necessary for the Party to mobilize the national bourgeoisie to join in the struggle while guarding against the latter's wavering and compromises. It was quite difficult for the fledgling CPC to resolve this conflict. Many Party members did not understand that as long as the proletariat firmly grasped political leadership in the national revolutionary movement, it would lead part, or even most, of the national bourgeoisie to adhere to the revolution, but its leaders needed to be frequently aware of events that might disrupt the revolution. Mao's analysis of the national bourgeoisie more objectively reflected the actual situation of the class struggle at that time, providing an important theoretical basis for the Party to deepen its understanding and correctly handle its relations with the national bourgeoisie.

The peasants were another important issue to be addressed in the Chinese revolution. Before the Fourth National Congress, the Party had already come to recognize the important position peasants would hold in the revolution. The Fourth National Congress affirmed that the peasants were allies of the proletariat. In May 1925, the Resolution on the United Workers and Peasants, passed by the Second National Labor Conference to guide the peasants in the democratic revolution and establish a consolidated coalition with the peasants, served as a sort of certificate guaranteeing victory in the democratic revolution. Later, in the May 30th Movement, though the working class was isolated because of the painful experiences of destabilization and compromises of the national bourgeoisie, it proved that the peasant struggle was an indispensable part of the success of the national revolution and that peasants were the most reliable coalition force for the working class.

The May 30th Movement enabled many Party members to further understand the role the peasants would play in the democratic revolution and the importance of establishing a worker-peasant alliance. In October 1925, the expanded meeting of the Executive Committee of the CPC proposed that the Party's program once it was in power should include the settling of the peasant's land, holding that "the Communist Party of China should make the larger body of democrats aware that land acquisition is an inevitable policy and an important step in completing the 1911 Revolution." The meeting emphasized that the Party's "only hope for doing its part in history is to be united with the peasants."[8] After examining the economic condition of Chinese peasants, Li Dazhao said, "If China's vast peasant masses can organize and join the national revolution, the success of the revolution is not far off."[9] Chen Duxiu emphatically stated that Chinese workers should not only expand and consolidate to form a united front within their own class, but that there was also an urgent need for the establishment and harmony of the Workers and Peasants League. Only in this way could a preliminary victory in the political and economic struggle be obtained for the working class.

Beginning in 1925, Mao Zedong took the lead in guiding the peasant movement, making peasant issues his focus. Following "An Analysis of All Classes of Chinese Society," he published an article entitled "An Analysis of the Chinese Peasantry in Various Classes and their Attitude Toward the Revolution" in the January 1926 issue of *The Chinese Peasant*. This was the first use of Marxist class analysis in which rural residents were divided into landlords, small land owners, self-employed farmers, semi-self-employed farmers, semi-dependent farmers, poor peasants, farm laborers, and rural handicraftsmen. A more in-depth analysis of the attitudes of these groups' attitudes toward the revolution was made, and on this basis an initial theory of class attitudes in rural areas was formulated. This provided the Party with a more accurate understanding of the peasant class and the status and role of the peasantry within the revolution, laying a solid foundation for the formulation of a policy for the peasant class.

In May 1926, Party leaders held the Guangdong Province Second Peasant Congress, issuing the Resolution on the Position of the Peasants Movement Within the National Revolution, which states, "The semi-colonial Chinese national revolution is a peasant revolution," and "peasant issues are central concerns in the national revolution. The success and progress of the Kuomintang is entirely dependent on the success and progress of the peasant movement."[10] Making peasant issues a core concern of the national revolution demonstrated that the Party's position on the role of the peasant classes in the revolution was based on a deep understanding of the importance of the peasantry.

Before the Fourth National Congress, to varying degrees, the Party had engaged in discussions regarding the leadership of the proletariat. However, it was only at the Fourth National Congress that it was made clear that the proletariat must take leadership over the democratic revolution. However, they lacked any real means to realize the dictatorship of the proletariat amidst the competition for leadership between the proletariat and the bourgeoisie.

During the May 30th Movement, China's working class once again demonstrated its full strength, while the bourgeoisie showed itself to be of two minds. These facts enabled the CPC to further recognize the importance of the leadership of the proletariat as an important asset. In summing up the experience of the May 30th Movement, Chen Duxiu pointed out that though the movement was a united national struggle of all classes, the real struggle with imperialism was actually taking place in workers' strikes in Shanghai, Hong Kong, Hankou, Jiujiang, Nanjing, Qingdao, Tianjin, and Jiaozuo. There was nowhere more solidarity than that seen in the working class. For this reason, though it would be an exaggeration to say that the Chinese workers were the only force in the revolution, they were undeniably an important, reliable force. Further, the bourgeoisie's attitude was one of hesitation and compromise, and they gained sufficient advantages from the imperialists and warlords. Liu Shaoqi noted that "the working class made the greatest sacrifice during the May 30th Anti-Imperialist Movement, and its advocates were the most radical, the most tenacious, and demonstrated great strength. Among all the various facts related to the struggle, one unmistakable point is that the working class has led the revolutionary movement." He continued, "The Chinese proletariat has always been oppressed by the imperialists and the warlords, and thus was fortified in its participation in the national revolution. The bourgeoisie, on the other hand, made compromises throughout their participation in the revolution, and thus could not see it through."[11] Qu Qiubai believed that the weaknesses and concessions the bourgeoisie made to the capitalists during the course of the strikes led to setbacks in the overall struggle, and that the compromises of the bourgeoisie and the cowardice of the petty bourgeoisie sufficed to prove once and for all the necessity of putting the leadership of the revolution into the hands of the proletariat.

Party members placed a heavy premium on the issue of the proletariat's struggle with the bourgeoisie, proposing the notion that this struggle could not be confined to questions of mass movements, but should also give attention to political issues. Deng Zhongxia explicitly stated, "We are engaged in a national revolution, which means we must gain political power." However, he added, "the fact that the power is not dropping from the sky into the workers' hands means that we must engage in political struggle to slowly siphon every drop of power to the proletariat." He particularly emphasized that "if we do not take power, the bourgeoisie is waiting to seize it," and it was only when the proletariat became increasingly politically established and influential that "we can prevent the bourgeoisie from compromising and softening the revolution, putting an end to its political independence," which "paved the way" for the establishment of the workers' government after the revolution.[12] Zhou Enlai pointed out that "revolutionary leaders should be peasant soldiers and should serve as the great alliance of workers, peasants, and soldiers, who together will overthrow the imperialists."[13]

Issued by the expanded meeting of the Executive Committee in July 1926, under the grim situation of the tightening of anti-communist rule by both old and new rightists, the Resolution on the Relationship between the Communist Party of China and the Kuomintang stated, "Our tactics in the national revolution must make it even more explicit that, on the one hand, the Party should more firmly manifest its political independence, establishing itself as a force among workers and peasants and obtaining political influence among the general revolutionary population, and on the other hand, organizing the tide of the petty bourgeoisie to gather in the Kuomintang and enriching its left wing to serve as an influence within the KMT on behalf of the proletariat and peasants in the revolution of the masses. In this way, the left wing of the KMT will become a powerful ally in the struggle, with great assets for the guidance of the class in the national movement. Only in this way can the proletariat achieve and maintain the leadership of the national revolution."[14] These expositions demonstrate that, guided by factual education, the CPC had deepened its earlier understanding of the power of proletarian leadership, and from that understanding and their debate regarding the struggle for leadership between the proletariat and the bourgeoisie, had formulated a guiding principle for its relations with the KMT.

Regarding the issue of armed struggle as the main force in the Chinese revolution, the Party made new progress at this juncture. Earlier, the CPC had criticized the KMT for its exclusive focus on military efforts, neglecting the work of mass movements. However, the Party committed the opposite error, focusing on mass struggle while neglecting military work. In the process of unifying the revolutionary base area in Guangdong, the Party had previously begun to pay attention to carrying out the work of military transport and intensifying propaganda efforts under the warlord forces in hope of promoting its message among those inclined toward revolution. In June 1925, in a speech on his way back to East China, Zhou Enlai referred to the army as a tool, saying, "Oppressors use this tool to oppress people," then going on to reason that "the oppressed class can likewise be used as a tool against their oppressors, overthrowing the oppressors." In terms of overthrowing the imperialists and warlords, he said, "the army is the vanguard of our theory."[15]

The Party likewise quite early on recognized the importance of arming workers and peasants. After the beginning of the provincial strike in Hong Kong, the Party noted the important role played by the Workers' Picket Corps in the struggle to consolidate the revolutionary base areas in Guangdong and to consider it a vanguard of China's national anti-imperialist movement. In October 1925, the expanded meeting of the CPC Central Committee discussed the issue of arming the working class, proposing that the bold preparations for arming working class loyalists should be organized.

Regarding the importance of the armed struggle and the revolutionary army during the period of the of the national revolution, Qu Qiubai offered a systematic exposition in his article "The Question of Armed Struggle in the Chinese Revolution." He pointed out that the Chinese people had already fought through demonstrations, boycotts, and strikes. "However," he wrote, "since the May 4th Movement, the February 7th Movement, the May 30th Movement, the March 18th Movement, the Battle of Guangzhou, and up until today, the tide of revolution has been swirling. This sort of action is preparation for waging an immediate decisive battle, and the time for us to enter a deadly battle is near." He continued, "Especially during this period, revolutionary military action is the way. All other methods are preparation, either directly or indirectly, for the revolutionary war." Qu said, "An official armed force and a civilian armed force are both extremely necessary for China's national revolution," since grassroots insurrections had always been able to defeat even powerful enemies. He insisted on gathering and training the masses of workers, peasants, and the petty bourgeoisie to build a formal revolutionary army, saying, "The revolutionary masses are the main political body, while the revolutionary army is the main military body engaged in revolutionary operations… This is the only hope civilians have for complete liberation."[16] This was the first article in the history of the Party dedicated to the question of armed struggle. It not only played a key role in swaying public opinion in favor of the Northern Expedition, but was also a pioneering theoretical work for the Party's later explorations of the revolutionary path.

The items discussed above constituted the early basic thinking of the CPC in regard to the question of the Chinese revolution. The key conclusions drawn included the need for proletarian leadership of the peasants, petty bourgeoisie, and other classes in the revolution, and the struggle against the national bourgeoisie, the necessity of a democratic revolutionary struggle against imperialism and feudalism, and the overthrow of the warlord regime as a representative of the imperialists and the compradors, and the necessity of establishing joint leadership of the revolutionary classes in opposition to the reactionary rule of the landlord class. Further, it was determined that China's current conditions would not lead to successful revolution if the movement were led by the bourgeoisie and a dictatorship of the bourgeoisie were established. In this world where there was as yet no revolution, part of the purpose of the bourgeoisie revolution would be to prepare China for the socialist revolution. At that time, these ideas were proposed and explored by many prominent members of the CPC. Though they were rather imprecise and incomplete, and though various Party members held differing views, the CPC made great efforts to apply the valuable gains Marxism had thus far achieved to China's current national situation, and these efforts were of great significance to the formation of the later theory of the new democratic revolution.

3. Disagreements in Revolutionary Practice and the Emergence of Erroneous Theories

The victory of the Northern Expedition and the vigorous development of the worker-peasant movement led to great changes, such as internal conflicts and struggles in the revolutionary camp and the intensification of political and military strife throughout the nation, especially in the South. It was at this time that the International Communists, the United Communists (Bolsheviks), and their representatives in China proposed a series of guidelines based on correct principles, offering much helpful guidance to the CPC. However, because they lacked vigilance in facing the danger of rebellion by Chiang Kai-shek and others, in their dealings with Chiang Kai-shek, Wang Jingwei, and Tang Sheng-chih, they opted for the wrong approach, which had a negative impact on the CPC Central Committee's decision-making. The most intense manifestation of this phenomenon was seen in the formation and development of Chen Duxiu's errors.

With the revolution expanding, the issue of a revolutionary regime had already come to the forefront of debate within the Party. Both rural and urban worker-peasant movements were deepening, promoting change in many county governments. In Hunan Province, some counties set up county affair conferences or joint meetings with public bodies. Attending these conferences and meetings were county peasant associations, county unions, and the representatives of other mass revolutionary organizations. Although they did not propose their own county magistrates, the former magistrates had no choice but to listen to the opinions of various mass organizations and actually form a situation in which mass organizations jointly held power. In Jiangxi Province, due to the support of the broad masses, in some counties, Party members served as county magistrates. At the provincial government level, Communist Party member Dong Biwu was part of the leadership of the Hubei provincial government, and Lin Zuhan and Li Fuchun were part of the Jiangxi Provincial Political Committee. Party members took part in the revolutionary regime, working alongside workers and peasants. This was a part of the new process initiated after the victory of the Northern Expedition.

Although the CPC's participation in the revolutionary regime had become a requirement for further development of the revolution, the central government's understanding of this issue lagged behind the actual development of the situation, leading to at least one error. In September 1926, the Central Government entrusted its representation at the Seventh Plenum of the Executive Committee of the Comintern to Tan Pingshan, who asked the Comintern whether the communists should join the government. However, before the Comintern could reply, the CPC Central Committee gave directions to the Party, severely criticizing and preventing CPC members from participating in the government and emphasizing that, during the period of national revolution, the CPC should establish its position as an opposition party and should always maintain its independence by expressing an opposition attitude.

The CPC Central Committee adopted the policy of maintaining its opposition party status. On the one hand, at that time, the mass movement was given primary position and held the mistaken idea that participating in the government was equivalent to fame and status hunting, which had a direct bearing on this policy. Influenced by this concept, the Central Committee proposed a severe ban on "opportunist officials" within the Party, ordering that those serving as county magistrates in Jiujiang and Yongxiu immediately resign, emphasizing that "from now on, our human resources are all to be used by the public and should not participate in government work."[17] On the other hand, what was even more essential was that the entire Party, especially its main leader, Chen Duxiu, had demonstrated a lack of understanding of how to make the transition from a democratic revolution to a socialist society. In July 1926, the Second Expanded Plenary Session of the Central Executive Committee stated in the Central Political Report that "building the capitalist nation" was the "future" of the "national revolutionary movement." In September, in an article entitled "Why are We Fighting Now?", Chen Duxiu stated that the realization of this future would be a victory "attributed to the civil government and army," and that "it is only then that capitalism truly distinctive to China can develop freely." The article plainly stated that during the period of national revolution, there would be no doubt of a Communist government, and that "the time the Communist Party comes into power will be the era of the proletarian revolution."[18]

It was in late 1926 that the CPC Central Committee first realized the importance of joining the government, leading it to decide that the Party "should strive to participate in provincial governments." The Comintern's Seventh Plenum of the Executive Committee made clear that Party members were to join the ranks of government agencies, a major step forward in the CPC's understanding of the importance, and even urgency, of Party members joining the government. In response, Party members such as Tan Pingshan and Su Zhaozheng each in turn began to serve in the national and local government. However, with the rapid deterioration of the situation, they did not actually play an important role in these bodies.

Chen Duxiu, like most other leaders in the CPC, did not give sufficient attention to establishing an armed force. Before the beginning of the Northern Expedition, Party members, graduates of the Whampoa Military Academy, and members of the Communist Youth League totaled about 2,000 people. The majority of workers and peasants from Hunan, Hubei, and Jiangxi Provinces were easily defeated at the hand of the enemy, and they desperately needed guns and ammunition with which to arm themselves. Many officers in the National Revolutionary army sent invitations requesting people from the CPC to come and help with the work. However, Chen Duxiu was opposed to capitalizing on these favorable conditions to bring the revolutionary forces together directly under one umbrella. After the beginning of the Northern Expedition, the Central Committee decided to cut back on the number of people it was sending to study at the Whampoa Military Academy, saying that comrades in the peasant movement "must not be allowed to abandon their work to study" in military academies. The central government also demanded that members of the CPC and Communist Youth League who engaged in political work in the National Army should "just pay attention to political propaganda, but not interfere in military administration."[19] For this reason, the Northern Expedition not only failed to establish more formal armed forces directly under CPC control, but also did nothing to consolidate and develop what could have been a considerable force of armed workers and peasants.

With the progress of the Northern Expedition, dangerous tendencies in the united front of the national revolution became increasingly apparent. In the face of a difficult set of changing circumstances, the main challenges before the CPC were, on the one hand, the need to overthrow the warlords in the north and, on the other, to address the conflicts within the revolutionary camp. Deciding how to address this was a complex question, with a variety of internal and external conflicts. The problem of how to respond to betrayal by allies and to sudden attacks had become an urgent problem to be addressed. To the still inexperienced Party, this was indeed a huge problem.

In an effort to analyze the various dangerous tendencies surfacing in the joint front of the national revolution, the Central Committee held a special meeting in Hankou in December 1926. Comintern representatives Grigori Voitinsky, Mikhail Borodin, and others attended the meeting, where Chen Duxiu pointed out in his political report that since he had won a victory on the battlefield in Jiangxi Province, many changes had taken place in the relationship between the CPC and the KMT, with many dangerous tendencies emerging, threatening to rupture the united front at any time. The report analyzed the source of these dangerous tendencies and admitted that the KMT was right-leaning and that, despite Chiang Kai-shek's occasional leftist remarks, his actions were in fact right-leaning beyond the extent that was deemed acceptable. No effective solutions to the problem were offered, only criticism of all the so-called leftists within the Party and an endorsement of the Kuomintang. In arranging the people's movement, he ignored the existence of the left, misunderstood the independence of the Party, initiated poor policy regarding the petty bourgeoisie, and so on. According to the report, at that time, "the most serious tendency was that, on the one hand, the people's movement had gradually shifted left and, on the other, that the military regime, which was moving right, fears the building of the people's movement." These "left" and "right" movements moved steadily apart, constituting "the very reason for the break of the general united front."[20] This statement exaggerated some radical actions in the worker-peasant movement as major threats, going so far as to call the correct approach "left-leaning." At the same time, it masked the fundamental problem, which was that the new right was then poised to betray the revolution, reversing the importance of these two issues. The report proposed as its central idea seven measures for avoiding the crisis, "preventing the rightist from taking over the Party, while also opposing left-leaning factions within the Party," clearly reflecting an erroneous understanding of the situation.

The Resolution on the Issue of a Leftist Faction within the Party stipulated that it should assist the leftists in the Kuomintang in every aspect, turning them into a powerful political force that could struggle against the reactionary tendencies of the rightist forces. The Resolution held that although the leftist wing of the KMT was weak, the CPC should still unite with and support it. This was essentially pinning all hopes of fighting against the rightist KMT on the leftist faction within it. Chen Duxiu and others also regarded some officers and politicians who had expressed leftist sentiments as reliable left-wing members of the Nationalist Party, particularly Wang Ching-wei, and thus placed too high hopes on the KMT. They not only sought to enable them to gain power within the KMT, but also gave them power within the general mass movements that had always been under the guidance and leadership of the CPC. This not only led to serious consequences at the critical moment, but was also a sudden reversal of the current situation.

The policy proposed at this meeting to avert the crisis was not only based on efforts to consolidate it on the basis of strengthening the CPC's own power, but also failed to make proper mental and practical preparations for the various incidents at the time, instead placing their hope entirely in Wang Ching-wei and other KMT military generals, under the illusion that such concessions would bring unity. Objectively speaking, there were two consequences of this policy. The first was that it made it possible for Chiang Kai-shek, who was already sharpening his sword, to set his heart on spreading his own dangerous ideas among the masses, turning them from left to right, while the relatively weak, volatile, suspicious Wang Ching-wei formed a strong leftist faction that was to assume the important task of completing the national revolution. The second consequence was that it poured cold water on the rapid development of the revolutionary workers and peasant movement then in full swing, clamping down on the enthusiasm of the masses and suppressing the mass movement. In essence, this policy sacrificed the basic interests of the workers, peasants, and masses, shifting the leadership of the KMT neatly into the hands of its right-wing under Chiang Kai-shek and Wang Ching-wei.

The special meeting at Hankou did not address the imminent danger facing the Party, nor the vitally important question of how the CPC might survive and fight in this struggle. Instead, it pointed the Party in the wrong direction, creating an opportunity for the gradual development of the errors of the right wing. The decisions of the meeting were received and approved by the Politburo of the CPC and the Comintern representatives. It was an important subjective factor that led to the failure of the Great Revolution.

II

Various Twists in the Process of Exploring the Basic Issues of the Agrarian Revolutionary War in the Early Stages of the Chinese Revolution

1. A Major Step Forward in Understanding the Basic Issues of the Chinese Revolution

After the failure of the Great Revolution, the domestic political situation underwent a tremendous reversal, with counter-revolutionary forces beginning to outnumber Communist-led revolutionary forces by a large margin. The peak of the nationwide revolution came to an end, and there was a downturn in the revolutionary situation.

The failure of the Great Revolution demonstrated to the Party leadership and the united front that armed struggle was the foundation of the revolution. It was only by settling this question and correctly understanding and resolving these issues that the promotion and development of the revolutionary cause would finally be successful. This harsh fact came as a profound teaching for the CPC.

In an effort to review and rectify the serious mistakes the Party had made in the later stages of the Great Revolution and decide on a new approach and new policies, on August 7, 1927, the CPC Central Committee held an emergency meeting in Hankou, Hubei Province (known as the August 7th Meeting), during which Comintern representative Lominadze's past mistakes were examined and a new approach was forged, with new conclusions drawn. On behalf of the Central Standing Committee, Qu Qiubai issued a report detailing the future of the Party's work. Many Party members spoke out, criticizing the central government for the right-leaning mistakes they made in dealing with issues related to the KMT, peasant land rights, and armed struggle. Some members of the CPC likewise criticized the errors made by the Soviet consultants and representatives of the Comintern.

The August 7th Meeting passed the Report of the CPC Central Committee Executive Party Members and Other Documents, demanding that resolute measures be taken to correct the Party's past mistakes and urging the majority of Party members and the revolutionary masses to continue fighting. The meeting criticized the erroneous opportunism of the rightists and other mistakes made by the Central Committee under Chen Duxiu's leadership in the late stages of the Great Revolution, while also pointing out other periods in which errors were made, such as 1) the issue of the relationship between the Central Committee and the KMT, in which the Central Committee completely renounced the political independence of the CPC and implemented a policy of compromise and concession, 2) the question of revolutionary armed forces, in which the Central Committee never considered the need to arm workers and peasants, not even contemplating the idea that it would be workers and peasant forces that would lead to a true revolution, and instead going so far as to voluntarily order the dissolution of the workers' picket lines, 3) the Central Committee's lack of active support and leadership in the peasant movement, hesitating because they were intimidated by KMT leaders, which prevented them from proposing a revolutionary platform of actions to address the land issue, and 4) the Central Committee's inability to supervise the masses, which led to a lack of democratic life within the Party. This report made clear to all Party members that "the Party's public acknowledgment of its errors is not a sign of weakness, but is made to correct its mistakes and eliminate them, which to the contrary, demonstrates the great strength of the Chinese communist movement."[21]

The August 7th Meeting summed up the lessons learned from the failure of the Great Revolution, discussed the Party's tasks, and established the approach to be taken in implementing the peasant revolution and armed uprising.

With regard to the peasant revolution, in the spirit of the instructions issued by the Comintern and the Central Committee of the CPC on July 20, 1927, in the document The New Stage of the Chinese Revolution: A Peasant Revolution, which clearly stated that the peasant revolution was a central issue in China's bourgeois democratic revolution and that the new phase would mainly be one of socio-economic reform, the meeting pointed out that it was essential to use "civil means" of revolution to address the land problem, confiscating the landlords' land, all so-called public ancestral shrines, and other land for production, redistributing it to tenants or landless peasants. For small landowners, rent would be reduced. The decision made at this meeting answered the key issue now facing the Chinese revolution. In China, the construction of a land system had been an important foundation for the reactionary rule of the forces of imperialism and feudal compradors. The issue of land was always fundamental to the revolution. After the founding of the CPC, though it had been noted that solving the issue of the people's land was of central concern, and in some areas rent had even been reduced, the problem had yet to be addressed. After the failure of the Great Revolution, the CPC had to independently abolish feudalism if it were to lead the revolutionary struggle against the landowners and implement a system in which "farmers own the land." It was only with the support and participation of the vast majority of peasants that armed struggle could be carried out and a revolutionary regime established with an extensive, reliable base. For this reason, the implementation of the peasant revolution not only reflected the roots of the Chinese revolution, but was in fact a requirement uniquely adapted to the needs of the actual struggle.

Regarding the question of armed uprising, the meeting made it clear that, given the situation, the Party's most important task was to systematically push as far as possible into the vast hinterland for a total insurrection of the peasants. The meeting considered poor peasants the main force of the peasant movement, and so decided to deploy the most active, strongest, and most experienced Party members to the major provinces and autonomous regions to mobilize and lead the peasant insurrection, organizing the worker-peasant revolutionary army and establishing the worker-peasant revolutionary regime to address the issue of the peasants' land. The meeting emphasized that the workers' movement and armed peasant insurrection must have close mutual ties, that attention must be paid to military training such as street warfare among workers, and that their riots must be prepared to respond immediately to the rural peasant uprisings. The working class had to be prepared to lead and participate in armed insurrection. The position of undertaking armed opposition and opposing the policy of the massacre of KMT reactionaries, as was adopted at the meeting, was the correct one, and it was a conclusion reached by the Party only after sacrifices had been made. These conclusions marked significant progress in the CPC's understanding of the Chinese revolution.

The meeting passed the Resolution on the Party's Organizational Issues, which was proposed before the Sixth General National Assembly and implemented by all the powers of the Central Committee under the Politburo. Given that covert close efforts would become the Party's main form of work in KMT-controlled areas, the resolution proposed that organization should be the main task at that time, and it should undertake the creation of a staunch, capable covert organ, and Party organizations at all levels should contribute to the covert efforts to build a strong Party. At the same time, it was important to pay attention to making full use of all possibilities that opened up, so as to expand the Party's influence.

At the conclusion of the August 7th Meeting, with the lessons learned from the mistakes made in the later part of the Great Revolution, it was determined that one important cause of these errors was that the leadership body of the Party was largely made up of intellectuals and members of the petty bourgeoisie. For this reason, it was noted that it was necessary to promote comrades who were workers to positions of greater responsibility. Influenced by this understanding, shortly after this meeting, the Central Committee Circular (No. 2) stated that the composition of the Party's leading organ should be based on work and that workers and peasants who performed well in the struggle were responsible for guiding the Party organs at all levels. Party members needed the workers and peasants, and thus needed to quickly absorb them into the Party in great numbers. This improper emphasis on leadership organs and the guiding ideology of the simple composition of workers and peasants in the Party was a departure from the actual conditions both in China and in the Party, which had a negative impact on Party-building. In particular, this "leftist" error came at a time of the Central Committee's dominance within the Party, repeatedly emphasizing "family background as the only yardstick," which seriously hindered the healthy development of the Party's organizations.

In his speech at the meeting, Mao Zedong not only criticized Chen Duxiu's rightist errors, but also proposed two very serious questions. One was related to the issue of military struggle. Mao criticized the Party for past mistakes, saying it "was not specializing in military campaigns, but in populist movements." He proposed "the need to pay greater attention to the military and to be aware that regimes are acquired through the use of guns." This assertion was taken from the lesson of the failed Great Revolution, which affirmed that the question of the role of military struggle in China's revolution was a weighty issue of central concern. The second question raised by Mao related to the peasants' land. He proposed that the standards for large- and medium-sized plots, suggesting 50 *mu* as the limit, and that land in excess of 50 *mu* would be confiscated, regardless of whether it were fat or lean land. The question of small landowners was central to the issue of land titles, and if the property of small landowners was not confiscated, "there will be many places without landlords, and the farmers will simply stop working. Therefore, it is necessary to abolish the landlord system entirely and a definite solution to the small landowner issue must be put in place. The main concern is always the security of the people."²² Autonomous farmers in rich and middle class peasant families had different land rights, so if the peasants attacked wealthy farmers, it would set a proper direction for the revolution. This proposal was suited to Hunan, Hubei, Jiangxi, and Guangdong Provinces, where the possession of land would lay a solid foundation for carrying out the peasant revolution in the future, forming a correct course and an accurate understanding as a foundation for the peasant revolution. However, the Comintern representatives did not adopt Mao's correct opinion, but counter-proposed that the fundamental solution to the problem of land expropriation was the state ownership of land.

Held amidst a serious crisis in the Chinese revolution, the August 7th Meeting was timely, and the guidelines formulated at the meeting were the correct path for continuing the revolutionary struggle, had the entire Party not been alarmed by the looming White Terror. The panic generated in the face of the White Terror re-ignited the courage of the Party to fight the KMT reactionaries and save the Party and the revolution. From that time on, the Chinese revolution began the peasant revolution, forged from the failure of the Great Revolution, marking a great change in the direction of the revolutionary effort.

However, because of the "leftist" thinking of the Comintern and its representatives, coupled with the leftist sentiment within the CPC itself, the August 7th Meeting failed to give attention to preventing and correcting leftist errors while opposing rightist mistakes. The lack of understanding, tolerance, and encouragement for the Party to organize amidst the low ebb of revolutionary activity led some to blindly mobilize workers to strike or even organize urban riots. Chen Duxiu did not notice this tendency at the meeting, instead wrongly accusing leaders of not focusing on the ideological or theoretical lessons extracted from previous mistakes, as outlined in the summary of the meeting. The meeting also inappropriately emphasized the simplistic composition of the workers as leaders for the Party organs and the main body of the Party's membership. The meeting objected to the idea that the completion of the bourgeoisie-democratic revolution (which included the peasant revolution), and especially the completion of the anti-imperialist revolution, was dependent on the realization of the bourgeoisie struggle. This understanding provided the theoretical basis for the future development of leftist errors, according to the report, bringing great harm to the Chinese revolution.

After the August 7th Meeting, many armed uprisings were carried out in succession. What sort of government was to be established after an armed uprising? The question of the nature of the post-revolution regime became an urgent issue for the Central Committee. The Proposal on the Coming Peasant Struggle and Resolution on the Coming Workers Movement passed at the August 7th Meeting proposed the slogan "the village government belongs to the Peasant People's Association" and the realization of the goal of a "worker-peasant dictatorship." On August 9, in a directive to the Hunan Provincial Committee, the Central Provisional Politburo stated clearly that a revolutionary political power should be set up in order to establish the democratic dictatorship of workers and peasants. Specifically, all power in the village should be held by the peasant associations, while in the city, power should rest solely with the revolutionary committee. It declared that, once the victory of the revolutionary committee was proposed, the representatives of the trade unions, peasant associations, and revolutionary small businessmen should be called for elections and establish a formal "civil government." In regards to when such a "civil government" could be organized, the letter fixed the time as the period after local revolutionary committees had consolidated power.

At this time, though the Central Committee had set forth the principle of establishing a worker-peasant democratic government, it still proposed to organize workers and peasant riots under the banner of the left wing of the Kuomintang. The Central Committee believed that the KMT was a special flag of the movement that would provide a national solution, and that if the Communists joined the KMT, they could move the KMT's left wing to its center. The actions and propaganda of grassroots organizations and Party members made the KMT a small asset in the city among the masses, even making them part of the mass workers' movement, with some revolutionary prestige already coming to be associated with the KMT. The Communist Party was not yet ready to lose this flag. At the same time, organizing a riot under the banner of the KMT could attract some small assets to the revolutionary classes. For this reason, the slogan of organizing for the soviets was not proposed at this time.

More than a month later, on September 19, the meeting of the Central Provisional Politburo passed the resolution, but under the changing circumstances, the resolution abandoned the banner of "the left wing of the KMT" and put forward the propaganda slogan of setting up the soviet (i.e. representative meeting).

2. The Nature of China's Revolution and Proposal of its Revolutionary Path

With the failure of the national revolution and the commencement of the peasant revolution, even as the Communist Party of China attempted to sum up the failure of the revolution, they also sought to re-examine and further explore numerous issues concerning the Chinese revolution, including the nature of society, the nature of revolution, revolutionary motives and class relations, the content and main methods central to the revolution, the revolutionary regime, the future of the revolution, and the revolutionary path. This inevitable undertaking had to be carried out after the revolutionary upsurge had passed. The crux of these issues was the nature of revolution and the revolutionary path.

The nature of society. To understand the nature of China's semi-colonial, semi-feudal society was to understand all the basic issues of the Chinese revolution. Among China's Communists and early Marxists, the first to use the phrase "semi-colonial" to describe China's social situation was Cai Hesen. In his September 1922 article, "Unification, Lending, and the Kuomintang," he pointed out that "China's international status is already semi-colonial."[23] In November 1922, the Fourth Congress of the Comintern reiterated that China was "a semi-colonial country," after which concepts such as "semi-colonial China," "semi-colonial society," and "semi-colonial Chinese society" began to appear widely in a range of Chinese Communist documents and Marxist theoretical works. Among Chinese Communists and early Marxists, Cai Hesen was likewise the first to use the phrase "semi-feudal." In September 1922, he wrote in his article "The United Front and the Self-Governing United Provinces: A Consideration of Politics and Warlords" that China was "semi-feudal and semi-democratic." By September 1924, Cai had already introduced this formulation in his article "Anatomy of Freedom in the Anti-Revolutionary Movement," but had not specifically demonstrated, defined, or explained it. The "semi-feudal" nature of China's economy and Chinese society was the topic at the Sixth National Congress of the CPC. The Sixth National Congress passed the Resolution on Land Issues, which states unequivocally, "The characteristics of China's economy are based on land relations, and it is clearly a semi-feudal system." It goes on, "The current economic and political system in China should indeed be regulated as a semi-feudal system."[24] On the basis of this clear understanding of the two aspects of China as a "semi-colonial," "semi-feudal" society, in February 1929, the CPC Central Committee issued Circular No. 28 of the Central Committee: A Strategy for Peasant Movements, marking the first wholesale use of the concepts "semi-colonial" and "semi-feudal" in official writings. The document stated, "According to precious experience gained through its study conducted over several years of economic relations and the peasantry in China's semi-colonial, semi-feudal society, the Sixth National Congress of the CPC has pointed out that the main idea of the peasant movement is to strive to build a united front among the anti-landlord class among peasants in rural areas, consolidating leadership and protecting the proletariat in the peasants' revolutionary struggle and, through the victory of the peasant revolution, to turn the future toward socialism."[25] Although the Sixth National Congress of the CPC demonstrated a definite understanding of the semi-colonial, semi-feudal nature of Chinese society, these concepts were still not completely formulated, so it was in Circular No. 28, issued at the Sixth National Congress, that the concepts first explicitly came into official use, being the first time the terms were used in a CPC document. For the purpose of this volume, it is sufficient to say that the terms were seldom used in any documents before this, and that the concepts of "semi-colonial" and "semi-feudal" had been proposed at various times with different connotations. After the beginning of the Great War in the 1930s, there was much debate about the nature of China's semi-colonial, semi-feudal society, with many different views proposed. After the controversy, the first to recall the formulation of a "semi-colonial, semi-feudal Chinese society" were Su Hua and Zhang Wentian. In September 1933, in his article entitled "The Development of the Chinese Capitalist Economy," Su Hua pointed out that at the time, Chinese society was "a semi-colonial, semi-feudal society."[26] This expression focused on "semi-feudal," with "semi-colonial" used to modify the phrase "struggle to build society." In January 1934, in his article "The Socio-Economic Basis for the Chinese Revolution," Zhang Wentian laid hold of the basic issue of China's land relations, persuasively concluding that the economic nature of Chinese society was "a semi-colonial, semi-feudal economy." At one point, he stated, "This economy determines the tasks and nature of the Chinese revolution and determines its progress in the relations between various classes, which is the impetus behind the Chinese revolution."[27] After this, in June 1934, in his article "A Study of the Early History of Chinese Society," Lu Zhenyu likewise clearly concluded that after the Opium War, Chinese society was "semi-colonial and semi-feudal." The above discussion offers a clear view of the CPC's thinking concerning Chinese society at that time. By the first half of the 1930s, after a lengthy debate regarding the nature of Chinese society, the understanding of China's semi-colonial, semi-feudal society was furthered and gradually solidified. By December 1936, Mao Zedong had begun to use the concept of "semi-colonial, semi-feudal." In his article "Strategies for China's Revolutionary Struggle," he wrote, "We are now at war. It is a revolutionary war, and our revolutionary war takes place in semi-colonial, semi-feudal China." This statement demonstrated Mao's agreement with leading Marxist theorists of the time.

The nature of the revolution. On August 1, 1927, in a speech entitled "China," delivered at a joint conference of the Central Committee of the Soviet Communist Party and the Soviet Central Commission, Stalin stated that there were three stages in the Chinese revolution. "The first stage was the revolution of the united front of the entire nation. This was the Guangzhou era, when the main revolutionary goal was to combat foreign imperialism, and with the national bourgeoisie's support of the revolutionary movement. The second phase came after the democratic class revolution. In this phase, after KMT forces reached the Yangtze River, the national bourgeoisie quit the revolution, but the land movement developed into a powerful revolution for millions of peasants. Today, China remains in the second phase of the revolution. The third stage of the soviet revolution has not yet come, but it is coming." On February 25, 1928, the Comintern Executive Committee issued the Resolution on Issue Concerning China, which clearly stated that "the current stage of the Chinese revolution is the stage of a bourgeoisie civil rights revolution."

The CPC's August 7th Meeting determined, "The Chinese revolution is still a bourgeoisie civil rights revolution, the socio-economic civil rights revolution, and the socio-economic and political legacy of the repressive imperial and feudal system."[28] The CPC Central Committee Politburo Circular on Resolutions by the Comintern, issued on April 30, 1928, stated, "The Central Committee Politburo has always clearly understood that the Chinese revolution is a bourgeoisie civil rights revolution." At the Sixth National Congress, the CPC pointed out more clearly that "the current stage of the Chinese revolution is the stage of a bourgeois civil rights revolution." Because "the current goal of the revolution" was to "expel the imperialist and complete the institution of a truly Chinese system and to complete the civilian overthrow of the private land ownership system of the landlord class, the revolution is the ground… on which all semi-feudal ties among local institutions will be completely destroyed."[29] In an article written by Mao Zedong, Cai Hesen, Qu Qiubai, Li Lisan, and many other Party members, it was frequently made clear that "the present stage of the Chinese revolution is a part of the bourgeois civil rights revolution." Party members, understanding that the Chinese revolution was still under the umbrella of the bourgeois democratic revolution, pointed out the "uniqueness" of the bourgeois democratic revolution in China. First, in China's bourgeois democratic revolution, it was urgent not just to oppose imperialism and feudalism, but also to oppose the national bourgeoisie. The political resolution of the Sixth National Congress stated, "China's current bourgeois civil rights revolution must oppose the victory of the national bourgeoisie […] because the bourgeoisie is an obstacle to the victory of the revolution, and in fact, one of its most dangerous enemies." The resolutions on the political issues of the Sixth Assembly of the Comintern likewise pointed out that "with the expansion of the mobilization of the masses and the intensification of the peasant revolution, the national bourgeoisie has gradually become anti-revolutionary. For this reason, China's anti-imperialist struggle cannot be separated from its opposition to the national bourgeois revolution."

The Party believed that "the land ownership of China's national bourgeoisie and feudal landlord class are linked together, heart and soul, even as they shamelessly surrender to imperialism."[30] Further, although "the bourgeoisie is engaged in an economic and anti-imperialist struggle, its strength is fundamentally at odds with the interests of the majority of Chinese workers and peasants."[31] It went on to say that "the Chinese bourgeoisie is driven by imperialist economic aggression, and it cannot resist imperialism while also enriching the imperialists. It is only able to make compensation by further aggravating the exploitation of the Chinese worker and peasant."[32] For this reason, it was necessary for the Chinese revolution to oppose the national bourgeoisie. For a long time after the failure of the Great Revolution, the CPC proceeded from the class standpoint, harboring hatred for the national bourgeoisie, who had rebelled against the revolution and rooted it in the political attitude of the national bourgeoisie and hostility toward the Communist-led peasant revolution, which was a rallying call for the national bourgeoisie. However, most Party members still understood that "opposing the bourgeoisie is not because the national bourgeoisie espoused capitalist ideology, but because it has become a tool of imperialism and an ally of the landlord class, betraying the revolution in favor of a counterrevolutionary leader opposed to the civil rights revolution. Thus, if the new task does not go beyond the nature of the bourgeois civil rights revolution and destroy capitalist methods of production, it will, on the contrary, become a starting point for the development of capitalism."[33]

A second unique feature of China's bourgeoisie democratic revolution was that it was a part of a worldwide movement of proletarian socialist revolutions. Cai Hesen pointed out that China's bourgeois democratic revolution "opposes international imperialism, and it is just one part contributing to the larger worldwide revolution."[34] The Sixth Assembly of the Comintern believed that "China's revolution is of tremendous worldwide significance." The Sixth National Congress of the CPC pointed out that the Chinese bourgeois democratic revolution was "opposed to imperialism… diminishing its power… and the Soviet Union and the working class revolts in all countries are helping to reduce imperialist oppression of the proletariat around the world, for the sake of a revolutionary future." It further stated that "it is a help and a major component of the worldwide socialist revolution."

A third unique aspect of the Chinese bourgeois democratic revolution was that it had to be led by the proletariat and jointly dominated by peasants from the general public. The Notes from the August 7th Meeting of the CPC pointed out that "based on objective conditions, China's working class is the strongest, most thorough, and most uncompromising force striving for the liberation of China. Such circumstances enable the Chinese proletariat to assume leadership of the national liberation movement." In his article "Why is China's Red Regime Able to Exist?", Mao Zedong wrote, "China urgently needs a bourgeois democratic revolution, and this revolution must be completed under the leadership of the proletariat." Qu Qiubai added, "The development of the Chinese revolution must be led by the peasant soldiers of the proletariat, based on class, leading the masses in a revolution to overthrow the landlord bourgeoisie of the gentry class and the bourgeoisie of international imperialism."[35] Cai Hesen emphasized that China's bourgeois class had betrayed the revolution, even turning its back on the key concept of "the dictatorship of the proletariat," which was "the core issue of the Chinese revolution." He added, "Victory can only be achieved… with a united peasantry."[36]

The fourth unique aspect of China's bourgeois democratic revolution was its non-capitalist future. In February 1927, the Resolution of the Seventh Meeting of the Executive Committee of the Comintern noted that the development of the Chinese revolution would lead to a non-capitalist (i.e., a socialist) future. The Sixth National Congress of the CPC similarly noted this same point. Some Party members pointed out that "the uniqueness of the Chinese bourgeois civil rights revolution lies in the fact that its victory will mark the early development of socialism."[37] Why was it necessary for China's democratic revolution to be non-capitalist? Party members addressed this question from different perspectives. "The driving force behind the Chinese revolution has only been among the proletariat and peasantry, and with the leadership of the proletariat at the bourgeois stage of the democratic revolution, it has been established amid the democratic revolution (since the proletariat can help and guide farmers to implement the peasant revolution and provide leadership in the anti-imperialist struggle). This can open the way for the future development of the Chinese revolution so that it will lead to a non-capitalist future, which is to say, a socialist future. World capitalism is now fearful, and in this period of panic and the dictatorship of the proletariat, ten years have passed since the establishment of socialism in the Soviet Union, and political and economic power are growing there, which is sufficient to help the Chinese proletariat in its revolutionary struggle to bring about the future of socialism and guarantee the possibility of victory."[38] Further, "China's industrial and agricultural crisis is a necessary transitional economic stage in the approach to socialism," and because the Soviet government had no foreign capital, "it confiscated the land of all the major enterprises to organize and direct the country's new economic life." Further, because "agricultural productivity is weak, when the peasant revolution is completely victorious and the development of capitalism begins, it must inevitably encounter other great obstacles, including imperialism and the domestic rectification of the landlord class, the bourgeoisie, and wealthy peasants." To overcome these obstacles, the only choice for peasants (except wealthy peasants) was to "prepare for the transition to the conditions suited to the socialist revolution, that is, eliminating the capitalist market economy and replacing the rate of large-scale organized state-owned industries under the rural collective economy. By the time such a change is complete, it is no longer the development of capitalism but a preliminary step toward the construction of socialism."[39] The consensus among most Party members was that the future of China's bourgeoisie democratic revolution was non-capitalist. However, there were serious differences between the timing of China's bourgeoisie democratic revolution and the socialist revolution. The Party was clearly aware of this problem, and so opted to take a detour. The CPC Central Committee Politburo held an expanded meeting in November 1927 in which it determined that the Chinese revolution was "a continuous revolution," and that "it is inevitable that we must completely settle the task of democratization and make a sharp turn to head straight into socialism."[40] Qu Qiubai said that this sort of "continuous revolution… cannot help but surpass bourgeoisie populism."[41] He even believed that "the current stage of the Chinese revolution has grown into a socialist revolution."[42] The Comintern, the Sixth National Congress of the CPC, and some Party members criticized this view, pointing out that "only when the civil rights revolution has been completely victorious can we begin the transformation to the socialist revolution."[43] They noted that the Party absolutely "cannot skip the stage of the civil rights revolution."[44] At the same time, it was emphasized that "the end of the civil rights revolution is the beginning of the socialist revolution."[45] It would not be possible to find a path of capitalist development midway between the two.

After the August 7th Meeting, the CPC led the uprising, carried out armed struggle, and achieved a change in the type of struggle employed. However, the CPC failed to note the downturn in the revolutionary situation, instead erroneously estimating the situation and disregarding both subjective and objective conditions and blindly demanding that some areas be armed. The result was a gradual increase in "leftist" sentiments within the Party.

3. The Circuitous Exploration of the Basic Issues of the Chinese Revolution

For a long time after 1927, many Party members still took preparations for an urban uprising and work in white areas as the Party's central task. Leftist mistakes were repeatedly committed in connection with this issue. The historical lesson learned from their mistakes was that they had not proceeded based on the realities of the Chinese revolution and had failed to research and investigate China's historical and social conditions. Situated in the big cities, they were stiflingly dogmatic. Having some experience in overseas studies, they had some one-dimensional knowledge, but in the end, they were unable to fit their theory with Chinese wisdom and apply it to the specific circumstances, leading them to underestimate the military struggle, especially peasant guerrilla warfare and the rural roots of the revolution. The theory of attacking "the countryside around the city" was the so-called "peasant awareness of local ideas and conservative concepts," harboring dreams that urban workers' struggles and other mass struggles would suddenly break through the enemy's line with great force. This hope led them to consistently mobilize armed uprisings in areas surrounding the cities, imagining that the city at the center would lead to what was called the first provincial victory to form the so-called height of national revolution and lead to victory across the entire country. Urban workers were always at the center of everything in such dreams.

This leftist error was a blind repetition of the experiences of the Russian Revolution. Under the guidance of the erroneous leftist theory of the Comintern, from November 9 to November 19, 1927, the CPC Central Committee held an Expanded Meeting of the Provisional Politburo in Shanghai. The meeting was presided over by Qu Qiubai and attended by representatives of the Comintern. The meeting adopted a resolution entitled "The Current Situation in China and the Task of the Party," drafted by Lominadze and addressing questions related to political organization, political discipline, and other similar issues. On the one hand, the resolution correctly called for all revolutionary forces to be made Communists under Communist leadership, resolutely opposing imperialism and overthrowing the KMT's reactionary rule, resolutely leading peasant uprisings and implementing rural separatism, confiscating the land of the landlord class for farmers to cultivate, and organizing the workers and peasant revolutionary army for guerrilla warfare. On the other hand, they also considered the Chinese revolution as a "continuous revolution" and held that "the current revolutionary struggle is going to have to go beyond the scope of populism if it is to progress." Further, it was inevitable that as the issue of democratization was completely settled, it would rapidly go along the path to socialism. In this way, the boundary between the democratic revolution and the socialist revolution was confused.

The meeting accepted Lominadze's leftist point of view, that Chiang Kai-shek's mutiny was the treason of the entire national bourgeoisie, while Wang Ching-wei's mutiny was the treason of the petty bourgeoisie. The meeting did not admit that the revolutionary situation was at an ebb, thinking rather that the new KMT warlords were already on the brink of collapse and the current situation in China was a direct revolutionary situation. The meeting set the general strategy for the implementation of the national armed insurrection and demanded that rural riots be carried out in the same way as urban riots, combining with the urban struggles as the "center and director," so as to form a complete urban and rural insurrection until victory in one or several provinces resulted in revolutionary conditions. The meeting also provided a series of overly leftist policies, such as those advocating the confiscation of large capitalists at home and abroad, and when demanding "control for the factory workers," they demanded that "extremist and heroic counterrevolutionaries should be killed without pity and with extreme severity" during the peasant uprisings.[46]

According to Lominadze's proposal, there were no armed insurrections after the August 7th Meeting, nor was any specific analysis made of the situation. Instead, one-sided accusations were made, suggesting that the leaders of the uprising "hesitated to take action" and, contrary to the Central Committee's policy, committed "opportunistic" errors. For this reason, disciplinary action was taken against the leaders of the Nanchang Uprising and activities along the borders of Hunan and Jiangxi Provinces, including upright leaders such as Zhou Enlai, Tan Pingshan, Mao Zedong, and Peng Gongda, along with the relevant provincial committees. The expanded meeting of the CPC National Congress affirmed the Party's organizational process after the August 7th Meeting, while also embodying the guiding ideology of the Party's organs in the process of making Party membership more representative of workers and peasants. The Resolution on the Important Task of the Recent Organizational Matters adopted at the meeting held that one of the major organizational weaknesses of the Party was that its leading cadres were not even workers or poor peasants, but petty bourgeoisie intellectuals, and pointed out that this gave rise to opportunism within the Party. To this end, the motion proposed that the Party's most important organizational task was to replace non-proletarian knowledge with new cadres of workers and peasants, and that the cadres of the armed forces taken from the proletariat and the poor should make up the largest proportion of the Party's leading cadres. The meeting suggested requiring the Party's guiding organ to be completely rehabilitated before the Sixth National Congress of the Communist Party of China was held.

From mid-November to mid-December, the spirit of the expanded meeting of the Central Committee Politburo began to be implemented everywhere. Some areas forcefully pushed workers' strikes, peasant uprisings, and indiscriminate killing and burning, putting the Party at some distance from the masses in those places. Only a handful of armed uprisings in rural areas were victorious, with the majority of such efforts either failing or faltering altogether before they even got off the ground. In Wuhan, Changsha, Shanghai, and other cities in which a small number of workers and activists went on strike, the movements were quickly suppressed. In late December, under Qu Qiubai's leadership, the CPC Central Committee issued a circular stating that it was too difficult to launch riots in so many areas all at once and instructing those areas that did not possess suitable conditions for insurrection not to immediately call for riots. It was decided that the revolts originally planned in Hunan and Hubei would be halted in hopes of preventing loss and correcting the error of indiscrimination that had thus far plagued the movement. However, at this time, the CPC Central Committee had not yet recognized that the mistakes in the guiding ideology and general strategy had arisen from leftist errors, making it impossible to completely correct the indiscriminate errors in the overall situation.

The leftist error that began with the failure of the Great Revolution and continued through the peasant revolution was a historical turning point in the rising war. It was rooted in anger at the KMT policy of massacring CPC members, leading to widespread agitation within the Party. At the same time, some who had committed rightist errors were so afraid of repeating those mistakes that they started to assume that "left" was better than "right," and in so doing, primed the pump for the development of leftist error. At this time, the CPC could not give urgent attention to and make accurate analysis of every pressing problem facing the Chinese revolution after the failure of the Great Revolution. Lacking experience in and understanding of Party struggle, they were unable to prevent the leftist errors of the anti-rightists while also finding a solution to every challenge the revolution faced. The Comintern representative Lominadze played a major role in the emergence of this leftist error. Through his lack of political discernment, his organizational penalties, and other measures, he became the main proponent or promoter of leftist policy. The Central Committee Politburo, under the guidance of Qu Qiubai was likewise in part directly responsible for this leftist error.

The line taken by Li Lisan was the "city as center" theory. On January 11, 1930, the Central Committee Politburo adopted the Motion Accepting the Letter of October 26, 1929. On February 26, the CPC Central Committee issued

Circular No. 70, which went beyond the revolutionary statement, holding that "at present, the crisis is intensifying each day and the new wave of revolution" was gradually carrying out mass struggle all across the nation in "a balanced path to development." According to this estimate, the circular stipulated that the Party's "current general political path" should be the convergence of the various struggles taking place and that "the nationwide struggle should move from an anti-warlord war to a class war, overthrowing the KMT and establishing soviet power." The circular pointed out that the Party was not to continue implementing the strategy of accumulating power during the revolutionary ebb, but should focus on concentrating active aggression, with local workers being organized for political strikes, revolts, and mutiny and concentrating the Red Army in major cities. In April and May, the Central Committee and the Central Military Commission likewise made concrete plans for these actions. In the past, Li Lisan had published many articles in *Red Flag*, *Bolshevik*, and other Party publications, such as one entitled "New Issues Facing the Revolutionary Upturn," in which he proposed a series of left-leaning points. After the outbreak of the Central Plains War and the Hunan-Guangdong-Guangxi Border War, Li Lisan and others believed that the revolution was complete and that the nation was mature. For this reason, at the June 11, 1930, meeting of the Central Committee Politburo, Li Lian passed three drafts of the "Resolution on the Current Political Mission" (i.e., "New Heights in the Revolution, with Early Victory in a Few Provinces"). The resolution was mistaken in its estimation of the revolutionary situation and considered "the fundamental dangers of China's economic and political situation, which continues to be sharpened equally all across the country without any basic difference." It further stated that "the overall conclusion is that the new height of the revolution is before us now," and "there is a great possibility that we can turn this into a victory for the entire country." The resolution also held that "unprecedented world events indicate that the time for change and the great worldwide revolution are upon us," and that when the Chinese revolution broke out, it would "set off a grand revolution throughout the world." The Chinese revolution would be completed with a full victory in this final battle.

On the basis of this erroneous assessment of the revolutionary situation, the resolution held that at the time, there was no need for the Party to gradually accumulate and prepare revolutionary forces, because the masses were already not a small force, but a large force, and if there were to be an armed insurrection, it had to be a nationwide insurrection. The resolution's application of Russia's October Revolution to the Chinese situation was too mechanical, holding that as long as a sudden outbreak occurred in an industrial area or a great workers' struggle occurred in the political center, there would be an immediate victory of an armed uprising throughout the provinces and a nationwide regime would be established, gaining victory in every province and region throughout the country. Although the resolution was correct in acknowledging the importance of the Party's commitment to organizing the Red Army in rural areas, the task of the Red Army was to "cooperate with the armed uprisings in major cities, seize power, and establish a revolutionary regime throughout the country." For this reason, "the guerrilla tactics used in the past [...] must be fundamentally changed." It also demanded that the Red Army should organize itself in a centralized way and conduct unified command and large-scale implementation of an offensive war.

The resolution's view of the nature of the Chinese revolution, the question of revolution, and the issue of revolutionary change similarly returned to the past policy of "continuous revolution," which was criticized at the Sixth National Congress as erroneous understanding. The resolution did acknowledge that at this stage the Chinese revolution was still a bourgeois democratic revolution and that its main task was still to oppose imperialism and feudalism, and it also affirmed that "the bourgeoisie is already a part of the reactionary alliance," and that, if the revolution gained early victory in one or several provinces, it would be necessary for the Party to confiscate the banks, enterprises, and factories in imperialist parts of China, and that it would even be "necessary to seize the banks, factories, and enterprises of the Chinese bourgeoisie." At the same time, politically speaking, it held that "it is necessary to go from a worker-peasant revolutionary government to the dictatorship of the proletariat." The resolution noted that "the beginning of the victory of the revolution and the founding of the revolutionary regime are the beginning of revolutionary change," saying further, "If we think that we can only start the revolution when it is possible to win it throughout the entire country, we are making a serious mistake," while the theory of stages of revolutionary change "is undoubtedly an extremely dangerous right-leaning concept."

Influenced by this erroneous line of thinking, Li Lisan and other leaders developed a plan with Wuhan as the focal point for the nationwide urban-centered uprising and the nationwide project of Red Army attacks on areas with cities at the center. In July, heavy deployments were made in Nanjing, Shanghai, Wuhan, and other cities in preparation for riots. At the same time, provisions were made for the Red Army troops to 1) block the Wuhan-Changsha Railway, 2) enter Nanchang and Jiujiang to cut off commerce to Wuhan and Changsha, 3) force their way into Wuhan, and 4) attack Liuzhou, Guilin, and Guangzhou. Red Army forces in these regions immediately put the instructions from the Central Military Commission into action. In late July, Red Army troops engaged in a battle at Pingjiang and, on July 27, they successfully captured Changsha.

When Li Lisan learned news of this victory, he became even more convinced that the Communists "would enter Wuhan," their "horses drink the waters of the Yangtze," and that this would bring them closer to national victory, making it a goal that could be quickly achieved. This led to further development of leftist error. From early to mid August, Li Lisan and other Party members adopted the slogan "Militarization" and set up the Central Action Committee as the highest command organ to lead the armed insurrection. This prompted leading organs at all levels, including those from the CPC, the Communist Youth League, and the trade unions, to merge into action committees (also called "commissions"), stopping the normal activities of the Party, regiment, and trade unions. They further proposed the launch of riots in Wuhan, the South Beijing Riot, the Shanghai General League Strike, and the establishment of the Central Soviet Government in Wuhan and the National Riot Plan, and also put forward the idea that "the soviets must prepare for war" and that hundreds of thousands of Chinese workers in Siberia should act quickly to accelerate the armed forces and "prepare for war against Japanese imperialism." In suggesting that Mongolia could gain victory in riots in China, they added that large numbers of troops should be sent to attack the reactionaries in northern China. Li Lisan and others in the Party called for all Party members to "be brave and daring, and to move forward courageously." Li Lisan's erroneous thinking in this area spread all the way to the top.

Wang Minglu's line of thinking was typical dogmatism. This was clearly manifested in a brochure he wrote entitled *Two Directions*. Though this pamphlet contains some criticism of Li Lisan's inappropriate leftist thinking, it mistakenly pointed to Li's thinking as generally rightist, which hid the actual opportunist right-leaning thread. If Li's error was so clearly leftist, why did Wang misidentify it as rightist? This was mainly due to the fact that Wang's own thinking was even further left than Li's. In his view, the driving forces of the Chinese revolution were strictly the workers and peasants, while the petty bourgeoisie and all other classes were "already moving into reactionary camps," and so no room was left for "third factions" or "middle ground." He lumped the bourgeoisie and petty bourgeoisie under the same umbrella with imperialism and feudalism, regarding them all equally as targets of the revolution. They declared that in its present stage, the bourgeoisie democratic revolution could only gain a complete victory if it engaged in a struggle against the bourgeoisie. He emphasized that the national revolution had arrived and an offensive line must be put in place nationwide. He believed, "Currently, we have not yet entered a direct revolutionary situation in China, but as the new upsurge in the national revolutionary movement has grown and given the current condition of unbalanced development, the direct revolutionary situation can include, first and foremost, one or a few key provinces." He advocated that Hunan, Hubei, and Jiangxi Provinces "must really achieve the first victory for one or several provinces, then promote and fight for victory across the nation." Li Lisan advocated urban workers' riots as the key to the Chinese revolution, an urban-centric view that Wang Mingle likewise held. Wang followed the resolution proposed by the Comintern, saying, "The most credible sign that the new upsurge has led to a situation in which China's revolutionary struggle is ripe is that the workers' struggle has reached its climax in the strikes." The leaders organizing the economic struggle of the workers did in fact prepare for a strike in the Allied League, even noting that armed uprising was the Party's most important task. Although Wang Minglu also said that attention should be given to the Red Army, he did not completely understand the laws and revolutionary base areas under which the Red Army fought nor the laws of development of revolutionary principles. He accused the Party and the Red Army of "failing to establish centers in the winter of 1930 as bases for a secure revolution," believing this was the very rightist action to be opposed. Regarding the issue of the peasant revolution, Wang proposed that it was necessary to "firmly fight wealthy peasants" and "make wealthy peasants give poor peasants land," along with other erroneous leftist ideas. At the organizational level, he called for "actively supporting and implementing the struggles of international cadres, especially the workers, to reform and enrich the leading organs at all levels."

Three leftist errors were committed within the Party in the seven year period before the Zunyi Meeting, spanning the time from the winter of 1927 to January 1935. Each of these errors shared a common feature – it was focused on an urban-centered theory. Why was this basic error not corrected, but instead repeated? One fundamental reason is that the ideological line of thought, which formed the basis for the political line of action, was not correct. It was impossible to formulate a positive political line of action when the ideological line of thought was wrong. In particular, Wang Minglu's view did not proceed from China's actual situation, but instead simply treated dogma as a sacred treasure that could not be violated. In all of his writings, he merely acted on instructions from the Comintern. In all the international Communist movements, there had never been an experience of rural peasants surrounding cities, and in all its writings the Comintern stated its belief that the Chinese revolution must make cities its focus. Their logic was that foreign uprisings had always experienced proletarian victory in the cities, and the Chinese revolution was led by the proletariat, which must always be associated with the city. In other words, if the Party's focus was on the peasants rather than urban areas, that meant "its rejection of the city is a denial of the proletariat's leadership over the peasantry, which will result in the Party becoming a party of the petty bourgeoisie."[47] At that time, the CPC Central Committee always worried that taking rural areas as the focus was straying too far from the cities, for without leadership from the cities, there could be no leadership of the proletariat. Growing from such one-sided erroneous thinking, armed urban uprisings were taken as the main symbol for promoting the peak of the national revolution, which led to repeated insistence that efforts in soviet areas "should be transformed from a simple village to an important city,"[48] taking workers as the focus of the city. This viewpoint neglecting the idea of using rural areas as revolutionary bases was obviously not suited to China's actual situation.

Marxism holds that there are common basic rules in the development of human society and that it is wrong to deny these basic laws. However, there are different historical aspects in different places and among different people groups, and a failure to proceed based on the actual situation in a specific locale, beginning from the specific characteristics to enact a specific revolution according to the universal truths of Marxism-Leninism, will make it impossible to guide the revolution to victory. The three left-leaning errors during this period are the most basic historical lesson demonstrating this principle. The entire historical experience of the Communist Party of China has repeatedly proven one truth: when the political line of action departs from the dialectical materialist line of thought, errors will be made and revolutionary causes will be harmed. On the other hand, adherence to the ideological line of dialectical materialism to formulate a political line of action that is in keeping with China's actual conditions allows for continuous development of the revolutionary cause.

CHAPTER 3

The Elucidation of the New Democracy Theory

I

The Initial Formation of the New Democratic Theoretical System

1. Proposal Regarding the Task of Incorporating Marxism into China

During the period of the Great Revolution and the Agrarian Revolutionary War, the Communist Party of China was guided by the principles of Marxism-Leninism and, with the help of the Comintern, led the Chinese revolution to a major victory. At the same time, the question of how best to incorporate the principles of Marxism-Leninism into the on-the-ground situation of the Chinese revolution still remained. There were also major mistakes made during this time, particularly in the period from 1931 to 1934, when "leftist" dogmatism, represented by Wang Ming, treated the question of theory as a separate issue from China's actual condition. Instead of applying the principles of Marxist-Leninist thought to the specific situation of the Chinese revolution, they treated it as a ready-made formula to be applied wholesale to the Chinese revolution, particularly in the form of instructions from the Comintern, demonstrating a sort of blind obedience and taking what they called an international route. It was registered as a golden rule, the standard by which all theoretical and practical work was measured. This led to ruination of the Party's early work in White territories, which in turn led to the failure of the Red Army, another setback in the Chinese revolution. These ups and downs in the revolutionary cause made the CPC deeply aware of the importance of connecting theory to practice and applying foreign experience and the directives of the Comintern according to national conditions. Mao Zedong's "Strategic Issues in the Chinese Revolutionary War," *Practical Theory, Contradictions*, and other works demonstrated that the correct ideological line had been re-established within the Central Committee. However, newly returned from the Soviet Union after the outbreak of the War of Resistance, Wang Ming once again committed the error of seeking to copy foreign experience and implement the instructions of the Comintern wholesale. The main difference now was that he had moved from left to right on the political spectrum.

At that time, the Comintern and the Soviet Union actively supported the Chinese people's War of Resistance, but once again, they overestimated the power of the Kuomintang, while underestimating the power of the CPC. It was mistakenly believed that Chiang Kai-shek's army could clamp down and combat Japanese imperialism on the Chinese battlefield. They advocated that the KMT should be accommodated, with more concessions made to them. They disagreed with the CPC's principle of independence with a united front and the policy of unity and struggle. They proposed that "all should obey the Anti-Japanese National United Front" and that "everything should go through the Anti-Japanese National United Front." They only looked at the regular and positional warfare of the Nationalist Army, ignoring the role of the Communist-led anti-Japan guerrilla warfare. Wang Ming made these views the basis for his observation of China's anti-Japan issues and sought to develop right-wing errors in these new historical conditions. He declared that both the KMT and the CPC were "made up of a large number of outstanding young Chinese people" and that Chiang Kai-shek would "become an immortal national hero of China." He advocated that "everything go through the United Front" and "all obey the United Front." He did not support the principles of "independence and freedom," but openly opposed the proposal of joining the leadership of the United Front. He despised the People's Army and the guerrilla warfare led by the CPC, neglected the work of defending the anti-Japan bases behind enemy lines, and pinned all hope of victory in the War of Resistance on the regular warfare of the KMT army. He advocated the implementation of a strategic approach of "competitive warfare and guerrilla warfare with positional warfare." He even proposed that the armies led by the CPC and KMT should be unified in preparation, armor, discipline, welfare, command, operational plans, and operations. As Wang Ming continued to work under the banner of "international communism," his erroneous ideas continued to hold some deceptive power and were implemented in some areas, causing certain losses in the development of the War of Resistance and the people's revolutionary forces.

At the Sixth Plenary Session of the Sixth National Congress of the Central Committee of the CPC, held from the end of September to the beginning of November 1938, Wang Ming's rightist error was basically overcome. It was at this plenary session that the CPC clearly stated that the task of "solidifying Marxism in China" would be based on the experience and teaching gained in the seventeen years since the CPC had been established.

In a report on the theme of "On a New Stage," prepared by Mao Zedong for the conference, there was is a section devoted to "Learning." In it, he pointed out that "the political party that directs a great revolutionary movement without revolutionary theory or revolutionary knowledge, and without a deep understanding of the actual movement, cannot possibly be victorious."[1] For this reason, he proposed three corresponding learning points. The first was to learn Marxist theory, the second to learn historical heritage, and the third to learn current practical movements. Regarding the first point, he said, "We are leading a large nation with a population of hundreds of thousands of people to carry out a great, unprecedented struggle. Thus, the general and in-depth study of Marxist-Leninist theory is a major problem for us to solve, and it requires our focused attention."[2] He called for all "to enter a Party-wide learning contest to see who can really learn something. For those who learn a good deal, that's even better."[3]

However, in the study of Marxism, it was important to first address the issue of attitude. And what sort of attitude would produce the correct approach to one's study? Mao Zedong believed that Marxism-Leninism should not be regarded as a dogma, but as a guide for action. It was not enough, he said, to simply learn the words of this school of thought, but it was necessary to learn it as a revolutionary science as well. Likewise, it was not enough to understand its conclusions and general principles, but was also imperative that it be studied from the perspective of Marxist-Leninist theory and its methods of observation and problem-solving be adopted. It was especially important to "learn to apply Marxist-Leninist theory to the specific environment of China" and "apply it according to Chinese characteristics" because "Marxism must be combined with the unique characteristics of China and be passed on to fit a specific ethnic group in order to become a reality." He added that "distancing oneself from Chinese characteristics to discuss Marxism is just abstract, empty Marxism." For this reason, he said, "Let Marxism be embodied in China in such a way that it has the necessary Chinese characteristics in each expression of it," calling this "a problem that the entire nation needs to solve." Mao pointed out sharply and sternly that, "The rigid, foreign, high-sounding style must be abolished and the empty, abstract tone proclaimed less, and dogmatism must be put to rest and replaced by a fresh, lively Chinese style that is popular with the Chinese people."[4] The arguments were later developed more fully by Mao in *Practical Theory* and *Contradictions*, where he indicated more clearly the attitude of the CPC toward both Marxism and the directives of the Comintern. It was only "making Marxism concrete in China" that was consistent with the spirit of Marxism.

In his article "On the Anti-Japanese National Front and Party Organization," Zhang Wentian expressed the same view as Mao Zedong. He believed that "the principles and methods of Marxism are international, but we are doing the organizational work in China. We must make a strict assessment of the characteristics of China's politics, economy, culture, ideology, national customs, and morality, and we must correctly understand these characteristics. Only then will we decide on the form of our struggle, the form of our organization, and our working methods." He went on to say that "in order to make the organizational work Chinese [...] and place it in a national environment" in the Party's efforts to realize the principles of Marxism, it was important to understand that "one will surely be frustrated if one hopes to transfer the decision of a foreign party into China." In the Sixth Plenary Session, the entire Party was called "to learn to apply Marxism-Leninism and international experience to every practical struggle in China."[5]

The application of the principles of Marxism according to Chinese characteristics and the process of making Marxism concrete in China formed a sort of sublimation of the understanding of Communism espoused by Chinese Communists represented by Mao, which they gained through a hard, torturous path. This sublimation went beyond the general revolutionary experience and became a basic principle guiding the Chinese revolution. It was a principle that was clear throughout the entire Party, indicating that the CPC's thinking had entered a mature stage of theoretical thought, which provided the most favorable internal conditions for the final formation of the New Democratic theoretical system. Throughout this process, external conditions were gradually becoming increasingly available.

2. The Elucidation of the New Democracy Theory

After the outbreak of the War of Resistance Against Japanese Aggression, the CPC came out of a narrow world that had been subjected to a tightly sealed lock to become a large national party, and as it publicly set out on the huge stage of national political life, it received more – and closer – attention. People were eager to understand the CPC's views of the current situation in and the future of China. The Party had to maintain independence in the Anti-Japanese National Front, and it had to present its own political propositions that distinguished it from other political parties before the people of the country, so as to attract the people by their own upright ways.

After the beginning of the war, the Kuomintang and the CPC launched a fierce debate on the issue of the Three People's Principles. The KMT and the CPC had just reached a cooperation agreement. Chiang Kai-shek stated in his "Talks on the Manifesto of the Communist Party" that the "Three People's Principles" were "the founding principles of the Chinese nation," and that "China only has one direction toward which it must work today," and that was the Three People's Principles. At the beginning of 1938, KMT diehards launched a propaganda campaign in Wuhan to advocate "one ideology" with "one political party" and "one leader." KMT-controlled newspapers, such as *Mopping-up Operation*, published articles attacking the CPC and Marxism. The KMT literally clamored, "The KMT is 'the golden child' in all parties, and no other party is equal to it," stating that both then and in the future "there is no need for independence."[6]

By the time the war had reached a sort of stalemate, this sort of propaganda had intensified even further. In December 1938, Zhang Junyi of the National Socialist Party published an "open letter to Mr Mao Zedong." While advocating the abolition of the border area, the Eighth Route Army, and the New Fourth

Army, he also discussed with Mao Zedong the "theory of the Communist Party," writing aggressively, "At the current stage, when Mr Mao and others are hard at work on foreign and national wars, it is better to put Marxism to one side and make the Chinese people think they are on one side or the other of a black and white issue, without resorting to gray areas or disingenuous overtones. Spreading all sorts of Chinese ideology is the starting point for saving the nation, and it is also the easiest step." A renegade member of the CPC, Ye Qing (Ren Zhuoxuan) was known as "the theoretician of the KMT." He advocated even more publicly that "The Three People's Principles can satisfy China's present concerns and all its future demands. With their realization, China does not need socialism, thus organizing a Party aimed at achieving socialism and socialist struggle is not necessary." He added that all parties aside from the KMT had no reason to exist independently, not only at that time, but also in the future. In January 1939, Chiang Kai-shek made a speech at the Fifth Plenary Session of the Fifth National Congress of the KMT, calling members "to wake up the Party spirit, carry forward the Party's morality, and consolidate." In a speech entitled "Organizing the Party's Essentials," the so-called "waking of the Party's spirit" and "promoting the Party's morality" were the realization of "one ideology," "one political party," and "one leader." On the pretext that it was necessary to avoid war, Chiang Kai-shek claimed that the people would not invoke their civil rights, and that it was impossible to implement "constitutionalism," but only "military politics" and "martial law" could be implemented. He emphasized that the KMT should "manage everything" and "implement a party to govern" and "a party to build the nation."[7] In September, he published a lengthy article entitled "The System of the Three People's Principles and its Procedures," advocating what he called "a party to govern the nation" and "a party to build the nation," saying that "the day victory is achieved in the War of Resistance is the day the founding of the nation is complete." This put the issue of "where China is going" in stark terms before anyone who cared about the destiny of the nation. At this point, it was imperative that the CPC systematically express its position and views on this question.

Though dissatisfied with the KMT's authoritarianism and the incompatibility of the war, some representatives of the national bourgeoisie had their doubts about the CPC's propositions and the future of the War of Resistance Against Japanese Aggression. Some were also trying to take a path outside the political propositions of the KMT and the CPC, hoping to establish a European-American style of bourgeois republic in China.

This made the question of China's future a theoretical issue of great importance. Mao Zedong, Zhang Wentian, Zhou Enlai, and other leaders in the Central Committee of the CPC and members of the Yan'an academic circle published a series of articles and speeches on the attacks the KMT diehards had made on Marxism and the CPC. They rigorously exposed and criticized all sorts of false Three People's Principles, discussed the difference between Sun Yat-sen's Three People's Principles and the older Three People's Principles and the relationship between the Three People's Principles and Communism, thus clarifying the theory and program of the CPC and answering the question of where China was going.

Mao Zedong strongly refuted the paradox which held that "recognizing the Three People's Principles will reap Communism." He analyzed the history of the development of the Three People's Principles, comparing the similarities and differences between them and communism and pointing out that Sun Yat-sen's reinterpretation of the revolutionary Three People's Principles was the same as the basic program of the CPC's New Democracy platform. For this reason, the CPC recognized the Three People's Principles as the political foundation for the Anti-Japanese United Front. However, the two were different. They were two different ideologies guided by different worldviews, and their specific policies at the present stage were not identical. Their revolutionary thoroughness was different, making the prospects of their revolutions different. After the completion of the new democratic revolution, there was still a supreme program for establishing a socialist and communist social system, but not the Three People's Principles. It was a mistake to ignore this difference. It was not only wrong for the KMT to expect the CPC to "retract" communism, but it also showed that the Three People's Principles they were talking about were not Sun Yat-sen's revolutionary Three People's Principles, but merely a counterfeit. They called for "one ideology," but in fact, they denied the united front and denied the status of the CPC, the workers, and the peasants, and adhered instead to authoritarianism in a "one-party dictatorship." This sort of retrogression was simply not feasible. Mao said that the CPC would always sincerely implement long-term cooperation according to the Three People's Principles, and that it would never abandon any of its allies.

The debate between the KMT and the CPC regarding the Three People's Principles further clarified the nature of Chinese society and the characteristics of its historical development, while also further clarifying the major issues of the nature, tasks, and basic strategies of the Chinese revolution and promoting the CPC's formation of a New Democratic theoretical system.

The CPC regarded the War of Resistance Against Japanese Aggression as a stage in China's New Democratic revolution. To carry out the War of Resistance, it was necessary not only to expel the Japanese aggressors, but also to create conditions suited to the construction of the new China. In an effort to explain to the entire Party and all the people in the country the views of the Party on the Chinese revolution and the construction of the new China, Mao Zedong engaged in a great deal of theoretical work in Yan'an and concentrated the collective wisdom of the whole Party, systematically summarizing the experience gained in the Chinese revolution.

In his article "The May 4th Movement," published on May 1, 1939, Mao wrote, "The May 4th Movement of twenty years ago showed that the bourgeois democratic revolution against imperialism and feudalism in China had developed to a new stage."[8] He added, "The completion of the Chinese democratic revolution relies on certain social forces. These forces are the working class, the peasant class, the intellectuals, and the progressive bourgeoisie, and the foundational revolutionary force of the workers, farmers, military, intellectuals, and merchants are the workers and peasants, and the leadership lies with the working class. If you depart from this fundamental revolutionary force and the leadership of the working class, it is impossible to complete the democratic revolution against imperialism and feudalism."[9] In his speech "The Direction of the Youth Movement" on May 4, he called the ongoing Chinese revolution "The Chinese people's revolution against imperialism and feudalism," saying, "The bourgeoisie has been unable to complete this revolution, so it must be completed by the efforts of the proletariat and all the people."[10] After the fall of imperialism and feudalism, it would be necessary to "establish a people's democratic republic" and "build a people's democratic system." This would be "different from the current semi-colonial, semi-feudal state, but not the same as the future socialist system." Even so, there was "no doubt that China will eventually develop into a socialist system. No one can overthrow this law."[11]

Mao laid out several points more clearly in these two articles. First, he made it plain that the May 4th Movement had ushered China's anti-imperialist, anti-feudal revolution into a new stage, and that this stage of the revolution had to be led by the working class. Further, the goal of this stage was to establish a people's democratic republic that was different from the semi-colonial, semi-feudal state and that would bring about the development of a future socialist state. Obviously, Mao's new democratic theory had already been brewing by this point, with careful consideration and formulation going into the process, but he had not yet put forward a clear concept of the "new democracy," nor had he had time to systematically demonstrate or explain it.

The scientific concept of the new democracy was first proposed in *The Chinese Revolution and the Communist Party of China*, written in December 1939, a textbook written by Mao Zedong and several other comrades in Yan'an. The second chapter, entitled, "The Chinese Revolution," was written by Mao, and the first, "Chinese Society," was drafted by Mao and revised by others. *The Chinese Revolution and the Communist Party of China* was first published from Yan'an in the journal The Communist. After the founding of the new China, this work was approved by Mao for inclusion in *Selected Works of Mao Zedong*. In the article, Mao first distinguished the bourgeoisie-democratic revolution from the old democratic revolution and the new democratic revolution, stating clearly, "The so-called new democratic revolution is the masses in an anti-imperialist, anti-feudal revolution under the leadership of the proletariat."

Why was China's current bourgeois-democratic revolution only considered a new democratic revolution? This was determined by China's actual national situation.

Mao wrote, "To recognize the nature of Chinese society – that is, to recognize China's national situation – is fundamental for recognizing all revolutionary issues." For this reason, *The Chinese Revolution and the Communist Party of China* began with an analysis of Chinese society, then, based on this analysis, went on to discuss the issues, tasks, motivation, nature, and future of the Chinese revolution in detail.

Mao pointed out that China's current society was a colonial, semi-colonial, and semi-feudal society. This social nature determined the main object or main enemy of the Chinese revolution at this stage, which was imperialism and feudalism. Among them, imperialist national oppression was the greatest oppression, and thus imperialism was the greatest and fiercest enemy of the Chinese people. After Japan's invasion of China by force, the main enemy of the Chinese revolution was Japanese imperialism and all traitors and reactionaries who colluded with, publicly surrendered to, or were prepared to surrender to Japan. The tasks of the Chinese revolution was to overthrow imperialist oppression and overthrow the feudal landlord's oppressive democratic revolution, with the most important being to overthrow the imperialist national revolution. These two tasks were interrelated.

The enemy of the Chinese revolution was extremely powerful. Who could accomplish an arduous task such as that faced by the Chinese revolution? This was the driving force of the Chinese revolution. Mao Zedong analyzed all the characteristics of the economic status and political situation of various classes of Chinese society in turn, then came to the conclusion that the Chinese proletariat had many outstanding advantages, so it could become the most basic driving force behind the Chinese revolution. He said, "If the Chinese revolution is not led by the proletariat, it will certainly not be victorious." But if it were impossible to win by the power of a single class, then it was essential that all potential revolutionary classes unite in a variety of ways, organizing a united front for the revolution. Among the various classes of Chinese society, the peasants were the most solid allies of the working class, and the urban petty bourgeoisie was also a reliable allied force. To a certain degree and at certain times, the national bourgeoisie could also be counted on as an allied force.

The Chinese bourgeoisie presented a complex issue. Mao Zedong made it clear that "the bourgeoisie is clearly distinguished between the upper bourgeoisie with comprador traits and the national bourgeoisie." This was an extremely important distinction. Mao pointed out that the national bourgeoisie class was subdivided into two classes. On the one hand, it was under the oppression of imperialism and feudalism, so it could become one of the revolutionary forces. On the other, because of their economic and political weakness, they did not completely sever their connection with imperialism and feudalism. For this reason, they lacked the complete courage necessary to oppose imperialism and feudalism. When the revolutionary forces of the people were strong, they were most obvious. Mao pointed out that the duality of the national bourgeoisie determined that they could participate in the revolution against imperialism and against the bureaucratic warlord government for a certain period of time, becoming a kind of revolutionary force. During another period, lying behind the comprador class was the danger of their becoming counter-revolutionary agents. During the anti-Japan period, they were not only different from the landlords and capitulationists of the upper bourgeoisie, but also from the die-hards within that class. They were still better revolutionary allies. For this reason, it was best to "take caution in dealing with the national bourgeoisie. This policy is absolutely necessary." At the same time, it was pointed out that China's comprador class belonged to several imperialist countries. In the anti-Japanese war, the pro-Japan upper bourgeoisie and the Anglo-American upper bourgeoisie should be distinguished. The former was capitulationist and should be defeated. The latter was die-hard and two-faced, and thus the Party should deal with them according to a revolutionary two-faced policy. Further, many enlightened gentlemen from the small and medium scale landlord class – that is, landlords who to a degree were capitalists, but who held enthusiastic anti-Japan sentiments – needed to be united to fight against Japan. (Distinctions made between non-pro-Japan and pro-Japan, Anglo-American, large scale landlords, small and medium scale landlords, and the enlightened gentlemen were not mentioned when *The Chinese Revolution and the Communist Party of China* was first published in *The Communist*. On March 11, 1940, Mao first mentioned this issue in "Strategic Issues Facing The Current Anti-Japanese United Front." After April of that same year, he made the corresponding changes to this part of *The Chinese Revolution and the Communist Party of China*. The article was collected, edited, and published by the Propaganda Department of the CPC Central Committee that November in *Party Construction Proceedings*.)

The colonial, semi-colonial, and semi-feudal nature of Chinese society, which was China's unique national condition, determined that "the nature of the Chinese revolution at this stage is not proletarian socialism, but a bourgeois democracy."[12] However, "at this time, China's bourgeois democratic revolution is no longer an old-style general bourgeois democratic revolution. Such models of revolution are outdated. This is a new style of special bourgeois democratic revolution. It is the sort of revolution that has developed in China and in all colonial and semi-colonial countries, and it is called the new democratic revolution."[13] This sort of new democratic revolution was "an anti-imperialist, anti-feudalist revolution of the masses under the leadership of the proletariat," and "Chinese society must go through this revolution before it can further develop into a socialist society. Otherwise, such development is impossible."[14] This was the most significant conclusion drawn by Mao in the article.

Mao also stated that the new democratic revolution would inevitably bring about two consequences. On the one hand, it cleared the obstacles on the road to capitalist development, and it would bring about a considerable degree of capitalist development. On the other, there were also factors related to socialist development. These socialist factors included the proportion of the proletariat and Communist Party members who held political power in the country, whether peasants, intellectuals, and the urban petty bourgeoisie recognized the leadership of the proletariat within the Party, and whether there was cooperation between the state economy and the people's movements in the democratic republic. With a favorable international environment added to this mix, the future of the Chinese revolution would move toward socialism rather than capitalism.

The publication of Mao Zedong's *The Chinese Revolution and the Chinese Communist Party* opened the eyes of the people in a huge way. It offered such a clear, systematic explanation of the nature of Chinese society and a series of fundamental challenges facing the Chinese revolution, that this dazzling, confusing social phenomenon suddenly seemed organized and easy to understand, allowing the people to respond with greater sophistication and adaptability. As the situation became increasingly clear, it was easier to keep a clear grasp of the basic direction and maintain a consistent pace. The huge impact it made at that time and beyond was difficult to calculate.

The "new democracy" banner was lifted high. However, what were the specific points of the political, economic, and cultural aspects of the new democracy, and what were their characteristics? These and many other issues needed to be further elaborated and explained.

In January 1940, the First Congress of the Shaanxi-Gansu-Ningxia Border Region Cultural Association was held in Yan'an. There, Mao Zedong delivered a lengthy speech entitled "The New Democratic Politics and New Democratic Culture." It was reported that "this long speech began in the afternoon and went on until after the gaslights were lit." Further descriptions indicate that "the five or six hundred listeners crowded in that venue were inspired by and drawn to his vivid, insightful words. They listened with great concentration and were very enthusiastic, even bursting into applause from time to time." A month later, this speech was published in the first issue of *Chinese Culture*. When it was reprinted in the 98th and 99th issues of *Liberation* a few days later, the title was changed to "New Democracy." Mao himself said that the main purpose of the speech was to refute the diehards, but its significance went well beyond this scope.

In the speech, Mao clearly addressed the question of where China was going. His purpose was stated clearly when he said, "We want to build a new China." He said, "For many years, we Communists have not only made up China's political revolution, struggled for its economic revolution, and fought for a Chinese cultural revolution, but we have done so for the purpose of building a new Chinese society and a new Chinese nation."[15]

During the speech, Mao systematically expounded on the theory and program of the new democracy and once again talked about the issue of integrating Marxism into China. He said, "Formulatively absorbing foreign things has brought great loss to China in the past. The same is true of the Chinese Communists' application of Marxism in China. It is necessary that we complete both the universal truth of Marxism and the practice of the Chinese revolution. The proper unification of the land means that we must combine communism with the characteristics of the nation and that it will be useful only in a particular national form. It must not be applied subjectively."[16]

In this way, Mao put the basic characteristics and the specific content of the political, economic, and cultural aspects of the new democratic state into a clear and thorough outline of what sort of "new China" was to be established by the CPC.

In the article, Mao refuted an argument spread by the diehards, which was that since the CPC had pushed the socialist system to a later stage and declared that "The Three People's Principles are necessary for China today and the Party is willing to strive to realize them," then Communism should be set aside for the time being. Mao wrote, "Communism is the entire ideological system of the proletariat and a new social system [...] Without communism to guide the democratic revolution in China, the revolution is sure to fail now, let alone at later stages of the revolution."[17] He also specifically analyzed the parts of The Three People's Principles that were similar to Communism, as well as those that were different.

"New Democracy" was an article that provided both a strict theoretical system and a very strong argument. Mao let the content of this article brew for a long time as he repeatedly revised it, soliciting opinions from various comrades throughout the writing process. Two decades later, he said, "When the first draft of 'New Democracy' was half done, China was in a particular century, the first eighty years of which constituted one stage, while in the last twenty years, we have seen a new stage emerge. For this reason, I have had to rewrite the original many times before finalizing the manuscript." Even the reactionary scholar Ye Qing, who had a habit of attacking the Communist Party without providing any theory of his own, could not help but say after reading "New Democracy," "As for

Mao Zedong, from now on I will take him as a Communist theorist." The article had greater repercussions, both inside and outside the Party, in that it enabled people to gain a clearer understanding of the current goals of the struggle and the direction of China's future, so that more and more people would come together in the new democracy.

The primary difference between the new democratic revolution and the old democratic revolution lay in the question of leadership by the proletariat. The issue of the dictatorship of the proletariat had long been raised within the CPC. However, in China's complicated environment, how could the proletariat take leadership? Mao Zedong also spent a long period considering and exploring this question before offering a comprehensive exposition in the article "The Communist Party," in which he stated, "The experience of the past eighteen years has taught us that the united front, armed struggle, and Party building are the three magic weapons the Communist Party of China may employ in defeating the enemies of the Chinese revolution."[18] Regarding the relationship between these three, Mao wrote, "The united front and armed struggle are the two basic weapons to defeat the enemy. The united front implements armed struggle. Party organization is master of the united front and armed struggle, while the latter two are the weapons used to carry out the heroic rush against the enemy."[19] He went on, "The correct understanding of these three things and the relationship between them is equivalent to correctly leading the entire revolution." Currently, he said, "we have been able to correctly address the issues of the united front and armed struggle, and are correctly handling the issue of Party organization as well."[20] This was an important summary of his view of the CPC's struggle over the previous eighteen years.

What enabled Mao Zedong to produce such a huge theoretical work was, on the one hand, the fact that he had always been rooted in the rich, infinite practice of the Chinese revolutionary struggle, allowing him to deepen his understanding one step at a time in a progression that grew out of his attention to the new situations and challenges he met in real life. As he observed and thought deeply about these things, and through repeated exchange of ideas with other thinkers who understood the actual situation, he was able to brainstorm new theories without falling into an inward, personal view of the situation that was detached from reality. On the other hand, he delved diligently and painstakingly into Marxist works. His approach was based on the assumption that theoretical study lay in application, and in order to apply it, one must read frequently and with great focus, studying classic works of Marxism-Leninism and learn the development process of Marxism. Through the debates and criticism of various theoretical viewpoints, his understanding of the universal truths of Marxism was deepened. He once said to Zeng Zhi, "When I was writing 'New Democracy,' I read *The Communist Manifesto* many times."

Mao always believed that it was important to indicate the direction and future of the revolution, but that this alone was not enough. It was also necessary to determine the policies and strategies by which these goals may be achieved. He said that only by "clarifying theory and actual policy" could the solution to the problem be completely achieved. Of course, at that time, this attracted more attention to Mao's work. It was also the actual policy issue facing the Anti-Japanese National United Front at the time, rather than the specific policies that needed to be addressed in all aspects of the new China, but there were many similarities between the two.

The end of 1940 marked the eve of the Southern Anhui Incident. The situation was grave, and Mao was busy with his work. Even so, he did not relax at all, but continued to make a comprehensive, systematic summary of the Party's historical experience, particularly its experience with the national united front strategy. On December 4 and December 13, the meeting of the Central Politburo held serious discussions on these issues. Mao pointed out at the meeting that summing up past experiences and lessons should be divided into three periods: the Great Revolution, the Soviet period, and the War of Resistance Against Japanese Aggression. The general mistake lay in a lack of understanding of the long-term, unbalanced nature of the Chinese revolution. Many "leftist" mistakes were made in the previous Soviet stage because Marxism-Leninism was not sufficiently linked to the actual situation on the ground. Mao proposed that a committee should be organized to summarize the Party's policy issues, and another appointed to formulate regulations.

On December 25, based on the comprehensive summary of the experience of the Central Committee of the CPC, Mao Zedong drafted a Party directive on the current situation and policies. (The policy part of this directive is included in *Selected Works of Mao Zedong*, under the title "Policy on Income.") The directive clearly stated, "In the current situation at the height of anti-communist sentiment, our policy has a decisive significance." It continued, "Throughout the period of the

War of Resistance Against Japanese Aggression, no matter what the situation, the Party's Anti-Japanese National United Front policy must not be changed. Many of the policies from the past decade of the Agrarian Revolution cannot simply be quoted now."[21] The directive criticized some "leftist" opportunist mistakes that occurred during the Agrarian Revolution, saying, "The current Anti-Japanese National United Front policy is neither a joint denial of struggle nor a struggle to deny unity, but a policy combining both unity and struggle."[22]

The directive clarified and stipulated a series of policies for the Anti-Japanese National United Front, including 1) independent and united policy of the unified front, 2) independent military strategy, which was essentially guerrilla warfare that did not abandon traditional warfare under the right conditions, 3) in the struggle against anti-communist diehards, the "Use of conflict, fighting for the majority and opposing the minority in order to break through" and insisting on "reasonable, favorable, restrained" treatment, 4) in enemy-occupied and KMT-controlled areas, adopting a policy of "shadowing, long-term ambushes, consolidating strength, and waiting for opportunities," and 5) developing progressive forces in domestic relations, striving in intermediate forces, and isolating stubborn forces. These and other such policies were part of the directive.

The directive was based on a specific class analysis, particularly emphasizing the need to make various distinctions, such as distinguishing between pro-Japanese and the British and American landlords of the upper bourgeoisie who advocated an anti-Japanese stand. A distinction was likewise made between the duplicitous, anti-communist upper bourgeoisie and the two-faced national bourgeoisie, small and medium landlords, and the enlightened gentry. Internationally, different imperialist countries also needed to be distinguished. Many other distinctions of this sort had to be made. The directive made clear that "our policies are built on these distinctions. The different policies mentioned above are derived from the differences within these class relationships."[23]

With regard to specific policies, the directive also set clear, specific policies on political organization, labor, land, taxation, eliminating traitors, human rights, economics, culture and education, and the military, all according to the strategic principles of the united front.

The final demand of the directive was that "the tactical principles in the above-mentioned united front and the many specific policies stipulated in these principles must be resolutely implemented by the whole Party. The Japanese invaders and the domestic large-scale landlords and upper bourgeoisie will implement high-pressure anti-communist, anti-people's policies and military offensives. During this time, it is only through implementation of the policies mentioned here that we will be able to persist in resisting Japan, develop a united front, gain the sympathy of the people throughout the country, and strive for a better tomorrow."[24]

The formulation of the new democratic theory and the adoption of a series of guidelines and policies for the Anti-Japanese National United Front marked the maturation of Mao Zedong Thought, which combined Marxism with the practical experience of the Chinese revolution. After eighteen turbulent years, Mao finally pointed the Chinese people along a correct path by which victory in the democratic revolution could be gained and a new China built that was suited to China's national conditions.

In his early years, Mao Zedong said, "Ideology is like a flag. Once the flag is set up, it is a signal for everyone to see. Only then can they know the way to go." This flag had to be vivid, clear, and simple, and had to have a connotation that was rich and certain. This would make it easier for more people to understand and accept. The Chinese people began to accept Marxism from around the time of the May 4th Movement. After twenty years of arduous exploration and a very circuitous route, they finally succeeded in combining Marxism with Chinese revolutionary practice. During the War of Resistance Against Japanese Aggression, they were able to raise the banner of the "new democracy," so that more and more people would "understand" and "accept" it. This was a major event in Chinese history. It not only had a major impact during the middle and late stages of the war, but also played a huge guiding role in the future Chinese revolution and construction of the new China.

II

Further Development of the New Democratic Theory

1. The Establishment of the Status of the New Democratic Theory and Development of its Policy

Building around the new democratic theory, the CPC enriched and gradually fleshed out its idea on the path to a revolutionary theory, the construction of the People's Army, the strategy and tactics of a people's war, the strategy of a united front, economic thought, and the direction of cultural work. This demonstrated that from the Party's failure in the Great Revolution to the rise of the Agrarian War, and from the failure of the fifth anti-encirclement campaign to the rise of the War of Resistance Against Japanese Aggression, it had accumulated much rich experience in revolution, especially during the War of Resistance. The Party faced an intricate international situation and domestic environment, appropriately addressing new problems arising in the national and class struggles, and gained much relevant experience in the process. This furthered their understanding of the principles of the Chinese revolution, as Mao pointed out when he said, "In the anti-Japanese period, we have only formulated the general line of the Party and set some specific policies. At this time, we recognized the inevitable kingdom of the Chinese democratic revolution, and thus we have gained our freedom."[25] It is evident that during the War of Resistance, Mao Zedong was already in the process of integrating Marxism-Leninism into the Chinese revolution. The combination of revolutionary practice and the leap to a new stage formed a New Democratic theoretical system. It was multi-faceted and multi-layered in terms of politics, economics, military, culture, and Party building, and now it had a complete form. The new democratic ideas and theories had been tested in practice and taken on the following ideas:

1) It systemically summarized the historical experience of work in the White Area and construction of the rural revolutionary base area, correctly formulated the Party's strategy for struggle in the Japanese occupation zone and KMT-ruled area, and the principles and policies of the economic, political, and cultural construction of the liberated area.

The struggle for encircling cities in the countryside was based on establishing rural revolutionary bases and conducting armed protest as the main form of struggle. Mao wrote, "Focusing on armed struggle does not mean that other forms of struggle can be abandoned. On the contrary, armed struggles cannot be won without support from other forms of struggle. Similarly, focusing on rural work does not mean that urban work can be abandoned while work is conducted in the vast rural areas under enemy control. Rather, there is no division between urban and rural work, for if the rural work becomes isolated, the entire revolution will fail."[26] For this reason, the CPC, under the leadership of Mao Zedong, systematically summed up the experience gained and lessons learned during the Party's work in the White Area since the founding of the CPC. Based on the semi-colonial and semi-feudal characteristics of Chinese society at that time, it creatively formed a suitable set of strategies for the Japanese occupied and KMT-ruled areas. At the same time, it systematically summed up the lessons learned from the construction of the rural revolutionary base areas since the outbreak of the Anti-Japanese War in 1927, and formulated guidelines and policies suited to the actual situation of economic, political, and cultural construction in the liberated areas during the Anti-Japanese War. The implementation of these strategies and guidelines for struggle, both directly and indirectly, alongside the guerrilla war launched by hundreds of thousands of soldiers and civilians behind enemy lines and in the liberated areas truly made the War of Resistance Against Japanese Aggression a national revolution.

2) The systematic summarization of the lessons learned through Party building and the creative launch of the rectification movement brought about a unified understanding throughout the Party that was based on Marxism-Leninism and Mao Zedong Thought.

On the eve of the Anti-Japanese War and the War of Resistance Against Japanese Aggression, the Central Committee of the CPC, under Mao's leadership, systematically summed up the lessons learned regarding the issue of Party building and further strengthened Party building from the ideological perspective. It proposed a summary of the experiences and lessons of the Chinese revolution with the basic principles of an epistemology of dialectical materialism, strengthening Party building along the CPC's ideological lines by linking political threads with Chinese characteristics, such as in the united front and the armed struggle. This led to the launch of the rectification movement, opposing subjectivism, sectarianism, the eight principles of the Party, and a unified understanding throughout the Party based on the combination of Marxism-Leninism and the concrete practice of the Chinese revolution.

3) Mao Zedong Thought was formally confirmed as the guiding ideology of the whole party.

The Seventh National Congress of the CPC was the most important Party Congress during the democratic revolution. That conference summarized the historical experience of the tortuous development of China's democratic revolution over a twenty-year period, formulated the correct program and strategy, overcame erroneous ideas within the Party, and unified the understanding of the entire Party on the basis of Marxism-Leninism and Mao Zedong Thought. It reached an unprecedented level of unity within the Party. That Congress laid the foundation for the victory of the new democratic revolution in China. The new Party constitution adopted at the conference also officially and solemnly stipulated that the CPC, as the symbol of Marxism-Leninism and the practice of the Chinese revolution, was a guide for Mao Zedong Thought and all his work. That is to say, Mao Zedong Thought had by this stage developed and matured as a guiding ideology that was recognized by the entire party. The Party achieved unprecedented unity and solidarity that was founded on Marxism-Leninism and Mao Zedong Thought. Since the Zunyi Conference, throughout the period of the Anti-Japanese War, the Party's thinking gradually unified from the level of loose unity to that of complete reunification, finally coalescing in Mao Zedong Thought, which reflected the objective principles of the Chinese democratic revolution. It was precisely because the whole Party acted in accordance with Mao Zedong Thought – that is, the objective principles of the Chinese democratic revolution – that the Party's ranks were neat and their pace completely in step, so that their strength would equal that of any enemy. In this way, the leaders of hundreds of millions of people were able to persist in the eight-year-long War of Resistance, which brought unprecedented development to the revolutionary forces of the CPC and the people as they cooperated with the anti-fascist wars waged by the people of the Soviet Union and other countries, finally culminating in the defeat of the Japanese aggressors. If we say that all the revolutionary struggles of the Chinese people over the previous century had suffered setbacks and defeats, then we must acknowledge that the War of Resistance Against Japanese Aggression was different, and that the Chinese people finally achieved victory. This was due partly to the more favorable conditions in the international and domestic arenas than had been seen before, and partly to the CPC's correct application of these favorable conditions under the guidance of Mao Zedong Thought, which allowed them to overcome any unfavorable conditions. Mao Zedong Thought led to the great victory in the War of Resistance Against Japanese Aggression and laid a solid foundation for the victory of new democracy in China.

2. The Victory of the New Democratic Revolution and the Expansion of the New Democratic Theory

After the victory of the War of Resistance and the founding of the new China, under the guidance of Mao Zedong Thought, the people of the entire country carried out a fierce, massive scale war of liberation, overthrew the reactionary rule of the Kuomintang, and established the people's democratic dictatorship over the new China, bringing all these endeavors to great success. The transformation of Chinese society from new democracy to socialism ushered in great achievements in socialist transformation and construction, which enabled Mao Zedong Thought to develop further in many areas.

a. Using Revolutionary Force to Defeat Counter-Revolutionary Force

Faced with a complicated situation after the victory in the War of Resistance Against Japanese Aggression, the CPC estimated that the influence of various factors both domestically and internationally would create a situation in which China's social and political reforms could be carried out in a peaceful manner, while at the same time speculating on the possibility that another situation might arise. In other words, it held that after the CPC took the steps to enter peaceful negotiations, the Chiang Kai-shek faction might launch a counter-revolutionary civil war, a natural outcome of that faction's class nature. For this reason, it was made clear that the two arms of the revolution should overcome the two counter-revolutionary arms. This would enable the CPC to seize the opportunity to fight for peaceful, legitimate struggles when the conditions of the first possibility arose, in order to win the support of the masses and the sympathy of the centrists. At the same time, if the second set of conditions arose, the Party would be fully prepared to meet the KMT's military offensive, and there were sufficient reasons to believe the KMT would expose the Chinese people to the crime of destroying peace and launch a counter-revolutionary civil war, which explained why it was necessary for the CPC to overthrow the Chiang Kai-shek government and establish a new China by means of a revolutionary war. The two-handed strategy of the revolutionaries would not only keep the Party clear-headed and with a vigorous, fighting spirit, but would ensure it was prepared to relax the defensive war, being bound by a desire for peace, and make the Party's struggle more flexible and always political. The active position, as much as possible, would fight for the masses in the middle, completely isolating the small reactionary faction led by Chiang Kai-shek and depriving him of an excuse to launch a civil war.

b. The Transition from Strategic Defense to Strategic Offense and the Development of the Ten Military Principles

Given the disparity between the enemy forces and the Chinese People's Liberation Army, how could the latter defeat the attacks of Chiang's troops? How could such an offensive be overcome? The Central Committee of the CPC, headed by Mao Zedong, had clearly addressed the major questions concerning the success or failure of the Chinese revolution. He stated, "We must not only must defeat General Chiang, but we are also able to do so."[27] Thus, the Central Committee correctly formulated and realized a strategic defense plan to defeat Chiang and determined that, after it was successfully launched, at the right time, they would turn to a strategic offense. At the end of December 1947, at a meeting of the Central Committee, Mao noted emphatically that the main force of the PLA had already reached KMT-held areas. This was a turning point in history, the turning point in fact, that prevented Chiang Kai-shek's twenty-year counter-revolutionary rule from developing further and brought it to extinction. It was also the turning point that brought about the eradication of more than one hundred years of imperialist rule in China.[28] In a push to allow the PLA to completely eliminate Chiang's reactionary army and finally gain national victory, Mao systematically proposed the Ten Military Principles of the People's Liberation Army. These principles were proposed during the transition from the strategic defense phase to the strategic offense phase of the People's Liberation War, offering not only a high-level summary of the long-term experience of the PLA, but also the scientific foresight of the war process and its development trend. Using these military principles, the PLA not only shattered Chiang's troops' mad attack on liberated areas, but also triumphantly shifted from strategic defense to a strategic offense, until the time that a decisive strategic battle could be fought.

c. *The Development of the Land Reform Movement and the Consolidation and Expansion of the People's Democratic United Front*

During the nationwide War of Liberation, the Central Committee, under Mao's leadership, launched a land reform movement of unprecedented scale to further consolidate the alliance of workers and peasants. At the same time, based on the alliance of workers and peasants led by the working class, they united and strove for everything that could be won. Not only the national bourgeoisie, but also all the patriots who had been divided by the ruling KMT group, had among them many enlightened gentlemen who had separated from the feudal landlord class. This enabled the people's democratic united front to see unprecedented growth and consolidation, while the Chiang Kai-shek faction had fallen completely into isolation and helplessness. In May 1948, the CPC proposed to convene a political consultation meeting without the reactionaries, at which they would discuss the call for the establishment of a democratic coalition government. This proposal immediately received enthusiastic responses from democratic parties, people's groups, and non-partisan democrats. They sent representatives to the liberated areas and worked with the CPC to prepare for the new government. At the height of the strategic decisive battle of the PLA, the democratic parties announced their agreement with the CPC's industrial, commercial, and land reform policies. The group recognized that the reactionary rule of the KMT was the root cause of the counter-revolutionary civil war and the fundamental obstacle to domestic peace and democracy, further pointing out that American imperialism was the enemy of the Chinese people. They jointly issued a public statement announcing the abandonment of the middle line and accepting the leadership of the CPC. This was a major victory for the CPC in its appropriate handling of relations with the bourgeoisie. In September 1949, the Chinese People's Political Consultative Conference was officially named as the specific organizational form of the Chinese people's democratic united front. Through this meeting, the CPC formulated a common program to unite the people of all democratic classes and peoples across the country into this organization in an effort to complete the great historical task of finally overthrowing the reactionary rule of the KMT and establishing the People's Republic of China. At this point, the people's democratic united front against imperialism, feudalism, and bureaucratic capitalism "developed to the point of establishing a country led by the working class and founded on an alliance of workers and peasants."[29]

d. Reorganizing the Party's Ranks and Strengthening and Improving Party Leadership

Throughout the War of Liberation, the Central Committee, under Mao's leadership, always regarded the issue of Party building as a central link in the success or failure of the revolution and adopted effective measures to do so. On the one hand, the Party movement was carried out and the Party's rural grassroots bodies reorganized. Strengthening the centralized, unified leadership of the Central Committee enabled the Party, government, and leading military organs to achieve a high degree of unity in the implementation of policies and discipline, while also paying attention to perfecting the Party's committee system, carrying forward the democratic traditions within the Party, and carrying out democratic movements within both the Party and the military. In this way, the work of the Party's grassroots organizations and leading organs of the Party at all levels had been strengthened and improved, further consolidating and developing the ideological, political, and organizational unity achieved by the entire Party at the Seventh National Congress. Political unity and unity within the leadership had truly guaranteed the victory of the national revolution.

e. The Party's Strategy for Struggle in KMT-ruled Areas and Policy of Taking and Managing Cities

During the nation-wide War of Liberation, the CPC-led mass struggle in KMT-ruled areas saw unprecedented developments, forming a truly important front behind the lines held by the Chiang Kai-shek faction. Primarily, the opening and development of a second front worked strongly alongside the PLA to shatter Chiang's invasion of liberated areas. This, coupled with the strategic offensive and defensive battles and the strategic pursuit of the PLA, constituted an effective cooperation between the CPC and the people. The PLA protected and took over central cities where the enemy had long been entrenched. This was the continuation of the work guidelines and struggle strategies of the New Democratic theory for the White Area.

f. Theories and Policies on the People's Democratic Dictatorship and the Transition from New Democracy to Socialism

The people's democratic dictatorship was the link between the lowest level and highest level of programs of the CPC and the political condition for the transition from a new democracy to socialism. It was both a regime of a new democratic nature and one that could be smoothly transformed into the dictatorship of the proletariat. This transformation could and should be done under peaceful conditions. There was no need, for instance, for an overthrow of the reactionary regime through violent revolution, as Russia had done in the February Revolution and October Revolution. Because the reactionary power of the KMT had been destroyed by the revolutionary war, the newly established people's democratic dictatorship in China, whether during the period of the new democratic revolution or during the socialist revolution, was the people's regime led by the working class and based on the alliance of workers and peasants. When shifting to the socialist revolution, the workers and peasants would certainly not rise up to overthrow their own power. This was another new development of the Communist Party of China under the leadership of Mao Zedong, based on the fundamental principles of Marxism-Leninism regarding the armed seizure of power. Mao specifically pointed out in his summation of the Party's experience that there was a single focal point, which was that the democratic dictatorship of the people (via the Communist Party) must be united with international revolutionary forces.[30] This was the Party's formula, as well as its main experience and program. It could only rely on the people's democratic dictatorship as a weapon to unite all the people in the country, with the exception only of the reactionaries, and steadily move toward its goal.

CHAPTER 4

The Basic Principles of the New Democratic Revolution

I

The Party's Understanding of Modern China's National Situation

1. The Concepts of "Semi-Colonialism" and "Semi-Feudalism"

In modern China's history, the country found it had become a semi-colonial, semi-feudal society, and this was the defining feature of its national situation. This being the case, it was determined that the revolution had to be carried out in two steps, employing armed struggle in rural areas and encircling the cities. Mao Zedong said, "Only by recognizing the nature of Chinese society can we recognize the objectives, mission, power, and nature of the Chinese revolution, along with its future and transformations." For this reason, "recognizing the nature of Chinese society, which means recognizing its national conditions, is the basic foundation for recognizing all revolutionary issues."[1]

In 1921, one of the major tasks of the CPC was to establish the Party and determine its nature. At this time, Chinese Communism had not yet gained a deep understanding of China's national conditions, particularly its revolution. It was only through analysis of the overall situation of revolution throughout the world after the victory of the October Revolution that the Party came to realize that China's own socialist revolution had to rely on the proletariat as the main force. In the year following the founding of the CPC, through the study and mastery of Marxism and the practice of revolutionary struggle, the Party began to gain a better understanding of the international and domestic situation and the social conditions in China. At the beginning of 1922, the CPC participated in the First Congress of the Comintern and the National Revolutionary Groups of the Far East, hosted by the Comintern, and there accepted Lenin's theory on the issues of national colonies. On June 15, 1922, the Central Committee of the CPC published *The CPC's Proposals on the Current Situation*. This document focused on the analysis of the history and current condition of international imperialism and the Chinese feudal warlords after the 1911 Revolution, pointing out that China was a "semi-feudal state" under the authority of imperialism internationally and feudal warlords and bureaucrats on the domestic front. Based on further analysis of the nature of Chinese society, the Declaration of the Second Congress of the CPC clearly proposed for the first time a democratic revolutionary program against imperialism and feudalism. After the Second National Congress, the CPC continued to explore the nature of Chinese society. In 1923, Chen Duxiu mentioned the concept of "semi-colonialism" in his article "The Chinese National Revolution and Social Classes." He believed that the revolution of semi-colonial countries held the dual significance of an external national revolution and the internal democratic revolution. The independence of the economy and the freedom of internal political affairs were part of the peculiar nature of the national revolution in semi-colonial countries. The Declaration of the Third Congress of the CPC refers to China's democratic revolution as the "national revolution," emphasizing that "semi-colonial China" should focus its work on the national revolution, which was distinct from the bourgeois democratic revolution in European countries. That summer, Mao Zedong also used the term "semi-colonial" in the political papers of "The Beijing Coup and Merchants," pointing out that the semi-colonial political situation in China was a dual form of oppression based on the collusion between the national warlords and foreign imperialism as a means of clamping down on Chinese nationals. The historical mission of the revolution was to use the nation's power to defeat the warlords and foreign imperialism. In 1926, Cai Hesen used the phrase "semi-colonial, semi-feudal China" in "The Historical

Development of the Communist Party of China." It was based very precisely on an accurate understanding of the nature and revolutionary condition of modern Chinese society and the revolutionary united front the fledgling Communists Party of China and Chinese Nationalist Party had formed under the leadership of Sun Yat-sen, launching a vigorous national revolution. However, at this time, the CPC's understanding of the principles of Chinese society and the development of the Chinese revolution was not all undertaken intentionally. In the summer of 1927, the national revolution finally failed. As the representative of the KMT's New Right, Chiang Kai-shek established a new regime in Nanjing.

What sort of political power was represented by Chiang and this regime? Was there a fundamental change in the nature of China's semi-colonial, semi-feudal state? This was the issue the CPC had to resolve first in order to revive the revolution. At that time, there were many different understandings of this issue among the general public. Some said that China was still a feudal society, while others said it had already become a capitalist society, and yet others believed it was a post-capitalist society. Of course, there were also some who believed it remained a semi-colonial society. There were countless different views on the issue in circulation.

The Sixth National Congress of the CPC, held in June and July 1928, analyzed Chinese society's political and economic situation after the failure of the national revolution. It was pointed out at this meeting that, on the one hand, the real reunification of China had not been completed and China had not yet been liberated from the iron grip of imperialism. The Chinese revolution thus remained a semi-colonial revolution. On the other hand, the private ownership system of the landlord class had not been overthrown and the final remnants of semi-feudalism had not yet been eliminated, meaning that the nature of the current stage of the national revolution was that of a bourgeoisie-democratic revolution. In February 1929, the CPC formally provided a comprehensive concept of "semi-colonialism and semi-feudalism" in its own writings. However, shortly after the Sixth National Congress, there was another dispute within the CPC regarding an issue that had already been fundamentally settled. Chen Duxiu and others, accepting Trotsky's misconceptions of China's issues, believed that the failure of the national revolution indicated that the bourgeoisie had won and the feudal remnants had been hit hard. The KMT's Nanjing government was led by the bourgeoisie, leaving political power in its hands. Thus, it was believed, China was already a society dominated by capitalism and would now see peaceful development. The proletariat, then, should move toward socialist revolution after capitalism had become more highly developed, and the legitimate movement could only be carried out with the "national meeting" as its central slogan. This misconception denied that Chinese society was still semi-colonial and semi-feudal, thus denying the necessity of continuing the anti-imperialist, anti-feudal democratic revolution and taking a wrong view that ultimately undermined the revolution. At the same time, some who had taken the lead in the Central Committee of the CPC were influenced by Stalin and the Comintern. They believed that the KMT right-wing rebellion against the revolution represented by Chiang Kai-shek was a rebellion of the entire Chinese bourgeoisie, and that the KMT was already a bourgeois regime. However, while opposing imperialism and feudalism, it was also imperative that the Chinese revolution oppose the bourgeoisie, even the upper levels of the petty bourgeoisie, rather than simply offering arbitrary opposition to capitalism, imperialism, and feudalism in a way that confused certain boundaries of the democratic and socialist revolutions, while the wrong views of the "leftists" led to adventurism. But whether it was the errors of the right or the left, the common feature was that they exaggerated the capitalist elements of Chinese society under KMT rule. They believed that the Chiang Kai-shek regime represented the interests of the bourgeoisie and made mistakes on the fundamental issue of the nature of Chinese society. It is worth noting that they had almost identical misunderstandings of the nature of society, but they came to two very different conclusions regarding the nature of the Chinese revolution. One abolished the national democratic revolution, while the other sought to transcend it. From this, it is evident that a correct understanding of the nature of Chinese society was very important for a revolutionary party.

2. Deepening the Understanding of China's National Conditions and the Debate on the Nature of Chinese Society

Just as the CPC had conducted new explorations on a series of issues such as the nature of Chinese society and of the Chinese revolution, some members of the literati inside the KMT also frequently published articles on the nature of Chinese society. Tao Xisheng was one representative. Writing many articles in 1928 and 1929, he said on some occasions that modern Chinese society was no longer a feudal society under imperialist rule, and that the relationship between the scholar-officials and the peasants during the period before capitalism had fully developed was mainly a socialist social structure. On other occasions, he said that Chinese society was still basically a feudal system, but a late-stage feudal society. In capitalist terms, he viewed it as a pre-capitalist society. The upshot of such vague, contradictory statements regarding the nature of Chinese society was to cause confusion in an effort to oppose the Agrarian Revolution led by the CPC, which was then booming.

It was in this context that the controversy concerning the nature of Chinese society occurred. The debate lasted from the late 1920s to the mid-1930s, a ten-year period. The focus of the debate extended from the nature of Chinese society to its history, and to the nature of Chinese rural society. Under the direct leadership or influence of the CPC, Chinese Marxist theorists and progressive social scientists actively engaged in this huge debate. They analyzed modern Chinese society and the Chinese revolution from Marxist-Leninist standpoints, views, and methodologies. Refuting all sorts of misconceptions, especially the views of Tao Xisheng and the Trotskyists, they preliminarily demonstrated the semi-colonial, semi-feudal nature of Chinese society. They stressed that, in order to understand the nature of the Chinese revolution, it was first necessary to distinguish the economic structure and special nature of Chinese society. The untenable views held by Tao Xisheng and other Trotskyists regarding the nature of Chinese society were obstacles to the Chinese revolution. On the one hand, the aggression of imperialism hit China's rural natural economy hard, causing the Chinese economy to start to develop toward capitalism. On the other hand, imperialism and Chinese feudal forces colluded to exhaust all other forces, hindering the development of the Chinese national capital, and the bankrupting of national industry became a common phenomenon at that time. In China, semi-feudal relations thus continued to hold a comparative advantage. Their arguments were only preliminary, but in the current debate regarding the nature of Chinese society, it basically made clear that Chinese society was still semi-colonial and semi-feudal, the result being that this scientific argument of the CPC spread among the masses through the current debate, having a far-reaching significance.

In December 1939, *The Chinese Revolution and the Chinese Communist Party*, co-authored by Mao Zedong, Zhang Wentian, and Li Weihan, marked the highest achievement of the Party on this front. It documented and analyzed the feudal society that had endured for more than 3,000 years in China, since the days of the Zhou and Qin Dynasties. It stated, "Since the Opium War of 1840, China has gradually become a colonial, semi-colonial, semi-feudal society. In the Japanese occupied area, China still remains a colonial society. In the KMT-ruled area, it is essentially a semi-colonial society. In both the Japanese occupied area and the KMT-ruled areas, it is a society dominated by feudalism or semi-feudalism. This is the current nature of Chinese society. It is the current national situation in China."[2]

It was no accident that modern Chinese society evolved from a complete feudal society into a colonial, semi-colonial, and semi-feudal society. This social change came about through a long, slow, complicated process. Understanding this not only helped develop a deep understanding of the nature of modern Chinese society, but also aided in generating a correct assessment and understanding of the role of foreign capitalism in China over the previous century.

The book *The Chinese Revolution and the Chinese Communist Party* analyzed the evolution of two aspects of modern Chinese society. First was the process of China's evolution from a complete feudal society to a semi-feudal society. The other was its evolution from an independent, sovereign state into a semi-colonial society. These two historical processes took place in the same time and space. The book argued that the main cause of this evolution was the intrusion of foreign capitalism. "The result of the imperialist powers' invasion of China was, on the one hand, to prompt the disintegration of Chinese feudal society and promotion of capitalist factors, turning China from a fully feudalist society to a semi-feudalist society. But at the same time, they ruled China brutally, turning an independent China into a colonial and semi-colonial state."[3]

What role, then, did foreign capitalism play in promoting China's evolution from a complete feudal society to a semi-feudal society? The book argued, "Foreign capitalism has greatly disintegrated China's social economy. On the one hand, it undermines the foundation of China's self-sufficient natural economy and destroys the handicraft industries in the city and the cottage handicraft industries of the peasants. On the other hand, it promotes the development of both the rural and urban commodity economy."[4] Regardless of the destruction of the natural economic foundation, or of China's urban and rural areas, the development of the commodity economy had created conditions for the emergence and development of the Chinese bourgeoisie. However, because the imperialists controlled China's economic lifeline and its politics, China's national capital, which had emerged after the middle of the previous century, was under extremely difficult conditions, preventing it from growing normally. It had always "not become the main form of China's social economy" and had not brought China into a Capitalist society. It was not only marginalized by foreign capital with various privileges, but was also unable to resist the pre-capitalist system of exploitation that still dominated Chinese society. In this way, modern Chinese society had changed its historical direction of development, gradually evolving into "a weak capitalist economy and a serious semi-feudal economy. At the same time, some modern industrial and commercial cities and stagnant rural areas co-exist" as semi-feudal societies.[5]

However, the above changes were just one aspect of the social changes that occurred in modern China. The book went on to say, "The purpose of the imperialist powers' invasion of China was not to turn feudal China into capitalist China. Quite to the contrary, in fact, their goal was to turn it into colonial and semi-colonial China." If the promotion of the development of Chinese capitalism and making China a semi-feudal society was not the original, conscious intention of the imperial powers, it is certain that turning China into their colony and placing it in an arbitrarily demeaning status that ultimately slaughtered the nation was. Marx and Engels pointed out in *The Communist Manifesto*, "The need to continuously expand the market for products and drive the bourgeoisie all around the world must be settled everywhere. This business must be established everywhere, and contacts must be made in every place." With cheap commodities, it could destroy "every single Great Wall." Just as it subordinated rural areas to urban areas, it subordinated uncivilized and semi-open states to countries, subordinated peasant nations to bourgeois nations, and subordinated the East to the West. In order to conquer China, a vast, powerful nation, over the previous century, the imperialist powers had tried their best to take a variety of measures and approaches. *The Chinese Revolution and the Communist Party of China* combined the previous century's history of Sino-foreign relations into a summary of ten modes of imperialist aggression and oppression against China, viewed from the perspective of military, political, economic, cultural, and diplomatic relations, noting that the imperialists had "turned feudal China into a bloody picture of China in a semi-feudal, semi-colonial, and colonial world."[6]

From this we understand that the imperialist powers' invasion of China, on the one hand, prompted the disintegration of China's feudal society, prompting

China to develop certain capitalist features and turning it from a feudal to a semi-feudal society. On the other hand, these powers ruled China cruelly, turning an independent nation into a colonial and semi-colonial nation. Combining these two aspects together, Chinese colonial, semi-colonial, and semi-feudal society developed the following characteristics:

a. *Its natural economic foundation for self-sufficiency in the feudal era was destroyed.* Despite this, the foundation of the feudal exploitation system, the exploitation of the peasants by the landlord class, was not only retained, but was further combined with the exploitation of the comprador and usury capital, which had a clear advantage in China's social and economic life.
b. *National capitalism had developed somewhat, and played a significant role in China's political and cultural life.* Even so, it had not become the main form of China's social economy, and it remained weak and, for the most part, connected to foreign imperialism and domestic feudalism.
c. *The authoritarian regimes of the emperors and nobles were overthrown and replaced by the rule of warlord bureaucrats at the landlord level and the dictatorship of the landlord class and upper bourgeoisie coalition at higher levels.* In enemy occupied territory, Japanese imperialism and its humiliating rule remained in place.
d. *Imperialism not only manipulated China's financial and economic lifeline, but also manipulated China's political and military power.* In enemy-occupied areas, everything was under the monopoly of Japanese imperialism.
e. *Because China was under the rule or semi-rule of many imperialist countries, and because China had long been in a state of disunity, and its land was so vast, China's economic, political, and cultural development were extremely unbalanced.*
f. *Due to the oppression of imperialism and feudalism, especially the massive attacks of the Japanese imperialists, the Chinese people, particularly the peasants, were increasingly impoverished and even bankrupted.* The people were hungry and cold, and they lived without any political rights. The degree of poverty and suffering of the Chinese people at that time reached unprecedented levels.

These were the characteristics of colonial, semi-colonial, and semi-feudal Chinese society. The situation had mostly been determined by the forces of Japanese imperialism and domestic feudalism.

Mao Zedong repeatedly emphasized that only by recognizing the nature of Chinese society could the Party recognize the nature and tasks of the Chinese revolution and distinguish the objectives and motives of the Chinese revolution in order to foresee the future and transformation of the Chinese revolution. In short, it was only by recognizing the social nature of China that the basic laws of social development in modern China could be grasped and the series of basic problems faced by the Chinese revolution be correctly and scientifically solved. From that time on, Mao Zedong repeatedly discussed the semi-colonial, semi-feudal nature of modern Chinese in *New Democracy* and other publications.

II

The "Two Stages" of the Chinese Revolution

1. Initial Understandings and Deficiencies of the Principles of the Chinese Revolution

The concept of the two-stage revolution divided the Chinese revolution into two distinct stages, the democratic revolution and the socialist revolution. Mao stated, "The first step is to change this colonial, semi-colonial, semi-feudal society into an independent democratic society. The second step is to move the revolution forward and build a socialist society."[7] In the course of history, this strategic thinking was elevated to a level of perfection, but only after undergoing an extremely torturous process. In fact, whether this strategic thinking could positively recognize and interpret the situation not only affected the practice of the Chinese revolution, but also directly affected the development of the CPC's revolutionary theory.

After the founding of the CPC, the basic principles of Marxism-Leninism were wielded as a tool to observe the destiny of the country, which initially answered the questions encountered in the course of the Chinese revolution. At the Second Congress of the CPC in July 1922, in its scientific analysis of the international and domestic situations and the nature of Chinese society, the Party concluded that imperialism and feudalism were the main enemies to be confronted at that time. It was imperative, then, to overthrow the rule of imperialism and feudalism if the democratic revolution were to be accomplished and in order for the victory of the socialist revolution to even be possible. According to this line of reasoning, the Congress proposed for the first time in a declaration a thorough anti-imperialist, anti-feudal democratic revolutionary program – namely, by eliminating civil strife, defeating warlords, building domestic peace, overthrowing the oppression of international imperialism and achieving the complete independence of the Chinese nation, and unifying the Chinese headquarters (including the three eastern provinces under its umbrella) to form a true democratic republic. The declaration of the Congress once again reaffirmed the Party's supreme program, as "organize the proletariat, use class struggle, establish the dictatorship of the proletariat, eradicate the private property system, and gradually reach the state of a communist society."[8] Closely related to the formulation of the democratic revolutionary program of the Chinese revolution was the Party's Declaration at the Second Congress of the CPC, which insisted on the notion of a two-step strategy. The Declaration at the Second Congress of the CPC pointed out that the struggle of the proletariat had to be divided into two stages. The first was "to help the democratic revolutionary movement," and the second "to implement the 'dictatorship of the proletariat' among the poor peasants." It stated, "If the proletarian organizations and combat forces are strong, the second step of the struggle can succeed immediately after the victory of the democratic revolution."[9] The Declaration held that the revolution should be divided into two stages, with the proletariat first striving to complete the bourgeois democratic revolution. Compared with the idea of directly engaging in the socialist revolution in China, this was a major step forward and played a role in promoting the Party and encouraging the working class to join the democratic revolution. However, the Declaration failed to clarify the relationship between the democratic and proletarian revolutions. Although the Declaration pointed out that "Workers are under the severe oppression of Chinese and foreign capitalists, so the revolutionary movement will develop itself. The result of this self-development will create the revolutionary leader that will see the world's capitalist imperialists overthrown in China."[10] However, the basic understanding of the Declaration was that the proletariat was merely "assisting" and "helping" the democratic revolutionary movement. Of course, this "assistance" and "help" are "not the proletariat surrendering to the bourgeoisie." It was, rather, "a necessary step to prevent the extension of the feudal system and to develop the true power of the proletariat." The Declaration held that "the democratic revolution has succeeded, the proletariat has gained freedom and rights," and "the childish bourgeoisie will continue its rapid development and clash with the proletariat." At this point, it would be necessary for the proletariat to carry out "the second struggle." Regarding this issue, Chen Duxiu went further in 1923, stating, "The proletariat likewise knows this sort of democracy. The success of the revolution is indeed the victory of the bourgeoisie. However, the naive proletariat has the opportunity only to gain certain freedoms and expand its abilities in this struggle for victory. For this reason, cooperation with the revolutionary bourgeoisie is also the only way for the Chinese proletariat." He continued, "Under normal circumstances, the victory of the national revolution is naturally the victory of the bourgeoisie," and "it is natural for the bourgeoisie to hold political power." What the Declaration was lacking was later developed by Chen Duxiu as The Second Revolutionary Theory, which became the theoretical basis for right-wing error within the Party.

The Fourth National Congress of the CPC, held on January 11–22, 1925, discussed the question of the relationship between the democratic and socialist revolutions – which is to say, the future of the Chinese revolution. The Fourth National Congress stated that the future of the Chinese revolution was a non-capitalist revolution, a point originally included in the draft resolution, but eventually deleted after further discussion. However, compared with the conclusions drawn by the Second National Congress, the Fourth National Congress had deepened its effects toward addressing the question of what two steps needed to be taken. First, it was basically clear that the proletariat must bear the responsibility of leadership in the Chinese revolution. It was pointed out that "China's national revolutionary movement must have the strongest participation of the majority of the proletariat, which must take leadership if victory is to be gained."[11] The second question was whether the bourgeoisie could assume power after the victory of the democratic revolution. These two points were interrelated. Taking them together, the clear conclusion could be drawn that the democratic revolution led by the proletariat was not a capitalist revolution. Yet, the resolution of the Fourth National Congress remained ambiguous. It stated, "Whether the victory of the nationalist revolution can be followed by the proletariat revolution is determined by its passage through the bourgeoisie-democratic system and to what extent the proletariat has prepared during its own national revolution and to what degree the social conditions of the time are fixed. The global political situation at that time will also have a great influence on domestic circumstances."[12] Here, the question of the connection between the victory of the democratic revolution and the proletarian revolution was obviously different from the view of that relationship contained in the "second revolution theory." However, this expression only raised questions about the stage of capitalism between the democratic and socialist revolutions, particularly the question of whether it was necessary to go through a bourgeois democratic system at all, with the proposal that it depended entirely on the circumstances. In other words, it did not rule out the possibility of a capitalist future. At the same time, the Fourth National Congress did not offer concrete answers concerning how to achieve the leadership of the proletariat, and especially how to properly handle the complex issues in the struggle for leadership among the bourgeoisie. Further, the extremely important questions of political power and armed struggle remained, and there was not sufficient knowledge to address them. These weaknesses were gradually manifested in the later development of the revolutionary movement.

Despite the events leading up to and following the Fourth National Congress, some Marxist thinkers within the Party, such as Deng Zhongxia, Zhou Enlai, Li Dazhao, Mao Zedong, Liu Shaoqi, Qu Qiubai, Yun Daiying, Cai Hesen, and Xiao Chunu, had published articles in which, under the guidance of Marxism, they offered criticism from various angles. The right wing of the Kuomintang and Chen Duxiu's erroneous theories analyzed the economic status and political attitudes of various classes of Chinese society, studying the practical issues and characteristics of the Chinese revolution and actively exploring the basic laws of the Chinese revolution. For example, Deng Zhongxia pointed out in his article "Several Important Issues in the Labor Rehabilitation Period," published in May 1925, "The proletariat participates in the national revolution and is not affiliated with the bourgeoisie, but participates in the purposes of its own class. Therefore, we in the national revolution should premise our acts on the interests of our own class." Mao Zedong published two articles in response, "Analysis of Chinese Social Classes" in the October 1925 issue of *Revolution* and "An Analysis of Various Classes of Chinese Peasants and their Attitudes toward the Revolution" in *Chinese Peasants* in January 1926, and in March he published "The Reasons for the Separation of the Kuomintang's Right-Wing and the Future of the Revolution" in *Political Weekly* and "An Analysis of Various Classes of Chinese Society" in *China Youth*. In these articles, based on the Marxist class analysis system, he analyzed the various classes of Chinese society, expounded the tasks, objectives, leadership, motivation, and future of the Chinese revolution, and put forward the basic ideas of the new democratic revolution. However, these correct opinions were not dominant among the Party's leadership at the time. Until the end of 1926, the "second revolution theory" was still the main view espoused by the majority, which meant voluntarily giving up or not striving for the leadership of the proletariat and the Communist Party in the revolution, constituting a right-wing error at the crucial moment of the revolution and ultimately leading to the failure of the first revolution.

2. Strategic Conception of the "Two Step" System

At the end of 1926, the Resolution on China's Situation, adopted by the Seventh Expanded Meeting of the Comintern Executive Committee stated, "Although the current nature of the revolution is, at this stage in history, still that of a bourgeois civil rights movement, it must take on the nature of a wide range of social movements. The Chinese revolution will not necessarily result in a socio-political environment that will promote the development of capitalism. The process of the Chinese revolution is set in an era of the decline of capitalism, which means a complete struggle to eliminate capitalism and build socialism. In part, the structure of the revolutionary state will depend on its class foundation. This revolutionary state will not be a purely bourgeois civil rights state, but will become a civil dictatorship of the proletariat, peasants, and other exploited classes. It will serve as a transition to non-capitalist (socialist) development during the period of the revolutionary anti-imperialist government."[13] It was further declared that "the Communist Party of China has decided to put forth all efforts to achieve the future transition to a revolution for a non-capitalist government."[14] The Comintern had thus highlighted the "non-capitalist future" of the Chinese revolution for the Communist Party of China.

From the end of 1926 to the beginning of 1927, the Politburo of the Central Committee of the CPC discussed the convergence of the two stages of the Chinese revolution and produced an intra-party document entitled "The Interpretation by the Central Politburo of the Resolution on China Passed by the Comintern Seventh Congress." The Politburo of the Central Committee of the CPC accepted the instructions issued by the Executive Committee of the Comintern, reviewed the mistakes of the "second revolutionary theory," and explained the international directions. The Politburo believed that the Central Committee's past understanding of the Chinese revolution "contained a fundamental error," which was "a big gap between the nationalists and proletarians that was 'impossible to transcend by mere human strength.'"[15] If the national and proletarian revolutions were completely separated into two unconnected stages and the old framework employed for the practice of revolution, it would be tantamount to "discarding the national revolution." According to the directives from the Comintern, and based on China's internal and external conditions, "The development of the Chinese revolution surpassed the democratic revolution of the bourgeoisie. The success of the national revolution under the leadership of the proletariat of course does not necessarily lead to the development of a political environment of capitalism, but creates a political environment of non-capitalism (socialism) from one of capitalism… moving toward socialism."[16] Further, the correct approach was to "regard the national and proletarian revolutions as a whole Chinese revolution," and "grasp the link between these two revolutions and join them as a single, solid chain" which was "not subjectively doomed or fated to have a second phase of revolution, or to be preparation for a second revolution."[17]

This interpretation offered by the Politburo officially disavowed the mistake of cutting off the relationship between the democratic and socialist revolutions as espoused by the earlier "second revolutionary theory," organically linking the issue of the leadership of the proletariat to the question of the two revolutionary stages and viewing the national and socialist revolutions as a whole without considering the question of how to generate non-capitalist development. In this, it was correct. However, this interpretation also included the notion that the democratic and socialist revolutions could be accomplished "in one go" without "preparing for a second revolution," which was wrong. This demonstrated that the Central Committee had not yet affirmed the differences and links between the two stages of the Chinese revolution, nor had it yet found the correct path to achieve a non-capitalist future.

The "one revolutionary view" confused the nature and the boundaries between the stages of the democratic and socialist revolutions and attempted to complete the two revolutionary tasks in one step, reflecting an eagerness for leftist tendencies. But at the same time, it contained valuable ideas that were later proven to be true. Specifically, it held that the proletariat must establish the power of the workers and peasants after the democratic revolution and seize the highest form of economic power from the imperialists, warlords, bureaucrats, and compradors, securing power for the proletariat. There would be only one stage in the revolution. The Chinese democratic revolution would not be like the French Revolution, where the bourgeoisie took power. In short, the future of the Chinese revolution was socialism, not capitalism. This indicated theoretical progress for the CPC. However, at that time, the erroneous aspects of the "one revolutionary theory" became increasingly prominent and continued to develop, forming a "leftist" error that simultaneously eliminated the bourgeoisie from the democratic revolutionary stage. After 1927, Qu Qiubai, Li Lisan, and Wang Ming, without exception, made the mistake of adopting the error of the "one revolutionary theory" in their own theories concerning the relationship between the democratic and socialist revolutions. The leading organs of the Central Committee had caused serious harm to the revolutionary cause.

During the Agrarian Revolutionary War, Mao Zedong pointed out in his article "The Struggle in Jinggangshan" the error of believing in the existence of an "inevitable revolution" and the Party's desire to skip the bourgeoisie civil rights revolution. "China is still in the bourgeois civil rights revolution stage of its own revolution," he writes. "The program of China's complete civil rights revolution includes the overthrow of imperialism and complete national liberation, the elimination of the comprador class in the city, the completion of the land revolution, the elimination of rural feudal relations, and the overthrow of the warlord government. We must go through just such a civil rights revolution before we can create a real foundation for the transition to socialism."[18] From there, Mao went on to demonstrate the economy of the policy for the Red region issued by the Second National Workers, Peasants, and Soldiers Congress held in January 1934. He says, "The principle of our economic policy is to carry out all possible and necessary economic construction, concentrate economic power to supply the war, and at the same time strive to improve the lives of the people, consolidate the economic union of workers and peasants, and ensure that the leadership of the proletariat goes to the peasants. Striving for the leadership of the state-owned economy will lead to the development of socialism in the future."[19] But at the same time, most of Mao's thought was triggered by the correct guidance of the Comintern, Marxism-Leninism, and the Chinese revolution. The preliminary results of the combination of concrete, actual circumstances and Mao's concept of the "two stages" of the Chinese revolution were still in their infancy and the early stages of formation.

However, in order to "take the work a step further," it was necessary to "further the great cause of combining the universal truths of Marxism-Leninism with the concrete practice of the Chinese revolution." After the anti-Japanese war came to a stalemate, the CPC's struggle on the ideological front was intense. The KMT diehards advocated that recognizing the Three People's Principles required a rejection of Communism. Though they were dissatisfied with the leadership of the KMT and the unsuitable state of the war efforts, some representatives of the national bourgeoisie still had their doubts about the CPC's proposition and the future of the War of Resistance Against Japanese Aggression. They attempted to find a political path that was in accord with the political views of the KMT and CPC, in hopes of establishing a Euro-American-style bourgeois republic in China. In the CPC and the revolutionary ranks, some people lacked understanding of the theories and policies of the Chinese revolution. For this reason, the task of explaining the Party's views of the Chinese revolution to the entire Party and the people of the whole nation was a serious challenge facing the CPC leadership. Mao's systematic research and exposition on the "two step" Chinese revolution was carried out in-depth under the conditions described above. In Yan'an, Mao did a great deal of theoretical research on this issue, systematically summing up the positive and negative experiences of the Chinese revolution, concentrating on the Party's wisdom, and writing *The Communist Party Reader*, *The Chinese Revolution*, *New Democracy*, and other works. The advent of these works marked the systematic formation of the "two step" strategy of the Chinese revolution.

III

The Nature and Basic Characteristics of the New Democratic Revolution

In order for a colonial or semi-colonial country to attain socialism, it first had to pass through democracy. This was a difficult and complicated proletarian path. Socially, the democratic revolution was bourgeois in nature, so why must a proletarian revolutionary movement take this as a first step in these countries? If after the victory of the proletariat-led democratic revolution, they failed to enter socialism, then what would their future be? If its direct future was not socialism, then why was socialism considered the inevitable direction of the new democratic revolution? These were some of the issues that the new democratic theory had to address and answer. The scientific clarification of these issues constituted the basic principles of the new democracy.

1. The Basic Implications of the Nature of the New Democratic Revolution

The new democratic revolution was a bourgeois democratic revolution in nature, not a proletarian socialist revolution. In *The Chinese Revolution and The Communist Party of China*, Mao Zedong raised the question of what type of revolution it was at that stage. Was it a bourgeois democratic revolution or a proletarian socialist revolution? Obviously, it was the latter, not the former. On the basis of his thorough understanding of the nature of Chinese society, Mao pointed out that because Chinese society was still colonial, semi-colonial, and semi-feudal, and because the main enemies of this revolution were colonialism and feudalism, and because the task of the Chinese revolution was to overthrow the national and bourgeois revolutions of its two main enemies, that meant that in the revolution waged by these two main enemies, even if the bourgeoisie betrayed the revolution and became its enemy, the main revolutionary blade would still not be turned toward capitalism and the domination of private ownership of property, but toward imperialism and feudalism, meaning that the nature of the current Chinese revolution at the time was not proletarian socialism, but bourgeois democracy. However, the current bourgeois democratic revolution in China was no longer the old-style bourgeois democratic revolution, which was outdated, but a new type of special bourgeois democratic revolution. This revolution was developing in China and in all colonial and semi-colonial countries at that time. This type of revolution was called a "new democratic revolution." This new democratic revolution was part of the world's proletarian socialist revolution, and it was resolutely opposed to imperialism and international capitalism. Politically, it was under the leadership of several revolutionary classes for the imperialists and traitors and against the bourgeois dictatorship of Chinese society. Economically, it accepted the large capital enterprises of the imperialists and traitorous reactionaries into the state, distributed the land to the landlord level of peasants, preserved the general private capitalist enterprises, and did not abolish the peasant economy. For this reason, on the one hand, this new type of democratic revolution cleared the way for capitalism, while on the other, it created the preconditions for socialism. The current stage of revolution in China was to end a transitional period between colonialism, semi-colonialism, and semi-feudalism and a socialist society. This was the revolutionary process of a new democracy.

So, when did this process begin? Mao believed it began only after World War I and the Russian October Revolution, and that it began in China with the May 19th Movement of 1919. The so-called new democratic revolution was the anti-imperialist, anti-feudalist revolution of the masses under the leadership of the proletariat. It was necessary for Chinese society to go through this revolution before it could further develop into a socialist society. Without doing so, it would be impossible for development to continue. Mao aptly pointed out that China's new democratic revolution was very different from the historical democratic revolutions in Europe and America. It would not result in the dictatorship of the bourgeoisie, but a dictatorship of the revolutionary classes under the leadership of the proletariat. In the War of Resistance Against Japanese Aggression, the anti-Japanese democratic regime established in the various anti-Japanese bases under the leadership of the CPC was the political power behind the Anti-Japanese National United Front. It was neither a dictatorship of the bourgeoisie nor a dictatorship of the proletariat. It was a dictatorship in which several revolutionary classes united under the leadership of the proletariat. As long as they were in favor of the anti-Japan and pro-democracy camps, regardless of party or faction, they all had a right to participate in the regime. On the other hand, this new democratic revolution was also different from the socialist revolution. It would only overthrow the rule of imperialism and the traitorous reactionaries in China, but not destroy any capitalist elements that could still participate in the anti-imperialist, anti-feudalist movements.

Mao emphasized that this new democratic revolution was basically consistent with Sun Yat-sen's revolution as stated in the Three People's Principles he had advocated in 1924. Sun said in the Declaration of the First National Congress of the Chinese Nationalist Party issued that year, "The so-called civil rights system in countries around the world is often driven by capitalism, and possession of this system, often unique to the bourgeoisie, is a tool suited to oppressing civilians. If the KMT's civil rights are to be shared by the general public, they cannot be the private possession of a minority." He went on, "All enterprises of foreign nationals and foreigners may have an exclusive nature, or may not be able to do so because of the power of private power, such as banks, railways, and routes. The capitalist system cannot manipulate the livelihood of the people, which is the key to controlling capital." Sun also pointed out in his will that "the fundamental principle of internal affairs and diplomacy must arouse the masses and unite people of the world, and I am waiting for them to fight together." All these aspects of the old democracy were adapted to the old international and domestic environment. The Three People's Principles were transformed into a new democratic theory and its new Three People's Principles adapted to the new international and domestic environment. The CPC issued a declaration on September 22, 1937, stating that "The Three People's Principles are necessary for China today, and the Party is ready to fully realize them." The term "struggle" here refers to this sort of Three People's Principles, not some other sort. This type of Three People's Principles were based on Sun Yat-sen's original principles, specifically the Three People's Principles of the Soviet Union, the Communist Party, and the support of agricultural and industrial policies. In the new international and domestic conditions, the Three People's Principles were something of a departure, and were not the revolutionary Three Party's Principles. This would make the Chinese revolution a bourgeoisie democratic revolution, regardless of its struggle (the united front) or its national composition. The status of the proletariat, the peasant class, and other members of the petty bourgeoisie could not be ignored. Who wanted to open China's proletariat? The peasant class and other members of the petty bourgeoisie could not solve the fate of the Chinese nation or any problems in China. The democratic republic in China's current revolution must include workers, peasants, and the urban petty bourgeoisie among its ranks, and a democratic revolution would play a particular role in a particular position. In other words, it would be a democratic republic of a revolutionary coalition of workers, peasants, the urban petty bourgeoisie, and all other anti-imperialist and anti-feudalist elements. The ultimate completion of this republic could only be possible with the leadership of the proletariat.

2. Basic Characteristics of the New Democratic Revolution

On the basis of a thorough understanding of the nature of the new democratic revolution, the Party systematically summed up the basic characteristics of this revolutionary nature and further deepened the understanding of the new democratic revolution.

a. *The New Democratic Revolution as "Part of the Worldwide Proletarian Socialist Revolution" and the "Allied Army of the World Socialist Revolutionary Front."*[20]

In the process of making a thorough, careful analysis of the historical characteristics of the new democracy, the CPC pointed out that as long as it continued to make careful study of the development of China and the rest of the world, it would understand the historical characteristics of the new democracy not just as it had formed since the Opium War, but also its later formation after the first imperialist war and the Russian October Revolution. Mao once again clearly emphasized the nature of China's current society, saying that its colonial, semi-colonial, and semi-feudal nature made it necessary for the Chinese revolution to be divided into two steps, and that the first step was to change the colonial, semi-colonial, and semi-feudal society, making it an independent society, while the second step was to move the revolution forward and make it a socialist society. China's revolution was currently taking the first step.

The preparatory phase for this first step had begun with the Opium War in 1840, when Chinese society first began to change from a feudal society to a colonial, semi-colonial, semi-feudal society. The Taiping Rebellion, the Sino-French War, the Sino-Japanese War, the Reform Movement of 1898, the Revolution of 1911, the May 4th Movement, the Northern Expedition, the Agrarian Revolutionary War, and the on-going War of Resistance Against Japanese Aggression were just many individual steps, spanning about a hundred years. At some point, the first step had been implemented, then the Chinese people had continued to advance that first step to varying degrees, opposing imperialism and feudal forces in order to establish an independent democracy and struggling to complete the first revolution. The Revolution of 1911 launched this revolution in a more thoroughgoing sense. According to its social nature, this revolution was a bourgeois democratic revolution, not a proletarian socialist revolution. Though it had not yet been completed, the revolution had expended a great deal of energy, primarily because the enemy of this revolution remained, even up to this point in time, a very powerful enemy. In reference to this sort of bourgeois democratic revolution, Sun Yat-sen said that "the revolution has not been successful and comrades must still work hard."

However, the Chinese bourgeois democratic revolution had changed since the first imperialist world war broke out in 1914, with the Russian October Revolution of 1917 having now established a socialist country that covered one-sixth of the earth's land. Before this, the Chinese bourgeois democratic revolution belonged to the category of an old-world bourgeois democratic revolution, and thus was an old style of revolution suited to that world. After this, the Chinese bourgeois democratic revolution moved to a new category of a new-style democratic revolution, and on the revolutionary front, it was part of the world proletarian socialist revolution. The most direct cause of this change, as Mao pointed out, was that the first imperialist world war and the first victorious socialist revolution, the October Revolution, had changed the direction of world history and moved history into a new era. In this era, the world capitalist front had collapsed in one corner of the earth (and this corner accounted for one-sixth of the land on the planet), while in the remaining corners, it had fully displayed its decadence. In this era when the remnants of capitalism had to rely on colonialism and semi-colonialism for its survival, socialism had been established and had declared its willingness to fight for all movements for liberation from colonialism and semi-colonialism. During this period, the proletariat in each capitalist country was steadily escaping the influence of the Social Democratic Party of social imperialism, announcing its support for colonial and semi-colonial liberation movements. In this era, if opposing the imperialists, which was to say, if engaged in revolution against the international bourgeois and international capitalism, any colonial or semi-colonial country would no longer belong to the old world bourgeois democratic revolution but to the new category. It was no longer part of the old world revolution of the bourgeoisie and capitalism, but part of the new world revolution, specifically, proletarian socialism. This revolutionary colonial and semi-colonial nation could no longer be regarded as an allied army of the world capitalist counter-revolutionary front, but changed to the allied army of the world socialist revolutionary front.

In the first stage of this colonial and semi-colonial revolution, though the first step was still largely of a bourgeois democratic social nature, there remained an objective requirement for clearing the way for the development of capitalism. It was not an old revolution led by the bourgeoisie to become a capitalist society under a bourgeois dictatorship, but was led by the proletariat, the first phase in the establishment of a new democracy. It was society and the revolution that were needed for establishing a dictatorship of the various revolutionary classes. For this reason, this revolution was precisely for the purpose of clearing the broader path for the development of socialism. In its progress, this sort of revolution was divided into several stages because of the changes in the enemy's situation and in the Allied forces, but its basic nature remained unchanged. This kind of revolution was a complete blow to imperialism, so it was not allowed by imperialism, and was in fact completely opposed by imperialism. By contrast, it was allowed by socialism and was aided by the socialist state and the international proletariat. For this reason, this kind of revolution could not be made a part of the worldwide revolution of the proletarian socialist world. In *New Democracy*, Mao reviewed the proposed process by which "the Chinese revolution is part of the worldwide revolution." He wrote that the proposition "the Chinese revolution is part of the world revolution" was correctly put forward during China's first great revolution from 1924 to 1927. It was proposed by Chinese Communists and was approved by all those who participated in the anti-imperialist and anti-feudal struggle at the time. However, the significance of this theory had not yet been fully asserted, so the people were only vaguely aware of the issue. Mao Zedong said that this "worldwide revolution" was no longer an old-world revolution. The old bourgeois worldwide revolution had long since ended. It was now a new worldwide revolution, a socialist revolution. This was a great change, unparalleled in global history and in Chinese history.

Mao Zedong also spoke in particular about the accuracy of the proposition proposed by the Chinese Communists, saying, "It is based on Stalin's theory." In 1918, in order to commemorate the first anniversary of the October Revolution, *The October Revolution and the Nationalist Issue* was published in which Stalin said, "The worldwide significance of the October Revolution is mainly 1) that it expands the scope of ethnic issues, bringing the struggle against national oppression from Europe to make it a global issue of liberation for all oppressed nations, delivering colonial and semi-colonial countries from imperialism; 2) it has opened up vast concrete possibilities for the liberation, greatly promoting the liberation of countries in both East and West and attracting them to the radical anti-imperialist struggle; and 3) it was thus in the socialist West and enslaved East that a bridge was set up to establish a new revolutionary front against world imperialism from the Western proletariat through the Russian Revolution to the oppressed nations of the East."[21] After this article, Stalin repeatedly played a role in discussing the colonial and semi-colonial revolution from the perspective of the old category and transforming it into a theory of the proletariat socialist revolution. The clearest explanation Stalin offered came in 1925, in an article published on June 30 entitled "Re-examining the National Problem," in which he argued against the Yugoslavian nationalists at that time. Thus, there were two worldwide revolutions, the first belonging to the bourgeoisie and to capitalism. The time for this sort of revolution had long ago passed, being at the end of the first imperialist world war in 1914, and particularly during the time of the October Revolution in Russia in 1917. From then on, the time had come for a second worldwide revolution, the revolution of proletarian socialism, which began with the proletariat of the capitalist state and the oppressed nations of the colonial and semi-colonial allies, regardless of in which oppressed nation, whatever kind of class, party, or individual was involved in the revolution, whether they knew it or not, and regardless of whether or not they understood it subjectively. As long as they opposed imperialism, their revolution would become part of the worldwide proletarian socialist revolution. In the face of the rapid development of the Chinese revolution, Mao Zedong said, "Today, due to the economic and political crisis of capitalism that dragged the world day by day into a Second World War, it is only in the Soviet Union that it has arrived by socialism." In the transitional period, Communism was capable of leading and assisting the proletariat and oppressed nations of the world, resisting the world of imperialism and combating the reaction of capitalism. The proletariat in various capitalist countries was preparing to defeat capitalism and realize socialism. At a time when the Chinese proletariat, peasant class, intellectuals, and other petty bourgeoisie under the leadership of the Communist Party of China had formed a greater independent political force, should it not be assumed that the Chinese revolution's significance to the world was even greater? Mao believed it should be. He held that the Chinese revolution was a great part of the worldwide revolution. The first stage of the Chinese revolution (which was divided into many small stages) was in nature a new-style bourgeois democracy. The doctrine of the revolution was not that of proletarian socialism, but it had early on become part of the worldwide revolution of proletarian socialism, and it had now become a great part of this world revolution and become a great allied force within it. The first step and first stage of the revolution were by no means a capitalist society for the dictatorship of the Chinese bourgeoisie, but a new democratic society with the dictatorship of China's revolutionary classes under the leadership of the proletariat. It must first complete the initial phase, then it would develop to the second stage of building a socialist society in China. This was the most basic feature of the current Chinese revolution. This was the new revolutionary process over the previous twenty years (starting from the May 4th Movement in 1919), and it was the vivid, concrete substance of the Chinese revolution of that time.

b. The Rise of the Proletariat's Leadership in the Chinese Revolution after the May 4th Movement (1919)

Mao Zedong pointed out that before the May 4th Movement in 1919, the political leaders of the bourgeois democratic revolution were the Chinese petty bourgeoisie and the bourgeoisie (meaning, their intellectuals). After the May 4th Movement, although the Chinese national bourgeoisie continued to participate in the revolution, the political leaders of the Chinese national bourgeoisie democratic revolution were no longer a part of the Chinese bourgeoisie, but of the Chinese proletariat. There were two reasons for this. First, the preparatory stage of the Chinese democratic revolution had begun after the Opium War, while the bourgeoisie-led Revolution of 1911 "began the revolution in a more thoroughgoing sense." The Revolution of 1911 overthrew the imperial system, established the Republic of China, and achieved many other notable things. However, it simply drove away an emperor and hung out a signboard reading, "Republic of China," while the nation still remained under the oppression of imperialism and feudalism and the anti-imperialist, anti-feudalist task was left uncompleted. The reason the Chinese bourgeoisie could not accomplish the mission entrusted to it, as the bourgeoisie in Europe and America had historically done – particularly the French bourgeoisie – was mainly that they were "economically and politically weak."[22] This weakness was formed during the process of China becoming a semi-colonial, semi-feudal society. It was "the old problem born of its mother," and it was a weakness that was difficult to overcome. Because of this weakness, they often compromised with the enemies of the revolution. China's national bourgeoisie "even in the revolution remained unwilling to completely split with imperialism, and they were closely related to land rent and exploitation in the countryside, and were even more reluctant to completely overthrow the feudal forces." Further, "in this way, the two basic problems of the Chinese bourgeois democratic revolution, its two basic tasks, could not be resolved."[23] As for China's upper bourgeoisie, represented by the Kuomintang, over the long period from 1927 to 1937, they constantly colluded with the imperialists and feudalists, opposing the People's revolution. In the War of Resistance Against Japanese Aggression, part of this group, represented by Wang Jingwei, publicly surrendered to the Japanese aggressors, "representing a new rebellion by the upper bourgeoisie." In short, "on the one hand, there was the possibility of participating in the revolution, and on the other, the compromise with the revolutionary enemy. These are the two faces of the Chinese upper bourgeoisie."[24] This duplicitousness was the fundamental reason the Chinese bourgeoisie could not lead the Chinese revolution to victory. On the other hand, the development of the revolutionary movement required and always found new leaders. Just as the Chinese bourgeoisie was defeated, the Chinese working class, which had matured, finally entered the stage of China's political struggle after the May 4th Movement. Although the Chinese working class had its weaknesses and shortcomings, it was the most progressive, most promising, and most combative class in Chinese society. Thanks to its organizational discipline, its natural connection with the peasants, and especially its pioneering team, the leadership of the CPC, the Chinese working class, without hesitation had taken the responsibility of leading the Chinese national revolution. Therefore, Mao said, "After the May 4th Movement, although the Chinese national bourgeoisie continued to participate in the revolution, the political leaders of the Chinese bourgeois democratic revolution are no longer a part of the Chinese bourgeoisie, but of the Chinese proletariat."[25] It can be seen that the change in the class of the leadership in the course of China's democratic revolution was the inevitable result of historical development and the choices made by history. Thus, the revolutions before and after the May 4th Movement, though both bourgeois democratic in nature, displayed "important differences." After the May 4th Movement, under the leadership of the Chinese proletariat and its political parties, and under the guidance of Marxism-Leninism, the Chinese democratic revolution quickly took on a new look. It was not only in the breadth and depth of the revolution, but particularly in the completeness and thoroughness of it, which was far different from before the May 4th Movement. Its political, economic, and cultural programs were all very different from the earlier versions. They not only fulfilled the established task of the Chinese bourgeois democratic revolution, but also created the preconditions and conditions for the next socialist revolution. It was in these senses that Mao Zedong called the democratic revolution before the May 4th Movement "the old-style general bourgeois democratic revolution," which was to say, the old democratic revolution. After the May 4th Movement, he termed it "a new-style special bourgeois democratic revolution," or the new democratic revolution.[26] For this reason, we can say that the change in the leadership class was the most important change in the development of China's democratic revolution. The leadership of the proletariat had become the most important feature of the new democratic revolution in China.

c. *The Ultimate Future of the Chinese Revolution Socialism and Communism, not Capitalism*

The question of the future of the Chinese revolution was also a question of the relationship between the Chinese bourgeois democratic and the proletarian socialist revolution and of the relationship between the current and future stages of the revolution. At the National Congress of the CPC held in Yan'an in May 1937, Mao Zedong said in response to questions about the future of the Chinese revolution that the bourgeois democratic and the proletarian socialist revolutions were like "two articles, the first and the next. If the first is done well, the next can be done well too. Resolutely leading the democratic revolution is a condition for winning socialism."[27] He said, "We are the agents of revolution," and "we advocate the transformation of the democratic revolution toward socialism," but that could only be when the time was right. Mao criticized the Trotskyists' "permanent revolution" theory that had caused harm to the Chinese revolution, along with tailism, adventurism, and a tendency toward radical revolution, calling on the Party to recognize the future of the revolution and the tasks at hand, and to work hard at those tasks. He said, "The current efforts aim at the big goals of the future. If you lose sight of this big goal, you will not be a member of the Communist Party. In the same way, anyone who relaxes in the tasks at hand is not a member of the Communist Party."[28] Later, in *The Chinese Revolution and the Chinese Communist Party*, *New Democracy*, and other works, Mao expounded on the ideas mentioned above more comprehensively and systematically, and the relationship between the democratic and socialist revolutions was summed up in an extremely succinct manner, and the question of China's future was given a clear answer.

Mao pointed out that since the Chinese bourgeois democratic revolution at this stage was not an old-style general bourgeois democratic revolution but a new-style special revolution, and because China's revolution was set in the new international environment of the 1930s and 1940s – that is, an environment of rising socialism and declining capitalism – and in the era of World War II and the revolution, then the ultimate future of the Chinese revolution was not capitalism, but socialism and communism. There was no doubt about this. Mao believed that since the current Chinese revolution was to change the status of the current colonial, semi-colonial, and semi-feudal society, which meant it was to complete a new democratic revolution, then after the victory of the revolution the obstacles on the development path would have been eliminated and a considerable degree of development would be attainable in Chinese society. This was not only imaginable, but also not surprising. There would be a considerable degree of development toward capitalism, which was the inevitable result in an economically backward China after the victory of the democratic revolution. But this was only the result of one aspect of the Chinese revolution, not its final result. The overall result of the revolution would be, on the one hand, the development of capitalist factors, and on the other, the development of socialist factors. What were these socialist factors? Mainly, the growth of the proportion of proletarian representation in the Communist Party and in the country's political leadership – that is, peasants, intellectuals, and the urban petty bourgeoisie, who have or may recognize the leadership of the proletariat in the Communist Party, or the Democratic Republic. The state economy and cooperative economy of the working class were likewise factors of socialism. The advantage of the international environment would determine the final result of the Chinese bourgeois democratic revolution, avoiding a future of capitalism and realizing a future of socialism. These were truly great possibilities.

This demonstrated that the relationship between the democratic and socialist revolutions was in fact the relationship between the present and the future. Their differences reflected the particularity of contradictions, while their links reflected the identity of the contradictions. The Chinese revolution was a complex contradiction that contained two such revolutionary stages. Faced with this situation, the CPC had to "recognize the difference between the democratic and socialist revolutions, while at the same time recognizing the connections between the two, in order to correctly lead the Chinese revolution."

In short, as far as the international front was concerned, the new democratic revolution was the allied army of the world's proletarian socialist revolution, not allied with the world's bourgeois revolutions. In terms of revolutionary leadership, the new democratic revolution was led by the proletariat, rather than by the bourgeoisie. In terms of the future of the revolution, the future of the new democratic revolution was socialism, not capitalism. These were the main features of China's new democratic revolution.

CHAPTER 5

The General Direction of the New Democratic Revolution

I

The Formation of the Party's Analytical View of China's Social Class Structure

1. A Correct Analysis of the Tasks of Various Social Classes

After the First National Congress of the CPC, the national and domestic political crises were deepening. The Party concentrated its efforts on launching and leading the workers' movement, and actually carried out the struggle against imperialism and feudalism, leading to rapid development of the revolution. However, there were great differences in social and political views, with an abundance of viewpoints expressed, including calls for a "unification with force," "provincial autonomy," and "good governance." The basic issues of the enemy, the motivation, the mission, and the nature of the revolution still needed to be clarified, all of which had to be based on a correct understanding and analysis of the various classes of Chinese society.

The Party's Declaration of the Second National Congress of the CPC (referred to hereafter as the Declaration) made an initial analysis of the bourgeoisie, the peasantry, the petty bourgeoisie, and the working class. It pointed out that the inexperienced bourgeoisie must rise up against imperialism in order to relieve the economic oppression of the imperialists and the feudal warlords. The peasantry was divided into three groups: wealthy peasant landowners, independent peasants, and tenants and agricultural laborers. The first was the smallest group, with the second and third accounting for about 95% of the peasantry. Oppressed and exploited, they had to rise up to fight, which constituted the "biggest factor" in the revolution. The petty bourgeoisie was numerous, and their lives were hard, with a noticeable rise in unemployment. This class was bound to join the revolution. The working class, "being under the extreme oppression of Chinese and foreign capitalists," would develop its own revolutionary movement and become the "great power" of the revolution, ultimately "leading the revolutionary army" against imperialism and feudalism. Based on the above analysis, the Declaration classified the feudal warlords and imperialists as enemies of the revolution, while the working class, peasants, petty bourgeoisie, and bourgeoisie were classified as revolutionary forces. It clearly proposed the overthrow of the oppression of imperialism, the defeat of the political power of the warlords, and the formulation of revolutionary democratic parties. In this way, during this period defined by political disagreement, the basic issues of the objects, motivation, tasks, and nature of the revolution were clarified for the first time.

At the Third National Congress, the Party passed the significant Resolution of the Third National Congress of the CPC (referred to hereafter as the Resolution), based on the analysis of the economic and political conditions of society and of the peasantry and working class. Focusing on the bourgeoisie and the KMT, it held that 1) the middle class was at odds with imperialism and the warlords. The Resolution divided the bourgeoisie into big businessmen (i.e., chaebols) and the middle class, pointing out the opportunism of the big businessmen and bureaucrats. The middle class was plundered by imperialism, which occupied the market and took away raw materials, nearly cutting off China's "development possibilities" altogether and turning its businesses to "uneven development." The rule of China was by "feudal warlords, not the bourgeoisie," and "the majority of the middle class" was politically oppressed. Therefore, "there must be conflict with international imperialism and the warlords." 2) Pointing out that of China's political parties, only the KMT was a national revolutionary party, it noted the difficulty of building a larger, more revolutionary party than the KMT, given the current situation of all classes of society. 3) The bourgeoisie "tended to feel content with its status quo" and "depended on the imperialist powers or warlords, subject to making compromises and selling out the civilians." The KMT also made the mistake of having illusion about imperialism and warlords, concentrating on military operations and being divorced from the people. The Resolution not only analyzed the revolutionary side of the bourgeoisie and KMT, but also offered initial analysis of its compromises and its non-revolutionary aspects. On this basis, a decision was made to cooperate with the KMT, thus formulating the Party's basic strategic policy regarding the democratic revolution. Although the Revolution was influenced by the Communist International and Chen Duxiu's right-wing thinking that the KMT was the "central power" and "leader" of the revolution and it had come to a wrong understanding of the issue of revolutionary leadership, the Third National Congress of CPC decided on the strategic direction of building a united revolutionary front line, which demonstrated that the Party had made a new leap in its own understanding.

During this stage, Chen Duxiu published three articles, entitled "Theories on Nation Building" (September 1922), "The Bourgeois Revolution and the Revolutionary Bourgeoisie" (April 1923), and "The Chinese National Revolution and the Social Classes." (December 1923). These articles were an important part of the Party's class analysis and understanding of the period. They shared three characteristics in their analysis of various classes of society. The first was that they pointed out that imperialism and the feudal warlords had always been enemies of the revolution. The second characteristic was that the articles divided the bourgeoisie into three groups, the revolutionary bourgeoisie, the counter-revolutionary bourgeoisie, and the non-revolutionary bourgeoisie. It pointed out that the emerging industrial and commercial workers were in favor of the revolution because the development of enterprise was hindered by imperialism and warlords, while the bureaucratic bourgeoisie had attached itself to the warlords and imperialists, and so opposed the revolution. The lives of small industrialists and merchants were uneasy, due to the small scale of their enterprises, and thus they remained neutral toward the revolution. The third characteristic of the three articles was that they analyzed both the advantages and shortcomings of the peasantry and working class. They pointed out that the peasantry accounted for the majority of China's population, and because of the looting of imperialism and the feudal bureaucrats, it was at least possible that they would join the revolution, forming the greatest revolutionary force. Without the participation of the peasantry, the democratic revolution would not succeed. However, the peasantry was scattered, not concentrated, uncultured, and conservative. In particular, self-employed farmers had a strong concept of privacy, and they opposed the landlords. "They cannot transcend the psychology of transferring private ownership of the landlords to their own private rights," Chen wrote. It was for this reason that it would be difficult for the farmers to join the revolution. The working class was "an important element" in the democratic revolution, and "its revolutionary tendency was greater than that of the bourgeoisie," so the small number of workers who had real class and political consciousness were the "bravest vanguard" in the revolution. However, some of the workers' minds continued sluggishly in the patriarchal society. The clans' local views were strong, and they had not left behind their superstitions and theocratic monarchs. Workers who possessed political consciousness were "too few in number." If the working class were merely carrying out a simple economic struggle, it was of "no major significance," as only a political struggle directly against imperialists and warlords would be of great significance. These analyses offered by Chen Duxiu played a positive role in the Party's analysis of the various classes of society.

However, Chen's class analysis had a wrong view of the right. This was mainly manifested in the wavering, compromising, non-revolutionary, and even counter-revolutionary aspects of the new industrial and commercial bourgeoisie. Without proper analysis, the affirmation of the merits and status of the working class was thoroughly inadequate. For this reason, based on the overall estimation, the bourgeois force was erroneously considered to be greater than the proletariat. The working class and peasantry were inferior to the bourgeois revolution, and the leader of the national revolution was not the proletariat, but the bourgeoisie. This resulted in a wrong conclusion of "two revolutions,"[1] and it caused serious fundamental errors in Chen's work, later leading to his rightist opportunism.

From this, it can be seen that the Party had begun to analyze the various classes of society. On the basis of its preliminary understanding of the economic conditions and political attitudes of these various classes, the boundary between the revolutionary objectives and revolutionary power was drawn, and the Party's democratic revolutionary program and strategic direction were set. However, the working class and peasantry had been underestimated, while the bourgeoisie had been overestimated, so the Party was still unclear about the issue of who their allies were, resulting in a right-leaning view on the issue of revolutionary leadership.

2. The Initial Development of the Party's Class Analysis

The establishment of the cooperation between the Kuomintang and the Communist Party of China had pushed the revolution into a new stage of development. In the united front, the class relationship between the proletariat and the bourgeoisie was highlighted. The fundamental problem of this relationship lay in who was leading the revolution. The CPC had yet to develop a correct understanding on this issue. There were, at this point, two erroneous tendencies. The leftist tendency was that the proletarian faction wanted to engage in a Soviet-style proletarian revolution, rather than having to lead a bourgeois revolution. The rightist tendency was to think that the bourgeois democratic revolution should be led by the bourgeoisie. In fact, both recognized that the bourgeoisie was leading the national revolution. In order to correct these two misunderstandings and clarify the leadership position of the proletariat in the democratic revolution, the Party conducted a good deal of class analysis.

On December 26, 1923, and in November 1924, Deng Zhongxia published two articles, entitled "The Situation of the Chinese Workers and Our Movement" and "The Power of the Chinese Working Class," both of which focused on analysis of the working class. The articles pointed out that the emergence and development of modern Chinese industry and the birth and growth of the working class illustrated the historical status of the working class and new modes of production. He first observed "China's proletariat has formed a strong, great team because of the progress of industry over the past thirty or forty years. When turning around, it could launch a 'betrayal' of imperialism and a counterattack on it." The power of the proletariat could then be "proved" and would not be difficult to be "anticipated" in the future, according to Deng, as "it will ultimately be the greatest force of the Chinese revolutionary movement." No one could deny its "leadership status." His second observation was not only to point out the advantages at the level of the workers, but also to point out their shortcomings, while continuing to focus on the revolutionary nature of the working class. Deng noted that the Chinese workers were cheap laborers for foreign capitalists. They worked long hours, "never seeing the sun," receiving low wages as an average income "amounting to mere cents," acting as a "beast of burden" for the sake of others. For this reason, the consciousness of the working class was determined by its oppressed, plundered position. "It would thus be wrong to deny the awakening of its awareness because of its patriarchal and feudal mentality." The third observation came in the form of a summary of the experiences and failures of the February 7th general strike and its full affirmation of the historical role of the working class. Deng pointed out that after the February 7th strike failed, it had been said that "the masses of workers have the status of the main force both in the democratic revolution and in the socialist revolution." For this reason, he said, "we should be extremely optimistic." He criticized some people who were overly skeptical about the power of the working class, pointing out that, simply because of a minor setback, they thought this path unreasonable and another preferable, but that the latter would never succeed.

Through his analysis of the proletariat, Deng Zhongxia clearly put forward the issue of the proletariat's leadership of the revolution, saying, "The leader of China's future socialist revolution is of the proletariat, and they are also the leader of the current national revolution." He added, "Only with the leadership of the proletariat can there be a national revolution."

In December 1924, Peng Shuzhi published an article entitled "Who is the Leader of the National Revolution?" In it, he divided the bourgeoisie into three parts – the bank bourgeoisie, the commercial bourgeoisie, and the industrial bourgeoisie. He said that the bank bourgeoisie was "by necessity counter-revolutionary." Within the commercial bourgeoisie, the comprador class was "against the revolution's fascists," and the local bourgeoisie was devastated by the various oppressions of the imperialists and warlords. They needed a revolution, but "there is no possibility of them leading other classes." The industrial bourgeoisie was in great conflict with the interests of the imperialists, and its development was hindered by the warlords. "They need the revolution," but "their economic foundation is weak," and "they lack power." For this reason, "there are many counter-revolutionaries among China's bourgeoisie. Revolution is already a difficult task for the bourgeoisie, so hoping that they will lead the national revolution would amount to daydreaming." The article went on to analyze the working class and peasants, pointing out that the working class was directly oppressed and exploited by imperialism and the warlords. Because it was more severely oppressed than any other class, its understanding of the imperialists and warlords was clearer and deeper than theirs. This was simply an objective condition and root cause for the working class to be able to shoulder the leadership of the Chinese national revolution. "The Chinese working class is naturally the leader of the national revolution." The peasantry would likewise be revolutionary, but it could only be led by other classes. The article held that the leader of the revolution was the proletariat, not the bourgeoisie. This was accurate, as the working class was naturally in a position of leadership in the revolution, and the bourgeoisie was naturally incapable of providing revolutionary leadership. This, then, abolished the struggle for leadership between the proletariat and bourgeoisie, relaxing the vigilance on the bourgeoisie's fight for revolutionary leadership and believing that everything was settled. The "natural theory" on the issue of leadership was thus mistaken.

In December 1924, Chen Duxiu also published an article entitled "Lessons from the National Movement Over the Past 27 Years." In it, he stated that the proletariat was the most uncompromising revolutionary class. It was the main force not only in the social revolution, or the national revolution, but was also its "supervisor."

The articles written by Deng Zhongxia, Peng Shuzhi, Chen Duxiu, and others showed that the CPC had numerous people carrying out class analysis. Moreover, their articles had one thing in common, which was the clear suggestion that the leader of the democratic revolution was not the bourgeoisie, but the proletariat, providing a broad ideological basis for the Party's confirmation of the "leadership of the proletariat" at the Fourth National Congress.

In January 1925, the Fourth National Congress passed the Resolution on the National Revolutionary Movement. Through the analysis of various social classes, the key issue of the leadership of the proletariat was clearly stated for the first time in a Party resolution. This clarified the issue of revolutionary leadership that had been left unresolved at the Second and Third National Congresses, and the Party's errors at the Third National Congress were corrected.

At this stage of development, through analysis of all classes of society, the Party had clarified the question of who was leading the revolution. This marked another major development of the CPC on the basis of clarifying the objectives and motivation of the revolution, thus indicating the initial formation of the CPC's basic thinking concerning the new democratic revolution. However, at this time, the Party had not analyzed the peasant issue as the central issue of the revolution. At the same time, there was still no correct understanding of the bourgeoisie. In the beginning, the entire bourgeoisie was considered revolutionary. Now, at this stage, the bourgeoisie was considered incapable of revolution. For instance, Deng Zhongxia's article argued that "the bourgeoisie cannot engage in revolution," and Peng Shuzhi's article argued that the bourgeoisie should be encouraged to participate in the revolution. The Resolution of the Fourth National Congress considered the bourgeoisie incapable of participating in the revolution, demonstrating that the Party had not yet gained a correct understanding regarding the issue of revolutionary allies.

3. The Party's Analysis of Social Classes Enters a Mature Stage

After the Fourth National Congress of the CPC, the revolution developed rapidly and the peasants movements in Hunan and Guangdong gained prominence, creating an air of excitement. However, after the death of Sun Yat-sen, the KMT split and the rightists began to plot to seize control of the revolution. All of this urged the Party to clarify who its allies were and bring the spirit of the Fourth National Congress into the Party's leadership by implementing proletarian leadership of the revolution. With this, the Party's analysis of all classes of society had entered a relatively complete, scientific stage of development.

From February to June of 1925, Qu Qiubai published three articles, "The Servants and the Chinese Civilian under Imperialism," "The May 4th Memorial and the National Revolutionary Movement," and "The May 30th Massacre of Imperialism and China's National Revolution." In these articles, he further clarified the issue of the necessity of proletarian leadership in the democratic revolution and addressed the implementation of the Resolution of the Fourth National Congress of the CPC.

In May 1925, Deng Zhongxia convened the Second National Labor Conference and published an article entitled "Several Important Issues in the Renaissance of the Labor Movement." In January 1926, at the reception held by the All-China Federation of Trade Unions to welcome the representatives of the Second National Congress of the Kuomintang, Deng offered a "speech" and a "response." Deng's article and speech raised the issue of "the combined worker and peasant class," expounding on the leadership position of the proletariat. He pointed out that peasants were the "natural allies of the workers." The "first" ally of the working class in the leadership of the national revolution was the peasantry. If the proletariat did not unite with the peasants, it would be impossible for them to obtain a leadership position in the revolution.

In December 1925, Li Dazhao published the article "Land and Peasants," which analyzed the many reasons why farmers were oppressed and exploited, pointing out that peasants and workers must unite to defeat the rule of imperialism and the warlord government.

These articles by Qu Qiubai, Deng Zhongxia, Li Dazhao, and others showed that, while the Party persisted in the notion of proletarian leadership, it only had a preliminary understanding of a basic issue of the centrality of the peasants to the task of realizing proletarian leadership. This issue involved the Party's recognition of its allies, which marked a new starting point in their understanding. In March 1926, Mao Zedong's article "An Analysis of the Various Classes of Chinese Society" developed this understanding to a new level. The main features of the article were:

1) The bourgeoisie was clearly divided into the comprador and middle classes, clarifying the vague concepts and viewpoints of the past. The article listed the comprador class alongside the warlords, bureaucrat, and landlord classes as representatives of the most reactionary and backward production relations, which were connected to imperialism and hindered the development of Chinese society's productive forces. It was clear that the comprador class was an irresistibly extreme counter-revolutionary class. This article made clear for the first time that the middle class was the national bourgeoisie, and that it was economically independent, but weak, while politically it swayed between contradictory positions. This was so vivid that anyone who examined this class would find it neither completely revolutionary nor completely counter-revolutionary, but rather wavering between the workers and peasants and the imperialists and warlords. It was an unreliable ally to the revolutionaries, and in any dealings with them, extreme caution was always necessary.

2) An extremely nuanced analysis of the petty bourgeoisie was offered in the article. It pointed out that the petty bourgeoisie included self-employed farmers, artisans, minor intellectuals, and small businessmen. The petty

bourgeoisie was divided into three groups, and a profound, vivid analysis of the characteristics of the "small" and "private" economic status of each group was offered, including items like the living conditions and political attitudes of each. It stated, "This class, because of both its numbers and its class nature, deserves great attention." This large revolutionary lower, private class was the greatest ally of the proletariat, and it must be united in leading the revolution.

3) The article made an unprecedented scientific analysis of the peasantry. It classified the semi-self-employed, poor peasants, small handicraft workers, clerks, and hawkers as semi-proletariats. It also offered a deep analysis of the economic status and political attitudes of the semi-agricultural farmers and poor farmers. It pointed out, "The so-called peasant problem is mainly the problem of the poor peasants and semi-self-employed farmers." This was because they then made up the largest sector of the population in the countryside. When considering the peasant problems, it was necessary to first consider their problems. They were a class exploited by the landlord class's feudal rent and usury. The main objective, therefore, was to make them the main force against the feudal forces in the countryside, encouraging their revolutionary spirit to become even greater than that of the farmers. It was easy for them to take revolutionary propaganda on board, especially for poor farmers. They were the group most fundamental to the realization of the proletarian revolution. Mao's analysis of the semi-self-employed farmers and poor peasants pointed out that they were the closest allies of the revolution, and were in fact central to the Party's consideration of peasant issues, especially the semi-self-employed farmers. Mao's keen observation and scientific analysis of the peasant problem was a prominent manifestation of his combination of Marxism-Leninism and the reality of the Chinese revolution.

With the issues of the bourgeoisie, petty bourgeoisie, and peasantry clarified, the question of revolutionary allies could be seen at a glance. This was another new contribution made after the Second National Congress and the clarification offered by the Fourth National Congress distinguishing groups of revolutionary enemies and revolutionary leaders.

During the Agrarian Revolutionary War, when faced with the more complex situation of class struggle, the CPC, represented by Mao Zedong, further distinguished Chinese society's class relations. In October 1933, Mao formulated a relatively scientific standard for the five classes of landlords, wealthy peasants, middle class peasants, poor peasants, and workers (including peasant farmers) in the document "How to Analyze Rural Classes." After arriving in Northern Shaanxi, the CPC summed up the lessons of history and made a more systematic analysis of class relations in Chinese society. In the article "The Chinese Revolution and the Communist Party of China," Mao Zedong offered a comprehensive analysis of various groups within the petty bourgeoisie, peasant class, proletariat, and nomads outside the landlord class, capital class, and peasantry. The purpose of these scientific analyses was for the formulation of Party lines, guidelines, policies, and strategies, providing a scientific basis for the development of the Party's analysis of Chinese society's classes to a new scientific level.

II

General Direction of the New Democratic Revolution

1. The Party's Understanding of and Conclusions Regarding the General Direction of the New Democratic Revolution

The "general line" of the new democratic revolution was a phrase used by the CPC to refer to a concentrated summary of the strategic objectives, main tasks, and means of achieving those goals and tasks at a particular historical stage – in other words, the general direction to be taken in the revolution. It embodied the Party's ideas and served as the basic principles for the Party's actions. It was a holistic approach that set the direction, goals, and channels for the Party's overall work. For this reason, the "general line" was the lifeline of the Party, playing the important role of unifying the entire Party's thought and action and uniting the people of all ethnicities. The formulation of the Party's general direction was based on the characteristics of the times and its tasks at various stages, and was thus an important tool for the CPC, under the leadership of Mao Zedong, to lead the revolution.

The general direction and general policy of the CPC during the stage of the democratic revolution was stated thus: "The revolution must be led by the proletariat and the masses against imperialism, feudalism, and bureaucratic capitalism." This general direction had undergone long-term theoretical exploration. The continuous practice of revolutionary struggle had been basically formulated up until the War Against Japanese Aggression, and was finally completed after further supplementation and development during the War of Liberation. It should be said that the process of forming the Party's general direction for the democratic revolution was the process by which the Party gained understanding of the three elements of the general direction of the revolution – revolutionary leadership, revolutionary power, and the revolutionary objective. It was built upon the CPC's knowledge of China's national conditions and Marxism-Leninism, a rare understanding that combined theory and practice, which wound its way through a circuitous route until it finally achieved national victory.

During the Party's founding period and the period of national revolution, the CPC made preliminary explorations of the basic issues facing the modern Chinese national democratic revolution and had formed a basic idea of the new democratic revolution. During the Agrarian Revolutionary War, the Party continued to explore the fundamental issue of what kind of revolution the Chinese revolution would be. It made significant progress, enriching theory concerning the path to revolution with the "encircling the cities with armed forces," the foundation for its new democratic revolutionary theory. During the War of Resistance Against Japanese Aggression, based on the systematic summary of the experiences and lessons learned since the founding of the Party, the CPC had comprehensively summarized and expanded the theory on the new democratic revolution. In many works from this period, Mao Zedong offered profound analysis of the basic issues of the international and domestic environment of the Chinese revolution and the nature of Chinese society. Based on this, Mao offered a comprehensive exposition on the historical characteristics of the new democratic revolution and the development principles of the Chinese revolution. The new democratic theory, program, and direction were a set of principles and policies by which the revolution completely and creatively addressed a series of major issues, such as the question of what type of revolution the Chinese revolution would be.

In "The Chinese Revolution and the Communist Party of China," Mao offered a comprehensive, profound discussion of the objectives, tasks, nature, and future of the new democratic revolution from the combination of theory and practice, stating clearly, "The so-called new democratic revolution is the anti-imperialist, anti-feudal revolution of the masses under the leadership of the proletariat."[2] This was the initial expression of the general direction of the new democratic revolution. After the victory in the War of Resistance Against Japanese Aggression, domestic class conflicts arose as the main conflict. A correct understanding of the nature and economic foundation of Chiang Kai-shek's regime became an urgent issue that the Party had to address. After making profound analysis of the nature of its political power and its economic foundation, Mao explicitly called the huge capital accumulated by "the four influential families" represented by Chiang Kai-shek relying on the state power as "bureaucratic capital," with the class that mastered bureaucratic capital being called the "bureaucratic bourgeoisie." Since bureaucratic capital relied on compradors, feudalists, and monopolies, "besides eliminating the privileges enjoyed by imperialists in China, the revolutionary task of the new democracy is to eliminate the exploitation and oppression by the landlord class and the bureaucratic bourgeoisie (upper bourgeoisie)." In April 1948, Mao explicitly listed bureaucratic capitalism as an object of the Chinese revolution, alongside imperialism and feudalism, in his "Speech at the Jincui Cadres' Conference," saying, "The new democratic revolution is not like any other revolution, and can only and must be led by the proletariat and the masses as a revolution against imperialism, feudalism, and bureaucratic capitalism."[3] This was the general direction and policy at that stage of the CPC's history. This general direction correctly addressed the basic issues of the leadership, power, objectives, tasks, nature, and future of the revolution, enriching and developing Marxist-Leninist revolutionary theory.

Why did the CPC lead the people to carry out the anti-imperialist, anti-feudal democratic revolution? What was the fundamental purpose of the CPC-led new democratic revolution? Answering these questions answered important questions such as what kind of revolution the Chinese revolution was to be. As the vanguard of the Chinese working class, the CPC generated China's advanced productive forces. The new democratic revolution, led by the CPC, aimed to change the feudal production relations of the comprador class and the decaying political superstructure to fundamentally liberate the bound productive forces. Mao had engaged in numerous brilliant discussions regarding these issues.

When Mao spoke at the work conference held by the Central Publicity

Department of the Communist Party of China in March 1944, he emphasized to the cadres that there must be a correct understanding of the revolution. He pointed out that many comrades were right to put politics and the military as top priorities, because if they did not manage to destroy the enemy, there was nothing else to talk about. However, it was also important not to forget that the purpose of politics and the military was to liberate and develop productive forces. Mao said that the power of politics and the military was to overthrow the forces that hindered the development of productive forces, with the aim of liberating productive forces and developing the economy. The economy was the foundation of politics and the military, while politics and the military were superstructures. The foundation was the economy, and the fundamental aim was to develop the economy. The reason politics and the military were placed as first priority was that, without them, productivity would not be liberated, making it impossible to address any other issue.[4] Here, Mao Zedong made profound analysis of the relationship between politics, the military, and the economy, and he clarified the fundamental purpose of the CPC-led new democratic revolution.

In April 1945, Mao clearly stated in the political report of the Seventh National Congress of the CPC that the fundamental criterion for judging the quality of a political party was the standard of productivity. He said, "The role and scale of the policies and practices of all political parties in China and among the Chinese people depend, in the final analysis, on whether they help the development of the Chinese people's productive forces and on the amount of help they offer. We can see it as the liberation of productive forces. The elimination of Japanese aggressors, the implementation of land reforms, the liberation of the peasants, the development of modern industry, and the establishment of a new China that is independent, free, democratic, unified, and prosperous can only be achieved through the liberation of China's productive forces. This will be greatly welcome to the Chinese people."[5] In December 1947, Mao developed an even clearer understanding of the issue of "The current situation and our mission" in the liberation of productive forces. He said that the most fundamental task of the new democratic revolution was to "change the feudal production relations of the comprador class and liberate the bound forces of production." In short, during the period of the new democratic revolution, the CPC's understanding of the relationship between politics, the military, and the economy, the purpose of the revolution, and the criteria for judging the quality of the Party were correct. In semi-colonial, semi-feudal China, it was only by carrying out the new democratic revolution and overthrowing the rule of imperialism and feudalism that the bound productive forces could be fundamentally liberated and developed. Throughout the period of the new democratic revolution, armed with just such a concept, the CPC embodied and practiced the requirements of advanced productive forces.

2. The Objective of the New Democratic Revolution

Victory in the revolution depended on having a correct direction and strategy. The basis for the general direction lay in a clear understanding of the national conditions, and the basis of the strategy was distinguishing between friends and foes. The latter was the primary issue facing the Chinese revolution. Who was the target of the revolution? This was determined by the nature, characteristics, and major social conflicts of modern Chinese society. Since modern China was a semi-colonial, semi-feudal society, and because the main conflicts in this society were between the imperialists and the people of China and between feudalism and the Chinese masses, the object of the revolution was naturally imperialism and feudalism, along with bureaucratic capitalism.

Mao Zedong raised the question of who the friends and enemies of the revolution were. It was not easy to distinguish between friends and enemies. Thirty years of Chinese revolution had brought little success, but it was not a problem of goals, only an error in strategy. This so-called strategic mistake was that it was impossible to unite true friends to attack one's enemies if it was unclear who was enemy and who was friend. After the Opium War, the Chinese people's struggle against imperialism and feudalism had never been interrupted. The fundamental reason for the repeated failures of these struggles was not a lack of scientific and theoretical guidance, nor was there any failing in the mobilization of the masses, particularly among the workers and the peasants. The problem was the failure to identify the friends and enemies of the revolution and formulate appropriate strategies.

Though the Taiping Heavenly Kingdom had the two characteristics of being both anti-feudal and anti-aggression, it failed to substantiate them from a theoretical perspective, and so, in practice, it was ultimately trapped in the quagmire of feudalism. The slogans and actions of the Boxer Rebellion, such has "helping the Qing Dynasty to eliminate foreign aggressors," showed that the peasants did not recognize the relationship between the feudalists and foreign aggressors. The bourgeois reformists attempted to rely on the feudal emperors to promote reform and restructuring, relying on British and American imperialists to aid and support those reforms, indicating that the reformists lacked a proper understanding of the nature of feudalism and Western powers. The 1911 Revolution overthrew the Qing government, but the fruits of the revolution finally fell into the hands of Yuan Shikai. The bourgeois revolutionaries did not explicitly oppose the imperialist program, nor did they completely oppose the feudalist program. Rather, they often used warlords to oppose warlords, and thus could not point the Chinese people to the appropriate object of the struggle.

After the founding of the Party, based on its understanding of the situation in Chinese society, the Second National Congress of the CPC clearly stated for the first time that the Party's most basic program was against imperialism and against the rule of the feudal warlords, carrying out a democratic revolution and addressing the problem of the revolutionary object, which had not previously been clarified. This pointed the way for the Chinese revolution. The Second National Congress proposed a thorough anti-imperialist, anti-feudal program and clarified the object of the revolution, marking a valuable first step for the CPC in the course of localizing Marxism in China.

a. *Imperialism as the primary target of the modern Chinese national democratic revolution*

Why was imperialism the primary target of the Chinese revolution? First, it was because imperialism directly hindered Chinese economic development and political progress. Modern China was bullied by all the world's major imperialist countries. Several powerful countries had tried to monopolize China, leaving it humiliated, damaged, and slaughtered. The purpose of the imperial powers in invading China was not to turn feudal China into capitalist China, but to turn China into a colonial and semi-colonial country. Although China did not perish under imperialism, and was in fact still semi-independent, it was actually ruled by imperialism.

Second, imperialism and Chinese feudalism together oppressed Chinese people. This was due to the inevitable fact that imperialism of a backward country always maintains power over the backward country, refusing to remove that power and changing the less developed country to facilitate the aggression and oppression. In the first seven decades of modern China, under the rule of the Qing Dynasty, the imperialists turned the Qing court into a taming tool for their own use. After the Qing Dynasty was destroyed, they supported warlord bureaucrats who represented the interests of the landlord class and the bureaucratic capitalists. The feudal forces and their superstructures were able to survive because of imperialism. Finally, the Chinese people opposed imperialism in order to eliminate the backing of the Chinese feudal system and complete the democratic revolution. In modern China, imperialism and feudalism were interdependent and closely connected. The imperialists used Chinese feudal forces to bully and oppress China, and the feudal forces were backed by the imperialists. Therefore, China's political arena was often subject to reactionary warlords and politicians, while the imperialist powers were always behind the scenes. In these circumstances, the Chinese people could only rid themselves of the shackles of the feudal system by carrying out the national revolution against imperialism, allowing the democratic revolution to be completed.

Opposing imperialism and striving for the independence of the Chinese nation was the fundamental premise for tackling the "salvation" and "development" of modern China, and it was the primary task of the revolution. It was certainly not an easy task to defeat imperialist forces that had already imposed their rule on China's backward society. But the experience of history proved that only by doing so could China's tragic fate be changed. That is to say, only by striving for the liberation of the nation and the independence of the nation could there be any discussion of the political, economic, and cultural construction of modernization.

Opposing imperialism remained a long-term task that ran through the entire process of the new democratic revolution. However, because of the different situations at each stage and the main target of the struggle, the main opposition to imperialism was different. The different forms of imperialist aggression and oppression of China at various stages likewise made the Chinese people's opposition to imperialism different. When the imperialists launched a war of aggression against China, the Chinese people's opposition to imperialism took the form of a national war, such as the War of Resistance Against Japanese Aggression. When the imperialists invaded China without the use of arms, including through political, economic, or cultural means, the domestic feudal army and reactionary politicians often formed alliances with the imperialists to oppress the people. In these cases, the Chinese revolution generally took the form of civil war to oppose the alliance between the imperialists and the feudalists, and to simultaneously engage the feudal forces indirectly while engaging the imperialists forces directly, such as in the national revolution, the Agrarian Revolutionary War, and the War of Liberation.

b. Feudalism as a major object of the modern Chinese national democratic revolution

Feudalism was another major target of the Chinese revolution because the exploitative feudal system was the main pillar of imperialism in China and the social foundation of the feudal warlords for implementing authoritarian rule. Although feudalism was the main cause of modern China's economic modernization and political democratization, it was an obstacle to the way forward for the Chinese nation.

In modern China, the landlord class controlled the grassroots political power of the vast rural areas and served as the bureaucracy of all levels of government. Many bureaucrats went to the countryside to purchase land and became landlords after seeking out the people's wealth. By supporting and fostering feudal reactionary regimes, the imperialists gained the greatest benefit in China, while feudal reactionary regimes relied on the landlord class to achieve national rule. This was true of both the Beiyang Warlords and the Kuomintang New Army.

In modern Chinese economic life, the feudal economy took the dominant position. The exploitative feudal system was premised on the landowners' possession of land, the exploitation of the peasants' surplus labor supply and even the necessary labor supply. In the old China, landlords and rich peasants accounted for less than 10% of the rural population and 70% to 80% of the land ownership, while poor peasants, farmers, middle peasants, and other workers accounted for more than 90% of the rural population and just 20% to 30% of the land ownership. The feudal landlord class collected high land rents by renting the land to farmers. This land rent exploitation not only encroached on the peasants' total surplus labor, but also encroached on a large part of their necessary labor. In addition to cruel land rent and exploitation, farmers were also exploited by commercial and usury capital, and were crushed by the reactionary government at all levels. This situation made China's productivity level extremely low and the people's quality of living extremely poor. Therefore, in order to realize China's economic modernization and political democratization, it was necessary to oppose feudalism. To do so, it was basically necessary to eliminate the exploitative feudal system economically, with the landlord's land tenure being the main focal point. To politically overthrow the imperialist's agents in China and the concentrated representatives of the landlord's comprador force, feudalism. The authoritarian rule of the warlords created conditions for the liberation of productive forces and the promotion of China's economic modernization and political democratization.

As with the opposition to imperialism, the opposition to feudalism also ran through the beginnings of the new democratic revolution, but employing different specific content and forms at different times. During the Great Revolution, the people opposed the rule of the Northern Warlords. The Party instigated the peasants to fight the local tyrants and divide up their fields. After its defeat in the Great Revolution, the Party raised the banner of the agrarian revolution and launched the Agrarian Revolutionary War, thus truly touching on the core substantive issues of feudalism, abolishing the feudal landlord class land ownership. During the War of Resistance Against Japanese Aggression, in accordance with the changes in major domestic conflicts and the need for a united front, the Party promptly changed the land policy of the confiscation of the landlord class to a policy of reducing rents and interest rates. After the War of Liberation, the Party implemented a land system that abolished feudal and semi-feudal exploitation, implemented a land system with arable land, and eventually overthrew the superstructure of Chinese feudalism and achieved a decisive victory against feudalism.

In short, the modern Chinese revolution had the dual character of anti-imperialism and anti-feudalism. These two aspects were inter-related. If the rule of the feudal landlords was not overthrown, the rule of the feudal landlord class could not be eliminated. Conversely, if the rule of the feudal landlord class was not eliminated and the foundation of imperialism not rooted out, the peasants could not be mobilized to form a powerful force for the Chinese revolution against the rule of imperialism. For this reason, though the two basic tasks of the national revolution and the democratic revolution were different from each other, they were linked.

c. Bureaucratic capitalism as the object of China's New Democratic revolution

In modern times, the development of Chinese capitalism emerged in two parts that were quite different, yet related. One was bureaucratic capitalism, and the other national capitalism. Correspondingly, modern China's bourgeoisie was divided into two groups, the bureaucratic bourgeoisie (known as the upper bourgeoisie or comprador class) and the national bourgeoisie (known as the middle bourgeoisie or the middle class). Bureaucratic capitalism and the bureaucratic bourgeoisie were the objects of the new democratic revolution. National capitalism had always been protected in the process of the new democratic revolution, and the national bourgeoisie had been one of the driving forces of that revolution. From this, it was evident that the Chinese new democratic revolution was not always against capitalism and the bourgeoisie. Rather, it allowed and encouraged the development of national capitalism, only opposing bureaucratic capitalism. The two parts of modern Chinese capitalism and the bourgeoisie were entirely a result of imperialist aggression against China and were unique to semi-colonial and semi-feudal societies.

The opposition to bureaucratic capitalism was not because it was capitalism, but because it was a combination of Chinese feudal landlord class and old-style wealthy peasants, and because it was a form of feudal state monopoly capitalism developed by state power. This sort of state monopoly capitalism was not developed on the basis of liberal capitalism, but was caused by the political representatives of the big landlords, which was a result of super-economic plunder. It had all the characteristics of a comprador, feudal, state monopoly. It was the economic basis of Chiang Kai-shek's reactionary regime and an important factor hindering the development of social productivity in modern China. Therefore, the confiscation of bureaucratic capital and the elimination of the bureaucratic bourgeoisie became one of the focal points of the new democratic revolution.

3. The Leadership of the New Democratic Revolution

The key issue in the new democratic revolution was the question of the leadership of the proletariat. Whether the leadership was in the hands of the bourgeoisie or the proletariat was the fundamental distinction between the old and new democratic revolutions and the touchstone for measuring the correctness of the

Party line. The right wanted to give up leadership, while the left was lacking it. But whether right or left, there was an error in leadership, so the issue was an important one, relating to the future of the revolution and determining its success or failure.

Generally speaking, it was necessary for the bourgeois democratic revolution to be dominated by the bourgeoisie and for the bourgeoisie to take responsibility in leading the revolution. However, the Chinese revolution took place in the environment of a unique era, and it was carried out amidst a special set of circumstances. Deciding who would lead the revolution was a new issue facing the people.

Judging from historical facts, the leadership of the Chinese revolution underwent a process of transformation. Since the emergence and development of national capitalism in China in the 1870s, representatives of the bourgeoisie had indeed set off a wave of revolution and led a great struggle of far-reaching significance, including the Revolution of 1911. At that time, the proletariat was small in number and politically immature. It had not yet formed as an independent class, so only bourgeois followers participated in the revolution. This situation changed with the May 4th Movement, during which the working class showed great political enthusiasm and maturity. This played an important role in allowing the proletariat to begin to enter China's political arena as an independent class. After the birth of the Communist Party of China, the leadership of the Chinese revolution gradually shifted from the hands of the bourgeoisie to the hands of the proletariat.

From the perspective of an ideological understanding, there was also a development process by which the issue of the leadership in the Chinese revolution was clarified. In articles published between 1923 and 1924, Qu Qiubai and Deng Zhongxia emphasized that the proletariat should occupy a dominant position in the current national revolution and must increasingly gain the leadership position in the revolution. The Resolution of the Fourth National Congress of the CPC also raised the issue of the leadership of the proletariat in the democratic revolution. However, the practice over the few years that followed showed that the CPC's understanding of revolutionary leadership had not been resolved. In 1925, when Mao Zedong analyzed the various classes of Chinese society, he proposed that the proletariat was thought of as the revolutionary leadership class. By the autumn of 1927, Mao had developed firmer ideas about the proletariat's leadership of the Chinese revolution. In 1930, while discussing the theory of the new democratic revolution, his theoretical exposition on the proletarian leadership of the revolution became an important part of his work.

The Chinese bourgeois democratic revolution could not be led by the bourgeoisie, because the changes of the times and China's national conditions had determined that the Chinese bourgeoisie was not able to take up this leadership role. China's bourgeoisie was completely different from its counterpart in the West, which did not have to complete the anti-feudal revolution. This unique trait determined the attitude of the bourgeoisie as unstable and irresolute, and even in the revolution, it was not willing to separate itself completely from imperialism, and it likewise remained closely linked to land rent and exploitation in the countryside. Therefore, the bourgeoisie was unwilling and unable to completely overthrow feudal forces. In this way, the two basic problems of the Chinese bourgeois democratic revolution and the two basic tasks would not be achieved by the Chinese bourgeoisie. This had been proven by the Reform Movement of 1888 and the Revolution of 1911. Objectively speaking, the Chinese revolution required a new leadership class and a new path. The Chinese proletariat had adapted to the requirements of history and the call of the times to become the leading class in the Chinese revolution.

The Chinese proletariat could shoulder the heavy responsibility of leading the Chinese revolution, mainly because of its own unique traits. The Chinese proletariat was relatively small compared to the peasantry, was younger than the proletariat in capitalist countries, and had a lower cultural level than the bourgeoisie. It also had an ideology of many small workers. Yet despite all this, it remained the representative of China's advanced productive forces. It was the most progressive, most promising, and most combative class. It had the basic advantage of the general proletariat, which was that it was associated with advanced economic forms and was rich in areas such as organization and discipline.

In addition to the advantages of the proletariat all around the world, the Chinese proletariat had many unique advantages as a class for revolutionary leadership. First, it was deeply oppressed by imperialism, feudalism, and capitalism. The severity and cruelty of their oppression was rare among the world's nations. For this reason, not only was the entire class the most revolutionary, but it was also more determined and thorough than any other class in the revolutionary struggle. Second, although China's working class was small in numbers, it was highly concentrated in large cities and large enterprises. They were easily organized and easily formed into powerful forces, and their situation was conducive to the widespread dissemination of Marxism. Finally, most of the industrial workers in China came from bankrupt farmers, giving them a natural connection with the much larger peasantry, which facilitated the formation of a solid alliance with the peasant class. These special advantages of the Chinese proletariat determined that it was the only class suited to revolutionary leadership. Without the leadership of the proletariat and its Communist Party of China, the Chinese revolution could not succeed, as already evidenced by the entire history of the Chinese revolution.

Recognizing that the proletariat should lead and was capable of leading the Chinese revolution did not mean that the issue of leadership had been resolved. Leadership did not fall naturally into the hands of the proletariat, but had to be vigorously pursued. For this reason, the CPC, represented by Mao Zedong, gradually formulated a set of policies and strategies for striving for and mastering revolutionary leadership in the long-term revolutionary practice. These were:

1) The establishment of a broad revolutionary united front based on an alliance of workers and peasants was the key to realizing the leadership of the proletariat. Mao Zedong once stated, "The Chinese proletariat should understand that although they themselves are the most conscious and organized class, they cannot win if they rely on the power of their own class. To win, they must form alliances in different situations with a variety of revolutionary classes and organize the revolution's united front."[6] Without a united revolutionary front, in fact, there would be no leadership of the proletariat. This united front must be based on the alliance of workers and peasants because "the proletariat is the most thoroughly revolutionary democratic class" and "the peasants are the greatest revolutionary democratic class."[7] The peasantry, which accounted for about 80% of the country's total population, was the basic force determining the success or failure of the Chinese revolution. For this reason, the key to realizing the leadership of the proletarian revolution lay in uniting the peasants and forming a solid alliance of workers and peasants.

2) When establishing a united front with the bourgeoisie, the principles of independence, unity, and struggle were the basis for the strategy for maintaining the leadership of the proletariat. Although the bourgeoisie

could not lead the Chinese revolution to victory due to its own political and economic weakness, that did not mean it would automatically give up leadership. They not only exerted great influence on the petty bourgeoisie and peasants, but also exerted great influence on the proletariat and the CPC, and even strove to turn the proletariat and the CPC into the bourgeoisie. The tailing factions of its political parties sought to attribute the fruits of the revolution to a group of bourgeois parties. Therefore, when the proletariat and its political parties established a united front with the bourgeoisie, they had to maintain a clear mind, adhere to the principle of independence and implement a flexible strategy of unity and struggle. Only in this way could they maintain the united front with the bourgeoisie without losing sight of the leadership of the proletariat.

3) The establishment of a strong revolutionary armed force was a strong pillar to guarantee the leadership of the proletariat. In a semi-colonial, semi-feudal China that lacked independence and democratic freedom, the main form of revolutionary struggle was to wage war, and the main form of revolutionary organization was the army. "Guns will bring power," so without a strong revolutionary armed force, the proletariat and CPC would have no status at all, not to speak of the leadership of the proletariat. Therefore, if the proletariat wanted to maintain its leadership in the democratic revolution, it must establish a strong revolutionary armed force.

4) Strengthening the efforts to build the proletarian party was the fundamental guarantee for realizing the leadership of the proletariat. The leadership of the proletariat in the Chinese revolution was achieved through its party, the Communist Party of China, which was essentially the leadership of the CPC. The CPC was the initiator and organizer of the proletarian revolutionary cause. Only under the leadership of the CPC could the proletariat complete its historic mission and realize its cause of human liberation. As the political representative of the proletariat, the CPC relied mainly on the correct program, direction, and policy, relying on the vanguard and exemplary role of the Party members and appropriate relationships with established allies, and depending also on the development of the Communist Party. The unity of thought, the strictness of discipline, and other conditions led to the achievement and guarantee of their own political leadership. To this end, it was necessary for

the CPC to comprehensively strengthen its own ideological, political, and organizational structure.

4. The Driving Force of the New Democratic Revolution

The driving force behind the new democratic revolution in the general line of the new democratic revolution was "the masses," which included the proletariat, the peasantry, the urban petty bourgeoisie, and the national bourgeoisie.

Most importantly, the proletariat was not only the most basic driving force behind the Chinese revolution, but also its leading force. This point has already been analyzed in great detail in the earlier discussion of the new democratic revolution.

The peasant class was not only the main driving force of the Chinese revolution, but also formed the main body of "the masses." Peasants accounted for about 80% of the country's total population, meaning that four out of five people in China were peasants. The so-called "masses," then, were mainly made up of peasants, so it followed that the main message of the revolution was an anti-feudal one. The most fundamental task was to eliminate the land ownership of the feudal landlords, and the main force that would accomplish this was the peasantry, the very class most oppressed under the feudal system. Therefore, the issue of the peasantry was "the basic theme of the Chinese revolution, and the power of the peasantry was the main force behind it." The Chinese revolution was characterized by armed revolution against armed counter-revolutionaries. The peasantry was the main source of manpower for the Chinese army, and the soldiers were simply peasants in military uniforms. To this end, Mao Zedong pointed out in his speech to the security forces of Northern Shaanxi in 1936 that whoever won over China's peasants would win the revolution. How should the peasant revolution be led? Mao said that the first step was to liberate the peasants, using the Agrarian Revolution as the central platform of the democratic revolution, and to completely eliminate the land ownership of the feudal landlords and implement the policy of "the cultivator having his own field." The second step was to educate the peasantry in Marxist theory, arming them with its advanced elements and inspiring them to recognize and overcome their own weaknesses. The Chinese revolution relied mainly on the power of two classes, workers and peasants.

The Chinese peasantry included wealthy peasants, middle peasants, and poor peasants. The wealthy peasant, making up about 5% of the rural population, were rural bourgeoisie with semi-feudal tendencies, though many remained neutral in the Agrarian Revolution against the landlords. The middle peasants, accounting for about 20% of the rural population, were economically self-sufficient, had no political power, could participate in the anti-imperialist, anti-feudal struggle, and could accept socialism. They could become a reliable ally of the proletariat and an important part of revolutionary dynamics. Poor peasants, along with farm laborers, made up about 70% of the rural population. They were a semi-proletariat group in the countryside, the most powerful force in the Chinese revolution, and the most natural, reliable ally of the proletariat. Although the Chinese peasantry was divided into three groups, it was mainly the poor peasants and middle peasants who were referred to as the main force of the Chinese revolution. It was only when the proletariat formed a coalition with the poor and middle peasants that victory would be achieved in the revolution.

Further, the petty bourgeoisie was one of the basic driving forces of the Chinese revolution. During the period of the new democratic revolution, the petty bourgeoisie included not only peasants, but also intellectuals, small businessmen, craftsmen, and other self-sufficient professionals. Their status was similar to that of the middle peasantry. They were increasingly oppressed by the imperialists, feudalists, and upper bourgeoisie. Therefore, the petty bourgeoisie was one of the driving forces of the Chinese revolution and a reliable ally of the proletariat. Among them, intellectuals and young students often played the role of pioneers and bridges within the Chinese revolution. In particular, the vast number of poor intellectuals could join and support the revolution alongside the workers and peasants. "The widespread dissemination and acceptance of Marxism-Leninism in China occurs first and foremost among intellectuals and young students. The construction of the revolutionary forces and of revolutionary undertakings cannot succeed without the participation of intellectuals."[8] Some of them were susceptible to the influence of the bourgeoisie, often subjectively and with an individualist impulse, so it was important to carry out the work of revolutionary propaganda and organization among them.

Finally, the national bourgeoisie was one of the driving forces of the Chinese revolution. The Chinese national bourgeoisie emerged in the 1870s, later than the Chinese proletariat. There were two main sources for the people making up this class. The first was the landlords, bureaucrats, and businessmen of modern enterprises in whom the government invested directly. The second group was made up of those transformed from manual workshop owner, who now used machines. Therefore, the Chinese bourgeoisie could be divided into upper and lower strata. The upper stratum owned large-scale enterprises and possessed relatively strong economic power. It had close ties to foreign capitalism and domestic feudalism. They had few conflicts, and often had a dual status as both official and businessman. The middle and lower strata usually owned smaller enterprises, and assets. Their ties with foreign capitalism and domestic feudalism were less, and their conflict greater.

In general, the Chinese national bourgeoisie was a two-strata class that possessed revolutionary hopes, yet also tended to vacillate. On the one hand, they were oppressed by the imperialists, shackled by feudalism, and caught in the conflicts with the imperialists and feudalists, and thus had a certain anti-feudal revolutionary nature and was thereby one of the driving forces of the revolution. On the other hand, they were economically and politically weak, and they could not completely cut their economic ties to imperialism and feudalism. They lacked courage to completely oppose feudalism and imperialism, and were thus easily shaken and compromised during the revolution.

The two sides of the Chinese national bourgeoisie were not the cowardly psychology of the primitive accumulation of capital nor the new problems that existed when workers' and peasants' risings threatened their own interests, but rather "the old problems they had been weaned on."[9] The two sides of the national bourgeoisie were not sometimes present and sometimes not, but rather, they were innate and inevitable. In the period of revolutionary dominance, they compromised with the enemy, were brought along reluctantly to the anti-imperialist and anti-feudalist program, and made early demands for the democratic nature of the Chinese revolution, though they lacked any real understanding of the issue. After the failure of the Great Revolution, the CPC's understanding of the nature of the revolution had been in a state of chaos. The Sixth National Congress of the CPC made an accurate assessment of the nature of the Chinese revolution, but leftist opportunism crept in, leading to the error of confusing the democratic and socialist revolutions. Through a combination of theory and practice, the CPC gained an accurate understanding of the nature of the revolution and offered a scientific interpretation, which culminated in Mao Zedong's *The Chinese Revolution and the Communist Party of China* and *New Democracy*.

Tied to the nature of the revolution was the question of its future. Generally speaking, the future of the bourgeois democratic revolution was to establish a capitalist system and a bourgeois dictatorship, but this was not the future of the Chinese revolution. The Chinese revolution no longer took the development of capitalism as its ultimate goal, but must instead follow the path of a new-style democratic revolution. Under the leadership of the proletariat, the people's democratic dictatorship would achieve the goal of socialism through the new democratic revolution. The question of the future of the new democratic revolution was actually a question of how to deal with the relationship between the democratic and socialist revolutions. To this end, Mao Zedong proposed the idea of a "two step" Chinese revolution, stating that the Chinese revolution had to be divided into first the change of social form from a semi-colonial, semi-feudal state to a new independent democratic state, and then to engage in a revolution to build a socialist society. He wrote, "The entire Chinese revolutionary movement led by the CPC is an overall revolutionary movement that includes two stages, a democratic revolution and a socialist revolution. This revolutionary process involves two different natures, and both are necessary if we are to complete the process."[10]

Strictly distinguishing the nature of the democratic revolution from that of the socialist revolution was not meant to separate the links between the two. The relationship between the two revolutions was like that between the first and second parts of an article. Only if the first part was well written could the second part be well done. In a nutshell, "The democratic revolution is a necessary preparation for the socialist revolution. The ultimate goal of the entire CPC is to strive for the final realization of a socialist and communist society." There were two types of wrong tendencies in the CPC's internal struggle. One was to completely separate the two closely related stages of the Chinese revolution, only noting the differences between the two. Failing to see the connections between the two resulted in the period of bourgeois dictatorship and the development of capitalism. The other tendency was to advocate that the democratic and socialist revolutions "accomplished the same work," attempting to collapse the two stages into one. Taking things too far in this direction confused the line between the democratic and socialist revolutions. These two erroneous tendencies were contrary to the laws governing the development of the Chinese revolution. For this reason, Mao Zedong drew the profound conclusion that only by recognizing the distinction between the new democratic revolution and the socialist revolution, while at the same time recognizing the connection between them, could the Chinese revolution be led correctly.

Chapter 6

China's Revolutionary Path Theory

I

The Impact of the City-centered Theory on the Communist Party of China

1. The Origin of the City-centered Theory

After its failure in the Great Revolution, the CPC established the armed resistance against the Kuomintang's reactionary rule, but how were they to go about winning this armed struggle? What path should the revolution take? This was another question the Party faced, much like the earlier question of who would lead the revolution. Establishing the understanding that armed struggle was the main form of the Chinese revolutionary struggle was historic progress for the Party. However, for a period of time, the Party fell into some misunderstandings regarding the theory of the centrality of cities in the course of its exploration of the revolutionary road.

In the Soviet Union, the violent proletarian revolution was achieved by directly arming the working class and organizing an uprising in the urban centers to gain a victory for the revolution. Having developed Marxism in the process of leading the Russian Revolution, Lenin suggested that the proletariat must take the city as its center. Lenin believed that only the proletariat, which was concentrated in urban centers, could completely demolish the bourgeoisie. "The city must lead the countryside, and the countryside must follow the city," according to Lenin. For this reason, it was thought that seizing political power in urban centers was of strategic significance for seizing national political power. At the same time, Lenin pointed out that once the proletariat launched an uprising, it must continue a bold, brave attack. The basic principles of Marxism-Leninism were undoubtedly correct, but the revolution of each country had its own unique characteristics. Therefore, when the Comintern guided the Chinese revolution according to the Soviet model and the Chinese Communists gave their blessing to the Comintern directive, they shifted toward a "leftist" dogmatic line to guide the Chinese revolution.

After the October Revolution in Russia, the city-centered theory was introduced into China alongside Marxism. After the Second National Congress in 1922, the CPC joined the Comintern and became its Chinese branch, which resulted in the theories and policies of the international party having a profound impact on the formulation of the CPC's major policies. During the Great Revolution, the Central Committee of the CPC took the city-centered path, in accordance with the directive of the Comintern. At that time, because the first cooperation between the KMT and the CPC had been achieved, the revolutionary KMT had not only had a unified revolutionary base in Guangdong, but also had a national revolutionary army of tens of thousands of people. Further, the revolutionary goals of the Northern Warlords was divided, lacking a unifying force or a central government. This led to a great victory for the Northern Expedition, which was jointly led by the KMT and the CPC, demonstrating that the path used in that expedition to capture the urban centers was fundamentally correct. This was determined by the special historic conditions of that time. After the failure of the Great Revolution, China's political situation had undergone a drastic change. The Party's former allies had become vicious enemies, and they had established a unified government and a powerful army, while occupying the urban centers and opposing Communist Party members and revolutionaries and exercising a policy of bloody slaughter among the masses. Under these circumstances, the foreign experience of the centrality of the city to the revolution was obviously not suitable for China's national conditions. Mao Zedong later said, "If the revolutionary team is not willing to compromise with the imperialists and their lackeys, it must persist in its struggle. If the revolutionary team is to prepare to save the nation and exercise its own strengths, it must not waste powerful forces on invincible enemies, but must rather fight for a decisive outcome. This requires a change of direction." In other words, it was necessary to leave the urban centers and go to the mountains and countryside, where they would re-establish a solid base "and launch an attack on our fierce enemy in the countryside rather than the city and, in the long run, emerge victorious through the arduous revolutionary struggle."[1] This change in the revolutionary path was not only allowed under the tenets of Marxism, but was also the most essential need and truest expression of it. However, at that time, a lack of understanding of Marxist theory and Chinese revolutionary practice prevented the CPC from escaping the influence of the city-centered theory, so it continued to take the city as central to the revolutionary struggle. In this way, the influence of the city-centered theory became a prominent obstacle encountered by the CPC in its exploration of this new path for the Chinese revolution during the Agrarian Revolutionary War.

2. The Impact of the City-centered Theory on the Chinese Revolution

The impact of the city-centered theory on the CPC was divided into several stages. The first was from the August 7th session of the Central Committee of the CPC in 1927 through the Sixth National Congress of the CPC in June 1928. During this phase, the impact of the theory of the centrality of cities was mainly manifested in two ways.

The first manifestation was seen in the several uprisings led by the CPC Central Committee before and after the August 7th Meeting, all of which sought to use rioting as the catalyst by which to launch the revolution. For instance, during the autumn harvest in Hunan, the CPC and the Hunan Provincial Party Committee advocated the Changsha riot as the starting point for the revolution. In a letter to the Central Committee, the Hunan Provincial Party Committee pointed out, "The Changsha riots and autumn harvest riots are the same thing. The Changsha riots were the starting point for the autumn harvest riots."[2] The Central government also believed that this was true "in principle." Another example was the Guangzhou Uprising. The Central Committee believed that it was "the beginning of all the riots in Guangdong and a signal of the nationwide workers' and peasants' riots to come."[3] In this way, the Central Committee's idea of taking cities as the starting points for riots was fully reflected in the uprisings after the failure of the Great Revolution. Since October 1927, in the directives of the provincial committees in Hunan, Hubei, Chongqing, Guangdong, and Fujian, it was also proposed that guerrilla warfare and general agrarian revolutions should be launched, creating an "independent separatist situation" and "establishing a peasant revolution." However, this was not an indication that the Central Committee had abandoned the idea of the centrality of the cities. On the contrary, the Central Committee still advocated the notion that "a rioting city can become the center and guide for spontaneous peasant riots." Under the guidance of such thinking, the Central Committee demanded that in Hunan, "the overall arrangement of riots should be centered in Changsha." In a letter to the Guangdong Provincial Party Committee, the Central Committee pointed out that the Chinese revolution had in fact formed a special means of "censoring peasant separatists," but the development of such separatists "must be obtained" in the larger cities in various regions so that the leadership of the proletariat could be seen "on the surface." This demonstrated that the urban-centered thinking had not changed, regardless of what changes the Central Committee had made in connection with the specific form of rioting and a measure of attention placed on rural separatism.

This situation in the Central Committee was mainly the result of the influence of the Comintern. On February 25, 1928, the Ninth Expanded Meeting of the Executive Committee of the Comintern issued its Decision on the China Issue, which emphasized that the Chinese revolution should continue to follow the path of making cities the center of its activity, while criticizing the rural guerrilla war being led by the Central Committee of the CPC. The Decision pointed out that rural riots must be "the starting point for national riots" at the peak of the urban riots, and that the Party's main task was to prepare cities and villages across several provinces and regions. In order to coordinate with this mobilization, it was necessary to not merely launch armed uprising and guerrilla warfare in rural areas while failing to treat urban areas as the center of the revolution. To do so would inevitably lead to the failure of the guerrilla wars. It was further suggested that "we must oppose the infatuation with guerrilla warfare, which will only lead to failure, as it is indiscriminate and disjointed."[4] This was an obvious attempt to guide the Chinese revolution according to the model provided by the Russian revolution with the city as the center. Such subjectivism, which was out of sync with the situation on the ground in China, had a serious impact on the Chinese revolution.

The second stage was from the Sixth National Congress through the Third Plenary Session of the Sixth Congress of the Central Committee in September 1930. During this phase, the Central Committee emphasized that the focus of the Party's work should be placed on urban centers and that it should be aware of the risk of "leftists" as urban uprisings and attacks in big cities were organized.

The Sixth National Congress of the CPC, held in June and July 1928, continued to refer to the city-centered theory of the Comintern as a guide for the Chinese revolution. In a report from the Comintern, Nikola Ivanovic Bukharin's representative did not recognize the guerrilla warfare led by the CPC as a means of accumulating and developing revolutionary forces. Starting from the real situation in China, a positive exploration of a new path for the Chinese revolution, it criticized the CPC's armed uprisings in some places and establishment of revolutionary base areas, calling it "emphasizing the peasants and paying less attention to the workers." In his conclusions presented to the General Assembly, he also proposed that the Chinese Red Army was "an unproductive mass" that simply sought to demolish. He stated that it was best for the Red Army to "be distributed in various places," sending guerrillas everywhere, and play the role of a peasant self-defense force. After the Sixth National Congress of the CPC, the Comintern expressed its concern that the CPC had no longer served as a "peasant party" in rural area. They believed that the Party's work was centered in the city and that only workers' movements could reflect the leadership of the proletarian party. However, with rural areas as the center, there were a large number of peasant Party members, and instead of becoming a proletarian party, they were becoming a peasant party. In fact, it emphasized the requirement that the CPC must follow the city-centered path. On October 26, 1929, the Comintern Executive Committee gave the Central Committee of the CPC the Letter on the Kuomintang Reorganization and the Task of the Communist Party of China, stressing that the CPC should adopt a policy of "concern about all the forces, aiming to develop political strikes and prepare for the general political strike. By October 1930, although the Comintern recognized the imbalance between the Chinese workers' and peasants' movements, it continued to emphasize to the CPC that "the establishment of the Soviet government means that the CPC intends to hold an armed uprising in the largest industrial center." This was based on the model typical of the October Revolution to guide the specific actions of the Communist Party of China.

On April 28, 1928, when the Politburo of the Central Committee of the CPC discussed the February Resolution sent by the Comintern, either in response to criticism from the international party or in an effort to express loyalty to the international path, many people spoke in support of the international directive. They believed that since the August 7th Meeting, the CPC had underestimated the strength of the urban working class, bringing negative results and the abandonment of urban work. "This is not right," they asserted. They held that the lack of the workers' movement suggested "the leadership of a peasant consciousness," which needed to be guarded against. Based on this discussion, on the 30th, the Politburo of the Central Committee issued the Notice on the Resolution of the Comintern, stating that the failure of the armed uprising in rural areas was "a result of the lack of urban leadership and a lack of proper cooperation and communication." It further criticized the Hunan and Hubei Provincial Party Committees for the Autumn Harvest Riots, stating that since the riots they had "subjectively only called for rural riots, not urban riots" and were "sinking into" guerrilla warfare. In addition, it called upon local Party departments to "restore urban workers' leadership of the countryside," emphasizing that "the city is the leader of the countryside."

With the above-mentioned guiding spirit, after the Sixth National Congress of the CPC, the city-centered theory continued to have a deep influence on the CPC. This was evident in the following ways:

1) *Emphasis that the Party's work should be focused on urban centers.* The Central Committee of the CPC held that after the failure of the Great Revolution, many party organizations were transferred back to the countryside, and it was the resulting peasant consciousness that put the CPC "in danger of departing from the proletariat." In order to guarantee the nature of the Party and create its proletarian foundation, the Central Committee of the CPC suggested the appointment of industrial regions and important cities as "centers of work." Because "the city is the center of the entire political economy, it can lead the countryside. When we get the cities and villages, we can proceed quickly... changing the general spirit of our work from a

simple village mentality to an urban mentality."⁵ Even if rural work were carried out, "the focus should be on rural areas near cities,"⁶ and should never become biased toward the development of the hinterlands. This urban-centric view seriously hampered the transformation of the Party's focus of work.

2) *Ignore the peasant war and the soviet base.* At that time, the Central Committee believed that in the new climax of the revolution, the peasant war was a major tributary and the symbol of the most important peak of the revolution, the revival of the workers' movement. For this reason, in the Party's work, it was important to hold to the firm belief that the establishment of a branch of several people in a heavy industry was more valuable than the development of more than a hundred comrades in the countryside. Li Lisan's "leftist" risk-taking period was even more serious. The Central Committee emphasized that the riots in the urban centers must be decisive, stating that the idea of the city being surrounded by rural separatists was "a fantasy" and "an absolutely wrong concept," while accusing the rural workers of holding "a peasant mentality." In this way, the idea of rural separatism that the CPC had previously endorsed was now criticized as something wrong. This sort of understanding was undoubtedly a regression.

3) *Propose an expedition to attack urban centers.* At the beginning of the 1930s, as the revolutionary forces were restored to a certain extent, the warlord warfare provided a good opportunity for the development of the revolutionary struggle. The central government made an erroneous estimate of the situation, believing that the revolutionary situation was mature and reaching its peak. In this situation, it was important to prepare a province or provinces to unite first, establishing a national revolutionary regime as the general policy of the Party's current strategy and emphasizing that the region first captured should be "a place that stood for national leadership both politically and economically," such as Shanghai or Wuhan. In this way, the capture of the big city was proposed as the primary task. The Central Committee emphasized that the capture of the big cities must involve armed riots by workers. This was the "most important" condition for the riots to succeed. Therefore, military efforts should allow armed workers to take "first place" on their agenda. The Central Committee insisted that the

general alliance strike, or even stage armed riots, in Shanghai and organize armed violence in Nanjing in an effort to cooperate with the first victory of the armed forces in Wuhan and neighboring provinces. At the same time, the Central Committee also suggested to the Red Army that it should attack big cities, insisting that it "develop strategically and tactically toward a focus on urban centers."[7] Clearly, the CPC Central Committee sought to establish an alliance between the urban workers' riots and the Red Army's offensive in an effort to capture the urban centers and achieve an early victory in the provinces, with Wuhan as its center.

4) *Deny the imbalance in the development of the revolution.* At that time, the Central Committee overestimated the development of the revolutionary situation, exaggerated the instability of the enemy's rule, denied the imbalance in the revolutionary development, and believed that "the fundamental crisis of China's economic politics is sharpening equally in all parts of China, with only slight variations." Further, "the most obvious aspect of the revolutionary situation is the development of the workers, peasants, and soldiers of the Red Army," which would "in any event, lead to a revolutionary climax." When the height of the revolution came, "the beginning of a riot in a province or provinces will be the beginning of a national riot," and "the first victory in a province or provinces will be the beginning of a national victory."[8] This estimate was actually completely dependent on the first victory in a province.

It was undeniable that after the Sixth National Congress the Central Committee also paid more attention to the development of the Red Army in rural areas and started to engage in guerrilla warfare. However, the Central Committee raised this issue from the perspective of striving for the masses and preparing for urban riots. The development of the Red Army and rural guerrilla warfare had always been lumped under the umbrella of urban riots. The Party's work had been greatly damaged by the adventurist policies of the leftists that focused on seizing the big cities. Though the Party's work was focused on urban centers, urban work did not achieve the results the Central Committee had expected, instead suffering great losses. Over the previous two months, eleven Provincial Party Committees had been destroyed by the enemy. There were few Party members in large enterprises, and the flow of large urban branches was uncertain, creating an overall unacceptable situation. At the same time, the Central Committee mobilized the Red Army to attack urban centers that were at some distance from the base areas, causing both the Red Army and the base areas to suffer damage to various degrees. The influence of the "urban center" theory had seriously hindered the development of the rural revolutionary struggle.

The third stage was from the Third Plenary Session of the Sixth Central Congress in September 1930 to the Sixth Anti-Encirclement Campaign. At this stage, the city-centered theory further harmed the Chinese revolution, practically bankrupting it. The Third Plenary Session brought a halt to Li Lisan's leftist adventurism (generally referred to as the "Lisan Road"), stopping the riots in and attacks on big cities, but the influence of the city-centered theory remained. After the failure of the Lisan Road, under the guidance of a directive from the Comintern, Wang Ming's "leftist" dogmatism, which was left even of the Lisan Road, once again dominated the Central Committee of the CPC. Under the Wang Ming Road, the risky activity of taking urban centers re-emerged, insisting that the Red Army attack urban centers and engage enemy troops there. The city-centered theory brought new forms of loss to the revolution.

During this period, the revolutionary situation had undergone some changes. On the one hand, the Red Army and the base areas had made great progress in the revolutionary war. On the other, the Party's work in White areas had suffered serious setbacks, with Party groups at all levels being destroyed and most of the struggles in the form of urban workers' strikes, mobile rallies, and even armed uprisings failing. Under these circumstances, it was imperative that the guiding ideology of the Central Committee not change, and it was even more important to pay attention to the battles of the Red Army and the rural revolutionary base areas. In the spring of 1933, the Central Committee moved temporarily from Shanghai to the Central Soviet Area, which should clearly have been a positive change. However, the move was forced and not well thought out. Although the Central Committee had moved temporarily to the countryside, it continued to hold to the city-centered theory. This basically demonstrated that:

1) *Advocating that the Red Army occupy the urban centers and achieve a first victory in one province.* Guided by Wang Ming's leftist ideas, the Central Committee failed to recognize the long-term and circuitous nature of the Chinese revolution. Although they criticized Li Lisan for ordering the Red Army to attack the big cities as a risky, premature act, their disagreement with Li was not over whether

they wanted to use occupation of the city to gain victory in a province or provinces, but rather in their estimation of the current situation, specifically, under what circumstances the city could be occupied. Therefore, if the situation changed, the Central Committee would repeat its mistake of attacking large cities. This was, in fact, what happened. Shortly after the September 18th Incident, the Central Committee proposed that "the past correct strategy of not taking the big cities no longer applies," and "with the current smooth political and military situation, we must take one or two important cities. The successful taking of a city will be the beginning of successful revolution in one province, as has been added to the overall agenda of the CPC during the soviet movement."[9] From that time on, the occupation of an urban center with the aim of gaining a first province or provinces became the general policy of the Central Committee. Even in the Fifth Anti-Encirclement Campaign, the Red Army was in an extremely passive situation, and the Central Committee repeatedly emphasized the need to occupy urban centers to achieve victory in a first province. Under this policy, the Central Committee had divided Mao Zedong's set of guidelines and policies for consolidating and developing the rural revolutionary base areas into "soviet theories for the mountains" and proposed that Deng Xiaoping, Mao Zedong, Xie Weijun, and Gu Bai "focus on the cities and set aside the impossible task of developing the soviet areas as major transportation networks." Directing their energy to developing vast rural areas with "weak enemy forces" was criticized as the "pessimism" of "proclaiming the abandonment of the soviet base areas." This was a struggle launched against Deng, Mao, Xie, and Gu.

The difference between this and the two early stages lay in the way it sought to capture urban centers to achieve the initial victory in a province. Although the Central Committee still proposed armed urban uprisings, its main emphasis was now on the occupation of the city through military attack by the Red Army and the first victory in a province or provinces. The main reason for this difference was that urban work had already been greatly diminished, while the strength of the Red Army continued to gradually increase. Circumstances had forced the Central Committee to take a new path in its urban-centric approach.

2) Use of the "active offense" approach and the strategy of regular warfare to command the Red Army's war. The left unilaterally understood the principle that the Marxist struggle should continue after the armed uprising, and proposed that the "main key" of all strategic tactics was to destroy the enemy "by an offensive line," through what was called an "all round attack" which "captured the city in the center" then "fought the enemy with both fists," and other similar tactics. In order to carry out the line of active advances, the Central Committee emphasized the use of formal warfare, mentioning its opposition to "the conservative guerrilla warfare strategy" and insisting on the formalization of the Red Army. It stated that "the main force of the Red Army must be concentrated and must act as quickly as possible" to enable it to be fully committed to a decisive battle." The Central Committee denied that the form of the Chinese revolutionary war was an ongoing repetition of the Anti-Encirclement campaigns. It believed that the Fifth Anti-Encirclement Campaign was the "decisive class war," and that this campaign could address the "soviet path and the colonial path." The question of who would win this battle still remained. Guided by erroneous thinking, the Central Committee directed the Fifth Anti-Encirclement Campaign according to the principle of so-called regular warfare, opposed "guerrilla tactics," opposed the enticement of the enemy, and advocated "defending against the enemy in the backcountry" while promoting inner maneuvers. This defense and fortress tactic led directly to the failure of the Fifth Anti-Encirclement Campaign.

Under the guidance of Wang Ming, the Central Committee led the work of the Red Army and the base areas armed with a wrong view of the cities, which brought great losses to the Chinese revolution. The failure of the Fifth Anti-Encirclement Campaign had objectively declared the end of the city-centered theory in China.

The failure of the Fifth Anti-Encirclement Campaign led to a crisis in the Chinese revolution. At this critical juncture, in January 1935, the Central Committee held the Zunyi Conference during the course of the Long March. The meeting focused on correcting military mistakes that had a decisive significance at the time, summing up the lessons of the defeat in the Fifth Anti-Encirclement Campaign and ending the dominance of Wang Ming's leftist doctrine within the Central Committee. According to a speech made by Mao Zedong entitled "The Summary Resolution on Opposing the Enemies Five Encirclement Campaigns," he stated, "The Chinese civil war is not a short-term struggle but a long-lasting one. The soviet revolutionary force constantly demolished the enemy, as developed in the Anti-Encirclement campaigns. Under the principles of a protracted war, it is necessary to oppose both conservatism and adventurism caused by the overestimation of one's own victory and the underestimation of the enemy's strength." The resolution specifically mentioned that the adventurism of "uncertainty and unnecessarily attacking the enemy's urban centers" had caused serious losses to the Red Army and the revolutionary war. This was actually a criticism of the city-centered theory, and it marked the beginning of a shift of focus in the work of the entire Party.

After the Red Army's Long March reached Northern Shaanxi, the Central Committee deployed work in the five provinces of Shanxi, Shaanxi, Gansu, Yunnan, and Ningxia, but no longer employed a strategy of attempting to gain a first victory among several provinces with a city as the center. Rather, the Central Committee believed that "the Chinese soviet revolution has achieved its first victory in certain provinces and regions."[10] The view that it must first take a city in order to take a province was declared "incompatible." After the Wayaobao Meeting, in his article "On Strategies for Resisting Japanese Imperialism," Mao Zedong discussed the imbalance in China's political and economic development and the resulting imbalance of revolutionary development. The resulting long-term characteristics of the revolution had led to the conclusion that "the victory of the revolution always begins with the areas where counter-revolutionary forces are weak. These areas must be developed first in order for victory to be gained."[11] This was why the Central Committee shifted its focus to the countryside. The idea of triumphing first in the areas where enemy rule was weak completely refuted and replaced the view that the provinces with the city as focus should be conquered first, bringing to fruition a significant change on the revolutionary path. This was mainly a result of Mao Zedong's efforts. Under his guidance, a group of Chinese Communists adhered to the long-term rural revolution, constantly summing up the experience gained and lessons learned there and fighting "leftist" error.

3. Summary of the Practical Results of the Party's City-centered Theory

The CPC was a party particularly skilled at summing up the lessons it had learned from failures and setbacks. The result of the painful practice of the city-centered theory enabled the Party to earnestly recognize that:

1) *The city-centered theory had a profound impact on the CPC*. No matter what form it took, the theory only brought harm to the revolutionary cause. In the first instance, it had enabled the Central Committee to adhere over a long period to the idea of focusing on the city, whether as the center of riots or the center of daily

work. Even when the Central Committee finally moved into the countryside, it continued to call for the capture of urban centers. The Red Army and the work of the base areas was guided by such thinking for a long time. In addition, it led the Central Committee to command the Red Army's maneuvers with the armed uprising principle of the European proletarian revolution, which lacked understanding of the rules and characteristics of the Chinese revolutionary struggle. In short, the city-centered theory seriously affected the shift of the focus of the work of the CPC, and for a long time the Party was not able to accept the correct revolutionary path presented by Mao Zedong. As a result, the revolutionary cause suffered repeated setbacks. Of course, in the practice of leading the revolution, the Central Committee's ideological understanding also underwent a change. For instance, the idea that victory had first to be won in the city then in the province was colored in such a way to fit Chinese circumstances and conform to China's situation. Therefore, when some failed to understand the characteristics of the Chinese revolution at a certain point in time, they would accept this view. In this sense, the idea of first gaining a victory in one province, then a number of provinces played a transitional role in the process of the Party ridding itself of the influence of the city-centered theory. However, the first point of victory in a province was the provincial capital or central city, which was in essence still urban-centric. At that time, the Central Committee was not able to grasp that the capture of the central cities was the final stage of the Chinese democratic revolution, and that it was not necessary in the short term to capture an urban center in order to capture a province. Here, the influence of the city-centered theory was clearly visible and had become an obstacle to the CPC's deepening understanding of the Chinese revolution. Facts had proven that no matter what form the city-centered theory took in China, it could only bring harm to the revolution.

2) *The reason the city-centered theory could not lead to victory in the Chinese revolution was that it was not a product of China's social, political, and economic development.* As such, it did not conform to the real situation in China. The soil in which the city-centered theory had been cultivated was that of a European capitalist society, and so it reflected the rules and characteristics of a European proletarian revolution. China's national conditions were different from those of Europe, and they were unique. From the perspective of China's social and economic development, it is evident that China had lost the opportunity to develop capitalism independently

because of imperialist invasion. China's social economy did not follow the normal rules of economic development, forming a unified market for cities and villages, with cities controlling the nation's economy. Of China's big cities, the ones that had survived this history, such as Beijing, were mainly centers of feudal political power, the consumer center rather than the center of production. Such cities were economically unable to control the countryside. The other category was the emerging economic and political centers, such as Shanghai, but the economic lifelines of such cities were in the hands of the imperialists. This sort of urban economy could only be found in a semi-colonial country, and it could not be compared with Western economies, in which cities were the center. As far as the rural economy was concerned, in China's vast hinterlands, feudal production methods were still predominant, so it was difficult to say that industrial cities would have a decisive influence over the vast rural areas. Throughout the process of China's capitalist development, peasants close to the commercial port areas would undoubtedly be affected by the commodity economy, accelerating the process of the separation of laborers from the means of production. However, this process of separation was mainly caused not by the prosperity of the industrial and commercial sectors, but by feudal factors such as feudal land ownership and super-economic forced exploitation. In the vast areas far from the trading ports and inaccessible areas, the natural economy was still predominant. In China, not only was there an imbalance between the economic development between urban and rural areas, but the economic development between various rural areas was likewise uneven. Therefore, China's cities and villages were not in a unified economic state. Cities could not control the vast rural areas, and villages could be self-sufficient without the cities. Under such conditions, cities could play an important role in the revolution, but they could not carry the same weight of authority as European cities. From the comparison of class power, it is evident that the absolute number of people making up the Chinese proletariat was not less than the number of Russian workers in the October Revolution. However, because of China's large population, the relative numbers of the Chinese working class were small. During the October Revolution, Russian workers accounted for one-sixth of the country's total population. Now, Chinese workers only accounted for one in two hundred of the total population. For this reason, the main force of the revolution could not be workers, but peasants. The leadership role of the proletariat could not be reflected in actions such as urban strikes and riots, but in the dispatch of its own vanguard to serve as the rural leadership of peasants in the agrarian revolution and the revolutionary war. The proletarian leadership of the peasants could not take the same form it had in Europe, where urban workers first took part in the revolution, driving the peasants.

Judging from China's political situation, it is clear that China had been a feudal autocratic centralized nation for thousands of years, and yet it had no democratic tradition. Since the revolution of 1911, although there had been some democratic propaganda, it had never penetrated very deeply because it had had such a short time to do so, particularly in the face of such old traditions, alongside other reasons. After Chiang Kai-shek came to power, he too inherited the tradition of feudal autocracy and participated in fascist methods of rule. The more central a city was the stricter his reactionary rule there was, and the more easily the revolutionaries were suppressed. Given such conditions, there was no established parliament like that in some European countries on which to rely, and it was impossible to launch activities and consolidate strength in the city. Therefore, the Chinese revolution could not use cities as its base, directly seizing supreme political power in a city. It could only use villages as a revolutionary base, then move from the village to attack the city, finally achieving national political power in this way.

The above social and historical conditions determined that the Chinese revolution could not take the same path taken by European revolutions, with the city as center, as it was not feasible to do so in China.

3) *The Central Committee of the CPC rid itself of the city-centered theory through a long, torturous process.* This demonstrates that the proper combination of Marxism and Chinese revolutionary practice was a complex, arduous undertaking. At the turning point after the failure of the Great Revolution, the Central Committee of the CPC could not yet fully understand the national conditions of the country in a way that allowed them to be revolutionized and the rules and characteristics of the revolutionary movement put into place in a short period of time, exploring the revolutionary road. Subjectively, an important cause was the dogmatic treatment of Marxism and the arbitrary application of foreign experience. Marx, Engels, and Lenin all attached great importance to the city's leadership role in the revolution. According to Marx and Engels, the leadership role of the city referred to the leading role the proletariat played for the peasantry. Lenin also said, "The bigger the city, the greater its role in the revolution." Of course, Marx, Engels, and Lenin did not neglect the role of the peasantry, but they all discussed the issue from

the perspective of fighting for the peasants' allied force. They did not say that the proletarian class should not focus its work on the countryside in the course of revolution. The Chinese Communists, who were adhering to Marxism-Leninism but were not good at applying its principles to the reality of the Chinese situation, naturally went on to apply the principles of Marxism-Leninism as a guide to action, and so the city naturally became the Party's center of work. Such thinking became a sort of fixed orthodoxy for a long period, and the new concept derived from China's actual situation was treated as a form of anti-Marxist "heresy." It was not easy to creatively apply the principles of Marxism in the context of Marxist dogma and the blessing of the resolutions and directives of the Comintern and Soviet experience. This was a part of the profound teachings history has left to us.

II

The Establishment of the Concept of an "Armed Division of Workers and Peasants"

1. Proposing a Different Model from the October Revolution

Through the entire Party's struggle to find a way to save the nation and a new path for the revolution, many members of the CPC, represented mainly by Mao Zedong, eventually found a way to promote the Chinese revolution, after a long process of creating and cultivating the Red Army and the rural revolutionary base areas. The path to revival was instrumental in formulating a set of theories that led to the victory of the Chinese revolution. The idea of an "armed division of workers and peasants" marked the beginning of this great theoretical construction.

Although the city-centered theory continued to dominate the CPC, when faced with the difficult situation and the complex national conditions of the Chinese revolution, the entire Party sought to explore and consider the future and its path.

Because of the inconsistent pace and degree of revolutionary development from one place to another, the Central Committee began to recognize the imbalance of China's social and political development, which caused an imbalance in the development of the revolution. The first was that because of the imbalance in the development of the workers and the peasants, the rural struggle had developed in the form of guerrilla warfare and some places had been organized and soviets established, while the cities had not developed to this extent. The second observation was that the development of regional revolutionary movements was unbalanced, with some provinces having developed to the extent of riots and seized provincial power, while many provinces had yet achieved this level. This being the case at this stage, the Central Committee proposed ideas that were a departure from the Russian October Revolution model.

The first of these was a strategic goal of "first victory in one provinces, then several." At the beginning of the Agrarian Revolutionary War, the Central Committee mainly instigated armed riots in the provinces of Hunan, Hubei, Jiangxi, and Guangdong. In fact, most of the uprisings led by the Party were concentrated in these provinces, and the riots in the north were not as vigorous as those in the southern provinces. This indicated that the Central Committee did not take approach of the French Revolution or the Russian October Revolution, which was to seize the capital in "a single stroke." In November 1927, the Central Committee clearly stated that it was necessary to "combine the power of the peasant riots, consolidate spontaneous labor and peasant riots everywhere, and seize power, eventually gaining victory in a province or provinces."[12] The central government believed that, faced with a general climax in the revolution, it was possible to first gain victory in areas where the enemy was weak, the trend of the workers and peasants was rising, and Party leadership was strongest. Such a victory would be the first step toward national victory, which would be guaranteed by the establishment of a soviet regime. After this, it was necessary to "extend this regime to other regions, even to all of the four hundred million people in China."[13] The Sixth National Congress of the CPC affirmed this strategic goal of gaining an initial victory in a province or provinces, pointing out that if the revolution reached a climax, it would be possible to win one or several provinces.

The second proposal was the idea that a rural-urban division would strengthen urban work, so that the first victory of a province would be completed through an urban riot. After the failure of the Guangzhou Uprising, the Central Committee emphasized in its instructions to all locales that "the occupation of large cities is the final step in the struggle of the workers and peasants that will lead the vast areas to a stage of maturity."[14] Prior to this, in the struggle to strengthen urban centers, the "zoning" of rural areas led to a sort of "separatism."[15] Further, it held that "when the division of the country is complete and the urban struggle reaches its climax, then the completely regional rural riots with cities at the center will be launched. Only then can the task of capturing these areas be achieved."[16]

In this way, by encircling the cities with rural divisions, while at the same time strengthening the urban work, and finally completing the revolutionary path of an initial victory in a province through rural riots, the city was replaced as the starting point for revolution, pushing it instead to the countryside, from which an initiative aimed at taking the capital would be launched. This was the Central Committee's first step toward starting to work from the actual situation in China and break through the shackles of the city-centered theory. It played an important role in shining a light on the Party's exploration and ultimate acceptance of the idea of rural encirclement of urban areas.

However, at that time, the Central Committee did not understand the imbalance of China's social and political development, particularly the imbalance between the political and economic development of urban and rural areas, making it impossible to break the shackles of the city-centered theory. At the same time, the goal of gaining a first victory in a province or provinces did not accurately reflect the principle of imbalance in the development of the Chinese revolution. The defects it contained would still bring losses to the Chinese revolution under certain conditions.

2. The Initial Form of the Concept of an "Armed Division of Workers and Peasants"

In the exploration of the Chinese revolutionary path, an ideological sprout of truly great significance was the proposal of the "climbing the mountains" idea within the CPC. This idea was the initial form the concept of an armed division of workers and peasants took.

Around the time of the August 7th Meeting, the Central Committee discussed several issues concerning the peasant movement and the peasant armed forces. It was at this time that Mao proposed the idea of "climbing the mountain." In June 1927, Mao convened a meeting in Hankou of the Party members from Hunan who had fled after the Mari Incident. At this meeting, he called on everyone to go back to their hometowns, suggesting those from mountainous regions go to the mountains and those from lake or river regions board boats, as they resolutely fought the enemy and defended the revolutionary ideal.[7] He then returned to Hunan as the Secretary of the Provincial Party Committee, where he presided over the committee's work and led the members of peasant association and peasant self-defense forces to "climb the mountain" and "go into the lake" to conserve the energy of the revolution and bide their time. On July 4, at the Expanded Meeting of the Standing Committee of the Central Committee of the CPC, Mao suggested that "the peasant armed forces can climb the mountain, or they can invest in an army that is connected with the Party," stating clearly that "if we don't conserve energy, we will have nothing in the future." He believed that "the peasant army can climb the mountain," and he expected that doing so "can create the basis for military power."[18] On the 13th, the Central Committee issued a declaration stating that this was "the point at which the revolution is in jeopardy." The Central Committee decided to hold peasant riots at the autumn harvest in four provinces, Hunan, Hubei, Chongqing, and Guangdong, to promote the implementation of an agrarian revolution. At the end of July, Mao actively engaged in the preparatory work for the autumn harvest riots and drafted for the Central Committee the Outline of the Hunan Movement (referred to hereafter as "the Outline"). The Outline reflects Mao's idea of starting a military riot, establishing an army led by the Party, forming an armed separatist group, establishing a revolutionary regime, and promoting an agrarian revolution. On August 7, the Central Committee of the CPC secretly held an emergency meeting in Hankou. At this meeting, Mao summed up four lessons learned from the failure of the Great Revolution: completely abandoning the Communist Party's stance on political independence, failing to pay attention to military issues, failing to propose a revolutionary solution to the peasants' land problem, and allowing the Party to be separate from the people, which highlighted the need for greater attention to military efforts in the future. It was essential to understand that political power was obtained by guns.[19] At the August 7th Meeting, Mao was elected to serve as an alternate member of the Central Provisional Politburo. Cai Hesen proposed that Mao remain involved in Central work, and Qu Qiubai asked him to go to the Shanghai branches of central organs. Mao disagreed. He said, "I want to go out and engage in armed uprisings. I don't want to stay in high-rise buildings. I want to go to the mountains and befriend our comrades there."[20] On August 9, Mao attended the meeting of the Provisional Central Politburo, where he criticized Hunan for organizing an army division for the Nanchang Uprising, following the errors of Guangdong. He believed that "Hunan's popular organizations are expanding beyond Guangdong, but they lack arms." He said pointedly, "We must form a division in Hunan, arm it, and occupy five or six counties, forming a political foundation upon which to develop an agrarian revolution." Concerning the autumn riots, he held that "even if they fail, there is no need to go to Guangdong. It is better to climb a mountain."[21] In mid-August, Mao went to Hunan to lead the Autumn Harvest Uprising as a special commissioner of the Central Committee. On August 18, he delivered important opinions in the riots and land issues at the Provincial Party Meeting held in Changsha. He advocated that the development of the autumn harvest efforts in Hunan were meant to address the issue of the peasants' land. He pointed out that the power of the peasantry alone was insufficient to launch a riot, and that military aid was necessary. The point of the riot was to seize political power. The mistake the Party had made in the past was to ignore the need for military power. Now, it must give 60% of its energy to the military movement, and it must seize power and establish its own political control through the use of guns. He believed that, in order for the peasants to be able to fully grasp power, the landlords' land had to be confiscated and handed over to the peasants.[22] On September 9, Mao launched the Hunan Autumn Harvest Uprising. The obvious feature of this uprising was that many armed peasants and workers participated, and the flag of the Workers' and Peasants' Revolutionary Army was publicly displayed. The uprising still aimed to capture the central city, Changsha. When the plans of various insurgents to attack Changsha were frustrated, Mao showed his unique ability to summarize lessons from earlier experience in a timely way, opting to make a decisive change in the original deployment. He decided to make a "transfer" at the Wenjia City Meeting, and led the troops to "climb the mountain," seeking to establish a foothold in the mountainous areas where the enemy was weak. As a result, the Autumn Harvest Uprising troops retreated toward Pingxiang and marched south along the Luojing Mountains. After the Three Bays Adaptation, at the end of October, Mao led the division to the nearby Jinggangshan region. After climbing the mountain, under Mao's leadership, the troops mobilized the masses to help the local residents restore, rectify, and establish Party organizations, carry out an agrarian revolution, establish the Red Army and the revolutionary regime of workers and peasants, carry out extensive guerrilla warfare, and vigorously strengthen the construction of the Red Army. Jinggangshan became the first rural revolutionary base in the country, and in practice, it lit the fire of the stars of the "armed division of workers and peasants."

However, the revolutionary practice of the CPC's founding of rural revolutionary bases, as represented by Mao Zedong, was not at that time accepted by the whole Party, nor was it accepted by the Comintern. Many in the Party expressed doubts about whether a small, or even a few small, revolutionary bases could exist for long. The dogmatists dismissed this great creation as "the peasant mindset," while the Comintern believed that "the workers' and peasants' revolution is moving toward a climax, and the official policy of the CPC was to prepare for that revolutionary climax, the main task of which was to prepare for a 'widespread launch' between the cities and villages and several neighboring provinces." Therefore, it was necessary to oppose the "disorderly, unrelated guerrilla war that is destined to fail." In order to implement the instructions of the Comintern regarding the adaptation of urban and rural areas and neighboring provinces, the Central Committee of the CPC specifically arranged for the road leading to Pingyue along the Hunan-Guangdong border to serve as the riot line that would bring the completion of victory to Hunan Province. They placed armed forces from the Jinggangshan Revolutionary Base in the Luojing Mountain Range as part of the province-wide riots Mao had initiated, then ordered Mao to lead the troops and "expand" the base areas and merge with the groups in southeastern Hunan and northern Guangdong. At the time, Mao also believed that the establishment of the base area in the countryside was for the purpose of accompanying the uprising in the central city. The difference was that he could proceed from the specific circumstances at the time to determine his work policy. Mao suggested different views on the instructions of the Central Committee and the Hunan Provincial Party Committee. He believed that in the period of temporary stability of the ruling class, the principle of separating the troops should not be adopted, but that only a consolidated approach should be taken. Mao summed up the experience of armed uprisings since the August 7th Meeting, offering six arguments against the Red Army driving Hunan to "expand" the base areas, suggesting instead that it should first consolidate the revolutionary base areas in the Luojing Mountains to prepare for a "long-term struggle with the enemy." He emphasized the importance of consolidating the revolutionary base areas, saying, "This sort of proposition is by no means a conservative concept. In the past, national riots have flourished all over. Once the enemy launches a counter-offensive, it is like we are washing a river, which is completely ineffective. On the one hand, this problem has established a large base for the military and on the other, offered a solid foundation for the riots in these two provinces."[23] But Mao's accurate observation was not adopted, resulting in the "August defeat" in Hunan. After that defeat, the leftist dogmatists who had failed to offer correct opinions continued to criticize Mao, saying that his views on consolidating the base areas was a conservative idea. They believed, rather, that the Red Army could only develop outwards, through expanding the soviets and other similar activities.

3. The Suggestion and Connotations of the Armed Division of Workers and Peasants

On the opposite end of the spectrum from the leftist dogmatists who were eager to seize power through uprisings in urban centers was a group of right-wing pessimists within the revolutionary base. Some Party members overestimated the strength of the enemy and could not see the conflicts within the enemy camps. They took such local setbacks and difficulties to heart, particularly when they encountered a defeat, were surrounded on all sides, or were pursued by powerful enemies. As a whole, they essentially raised the question, "how long can the red flag last?" Mao said that this was a fundamental issue, and that it was impossible to take a step forward without addressing the question of whether the revolutionary base areas and the Red Army could exist and develop. Applying the basic principles of a Marxist violent revolution, Mao summed up the positive and negative experiences of Jinggangshan and the construction of the revolutionary base areas. He wrote articles entitled "How May China's Red Political Power Exist?" and "The Jinggangshan Struggle," in which he proposed the "armed division of workers and peasants."

Primarily, in these articles, Mao discussed the reasons and conditions for the existence and development of the Red regime. He wrote, "In a country where we are surrounded on all sides by the White regime, there is a small, or perhaps a few small, Red regimes that can exist for a long period. This is something that has never been seen in the world before. This sort of wonder is unique. The reason for its existence and development must also have particular conditions."[24]

1) *China's uneven political and economic development.* China was a semi-colonial, semi-feudal country with unbalanced political and economic development. The power of the ruling class was concentrated mainly in the cities, while the rural areas were relatively weak. Because it was a semi-feudal country, the local self-sufficient economy made China's rural areas relatively independent, with rural areas not being overly dependent on the cities. This provided the proletariat with the necessary economic conditions for launching the peasant movements in the countryside and implementing armed struggles there to establish Red power. Because it was a semi-colonial country, many imperialists competed for and divided the sphere of influence in China, manifested in the long-term continuous division and fighting between the warlords. The proletariat could use such conflicts, divisions, and fighting between the warlords to establish and develop revolutionary base areas, so that the Red regime could exist and persist in the midst of the surrounding White regime. Mao stated, "We only need to know that the division and fighting of China's White regime is continuing, and the Red regime's existence and development will be beyond doubt."[25] At the same time, because China was a big country, its revolutionary forces had room to maneuver, which was conducive to the establishment of Red political power and provided a good terrain for the Red Army to fight. Mao's selection of the Luojing Mountain Range as the site for the base area was an exemplary move.

2) *A good foundation with the masses.* The places where the Red regime first came into being and could exist for a long time were in those areas that had been affected by the first domestic revolutionary war and had high involvement from the revolutionary masses. Such areas, including Hunan, Anhui, Hubei, and Guangdong, had been the main areas where the Northern Expedition had been fought. There, they had Party organizations, and the Party had had considerable influence among the masses. It had organized trade unions and peasant associations among the workers and peasants, and had urged a struggle against the landlord class. In such places, the people and the army had been trained politically during the democratic revolution, so it was easy for the Red regime to come into being and exist there for a long period.

3) *Progress in the revolutionary situation.* Whether a small local people's political power could continue for a long time depended on whether the revolutionary situation was moving forward. Mao believed that if the revolutionary situation was progressing, there was no doubt that the development and long-term existence of the fledgling Red regime would continue. The opposite was not possible. So the question of whether the revolutionary situation was progressing and developing remained. Mao believed that after the failure of the Great Revolution, the basic conflict that caused the Chinese revolution had not been resolved. Therefore, "The current situation of the Chinese revolution is following the continued division of and fighting with the domestic comprador class and the international bourgeoisie, and it must continue to move forward."[26] This meant that the Red region would continue to develop, and was in fact drawing closer to obtaining national political power.

4) *The existence of a relatively powerful Red Army.* Mao believed that the presence of a relatively powerful formal Red Army was a necessary condition for the existence of the Red regime. If there was only a Red Guard and no formal Red Army, they would not be able to deal with the reactionary forces, and they would not be able to generate a separatist movement, even if the separatist movement were not long-term and became increasingly separatist. He emphasized, "The idea of 'an armed force of workers and peasants' is an important idea that the Communist Party and the workers and peasants must hold to fully."[27]

5) *Correct leadership of the Communist Party.* The "armed division of workers and peasants" was a division under the leadership of the CPC. The correct leadership of the Party was a key factor in the existence and development of the Red regime. The Special Committee on the border between Hunan and Jiangxi under Mao Zedong and the Military Committee, with Chen Yi as secretary, implemented a correct border policy, resolutely fought against the enemy, established the political power in the Luoxiao Mountain Range, opposed escapism, and deepened the agrarian revolution in the area. The Party helped with the development in the local area, and the armed forces helped develop local troops. They reinforced the defensive strength of Hunan, which had a relatively strong ruling power, and the offensive strength of Jiangxi, which had a weak ruling power. With great effort, they

created a force among the masses and the division of the masses, so that in the long-term struggle, the Red Army's forces could be concentrated to face the current enemy and avoid being crushed. The expansion of the separatist region adopted a wave-like policy, opposing an aggressive policy. In this way, there had been military victories in the Jinggangshan base area from April through July, while the "leftist" sectarian commander led the "August defeat" in Hunan.

Of the five conditions recounted above, the first was most important. It was precisely because of the social nature of China's semi-colonial, semi-feudal society that the imbalance of its political and economic development had made it possible to establish Red political power. Based on the characteristics of Chinese society, Mao proposed a correct analysis of the existence and development of the Red regime.

In addition, Mao proposed the basic content of the idea of the "armed division of workers and peasants." What was this division? Under the leadership of the proletariat, armed struggle was the main form the revolution took, and the revolutionary base was the main support for it, while the rural and agrarian revolutions were its substance on which the construction of Red regions and Red political power were based.

Armed struggle was the main form of struggle the armed division of workers and peasants would undertake. Mao pointedly commented that China was a semi-feudal, semi-colonial country lacking a democratic system, being instead oppressed by the feudal system. There was no national independence, as it was under the weight of imperialism. The enemies of the Chinese people, which included the warlords, tyrants, and imperialists, were all heavily armed for killing. In the face of such an enemy, the main body of the Chinese revolution must also be armed. The Chinese revolution, whose main economy was agricultural, featured riots and military activity, because in the siege of the White regime, there were no armed forces and no armed struggle. Such a divided situation could not be supported all in one day. Mao stated that the struggle on the border was entirely a military struggle, and the Party and the masses all needed to be militarized. How to deal with the enemy and how to fight against it had become the central issue in their daily lives. The so-called separatists must be armed. Without sufficient arming, and without an appropriate strategy for dealing with the enemy, the place would immediately fall into enemy hands. Without armed struggle, there would be no revolutionary bases, no status for the people, and no other Party work. It was only by thoroughly mobilizing the masses and carrying out extensive armed struggles that the Party could safeguard the peasants' agrarian revolution, expand the area of the separatists, and build and develop rural revolutionary base areas.

The agrarian revolution was central to the armed division of workers and peasants. It was necessary to mobilize the peasants to carry out an in-depth agrarian revolution in the effort to carry out the anti-feudal, anti-imperialist democratic revolution, because the imperialists' exploitation and oppression of the Chinese people basically depended on the backward feudal relations in the countryside. The destruction of the feudal system was a deadly blow to imperial rule in China. When Mao Zedong participated in the Hunan Provincial Party Committee Meeting in Changsha to discuss the plan for the autumn harvest uprising, he pointed out that the purpose of the Autumn Harvest Uprising was to completely implement the agrarian revolution and address the issue of the peasants' land through military force. After the armed division of workers and peasants was created at Jinggangshan, the agrarian revolution became a major component of the separatist work in the region. When the Red Army first arrived at Jinggangshan, Mao mainly led the Red Army, mobilized the peasant masses, defeated local tyrants, divided the wealth, and canceled debts to prepare for the distribution of the land. On May 20, 1928, when Mao presided over the First Congress of the Hunan-Jiangxi Border Party, he proposed the task of intensifying the agrarian revolution. After the conference, under the leadership of the CPC Special Committee for Hunan-Jiangxi border and the government of the workers, peasants, and soldiers on the border, the agrarian revolutionary committee was established in counties, districts, and townships, and the policy of distributing land as units by townships and by population was established. In this way, the Jinggangshan agrarian revolution was carried out with gusto in the base area. The agrarian revolution liberated the rural productive forces and greatly stimulated the enthusiasm of the peasants for revolution and production. It not only gave the Red Army a supplementary source, but also created the material conditions for the Red Army's war. This served to further consolidate and develop the armed division of workers and peasants along the Hunan-Jiangxi border.

The rural revolutionary base area was basically an armed division of workers and peasants, the foothold and starting point of revolutionary development, and the support for carrying out armed struggle and launching the agrarian revolution. The fundamental issue of the revolution was the question of political power. In accord with China's national conditions, the Party shifted its focus from urban to rural areas, establishing revolutionary base areas in rural parts, and gathering and developing forces. The question of opening up and establishing a rural revolutionary base was essentially an issue of seizing power. First, the countryside was taken, then the city was occupied, just as the local government was seized first, then national political power. The establishment of the force of workers and peasants led partially by the proletariat was the starting point for promoting the climax of the national revolution and gaining the ultimate victory, and the correct way to do this was to seize and master national political power. Mao attached great importance to the construction of revolutionary base areas. He believed that the consolidation and development of this Red political power was not only conducive to the development of the agrarian revolution and armed struggle, but also to creating a talent pool for the Party. Mao specifically opposed the "mobile guerrillas" that did not want revolutionary bases. When he wrote a letter criticizing Lin Biao's mistaken prediction, he pointed out that it seemed futile to do such work to establish political power in a period so far removed from the climax of the revolution, and he hoped instead to use relatively light mobile guerrilla tactics to expand political influence and wait until the masses throughout the entire country had completed their work, or at least come close to completing it, then stage a nationwide armed uprising. At that time, the strength of the Red Army would have increased, and it would be a nationwide revolution, including every locale. The theory of establishing political power first then mobilizing the masses was not suitable for China's revolutionary situation. Mao said that he, Zhu De, and Fang Zhimin had established a base and planned to build political power, intensify the agrarian revolution, and expand the people's armed approach through the township Red Guards, district Red Guards, county Red Guards, the local Red Army, and the regular Red Army. With such measures, the development of political power was expanding in waves, and these policies were beyond dispute.

In short, Mao's idea of an armed division of workers and peasants was meant to demand that armed struggle be the main form of struggle under the leadership of the proletariat; the agrarian revolution would be its basic substance, and the revolutionary bases would serve as its strategic positions, and this would be used as the starting point for seizing national political power, which was the fundamental purpose of the armed struggle. Under the guidance of the armed division of workers and peasants, the armed struggle, the agrarian revolution, and the construction of the base areas would be organically integrated and interconnected. Without an armed struggle under the leadership of the proletariat, an effective agrarian revolution could not be carried out, nor could a revolutionary base area be established and developed. Without an agrarian revolution, the peasants could not be fully mobilized, the armed struggle could not attain the support of millions of people, and the base area could not be consolidated and developed. Without the revolutionary base areas, the armed struggle would lose support and eventually fail, and the achievements of the struggle and the agrarian revolution could not be maintained. The idea of the armed division of workers and peasants combined the inseparable content of these three items, including the basic notion of the Chinese democratic revolution and its main form and fundamental purpose, which guided the Chinese revolution after the failure of the Great Revolution.

Mao's exposition on the conditions of Red political power, the idea of the armed division of workers and peasants, and his specific clarification of the separatist policy had great theoretical and practical guiding significance. Mao answered the question of how long the Red flag could endure on the basis of a scientific argument. He adopted the main means for the Party to lead the revolutionary struggle and consolidate and develop revolutionary forces, which included relying on the strength of the workers and peasants (mainly peasants) for armed struggle and establishing and developing rural revolutionary base areas. This was concisely summarized as a formula, which was not merely a summary of the achievements of the Party's exploration of the revolutionary road in earlier stages, but also laid the foundation for the subsequent formation of the theory of the policy of "encircling the city." The provisions served as a reference for the consolidation and development of other revolutionary base areas.

In April 1929, Mao drafted a letter to the Central Committee for the former Red Army, proposing a plan to fight for the whole of Jiangxi through the divisions of four regions. With the situation being that revolutionary forces in northern Fujian, western Yunnan, southern Fujian, and eastern Fujian had "encircled Nanchang," the plan was to cause havoc for the KMT in the early stages in a large area of more than twenty counties in Fujian. For the entire area, guerrilla tactics would be used to mobilize the masses, openly forming them into divisions, intensifying the agrarian revolution, and establishing the political power of the workers and peasants. From this, the separatist network would be connected to the separatists at the Hunan-Jiangxi border, forming a solid force and laying the foundation for progress. After this, the troops would struggle for the whole of Jiangxi, while also expanding to Yunnan and Zhejiang, all in the span of one year. In September, the First Congress of the CPC in Western Fujian made plans for the "first wave of armed divisions of peasants and workers," including the "way to develop the Party and its political power among the masses." Emphasis was placed on three points. First was "establishing a central work area" and "considering how the base area could continue to develop." It also held that "there should be a central work area in each county, which will be considered the basis of development for the county." The second point was to eliminate the gaps between Red areas and "connect them." The third was to "maintain the place where work has already been done, like waves, and not be disjointed." These two documents laid out specific plans for how to implement the armed divisions of workers and peasants in a region or province. They mentioned that it was necessary to pay attention to the establishment of a "central area" as a base for further progress. The development of a base area must "follow" existing areas, and the principle of connecting adjacent areas must be gradually enacted. The provisions concerning the struggle in separatist regions were summaries of actual experiences of struggles, enriching the idea of armed divisions of workers and peasants.

III

The Theory of Encircling the City

1. The Beginning of the Theory of Encircling the City

The division of workers and peasants was an important part of the strategy of surrounding the city with rural strongholds, but its establishment was not the equivalent of completing the formation of that revolutionary path, because there still remained two problems to be addressed. The first was the question of where the Party's work should be focused, on the urban struggle with the aim of ushering in the revolutionary climax, or on rural workers and peasants in the surrounding rural areas. The second question was how to evaluate the rural base area's role in capturing national political power, whether it should be a vital factor or merely in a supplementary role. If these two issues were not addressed, the continuation and development of the new path would not be possible.

The development of the revolutionary road had promoted deeper understanding of the Chinese revolutionary path by the CPC, as represented by Mao Zedong. The Sixth National Congress of the CPC affirmed Mao's practice of establishing bases. Subsequently, in September 1929, Zhou Enlai issued a letter of instruction to the former Fourth Red Army (referred to hereafter as the September Letter). He affirmed Mao's idea of "the armed division of workers and peasants," saying, "First is the Red Army, and later urban political power. This is a characteristic of the Chinese revolution, which is a product of China's economic foundation." The letter supported Mao's strategy for Red Army action and strengthening the construction of the Red Army, correcting the lack of a proletarian ideology in the Party, and the establishment of a strong people's army under the leadership of the CPC. According to the spirit of the Central Committee's September Letter, in December 1929, the Fourth Red Army held a Gutian Congress (the 9th Party Congress of the 4th Army of the Chinese Workers' and Peasants' Red Army) in Fujian which pointed to a clear direction for the construction of the army and the Party. In the process of moving the base area to southern Jiangxi Province, and western Fujian, the experience of other base areas (such as the Fujian-Zhejiang-Jiangxi base under the leadership of Fang Zhimin and the Hunan-Hubei western border base under the leadership of He Long) continued to spread among the Fourth Red Army. These experiences greatly expanded Mao's vision, bringing about a new leap in his understanding of the Chinese revolutionary road, which in turn greatly strengthened his view that the Chinese revolution had to follow the strategy of encircling cities with rural strongholds.

However, there was a wrong tendency within the Party of reversing Marxist-Leninist dogma and the Comintern directive. Because of the general lack of understanding of the strategy of surrounding cities with rural strongholds, at one point the Comintern and some leaders in the Central Committee of the CPC adopted a relatively pessimistic view, as reflected in a letter from the Central Committee in February, which suggested that the climax of the revolution would not come, so the Red Army should be divided into smaller units and scattered across the countryside. This sort of pessimistic view likewise had an impact on the

Fourth Red Army. Lin Biao (then commander of a division in the Fourth Red Army) was one of them. His sentiments became more apparent at a meeting in Ruijin on May 18, 1929, when he made clear that he believed "the revolutionary situation is not optimistic," and "the future is not promising." At the time, he believed, the hard work of establishing Red political power and deepening the agrarian revolution in the countryside was "in vain." He proposed the use of "mobile guerrillas" to influence the masses, instead of establishing revolutionary bases. In mobilizing the masses to a certain extent, he hoped that a revolutionary victory would be achieved when a national armed riot was held. This demonstrated his lack of a correct understanding of the development of the Chinese revolution and the road to victory for the military and the Party. In order to address this issue, Mao wrote a long letter to Lin Biao in January 1930. This article entitled "A Single Spark Can Start a Prairie Fire" systematically laid out the strategic significance to the Chinese revolution of establishing rural base areas. The main ideas presented in the article were as follows:

a. It was appropriate to assert that China's national conditions were not suited to launching armed uprising focused on the cities; China merely needed to take its own path in doing so.

At the beginning of the article, Mao proposed that "in the assessment of the current situation and the accompanying actions we have taken, some comrades in the Party still lack a proper understanding."[28] He explained that these comrades did not believe that the climax of the revolution could come soon, and they lacked a deep commitment to establishing a Red regime in the guerrilla zone and promoting the arrival of the climax of the national revolution. He wrote, "They seem to think that it is futile to do this sort of hard work to establish political power at a time still far removed from the climax of the revolution, and thus hope to employ relatively light mobile guerrilla tactics to expand political influence, then wait until the work among the masses is completed nationwide, or at least in most areas, and stage a national armed uprising at that time so that, when reinforced by the Red Army, it will become a nationwide revolution. Their theory of nationwide, including all localities, fighting among the masses to build political power is not suitable for the actual situation of the national revolution."[29] Mao's analysis suggested that this theory arose mainly because they did not understand China's national conditions, so their theory could not proceed from the actual situation.

b. It further demonstrated the necessity of establishing and developing revolutionary base areas and Red political power, and proposed the idea of a rural-focused strategy.

Mao's analysis found that China's national situation was that of a semi-colonial, semi-feudal country in which many imperialists competed with one another. He pointed out that this had created a state in which factions within the Chinese ruling class had long been entangled with each other, making it possible to establish revolutionary base areas and enable the Red Army and Red regime to exist and develop in the countryside over a long period. Mao emphasized the necessity and significance of building political power in a systematic, well-planned manner, intensifying the agrarian revolution, and expanding the people's armed forces. He pointed out that this sort of armed division of workers and peasants was "the ultimate result of the semi-colonial peasant struggle under the leadership of the proletariat and the development of the struggle of semi-colonial peasants, and it is undoubtedly the most important factor in promoting the national revolutionary climax… This must be done in order to establish the confidence of the revolutionary masses, such as those in the Soviet Union and throughout the world. It must be done to create difficulties for the ruling class, shaking its foundation and fostering its collapse from within. It must be done so that the Red Army can become the main tool of the future great revolution. In short, it must be done to promote the climax of the revolution."[30] This was because peasants accounted for more than 80% of the country's population and were the main force of the Chinese revolution. It was imperative that the Chinese proletariat complete the anti-imperialist, anti-feudalist work and settle on the central message of the democratic revolution, the issue of the peasants' land. It was necessary to organize and rely on the peasants, and to raise the peasant struggle to the highest form of armed seizure of power. The revolutionary war led by the Chinese proletariat was actually a war dominated by peasants. One of the "most important factors" and four "must-do tasks" proposed by Mao had already made clear that the relationship between the workers and peasants' armed forces had gained victory in the national revolution. As Zhou Enlai said in his article "On the Studies of the Sixth National Congress," Mao's idea – meaning his advocacy of focusing on the village – required the entire Party to shift its focus from urban to rural areas and make them the starting point for a new revolution.

c. It analyzed a series of conflicts in China at that time, indicating that the idea that "A Single Spark Can Start a Prairie Fire" of the Chinese revolution was inevitable.

Mao pointed out that in judging the political situation in China, it was necessary to analyze it from the perspective of developing overall cohesiveness, grasping the essence of things, and avoiding becoming confused by various phenomena. He specifically analyzed the subjective power and counter-revolutionary forces of the Chinese revolution, pointing out that though the subjective power of the Chinese revolution was not great, the counter-revolutionary forces based on China's backward, fragile social and economic organizations was relatively weak, so when the Chinese revolution reached a climax, it would happen more quickly than it had in Western Europe. Moreover, it was important to look at the essence of things. As long as one examined in detail the various conflicts that had caused the Chinese revolution, it was evident that the climax of the revolution was undoubted. There could be no confusion on this issue. Mao offered specific analysis of the events following the defeat of the Great Revolution in 1927, noting that the conflicts between the people and the imperialists and feudalists had not been resolved, and the conflicts between the ruling classes could not be reconciled. The masses of workers and peasants, petty bourgeoisie, and young students were all revolutionary, including the transformation of soldiers in the reactionary armies of the KMT. China was full of good wood throughout the country, and it would soon catch fire. The trend "A Single Spark Can Start a Prairie Fire" was unstoppable. Mao wrote, "Undoubtedly it is not long before 'a single spark' will 'start a prairie fire,'" criticizing the pessimistic ideas concerning the Red Army and the Party, including the letter from the Central Committee in February, because they failed to grasp the essence of the situation. At the same time, he pointed out that Marxists were not fortune-tellers, so could only point the way to large shifts and future developments and changes, but these could not and should not be stipulated mechanically. Looking eastward, one could see the radiant sun rising in all its splendor above the horizon.

It was not difficult to see that Mao had at this point made a new leap in his understanding of the characteristics of Chinese society and of the Chinese revolution and its principles. He further answered the possibility of the existence and development of China's Red regime. The Chinese revolution was pressed from both sides in the city, so could not make urban centers the focus of its work. In order to win a central stronghold for the national revolution, the Party's work had to focus on the countryside rather than the city. This marked the beginning of Mao's strategy of encircling the cities with rural strongholds.

2. A Comprehensive Analysis of the Theory of Encircling the Cities with Rural Strongholds

In May 1930, Mao wrote an article entitled "Objections to Pedantry," further offering Marxist responses to the debate concerning the Chinese revolutionary path within the Party from the perspective of an overview of Party thought. To the "leftist" dogmatists at the time, the dogmatization and revering of the armed rebellions, urban-centric path of the Russian October Revolution, and the mistake of opposing the approach of surrounding the cities with rural strongholds were exposed and criticized, and it was stated definitively that the strategy of surrounding cities with urban strongholds was the correct path. The article said, "The victory of the Chinese revolutionary struggle depends on Chinese comrades understanding the Chinese situation," and "those who have not investigated the situation have no right to speak."[31] It criticized the idea that was to be found within the Party at the time, calling it a negative behavior of "speaking with one's eyes closed."[32]

Mao took the first steps to establish the Party's work in the countryside, building rural revolutionary bases and, after expanding the theory of encircling the cities with urban strongholds with items such as the agrarian revolution in rural revolutionary bases, he further summarized the experience of Party-building, political construction, and building the army, while also proposing a series of new principles and policies, which constituted the complete theory of encircling the cities with urban strongholds. In January 1935, the Zunyi Conference determined that Mao's leadership was right, and that it opened new possibilities for the Chinese revolution. In December 1936, Mao wrote *Strategic*

Issues in the Chinese Revolutionary War, in which he offered a comprehensive exposition of the characteristics of the revolutionary war, expounded on the principle of imbalance in China's semi-colonial political and social development, and concluded that for the Chinese revolutionary war, development and victory were possible conclusions. From there, he determined a set of military strategies and tactics for encircling cities with rural strongholds, such as active defense, anti-encirclement preparation, strategic retreat, strategic counter-attack, concentrating strength, mobile warfare, quick battles, and annihilation warfare. In this book, Mao expounded on the objective and subjective conditions for the existence and development of China's revolutionary base areas, saying, "China is a huge country, so that even 'when it is not bright in the east, it is bright in the west.' We will not lack space for maneuvering."[33] This was an important geographical condition. Due to the implementation of the agrarian revolution and the equality of the officers and men, it was possible to obtain the peasants' assistance in support of the Red Army, forming an important base among the masses. The CPC adopted the correct strategy, which was to subvert the subjective initiative and obtain a fundamental guarantee of victory in the revolution. These statements by Mao also constituted an important part of the strategy of encircling the cities with urban strongholds. In July 1937, Mao wrote *Practical Theory* and completed *Theory of Conflict* the following month. In these works, he explained theory's dependence on epistemology and analyzed how best to address the issues, while firmly opposing dogmatism. The deep-rooted dogmatism and the serious harm it had brought to the revolutionary cause had laid a philosophical foundation for the strategy of encircling the cities with urban strongholds. At this point, Mao's thorough, systematic elaboration of the strategy marked its complete formation.

In the late August 1937, after the outbreak of the War of Resistance Against Japanese Aggression, the Luochuan Conference of the Central Committee of the CPC correctly formulated the principle of independent guerrilla warfare in the mountains, deciding to enthusiastically organize guerrilla warfare behind enemy lines and release the masses to establish rural anti-Japanese military bases more extensively. The Central Committee, under the leadership of Mao Zedong, proceeded from the actual situation of the War of Resistance Against Japanese Aggression, resisting Wang Ming's efforts to re-introduce right-wing error and put the Party's focus back on urban-centric work. Instead, Mao made concerted efforts to shift the entire Party's focus to the vast rural areas. In May 1938, Mao emphasized the establishment of a base area for the anti-guerrilla war in the "Strategic Issues of the Anti-Japanese Guerrilla War." In settling on the necessity and importance of establishing areas of anti-Japanese guerrilla warfare, he pointed out that, due to the long-term and cruel nature of the War of Resistance Against Japanese Aggression, guerrilla warfare behind enemy lines could not be supported without a base. The guerrilla bases could rely on their own strategic missions for self-preservation and development, as well as elimination and expulsion of the enemy. Without such a strategic base, the implementation of all strategic tasks and the realization of the goals of the war would have lost their support. For this reason, completely eliminating gangsterism from the minds of the leaders of the guerrilla war was a prerequisite for establishing a policy by which to construct bases. It was also suggested that temporary base areas or relatively stable base areas should be established in the mountains and planes and around rivers and lakes, where the enemy's hold was weak. From the local point of view, each isolated base was surrounded on all sides by the enemy, but if each base was linked to others, the enemy's urban strongholds would then be surrounded by rural revolutionary bases.

That October, Mao made careful analysis of the conditions for China's three-in-one approach in an article entitled "New Stage." The first condition was that semi-colonial cities could not completely rule the countryside, the second that China was a huge country with a large amount of guerrilla activity, and the third that the people's masses must be led by the CPC. Using the long-term organization that the Party adhered to, such as opposing enemy-occupied cities, surrounding the cities, and isolating the cities, these three conditions gradually led to a change in the enemy and its situation. When adding the changes taking place around the world, it was evident that the enemy could be expelled from the cities and the cities liberated. Mao also pointed out that these three conditions made it possible for the villages to defeat the cities.

It was necessary for China's armed struggle to follow the path of surrounding the cities with rural strongholds. This hallmark of the Chinese revolution was determined by China's economic base, which was different from that of capitalist countries. The economic foundation of capitalist countries was that the capitalist mode of production predominated, and the center of this economic base lay in cities. By contrast, China's economic base lay mainly in backward feudal modes of production in rural areas, while the more advanced, modernized cities had long been occupied by powerful imperialists and domestic reactionaries, making them the centers of enemy rule. After the defeat of the Great Revolution, the urban revolutionary forces were devastated repeatedly and severely, due mainly to the brutal rule of the Kuomintang's new warlords. For this reason, the weak revolutionary forces in the cities could not engage in a decisive battle with an enemy that held absolute superiority. The main object of the proletarian revolution in capitalist countries was the bourgeoisie concentrated in urban centers, and the main driving force was the working class concentrated in cities. One of the main objects of the Chinese revolution was the feudal landlord class scattered across the countryside, and the main driving force was the peasant class dispersed in rural areas, under the leadership of the Party. This determined that the revolution in China must first involve the rural Red Army, and only later move to the city. It was for this reason that Mao made a clearer summary of the issue of the Chinese revolutionary path in his article "War and Strategic Issues," published in November 1938. There, he pointed out that a proletarian party in a capitalist country could fight for the masses through long-term legal struggle. When it came to war in such countries, it was best to first occupy the big city, then attack the rural areas. China was different. The characteristics defining China were that it was not an independent country, but semi-colonial and semi-feudal. Further, there was no democratic system in China, as it was under imperialist oppression. Therefore, there was no parliament that allowed the revolution to take advantage of the legal right of unorganized workers to strike. Here, the task of the Communist Party was basically not to engage in uprising and war only after a long period of legal struggle, nor to take the countryside after first taking the city, but rather to take the opposite path.

In December 1939, Mao continued to clarify the path of the Chinese revolution in *The Chinese Revolution and the Communist Party of China*. He stated that the Chinese revolutionaries should be prepared to conserve and exert their strength as appropriate, avoiding fighting against powerful enemies when they were not strong enough to do so. "Thus we must use backward rural areas to create advanced, consolidated base areas."[34] The military, political, economic, and cultural revolutionary positions were used to oppose the use of the city to attack the fierce enemy in the rural areas, so as to gradually strive for the full victory of the revolution in the long-term battle. At the same time, the book also pointed out, "Because of the imbalance of China's economic development (not a unified capitalist economy), due to the vastness of China's land (allowing revolutionary forces space to maneuver), and due to the inconsistency and numerous conflicts within China's revolutionary camps, and because the peasants, under the leadership of the CPC, are the main force in the Chinese revolution, victory in the Chinese revolution is first possible in the rural areas. On the other hand, the imbalance of the revolution has brought long-term enthusiasm for the cause, so it is understandable that the long-term revolutionary struggle and the peasant guerrilla warfare in the revolutionary bases should be under the leadership of the CPC. Therefore, ignoring the idea of rural revolutionary bases, the viewpoint of the enthusiastic work done by the peasants, or the necessity of guerrilla warfare is all wrong."[35] However, focusing on the work in the rural base areas did not imply that urban work or work in rural areas under enemy rule could be abandoned. On the contrary, if there was no work in the cities or enemy-occupied rural areas, leaving the revolutionary bases isolated, the revolution would fail. Moreover, the ultimate goal of the revolution was to seize the cities currently serving as the enemy's base. Without sufficient urban work, this goal could not be achieved. These arguments had enriched Mao's theory of surrounding cities with rural strongholds. This approach taken by the CPC, under Mao's guidance, in an attempt to seize political power in the urban centers during the War of Resistance Against Japanese Aggression, spread through numerous regions in China, becoming the only appropriate path by which to lead to the final victory in the War of Resistance. With regard to this approach, the theory of armed seizure of power had been comprehensively elucidated. Its main ideas were:

a. China's national conditions meant that the Chinese revolution had to take the approach of encircling cities with urban strongholds if it was to seize power.

Mao pointed out that the central task and the highest form of the revolution were the armed seizure of power to address the issues. This Marxist-Leninist revolutionary principle was always correct. In capitalist countries, there was no feudal system, and some were bourgeois democratic systems. There was no external national oppression, and some even oppressed other nations. Based on these characteristics, the task of the proletarian party in capitalist countries was to educate the workers and harness the power of long-term legal struggle to prepare for the final overthrow of capitalism. However, China was not an independent democratic country, but semi-feudal and semi-colonial, lacking a democratic system and oppressed by imperialists. No discussion could prevail, and unorganized workers did not have the right to strike. Therefore, in China, the main form of struggle was war, and the main form of organization was the military. The task of the CPC was basically not to engage in uprising and war in a long-term struggle, nor to first take the city, then the countryside, but to use the opposite approach. In other words, their approach had to focus on the rural areas, conserve and develop power in the vast rural areas where the enemy was weak, and prepare to finally seize power through armed struggle.[36]

b. To employ the approach of encircling the cities with rural strongholds, it was necessary to establish a solid rural base.

Mao pointed out that if the revolutionaries were not willing to compromise with imperialism and its lackeys, they must persist in their struggle, if the revolutionary force was to prepare to conserve and exert its strength as appropriate and avoid taking decisive action against powerful enemies if its own strength was not sufficient. In a battle, it was necessary to create an advanced, consolidated base area in backward rural regions and to create a military, political, economic, and cultural revolutionary position, so as to oppose the fierce enemy's use of the city to attack the rural areas, allowing the revolutionaries to gradually strive for full victory through long-term struggle.

c. It was necessary to correctly handle the relationship between urban and rural struggles.

Mao pointed out that focusing on rural areas did not mean abandoning urban work, nor was it something other than armed struggle. Similarly, without urban work and other efforts in enemy occupied rural areas, the rural revolutionary bases would become isolated, and the revolution would fail. In the relationship between urban and rural areas, the rural areas would take precedence, their work supplemented by the cities, and urban struggles would complement rural struggles. The Party's urban struggle should be based on defense, and efforts should be made to organize the masses to carry out struggles. The Party's work policy in White areas was "shadowy and lean, long-term ambushes, consolidating strength, and waiting for opportunities."[37]

Later, during the War of Liberation, the People's Liberation War entered the stage of a strategic decisive battle. According to Mao's thinking regarding encircling cities with rural strongholds in order to eventually win the city, the Chinese People's Liberation Army gradually gained several points across the country, completing the task of taking cities that had been surrounded by rural strongholds. The PLA employed two methods for seizing the cities. The first was armed capture, and the second peaceful liberation. Mao's strategic thinking and revolutionary practice during the War of Liberation further enriched and developed the idea of encircling the city and finally winning it.

The CPC, led by Mao, proceeded from China's actual semi-colonial, semi-feudal situation and, by seeking the truth from facts and breaking the shackles of dogmatism, it creatively formed an armed division of workers and peasants and established Red political power through the combination of theory and practice. In the rural environment, the establishment of the Party and the army, the implementation of an agrarian revolution and the strategies to be adopted, forming a relatively complete set of cities surrounded by rural strongholds, and the theory of armed seizure of national political power constituted the objective principles of the development of the Chinese revolution and opened the way for victory. The newly gained political power guaranteed the victory of China's new democratic revolution and realized the first historic leap in combining Marxism-Leninism with Chinese revolutionary practice during the Chinese democratic revolution. China's approach of surrounding the cities with rural strongholds as a path to seizing national power was never mentioned by Marx, Engels, or Lenin, and thus forged a new path in the history of the proletarian revolution. It was a shining example of Marxism-Leninism's basic principles, such as violent proletarian revolution, state power, the union of workers and peasants, and the imbalance of political and economic development in imperialist countries, combined with the concrete practice of the Chinese revolution. It was a great pioneering work in the class revolutionary movement, much like Russia's October Revolution. China's theory of surrounding cities with rural strongholds for the purpose of armed seizure of national political power occupied an extremely important position in Mao Zedong Thought.

IV

The Theory of Constructing Revolutionary Base Areas

1. The Initial Period

After the defeat of the Great Revolution in 1927, the focus of the CPC's work shifted from the city to the countryside, and the armed divisions' base areas were begun. After the CPC, under Mao's leadership, opened the first revolutionary base area in Jinggangshan, it carried out the difficult task of exploration and offering theoretical analysis in the construction of the base areas and proposed a series of unique ideas related to political, economic, and cultural construction. The insights they offered formed a relatively accurate theory for construction of the bases.

a. *Ideas Concerning the Construction of Political Power*

After the troops arrived in Jinggangshan for the Autumn Harvest Uprising, they started building political power. On November 28, 1927, the Government of the Workers and Peasants of Chaling County was established, and Tan Zhenlin was appointed chairman. In January 1928, the Government of the Workers, Peasants, and Soldiers of Suichuan County was established, which was followed by the establishment of the Government of the Ningkang County Workers, Peasants, and Soldiers in February. Subsequently, the Government of the Yongxin and Lianhua County Workers, Peasants, and Soldiers were also established, and the people's political power had been established in the districts of townships of the counties. In May, the Soviet Government of the Workers, Peasants, and Soldiers had been established on the basis of various people's governments on the Hunan-Jiangxi border. On November 25, Mao Zedong concentrated on the collective wisdom of these experiences and, in summing up the year's work in constructing political power, wrote a report entitled "Jinggangshan Struggle," which he sent to the Central Committee of the CPC. The report expounds of the following ideas:

1) *A system of people's congresses must be implemented*. Mao pointed out that the political power of the people had been generally organized at the county, district, and township levels, but not properly organized. In

many places, there was no representative body of workers, peasants, and soldiers at the township, district, or even county level. The government's executive committees were instead elected through a sort of mass vote. A mass gathering could not discuss issues, nor could a mass receive political training. Further, a mass gathering was much more easily manipulated by spectators. Even though some places had called representative meetings, when the elections were complete, power was taken over by a committee without discussion among the representatives. Mao suggested that this was a result of the lack of public education concerning the new congressional political system. In the feudal era, arbitrary dictatorial habits had been ingrained in the minds of the masses, and even the general Party members. When they were wiped out, they still remained greedy and poised to take over. They did not like the troublesome democratic systems.[38] For this reason, Mao proposed that it was imperative that democratic systems be implemented and detailed organization laws for representatives at all levels be formulated. This was the earliest of Mao's ideas concerning the implementation of the people's congress system.

2) *The principle of democratic centralism must be upheld.* Mao pointed out that the dictatorship of the proletariat and peasants was "the people's own political power. It relies directly on the people [...] and its relationship with the people must be maintained at the highest level." He added, "It also depends entirely on the people." At that time, the system of democratic centralism was used not only in congress, but also in the executive committee, which was to say, "we are not in the habit of employing it for government work." Mao stated, "the system of democratic centralism must show its effectiveness in the revolutionary struggle, so that the masses understand that it is the system most capable of mobilizing the masses and the most conducive to the struggle and that mass organizations can be applied universally."[39] He summed up the experience of implementing the system of democratic centralism in the revolutionary base areas over the previous several years, particularly focusing on the experience of developing a people's democracy during that time. He emphasized the importance of adhering to the principle of democratic centralism in the construction of political power in the base areas.

3) *The principle of separation of the Party and government must be implemented.* Through the construction of political power in the Jinggangshan area, the prestige of the CPC was relatively high, but the government functions were not well performed. As a result, the phenomenon of Party-government emerged. At the same time, in some places, there were no Communist organizations in the political organs. To overcome these two phenomena, Mao suggested that "the Party must implement the task of leading the future government. The Party's proposition, in addition to propaganda, must be implemented by the government when it is installed."[40] In November 1931, the Chinese Soviet held the first National Congress of Workers, Peasants, and Soldiers, establishing a government of the dictatorship of the proletariat and peasantry. The Provisional Central Government of the Chinese Soviet Republic elected the Central Executive Committee and the People's Committee, chaired by Mao Zedong, and adopted the first constitution in the history of the revolutionary bases, entitled Outlines of the Chinese Soviet Constitution. The Constitution stipulated that "all regimes in the soviet belong to the workers, peasants, and soldiers, the hard-working people." It also stipulated that it did not recognize the privileged position of the imperialist in China, that all unequal treaties were abolished, that all property of colonial forces in China were "returned to the state," and so on. At the close of the Conference, the National Workers, Peasants, and Soldiers Congress was named the highest authority of the soviet regime, and the National Soviet Central Executive Committee was the highest political authority. The Central Executive Committee organized people's committees to handle daily government affairs. In January 1934, the Second National Congress of the Chinese Soviet Workers, Peasants, and Soldiers was held in Duanjin. Mao Zedong delivered the "Report of the Central Executive Committee and the People's Committee of the Chinese Soviet Republic on the Second National Soviet Congress" and "Caring for the Masses, Attention to the Conclusions of the Working Methods." The Outline of the Chinese Soviet Constitution was passed and the Executive Committee of the Chinese Soviet Government re-elected, with Mao continuing to serve as chairman.

In the period during which he presided over the government, Mao emphasized several ideas for the construction of political power. The first was the idea of combining democracy and dictatorship. Mao pointed out that the most extensive democracy of the soviets was manifested first of all in their own elections. The soviets gave all the people who had been exploited or oppressed in the past an absolute right to vote and to be elected, so that women's power was equal to men's. Further, soviet democracy was seen in the representatives of cities and townships. The system of city and township representatives was composed of soviets. The basis was to ensure the soviets remained close to the organs of the general public. And finally, soviet democracy was also evident in that all people were given the freedom to publish and to strike, with complete freedom of assembly and speech, to allow the people to supervise and criticize their work. Mao paid special attention to the role of the people's congress and let the people fully exercise their right to be the masters of the country. He believed that, in general, the soviets had a very broad revolutionary democracy for the general public, but at the same time constituted the vast majority of its power in this kind of democracy, built upon millions of workers and with an awareness of the need for stability and power. With this power, the soviets formed their own dictatorship, organized the revolutionary war, organized the soviet courts, and carried out fierce attacks on class enemies on all sides, while the soviet courts played a key role in suppressing counter-revolutionary activity within soviet territory.

The second idea was a concern for the thoughts of the masses. Mao pointed out that the central tasks of the CPC at that time were to mobilize the masses to participate in the revolutionary struggle, to defeat the imperialists and the Kuomintang in the revolutionary war, to develop and revolutionize the whole country, and to drive the imperialists out of China. Therefore, it was necessary to get the support of the masses. He said, "Do you want the support of the masses? Do you want them to put their full strength on the front line? If so, then we must be with the masses, to mobilize their enthusiasm, and care about their suffering. We must do practical work for the sake of their interests and solve the problems of production and of their livelihood – the problems of salt, rice, housing, clothing, childbearing – we must solve all their problems. When we have done this, the masses will certainly support us, and will even regard the revolution as their whole lives, taking it up as a glorious banner." He went on, "What is the real impregnable wall? It is the masses, which number in the millions, who sincerely support the revolution. The real impregnable wall is a power which cannot be broken. It is completely unbreakable. The counter-revolution cannot break us, but we must break it." Mao said with great confidence that, in order to unite the millions of people around the revolutionary government and develop the Party's revolutionary war, it was necessary to eliminate all counter-revolutionaries and win all of China.

The third idea was to pay careful attention to working methods. Mao pointed out that the Party was the leader and organizer of the revolutionary war, and also of the lives of the masses. Here, the problem of working methods was placed seriously before the Party, thus "we must not only propose tasks, but also answer the question of how to complete them," and, "if you don't address the issue, the task will be just groundless talk. If you don't pay attention to expanding the leadership of the Red Army and to the method of its expansion, then even if you expand it a thousand times, it will not bring successful results."[41] Mao also proposed the working method of the more advanced leading the less advanced. He said, "In all the places we lead, there are undoubtedly many active cadres, good working comrades emerging among the masses. These comrades have a responsibility to help those places where the work is weak and help those who are not yet comrades but who are working hard." He added, "We must use practical methods to improve our work. More advanced places should continue to advance, and those which are less advanced should strive to catch up."[42] Only in this way could the enemy's encirclement campaign be destroyed and the imperialist and KMT rule throughout the country be toppled.

b. Ideas Concerning Economic Construction

Economic construction was the main work involved in the construction of the revolutionary base areas. Mao began from the actual situation of the production status, production level, and economic structure of the rural revolutionary bases, taking into account the needs of the revolutionary war, summing up the experience of the economic construction in the revolutionary base areas while carrying out the construction of political power and proposing some valuable ideas regarding the economic construction of the revolutionary base areas. In October 1928, the Second Congress of the Hunan-Jiangxi Border Party passed a resolution drafted by Mao. The first part of the resolution was entitled "How Can

China's Red Political Power Last?" It put forward the idea that the experience of the revolutionary base areas surrounded by White forces was "worthy of the notice of every Party member." At that time, at the revolutionary bases, "the lack of daily necessities and funds for the military and civilians is a huge problem." He stressed that "if the border party cannot generate an appropriate solution to the economic problem, under the condition that the enemy's power remains stable for a relatively long period, the bases will encounter great difficulties. The economic problem must be resolved. It deserves the attention of every Party member."[43] During his work with the interim central government of the Chinese Soviet Republic, Mao Zedong led the economic construction of the central base area, summed up the experience of the work in economic construction, and published "The Necessity of Paying Attention to Economic Work," "Our Economic Policy," and other important works elaborating on the idea of economic construction in the revolutionary base areas.

Primarily, he expounded on the importance of economic construction in the revolutionary base areas and criticized the misconceptions about economic construction. Mao pointed out, "The fierce development of the revolutionary war requires us to mobilize the masses, immediately carry out the movement on the economic front, and carry out all necessary and possible economic construction. This is because all work at this time should be in service to the revolutionary war. The first tasks are the complete smashing of the enemy's Fifth Anti-Encirclement Campaign, to ensure the supply of the Red Army's material needs, and to further improve the lives of the people, inspiring them to participate in the revolutionary war. Economic construction is needed in order to organize the masses of the people on the economic front and educate them to make new gains in the mass forces, to consolidate the alliance of workers and peasants, to consolidate the dictatorship of the proletariat and peasantry, and to strengthen the leadership of the proletarian class."[44] To this end, Mao criticized two misconceptions concerning economic construction. The first was the view that the environment of the revolutionary war need not undertake economic construction, which he saw as an extreme error. He pointed out that they did not understand that if economic construction was not carried out, the material conditions of the revolutionary war would not be guaranteed, and the people would grow weary of the long-term war and be unable to break the enemy's blockade of the base areas, which would result in no improvement to the people's lives. In this way, the revolutionary war would not proceed smoothly and the workers' and peasants' alliance would be affected. The second view refuted by Mao was that economic construction was already central to the current tasks, and that it was thus wrong to leave off the revolutionary war for the sake of economic construction. Mao pointed out, "At this stage, economic construction must be built around the revolutionary war, which is our central task. The purpose of economic construction is the revolution, and it must be surrounded by and subjected to the revolution." He added, "Only after the end of the civil war can it be said that economic construction is our central task."[45] Mao carefully clarified the dialectical relationship between economic construction and the revolutionary war.

Mao went on to correctly define the revolutionary base areas' economic policies and their source. After 1931, the labor and taxation policies promoted by the adventurists on the left, as represented by Wang Ming, caused great damage to the industrial and commercial sectors in the rural revolutionary bases and caused serious difficulties for the military and civilians. This caused doubt and dissatisfaction among many Party members. In 1933, Zhang Wentian and Chen Yun each published articles criticizing this leftist error, pointing out that at that time, the policy of "capitalizing on the current assets alone" would inevitably lead to the demise of the soviet economy, unemployment of workers, and the deterioration of the workers' quality of living. The policy was actually an expression of a petty bourgeois mindset that represented a group of backward workers and the narrow interests of a small sector of the working class. In January 1934, Mao made a report at the Second National Conference of Workers and Peasants, in which he further elaborated on the economic policies of the rural revolutionary base areas, saying, "Now, our state-owned economy is composed of three parts: state-owned enterprises, cooperative enterprises, and private undertakings." He added, "For the private economy, as long as it is not outside the scope of the government's law, it will not only not be prevented, but will be instead promoted and rewarded, because the development of the private economy is now required by the interests of the people. That to to say, the economy is now an absolute advantage, and it will be for a long time." He further stated that it was necessary "to develop the state-run economy as much as possible and develop the cooperative economy on a large scale, which will in turn reward the private economy [...] The cooperative and state-run economies will work together and, after long-term effort, will become a huge force in the economy." And finally, "the principle of our economic policy is to carry out all possible and necessary economic construction and concentrate economic power, supply the war, and at the same time, try to improve the lives of the people and consolidate the workers and peasants. The combination of the economy guarantees the leadership of the proletariat over the peasantry and strives toward its leadership in the state-owned and private economies, which will, in the future, lead to the development of socialism."[46] It could be said that Mao proposed these three key parts of the new democratic economy (the state-owned, cooperative, and private economies) and the concept of their inter-related nature. These ideas on economic policy guided the development of the economy in the base areas from that point on.

Mao further expounded on the status of agricultural production as a central concern for the economic construction in the revolutionary base areas. China was home to one of the world's earliest developed civilizations, and it was also the country with the most developed natural economy in rural regions. In China's more than 2,000 years of feudal society, its dominant economic form had always been the natural economy combining agriculture and cottage craft industries. Its production was not for exchange, but for the needs of the producer or production unit itself. This form of economy continued into modern China. For this reason, Mao Zedong stated, "The center of our economy is the development of agricultural and industrial production and the development of foreign trade and cooperatives." He particularly emphasized that "under current conditions, agricultural production is the first priority in our economic work," because China had been an agricultural society since ancient times. The Party was based in rural areas, which were mainly dedicated to agricultural production. It not only solved the most important issue of food, but also provided the raw materials for other daily necessities such as clothing, sugar, paper, and so forth. To this end, it was necessary to lead peasants to seek solutions to problems such as "labor issues, cattle farming, fertilizer problems, seed problems, water problems, and so on."[47] He pointed out that mobilizing women to participate in production, organizing mutual assistance for labor, and organizing farmers' cooperatives were important measures that could be taken to address these issues. In particular, he put forward the idea that water conservation was the lifeblood of agriculture.

Finally, he pointed out the basic policy guidelines for the financing of the revolutionary base areas. The purpose of soviet funds was to guarantee the supply of the revolutionary war and to guarantee that all revolutionary costs would be covered by the Soviets. However, at that point, the Soviet Republic still only occupied a small part of the country, and even that was a place with a relatively backward economy. Facilitating a people's taxation policy, along with a Soviet fiscal policy, had to be built on the principles of class and revolution. Thus the soviet financial sources were 1) confiscation and collection of the property of all feudal exploiters, 2) taxes, and 3) development of national economic undertakings. Mao pointed out that "increasing our fiscal revenue through the development of the national economy is the basis of our fiscal policy." It was important to make financial work serve the development of production so that "the national bank-issued banknotes will be essentially based on the demands of our national economic development. The need for pure finance can only be a secondary consideration." At the same time, he stated, "Financial expenditure should be based on the principle of saving." It was necessary to "save every copper plate for war and revolution, for our economic construction and the principle of our accounting system." Further, it was necessary for every government worker to understand that "corruption and waste are great crimes,"[48] thus it was necessary to fight against corruption and waste.

Guided by Mao's thoughts on economic construction, the work of building the economy in the revolutionary base areas was carried out by the soviet government with great diligence and through avid attention to developing production, which not only supported the revolutionary war, but also improved the lives of the people in the revolutionary base areas.

c. Ideas Concerning Cultural Construction

China was a country with a backward culture. Under the reactionary rule of the Kuomintang, about 80% of the country's population was illiterate, trapping the people in ignorance. Regarding this issue, Mao pointed out that the soviets must implement a cultural education reform in order to gain victory in the revolutionary war, consolidate and develop the soviet regime, mobilize the forces of the people, join the revolution, and create a new revolutionary era, lifting the shackles of the reactionary ruling class and raising the spirit of the proletariat and peasantry to create a new soviet culture among the workers and peasants. After the construction of the revolutionary base areas, great emphasis was placed on cultural construction. Primary schools were established throughout the base areas to enable the children of the workers and peasants to go to school, to carry out literacy work, to organize various forms of evening schools and study classes, and to carry out literacy campaigns. The government also developed a publishing enterprise, publishing a variety of newspapers and books and developing the revolutionary literature and art of the masses. Its sports and health work likewise achieved great results. Mao summed up the experience of cultural education work in the revolutionary base areas and put forward two basic items for cultural education. The first item was the policy of cultural education. Mao pointed out that the Party's policy of cultural education was "to educate the great masses of laborers, in the spirit of Communism, to make cultural education serve the revolutionary war and class struggle, to link education with labor, and to allow the vast majority of Chinese people to partake in the enjoyment of civilized people."[49]

The second item was the central task of cultural education construction. Mao pointed out that the central task of education in the revolutionary base areas was "to implement compulsory education, develop a broad range of social education, eliminate illiteracy, and create a large number of senior cadres to lead the revolutionary struggle."[50] Regarding existing intellectuals, Mao said they should serve the people, train revolutionary intellectuals, and serve in cultural education.

2. Period of Development and Maturity

After the outbreak of the War of Resistance Against Japanese Aggression, the CPC-led People's Army advanced behind enemy lines and launched an independent self-defense guerrilla war, seeking to mobilize the masses and establish anti-Japanese base areas. With the development of the anti-Japanese guerrilla war, the anti-Japanese democratic base areas were likewise increasingly consolidated and expanded. The anti-Japanese democratic base area was an advanced position for implementing and realizing the new democratic theory of the CPC. The various new democratic policies adopted by the CPC-led regimes of the united front in each base area fully demonstrated that the base areas had begun to change their semi-colonial, semi-feudal social nature and were gradually becoming, in embryonic form, a new democratic society. In the base areas, the people really lived a new life as masters of their own affairs. Their spirits were lifted, united under the leadership of the CPC, and they fought for victory against Japanese aggression, achieving a better future for themselves. At the same time, the Party's ideas for laying the foundations for the country were developed more fully through this process. In the various construction efforts of the anti-Japanese democratic base areas, the construction of political power formed the central link. The basic guiding ideology for the construction of political power in the anti-Japanese democratic base areas was the "Ten Principles for Anti-Japanese Salvation," formulated by the CPC in the early days of the Anti-Japanese War, alongside the political program of the new democratic revolution as laid out by Mao Zedong in *New Democracy*. The specific content of this ideology included:

a. *The Construction of the Regime*

The first principle implemented universally was the "3-3 System." Political power in the anti-Japanese democratic base areas lay in the united front. In constructing political power, the Party earnestly implemented the 3-3 System, which was a practice and system by which the Party implemented democracy. On March 6, 1940, the Central Committee of the CPC clearly stated in the directive Issues of Responsibility in the Anti-Japanese Base Areas that among the public opinion organs or political organs at all levels, "CPC members must account for one-third, left-wing progressives for one-third, and non-left, non-right centrists for a third."[51] On March 11, at the Yan'an Senior Cadre Conference, Mao reiterated that the distribution of personnel in the regime should be "one-third CPC members, who represent the proletariat and poor peasants, one-third left-wing progressives, who represent the petty bourgeoisie, and one third non-left, non-right centrists, who represent the middle bourgeoisie and enlightened gentlemen. Only traitors and anti-communist elements are not eligible to participate in this regime."[52] On December 25, 1940, Mao's instructions to the Central Committee marked the first time the name "3-3 System" was officially proposed. On May 1, 1941, the Central Bureau of the Shaanxi-Gansu-Ningxia Border Region proposed that the Shaanxi-Gansu-Ningxia Border Region Policy Agenda be approved by the Politburo of the Central Committee. The Agenda stipulated, "Those shortlisted Party members may account for just one-third. All Party members and non-members can participate in the activities of public opinion organs and in the administration of border areas." On November 21, 1941, in his Speech on the Central Bureau of the Shaanxi-Gansu-Ningxia Border Region, Mao again explained the implementation and importance of the 3-3 System, stating that "state affairs are the official affairs of the state, not the private matters of one party, so the CPC is obligated to cooperate with non-party personnel and is not to exclude others or monopolize all rights."[53] He solemnly declared to non-party members, "The principle of democratic cooperation between the CPC and non-party members is fixed and will never change." He expressed hope that "this sort of cooperation will be implemented at this meeting."[54] The 3-3 System's principle of constructing political power was an effective democratic system explored by the Party in the anti-Japanese base areas. On April 15, 1941, Deng Xiaoping published an article in the journal *Party Life*, in which he pointed out that "The essence of the 3-3 System is democracy."[55] The firm implementation of such a democratic system came about, on the one hand, because there were common enemies who needed to be confronted by a united front. On the other hand, because all these classes had considerable strength, they were mutually constrained. If they did not give way to one another, as had been proposed by the 3-3 System, some CPC members felt this would weaken the Party's leadership. However, this policy was, on the one hand, precisely what guaranteed the leadership of the CPC political power and firmly united the masses of the petty bourgeoisie. On the other, it consolidated all the forces that could be united by the enlightened members of the middle bourgeoisie and landlord class. The CPC-led Anti-Japanese National United Front consolidated the anti-Japanese base areas and showed the extraordinary leadership and organizational skills of the CPC under Mao. The 3-3 System was a specific policy for the construction of political power in the anti-Japanese base areas, a special form for a specific time and specific conditions, and thus having distinct features. But in its basic spirit, it was an attempt to unite Party members and non-Party members under the regime's leadership for a democratic cooperation.

Second, it was important to fully guarantee the rights of the people in the base areas. After the organizational principle had been determined, ensuring the implementation of that principle depended entirely on the extraordinary character and serious spirit of the Party. During the War of Resistance Against Japanese Aggression, the general masses in the various anti-Japanese base areas were generally able to participate in the election activities, to truly implement their most sacred human rights, and to establish a government in which the Communists and trusted, capable anti-Japanese Party and non-Party members cooperated. Those who had experience and could represent the interests of the people were elected to leadership positions at all levels. This served as an important symbol of the implementation of democratic politics. The leaders of the Shaanxi-Gansu-Ningxia border region and other anti-Japanese base areas all came from the masses. Article 2 of the Regulations on the Election of the Senate of the Shaanxi-Gansu-Ningxia Border Region stipulated, "The general, direct, equal, and secret ballot voting system shall be adopted." Article 3 stipulated, "All people living in the border area who are at least 18 years of age, regardless of class, party affiliation, occupation, gender, religion, nationality, property ownership status, and education, has a right to vote and to be elected. Only those who have been found guilty of treason by the courts and those who are mentally ill will be deprived of their rights to vote and to bear office." According to these regulations, all anti-Japanese classes, whether peasants, workers, landlord, or capitalist, all anti-Japanese parties, whether CPC, KMT, or any other party, and all ethnic groups, whether Han, Manchu, Mongolian, Hui, or Tibetan, provided they were of sound mind and body, would be given the right to vote, to be elected, to dissent, and to participate in all political activities in the anti-Japanese base area. During the election, all parties, groups, and individuals were free to campaign, and their campaign platforms were to be included in each election. It was not only laborers who would participate in the election, but also landlords and wealthy peasants who also enthusiastically invested in the election activities. In order to reflect the nationwide equality of the Anti-Japanese National United Front, the anti-Japanese democratic regime had clearly defined the right to vote for ethnic minorities. The ethnic groups with a sufficient quorum of the Senate would have separate election, while those without a sufficient quorum but with one-fifth of the quorum in a township, a county, or a city election, or one-eighth in an election in the border region, would also have separate election. One representative would be elected at each level. In terms of the proportion of voters who participated in the election, it indicated that the principle of democratic equality must be enforced in the anti-Japanese democratic regime. Taking the Shaanxi-Gansu-Ningxia border region as an example, three democratic elections were held from 1937 to 1946. The first was from May to November 1937, and voter turn-out accounted for more than 70% of eligible voters. During the second election in 1941, voter turn-out accounted for 80% of eligible voters, and in the third election, held from March 1945 through March 1946, the average turn-out in each electorate was 82.5% of eligible voters, while some districts reached as high as 96%. These figures are similar to those seen in other anti-Japanese base areas during that period. In the election of seven counties in Jinchaji (parts of Shanxi, Hebei, and Inner Mongolia) in 1940, the citizens who participated in the county election, both men and women, accounted for 78.3% of the total number of citizens, while those who participated in the district elections accounted for 81.4%, and those who participated in township elections accounted for 83.9%. Even in certain guerrilla areas that had been "swept" by the enemy, the people's elections were not disrupted. Sometimes they could not be carried out in the daytime, so they were carried out in the evening, and if a general assembly could not be held, the people were divided into small groups. In short, great effort was put into finding ways to achieve the goal. Further, women's participation in politics was one way of measuring social progress. In the elections in the anti-Japanese base areas, the proportion of women's participation was very large, generally about 80%, and even hitting highs of 90%.

The election activities in the anti-Japanese base areas truly embodied the principles of universality, directness, and equality, and they ensured broad representation at all levels. Through the elections, political power at all levels was improved and consolidated, and the united anti-Japanese spirit among all ethnic groups and parties was further strengthened, the process of democratization of the anti-Japanese base areas promoted, and the development of the War of Resistance furthered.

Third, it was necessary to implement simple administration in the military. From 1941 to 1943, the anti-Japanese base areas led by the CPC entered their most trying stage. The region in which the base areas were located had been reduced by half and its population dropped from 100 million to less than 50 million, and the Eighth Route Army and New Fourth Army had been reduced from 500,000 soldiers to 300,000. The soldiers and civilians in the base area had almost no clothing, oil, or paper, and the soldiers had no shoes or socks. Their personnel had no shelter in winter and faced extremely difficult circumstances. Faced with such a severe situation, the Party began to implement the policy of "skilled, simple administration." In November 1941, Li Dingming proposed a policy of "skilled, simple administration," pointing out that under the present circumstances of hardship and a lack of resources, "the government should first propose a planned economy based on the objective material conditions and subjective economic needs, in an effort to improve overall productivity, economic conditions, and the economic base. Then, on the basis of the existing economy, the government should have a united economic plan that is within its means of expenditure. The following step, under conditions of financial and economic strength and without disrupting the anti-Japanese forces, is to implement militarism for the army, strengthen its combat effectiveness, and fight with the soldiers. Victory will be gained on this principle, avoiding the use of the old, weak, or disabled in battle. The government should implement simple administration, enrich government institutions, and operate under the principle of compactness and precision, always being competent, avoiding large institutions, redundant staff, and the waste of manpower and financial resources. Next, it should stipulate supply regulations and avoid unnecessary supply and consumption. Finally, it should promote conservation and cleanliness, and should avoid unnecessary waste."[56] Mao commented on this proposal, saying, "This approach is very good. It is precisely the sort of transformation our institutionalism, bureaucracy, and formalism needs." In December 1941, the Central Committee of the CPC issued instructions to the anti-Japanese democratic base area. The *Liberation Daily* published many editorials and organized numerous discussions. Many of the Party's directives and editorials were drafted by Mao personally. He said, "This simple administration must be strict, thorough, and universal, not perfunctory, careless, or partial. In this simple administration, we must achieve five key things: streamlining, unity, effectiveness, economy, and opposition to bureaucracy."[57] Beginning in the winter of 1941, the anti-Japanese base areas began to implement "simple administration." The Shaanxi-Gansu-Ningxia Border Region had been streamlined three times, and the internal institutions of various offices, organs, and institutions had been cut by a quarter, and its subsidiary organizations had cut down from 1140 to 991 people, the number of departments from 35 to 22, and the number of personnel from 469 to 279. After the second reorganization, the total number of county (or municipal) governments was reduced 1,189 to 397 people, about 33% of the original number. The original staff of the district offices was cut from 1,250 to 955, about 75.6%. The other bases were similarly streamlined to a third or quarter their original size. This streamlining lasted from the end of 1941 until sometime in late 1943, when it was basically completed. The various anti-Japanese democratic bases and regimes claimed to have achieved great result, and some of their personnel returned to the front lines of production. Through this work, various forms of old-style cronyism in the political system were corrected. The system of unified leadership had been determined, the bureaucratic tendency in the work had been opposed, and the work efficiency had been improved. The simplification of the administration had played a positive role, reducing the number of non-working personnel and greatly saving on expenses. Further, the number of public debts collected in each base area had correspondingly decreased, with each locale dropping by a third, which greatly reduced the burden on the people, raised the level of integrity in the CPC-led anti-Japanese democratic regime when faced with great difficulties, and strengthened the most basic ties between the Party and the people, having consolidated the Anti-Japanese National United Front and created good social conditions and material foundations for the victory of the revolution.

b. On Economic Construction

The period of the War of Resistance Against Japanese Aggression was an important time for the Party's ideological and theoretical policies to mature. During this period, the Central Committee formulated a series of appropriate economic policies and accumulated rich experience for guiding economic construction.

The first was the establishment of the general policy for fiscal and economic work, a policy of "developing the economy and guaranteeing supply." In order to supplement the financial and economic deficiencies and improve the lives of civilians and soldiers during the early days of the War of Resistance Against Japanese Aggression, Party leaders in the Shaanxi-Gansu-Ningxia Border Region took the lead in the production movement and achieved great results, which enabled the Party to successfully pass through its most difficult period. However, at the time, there were still different understandings both inside and outside the Party regarding how to fundamentally address the problem of financial supply in the border areas. Some people were bound by outdated, conservative fiscal views, forgetting the need to develop the economy and open up financial resources, and thus only fighting on the issue of simple revenue and expenditure, in an attempt to solve financial problems by shrinking expenditures that were in fact indispensable. Although some advocated the development of production, they proposed many risky, unrealistic plans, such as the construction of heavy industry and the development of a large salt industry and military industries. In an effort to correctly guide the economic construction of the border areas, Mao made an important report on the economic and financial problems during the anti-Japanese period in the Northwestern High-level Conference in December 1942, accurately summarizing and criticizing the experiences and lessons of the financial and economic work in the border areas. The two errors mentioned above tended to put forward a general policy of "developing the economy and guaranteeing supply." Mao stated that the quality of a fiscal policy was sufficient to affect the economy, but fiscal policy should be determined by economics. If there was no economic foundation and the policy could not address financial hardships, then there would be no economic development to generate abundant finances. Financial difficulties could only be solved through tangible, effective economic development. Forgetting to develop the economy and open up financial resources and attempting to resolve fiscal problems by shrinking unnecessary expenditures would not solve any problems.[58] Here, Mao clearly pointed out that the fundamental way to resolve financial and economic difficulties was to develop the economy, open up financial resources, and increase revenue. In view of this, the Central Committee placed great emphasis on the practical benefits of developing production in the border areas. It pointed out that all organs, schools, and troops must enthusiastically grow vegetables and grains, raise pigs, burn charcoal, develop handicrafts, and engage in other similar activities during the war. For production activities, all factories should base the growth and decline of their business strictly on their own economic profits and losses. The common goal of the Party branches, the executive leadership, and the trade unions in the factories was to create as many products and of as high quality as possible and sell them as fast as possible, all for the greatest possible benefit. In other words, the measure of the economic construction in the base areas was not only about how much wasteland remained, how much land had been planted, or how many factories set up, but also about how many products were produced for the benefit of society and how well the production of individuals and groups was aligned with the needs of society.

Mao's general policy for fiscal work also clearly pointed out the fundamental purpose of developing the base areas, which was to guarantee the supply of funds for the war of resistance, to address the needs of Party and government personnel, and to improve the people's lives. In this way, the general policy offered a profound clarification of the fundamental guiding ideology of economic construction in the base areas from the aspects of both means and objectives.

In addition, focusing on agriculture while also developing production was a strategic policy proposed by the Party as a means of developing the economy in the base areas. What should the focus of development for the rural base areas' economy be? This was a major question, and it was not immediately clear to the Party. In the first phase of the production movement in the Shaanxi-Gansu-Ningxia Border Region, the troops, institutions, and schools all focused on the development of agricultural production, while government's investment in production was more industrial and commercial than agricultural. This situation created a heavy commercial agriculture that was very unfavorable to the economic development of the entire border region, and it was imperative that it be corrected. To this end, Mao Zedong proposed the development of various economic undertakings in the border areas, saying, "It should be established that agriculture is primary, industry, handicrafts, transportation, and animal husbandry secondary, and business tertiary,"[59] thus indicating the priorities for the economic development of the base areas, offering focus and direction for the economy. In order to vigorously develop agricultural production in the base areas, Mao also proposed a series of major economic and technological measures based on the actual situation. Mainly, he intended to 1) reduce rents and interest rates, reduce feudal landlords' exploitation of farmers, and stimulate the production interests of the peasants, 2) organize and establish various forms of agricultural labor mutual aid organizations, implement collective production, and improve labor productivity, 3) reward production, carry out the model labor movement, reward labor heroes, and promote wealth among laborers, 4) adapt to local conditions, proceed from actual conditions, and realistically determine measures to increase production, and 5) improve and transform agricultural technology, such as the development of water conservancy, and promote a variety of excellent practices. All of these measures played an important role in the development of agricultural production in the base areas.

Further, the Party put forward two important guidelines for correctly handling economic relations between the two types of bases – the guidelines of "public-private considerations" and "military-civilian considerations." In the rural areas during the War of Resistance Against Japanese Aggression, there were generally two different economic components, the public economy and the people's economy (i.e., the private economy). The public economy was the agro-industrial enterprise operated by the government, military, organs, and schools. The people's economy referred to agro-industrial businesses operated by private individuals. How to correctly handle the relationship between these two types of economies in the economic development of the base areas was an important issue. At the beginning of the Anti-Japanese War, the Party adopted a policy of "striving for foreign aid and recuperating the people" in the Shaanxi-Gansu-Ningxia Border Region. On the one hand, organizations helped the people develop production. On the other, efforts to alleviate the burden on the people had resulted in the people's economy being mostly restored and developed. In terms of agriculture, from 1937 to 1940, the area of cultivated land expanded by about one-third in a three-year period, and food production increased by about 45%. Later, with the serious difficulties in the financial economy and the implementation of self-sufficiency tasks, especially from 1941 to 1942, more attention was given to the establishment and development of the public economy, while the development of the people's economy was neglected, with the government's investment in economic development going mainly to the public sector. There were few investments for private enterprises, and the burden on the masses had increased too much, resulting in widespread dissatisfaction. In order to mobilize both the public and private sectors and jointly develop the life of the economy in the base areas, Mao proposed the principle of "public-private consideration" or "military-civilian consideration," which was, on the one hand, the development of the public economy, and on the other, the development of the people's economy and the implementation of both public and private investment.

The implementation of the principle of "public-private considerations" or "military-civilian considerations" handled the relationship between the public and private economies in an appropriate manner for that time, making great strides toward mobilizing the enthusiasm of the public and private sectors to develop the economy of the base areas, improving both the public and private economies.

Finally, "unified leadership and decentralized management was an important principle put forward by the Party to organize and lead the economic life of the base areas." The public economy was an important component and leading factor in the new democratic economy. Its establishment and development was to play a decisive role in the development of the economy in the base areas. In order to organize and lead the development of the public economy in the Shaanxi-Gansu-Ningxia Border Region, the Central Committee put forward the principle of "concentrated leadership and decentralized management" in 1942, distributing some production expenses to all units, requiring each unit to decentralize independent operations and introduce self-sufficient production. However, at that time and for a while thereafter, this principle was not fully implemented. As a result, there were too many decentralized operations, insufficient centralized leadership, or even no centralized leadership, which brought great confusion to the economic life of the border areas. People paid more attention to industrial, while ignoring agricultural production. Commercial speculation was quite serious, and some even smuggled arms, evaded taxes, and continued industrial construction without regard for regulations, so that some factories were built but could not be started up or were soon out of commission. Each unit focused on its own gain, creating bitter rivalries and consuming all they earned, leaving no way for district or county cadres to send a couple of pounds of cotton for making their own clothes. This situation was incompatible with the Party's general policy of "developing the economy and guaranteeing supply." Therefore, in a report entitled "Economic and Financial Issues," Mao emphasized, "The development of the public economy must be implemented on the principle of 'concentrating leadership and decentralizing management.' This is true not only for industry, but also for agriculture and commerce." After that, Mao again further summarized this principle as "unified leadership, decentralized management." The development of the public economy in the Shaanxi-Gansu-Ningxia Border Region had been fully implemented since 1943. The business direction of the enterprise was unified according to the system, and the mutual relationships between the enterprises were adjusted, allowing for a considerable portion of the revenue to be retained. Under the conditions in the unit, the production profit was unified, and the various parties were allowed to follow a unified plan, policy, and governance. By tackling the problem of self-reliance and problem-solving, it quickly reversed the chaos of the past, allowing the economic development of the border region to be relatively smooth and overcoming the shortcomings in various aspects. For this reason, Mao said, "The principle of 'unified leadership, decentralized management' has proven to be the appropriate principle for the organization of all economic life under the current conditions in our liberated areas."

c. *On Cultural Construction*

As the leader of cultural construction in the base areas, the CPC was directly responsible for cultural construction. Because construction of the base areas was to be fully carried out, questions of what principles should be followed in cultural construction, what tasks to accomplish, what methods to adopt, and what direction to develop were not only theoretical issues, but had also become practical issues. To this end, the CPC conducted a multi-party exploration and formulated a more complete policy.

Primarily, the basic policy of emphasizing cultural construction in the base areas was to focus on the War of Resistance Against Japanese Aggression. In the early days of the war, in his article "Policies, Measures, and Future Opposition to the Japanese," Mao proposed a fundamental reform of the earlier education policy and system. Anything that was not urgent and reasonable was abandoned. News, publishing, film, drama, literature, and art were all utilized for the benefit of national defense. In October 1938, after the War of Resistance entered a stalemate, Mao further stated in his political report to the Sixth Plenary Session of the Sixth National Congress of the CPC, entitled "On the New Stage," that "According to the principles of all wars, all cultural and educational undertakings should be adapted to the demands of war. Therefore, the following cultural and educational policies must be implemented: 1) change the academic system, abolish unnecessary courses, change management systems, teach the courses necessary for war, and promote enthusiastic student learning, 2) create and expand various cadre schools and train a large number of anti-Japanese cadres, 3) extensively develop people's education programs, organize various tutorial schools, literacy activities, drama activities, singing activities, sports, and create newspapers in various places behind enemy lines to improve the people's national culture and consciousness, and 4) make primary education compulsory and educate the new generation in the national spirit."[60] The above principles and policies highlighted the fundamental principle of cultural construction. It was necessary for the Party to focus on the War of Resistance Against Japanese Aggression and serve as the comprehensive and ongoing force of the war.

A basic direction for cultural development was also proposed. In January 1940, Mao delivered a speech at the First Congress of the Shaanxi-Gansu-Ningxia Border Region, entitled "The Politics and Culture of the New Democracy" (from *New Democracy*), in which he discussed the historic process by which modern Chinese culture had developed and its characteristics. He went on to propose the task of "turning China, which is ruled by an old culture and is thus ignorant and backward, into a civilization that is ruled by a new culture and is thus advanced." This "new culture" was to be "a culture of the scientific masses of the nation, that is, an anti-imperial, anti-feudal culture." This actually pointed the way for the development of a new democratic culture and served as an invaluable guide. After the beginning of the rectification movement in May 1942, Mao published his "Speech at the Yan'an Forum on Literature and Art," expounding on the relationship between literature and politics, literature and art, and the entire revolutionary cause, not only suggesting that literature and art must be used to serve the workers, peasants, and soldiers, but also going on to discuss how it may be made to do so. These would inevitably have a major impact on the cultural construction of the anti-Japanese base areas and become a powerful driving force for the literary and arts movements in the anti-Japanese base areas.

Further, the key to the cultural construction of the anti-Japanese base areas was to have a large number of intellectuals there and allow them to play their role to the fullest extent. With the consolidation and expansion of the anti-Japanese base areas, the task of propaganda, organization, and arming the masses were extremely arduous, and the brutal confrontation of cadres and soldiers in the struggle with the enemy had resulted in a large number of sacrifices and loss of personnel. It was necessary to absorb a large number of intellectuals to take part in the Party and the army. The CPC under Mao's guidance had a very clear understanding of this matter. In December 1939, in the article "Absorbing a Large Number of Intellectuals," Mao pointed out, "In the long and cruel war for national liberation, during the great struggle to establish a new China, the CPC must excel at absorbing intellectuals into the Party so that we may organize a great war of resistance, organize millions of peasant masses, develop revolutionary cultural movements, and develop a revolutionary united front. Without the participation of intellectuals, victory in the revolution will be impossible."[61] In December 1940, Mao's instructions for the Central Committee also stated that "educators, cultural figures, journalists, scholars, and technologists of bourgeois liberalism should be allowed to cooperate with us in the base areas to run schools and newspapers and to carry out various tasks. We should absorb all intellectuals who are active in the anti-Japanese spirit into the schools we run for short-term training and to participate in military, government, and social work."[62] During the War of Resistance Against Japanese Aggression, the anti-Japanese bases centered around Yan'an could come to be made up of mainly patriotic intellectuals, young students, and cultural elites, attracting them to beware of the dangers and stay on the straight path of the policies set by the CPC.

Finally, specific policies suited to the demands of cultural construction in the base areas were formulated. Along with the gradual implementation of these principles and policies and the continuous expansion and consolidation of the base areas, the cultural propaganda activities of the base areas had become increasingly active, and cultural associations had been established. The CPC regarded "cultural propaganda as an important weapon for educating and organizing the masses and attacking the enemy, and thus necessary for the general front."[63] The Party had a cultural management department in its own organization, and the government likewise had a cultural management organization that used various means to promote the development of cultural undertakings. In September 1940, in an effort to carry out its cultural movement in the War of Resistance, the Central Committee of the CPC issued the Directive of the Central Committee Regarding the Development of Cultural Movements, requiring the Party organizations and armed forces of the various base areas to "organize the planning and implementation of all propaganda, educational, and publishing undertakings. We must popularize and improve the theoretical and political level of the cadres inside and outside the Party, as well as in the anti-Japanese army. It is necessary to raise the theoretical, political, and cultural levels of the cadres, army, and people in the base areas, and to expand them to the entire country. It is important that we give as much attention to transporting cultural nourishment as we do to transporting ammunition."[64] In January 1938, the Military and Civilian Congress of the Jinchaji Border Region passed the Resolution on Cultural Education, which stipulated the basic principles of cultural education. These principles included exerting a high level of national spirit and strengthening the War of Resistance, cultivating sound military and political cadres to lead the War of Resistance, creating expertise and building various undertakings during the war, cultivating enthusiastic new youths to expand the basic forces of the national revolution, and improving the cultural standards of the general public and enhancing their health. In January 1939, the First Session of the Shaanxi-Gansu-Ningxia Border Region passed the Government Program for the Anti-Japanese War in the Shaanxi-Gansu-Ningxia Border Region, which offered a comprehensive exposition of the cultural education and cultural construction policies in the border area. That November, the Second Congress of the Shaanxi-Gansu-Ningxia Border Region made the following resolution on the cultural work in its border region: "Cultural education in the border region must strive to remove the cultural backwardness left by the old system before the revolution of the masses – illiteracy, superstition, poor hygiene, and so on. It must be based on scientific theories of progress on the basis of establishing a new culture for which the Chinese nation must struggle."

CHAPTER 7

Thoughts on the United Front

I

Ideas Concerning the Establishment of the United Front

1. Basic Strategy for Establishing the Democratic United Front

The Party's theory on the united front was derived from the Marxist principle of the proletarian revolution strategy, which underwent a logical development process in the specific environment of the Chinese revolution. Its earliest theory and practice during the Chinese revolution was the Party's concept of the democratic united front and its realization in the first cooperation between the KMT and the CPC.

At the time, the object of the united front, as understood by the CPC, was extremely broad. In January 1923, an article in *Guide* stated that regardless of whether the "one class, one party" revolution was fixed, under certain historical conditions, the proletariat could rise "together with any party... and any army, bringing a revolutionary force to it." But, the article insisted, it could only be a "revolutionary union" and "not a compromised union."[1] Specifically, among the various classes of Chinese society, the CPC believed that the national bourgeoisie was an aspect of the revolutionary dynamic during the democratic revolution. The petty bourgeoisie was the basic force of the revolution, while the comprador class was fundamentally counter-revolutionary, and because they were the agent of the imperialists, the compradors of various factions would have different interests and conflicts. Therefore, "the Anfu Political Group of Japan's comprador could be attached to the anti-British movement in the national revolution."[2] The "Research Department" was "often opposed to Fengtian warlords."[3] Thus the proletariat "should try to use" this "internal conflict" to weaken "the enemy's power."[4]

With these principles in mind, the CPC analyzed the situation of the political forces in the various Chinese factions before and after the Second National Congress of the CPC, coming to the conclusion that "only the KMT is a revolutionary democrat, and it is a true democrat."[5] For this reason, in its Proposal on the United Democratic Front, the CPC proposed "to invite the KMT and the Socialist Youth League to hold a representative meeting at a suitable location, where we will discuss how to invite other innovative groups and how we might proceed." This demonstrated that the Party also joined other "innovative groups" at the same time it was aligned with the KMT to form a broad united front. At that time, in view of Wu Peifu's support for the populist movement, the CPC believed that it was worthwhile to unite Wu at the point of "annihilating the red beard" ("red beard" referring to Zhang Zuolin).[6] Therefore, while the revolutionary party "proposed... to unite with the people," it did not rule out a certain amount of "meaningful unilateral relations"[7] with Wu Peifu.

In 1923, Wu Peifu instigated the February 7th Massacre, and the CPC immediately changed its stand to one of resolutely and directly defeating the warlords. From that time on, with the help of the Comintern, the CPC successfully launched a cooperation with the KMT in early 1924. However, the Party's joint objective at the time was not one-dimensional. In October 1924, after Feng Yuxiang initiated the Beijing Coup, the CPC took a period of time to observe, adopting the policy of uniting with Feng Yuxiang and the National Army. After the outbreak of war, the democratic tendency of Feng Yuxiang's National Army was clarified, and other political forces also put forward the ideal of democratic politics. In this special situation, the CPC proposed that the Guangzhou National Government, the National Army, the workers and peasants, the nationalists, the KMT right, the KMT left, and the CPC "join together" to jointly promote the National Conference and create "a real republic."[8] However, due to the rapid reversal of the fighting situation in the Anti-Japanese War, the above propositions of the CPC were not realized. Even so, the National Army became the joint objectives of the CPC and KMT. These principles and policies of the CPC embodied the basic principles of using conflict, striving for the majority, and uniting all forces that could be united under specific historical conditions to combat the most important enemies.

Of the two main joint objectives at the time, the CPC believed that the Feng faction was an "anti-rural bourgeois group."[9] The understanding of the KMT presented further complications. At the beginning of the Party's agenda, the CPC pointed out that KMT-based democrats were "representative assets." However, the so-called bourgeoisie at that time had no definite ideology.

From an analysis of the Declaration of the Second National Congress of the CPC, the "bourgeoisie" included both "the bourgeoisie of commercial industry" and the "petty bourgeoisie." When discussing the issue of the union between the proletariat and the bourgeoisie, it only said that it was necessary "to establish a democratic front with the petty bourgeoisie." It appeared that the so-called democratic bourgeoisie represented by groups such as the KMT was referring specifically to the petty bourgeoisie.

First, it pointed out that the KMT was a multi-class party representative of the Comintern leader Marin,[10] who stated in his July 1922 report to the Executive Committee that the KMT was composed of four elements: intellectuals, emigrants, soldiers, and workers. The emigrant was the "capitalist factor" in the KMT. The following January, the Executive Committee of the Comintern, in its Resolution on Relations between the KMT and the CPC, pointed out that the KMT's class base included the "free bourgeoisie," "petty bourgeoisie," and "intellectuals and workers." The CPC quickly accepted the Comintern's view that the KMT was a temporary alliance of four classes, pointing out that the interests of the bourgeoisie and that of the workers and peasants in this alliance were fundamentally in conflict. In May 1924, the Third Plenary Session of the Third General Meeting of the Communist Party of China analyzed this objective fact and began to divide the left and right factions within the Kuomintang. However the specific class make-up of the left and right parties had yet to be defined.

In the second half of 1924, the CPC further divided the left, centrist, and right factions within the KMT. There was no unified view on the class make-up of the three factions.

In July 1926, the Third Plenary Session of the Fourth General Meeting of the CPC further discerned four forces within the KMT – warlords, compradors, bureaucrats, and other semi-feudal forces. They represented the right. The representative of the workers and peasants was the CPC, and the petty bourgeoisie represented the left. The national bourgeoisie formed the new right or center. This basically clarified the factions within the KMT. On this basis, the Plenary proposed a strategy of "joining the left and centrist factions to attack the reactionary right." It clearly recognized the Party's main united front was the petty bourgeoisie on the KMT's left and the centrist national bourgeoisie.

Of the two classes that could be united, the CPC believed that the petty bourgeoise was the more reliable force for the revolution, while the national bourgeoisie held a "contradictory" attitude toward the revolution and its special status. Before and after the Second and Third National Congresses of the CPC, the Party pointed out that the bourgeoisie was still "naive" and could not be an "independent class power." In the revolution, there would inevitably be a tendency to "compromise" with a "complaisant mentality" and to "feel contented with the status quo."[11] But the Party believed that the bourgeoisie should occupy the leading position in the democratic revolution, saying that "any revolution that recognizes democracy is of course in the interests of the bourgeoisie." Obviously, this was assigning too high a position to the bourgeoisie.

In May 1924, after the Third Plenary Session of the Third General Meeting of the Executive Committee of the CPC, the Party further pointed out that the revolutionary nature of the bourgeoisie was "always intermittent" and "the more wealthy bourgeoisie in the upper class, the more the compromises."[12] Its participation in the revolution "cannot persist, in the end."[13] However, the CPC had too long neglected the reality of the power of the national bourgeoisie, arguing that it was in a transitional stage from a comprador class to that of the national industrial bourgeoisie, and thus could not participate in the revolution, nor did it have any desire to seize revolutionary leadership.[14] This view had been in circulation for a long time, and it proved to be the theoretical root of the Party's prolonged failure to propose the issue of vying with the bourgeoisie for leadership in the revolution. It was not until the first half of 1926 that Mao Zedong actually pointed out in his article "The Cause of the Separation of the KMT Right and its Influence on the Revolution," the actions of the Chinese bourgeoisie and its attempts to grasp exclusive leadership in the revolution and achieve a future of capitalism. That July, the Fourth Plenary Session of the Third General Meeting of the Executive Committee of the CPC pointed out that "the Chinese bourgeoisie has gradually become an important component of the national movement, and it has a tendency to lead the movement." Its armed forces had gradually "formed," but its "fundamental compromise" was still a serious matter. "As soon as it gains some small victories," it was bound to "betray the revolution and cooperate with the enemy." For this reason, on the one hand, the Party should "promote the bourgeoisie to revolutionize" and regard it as "an ally." On the other hand, it was necessary to prevent future dangers and strive to compete with the bourgeoisie for the leadership of the revolutionary movement. It was believed that the national bourgeoisie had had two sides throughout this stage in the democratic revolution. Its weakness was not manifested in its lack of desire to seize leadership, but in the fact that it was sure to fail to lead the revolution because of its own weak will. It was pointed out that the proletariat must not only unite with the national bourgeoisie, but must also be wary of its betrayal and strive to compete for revolutionary leadership. This was completely correct in theory, but when the Third Plenary Session of the Fourth General Meeting corrected its mistake in neglecting the existence of the power of the bourgeoisie, it was described as a force that was inseparable from the revolution, and the special role of the Chinese national bourgeoisie was still not fully recognized.

From the above analysis, the CPC basically clarified the correct attitude of the proletarian order of the alliance during the Great Revolution. However, the issue of determining the political representation within the coalition was seriously affected by the "stereotypes" set by the Comintern. At that time, the CPC regarded the left, centrist, and right factions of the KMT as the political generations of the petty bourgeoisie, the national bourgeoisie, and the landlord's comprador class. This seemed reasonable, but in fact, it was simplistic and absolute. The mistake lay in the fact that the Chiang Kai-shek group was regarded as the fixed core of the party, while Wang Jingwei was regarded as the representative of its "left" faction, failing to realize that in semi-colonial, semi-feudal China, the boundaries between the various parts of the bourgeoisie and imperialist feudal forces could not be delineated. For this reason, it was impossible for the KMT's factions and their representatives of all classes of the bourgeoisie to have completely different positions. The Party failed to see the complexity and variability of Chiang Kai-shek and Wang Jingwei, these two politicians who originated from the complexities of Chinese society, misunderstanding their complex relationship with the landlord's comprador class, and thus being unable to grasp the complexity and variability of their class attributes. Thus, before April 12, the CPC, under Chen Duxiu's auspices – and especially the Comintern – always gave way to Chiang Kai-shek. After April 12, the CPC accepted the Comintern's "three stage" theory of the revolution, regarding Chiang Kai-shek's betrayal as a sign of the reaction of the entire national bourgeoisie, and as a result, put forward the slogan "crush the bourgeoisie," with the intention of obliterating both sides of the national bourgeoisie. This was fundamentally limited to the so-called left wing of the KMT, which centered around the Wang Jingwei Group, placing unrealistic hopes on it.

2. Initial Proposals Regarding Leadership of the United Front and the Issue of Independence

At this stage of the democratic revolution, with the basic principle of the alliance between the proletariat and bourgeois democrats, Marxism-Leninism held that there were two principles. First, the proletariat must have leadership of the union, and second, the proletariat must maintain complete independence. The understanding of these two principles during the initial establishment of the united front by the CPC had undergone a complicated process.

The Second National Congress of the CPC made provisions on the principle of unity, stating that the proletarian coalition could only "assist in the democratic revolution" and "not surrender to the democrats representing the bourgeoisie or become their accessory." At the same time, it was necessary that the proletariat gather under the banner of the CPC and act independently as its own class. Here, the independence and the independent thinking of the proletariat in the revolutionary united front were distinct, but the CPC did not point out the fact of the leadership of the proletariat at the meeting, understanding that its independence as a class could not be won completely during the democratic revolution, thus creating the necessity of an independent class struggle, without a union as master, but only as an aid in gaining some benefits.

In August 1922, with the help of the Comintern, the CPC established a policy for cooperation between the CPC and the KMT in a united front. At the end of the year, the Party's spokesperson pointed out at the Fourth National Congress that when the CPC cooperated with the KMT, it must "compete rigorously with the KMT" in organizing and educating the masses and must "divide the KMT."

This demonstrated that even from the beginning of establishing cooperation within the KMT, the Party held onto the idea of seeking leadership within that cooperation. However, the Fourth Congress of the Comintern denied this principle, and on this basis, it passed a resolution on the cooperation between the KMT and the CPC. Thus, at all three major levels within the Party, the CPC waged heated debates on the principles of cooperation between it and the KMT. Some members, such as Chen Duxiu, fully accepted the resolution of the Comintern, advocating that all CPC members and all industrial workers join the KMT, saying, "All work should go to the KMT." This faction had a positive attitude toward the issue of cooperation, but it mistakenly believed that there would be "no problem" in connection with the independence of the Party in the future, and thus tended to ignore the Party's independence. Some leaders, such as Cai Hesen, believed that they must wholly "maintain the independence of the Party" after joining the KMT. However, this faction also interpreted independence according to membership in the CPC, and did not recommend all joining the KMT, saying that industrial workers "should not join the KMT." The idea of "independence" was still limited to a truncated, simplistic understanding.

The two opinions explored above were united in the Resolution of the Third National Congress of the CPC. The principles of cooperation between the KMT and CPC as laid out in the Resolution were 1) political independence, which meant maintaining the political face of the revolutionary proletarian party and "not compromising with any warlord or imperialist," 2) organizational independence, which implied that even in joining the KMT, the Party's "organization" must remain "strictly enforced" and its discipline should further "expand" its organization, 3) independence of the workers' movement, which meant that while engaging in the national revolution, it was important not to abandon the "special work" of the CPC, which was to independently carry out the trade union movement and the class struggle of the working class, 4) resist wrong policies and actions of the KMT, and 5) recognize that the leader of the national revolution was the KMT. These principles were basically correct in theory, except that the fifth item required a more complex understanding. The main shortcoming was that the third article emphasized the independence of the workers' movement, but did not point out that the Party should also maintain the right to independent activities in mass movements among the peasantry and petty bourgeoisie. At the same time, the thrust of that independence was that the Party must maintain independence in terms of organization, propaganda, and mass movements, and did not involve the issue of independent political and military work. The principle of cooperation thus retained a good deal of one-sidedness.

In November 1923, at the Third Plenary Session of the First General Meeting of the CPC, new decisions were made regarding the principles of cooperation. CPC and Youth League members were required to "work hard to stand in the center of the KMT." Theoretically, this involved the CPC striving for full dominance within the united front. However, they failed to adhere to and develop this idea, and in the specific work after cooperation between the KMT and CPC had been established, even the independence of the Party organization and the mass movement proposed by the Third National Congress had not been implemented, leaving the KMT to take all the work. The Third Plenary Session of the Third General Meeting eventually corrected this error. The Fourth National Congress of the CPC carefully summarized the practical experience of the cooperation between the KMT and the CPC, expanding the principles of this cooperation to include 1) confirming the proletariat in the leadership of the democratic revolution, 2) placing more explicit emphasis on the independent work on the principle that "the industrial workers' movement is the foundation of the proletarian party," 3) the principle that industrial workers "must only join the KMT if there is a need" was proposed, and 4) the notion of independently organizing the peasant movement was proposed. The resolutions proposed at the Fourth National Congress regarding the peasant movement noted that in the peasant movement, the CPC "must be separate from the KMT, and must act independently… carrying out the work of propaganda and publicity."

The above-mentioned principles suggested that the CPC had a clearer understanding of the special status of the proletariat within the cooperation. However, these principles still fell far short of being translated into correct practical policies. The leadership of the proletariat was only the proletarian party's leadership of the populist movement, and "independence" still only referred to the independent development of the workers and peasants. Furthermore, the whole Party was required to maintain a certain distance from the allies in the industrial and agricultural movements, especially in the industrial workers' movement, and the policy of allowing industrial workers to join the KMT only as necessary was implemented. They lacked independence in conducting and leading political and military work, to change the balance of power in the cooperation, to ensure that the united front functioned according to the will of the proletariat and its political parties, and thereby to transform the victory of the democratic revolution into a victory for the proletariat and realize a future of socialism.

The KMT's new right could not tolerate even the very moderately independent activities of the CPC. Such occurrences as the Zhongshan Shipping Incident and the case of the preparation of Party affairs indicated that the rightist faction had begun to gradually restrict and eliminate the independent activities of the CPC. After the establishment of the Northern Expeditionary General Command, Chiang Kai-shek also publicly issued a series of decrees restricting the struggle for the independence of workers and peasants under the pretext of the Northern Expedition. In view of these things, the CPC put forward the idea of "exiting the KMT" and "preparing military forces for independence," confronting Chiang Kai-shek. However, the Comintern did not support the CPC's independence in military affairs, and it also "resolutely opposed demands for withdrawal from the KMT" and did not allow "such positions as inevitably lead to the withdrawal from the KMT." It also clearly stated that the "independence of the CPC" could not be understood in this way.[15]

In July 1926, the Third Plenary Session of the Fourth General Assembly of the Executive Committee of the CPC raised the issue of the proletariat vying for leadership with the bourgeoisie. It pointed out that the Party must "enhance the political demonstration of its own independence" and "establish its power among the majority of workers and peasants." This indicated that the entire Party was increasingly aware of the significance of the proletariat's revolutionary leadership and independence after a series of betrayals by Chiang Kai-shek. The problem remained that neither "leadership" nor "independence" were directly linked to military or political issues, and it was clearly stated that they could help the left as long as they did not "replace the left wing." This proposition was practically a wholesale copy of the Comintern's understanding that "attempting to replace the 'left wing' is not the job of the Communists."[16] The direct source of this error was clearly the Comintern.

After the Northern Expedition had spilled over into the Yangtze River Valley area, the KMT's right-wing anti-proletariat activities became more apparent. The report of the CPC pointed out that after the Zhongshan Warship Incident on March 20, 1926, the Chiang Kai-shek faction gradually crowded out the CPC and the KMT's left-wing, forming "the center of the Chinese regime" and leaving leaders on the left "partly shaken." In this situation, the Communists in turn believed that they could not replace the left in the leadership efforts, but could help the left "regroup" and "be responsible for themselves." In December 1926, the Hankou Special Meeting (also called the December Special Meeting) more clearly pointed out that the Party could not monopolize "all popular movements" and "political struggles" such as those in business and agriculture, and explained that the independence of the Party only referred to independent organization of "political propaganda and Party work." The independence of the workers and peasants that had before been emphasized was now also abandoned. Of course, this change made by the Hankou Special Meeting emphasized the necessity of cooperating with the leftists in the workers' and peasants' movements and political struggles to avoid "conflict between the whole Party and the KMT," which was not completely unreasonable. The problem was that the meeting did not propose specific measures for the Party to achieve full leadership of the democratic revolution by strengthening the left, but instead believed that the Party should give some power to the left, then distance itself from the democratic faction, which led to a reduced principle of "cooperation."

In the spring of 1927, after the Seventh Expanded Meeting of the Comintern sent its resolutions to China, and particularly after Chiang Kai-shek rebelled against the revolution, the CPC accepted the "three-stage" theory of international revolution, which held that the Chinese revolution had entered a period of a three-class alliance of the petty bourgeoisie, workers, and peasants. The task of the KMT-CPC cooperation was to form and lead the democratic dictatorship of the petty bourgeoisie, workers, and peasants into a "closer" alliance. But this was not, in fact, the case. The closer one drew to the late period of the Great Revolution, the more rapidly the so-called leftists under Wang Jingwei became representatives of the landlords' comprador class. The signs of betrayal became increasingly apparent, and the situation grew more serious. Although the CPC and the representatives of the Comintern had theoretically considered the cooperation to be closer, they also saw the seriousness of the situation from a realistic perspective. However, they did not have a realistic response to the question of how to maintain the independence of the proletariat under such conditions. Although the Comintern representative, Manabendra Nath Roy, made a report to the CPC Central Committee Politburo on the relationship between the CPC and the KMT and the independence of the CPC, he emphasized that after Chiang's betrayal, the CPC must continue to maintain "independence" within the KMT. However, when it came to specific measures for maintaining independence, he only repeatedly proposed the three principles of "developing the agrarian revolution, strengthening the workers' movement, and fighting the petty bourgeoisie for power," without offering any specific suggestions. Later, he proposed overthrowing the KMT through a coup, thus changing the cooperation altogether and maintaining the independence of the CPC. This plan was obviously not realistic. The Comintern delayed the issuance of the May Instructions, proposing the establishment of "eight to ten military divisions with reliable leaders," and of a "revolutionary military court" to punish revolutionary officers. In terms of basic theory, this was clearly correct. However, under the conditions of that time, this path would obviously not work.

At the same time, the CPC's principles of the united front had also changed. In the process of leading the Shanghai workers' armed uprising, the Party clearly put forward the principles of armed uprising by workers, seizing power and convening congresses of people from all walks of life to establish the principles of civilian democratic power, and turning this principle into a reality. Here, "leadership" and "independence" were linked to military and political issues for the first time. However, the way in which power was seized in Shanghai was not itself suitable for the objective situation of Chinese society or the disparity of power, causing the uprising and the struggle to establish a democratic regime to fail. At the same time, the Comintern did not agree with the way in which the Shanghai workers' armed uprisings seized power and advocated that the CPC participate in the Wuhan Kuomintang government. Accepting the opinion of the Comintern, the CPC decided to participate in the local government in Wuhan at various levels, transforming it into a petty bourgeois democratic dictatorship of workers and peasants. In theory, there were still independent political activities, but because the CPC failed to propose fundamental and effective measures to transform the army into the mainstay of the regime, the goal of reforming the KMT was defeated, and the Party's independent activities were increasingly threatened, eventually costing it its independence and leadership.

3. Establishing the Form of Intra-Party Cooperation

At the beginning of the work of establishing a united front, the CPC and the Comintern had very different ideas on the form of "cooperation." It was not until

August 1922 that the West Lake Conference made a preliminary determination regarding the form of cooperation within the CPC. Judging from the Party's activities after the First National Congress of the KMT, the form of cooperation between the Comintern and the Communist Party of China was understood to encompass three aspects.

The first aspect was that members of the CPC joined the KMT in their personal capacity. Throughout the history of the international Communist movement, there had been precedents for Communists joining united forms of democratic parties. During the European revolution of 1848, Marx and Engels led Communist allies to participate in democratic organizations such as the bourgeois German Democrats. In 1917, Marin once again instructed members of the Indies Social Democratic Alliance to join the bourgeois Islamic Union. The CPC's direct experience of its first cooperation with the KMT grew out of the latter. Even so, the two unions had few similarities. Although Indonesia was also a backward colonial country in Asia, its political environment at the time was characterized by the presence of numerous Western powers with great reach. Thus, though the Indonesian revolution was also a national revolution, it could adopt the methods of democratic revolutions in Western countries, to a large extent. China was semi-colonial and semi-feudal, and lacking a democratic tradition. Without a bourgeois democracy, it was determined that the CPC's cooperation with the KMT must adopt a special form that conformed to China's situation. Members of the CPC joined the KMT in their personal capacities, then under the guidance of the Comintern, helped the KMT build a party in the style of Soviet Russia, later to establish a strong government. This was an unprecedented move in the history of the international Communist movement, and was completely necessary for China's special national conditions.

Since the cooperation between the KMT and CPC had taken a special form, it was necessary to adopt a corresponding strategy to ensure that the cause of cooperation was victorious, because under the conditions in China at the time, a party with strict organizational discipline and a strong armed force, a party that combined politics and the military in this way, could become a powerful force for the people's liberation struggle and the exercise of their rights, provided that party were in the hands of the proletariat. On the other hand, if it were in the hands of a dictatorship, it would become the tool of a fascist-style personal dictatorship. Sun Yat-sen, a loyal fighter for democracy, personally regarded this as a republican tool. However, in the end, the KMT was not Sun Yat-sen's personal party. In the KMT, various classes were intermixed, and the anti-communist, anti-soviet faction had been made manifest from the beginning. The use of the KMT's party and government organizations to establish an individual fascist dictatorship occurred clearly, and it gradually developed over time.

The CPC, and particularly the Comintern, the architect of the CPC-KMT cooperation, aimed to help a non-proletarian party establish a strict organization, a strong army, and a strong government. How could it, then, ensure that it could help build the political system to play the role according to its direction and not become an alien force? To this end, it needed to have a clear, unwavering general policy from the beginning.

However, the Comintern did not do so when determining a path for cooperation with the KMT. The strategy of the CPC likewise had its shortcomings. As mentioned above, since the Second National Congress, the Party had formed according to the basic understanding that after the success of the democratic revolution, the proletariat would not be completely liberated, so a second step of revolution against the bourgeoisie must be carried out. Therefore, cooperation between the proletarian party and the democratic KMT was a temporary strategy. The proletariat's participation in the democratic revolution was a boon to the democrats, and this idea of "aid" had been in circulation for some time. The Fourth National Congress of the CPC proposed that the proletariat should join the KMT as needed, but that it would not expand the organization of the KMT when necessary, narrowing its scope as helper. This essentially meant maintaining some distance from the democrats. The Comintern regarded the change in the principles of cooperation as stated by the Fourth National Congress of the CPC as a change from the earlier "close alliance" to a "political alliance" between the KMT and the CPC. This statement was very vague, failing to clarify the exact meaning and specific form of "political alliance," nor did it point out the specific differences between a "close alliance" and a "political alliance."

Since the Comintern and the CPC did not adopt special strategies to guide the special cooperation during the implementation of the cooperation between the CPC and the KMT, they did not formulate specific guidelines for firmly grasping the direction of cooperation and development. Therefore, the leading organs in the cooperation gradually evolved after the death of Sun Yat-sen, and were beginning to convert into authoritarian tools. After Sun's death, the Xishan

Conference Faction flagged against "Sun Yat-sen's Three Policies (of making alliances with Russia and the Communist Party, and of supporting workers and farmers)." Chiang Kai-shek used these anti-communist forces to gradually display his dictatorship conspiracy. The Northern Expedition took advantage of the opportunity to fully capture the political machinery of the KMT and began to restrict the independent activities of workers and peasants. In the face of the increasingly obvious signs of the new warlord's dictatorship, the Comintern still did not remind or warn the CPC to take effective measures to stop this dangerous development, its own strategy remaining blind to the precariousness of the situation. Clearly seeing this danger, the CPC proposed a slogan of opposing the dictatorship of the Northern Warlords and opposing the new military dictatorship.

In response to the trend toward military dictatorship embraced by the KMT's new right, the CPC proposed to change its form of cooperation. After the Zhongshan Warship Incident, the CPC advocated "exiting the KMT," which was actually a move that completely changed the cooperation from internal to external within the Party. After this suggestion was rejected by the Comintern, the executive committee of the Third Session of CPC's Fourth National Congress proposed a partial revision of the form of cooperation, pointing out in the resolution, "The KMT's organization cannot be a centralized party with strict discipline. Thus, it is now necessary to introduce great revolutionary masses of the petty bourgeoisie into the KMT, so that the Party's organizational form can be more liberal… something like a political club." Tan Pingshan submitted this to the Comintern on behalf of the CPC Central Committee. The written report of the Executive Committee further pointed out, "The KMT's organizational charter is almost identical to the CPC's Constitution. These are strict, rigid regulations, which are not in line with the needs of the Chinese situation. This strict charter is not only unhelpful, but harmful."[17] The Comintern did not officially recognize this view of the CPC until May 1927. The Eighth Executive Committee of the Comintern's Resolution on China said, "The KMT's task requires that its organizational form be changed accordingly. It must be recognized as soon as possible based on the path of closest proximity to the masses… It is necessary for peasant, military, and artisan organizations… to join the KMT."[18] This proposal was the same organizational plan as the 1924 reorganization of the KMT, but none of these programs were implemented, nor was it possible to implement them.

Faced with such a serious situation, the CPC and the Comintern did not take effective measures to reverse the transformation of the united front's institutions into dictatorial tools. After the Zhongshan Warship Incident, the CPC Central Committee, chaired by Chen Duxiu, adopted a policy of concession. During the Northern Expedition, the Central Committee proposed the use of a wide-scale National Conference movement to resist the dictatorship. In the KMT, the "Party Movement" and the "Welcome to Reinstatement" campaigns and the "balance of power" among various military factions were attempted in an effort to prevent Chiang Kai-shek's dictatorship, but none of the proposed means were effective. The Comintern advocated the rapid entry to the KMT by large numbers of the revolutionary mass to eliminate this trend toward dictatorship. In the Seventh Expanded Meeting of the Executive Committee, the Comintern also proposed the principle of CPC members participating in the Nationalist government, expanding the scope of "intra-party cooperation," from within the party to within the government. This was a major evolution from the first form of cooperation between the KMT and the CPC. The Eighth Executive Committee further emphasized this principle and proposed the task of the CPC seizing leadership within the KMT. However, this would not change the balance of power within the united front and thus ensure a smooth transition of the democratic revolution to a socialist revolution. Based on the experience of the October Revolution, Stalin asserted that the transformation from the democratic revolution to a socialist revolution would be achieved by transforming the KMT government into a democratic dictatorship of the proletariat and peasantry, which was actually impossible. He believed the transitional regime established by the democratic revolution could be overthrown through armed conflict at the end of the October Revolution. However, the Comintern still did not propose a clear policy to the CPC to independently engage in the armed forces, and its strategy was contradictory. Under the guidance of this blind policy and the direct environment of military exchange, under the auspices of Chen Duxiu, it was even more impossible for the CPC Central Committee to take the initiative and take effective measures to recover from the crisis.

In the context of semi-colonial, semi-feudal China, the CPC adopted a form of cooperation with the KMT to establish a revolutionary united front, helping the KMT build a centralized, unified party, a strong armed force, and a strong cooperation with Soviet Russia and its army. The effective governing policy was correct in itself, and it played a huge historic role. However, under the guidance of the Comintern and Chen Duxiu, the CPC Central Committee focused only on the independence of the party organization and the mass movement. It did not seize overall leadership within the united front, and it did not adopt a strategy of surpassing its allies in the overall competition for power. There were sharp contradictions between content and form, which was undoubtedly one of the key reasons for the loss in the Great Revolution.

During the Great Revolution, the CPC was still in its infancy. The whole Party, including Mao Zedong's theoretical strategy, inevitably bore the characteristics of youth. Therefore, the Party could not fully and correctly resolve all the theoretical and strategic issues within the united front. Only in the new era of the War of Resistance Against Japanese Aggression, under the leadership of Mao Zedong, was the entire Party concentrated to develop and enrich the theory and strategy of the first united front, establishing the main symbol of cooperation between the KMT and the CPC. The broader Anti-Japanese National United Front played an important role in gaining the victory in the War of Resistance Against Japanese Aggression.

II

Ideas and Strategic Policies for Establishing the Anti-Japanese National United Front

1. Establishment of the Principle of Independence and Autonomy Within the Anti-Japanese National United Front

The Anti-Japanese National United Front was a broad alliance advocated by the CPC, based on the cooperation between the CPC and the KMT and including all social and economic classes, political parties, groups, patriots, ethnic minorities, compatriots in Hong Kong, Macau, and Taiwan, and overseas Chinese. During this period in the War of Resistance Against Japanese Aggression, it mobilized the army and the people to the maximum extent, becoming the most effective form of organization for the national resistance and a decisive factor in defeating the Japanese aggressors. The formation and application of the thought and strategic policies behind the Anti-Japanese National United Front were the crowning achievement of the CPC's strategic thinking in connection with the proletarian revolution and the concrete practice of leading China's War of Resistance Against Japanese Aggression.

The CPC's principle of "independence and autonomy within the Anti-Japanese National United Front" was intended to uphold the political, ideological, and organizational independence of the CPC and to maintain this as a first priority throughout its participation in the united front. The essence of this principle was to uphold the leadership of the CPC during the period of its participation in the united front and the war against Japan.

From December 1935 through July 1937, the CPC Central Committee and Mao Zedong put forward the principle of establishing the Anti-Japanese National United Front, emphasizing the leadership of the CPC within the united front, thereby asserting the theoretical basis for the principle of "independence and autonomy within the Anti-Japanese National United Front."

In mid- to late December 1935, the Central Committee of the CPC held a meeting of the Politburo in Wayaobao, in northern Shaanxi. On December 25, the meeting adopted the Resolution on the Current Political Situation and the Party's Tasks (hereafter referred to as the Resolution). The Resolution proposed that the Party's approach was to "launch, unite, and organize all revolutionary forces of the entire Chinese nation" and establish "the most extensive Anti-Japanese National United front."[19] Alongside emphasizing the establishment of the Anti-Japanese National United Front, the Resolution also emphasized the leadership of the CPC within the united front. The Resolution stated that the CPC should "resolutely and unwaveringly fight against all tendencies toward vacillation, compromise, surrender, and rebellion within the Anti-Japanese National United Front," and should "face our own responsibility to resist Japan and rid ourselves of all traitors as we take leadership in the anti-Japanese united front." It added, "Only under the leadership of the Communist Party of China can the anti-Japanese movement become completely victorious."[20] After the meeting, Mao presented a report entitled "Strategy for Opposing Japanese Imperialism" at the Party's activist meetings, systematically clarifying the Party's views on the issue of leadership in the Anti-Japanese National United Front. Mao pointed out, "The CPC and the Red Army must not act as a catalyst for the Anti-Japanese National United Front, but must also become a strong pillar in the future anti-Japanese government and army." He went on to say, "As long as the CPC and Red Army exist and develop, the Anti-Japanese National United Front will inevitably exist and develop. This is the leadership role of the CPC and the Red Army in the national united front."[21] Mao also cited the failure of the 1927 revolution as an example, emphasizing the importance of Party leadership in the united front.

In his article published on April 20, 1936, entitled "Several Issues on the People's United Front in the Anti-Japanese War," Zhang Wentian emphasized that "the Soviet and Red Army must be the core of the united front in the struggle to promote, create, and expand the Anti-Japanese People's United Front."[22] On September 1, 1936, the Central Committee issued the Instructions on the Issue of Chiang's Anti-Japanese Resistance, pointing out on the one hand that "our policy should be to force Chiang to resist Japan," while emphasizing on the other hand that "we are the organizers and leaders of all parties and factions across China in the Anti-Japanese National United Front (including Chiang's KMT)."[23]

In mid-May 1937, the Central Committee of the CPC held a meeting of national Party representatives in Yan'an. At the meeting, Mao Zedong presented reports entitled "The Tasks of the Communist Party of China in the Anti-Japanese War" and "Striving for Millions to Enter the Anti-Japanese National United Front." He said, "Does the proletariat follow the bourgeoisie, or does the bourgeoisie follow the proletariat? This issue of leadership responsibility in the Chinese revolution is the key to the revolution's success." He went on, "Today, the bourgeoisie represented by the KMT is very passive and conservative," and "This situation aggravates the problem of the leadership responsibility of the proletariat and its political parties."[24] He further asked, "How does the proletariat achieve political leadership over the revolutionary classes of political parties across the country? First, it introduces basic political slogans rooted in historical developments, pointing to new stages of development with these slogans, utilizing a new slogan for each major event […] as a means of specifying the goal of the concerted actions of the people throughout the country […] Second, when acting for the entire nation in accordance with a specific goal, the proletariat, and especially its pioneering Communist Party, should manifest its infinite enthusiasm and loyalty as a model for achieving these goals […] Third, based on the principle of not losing the designated political goal, the proletariat should establish appropriate relationships with allies, or develop and consolidate the alliance […] And finally, it will be achieved by the development of the CPC, its unity of ideas, and its strict discipline."[25] Mao also pointed to Chen Duxiu's rightist error of capitulating, "reducing the Party's position, obscuring the Party's face, and sacrificing the interests of the workers and peasants,"[26] using it as an instructive example of revolutionary failure and an illustration of the importance of upholding the leadership of the proletariat within the united front.

From August through November 1937, the CPC Central Committee and Mao Zedong clearly proposed the principle of independence and autonomy in the united front, offering a preliminary explanation of this principle.

After the beginning of the national anti-Japanese war in July 1937, representatives of the CPC, including Zhou Enlai, Qin Bangxian, and Lin Boqu, continued to negotiate with KMT representatives on the cooperation between the KMT and the CPC, and the reorganization of Red Army. On August 1, Mao Zedong and Zhang Wentian pointed out in a telegram to Zhou Enlai, Qin Bangxian, and Lin Boqu that the Red Army should "execute a guerrilla war of independent, decentralized operations under an overarching strategic policy" after the reorganization of the Red Army, saying, "You cannot be bound by traditional battle tactics," and "only in this way can the special strengths of the Red Army be exerted and the Japanese be hit hard." On August 4, Mao Zedong and Zhang Wentian again sent a telegram to Zhou Enlai, Zhu De, and Ye Jianying, asking them to point out at the Nanjing National Security Conference that "The combination of regular warfare and guerrilla warfare by the Red Army and other appropriate forces should be executed under independent, autonomous command under an overall strategic deployment." In late August 1937, the Politburo of the Central Committee held an expanded meeting in Luochuan, in northern Shaanxi. The meeting determined that the Party must adhere to the leadership of the proletariat in the united front, launch an independent guerrilla campaign in the mountains behind enemy lines to open up a battle line at the rear and establish anti-Japanese bases in enemy-occupied territory, and in KMT-ruled areas, to mobilize the anti-Japanese mass movement and strive for the political and economic rights of all the people in the nation, seeking to reduce land rents and interest rates as a basic policy for solving the peasants' problems during the War of Resistance Against Japanese Aggression. In October 1937, Mao once again explained his stand in an interview with British journalist James Bertram, saying, "The tactics used by the Eighth Route Army are now known as independent guerrilla warfare and mobile warfare."[27] Obviously, from early August through October 1937, the CPC Central Committee and Mao Zedong had clearly put forward the principle of "independence and autonomy." However, at this time, it only referred to military independence.

On November 12, 1937, at the Party activist meeting in Yan'an, given the trend of class capitulationism in the CPC and national capitulationism in the KMT at that time, Mao made it abundantly clear that "we must firmly uphold the principle of independence in all work of the united front," pointing out that "the explanation, practice, and persistence of the principle of independence and autonomy in the united front is central to the path to victory in the anti-Japanese revolutionary war."[28] In this way, the principle of the independence of the Anti-Japanese National United Front was clearly and completely presented.

From November 1937 through November 1938, the Central Committee, led by Mao Zedong, fought against Wang Ming's rightist errors, further establishing the principle of independence and autonomy of the Party in the Anti-Japanese National United Front.

By the end of November 1937, Wang Ming, the CPC's representative to the Comintern and also a member of the Comintern Executive Committee and member of its delegation, returned to China from the Soviet Union. He proposed that the Luochuan meeting's emphasis on independence, democracy, and the people's livelihood was wrong. He opposed the principle of independence and autonomy of the Party within the united front, insisting that "all must go through the united front" and "all must obey the united front" and advocating a relatively systematic right wing error. Wang Ming's mistaken prediction held certain influence within the Party, making it impossible to fully implement its independence and autonomy within the Anti-Japanese National United Front, which resulted in certain losses to the Party's work. The CPC Central Committee, under the guidance of Mao Zedong, carried out a struggle against Wang Ming's rightist error, preventing these wrong claims from formulating into a resolution. In the actual work of leadership, the Central Committee and Mao Zedong continued to adhere to the principle of independence and autonomy within the united front, enabling the Party's work to continue to develop.

From late September to early November 1938, the Sixth Plenary Session of the Sixth General Assembly of the Central Committee of the CPC was held in Yan'an. The meeting passed the Political Resolution of the Sixth Plenary Session of the Communist Party of China, which approved the approach of the Central Committee Politburo, as presented by Mao Zedong. The meeting criticized rightist sympathies, basically overcoming Wang Ming's right-wing error. In his concluding remarks at the meeting, Mao particularly emphasized and specifically elaborated on the issue of the independence and autonomy of the Party within the united front. He stated, "In short, we must not break with the united front, but we likewise must not bind our own hands and feet." He added, "Our policy is one of independence and unity in the united front – we will be both unified and independent."[29] In the Plenary Session's Political Resolution, it was also emphasized that "the political independence of the CPC must be upheld." In this way, the principle of independence and autonomy within the Anti-Japanese National United Front was established throughout the Party.

2. Establishment of the Anti-Japanese National United Front as a Broad Alliance Based on Cooperation between the KMT and the CPC

In speaking of the composition of the Anti-Japanese National United Front, Mao Zedong said, "The Party's task is to bring together the activities of the Red Army and all the activities of the workers, peasants, students, petty bourgeoisie, and national bourgeoisie across the country and become a unified national revolutionary front."[30] In order to achieve this task, it was necessary, in light of the specific situation in China at the time, to carry out extensive work at the upper level of the united front.

To achieve this, the Party would first strive to unite the patriotic leaders of various parties and groups as a breakthrough in the work of the upper class. On behalf of the CPC Central Committee, Mao wrote letters to Shen Junru, Zou Taofen, Tao Xingzhi, Zhang Naiqi, Song Qingling, and Cai Yuanpei, expressing enthusiasm for their patriotic anti-Japanese ideas and activities, publicizing in this way the CPC's political proposition of fighting against Japan and saving the country. Responding positively, Lu Xun, Mao Dun, and Song Qingling all wrote letters to the Central Committee, expressing their support for the CPC's united fight against Japan. Fang Zhenwu, Chen Mingshu, Cai Tingkai, Tao Xingzhi, and others all published articles or speeches in the *National Salvation Times*, expressing their support for the establishment of the Anti-Japanese National United Front. The Chinese National Liberation Action Committee (a third party), led by Zhang Bojun and others, publicly issued two declarations on the organization of the Anti-Japanese front, responding to the CPC's call to establish a united front against Japan. The above facts demonstrate the effectiveness of the Mao-led CPC in fighting for a united front in the struggle between the national bourgeoisie and the upper petty bourgeoisie.

The Party's second task was to strive to lead local strength to participate in the Anti-Japanese National United Front, which was in fact to be the core of the united front. Mao Zedong, Zhou Enlai, Zhu De, and other leaders in the Central Committee used letters or public conversations, approaching figures such as Zhang Xueliang, and Yang Hucheng in Shaanxi, Yan Xishan in Shanxi, Chen Jitang, Li Zongren, and Bai Chongxi in Guangdong and Guangxi, Liu Xiang and Liu Wenhui in Sichuan, Long Yun in Yunnan, Feng Yuxiang, Song Zheyuan, and Fu Zuoyi in Northern China, and many others, inviting them to actively participate in the united front. In particular, they sought to strengthen the work of the 17th Route Army of the Northeast Army and Yang Hucheng and Zhang Xueliang's institute in Shaanxi. In November 1935, Mao Zedong wrote to Dong Yingbin, the commander of the 57th Army of the Northeast Army, explaining to him the CPC's Anti-Japanese National United Front policy. The Central Committee also set up the Northeast Military Work Committee, naming Zhou Enlai its director. On January 25, 1936, Mao Zedong and Zhou Enlai published "To the Generals of the Northeast Army" in the name of the leaders of the Red Army, pointing out that the enemy of the Northeast Army was Japan, and that Chiang Kai-shek was a traitor, which meant that the only way out for the Northeastern Army was to oppose both Japan and Chiang. At the same time, they made it clear that the Red Army was willing to join the Northeastern Army in a united resistance against Japan, and that they hoped to send representatives to the Northeast to discuss such a cooperation. Through the Party's diligence, the officers and men of the Northeast Army first accepted the invitation to join in a united anti-Japanese effort. After Zhou Enlai, Li Kenong, and Zhang Xueliang held talks, Zhang embarked on the path of the CPC's anti-Japanese war. At the same time, the CPC considered the good relationship Yang Hucheng had had with the Party during and after the Great Revolution, and so sent Wang Feng to see Yang, carrying with him a personal letter from Mao Zedong, and also sent the Party cadre Wang Bingnan to the 17th Route Army. The work with Yang Hucheng soon prompted him to sign an agreement with the Red Army, putting a halt to the civil war in favor of launching a united resistance against Japan. In this way, the CPC's policy for the Anti-Japanese National United Front achieved its first major victory in the Northwest Region.

The third item was to carry out work with Chiang Kai-shek's clique. In the winter of 1935, the CPC sent representatives to conduct initial negotiations with the KMT in hopes of establishing an Anti-Japanese National United Front. The negotiations were first proposed by the KMT, and the representatives of the two sides met under conditions of greatest secrecy. The main issues in the negotiations included the cessation of civil war, the establishment of a national defense government, and an anti-Japanese coalition. Others concerned the reorganization of the Red Army, the issue of the southern guerrilla troops, the dissemination of the public opinion on anti-Japanese efforts, the release of political prisoners, and the halt on land reforms, etc. Due to the Chiang faction's lack of sincerity, the negotiations continued until the Xi'an Incident, without any specific agreement being reached. However, the Mao-led CPC made tremendous efforts to achieve a second cooperation between the KMT and the CPC. On April 25, 1936, the CPC Central Committee issued the Declaration of the Anti-Japanese People's Front for the Establishment of Various Parties in the Country, and for the first time, it publicly included the KMT in the united front. On May 5, the Red Army's eastward anti-Japanese fighting was blocked by heavy KMT forces. It decided to return to the division to regroup, where it issued the "Telegraph on a Cease Fire for Peace Talks and Launching Anti-Japanese Efforts" and let go of the slogan of "opposing Chiang." On August 12, in "On Strategic Plans," the Central Committee identified for the first time the Nanjing administration as the "primary and essential opponent" of the united front, proposing the issue of "requiring Chiang to resist Japan." On August 25, the Central Committee issued a "Letter from the Communist Party of China to the Kuomintang," officially proposing that the CPC and KMT form a solid revolutionary united front. On September 1, the Central Committee issued the Instructions Insisting on Chiang's Resistance of Japan to the whole Party. From then on, the CPC's policy officially changed from an "anti-Japanese, anti-Chiang" stand to one of "forcing Chiang to resist Japan." The Central Committee had firmly grasped the theme of the ethnic conflict between China and Japan and decisively implemented the adjustment and transformation of the Party's policy. Mao pointed out that the China-Japan conflict had changed the situation and policies of the people, the entire nation, and the Communist Party of China, saying, "This is what our Party's August 1935 Resolution, our December Decision, our May 5, 1936, letting go of the 'oppose

Chiang' slogan, our August letter to the KMT, our September Democratic Republic Resolution, our December insistence on a peaceful resolution to the Xi'an Incident, and our February 1937 Telegraph to KMT Third Plenary Session were all aiming to achieve."[31]

After the Xi'an Incident, which caused great alarm both domestically and abroad, the country was suddenly thrown into an extremely complicated, tense situation. The Mao-led Central Committee formulated a policy for peacefully resolving the Xi'an Incident, through outstanding political foresight and concern for the interests of the Chinese nation. The diligence of the CPC delegation finally forced Chiang Kai-shek to agree to six conditions, including a cessation to the civil war and uniting with the Red Army to fight Japan. From then on, the decade-long civil war was basically ended and the foundation laid for the formulation of the cooperation between the KMT and the CPC in the Anti-Japanese National United Front.

3. Strategy and Comprehensive Elaboration on the Basic Policies of the Anti-Japanese National United Front

In the struggle to uphold the cooperation between the KMT and the CPC and oppose the "hardcore" elements in the KMT, the strategic principles and basic policies of the Anti-Japanese National United Front were fully laid out and explained. The CPC's strategic thinking on the Anti-Japanese National United Front correctly resolved several basic problems, as described below.

a. *Correct handling of the relationship between the national struggle and the class struggle within the united front*

Firmly grasping that the main conflict was the national conflict between China and Japan, Mao offered specific analysis of the particular conflicts within the national united front. He wrote, "In the first analysis of the characteristics of the war, the primary conflicts are the Sino-Japanese conflict and the domestic conflicts." He studied the norms and characteristics of the Anti-Japanese National United Front as a basis for formulating strategies. In the struggle against Japan, there were struggles on both the national and the local level, though it was generally a national struggle. Making class struggle serve the national struggle against Japan was a fundamental principle of the Anti-Japanese National United Front. Mao emphasized the consistencies between the two, pointing out, "In the national struggle, class struggle has emerged in the form of national struggle. This form shows the consistencies between the two. On the one hand, the political and economic demands of the class struggle area, in this particular historical period, depended on not breaking cooperation. On the other hand, the requirements of all class struggles have to be based on the needs of the national struggle (i.e., the anti-Japanese war). This will bring unity and independence within the united front, while ensuring that the national and class struggle are consistent."[32] The relationship between the anti-Japanese struggle and democracy was essentially the same as the relationship between the national and class struggles. Fighting for democracy was anti-Japanese. The government gave the people the necessary democratic and political freedom, particularly the freedom to arm and train themselves, in an effort to mount an effective anti-Japanese war. However, if there was appropriate class struggle within the national struggle, such as preserving the independence of a party or class, adhering to certain limits of party and class, the freedom to criticize the improvement of people's political and economic conditions, and so forth, then the struggles of the people and the masses they led would be conducive to uniting to oppose Japan. What could and should be stopped in the struggle against Japan was those activities not conducive to uniting to oppose Japan, such as civil wars, partisanship, local separatist movements, feudal politics, and economic oppression, along with riot policies and excessive economic restrictions. According to this line of thinking, the CPC Central Committee proposed:

1) *The necessity of distinguishing the two-faced big landlords and upper bourgeoisie who advocated opposition to Japan, yet wavered, or advocated unity, but were anti-communist, from the national bourgeoisie, small landlords, or enlightened gentlemen.* When the KMT launched the first anti-communist campaign, it had not been verified what the attitude of the national bourgeoisie was, whether it was different from the upper bourgeoisie and big landlords. Therefore, Mao Zedong made important changes to *The Chinese Revolution and the Communist Party of China*, writing that the national bourgeoisie was "not only different from the compromising big landlords of the upper bourgeoisie, but also different from the diehards of the upper bourgeoisie.

They are also better allies for us. Therefore, it is absolutely necessary to adopt a prudent policy toward the national bourgeoisie."[33]

2) *The necessity of distinguishing between the pro-Japanese upper bourgeoisie from the anti-Japanese, pro-Europe and America big landlords of the upper bourgeoisie.* Mao stated, "The pro-Japanese upper bourgeoisie (the compromisers) have already surrendered. The Euro-American bourgeoisie (diehards) have remained in the anti-Japanese camp, even though they have wavered to a great extent. They are two-faced, in that they are both anti-Japanese and anti-communist. Our policy for the upper bourgeoisie compromisers is to treat them as enemies and resolutely defeat them. For the diehards of the upper bourgeoisie, they must be treated with a two-sided revolutionary policy, which is to say that, on the one hand, they are united with us because they resist Japan, and we should utilize them in the conflict with Japanese imperialism. On the other hand, we must struggle resolutely against them, because even while they are opposing Japan, they are carrying out a high-pressure policy of destroying communism, which is opposed to the Anti-Japanese National United Front and to the people. A failure to struggle against them will endanger our unity."[34]

3) *The necessity of distinguishing between the factions within the KMT, which was dominated by pro-British and pro-American upper bourgeoisie.* The KMT was a party composed of a complex variety of elements, including diehards, centrists, and even progressives. Because of their different statuses, interests, relationships, and historical situations, their attitudes toward the conflict with Japan and toward the CPC were also different, and they varied according to time and place. Therefore, it was necessary for the CPC to also treat them differently. On July 6, 1940, Mao Zedong pointed out in his report at a cadre meeting that only a few within the KMT were actually true diehards. On April 12, the Central Secretariat and Central Military Commission likewise pointed out that only some of the officers and political training systems among the Central Military Commanders were diehards, while others were centrists or even progressives, and that the Central Military Command at Chengdu should not be regarded as diehard. On November 16, Mao Zedong, Wang Jiaxiang, Zhu De, and other leading comrades of the Central Committee pointed out once again that the traditional concept of the CPC and its armed forces, which

had previously regarded students of the Whampoa Military Academy as generally anti-communist, was misguided and harmful. Given the current serious situation, there was a need to correct this concept and use every opportunity to carry out the work of the united front alongside the Whampoa soldiers. They should not be agitated, but should rather have the notion of putting the country first firmly impressed on them. On April 23, 1941, the Central Military Commission issued the *Instructions on the Different Treatments for Various Elements within the Kuomintang Army for Maximum Benefit*, which divided the KMT army into four categories. The first were those already colluding with Japan and resolutely anti-communist (hidden traitors), the second those who were not colluding with Japan but were resolutely anti-communist (true diehards), followed by those who were neutral toward communism, and finally the communist sympathizers. It further pointed out that the CPC's policy was to unite with sympathizers, fight for those who were neutral, weaken the diehards, and eliminate the traitors, all while striving and persisting in the war effort.

4) *The necessity of distinguishing between the traitorous pro-Japanese faction and determined traitors such as Wang Jingwei, Wang Yitang, and Shi Yousan.* Mao stated, "There are two elements among the traitor group. We should treat them with a two-sided revolutionary policy, which is to say that if they are pro-Japanese, we must combat and isolate them. If they are still wavering, we must woo and fight for them, distinguishing them from traitors such as Wang Jingwei, Wang Yitang, and Shi Yousan."[35]

b. Unity in struggle; struggle in unity

In discussing the policy of the Anti-Japanese National United Front, Mao said, "The current Anti-Japanese National United Front is neither a joint denial of unity nor a joint denial of all struggle, but is a combination of both unity and struggle. It is a basic policy of the CPC toward the bourgeoisie and the general policy of the Anti-Japanese National United Front. This general policy is an invaluable experience that our party has summed up through a circuitous route, and through both our successes and failures. The progress and setbacks of our party and the successes and failures of the revolution are closely linked to this policy."

The unity and struggle within the Anti-Japanese National United Front was a dialectical relationship, and the two were relative rather than absolute. Mao said in a speech delivered to the Politburo of the CPC Central Committee on September 24, 1938, that in the united front, reunification was a basic principle. It had to be implemented in all localities and in all work. At no time and in no place could this principle of unity and struggle be forgotten, because the struggle was for the sake of unity, and without unity, the struggle could not develop. The struggle was needed on the front line. In his *Outline for Opposing Capitulationism*, he likewise said, "Unity does not forget the struggle, and the struggle does not forget unity. Neither can be neglected, but they are based on unity, 'with friction but no breakdown.'"[36] Mao summed up the relationship between unity and struggle in one sentence, saying, "The struggle is the means of unity, and unity is the purpose of the struggle. Unity is the unity of struggle, not that of compromise."[37] In July 1940, Mao drew the following conclusions at a cadre meeting in Yan'an: 1) the Party had always emphasized unity, and the future was always for all resistance fighter groups, 2) the Party had always emphasized struggle, and its future was always dealing with capitulationists, 3) the Party emphasized both unity and struggle against the diehards and those anti-communists who opposed Japan, 4) alternating between emphasizing struggle and emphasizing unity, depending on whether dealing with a diehard who was united or one who was anti-communist, 5) the struggle was for unity, in order to extend the period of cooperation, and 6) in any case (political, military, or cultural), in the current period, the dominant need was for unity, but struggle was also necessary. Correct handling of unity and struggle was very complicated, and a difficult issue to grasp. The correct handling of the two became a dividing line between correct policy and wrong policy in the course of the CPC's history.[38]

During the War of Resistance Against Japanese Aggression, the CPC had grown from a party in its infancy to an ideologically and politically mature party, and it had mastered Marxist leadership. Not only did it offer a deep analysis of the national bourgeoisie – particularly the big landlords and upper bourgeoisie – but it had also formulated a strategy of unity and struggle, and it had successfully put this strategy into practice. In the Anti-Japanese National United Front, the CPC adopted a strategy of uniting and fighting against the big landlords and the upper bourgeoisie. In doing so, it had on the one hand defended against attack from the diehards, protected the progressive forces from loss, and enabled the progressive forces to continue to develop, while on the other hand extending and maintaining their anti-Japanese cooperation and avoiding the outbreak of large-scale civil war. For this reason, Mao said, "If there is no struggle, the progressive forces will be eliminated by the diehards and there will be no united front, nor will the diehards put up any resistance to the enemy, and civil war will follow."[39] The main reason the Anti-Japanese National United Front was able to insist on victory in the War of Resistance was because the CPC adhered to the general policy of unity and struggle within the united front.

4. Developing progressive forces, fighting for neutral forces, and isolating diehard forces

The united force was by definition the union of several classes or political groups. Because the interests and positions of the various classes and political groups participating in the united front were different, they were inevitably divided into three forces, the left, right, and center. Mao Zedong stated, "The basic requirements to achieve victory in the War of Resistance Against Japanese Aggression include the expansion and consolidation of the anti-Japanese National United Front. To achieve this goal, we must adopt a strategy of developing progressive forces, fighting for neutral forces, and opposing diehard forces. These three things are inseparably linked, and we must struggle to achieve unity among all anti-Japanese forces."[40] Developing progressive forces, fighting for neutral forces, and opposing diehard forces were not only the CPC's basic strategy in connection with the national united front, but also in its entire political platform throughout the War of Resistance Against Japanese Aggression.

1) *Developing progressive forces.* At this time, it was necessary for the Party to develop seven forces: the proletariat, the peasantry, the urban petty bourgeoisie, the expanded Eighth Route Army and New Fourth Army, the extended establishment of anti-Japanese base areas, the organization of the CPC throughout the country, and the development of national workers, peasant, and youth organizations. The popular movements among women, children, intellectuals, and other groups, alongside movements for the expansion of constitutional democracy among the masses, were the basic central links of the three strategic principles. Mao said, "Only through systematic development of the progressive forces can we prevent the reversal of the situation, prevent surrender and division, and establish a solid foundation for the victory of the anti-Japanese war."[41]

2) *Fighting for neutral forces*. Mao asserted that "we must understand that Chinese society is one with a small proportion in the lower and upper classes while a large percentage are in the middle class. If the CPC cannot fight for the masses of the middle class and give them a proper place in accord with their circumstances, it will not solve the Chinese problem."[42] He later added, "In China, the neutral force is very large. Power can often become a factor in our decision to win or lose with the diehards. This makes it all the more essential that we take a very cautious approach to the neutral forces."[43] The neutral forces were characterized by political vacillation, therefore, under certain condition, it was possible to win them to the Party's side. The fight for the neutral force was specifically a fight for seven groups: the national bourgeoisie, enlightened gentlemen, miscellaneous armed forces, the centrists within the KMT (referring to factions with the KMT who were not active or neutral for a certain period of time), centrists within the Central Army (the Central Army was Chiang Kai-shek's squadron, but some who were anti-Japanese were not actively anti-communist, or took a neutral stance), the upper petty bourgeoisie, and various small parties. The CPC did a good deal of work related to these seven groups during the War of Resistance Against Japanese Aggression, and it achieved great results, not only leading them to cooperate with the Party in the anti-Japanese effort, but also to join in the struggle for democracy.

3) *Isolating diehard forces*. The "diehards" were the anti-Japanese faction of the big landlord, upper bourgeoisie class, or more specifically, Chiang Kai-shek's clique within the KMT. During the war, they adopted a two-faced policy, on the one hand opposing Japan, and on the other, implementing an extremely reactionary policy that devastated progressive forces. The isolation of diehards discussed here referred to a two-pronged approach to this class. One prong involved fighting to keep them engaged in the anti-Japan effort, with the understanding that the longer they could be persuaded to stay involved, the better it would be for the war effort. The other prong acknowledged the negative impact of their attitude toward progressives, and thus waged a resolute struggle against the anti-communist agenda. This was the approach of seeking unity through struggle and struggling for unity, a combined push-and-pull strategy.

How could the Party fight against the diehards? Mao proposed principles of rationality, advantage, and temperance. The principle of rationality was a self-defense approach. In other words, as long as no one offends me, I don't offend them, but if they offend me, I may launch a counter-offensive. The principle of advantage was a "winning" approach, which stated that one should not fight a battle one could not win, or in other words, one must never wage an unplanned, unpredictable struggle. The policy of temperance was a policy of truce, which meant only struggling when the situation was right. The successful application of these three principles would achieve the ultimate goal of isolating the diehards.

5. Use conflicts, fight for the majority, oppose the minority, and destroy one by one

Under imperialism, in the relationship between the colonizer and the exploited classes, groups, and factions, there will always be those who give in and collude with the colonizer to exploit and oppress the people. In one way, this happens because of the vying interests between them and their internal conflicts. This is especially true in a revolutionary situation in which the conflicts between the various groups grow more acute. The conflicts that exist within the exploiting classes and their continuing expansion are beneficial to the revolutionary people's struggle led by the proletariat. In his book *On the Strategy for Opposing Japanese Imperialism*, Mao suggests the strategy of "collecting all the struggles, gaps, and conflicts within the enemy camp and using it to oppose our main enemy."[44] Later, he summarized this in the pithy statement of strategy, "Use conflict, strive for the majority, oppose the minority, and destroy one by one,"[45] an approach Party leadership managed to apply successfully, first through the establishment of the second cooperation between the KMT and the CPC and the formation of the Anti-Japanese National United Front, both of which were the result of the CPC capitalizing on the conflict between the upper bourgeoisie and the Japanese imperialists. In 1956, when Mao shared with his foreign allies his experiences in winning China's democratic revolution, he once said, "In the past, China's comprador class was pro-British, pro-American, and pro-Japanese. We used the conflict between Britain, the US, and Japan to first strike against Japanese aggression and the comprador group attached to it, then we went against British and American aggressor forces and defeated the pro-American and pro-British comprador groups."[46] Similarly, the CPC first used the conflicts between the local forces and the Chiang Kai-shek group to fight for power in various localities, isolating the Chiang faction and forcing it to embark on the path toward cooperation with the CPC against Japan. After this, the CPC was united with the Chiang faction of the KMT. In the struggle for eliminating anti-communist activities, they also made full use of the conflicts among the various groups and factions within the KMT, winning the majority and isolating the minority, and ultimately winning the struggle. During the War of Resistance Against Japanese Aggression, in many places, the people's revolutionary forces were at a comparative disadvantage in relation to the KMT, incapable of winning a large-scale battle against them, yet they managed to gain victory first through the political superiority of the CPC, and secondly through its proper application of strategy. Finally, the Party also made use of the conflicts between the national bourgeoisie and the big landlord upper bourgeoisie, uniting the former and isolating the latter.

III

Thoughts and Policies on the People's Democratic United Front

1. Proposal of the Concept of the People's Democratic National Front

The War of Liberation was the final stage of the Chinese democratic revolution, and one of the most spectacular chapters in the history of the Chinese revolution. The Chinese revolutionary united front formed against the backdrop of China's choice between two fates and two futures, each with its own characteristics. It was based on a common political foundation of the struggle for a people's democracy and the realization of peace within the country. The Party's principles and policies were completely determined and implemented independently by the CPC, and it had a perfect organizational form in the Chinese People's Political Consultative Conference, among other factors. However, the most prominent feature of the united front during the War of Liberation was that its scale and deep roots were beyond the reach of what had been known before. During the War of Liberation, Mao Zedong repeatedly discussed the grand scale and deep roots of the united front. In February 1947, he said in the Party's instructions drafted by the Central Committee of the CPC, "This is an extremely broad united front, spanning the entire nation. Compared with the united front during the anti-Japanese war, it is not only as widespread, but has even deeper roots."[47] That the roots of the united front were deeper than during the anti-Japanese war had already been mentioned, but at the end of 1947, with the development of the practice of the united front, Mao drew further conclusions, saying, "The united front is now greater than ever before, and more consolidated than at any time in the past."[48] He explained in particular that "On the surface, in the present, our united front seems smaller than it was during the anti-Japan period, but in reality, it is only in the present period, after Chiang Kai-shek sold our national interests to American imperialism and launched a nationwide civil war against the people, that the evils of the reactionary groups of the American imperialists and Chiang Kai-shek have been exposed before the eyes of the Chinese people, ultimately causing the united front to expand."[49] In saying this, Mao clearly affirmed that the scale of the united front was greater during the War of Liberation than during the previous period, particularly in terms of scale, scope, and influence.

The concept of the people's democratic united front appeared during the later stages of the War of Liberation. The democratic figure Zhu Xuefan first proposed the term "people's democratic united front." In January 1948, Zhu, who was serving as the chairman of the China Labor Association in London, accepted an invitation from the CPC Central Committee to issue a statement to workers around the world when he visited liberated areas of the country. The statement made clear that it fully accepted the CPC's proposition, supported the democratic revolutionary movement, advocated the implementation of land reforms, and upheld all political forces that struggled for democracy and formed a people's united front. On July 1, 1949, the Central Committee of the CPC issued a slogan to commemorate the 12th Anniversary of the July 7th anti-Japanese battle, a slogan proposing to "consolidate the people's democratic united front," thus marking the original formulation of the CPC's concept of the front.

2. Systematically Clarifying the Main Objectives of the Revolution in the New Situation

The CPC's successful policy for the united front prompted the formation of new thoughts and strategies for a whole new people's democratic national front with its own characteristics. In order to lead the entire Party and all the people throughout the country to further recognize the current direction of the struggle, in April 1947, Mao Zedong more clearly proposed that the three major tasks of the new democratic revolution were opposing bureaucratic capitalism, opposing imperialism, and opposing feudalism.

In December 1947, Mao Zedong analyzed the economic reality of the bureaucratic bourgeoisie agglomeration's monopoly on social wealth and the national economic lifeline in the report "The Current Situation and Our Mission," stating, "This monopoly capital is combined with state power, and it became a form of state monopoly capitalism. This monopoly capitalism was closely linked to foreign imperialism, the native landlord class, and the old wealthy peasantry, and it became a feudal state monopoly capitalism. This is the economic basis of Chiang Kai-shek's reactionary regime."[50] For this reason, the task of the new democratic revolution was "not only for the special task of abolishing imperialism in China, but also, internally, for the elimination of the exploitation and oppression of the landlord class and the bureaucratic bourgeoisie (the upper bourgeoisie), changing the feudal production relations of the comprador class and liberating the bound productive forces."[51] Because the bureaucratic monopoly bourgeoisie held power over the country, the national economic lifeline had a huge amount of social wealth. Mao stated "It has prepared sufficient material conditions for the new democratic revolution."[52] He explicitly advocated "confiscating the monopoly capital headed by Chiang Kai-shek, Song Ziwen, Kong Xiangxi, and Chen Lifu and making it the property of the entire new democratic state," and "confiscating the land of the feudal class and distributing it to the peasants," while "protecting the national industry and commerce," listing these as the three major economic programs of the new democratic revolution. This was Mao's new political and economic environment after the victory of the anti-Japanese war. A closer look at these new tasks and programs of the new democratic revolution is warranted.

During the War of Resistance Against Japanese Aggression, Mao once said, "The upper bourgeoisie and its comprador class have never been the driving force of the Chinese revolution, rather, that are the object of the revolution."[53] However, during the War of Resistance, the Party did not directly propose the confiscation of bureaucratic capital and the elimination of the bureaucratic bourgeoisie slogan, mainly because the bureaucratic bourgeoisie was a part of the anti-Japanese camp. It was important at that point to adopt a unified strategy, as befitted a united front, and not a program of action. Further, the monopoly groups of big bankers and compradors were formed gradually before the War of Resistance Against Japanese Aggression. The period during the war was a time of developing and expanding the monopoly power from the financial industry to other economic sectors and accelerating the concentration of capital. After the victory in the War of Resistance Against Japanese Aggression, bureaucratic capital developed to its highest point, bringing an unprecedented disaster to the Chinese people. Its feudal, comprador, military, and reactionary nature as a state monopoly were exposed before the people. As Mao pointed out, "On the basis of the Sino-American commercial contract, the exclusive capital of the US and Chiang Kai-shek's bureaucratic capital are tightly integrated into the control of the economic life of the country. The result is extreme inflation at unprecedented levels and high prices. National industry and commerce are increasingly bankrupt, and the lives of the working people and public officials are deteriorating. This situation forces people from all walks of life to unite in a fight to the death."[54] In short, the production, development, and demise of bureaucratic capital and its reactionary nature had gradually been exposed. The Chinese people's understanding and struggle against it also went through a gradual process of development. After the Chinese People's Liberation Army turned to a strategic offensive in 1947, the CPC promptly introduced the slogan regarding confiscating the bureaucratic capital of the four major families and it naturally and immediately received the heartfelt support of the broad masses of the people in China.

Mao brilliantly noted that "the proletariat-led revolution and the people's masses oppose imperialism, feudalism, and bureaucratic capitalism. This is China's new democratic revolution. This is the general line of the CPC at this current historical stage."[55] In view of the concentrated representatives of the three major enemies of the revolution – imperialism, feudalism, and capitalism – Chiang Kai-shek's ruling reactionary group, Mao vividly proposed the slogan of "overthrowing Chiang Kai-shek and liberating the whole of China." This slogan concentrated on the entire revolutionary program of the CPC at the time, pointing to clear goals and political directions for the whole Party, the whole army, and all the people of the whole country. The masses were extremely important to maximizing the isolation of a small enemy and uniting the vast majority of the country, especially the centrists.

At various stages during the development of the revolution, Mao consistently paid close attention to correctly noting the main enemy of the revolution according to the changes that came in the objective situation at each stage of the revolution, in order to formulate corresponding specific programs and policies. Under this premise, Mao always attached importance to the use of conflicts among the various factions within the ruling reactionary clique, disintegrating and scattering the enemy and emphasizing the need to "collect all struggles, gaps, and conflicts in the midst of the enemy camp as a major weapon against the current enemy."[56] At the beginning of the War of Liberation, Mao pointed out that in order to smash Chiang Kai-shek's offensive "in the KMT army, we should fight for all those who oppose civil war and isolate the militants."[57] He adds, "On the one hand, our army must conduct an extensive public propaganda and political offensive against the KMT army in an effort to disintegrate the KMT forces' will to carry out the civil war. On the other hand, it is necessary to prepare and organize an uprising from within the KMT army and carry out the Gao Shuxun Movement so that at the critical moment of the war, the KMT would follow the example of Gao Shuxun and stand on the side of the people."[58] For this reason, the Central Committee set up a special department for deploying cadres to engage in the differentiation of the enemy. After the PLA turned to a strategic attack, Chiang Kai-shek's military failure caused an extremely deep crisis in the enemy's camp. Between the various factions within the KMT, the conflict between Chiang's military and local military groups became increasingly acute. Accordingly, the Central Committee further pointed out, "In the use of enemy conflict, when it is only an internal opposition of reactionary forces against a local anti-Chiang force, we can only see it as an indirect allied army, but when it changes its position and openly opposes the US and Chiang Kai-shek, we must adopt a welcoming attitude and urge them to transform themselves through action and prove that they are our direct allies."[59] Under this correct policy, the CPC was able to differentiate the anti-Chiang factions within the KMT, and through great patience and meticulous work, accelerate their efforts.

Under the influence of the CPC, in January 1948, the anti-Chiang factions within the KMT jointly established the Kuomintang Revolutionary Committee, headed by Li Jishen and Feng Yuxiang, and publicly announced their participation in the struggle to overthrow Chiang's dictatorship. At the same time, under favorable conditions that the KMT defeat had been set in motion and conflicts within the enemy's camp were rapidly expanding, the PLA had adopted a policy of closely uniting with military strikes and political struggles, launching a strong political offensive on several fronts. This not only prompted many divisions within the KMT, but also won the peaceful reorganization of General Fu Zuoyi's troops, who had been given heavy responsibility under Chiang Kai-shek and was in command of more than 600,000 troops. In the great march of the 1 million-strong army of the CPC across the Yangtze River and straight to Nanjing, even Zhang Zhizhong, the chief representative of the KMT government, was won over by the people's revolution and joined the ranks of the people's democratic national front.

3. Consolidating and Expanding the Strategic Thinking of the Workers' and Peasants' Alliance

The feudal landlord class had always been one of the main targets of the Chinese democratic revolution. During the War of Resistance Against Japanese Aggression, in an effort to establish a broad Anti-Japanese National United Front, the CPC took the initiative to change the policy of confiscating the landlords' property after 1927, turning it into a policy of rent and interest reduction, in order to secure the landlords' participation in the anti-Japanese war. At the end of the War of Resistance, the ethnic conflicts between the Chinese and Japanese eased, while the conflicts between the peasant masses and the feudal landlord class intensified. In the liberated areas of Shanxi, Hebei, Shandong, and Central China, there were large-scale mass movements. In the struggle against oppressors and traitors, liquidation settling accounts, rent reduction, and interest rate cuts, land was obtained directly from the landlords, and the cultivators of the fields owned the land. Some traitors, bullies, and landlords fled to the city, and the peasant movement swept through liberated areas. Under the influence of reactionary elements, some intermediaries expressed doubts about the peasants' struggle, and even a few voices within the Party suggested it was "overkill." In response to this situation, Mao Zedong and Liu Shaoqi made clear at that time that "now, like the period of the Great Revolution, the peasants have reached out to take the land, and the CPC must be clear about whether it approves of this."[60] They added, "The KMT currently has the big cities and the aid of the imperialists. In a region home to three-quarters of the population, we can only change the situation of our relative size by relying on the strength of the broad masses, and if the land issue is resolved among the liberated areas of tens of millions of people, it will win the support of the people in those liberated areas for a long time […] This is a fundamental issue, and it is the basic idea linking all our work. All the cadres throughout the Party must be made aware of its importance."[61] For this reason, on May 4, 1946, the CPC Central Committee issued the *Instructions on*

Land Issues (hereafter referred to as the May 4th Instructions) requiring local Party committees to "resolutely support all legitimate landowners who approve the acquisition of land by the peasants. The oaths of traitors, the rich gentry class, and landlords should be refuted and the suspicions of the centrists addressed. For the incorrect views held by those in the Party, we should offer education."[62] From that time on, the Party's anti-Japan war era policy of reduced rents and interest rates was modified to a policy of confiscating the land of the landlord class and reallocating it to the peasants. The liberated areas saw land reform movements launched one after the other. However, in view of the fact that the overall civil war had not yet erupted and the door to peace talks had not yet closed, the May 4th Instructions also pointed out that for wealthy peasants and certain landlords, the issue was mainly taken care of, such as stipulations that "the land of the wealthy peasants will remain generally unchanged," the landlords who "had earned merit for resisting Japan" would be "left with more land," and so forth. The purpose of these regulations was to win the landlords, and people from all walks of life who might be connected to them, over to the opposition against Chiang's policy of civil war and dictatorship.

After the outbreak of full-scale civil war, Chiang's aggressive attack on the liberated areas fueled the reactionary arrogance of the landlord class, and they hoped for the victory of Chiang's government. The landlords who fled to Chiang Kai-shek were an organized group for "returning home" and alongside Chiang's army, they attacked liberated areas. They carried out extremely cruel counter-attacks against the peasants and stubbornly opposed the land reform movement led by the CPC. At the same time, the wealthy peasants also took a hostile attitude toward the land reforms. In essence, within Chinese society, the key purpose of the Chiang faction's launch of a counter-revolutionary civil war was precisely to preserve the feudal land system and the feudal privilege of the landlord class in order to maintain the economic foundation of its reactionary rule. Accordingly, the CPC held a national land conference from July to September 1947 to formulate the Outline of the Chinese Land Law. On October 10, the Central Committee solemnly announced, "China's land system is extremely unreasonable. Generally, landlords and wealthy peasants, who account for less than 10% of the rural population, own about 70% to 80% of the land, and they cruelly exploit the peasants. The farmers, poor peasants, middle class peasants, and other groups, who together account for 90% of the rural population, own only about 20% to

30% of the land, and they work year-round, but are not even given sufficient food and clothing. The seriousness of this situation is the root cause of national aggression, oppression, poverty, and backwardness, and it is the basic obstacle to the democratization, industrialization, independence, unity, and prosperity of our country."[63] In order to change this grave situation, the *Outline of the Chinese Land Law* (hereafter, the Outline) further developed the revolutionary spirit of the May 4th Instructions, clearly declaring, "We must abolish the land system of feudal and semi-feudal exploitation and implement a system in which the fields are owned by those who cultivate them."[64] The Outline clearly stipulated everything that was to be confiscated from the landlords and the policy of collecting surplus land and property from wealthy peasants, and it proposed that "the land will be properly distributed in terms of both quality and quantity" as a specific method of land distribution. In accordance with the Outline, a thorough land reform that destroyed the feudal and semi-feudal systems of exploitation and eliminated the landlord class was carried out on an unprecedented scale in various liberated areas.

After the Central Committee issued the May 4th Instructions, the land reform movements carried out in liberated areas showed more concern for wealthy peasants and certain landowners, while in some areas, rightist biases such as daring to let go of the masses or seeking to avoid meeting the needs of the poor peasants prevailed. After the National Land Conference formulated a thorough land policy, the liberated areas overcame these right-wing biases and promoted vigorous land reform. At the same time, there were also some leftist errors. For instance, some places lacked correct standards for class division, and some people were misidentified as landlords or wealthy peasants. The distinctions between various enemy groups were unclear. In some places, the interests of the peasants were infringed or destroyed by national industry and commerce. In some places, over-emphasis on discovering landlords and wealthy peasants led to the use of the same methods to fight against the two groups, even adopting the method of "sweeping them out of the door," leaving them without a livelihood, perhaps even resulting in riots and killings. In this regard, the Mao-led CPC Central Committee attached great importance to it. Before and after the December 1947 Central Committee meeting, it further elaborated on the basic principles of land reform and a series of specific policies correcting leftist error.

At the end of November 1947, the Central Committee reissued two documents entitled "Dividing the Rural Classes" and "Decisions on Various Issues in the

Land Struggle," both written by Mao Zedong in 1933 as the basis for class division and the implementation policy. The issuance and implementation of these two documents corrected the leftist bias of the land reform policy which had led to some people mistakenly being classified as landlords or wealthy peasants. At the December meeting of the Central Committee, Mao pointed out, "In order to resolutely and thoroughly carry out the land reform, villages must not only organize the broadest masses of peasant associations, including poor and middle class peasants and their elected committees, but must first organize poor peasant groups and their committees and implement the legal organs of land reform, making poor peasant groups the backbone of all rural struggles. Our policy is to rely on poor peasants and consolidate the cooperation with the middle class peasants and to eliminate the feudal and semi-feudal exploitation system of the landlord class and the former wealthy peasants. The land and property of the landlords and the wealthy peasants should not exceed that of the peasant masses. However, those categorized as 'landlords who did not divide their land and wealthy peasant who spoiled the land' under the wrong policies during the years from 1931 to 1934 should not be made to repeat the exercise."[65]

In order to persuade 90% of the people in the village to participate in the land reform of the united front, Mao suggested that two basic principles should be given attention, saying, "First, we must meet the needs of the poor and middle class peasants, which is the most basic task of the land reforms. Second, we must resolutely unite the middle class peasants and avoid harming their interests."[66] In order to complete this strategic task of consolidating and uniting the middle class peasants, Mao issued a policy with specific provisions for them, stating that in the process of confiscating and dividing the land and property of the feudal class, it was important to respect the opinions of the middle class peasants and pay attention to certain of their demands, such as allowing them to maintain a higher amount of land relative to the average peasant. In the peasant committees and rural democratic regimes, it was necessary to recruit the middle class peasant activists to participate in the work and to avoid mistaking those who belonged to the middle class peasantry for wealthy peasants. At the same time, it was necessary to ensure that middle class peasants bore the land tax and supported the war. With the implementation of the above principles, the workers' and peasants' coalition led by the proletariat (via the CPC) had been consolidated and developed in an unprecedented manner, allowing the main peasant force to play its role more fully.

In the land reform movement, the Mao-led CPC not only relied on the poor peasants, but also united the middle class peasants and gave attention to other classes that could be won to the cause. In an effort to isolate the most stubborn hostile elements in the feudal class, based on the actual situation of the feudal relationships in rural China, Mao suggested that a distinction should be made between the landlords and the wealthy peasants, between the large, medium, and small landowners, and between the bullies and non-agitators among the landlords and wealthy peasantry, and non-interference policies towards the landlords and wealthy peasants who made investment in business and industry as it was a form of non-feudal exploitation should be created. In the struggle to overthrow the feudal system, Mao and the Central Committee paid particular attention to the enlightened gentlemen who had split from the feudal classes. The Central Committee reiterated the strategic principle of "striving for the majority, opposing the minority, using conflicts, and destroying one by one," emphasizing the need "to understand the few enlightened elements of the majority that have always been included in enemy camps (that is, the enlightened gentlemen in the feudal comprador class, the patriots, etc.)."[67] Mao Zedong offered a profound explanation of this issue, saying, "The enlightened gentleman is a democratic individual in the landlord or wealthy peasant class. These people are in conflict with bureaucratic capitalism and imperialism, and they have some conflicts with feudal landlords and wealthy peasants."[68] They "gave us considerable help during the difficult period after the War of Resistance Against Japanese Aggression. When we implemented land reforms, they did not hinder or oppose the agrarian reforms. Therefore, we should continue to adopt a policy of unity toward them."[69] Since most of China's intellectuals came from landlord or wealthy peasant households, and because most of China's national bourgeoisie was tied to the land, there were hundreds of thousands of enlightened gentlemen throughout the country. If the Party united without exception those who were anti-American, anti-Chiang, and pro-democracy (while not anti-communist), and the enlightened gentlemen who were in favor of the agrarian reform, then educated them by unifying them, it would help the CPC win the support of the intellectuals, the national bourgeoisie, and the enlightened gentlemen throughout the country, which benefited the efforts to isolate the main enemies of the revolution, Chiang Kai-shek and his reactionaries.

According to these guidelines, the CPC united in the land reform to win a large number of enlightened gentlemen and patriots, leaving the big landlords, bullies, and local tyrants in the feudal class extremely isolated. Under the united education of the CPC, many representatives of the enlightened gentleman class each stood in turn on the side of the people's revolution and participated in the struggle against the American-Guangdong reactionaries and played a certain role in the people's democratic united front.

In January 1948, after thorough investigation and study, the CPC Central Committee entrusted Ren Bishi with the task of delivering a speech entitled "Challenges in the Agrarian Reform," in which he accurately said that "based on the criteria used to divide the rural classes," the Party "should strongly unite all classes of the middle peasantry" and introduce "methods for the struggle against the landlords and wealthy peasants, [...] the policy on commerce and industry, [...] and the issue of intellectuals and enlightened gentlemen" while "resolutely opposing rioting and killing." This important speech by Ren Bishi clarified more specifically Mao's above-mentioned principles and policies on land reform and played a positive role in correcting the leftist bias.

In short, the Mao-led Central Committee learned lessons from the Agrarian Revolutionary War period, gave attention to correcting both rightist and leftist biases in the agrarian reform movement after the May 4th Instructions, and formulated land reform policies that were in line with the actual situation. The implementation of these principles and policies had mobilized the majority of poor and middle class peasants, consolidated and united all middle class peasants, and strove for the enlightened gentlemen and other patriots, so that the team of the rural, anti-feudal people's democratic united front was not narrowed, but consolidated and expanded.

With the advancement of the PLA into Kuomintang areas, the newly liberated areas increased rapidly. In view of the fact that the remaining enemies in these areas had not been cleared and the masses were generally low, unlike the actual situation in the traditional and semi-traditional liberated areas, in February 1948, Mao proposed that different methods should be adopted to implement land laws in different regions. In the old liberated areas, the land issue had been largely resolved. It was necessary not only to adjust a part of the land without reallocating it, but also to focus on rectifying the Party's ranks and resolving the conflicts between the Party and the masses. In the semi-traditional liberated areas, the land issue had not yet been thoroughly resolved, so the land had to be distributed more generally and thoroughly. In the new liberated areas, the land law was to be implemented in two stages. The first stage would be that of leaving middle class peasants alone while fighting the landlords, seizing and redistributing the latter's land and property. In the second stage, the surplus land and property of the wealthy peasants would be redistributed. Before long, Mao introduced new regulations based on the actual situation in the rural work in newly liberated areas. He pointed out that in the rural parts of newly liberated areas, "premature disbursement of wealth is welcomed by only a few bold individuals, but wealth is not fundamentally divided up between the masses, so they may express their dissatisfaction. Moreover, if social wealth is rapidly dispersed, the soldiers will be at a disadvantage. If the land is divided, the burden of the military will fall prematurely on the shoulders of the peasants, rather than the landlords and wealthy peasants."[70] For this reason, it was necessary to first implement the reduction of rents and interest rates and the corresponding social and fiscal policies, so that "social wealth will not be dispersed and social order will remain relatively stable, which is conducive to concentrating all our forces to eliminate KMT reactionaries."[71] The above-mentioned strategy proposed by Mao Zedong allowed the land reform to be adapted according to the strength of the feudal forces in different types of liberated areas, as well as the level of awareness and the level of organization of the masses. The policies were meant to be carried out in stages, which led to a more complete land reform.

In April 1948, Mao summarized the basic principles and policies of the land reform laid out above as a general approach to land reform, which was stated as "reliance on poor peasants, uniting middle class peasants, and systematically and separately eliminating the feudal exploitation system and developing agricultural production."[72] After that, the large-scale land reform movement progressed healthily along the correct path of this general approach. In a span of more than a year after the publication of the Outline of the Chinese Land Law, the CPC completely resolved the land problem in a vast area that was home to about 100 million people. The land of the feudal class was redistributed to the rural people, especially the poor and working farmers. This greatly stimulated the revolutionary enthusiasm of the peasants and the proletariat. The peasants who had been politically and economically liberated worked hard to participate in the military activity, actively supporting the front line and providing a solid rear line and inexhaustible reserve forces for the national War of Liberation. In the recruitment of soldiers, supplying military stores, and transporting war materials, the peasants played an unprecedented role in the war. The general, thorough, systematic, and separate implementation of the land reform movement mobilized the enthusiasm of hundreds of millions of peasant masses, while at the same time striving for all the forces that could be won, so that the Party could obtain what was necessary to defeat all its enemies, expanding and consolidating the people's democratic united front.

4. Promoting the Formation and Development of the Second Front

After the outbreak of full-scale civil war, with the heroic fighting and resolute resistance of the PLA, the KMT forces turned from a comprehensive offensive to more targeted attacks, and the KMT's Nationalist government suffered a heavy military blow. At the same time, the Nationalist government had also fallen into a serious political and economic crisis. Economically, Chiang Kai-shek signed a series of treaties and agreements with the US, allowing the US military to run rampant in China without in fact doing anything constructive. According to incomplete statistics from Shanghai, Nanjing, Beijing, and Tianjin, from August 1945 through the end of 1946, the US military was responsible for at least 3,800 atrocities, causing more than 300 deaths and injuries to Chinese military personnel and civilians, including raping more than 300 women, resulting in the KMT-ruled area being re-colonized. The KMT destroyed the people and churned out countless banknotes, causing inflation to expand and prices to soar, making it impossible for the people to earn a living and plunging them headlong into the fire. Politically, on the other hand, the KMT unilaterally held a divided National Assembly, undermining the Nanjing Peace Talks and forcing CPC representatives to retreat from KMT-ruled areas, completely exposing the real nature of the false peace. The general masses and the democratic parties were instructed concerning the KMT's backward ways, and they grew even more dissatisfied with the KMT, pinning their hopes instead on the Communist Party of China. Mao stated, "On the basis of the Sino-American commercial contract, the exclusive capital of the US and Chiang Kai-shek's bureaucratic comprador capital are tightly integrated as a means of controlling the economic life of the country. The result is extreme inflation and unprecedented price hikes. National industry and commerce are increasingly bankrupted, and the lives of the working people and public officials are deteriorating. This situation forces people from all walks of life to unite and fight to the death."[73]

The CPC Central Committee, correctly analyzing the situation at that time, believed that they were on the doorstep of the climax of a new nationwide people's revolution. To this end, on February 1, 1947, Mao drafted a directive on behalf of the Central Committee, which stated, "The current situation indicates that the Chinese revolution will develop to a new stage, moving from the stage of the nationwide anti-imperialist, anti-feudal struggle to a new people's revolution. The Party's mission is to fight for the arrival of the climax and its victory."[74] For this reason, on February 28, 1947, Zhou Enlai also drafted the Measures for the Kuomintang in the White Area on behalf of the Central Committee and sent it to Dong Biwu, Liu Xiao, Qian Ying, Wu Yuzhang, Fang Fang, and others. The Measures stated that the mass struggle in Chiang-controlled areas must necessarily go through a series of gains and setbacks, but that the general trend would inevitably continue to grow. In response to Chiang's then current policy of repression, the Party should expand its publicity work, avoid being hit hard, fight for intermediaries, use legal methods, and strive to build a broad front against terror tactics, oppose civil war, authoritarianism, and special agent terror groups, and continue the struggle to survive. The Measures emphasized that "in this struggle, we must remain united, and sometimes we must transfer our efforts to economic struggle, so that we can mobilize more people and more easily gain control of legal forms. With economic struggle as our broad foundation, it will be easier to be linked to anti-special-agent, anti-civil war groups."[75] On May 5, Zhou Enlai drafted instructions on behalf of the Central Committee and sent them to Liu Xiao, Liu Changsheng, and Qian Ying. In response to the KMT government's plot to fabricate the so-called CPC policy of underground struggle and attempts to suppress the people's movement in KMT-ruled areas, the directive pointed out that in KMT areas, the Party's work policy was "to protect the Party and various democratic and progressive forces in order to continue to strengthen the development of the people's movement," and "for the sake of this goal, we must be firm and brave, but also cautious."[76] It was necessary to adhere to the principle of putting the Party's anti-American, anti-Chiang movement into the hands of the people and carry out both "legal and illegal struggles." The instructions declared, "The work in the cities in Chiang's area must be thoroughly planned with a long-term view of promoting the mass struggle and carrying out the work of the united front. In this way, it can cooperate with the victorious groups in liberated areas and accelerate the arrival of a new national climax."[77] Those in the KMT-controlled areas who were under the specific guidance of the CPC and the united front had launched a patriotic and democratic movement against the KMT's reactionary rule, both in the cities and in rural areas.

By adopting a policy of transforming China into a US colony, launching a civil war, and strengthening a fascist dictatorship, the US and Chiang Kai-shek declared themselves enemies of the people of China and placed people from all walks of life throughout the country on a path toward hunger and death, compelling the people to unite, fighting the KMT government for their lives. Further, they had no way out. Mao pointed out, "People from all walks of life in China, who are oppressed by the reactionary policies of the Chiang Kai-shek government and are united to help their own cause, include workers, peasants, the urban petty bourgeoisie, the national bourgeoisie, enlightened gentlemen, other patriots, ethnic minorities, and overseas Chinese. This is an extremely broad united front."[78] On May 30, 1947, Mao stated, "There are two fronts in China. Chiang Kai-shek has initiated a war between his army and the People's Liberation Army. This is the first front. The second front that has now formed is the sharp struggle between the great student movement and the reactionary government of Chiang Kai-shek."[79] The second front, based on the student movement, included the KMT's rule and oppression, putting pressure from democracy movements on all levels.

The starting point for the formation of the second front was the December 1942 student movement in Beiping, protesting US military atrocities. On the evening of December 24, 1946, an American soldier raped Shen Chong, a female student at Peking University. When word came out regarding the incident, it caused great indignation among the people of Beiping, particularly students. The underground Party organization believed that this was a good opportunity to mobilize the masses to carry out the struggle. It immediately decided to raise the banner of safeguarding national dignity through the Shen Chong Incident, inspire national outrage, and launch a campaign against military atrocities among the students of Beiping. The Party organization decided to unite broader groups of students, so they mobilized the city's university students to strike. In an attempt to use "legal settlements" to blur the political nature of the struggle, the KMT government undermined the student movement. In response to the conspiracy of the US-Chiang reactionaries, the CPC organization suggested they persist in the struggle, introducing the slogan "American soldiers, roll out of China." The political struggle in the slogan was clear, and it was easy to rally the masses around it to expand the patriotic united front. On December 29, the Peking Party School Committee decided to take to the streets. On December 30, students in Beiping marched on the streets, first shouting slogans such as "American soldiers, roll out of China." The movement quickly expanded throughout the entire country, with half a million students participating in protests. The protests aimed directly at the US-Chiang reactionaries, which marked a new upsurge in the people's struggles in KMT-controlled areas and became the starting point for the formation of the second front. From then on, the CPC's underground movement took the initiative to unite the masses and lead the people in KMT-ruled areas to carry out one anti-American, anti-Chiang struggle after another.

In 1947, the May 20th Movement became the symbol of the formation of the second front. After the protests, mass struggles popped up one after another and the patriotic, democratic united front started to expand, mainly in response to the KMT government's moves to step up its economic rule and political oppression. In response to this situation, the Shanghai Bureau of the CPC made a report to the Central Committee on April 28, 1947, stating that "the mass movement in the Chiang-ruled areas will follow the second climax of the protest movement, which will arrive soon. In fact, it might come as early as May."[80] The Shanghai Bureau decided to mobilize the masses to first "break through the continuous development in this life or death struggle" and gradually develop the opposition to the KMT's "borrowing foreign debts and fighting civil wars," concentrating on "organizing several central movements as the backbone of the overall movement."[81] On May 5, Zhou Enlai drafted a telegram to Liu Xiao and others on behalf of the Central Committee, emphasizing that "we must protect our Party and the various democratic and progressive forces if we are to continue to strengthen the people's movement."[82] It was decided that they should release the masses and expand the united front to carry out the anti-America, anti-Chiang struggle. In the spirit of these instructions, the Shanghai Bureau decided that from the beginning of May 1947, university students from all over the republic and the KMT areas would hold various events to commemorate the May 4th Movement. In this way, the prelude to the second front's struggle was unveiled.

The Shanghai Bureau believed that, as the "capital" of KMT-ruled areas, Nanjing held great political influence. For this reason, it decided to break out in Nanjing and launch an anti-civil war, anti-hunger campaign that shocked China and other nations. Under the leadership of the Shanghai Bureau, on May 20, universities and colleges in Shanghai, Hangzhou, Suzhou, and other cities sent representatives to meet the students of Nanjing University, where a total of more than 6,000 students launched a massive anti-hunger, anti-war march. The march was suppressed by the KMT army, police, and special forces, which was known as the May 20th Massacre. The movement was characterized by its development from an economic to a political struggle, and from its gradual merging of several decentralized struggles into a unified national struggle. The students' patriotic, democratic movement was supported by the people across the nation, and the anti-American, anti-Chiang struggle developed rapidly in more than 60 large and medium-sized cities across the country, creating a wave of anti-American, anti-Chiang sentiment.

In the struggle, the CPC paid great attention to the use of the united front strategy, emphasizing the mobilization of the masses, uniting the majority, utilizing the conflicts of the enemy, dividing and scattering the reactionary forces, and grasping the principles of nationality, benefit, and unity. At the time, within the KMT ruling group, there were differences in the responses to the student movements. The KMT Legislative Body, the Shanghai Mayor Wu Guozhen, and some presidents of universities feared that the KMT's army, police, and special forces would expand and make it difficult to clean up the situation and advocate for mediation or negotiation. The Shanghai Bureau guided the masses to demand the release of all arrested students, punish the murderers, and aim at the KMT's army, police, and special forces. At the same time, in order to reduce the persecution by the KMT military and police forces, on May 23, Zhou Enlai pointed out in the Directive of the CPC Central Committee on the Work of the Youth Army and the Police Forces in the Communist Movement, which he drafted on behalf of the Central Committee, "To avoid confrontation, the youth army, police, and soldiers have striven to gain sympathy for the student movement. In order to dispel the power behind Chiang Kai-shek's suppression, you should go through various organizations and activists from all walks of life to quickly carry out the work of soldiers in the youth army and military police." He added, "The slogan will generate sympathy for the students' desire for food and for peace, and will allow them to reintegrate their struggle."[83] At that time, some schools sent teachers and students to join the youth army, in accordance with the instructions from the Central Committee. When Shanghai and other places were obstructed by the military and police, they shouted at them, pointing out that their salaries were meager and that their consciences should be pricked. In this way, the opposing sentiments of the other side were reduced, to a degree. At the same time, the Shanghai Bureau also clearly pointed out that when the masses were mobilized and the struggle had achieved certain results, it would certainly be appropriate. It was necessary to persuade the activists to modify their excessive demands of indefinite strikes and prevent them from retreating from the masses. As a result, the strategy of temporarily suspending the strike, resuming classes, and continuing the struggle was promptly proposed, and the students gained broad sympathy from the public.

In an effort to promote the national student union and prepare for new battles, the National Student Federation was established in mid-June 1947. The Federation issued a call to the entire nation, calling for all to fight against hunger, and for peace, to fight against persecution and for freedom, and to unite, forming a solid united front to oppose reactionaries, regardless of party, faith, or geography.

Fighting on the second front cooperated directly with the front line of the People's Liberation Army, causing disruption behind the lines in KMT-ruled territory, draining and weakening Chiang's power, and accelerating the process of the people's revolution. The student movement had aroused widespread sympathy across society, and workers, peasants, members of the urban petty bourgeoisie and national bourgeoisie, enlightened gentlemen, and patriotic overseas Chinese all stood on the side of the CPC and actively supported and participated in the patriotic democratic movement. The face of the Chiang-led Kuomintang had been exposed, leaving it completely isolated and surrounded by the people's movement as the people's democratic united front continued to consolidate and expand, bringing victory to all the people of China.

5. Forming a New Form of Organization in the United Front Under the People's Democratic Dictatorship

As early as the War of Resistance Against Japanese Aggression, given the persistence of the war and the KMT's tyrannical proposition to "merge, limit, and oppose the communist," the CPC proposed that all major parties should form a long-term cooperation on the basis of mutual respect and mutual aid, while adhering to their own independence. In practice, the CPC was the leader of the anti-Japanese base. It also established the 3-3 System, in which Party members, leftist progressives, centrists, and other elements accounted for a third of the coalition. After gaining the victory in the War of Resistance Against Japanese Aggression, in what direction was China to go? What sort of government should it establish? Various political parties formed and affirmed their own views and opinions, and for a time, there was great multi-party competition in China's political arena. After the War of Liberation was fully launched, the CPC considered the correct handling of relations with various parties as it established and consolidated its base, one of the major issues related to the development of the people's democratic united front, and proposed principles and policies for correctly handling the relationship between democratic parties, thus forming a fuller cooperation under the leadership of the CPC and initially establishing a multi-party cooperation and political system of consultation.

To correctly handle partisan relations, it was necessary to first scientifically analyze the nature of each party. Mao and the other members of the CPC conducted serious research on the democratic parties that were active in the Chinese political arena at that time. They made scientific analysis of their organizational components and political tendencies, which provided a theoretical basis for correctly handling their relationships with other democratic parties. Zhou Enlai pointed out in the *Opinions on the Work of Today's Democratic Parties* that although the organizational components of the democratic parties were more complex, encompassing those from the opposition ruling class to the progressives, they mainly came from the upper petty bourgeoisie, national bourgeoisie, and the political representatives of the intellectuals. They opposed the one-party dictatorship of the KMT, and the democratic parties and democrats associated with them were an important force in the Chinese political arena, one that should not be ignored. Zhou also offered an analysis of non-partisan democrats, stating his belief that though non-partisan democrats did not form official parties, they were essentially partisans. They participated in democratic political movements and participated in anti-imperialist and anti-feudalist activities. Judging from the struggles against bureaucratic capitalism, this was in itself a partisan activity. However, some democrats did not have partisan organizations, meaning that non-partisan democrats were actually partisan democrats without party organizations. Their political inclinations were basically consistent with the political inclinations of various democratic parties.

According to this analysis of democratic parties and democrats, the CPC proposed to unite with them during the War of Liberation and cooperate with them in the long-term to build a new China. At the same time, in its long-term cooperation with these parties, it was necessary to uphold the leadership of the proletariat and its political parties, and to criticize or struggle against their shortcomings and errors. Before the outbreak of full-scale civil war, the CPC actively sought the joint action of the democratic parties in the political struggle for negotiations with the KMT. After the outbreak of the full-scale civil war, the CPC formulated and implemented a series of correct policies for further cooperation with democratic parties and democrats. On the political front, the Party had absorbed the majority of non-Party elements and intermediaries to participate in political work and social undertakings, and it often communicated with them on major issues such as land reform and negotiations between the KMT and the CPC. On the economic front, it was necessary to resolutely implement policies to protect national industry and commerce, and to take care of and assist in protecting their health and security. Through extensive contact and cooperation with democratic parties and democrats, the CPC carried out meticulous in-depth work to help them elevate their understanding of US imperialism and the nature of the KMT, and also to make them aware of the trends and directions of the development of the Chinese revolution, embarking on the path of the new democratic revolution.

The principles and policies of the CPC for the implementation of cooperation and education for the democratic parties were correct and achieved great success. When the Chinese PLA's strategic counterattack had already gained a clear advantage, the call of the CPC to establish a democratic coalition government received a positive response from democrats from all walks of life.

On April 30, 1948, the CPC Central Committee issued the slogan "Commemorating May 1st as Labor Day," calling on "the nation's working class to unite, and to unite its intellectuals, the national bourgeoisie, the free bourgeoisie, democratic parties, the social elites, and other patriotic elements, and to expand the united front against imperialism, feudalism, and bureaucratic capitalism, and to work together to defeat Chiang Kai-shek and establish a new China." It further called for "democratic parties, various people's organizations, and various social leaders to quickly convene a political consultation meeting to discuss and form people's congresses for the establishment of a democratic coalition government."[84] The call of the CPC received a positive response from democratic parties and democrats. Several people from various groups – including Li Jishen and He Xiangning of the Chinese KMT Revolutionary Committee, Shen Junru and Zhang Bojun of the China Democratic League, Ma Xulun and Wang Shao'ao of the China Democracy Promotion Association, Chen Qiyou of the Chinese Zhi Gong Party, Peng Zemin of the Chinese Peasant Workers' Democratic Party, Li Zhangda of the Chinese National Salvation Congress, Cai Tingkai of the Chinese KMT Democratic Promotion Meeting, Tan Pingshan of the Comrades Union of the Three People's Principles (Nationalism, Democracy, the People's Livelihood), and the non-partisan democracy activist Guo Moruo – jointly called Mao Zedong to respond to the CPC's May 1st call and considered the "May 1st Labor Day slogan… suitable for the people's current situation, equal to the need of the people," adding that they would work with the CPC and together accomplish this great feat.[85] From that time on, the leaders of democratic parties and non-partisan democrats were invited by the CPC to enter liberated areas in groups to prepare for a new level of political consultation. On January 22, 1949, fifty-five leaders of democratic parties and non-partisan democrats, including Li Jishen and Shen Junru, who had traveled to the liberated areas, jointly published "Our Opinions on the Current Situation," saying that they "wish to make consistent contribution under the leadership of the CPC." At the same time, they also believed that there was "no possibility of compromise or reconciliation between the revolution and the counter-revolution," and that "there is no room for reactionaries to stand in democratic parties, nor is there any room for a so-called middle line."[86]

The May 1st call for support and response from various democrats not only shows the leadership of the CPC in the cooperation between various parties, as has previously been noted, but also indicates that the CPC's leadership in the initial formation of the multi-party cooperation and the people's democratic united front had entered a new historical stage. Recognizing the leadership of the CPC, democratic representatives entered the liberated areas for further cooperation in dealing with the principles and guidelines of relations between the democratic parties. On January 22, 1949, the CPC Central Committee issued the

Instructions on the Treatment of Democrats, which pointed out that the Party's policy toward democrats should be to explain the political and relevant parties to them in a completely frank and sincere manner. In all issues related to the policy, the Party should actively educate them and fight for them. Regarding policy questions, they were to answer frankly and not evade any question. Apart from the Party's secrets and certain specific strategies, nothing was off limits in their discussions. The implementation of the policy should also be reported according to the facts, and they should be invited to fully express their opinions and offer criticism in order to strengthen the spirit of cooperation. The methods adopted could be based on their proposals, and various heads of department within the CPC could make reports, hold talks, organize visits, or organize some Party members to conduct daily contacts and conversations. They were also welcome to express negative opinions within the Party, and to talk and exchange opinions with those in positions of responsibility.

Regarding how to deal with the development of local organizations and the structuring of various democratic parties and groups, the CPC offered clear instructions. In February 1949, the CPC Central Committee stated in its Instructions on How to Treat Local Organizations and Various Democratic Parties and Groups that all those who had established themselves as anti-imperialist and anti-feudalist before the May 1st call and had joined the struggle against bureaucratic capitalism and the KMT's reactionary rule, along with those democratic parties who had done most during the War of Liberation, as testified by PLA headquarters, would have their legal status recognized and protected. They could also carry out activities in the names of their parties, with the aim of developing their membership. It likewise pointed out that any party, including democratic parties, must abide by the PLA's notices and those of the People's Government and Military Commission.

These principles and policies for dealing with inter-party relations laid the foundation for the CPC's policy of "long-term coexistence and mutual supervision" after the founding of the new China.

With the initial formation of the multi-party cooperation under the leadership of the CPC, it was necessary to establish a united front organization to negotiate and handle differences of opinion between them. After the May 1st call in 1948, the CPC introduced a new slogan, "the meeting of the CPC and the democratic parties," indicating the active convening of a political consultative meeting between the CPC and the democratic parties, a meeting that gradually evolved into a broad united front organization led by the CPC with representatives from various democratic parties, various people's organizations, democrats from all walks of life, ethnic minorities, and overseas Chinese.

The term "political consultative conference" had been in circulation before the May 1st call. In January 1946, under pressure from those throughout the country who demanded peace and democracy, the KMT government convened a political consultative meeting. Finally, under the concerted efforts of the CPC, five resolutions conducive to democracy, peace, unity, and solidarity were adopted. However, the KMT government quickly tore up the Communist Party Political Consultative Conference resolutions and launched a comprehensive civil war. However, the form of democratic consultations seen in the conference left a great impression on the people throughout the country. This was precisely what Mao pointed out in the opening speech of the First Plenary Session of the CPPCC, saying, "This meeting is called the Political Consultative Conference because three years ago we had a political consultative conference with Chiang Kai-shek's Nationalist Party. The achievements of that meeting were destroyed by Chiang's KMT and their accomplices, but it has left an[87] indelible impression on the people." In order to distinguish it from the political consultative conference held in January 1946, in November 1948, after discussion, CPC representatives and representatives of the traditional democratic parties decided to refer to the earlier meeting as the "Old Political Consultative Conference" and the current preparatory meeting as the "New Political Consultative Conference." When the second preparatory meeting was held on September 17, 1949, it was decided that the later meeting would be renamed the "Chinese People's Political Consultative Conference." The lineup of the CPPCC was strong. It was only after several months of consultations and negotiations regarding the quotas and lists of units and representatives that it was agreed who would participate in the CPPCC. The CPPCC representatives included advisors from parties, regions, the military, groups, and specially invited representatives. Compared with the Old Conference, the lineup of the CPPCC had three salient features. The first was extensive representation that included all democratic parties, various people's organizations, regions, the PLA, ethnic minorities, overseas Chinese, and religious groups. The representatives fully reflected the great unity of various ethnicities, various democratic classes, and all patriotic forces in China's new democratic revolution. At the same time, it included celebrities and representatives who had contributed to the people's cause in various historical periods of the Chinese national democratic revolution. Key figures from the Revolution of 1911, the Northern Expedition, the May 4th Movement, the War of Resistance Against Japanese Aggression, and the War of Liberation were absorbed, representing all the revolutionary periods in China's recent history, and even stretching as far back to include those from the late Qing Dynasty and the Beiyang government who later sympathized with the revolution, absorbing many good people into the movement. The second factor was the seriousness of the political standards. Although the lineup of the CPPCC was extremely large and comprehensive, it was also based on serious political ethics strictly delineating one's own party, one's enemies, and one's allies. In accordance with the provisions of the Regulations for Organization, those who did not fully meet the criteria for participating in the CPPCC were not invited, but were instead asked to disband or cease their activities. At the same time, attention was given to the extensiveness of the solidarity, the history of democratic movements in these organizations, and the War of Liberation. Democrats with actual performance and certain representatives were invited, upon the disbanding of their groups or activities, to participate in the CPPCC in their personal capacities or to make appropriate working arrangements within the coalition government. The third factor was that it not only generated membership for the CPC, but also reflected the unity and cooperation between the CPC and those outside the Party. The leadership of the CPC did not overwhelm the minority with a simple majority. Instead, it cooperated with the democrats in a sincere manner and adopted democratic consultations to achieve political consensus. As a party unit, the CPC had the same number of delegates as the representatives of the National Revolutionary and the Democratic League. If the Party members in the liberated areas and various regions and the representatives of the foundational masses of workers, peasants, youth, and women were added together, they made up a majority. In this way, the CPPCC reflected both the leadership of the proletariat and various advantages based on the alliance of workers and peasants. A considerable number of non-Party members participated, giving attention to the extensiveness of the solidarity.

In September 1949, the First Plenary Session of the CPPCC was held in Beijing. The meeting adopted the Organic Law of the CPPCC. It stipulated that the CPPCC, composed of representatives of the CPC, various democratic parties, various people's organizations, various regions, the PLA, various ethnic minorities, overseas Chinese, and other patriotic democrats would take the organizational form of the people's democratic united front. This organizational form would exist for a long time, and before the universal election of the National People's Congress, the functions and powers of the Congress would be implemented. After the convening of the Congress through a universal election, the fundamental plans for the country's construction and other important measures would be proposed to the National People's Congress or the Central People's Government, beginning with the consultation, staff, and promotion. In the Organic Law of the CPPCC, it was stated that the purpose of the Conference was to unite all democratic parties and peoples through the unity of various democratic parties and people's organizations. Everyone would work together to implement the new democracy and oppose imperialism, feudalism, and bureaucratic capitalism, overthrow the KMT's reactionary rule, eliminate both the open and covert counter-revolutionary forces, heal the wounds of war, restore and develop the people's economic cause and cultural and educational undertakings, consolidate national defense, and unite with the world. The country would establish the independence, democracy, peace, unity, and prosperity of the People's Republic of China, led by the working class and based on the alliance of workers and peasants. The organization of the CPPCC also stipulated its organizational structure, which was a national committee produced by the plenary and local committees established in central cities, important regions, and provincial capitals. These organizations were highly democratic.

The common program of the CPPCC played the role of an interim constitution. Its formulation and adoption confirmed the party system and the politics of a multi-party cooperation led by the CPC in the legal and political system, which confirmed that the CPPCC was the organizational form of the people's democratic united front. This was not only the historical fruit of China's new democratic revolution, but also an inevitable outcome of the development of the revolutionary united front led by the CPC. It had created a people's democratic dictatorship with Chinese characteristics, a new form of organization for the united front.

6. Correct Handling of the Relationship Between Leaders and those Led

During the national War of Liberation, the people's democratic united front, led by the proletariat (via the CPC) and based on an alliance of workers and peasants, was able to consolidate and expand to an unprecedented degree. One of the important reasons for this was that the issue of the relationship between leaders was handled correctly. In January 1948, Mao Zedong offered an in-depth summary of the Party's historical experience in realizing the leadership of the proletariat in the united front and proposed that the working class and people's organizations be led by the working class. It was thus necessary that two conditions be met: "1) lead the coalition (the allies) to fight resolutely against the common enemy and be victorious, and 2) give material benefits to the leader, or at least to not harm his interests, while at the same time offering him political education. Without these two conditions, one will not achieve leadership."[88] Mao also specifically pointed out that "to achieve leadership among the middle class peasants, the CPC must lead them against the feudal classes, and we must fight resolutely and win (eliminating the landlord's armed forces and dividing his land). If there is no determined struggle, or if there is no struggle, there will be no victory, and the middle class peasants will waver. In addition, it must be distributed among the poorer of the middle class peasants as part of the landlord's property. The interests of the wealthy middle class peasants should not be harmed."[89] At the same time, politically, the middle class peasants also had to have certain rights and be educated. Similarly, "the same is true of the working class and the CPC in the cities, who must take leadership of the middle class, democratic parties, and the people's groups that have been oppressed and damaged by the reactionary forces."[90] That is to say that, on the one hand, it was necessary for the Party to try to guide them to join the ranks of workers, peasants, and petty bourgeoisie in opposing Chiang Kai-shek and the US, or at least to remain neutral, while also continuing to use the victory of the people's revolution in all aspects to strengthen their revolutionary nature and overcome their tendency to compromise and vacillate. On the other hand, it proposed an economic program for protecting national industry and commerce and a series of economic policies to protect their material interests from harm, while also educating them in the hopes of raising their awareness of the new democratic revolutionary program. In this way, the

CPC had put in place the basic conditions for leading the national bourgeoisie and its political parties.

Mao further stated, "The upper petty bourgeoisie and the middle bourgeoisie in the Chiang-ruled areas, which includes a small number of people – the right-wingers of these classes – have reactionary political tendencies toward the US and Chiang. The reactionary group spreads false hopes, and they oppose the people's democratic revolution. As long as their reactionary tendency is still capable of influencing the masses, it is necessary for us to expose the work to the people they are taking in, stamping down on their political influence among the masses, and enabling the masses to instead influence them, allowing liberation to come about."[91] However, the historical lessons from 1927 through 1931 indicated that when the right wing of the upper petty bourgeoisie and the middle bourgeoisie, alongside Chiang's group, opposed the revolution, the CPC correctly combated their reactionary tendency through political means. At the same time, it was often eliminated economically, which caused serious losses to the revolution. In view of this, Mao clearly pointed out in 1947, "The political blow and the economic elimination are two separate things. If we mix the two, we will surely make some mistakes." He added, "Because China's economy is so backward, the vast majority of the capitalist economy represented by the upper petty bourgeoisie and the middle bourgeoisie must allow them to continue for a long period even after the national victory, and according to the division of labor of the national economy, all need to work for the benefit of the national economy, playing their part for development."[92] Therefore, for the economic status of the national bourgeoisie, upper petty bourgeoisie, or middle bourgeoisie, "the policy must be treated with care and protected in principle."[93]

In line with Mao's thoughts as laid out above, the CPC formulated a business and industrial policy of "developing production, prospering the economy, taking care of both public and private interests and both labor and capital" to protect the property of businesses and their legitimate enterprises, allowing for a measure of economic development. However, in the process of implementing this policy, there were still some phenomena that destroyed business and industry in some areas. The main manifestations were unilaterally emphasizing the immediate welfare of workers in the employee movement, infringing on the interests of the national bourgeoisie, invading the landlord and wealthy peasants in the land reform's business and industry operations, exceeding the scope of inventory when surveying the economic counter-revolution, using the tax policy to combat business and industry, and so on. In this regard, the Central Committee and Mao Zedong attached great importance to it and resolutely corrected it. Mao pointed out that the Party's organization at all levels should "pre-empt the application to cities of the methods of fighting the landlords and enriching the peasants in the rural areas and destroying the feudal forces, strictly differentiate between eliminating the feudal exploitation of the landlords and rich peasants and protecting the landlord's business operations. We should also distinguish the correct policy of developing production, prospering the economy, considering public and private interests, and benefiting both the laborer and the capitalists from the polices that were supposed to add to the advantages of labor but were actually one-sided, narrow, practically damaging trade and industry and undermining the cause of the people's revolution."[94] It was necessary to establish policies based on these distinctions in order to eliminate the national bourgeoisie's doubt about the new democratic revolutionary program and bring them closer to the political and policy level required by the revolutionary struggle at that time, or to work with the workers and peasants. The cities' petty bourgeoisie was opposed to the common enemy or remained neutral. As the people's revolution approached victory, the CPC, through more in-depth political education, helped the democratic parties rid themselves of their neutral status and raise them to the level of accepting the new democratic revolutionary program. In short, after the bureaucratic bourgeoisie, represented by the Chiang Kai-shek faction, broke into the united front, the Central Committee and Mao Zedong continued to implement this theory and practice of unity and struggle against the national bourgeoisie, creating a favorable position for the national bourgeoisie to finally accept the condition of proletarian leadership.

In summary, during the national War of Liberation, the Mao-led CPC Central Committee launched a land reform movement of unprecedented scale, in an effort to further consolidate the alliance of workers and peasants. At the same time, based on the worker-peasant alliance led by the working class, everything could be won through unity. The people would unite and fight for it – not only the national bourgeoisie, but also the patriots who had separated from the KMT ruling clique and the enlightened gentlemen who had been separated from the feudal landlord class. This enabled the people's democratic united front to gain unprecedented ground in both consolidation and growth, leaving the Chiang clique completely isolated and helpless. In April 1948, the CPC proposed to convene a political consultative meeting without the reactionaries, where they would discuss the call for establishing a democratic coalition government. It immediately received enthusiastic responses from the democratic parties, people's groups, and non-partisan democrats. They sent representatives to the liberated areas and worked with the CPC to prepare for the CPPCC. During the climax of the PLA's strategic decisive battle, the democratic parties announced their agreement with the CPC's industrial and commercial policies, recognizing that the reactionary rule of the KMT was the root of the counter-revolutionary civil war and the fundamental obstacle to domestic peace and democracy, and pointing out that US imperialism was the enemy of the Chinese people. They jointly issued a statement, publicly announcing the abandonment of the middle line and accepting the leadership of the CPC. This was a major victory for the Party in its efforts to correctly handle its relationship with the bourgeoisie.

CHAPTER 8

The Theory of Armed Struggle

I

Armed Struggle as the Main Form of Struggle in the Chinese Revolution

1. Proposing and Establishing the CPC's Armed Struggle

The doctrine of armed struggle formed an important part of the CPC's ideological theory and one of the three main weapons of the Chinese revolution. Based on China's specific environment and conditions, the CPC gradually enriched and developed the Marxist-Leninist theory of armed struggle in the process of revolutionary practice.

In the period after the CPC was established, it was not enough to understand how crucial armed struggle was to the revolution. When summing up the Party's experience, Mao correctly asserted, "Concerning this point, we did not sufficiently acknowledge during the first five to six years from the founding of the CPC in 1921 to its participation in the Northern Expedition in 1926 how crucial armed struggle is in China, and thus we failed to organize the army and prepare for war, nor did we focus on military strategy and tactical research."[1] Of course, this did not mean that everyone in the Party was ignorant of how important armed struggle was, and in fact, many Party members did have outstanding ideas regarding this issue.

Zhou Enlai, for instance, had a long-standing definite understanding of the importance of armed struggle. In his article "Evaluating Hu Shih's 'Efforts,'" published on December 15, 1922, on a trip to Europe, he stated, "The real revolution must be extremely powerful. Without a highly organized revolutionary army, the revolution cannot defeat the warlords."[2] This was the initial expression of the idea of armed seizure of power. At the beginning of 1925, Zhou actively participated in and led the Huangpu Student Army to go east with the armed forces against the main force of the reactionary warlord Chen Jiongming. Later, in his report entitled "The Political Work of the Army," delivered to the Huangpu Student Army, he emphasized that, "The workers and peasants have been subjected to oppression and will inevitably resort to the use of force to resist the oppressors." He referred to the October Revolution as an example, encouraging everyone by explaining that it was a case of "workers and peasants using force to overthrow the Russian royal family." He went on, "When China's oppressed people and the weak realize that the imperialists and warlords were the oppressors, they will use the force they have created for themselves to defeat the imperialists and the warlords."[3] Obviously, Zhou made important contributions to the discussion concerning the issue of armed struggle, both in theory and in practice.

In January 1924, Deng Zhongxia also said that when the people's revolutionary ideas and actions had grown extremely fierce, military activity was not only indispensable, but was also one of the main tasks. Yun Daiying also said during this period that the revolution could absolutely not be separated from fighting by force. These insights were very valuable.

In particular, Qu Qiubai offered many insights on the issue of armed struggle, becoming a leader in the early development of the Party's understanding of the importance of armed struggle. In 1925, after the May 30th Movement, the importance of armed struggle was underscored in a series of articles published by Qu. He stated that "people should have the right to defend themselves." In October 1925, Qu attacked the current anti-war movement, saying, "If the people are armed and practice a war of rebellion, this is naturally the beginning of the national revolution, marking a new era in the revolutionary movement." Armed struggle became a symbol of a new stage in the revolution. Without armed struggle, there could be no real revolution. This was one of Qu Qiubai's important contributions. He also pointed out that the proper attitude of a revolutionary armed struggle was to not be afraid of armed struggle, but to "actively unite all forces against the warlords' imperialists and carry out revolutionary fighting," and to "prepare the people for armed struggle" so that "a central government can be established." Qu linked the armed struggle to the seizure of power. On the eve of the Northern Expedition, his theory of armed struggle rose to a new height. With repeated emphasis, he said the revolution should use "the fighting of the revolutionary army and the riots of the people's armed forces" to deal with the imperialist offensive and "remove all counter-revolutionary warlords." Further, he particularly highlighted the idea that armed struggle was the main form of struggle in the Chinese revolution, saying, "At present, the central issue of the revolutionary movement is preparing for the revolutionary war." Other forms of struggle were "either direct or indirect preparations for the revolutionary war," and "only revolutionary fighting is the main way."

With the development of the situation, the Party's understanding saw new advancements on the eve of the Northern Expedition. In February 1926, at the special meeting held by the CPC Central Committee in Beijing, the Party determined its main course. It prepared every aspect of the Northern Expedition of the Guangdong government to overthrow the rule of imperialism and the warlords through revolutionary war. In May 1926, the Ye Ting Independent Military Troop, under the CPC's guidance, first entered Hunan as the advance team of the Northern Expeditionary Force, which served as a prelude to the Northern Expedition. In an effort to cooperate closely with the Northern Expedition, in July 1926, the Party held the Third Expanded Meeting of the Executive Committee. The Military Movement Resolution, adopted at the meeting, clearly stated, "The CPC is a proletarian revolutionary party, and it is ready to be armed for riots and should participate in the work of armed struggle and contribute to the progressive military forces in the process of the national revolution. At the same time, this work aims to enable the Party to systematically prepare for armed uprisings." The meeting clearly pointed out that the armed uprisings were an important item on the agenda of the Party leadership, indicating that the Party's understanding of the importance of armed struggle had made an important leap. The resolution immediately reminded the whole Party that "the CPC's comrades have recently begun to give attention to the military movement," which was a significant improvement over the situation in which "our comrades do not pay attention to the military movement," but it must be pointed out that even this progress was limited, mainly in its "failure to understand the Party's current responsibilities in military work, and the significance of structured preparation for armed uprisings."

Guided by the relevant ideas in the resolution, Party leaders from the proletarian class in Shanghai staged three armed uprisings in October 1926, February 1927, and March 1927. The first two failed in the face of the enemy's furious counter-attack, but in the third uprising, the lessons learned from the two previous defeats led to a brilliant success under the leadership of Zhou Enlai, Luo Yinong, and Zhao Shiyan. This was an important part in the leadership of the Party's practice of armed uprising. Zhao Shiyan praised the armed uprising of Shanghai's working class in his article "A Record of the March Workers' Riot," written in April 1927. He held that "for the first time since the October Revolution in Russia, the revolutionary record of the proletariat has added a new chapter with the workers' riots in Shanghai. In the history of China's revolution, the hard-earned achievements of the working class are even greater because of the workers in Shanghai. The March riots have set the place of the proletariat in the revolution, and the place these riots will hold in the world's revolutionary history is written on the page following the October Revolution. The place of the March riots in the history of the Chinese revolution has been determined, and the nature of the Chinese revolution guarantees its victory, marking the beginning of a new chapter in China's revolutionary history." He also emphasized that "the riots of the proletariat are the most serious lesson in the teachings of Marxism-Leninism." Zhao's expressive statement that violent revolution is an important idea and one of the basic principles of Marxism-Leninism was a creative approach to the issue of armed struggle.

In the summer of 1927, the domestic political situation changed dramatically. On April 12, Chiang Kai-shek launched a counter-revolutionary coup. In mid- and late May, the reactionary officers Xin Douyin and Xu Kexiang each in turn launched an attack on the revolution. In the face of serious danger, Mao Zedong and Cai Hesen proposed many appropriate emergency measures. Cai Hesen repeatedly recommended to the Central Committee the path of resolute counter-attack, proposing that "only with a counter-offensive and riots can the rioting be addressed." On June 25, he wrote a letter to the Standing Committee, urging, "we sit here, waiting for others to dispose of us, like fish in a tank." He suggested that "the central government and the army should immediately check their forces and formulate a military plan, just in case." However, despite the fact that all of these plans were appropriate, they were rejected by Chen Duxiu, which ultimately led to the failure of the Northern Expedition.

After the failure of the Northern Expedition, the Party learned its lesson and took a major step toward understanding the armed struggle. In 1927, the Party's August 7th Meeting dissolved Chen Duxiu's errors of rightist opportunism and determined the general policies for the agrarian revolution and armed rebellion against KMT reactionaries. From that time on, the Party entered a new phase of creating its own armed forces and leading a large-scale armed struggle.

2. The Fundamental Implications of the CPC's Theory of Armed Struggle

a. Seizure of Power as the Central Task and Highest Form of Revolution

1) *The Central task and highest form of revolution is the armed seizure of power.* Any social revolution is a product of class struggle arising from certain historical conditions, related to a specific social and political environment. Its form of struggle and organizational structure must be compatible with these social characteristics. In his article "Issues Related to War and strategy," Mao Zedong offered a profound, detailed analysis of the differences between capitalist countries and Chinese society and the forms of revolutionary struggle that arose from each.

In capitalist countries of that time and before, violent revolution was a form of extreme struggle based on legal struggle. Capitalist countries had no feudal system, nor were they oppressed by imperialist nations, and they had an established bourgeois democratic system. The proletariat had some degree of freedom of speech, association, and assembly, the right to form trade unions and carry out political and economic strikes, and the possibility of using the parliamentary forum to fight for certain of the working class's political and economic interests. Therefore, as long as there was no fascist war, the main task lying within the scope of a proletarian party's work was to organize the masses and workers to carry out legal struggle without bloodshed, so as to educate the workers and harness the power of life in order to make long-term preparation for overthrowing capitalism. On the issue of war, the CPC noted that there was an imperialist war being waged against its own country, so the only war it hoped to see was a civil war. "But," it was noted, "when the bourgeoisie is particularly incompetent, when the majority of the proletariat is determined to engage in an armed uprising and wage war, and when the peasant masses have volunteered to assist the proletariat, the uprisings and war should not be held back."[4]

In analyzing the characteristics of China's political environment, Mao pointed out that China was different from capitalist countries. Internally, it was not a democratic country, but a semi-colonial, semi-feudal one, and it had no democratic system, but was oppressed by feudalism, nor was it independent in its external relations with other countries, since it was oppressed by imperialists. It had no parliament to use, and its workers did not have the legal right to strike. Moreover, there were warlords and separatists in the country, and all of these landlords – large, small, or local – had their own armed forces, which were more powerful than the proletariat, and they exerted a bloody suppression and policies for slaughtering the workers. In such a political environment, "the task of the CPC is basically not a long-term legal struggle to usher in an uprising and war."[5] The main, and essentially the first, step was to unite as many confederates as possible, organize an armed resistance, and depending on the situation, oppose both internal and external counter-revolutions in a fight for national and social liberation.

Based on these differences between China and capitalist countries, Mao Zedong always insisted that "in China, the main form of struggle is war,"[6] and in organizing for elucidating the basic principles, "the central task of the revolution and highest form of revolution is the armed seizure of power."[7]

2) *The Chinese revolution must put armed struggle first in any situation and insist on using military action to solve problems.* At various stages in the history of the development of the Chinese revolution, Mao Zedong consistently emphasized that armed struggle was the main form of the Chinese revolution, gradually formulating a complete theoretical system.

During the Great Revolution, Mao suggested that the CPC should have its own independent armed force and should help build armed forces among the peasants. On July 4, 1927, at the meeting of the CPC, he raised issues regarding the situation and the Party's policies that the peasant self-defense forces must be retained and, if necessary, go into the mountains and build a base of military power there. Later, when summing up the lessons learned from the failure of the first cooperation between the KMT and the CPC, he pointed out that the Party was not fully aware of any armed struggle within the years between its establishment in 1921 and the Northern Expedition in 1926. He added, "at that time, we did not understand the extreme importance of armed struggle in China. We did not seriously prepare for the war and organize the army, nor did we pay attention to military strategy or tactical research. In the course of the popular movement, as soon as the KMT reacted, all popular movements collapsed."[8]

During the Agrarian Revolutionary War, for some time, Mao Zedong was in the process of creating armed forces and revolutionary bases (particularly before the Party's central organs moved into the base area), though the Central Committee had yet to raise the issue of armed struggle. He wrote a series of articles on the loss of confidence in the victory of the armed struggle and various misunderstandings regarding the form of armed struggle within the Party and the military who "doubted how long the Red flag can last." He focused on the possibility and the necessity of separating workers and peasants and its significance for seizing national political power, and he held that the agrarian revolution must be combined with armed struggle, which in turn must be combined with the establishment of the power of the proletariat and the peasantry and the establishment of a revolutionary base. He wrote, "The establishment and development of the Red Army, the guerrillas, and the Red areas are the ultimate form of struggle for the peasantry under the leadership of the proletariat in semi-colonial China, and are the inevitable result of the development and struggle of semi-colonial peasants. This undoubtedly promotes the national revolution and is an important factor in it."[9] The entire Party's determination to cling firmly to the armed struggle played a decisive role in leading the Party's Work Committee to lead the revolutionary war. In 1936, Mao wrote "Strategic Issues in the Chinese Revolutionary War," in which he used the Marxist view of war in a comprehensive summary of his experience in the Agrarian Revolutionary War, systematically expounding on the fundamental views and attitudes of the CPC in dealing with the war and offering a profound analysis of the Chinese revolution. The characteristics, laws, and proper guidelines of the war further emphasized the importance of the Party's research on the revolutionary war and its leadership, as well as the use of armed struggle to defend against counter-revolutionary forces. This was an important symbol of the maturity of the Party's theory on armed struggle.

During the War of Resistance Against Japanese Aggression, Mao Zedong pointed out that when China was subjected to foreign imperialist aggression, all its forces that could do so united to wage a national war. This did not mean the principle of armed seizure of power had been abandoned, but was merely a step to realize this principle. It was, in other words, part of the armed seizure of power. He eloquently discussed the relationship between the overthrow of imperialism and feudalism, noting that they were interrelated. He said, "If you do not overthrow imperialist rule, you cannot eliminate the rule of the feudal landlord class, because imperialism is the main supporter of the feudal landlord class. Conversely, because the feudal landlord class is the main social foundation of the imperialists' rule in China and the peasantry is the main force in the Chinese revolution, if we do not help the peasants overthrow the feudal landlord class, they cannot form a powerful team of the Chinese revolution and overthrow imperialist rule."[10] Mao Zedong insisted on opposing national capitulationism, publishing a series of brilliant works, such as "Guidelines, Methods, and Prospects for Opposition Against Japan" and "On Protracted Wars," in which he expounded on the theory of a comprehensive and enduring war of resistance, thus providing powerful ideological and theoretical weapons for the formation of a national war of resistance and its ultimate victory. On the other hand, it also opposed surrender, insisted on the principle of the Party's independence and autonomy in the united front, and criticized and overthrew the right-wing errors of Wang Ming. It pointed out that adherence to independence and autonomy would allow the Party to maintain its original status, and even to gain new status, which was central to the path to victory in the anti-Japanese national revolutionary war. For the KMT, Mao proposed three principles of rationality, advantages, and restraints. The first was the principle of self-defense, which was essentially the notion that if no one committed any offense against me, I would commit no offense against them, but if they did commit an offense against me, I would strike back. This applied to things such as military attacks against the diehards, which required the Party to be resolute, thorough, and clean as it eliminated its enemies. The second was a principle of victory, which stated that if one fought, one must fight to win. The third was a principle of truce, which said that after retreating from the diehards for a period of time, the efforts should stop, so as to ensure the development and growth of the PLA during the War of Resistance Against Japanese Aggression, preparing a strong force for both gaining victory in the war and overthrowing KMT reactionary rule.

At the end of the War of Resistance Against Japanese Aggression, on August 13, 1945, Mao Zedong delivered a speech at the Yan'an Cadre Conference, entitled "The Situation After the Victory of the Anti-Japanese War and Our Policy," in which he offered a profound analysis of the basic situation in Chinese politics after the anti-Japanese War. Chiang Kai-shek hoped to seize the fruits of that victory, launching an anti-people's civil war and seeking to slaughter the inevitable trend of the people throughout the country. He was, in fact, already sharpening the sword for battle. Thus, it was necessary for the Party to likewise sharpen its sword. Chiang would take his authoritarian rule to the people, and he would gain ground. The Party's job was to keep pace and ensure the people's rights were not easily lost, and indeed, to fight to defend those rights. In the period that followed, there was an unprecedented trend toward peace and democracy in the international arena. There were also some signs pointing toward the possibility of peaceful coexistence between the KMT and the CPC. Some Party members were too optimistic about the prospects for peace, believing that parliamentary struggle would become the main form of struggle. In response to this tendency, Mao reiterated that the Chinese revolution should take the path of armed seizure of political power, pointing out, "Our principle is that the reactionary forces who oppose the democratic will of the people must be eliminated where possible. Those who cannot presently be eliminated will be eliminated in the future. This being the case, the democratic forces of the people should adopt this same principle toward the revolutionary forces."[11] Before attending the Chongqing negotiations, Mao pointed out to the Party that it certainly should not put too much confidence in these negotiations, since it was an absolute certainty that the KMT was not acting out of good will, and thus it was necessary to rely on the strength of their own hands. During the negotiations in Chongqing, the army was instructed to resolutely counter the invasion of the KMT. The more the Party fought, the safer and more proactive the negotiations would be. After the Chongqing negotiations, when Mao spoke of countermeasures to oppose the downsizing of the army, he emphasized, "The people's armed forces, our guns, and our bombs must be preserved and cannot be handed over."[12] The People's Liberation Army won three major, decisive battles. After that, the KMT ruling clique launched a peaceful offensive with the support and planning of US Ambassador to China John Leighton Stuart, in an attempt to use peaceful negotiations to achieve the goal of "rule based on the division of the Yangtze River" in an effort to gain a bit of breathing space while maintaining a residual counter-revolution, with the forces then waiting for an opportunity to return. In response to this situation, Mao issued a great call to the entire Party and military, along with all the people in the country, to "carry the revolution to the end," pointing out that no enemy would simply eliminate itself, whether it be China's own reactionary forces or the aggressive American imperialist forces in China. They would not give up this historical stage on their own, so it was necessary to employ revolutionary methods to resolutely and thoroughly eliminate all reactionary forces, overthrowing the reactionary rule of the KMT nationwide and establishing a republic of a people's democratic dictatorship led by the proletariat and peasantry. Under the guidance of Mao's theory of armed struggle, the CPC insisted that armed struggle be placed first in any situation and under any circumstances, thus achieving the victory of the Chinese revolution.

3) *All forms of unarmed organizations and struggle must be coordinated and must serve the armed struggle.* While emphasizing that armed struggle was the main form of the Chinese revolution, Mao also pointed out that "all other things, such as the organization and the struggle of the people, are very important. They are indispensable and cannot be ignored, but they all serve the armed struggle."[13] He further emphasized that this cooperation and service were comprehensive processes that should continue throughout the revolution.

By the term "comprehensive processes," he meant that all forms of the Party's organization and struggle had to serve the revolutionary war, regardless of whether before or during the war. Before the outbreak of the war, all organization and struggles had to be carried out around the preparation and mobilization for war, such as the national salvation campaign launched by the Party before the anti-Japanese war, the civil war movement, and several student movements. It was these movements that promoted the rise of the national anti-Japanese patriotic enthusiasm, which prompted the initiation and peaceful resolution of the Xi'an Incident. After the outbreak of the war, all forms of organization and struggle had to be directly or indirectly coordinated with the revolutionary war. For instance, during the War of Resistance Against Japanese Aggression, the rectification movement within the CPC, the mass production movement in liberated areas, and the popular movement in KMT-ruled areas were all carried out for the sake of winning the anti-Japanese War.

The idea of "comprehensive" indicated that, whether in the front or rear, liberated or enemy-occupied area, urban or rural, political and cultural center or remote areas, the Party's organization work and the popular movement in most of China's territory was directly related to armed struggle and could only follow the needs of the front line.

b. Armed Struggle as a Trait and an Advantage of the Chinese Revolution

In his article "On the Future of the Chinese Revolution," Stalin noted, "In China, it is an armed revolution against an armed counter-revolution. This is one of the characteristics of the Chinese revolution, and one of its advantages."[14] Mao Zedong fully affirmed the correctness of this argument, and in his concluding remarks at the Sixth Plenary Session of the Sixth General Meeting of the Central Committee in November 1938, he offered an analysis of the nature of the Chinese revolution after the Northern Expedition and the common features of each stage, pointing out that Stalin's view was in complete accord with the actual situation in the Chinese revolution. China's problems could not be resolved without armed struggle, and without armed struggle, the revolutionary task would not be completed. In 1939, he published an article in the first issue of *The Communist*, stating that armed struggle was one of the two basic features of the Chinese revolution, alongside the united front, and that these two features together formed the basic building blocks and the three key weapons of the Chinese revolution.

1) *The nature and mission of the Chinese revolution were closely linked to armed struggle.* In his analysis of the characteristics of the Chinese revolution, Mao said, "Since China is a semi-colonial, semi-feudal country, a country with uneven political, economic, and cultural development, and a country whose vast land is dominated by a semi-feudal economy, this not only demands that the nature of the current revolution in China is a bourgeois democratic revolution, but also that its main targets are imperialism and feudalism. The basic revolutionary impetus is the proletariat, the peasant class, and the urban petty bourgeoise. For a certain period and to a certain extent, there is participation by the national bourgeoisie, which means that the main form of the Chinese revolutionary struggle is armed struggle."[15] The armed revolution was opposed to an armed counter-revolution, which was a special feature of semi-colonial China, setting it apart as a different sort of revolution from those that had historically occurred in capitalist countries.

The enemy and target of the Chinese revolution – feudalism, imperialism, and bureaucratic capitalism – had powerful anti-revolutionary forces, all of which relied on rule by force and counter-revolutionary wars to achieve their political goals. The proletariat and the vast majority of oppressed and exploited laborers demanded liberation. In an effort to defeat this enemy, who was armed to the teeth, the revolutionaries likewise had to arm themselves. From the birth of the Communist Party of China to the establishment of the People's Republic of China, the Chinese revolution went through four historical stages, the Northern Expedition, the Agrarian Revolutionary War, the War of Resistance Against Japanese Aggression, and the War of Liberation. The opposition in these wars were armed counter-revolutionaries, facing the main force made up of the armed revolutionary masses. Mao observed that "the only difference was whether it was a domestic or national war, and whether the CPC waged war on its own or in coordination with the KMT… In either case, it was an armed revolution against an armed counter-revolution, and in both instances, it was a revolutionary war that expressed the characteristics and advantages of the Chinese revolution."[16] The history of the Chinese revolution fully proved that without the status of the proletariat in the armed struggle of China's left, the people and the CPC would have had no status, and there would have been no revolutionary victory.

2) *The development and growth of the CPC were tied to armed struggle.* A striking difference between the CPC and the proletarian parties in capitalist countries was that the CPC developed through armed struggle, while proletarian parties in capitalist states developed through long-term legal struggles. An armed uprising could only be the result of the growth and development of the proletarian party in a capitalist state, not the means and rationale for the party's development and growth. The CPC was different from this norm. Before it seized power, the history of the Party was actually a history of armed struggle. Mao stated clearly that "the development, consolidation, and bolshevization of our Party were carried out through the revolutionary war. Without the armed struggle, there would be no Communist Party today."[17]

Although the Party had begun to understand the importance of armed struggle during the Great Revolution, this understanding was still not a full comprehension. It had yet to grasp that armed struggle was, in fact, the main form of struggle in the Chinese revolution, and it had not used its main energy to gain hold of armed revolutionary forces. When Chiang Kai-shek rebelled against the revolution, a large number of Party members were killed, and party-building and the Party's cause suffered serious losses. In the Agrarian Revolutionary War, the Party established an independent armed force and a revolutionary base. The Party's ranks and their combat effectiveness developed greatly, and the Party clearly announced that its military was to assist in local Party development efforts. During this period, because they did not understand the characteristics and rules of China's armed struggle, Wang Ming and Li Lisan committed leftist errors, and as a result, the Party's cause suffered more serious losses. The Zunyi Conference established Mao's leadership over the Party and the Red Army. The entire Party gained some understanding of the guiding role of armed struggle, resulting in the redevelopment of party-building and the Party's ranks. During the War of Resistance Against Japanese Aggression, the Party had a deep understanding of armed struggle. With the development of the Eighth Route Army and the New Fourth Army, now under CPC leadership, Party construction achieved unprecedented development. Mao pointed out, "With guns, party-building is made possible. The Eighth Route Army has created a large party in Northern China."[18] He added, "Party organization has emerged from a small circle and become a large national party... The Party's influence on people throughout the country has been further expanded."[19] During the War of Liberation, the Party's understanding of the principle of armed struggle and its ability to control the revolutionary war reached a new stage. The numbers in the PLA rapidly increased, and unprecedented combat effectiveness finally led to the overthrow of the rule of feudalism, imperialism, and bureaucratic comprador capitalism in Mainland China and established the People's Republic of China, which became the ruling party holding national political power. For this reason, it can be said that the success, setbacks, advancement, and retreats of the Party were all linked to armed struggle. Any departure from the armed struggle and revolutionary war would make it "impossible to understand our political line and the construction of the Party. Armed struggle is a vital part of our political line."[20]

3) *The understanding and participation of the Chinese people in the Chinese revolution was closely tied to armed struggle.* Any social revolution must be based on the people's full understanding and active participation, and the way in which the people gain such understanding and participation is a significant sign that reflects the characteristics, breadth, and depth of the revolution. In the proletarian revolutionary struggle in capitalist countries, a legal mass movement without bloodshed (mainly a workers' movement) was not only the most basic way to raise the consciousness of the working masses, but also the main way for them

to participate in the revolutionary struggle. Armed struggle could only be carried out after the legal struggle and mass movements had reached the widest and deepest extent throughout the whole society. At that time in China, by contrast, the people did not have any democratic rights in the political sphere, and 90% of the population were peasants in a closed, scattered, small-production state. It was impossible to mobilize and organize the broadest masses of people to join the ranks of the revolution through a legal, peaceful struggle. In the Chinese revolution, the people's understanding and participation in the revolution was mainly linked to the armed struggle. On the one hand, since armed struggle was the main form of struggle in the Chinese revolution, the revolutionary mobilization of the masses was actually the mobilization for the revolutionary war. The people's understanding of the revolution was initially linked to a violent means of revolution. Although the propaganda and mobilization work of the Chinese revolution was multi-channel and multi-faceted, it was mainly carried out through the military. Mao always regarded the propaganda team (work team) as an important part of the people's army. In China's rural areas, most of the peasants' understanding of the revolution came mainly from the military propaganda of the Red Army, the Eighth Route Army, the New Fourth Army, and the People's Liberation Army. As a result, the people's participation in the revolution was always proportional to the progress of the revolutionary war effort. In regions where the revolutionary war advanced and won battles, the people there were quickly mobilized and organized to take their stand. That is why Mao once compared the 25,000 *li* Long March of the Red Army to the propaganda team and sewing machine. In the same sense, through the progress of the armed struggle, the people worked for their own interests and, seeing their great power, understood that only the Communist Party could lead them to victory in the revolution, and thus actively and heroically participated in the revolutionary struggle. It was also in the practice of revolutionary armed struggle that the people were educated, trained, and ultimately liberated.

c. *China's Armed Struggle as Essentially a Peasant War Under the Leadership of the Proletariat*

China's armed struggle was essentially (or fundamentally) a peasant war under the leadership of the proletariat, for these reasons:

1) *China was a country in which peasants formed the main masses, accounting for 80% of the population.* From the perspective of manpower and material resources, peasants were the broadest and deepest source of strength for China's armed struggle. The peasants were the source from which the Chinese army could recruit, so much so that the soldiers were actually peasants in military uniforms.
2) *Chinese peasants were heavily oppressed by imperialism, feudalism, and bureaucratic capitalism.* They had no rights politically and were in extreme difficulty economically, living in dire straits, and thus having a strong desire for revolution. They were the most reliable allies of the proletariat and the main force of the Chinese revolution.
3) *China was a country with a long history and glorious tradition of peasant uprisings and peasant wars.* The CPC summed up the lessons learned from the peasant revolutions of past dynasties, inheriting and carrying forward the glorious tradition of past peasant wars, combining it with Marxist-Leninist theory of violent revolution with Chinese history to produce a new peasant revolution with Chinese characteristics. War was the essence of the armed struggle under the leadership of the Chinese proletariat. The main form of struggle was armed struggle, though "this does not mean that we can give up other forms of struggle. On the contrary, without the cooperation of various forms of struggle alongside it, the armed struggle cannot be victorious."[21] However, the purpose of other forms of struggle was to serve the war and armed struggle. Before the outbreak of war, all organizations and struggles were preparations for war. Armed struggle and all other forms of struggle were unified, and armed struggle could not be left out of other forms of struggle. Indeed, other forms of struggle must serve armed struggle. Only a correct understanding and treatment of the relationship between armed struggle and the struggles of workers, peasants, youth leagues, and women, along with struggles on the economic or ideological front, could all struggle be made compatible with the Chinese revolutionary war.

II

The CPC's Theory of Military Dialectics

1. Views on Establishing the Proletarian War

Zhu De once pointed out that "Comrade Mao Zedong systematically studied the principles of the Chinese revolutionary war. Of particular importance was his focus on the development of the theoretical basis and methodology of Marxist-Leninist military science, specifically military dialectics, in his military writings."[22] During the Agrarian Revolutionary War, the leftist adventurists employed a dogmatic approach to study and guide the Chinese revolutionary war, with disastrous consequences. This situation prompted the Mao-led CPC to focus on the methodologies of war in order to unify the military thought of the entire Party, from the heights of a global perspective. In 1936, Mao delivered a lecture entitled "Military Dialectics" at the Red Army University in northern Shaanxi. Most of the content of this lecture is included in the article "Strategic Issues in the Chinese Revolutionary War." Later, he also discussed a series of important ideas about military dialectics in his book *On Protracted Wars*.

a. What is War?

The CPC examined war from the perspective of class struggle. Historically, war has been derived from the creation of private ownership and the struggle between classes. Mao looked carefully into the peasant wars in Chinese history and concluded, "The cruel economic exploitation and political oppression of the peasant class forced the peasants to repeatedly stage uprisings to resist the rule of the landlord class… In feudal Chinese society, only the peasant class struggled, staged uprisings, and waged war, serving as the real driving force of historical development."[23] He likewise considered the national struggle and concluded, "In the final analysis, the national struggle is a class struggle. The oppressors of black people in the US are nothing more than the reactionary ruling cliques of the white race. They do not represent the majority of workers, peasants, revolutionary intellectuals, and other enlightened members of the white race."[24] Mao held an insistent view of class struggle. He added, "Because of the emergence of classes, human life has been filled with war for thousands of years. There have been countless fights in every nation, within ethnic groups, and between ethnic groups. In the period of imperialism in capitalist societies, the fights were particularly broad and particularly cruel."[25] It was evident that war was a social phenomenon based on class struggle. The forms of struggle that existed between various classes of humans in a class society were diverse, including economic, ideological, cultural, and diplomatic, and for the oppressed people and nations, the central task and highest form of revolution was the armed seizure of power. When economic, ideological, cultural, diplomatic, and other forms of peaceful struggle could not solve a problem, there was no other option but to resort to the use of force and war to address the problems. For this reason, war became the highest form for solving the problems of class struggle. This was an inevitable law, as Mao profoundly revealed. He suggested that "wars have been the highest form of struggle in any conflict at certain stages of development after the beginning of private ownership of property and class, and it is used to solve problems between classes, nations, countries, and political groups."[26] This was a perfect science for accurately revealing the origins and essence of war, and it clearly stated that war was not a super-level phenomenon, but a social phenomenon deeply rooted in class conflict.

The class nature of war was clearly manifested in the close relationship between war and politics. As early as the Gutian Meeting Resolution, Mao criticized the error of adopting purely military views, clarifying the relationship between war and politics. In the book *On Protracted War*, he further elaborated on the relationship between war and politics. Lenin had repeatedly acknowledged Clausewitz's assertion of war as a continuation of politics. In line with this view, Mao emphasized that war is politics, and war itself is a political action. The occurrence and development of any war is closely related to the social politics that produced it, and it is carried out for a specific political purpose. For instance, China's War of Resistance Against Japanese Aggression was carried out in order to achieve the political goal of expelling Japanese imperialism and building a new, peaceful China, which was closely related to the consolidation and development of the Anti-Japanese National United Front. In short, the moment of war was inseparable from politics. It was subordinate to politics and served political purposes.

Even so, war is not equivalent to general politics. It is a bloody politics and a continuation of politics for a special purpose. When political development reaches a certain stage and can no longer develop in the same way, war breaks out. For instance, China's independent and semi-independent status was an obstacle to Japan's aggressive political development. In order to remove this obstacle, Japan launched a war of aggression in China. Similarly, Japan's aggression was an obstacle to the development of China's democratic revolution. In order to remove this obstacle, the Chinese people launched their War of Resistance Against Japanese Aggression. Once Japan was expelled from China, the War of Resistance ended. This indicated that war and politics were intrinsically connected and were manifestations of class struggle, but there were differences between the two. Mao commented that "politics is a bloodless war, and war is bloody politics." The particularity of warfare produced a special organization and method of war, and the rules of war were different from the general rules of political struggle. Therefore, any view that ignored the military and the study of military science was flawed.

b. Factors Contributing to Victory

Mao Zedong's military thought was based on the notions that war is the highest form of class struggle and that war is the continuation of politics. In 1946, Chiang Kai-shek relied on his superior military strength and aid to attack the liberated areas. At that time, the advantage of Chiang Kai-shek's military strength was only a temporary phenomenon and the aid from the US only a temporary factor, but the anti-masses nature of Chiang's war, which underlay all his efforts, was a factor that was always at work. In this respect, the PLA had an advantage. The patriotic and just revolutionary nature of the PLA war had to gain the support of the people throughout the country. This was the political basis for defeating Chiang Kai-shek.

However, war is also a contest of material power. The outcome of a war depends not only on its political foundation, but also on factors related to the military, economy, science, and national geography. These are all qualitative conditions, and military strategists cannot win a war outside the scope of the material conditions. Therefore, during a war, efforts must be made to create conditions that are conducive to defeating the enemy, being unfavorable to the enemy's military, economic, scientific, technological, and natural environment, to lay the foundations for winning the war. With a certain material basis, subjective guidance becomes the decisive factor in who wins the war. The building stage of the strategist's activities is based on objective material conditions. However, with this stage, he can direct many vivid and colorful dramas, using flexible and strategic approaches and tactics to defeat the enemy and win the war.

Mao also pointed out that weapons are an important factor in war. At the time, China's weapons and equipment were relatively backward. This was a major shortcoming that needed to be improved. Even so, it was not weapons alone that would be the determining factor in the war, as the people, not things, would decide the outcome. That is to say, the contrast in power was not only about military and economic power, but also about human resources and the human heart. Military and economic power were to be generated and mastered. The practice of the Chinese revolutionary war proved that the soldiers and the people were the foundation of victory, and the courage and the wisdom of the people and the army were the factors that would determine the outcome of the war. China's revolutionary war, though equipped with inferior equipment to defeat superior equipment, relied mainly on the people, mobilizing and arming them to carry out a people's war. This was the essence of Mao Zedong's military theory for defeating the enemy.

c. Ways to Eliminate War

War is a peculiar phenomenon of a class society. When human society eliminates classes and countries, war will also disappear, and human society will enter an era of permanent peace. How could the CPC achieve this goal? Mao stated that there was only one method. After the war, war had to be eliminated. The purpose of the revolutionary war was to eliminate counter-revolutionary fighting, and the purpose of just war was to eliminate unjust war. Lenin once said, "The nature of war (reactionary warfare or revolutionary warfare) does not depend on who is attacking or in which country the 'enemy' is, but on which class is going to war and what politics this war is continuing."[27] Based on the class nature and political purpose of war, historically, wars could be divided into two categories, just and unjust wars. Mao pointed out that a just war was like an anti-toxin or a bridge to a new era in the world's history, without which it was impossible to make a new leap in social development, while an unjust war was a hindrance to social development and progress. For this reason, the CPC could not simply support all war, nor simply oppose all wars. Instead, it had to distinguish between just and unjust wars. Bourgeois pacifists did not distinguish between just or unjust wars, but opposed all wars, failing to note the social roots of a war and seeking unconditional peace from the imperialists. They believed it was possible to achieve universal, lasting peace under imperialism. This was a completely unrealistic fantasy. The experience of history already proved that to eliminate all wars in all countries and the world, it was necessary to overthrow imperialism and all forms of exploitation and build a socialist and communist system. Mao said, "We are the annihilators of war. We don't want war, but we can only eliminate war through war. If we want to rid ourselves of guns, we must first take them up."[28] The Party studied the principles of war and carried out the revolutionary war out of a desire to eliminate all wars. This was the CPC's fundamental position and attitude toward war.

2. The Economy as the Material Basis for War

War is inseparable from the economy, and the economy is the material basis for war. Mao stated, "War is not only a military and political contest, but also an economic contest."[29] He added, "If economic construction is not carried out, the material conditions of the revolution cannot be guaranteed."[30] As it was leading the Chinese revolutionary war, the CPC always considered economic construction as a necessary condition for defeating the enemy. In the early days of the CPC's leadership in the war, how could a region with a small Red regime or a few small Red regimes survive in a country surrounded by White regimes? How did the revolutionary war promote the arrival of the Chinese revolution? Mao analyzed the imbalance of China's political and economic development at the time – a weak capitalist economy co-existing alongside a serious semi-feudal economy, with several modern industrial and commercial cities co-existing alongside stagnant rural areas, and millions of industrial workers and tens of millions of old systems under which peasants and handicraft workers toiled. Large warlords managed the central government, while small warlords managed the provinces. The reactionary army had two so-called central troops belonging to Chiang Kai-shek and what was termed miscellaneous military forces belonging to the provincial warlords. Of the railways, cart paths, roads, and various thoroughfares meant for smaller modes of transport, some were traveled with ease, while others were in disrepair. Based on such imbalances in economic and political development, there were conflicts between the imperialist powers competing for China and the warlords within China. The Chinese reactionary government imposed heavy taxes on workers, peasants, and national labor and commerce. Many conflicts formed, as well as sharp conflicts between Chinese workers, peasants, intellectuals, the urban poor, and the soldiers of the reactionary army who had been exploited and oppressed, the reactionary rulers, the landlord class, and the bourgeoisie. Like a land full of dry wood, it would inevitably burst into flames. These economic conditions were the most fundamental reason for the inevitable occurrence and development of the Chinese revolutionary war. Mao's military thought provided a way to scientifically analyze the economic causes of the war that was instructive, no matter what type of war was being considered. In the current moment, whether it was between countries or within a single country, the question was why war had occurred at all. It would not be difficult to find the main cause if the question were analyzed economically.

The economy was the material basis for war. In China, a 22-year-long revolutionary war was waged in a vast land that was poor and underdeveloped. It could be attributed to the economic development, productivity boosting, and the adjustment of production relations, even during the course of fighting the war. Mao's military thought was an important contribution to the theory of developing the relationship between war and the economy. He wrote many books, and in different historical periods, he explained the importance of the economy to war and the guidelines for economic work at each specific point in time. He pointed out that, though war must remain focused on military struggle, economics was likewise a "great class struggle." It was necessary to carry out economic construction around the war effort. To abolish economic construction was to weaken the war. The Party must represent the interests of peasants and workers to help them develop production. It was necessary to implement policies to reduce rents and interest rates and to introduce land reforms, increase wages as appropriate, and give the masses visible physical benefits, stimulating their enthusiasm for advocating and participating in the revolutionary war and opposing the enemy's offensive. Otherwise, the masses could not distinguish between which was inferior, the KMT or the CPC, resulting in an unfavorable situation. The simple administration of politics was an important policy for overcoming difficulties, making war institutions suitable for war situations and enabling the Party's strength to increase. Not only would it not be defeated by the enemy, but it would ultimately defeat the enemy. Just as Sun Wukong, in *The Journey to the West*, went into the heart of the Princess of the Iron Fan in the form of a worm, the CPC would be able to defeat an invader that was much stronger than the communist forces. Rent reduction and production were two major parts of the defense of the liberated areas, allowing the completed rent reduction and production to determine the outcome of the political and military struggle in the liberated areas. These arguments were proven by the practice of revolutionary war to be scientifically correct.

As for peacetime, what was the relationship between economic construction and the construction of national defense? Mao stated, "There cannot be no national defense… The reliable method is to reduce the cost of military and political affairs to an appropriate proportion and increase the cost of economic construction. Only with economic construction can the rate of development be increased, in turn allowing construction of national defense to make greater progress." He continued, "Do you really want what you say you want, or are you half-hearted in your desire for it, or perhaps even only affording it a passing thought? If you really want it, you will reduce the proportion of military and political expenses and engage in economic construction. If you don't really want it, you will continue to work according to the old regulations."[31] He also asked, "Have the troops been cut off? It is good, because there are still enemies, and we are still being bullied and surrounded by enemies. We must strengthen the national defense, which means we must first strengthen economic construction. This is my understanding of the relationship between the economy and national defense in peacetime, and it is an important guideline for directing the construction of our national defense."

3. Seeking Truth from Facts and Using the Principles of War

a. War is an Inevitable, Recognizable Material Movement

A basic requirement of dialectical materialism is that everything begins from reality, which means that that which is subjective conforms to that which is objective. Mao Zedong applied dialectical materialism to military matters, noting that, historically, it was the same as any other social phenomenon. It was an inevitable material movement, which grew out of internal conflicts and objective realities that did not conform to the will of the people. Studying and guiding war had to proceed from the actual situation and a realistic understanding and application of the principles of war. This was a basic requirement and characteristic of military practice. Regarding the question of whether the principles of war and fighting could be recognized by the people, the bourgeois strategists often exaggerated the fluidity and inappropriateness of war from the perspective of idealism, believing that war and who would emerge victorious were unpredictable, determined by arbitrary factors such as "divine will." This was a sort of military agnosticism. Based on the principles of dialectical materialism and the practical experience of the Chinese revolutionary war, Mao completely denied such agnosticism. He pointed out that although war was highly mobile, there were various relatively stable stages throughout the flow of a war, when viewed overall. For example, in a strategic phase, there would be some changes in the number of battles fought from one war to another, but in the basic situation of the two opposing parties involved in the war, there would be no qualitative changes, making it a relatively stable period. The same is true of uncertainty in war. Since both sides in a war are made up of armed, living people, with each side seeking to keep its movements secret and creating illusions to deceive their opponent, there are certain unsettled characteristics within a war. However, the relative stability of the war cannot be denied. On the one hand, one side is relatively stable, while its enemy is not, but there are also numerous links or clues with many things to think about on every side, which results in a degree of relative certainty. In short, though war is greatly influenced by chance, the underlying stability hides a degree of inevitability. People can see the essence through various phenomena and grasp the inevitable through contingent events, allowing them to recognize and apply the principles of war.

b. Comprehensive Analysis of the Actual Situation of Oneself and the Enemy and Mastering the Guiding Principles of War

How does one know the principles of war? When Mao discussed "how to study war," he once pointed out, "There is a way to learn, and you should use this method when you study, and when you use it, there is a method you should employ. What is that method? It is to know the enemy's situation in all aspects, discover principles of action, and apply these principles to your own action."[32] This means that a war must follow the principles of war, and to understand these principles, one must make an objective, comprehensive analysis and comparison of all the complex phenomena, discerning what is smooth and what is rough, and what is true or false, and consider the matter accordingly. This is the fundamental way to resolve the subjective and objective conflicts in a war. Because war is a bilateral activity between two sides, it is a political, economic, military, and geographic competition that requires subjective guidance. The principles of war are the inherent connection between the objective, actual conditions of both sides. Therefore, the study of war must regard both subjective and objective conditions as the object of study and a starting point for comprehensively analyzing the subjective and objective conditions of both sides, in order to correctly understand the entire picture of a war and discover the guiding principles for that war. It is impossible to correctly understand the principles of war by arbitrarily emphasizing one point in isolation and neglecting other methods of research. Mao said, "There is a kind of person who knows himself and who does not know others, and there is another type of person who knows others but does not know himself. Both types are unable to address the question of how to study and use the principles of war."[33] He stressed the necessity of bearing in mind the famous phrase of Sunzi, "Know thyself and know thy enemy, and you will emerge victorious in every battle." Historical experience proved that Mao's argument was completely correct. During the second revolutionary civil war, both leftist opportunism and rightist adventurism came about precisely because those involved only saw the short-term victories of the Red Army and defeat of the enemy, or only examined the strengths and weaknesses of the Red Army, resulting in the errors of leftist opportunism and rightist adventurism. The subjugationists only saw the enemy's weak side, while those looking for a quick win only saw the enemy retreating before their advances, or other factors that determined only their own or the enemy's weakness in isolation. By contrast, Mao always analyzed and compared the situation between himself and the enemy in a comprehensive manner, seeing both favorable and unfavorable conditions, and both domestic and international conditions, while also seeing the actual situation, but focusing on development, leading him to discover the principles of war. During the Agrarian Revolutionary War, he comprehensively analyzed the enemy's situation and discovered four basic characteristics of the Chinese revolutionary war. Based on this, he revealed the fundamental principles governing the development of the Chinese revolutionary war and formulated its strategies and tactics. During the anti-Japanese fighting, he also made a comprehensive analysis of the situation between China and Japan, discovering four conflicts in the course of his comparison of China's power versus Japan's. On this basis, he argued for the fundamental principles governing the development of the War of Resistance Against Japanese Aggression and formulated the strategic principles, approaches, and tactics for a lasting war of resistance. In order to fully understand the situation of both China and the enemy, Mao systematically clarified the importance of understanding the dialectical development process of war through investigation and research. Mao applied the principle of dialectical materialist epistemology to the military. He pointed out that the commander's understanding of each war or each battle consisted of two stages, namely, the stage of perceptual recognition of rational understanding and the stage of practical recognition. The first phase mainly involved investigation and research, on which basis appropriate judgments and operational plans were formulated. The key at this stage was investigation and research. Mao stated, "The correct deployment of the commander comes from correct determination. Correct determination comes from correct judgment, which in turn comes from thoughtful and necessary investigation that gives careful consideration to the coherence of various probative materials."[34] He went on to point out that investigation and research were not only extremely important in the first stage of formulating an understanding, but were also extremely important in the second stage. Because the understanding obtained in the first stage was realistic, it needed to be re-examined in the second stage if it did not align with the actual situation. In the case of most discrepancies, it was necessary to revise the plan to adapt to the new situation. This was part of the process of gaining an understanding of the principles of war. To explore a universal application of these principles, one must deepen his understanding through practice and recognize the repeated iterations of it in his practice.

c. *Focus on the Characteristics and Development of War and on the Special Principles of War*

To study and lead a war, it is necessary to focus not only on comprehensive analysis of the enemy and its situation, but also to oppose idealism in relation to the issue of war. In addition, one must focus on the characteristics and development of war and oppose a mechanistic theory of war. One should not concentrate on general principles of war, but on the special principles of revolutionary war, or even more specifically, of the Chinese revolutionary war. This was the fundamental methodology Mao put forward by applying the principle of the general and the special – that is, commonality and individuality – to war.

First, based on the nature of war, it was evident that revolutionary war was different from counter-revolutionary war, thus its guiding principles were different and could not simply be applied mechanically. In the early days of the Agrarian Revolutionary War, some people in the military blindly duplicated bourgeois military teaching, opposing the Party's absolute leadership over the military, opposing the Red Army's three major tasks, and opposing military democracy. The root cause for this was that the fundamental difference between China's revolutionary war and the counter-revolution were overlooked, with that fundamental difference being a proletariat army as opposed to a bourgeois army.

In addition, from the perspective of war zones, various countries and ethnic groups, particularly large countries and ethnic groups, have their own characteristics. For this reason, the principles governing war likewise have their own characteristics. The Chinese and Russian revolutionary wars were both revolutionary in nature, but the two countries had different national conditions and characteristics, and thus the principles for guiding the wars were also very different. In spite of these differences, dogmatic factions bluntly transferred the experience of the Russian revolutionary war to China, blindly demanding complete "regularization" and opposing so-called "guerrillas." As a result, the Agrarian Revolutionary War suffered severe setbacks.

Finally, based on the conditions of timing, just as conditions of wartime change, the objective conditions and tasks likewise change one after another. For this reason, the guiding principles for war will have different characteristics for different stages. Compared with the era of firearms, the cold weapons era had a very different approach and set of principles in warfare. The same was true of the Chinese revolutionary war. Because of the different stages of military development, the guiding principles were different. For instance, in the later period of the Agrarian Revolutionary War, the PLA was mainly engaged in mobile warfare. During the War of Resistance Against Japanese Aggression, it turned to guerrilla warfare as the main form of fighting. Faced with a changing situation, the PLA again transformed its military strategy, going from the anti-Japanese guerrilla war to a revolutionary civil war. In short, as the war situation changed, the principles guiding the war changed accordingly. Therefore, Mao Zedong always emphasized that it was necessary to excel at using the guiding principles of war flexibly according to the changing military situation.

III

Thoughts on the Construction of the People's Army

1. The Sole Purpose of the People's Army

The idea behind the building of the people's army was that the CPC insisted on combining Marxist principles of military construction with the actual situation in the Chinese revolution in the long-term revolutionary war and the practice of military construction. It creatively proposed a new ideology and theoretical principles for constructing a people's army.

a. Serving the People Wholeheartedly

As early as November 1927, the CPC Central Committee formulated a report entitled "China's Current Situation and the CPC's Mission," in which it identified the nature of the "worker-peasant revolutionary army, which is completely different from a mercenary force," as the sort of Chinese army that was to be created. The worker-peasant revolutionary army mentioned here actually corresponded to the national revolutionary army. It excluded the Chinese bourgeoisie and other classes that went against the revolution and further revolutionized the revolutionary camp, thus affirming the nature of its proletarian army and serving the workers and peasants. At the beginning of 1929, Mao Zedong and Zhu De led the Red Fourth Army to the southern Jiangxi Province and the western Fujian Province. In the Red Fourth Army Command Notice, they proposed the idea that the "purpose of the Red Army is a civil rights revolution." This was the first time the CPC's military had applied this concept and stated its purpose. Taking the gaining of civil rights as the purpose of the Red Army, it was apparently still following Sun Yat-sen's idea of building a military. However, because the Red Army limited the concept of "people" to "workers, peasants, and all oppressed classes," it was not in line with Sun Yat-sen's original concept of "national." For this reason, the Red Army's purpose of a "civil rights revolution" was essentially the liberation of the broad masses of the working class. The notion of purpose was central to the Red Army's political education. The outstanding achievement of the Red Army's political education lay in its cultivation of the spirit of self-sacrifice and sacrifice of the officers and men who fought for the interests of the workers and peasants.

After entering the War of Resistance Against Japanese Aggression, because of the changes in tasks and environment, the mission of the military faced severe challenges. On the one hand, the purpose of the Red Army was obviously not fully adapted to the needs of the new situation in the Anti-Japanese National United Front. On the other hand, the CPC's armed force, which had been freed from the isolation of civil war, had been eroded by various non-proletarian ideas and was in danger of losing its fundamental revolutionary direction. This being the case, the army had invested more energy in the cause of education. Mao and others began to explore a form of expression that could maintain the essence of the Red Army's purpose and adapt to the demands of the new military situation. In May 1942, Mao first used the phrase "serving the people," in his speech at the Yan'an Forum on Literature and Art, to explain the fundamental purpose of the Party and the army in the revolutionary struggle. In September 1944, in his speech "Serving the People," Mao made further reference to the army's "complete" and "total" service to the people. On this basis, in April 1945, Mao formed a complete, accurate, scientific expression of the purpose of the military in the Party's report to the Seventh National Congress, entitled "On the United Government," in which he said, "We must firmly stand with the Chinese people. The sole purpose of the Chinese army is to stand beside the Chinese people and serve them wholeheartedly."[35] From that time on, serving the people wholeheartedly became a fundamental starting point for all the actions of the army, and adhering to this aim became an important guiding principle for the military's political work. Under the guidance of this aim, the CPC's military commanders could carry forward a revolutionary spirit that was not afraid of suffering, nor of death, and this revolutionary heroic spirit would overwhelm all who opposed it. It would enable the army and the people to share their common pains and sorrows, just as it would help the people to think, building a heartfelt bond with the people, even becoming a child loved by the people. It could act on all directions and obey the commands of the Party, becoming a model for implementing the Party's line, principles, and policies. In this way, the CPC's armed force could become invincible and heroic.

b. Reflecting the Essence of Class and of the New People's Army

The military is always subordinate to a certain class and serves the interests of that class. Therefore, it must have a distinct class nature. The purpose of an army determines the code of conduct of this army, and it is a concentrated expression of the class nature of this army. The CPC's military consciously adhered to the principle of "serving the people wholeheartedly," which demonstrated that the CPC's force was thoroughly committed to fighting for the interests of the people. The pursuit of this purpose was determined not only by the proletarian nature of the CPC's military, but also the fact that the army must maintain its proletarian focus.

The CPC's military was a new type of army, different from the anti-peoples armies that served the interests of the reactionary and bourgeois classes. It was also different from those historical forces of the oppressed classes or which emerged for the purpose of overthrowing the decaying ruling classes that were exploiting the masses. In the first place, it originated during China's new democratic revolution for the purpose of making this revolution a reality and to consolidate the fruits of this revolution. In its essence, the revolution was a bourgeois revolution led by the proletariat. Its ultimate goal was to clear the way for the establishment of a socialist, and even a communist, society that eliminated all exploitative systems and exploiting classes. Mao Zedong pointed out, "The new democratic revolution is an anti-imperialist, anti-feudal revolution of the masses under the leadership of the proletariat." He went on to say, "This revolution is for the precise purpose of clearing the broader road for the development of socialism."[36] This indicated that China's new democratic revolution was a necessary preparation for China's socialist revolution to eliminate exploitation and the exploiting classes. It was different from any previous revolution in history. It stood on a new historical starting line and had to reach new historical heights. The army that was born during and fought for this revolution would inevitably have a new ideological scope. In addition, the CPC's military was a Party-led army that carried out the Party's tasks. The CPC was the leading group of the proletariat, and as a conscious actor in the struggle to realize humankind's greatness, it was completely dedicated to working for the interests of the people. It stipulated that wholehearted service for the people was the purpose of the army under its leadership. Further, the CPC's army was armed with Marxist thought, applying dialectical materialism and historical materialism as tools to understand the world. One of the basic principles of Marxism was that the masses of the people are the creators of history. Without the support of the people, no one would accomplish anything. According to this principle of Marxism, Mao emphasized that the revolutionary war must have the support of the people, saying, "The deepest root of the great power of war lives among the people." The CPC's military had set itself up as an instrument in service of the people. The guiding principle of all its actions was to consciously practice this basic principle of Marxism, placing itself among the masses of the people, not breaking away from the masses, but relying on them.

Serving the people wholeheartedly was the source of the army's strength. In his article "On the United Government," Mao pointed out that "the reason our army has power lies in its conscious discipline and its purpose of wholeheartedly serving the people. Because of this purpose, the army has a persistent mindset, a dedication to overwhelming all enemies, and a firm commitment to never surrender. Because of this purpose, internally, there is great unity between officers and soldiers, command and rank and file, and political and logistical work, while externally, there is great unity between the military and civilians, and between political and military works. Because of this purpose, our military has a correct policy toward fighting the enemy and toward handling prisoners. Because of this purpose, our military has formed a series of strategic tactics necessary for the people's war. Because of this purpose, our military consciously performs the tasks as a production team."

Following by the purpose of wholeheartedly serving the people, the officers and soldiers clearly indicated that they were fighting for the interests of the people, including their own interests, and that the cause they were engaged in was great and lofty, and thus became a strong spiritual pillar for them. It was precisely because of this that they were consciously, courageously dedicated to sacrificing their lives to defeat the enemy. Even if meant fighting to the last man, they would never yield. It was this spirit that made the CPC's armed force such an unyielding, unrelenting army.

Guided by this purpose, the CPC's military established a good tradition of both internal and external unity. Internally, whether officer, soldier, or even cook, each came from different corners of the country, serving the people, and forming a class-based brotherhood. Only on the basis of a united dedication to the interests of a common class could this new relationship between officers and men be formed. Externally, the army shared a relationship to the people that was like a fish's relationship to water. The army regarded the interests of the people above everything else and always protected the interests of the people. The masses of people regarded this army as their own children and provided continuous support from their own human, material, and spiritual resources, supporting the troops at all costs. For the sake of the army, they stood guard, sent out alarms, acted as guides over the terrain, donated food and ammunition, aided the wounded, coordinated operations, and offered countless other forms of support to the army, which laid a solid foundation for its survival and development. The officers loved the soldiers, and the soldiers respected them. The army loved the people, and the people supported the army. This was an inexhaustible source of strength for the army.

In line with the purpose of wholeheartedly serving the people, the CPC's army was able to effectively disintegrate the enemy. Because the army was able to correctly distinguish the upper and lower levels of the enemy's forces and carry out targeted work, particularly for the lower ranks, the CPC's military employed actions of its own to serve the people, which helped the masses understand that the war the CPC's forces were waging were aligned with the people's own interests. Once they understood this, they broke away from the old camp and join the ranks of the CPC's army. In addition, guided by the purpose of serving the people, the army pursued a humanitarian policy for the captives, treated the injured, respected their individuality, and welcomed them as guests, then bid them farewell. This was an appropriate policy toward captives, and was decidedly different from the enemy's approach.

With the goal of serving the people firmly in mind, the CPC's army had formed strategies and tactics for war that were unique to it. Such strategies and tactics were based on the support of the people, and these strategies and tactics could only be effective with the support of the people.

With its unwavering commitment to serving the people, the army's political work was based on the principle that the officers and men were one, the army and the people were one, and the enemy was to be demolished. The political work carried out in accordance with this set of principles had basically mobilized the ingenuity and courage of the officers and men of the CPC's army, ensuring good relations between the army's internal and external forces and effectively demolishing the enemy.

As a force that existed for the purpose of serving the people, the CPC's military actively used the gap between combat and training to carry out production activities, starting from the principle of alleviating the burden on the people. The development of this activity not only greatly improved the lives of the officers and soldiers, but also won the support of the people and made them truly regard this army as their own army.

Persevering in the wholehearted service of the people enabled the army to gain great spiritual strength and won the people's support for the war. This was where the strength of the army lay. As Zhu De once pointed out, the army generated the Chinese people's revolution. Like a son loyal to his mother, the army was loyal to the people, so the people loved and supported the army, helping it to overcome difficulties while constantly consolidating and maturing in an extremely difficult environment.

c. *Performing The Three Major Tasks*

As the main military tool, the army is naturally responsible for war, and there have been no exceptions to this in ancient or modern China, nor in other countries. However, because the people's army was created by the CPC, its duties were not limited to war. From the beginning of this period, it carried out the task of fighting, working among the masses, and raising funds for the trio of military, political, and economic work. In September 1929, the Directive from the CPC Central Committee to the front forces of the Fourth Red Army pointed out that the basic tasks of the Red Army were "1) mobilizing mass struggle, implementing the agrarian revolution, and establishing the soviet regime, 2) implementing guerrilla warfare, arming the peasants, and expanding its own organization, and 3) expanding the guerrillas' territory and political influence throughout the entire country." It also stated that "if the Red Army cannot carry out these three tasks, it is no different from an ordinary army." Mao presided over the drafting of the resolution of the Gutian Meeting, in the spirit of the directive mentioned above, adding that the Red Army was "an armed group that carries out the political work of the revolution." He went on to say, "In addition to fighting to destroy the enemy's power, it must also bear the burden of propagating, organizing, and arming the masses and helping them establish revolutionary regimes and even build the Communist Party."[37] Lest this point be overlooked, Mao added, "This is the whole purpose behind winning the war, and the very purpose for which the Red Army exists."[38]

During the War of Resistance Against Japanese Aggression, the task of raising funds shifted to that of production. In other words, it focused on "using the gap between combat and training to engage in the production of food and daily necessities, achieving the goal of self-sufficiency, semi-subsistence, or partial self-sufficiency for the military."[39] Mao once wrote about the great significance of the army's self-sufficiency in production. He pointed out, "The self-sufficiency of production in the military seems regressive in its form, but it is essentially progressive and has great historical significance."[40] It "allows our army to overcome the difficulty of obtaining materials for our livelihood. It has improved our lives, while also being strong enough to relieve the people's burden incurred because of those difficulties. Therefore, it has won the support of the people and is sufficient for supporting the long-term war, expanding the army, and thereby expanding the liberated areas and narrowing enemy-occupied territory. Wouldn't achieving the goal of finally destroying the aggressors and liberating all of China be a matter of great historical significance?"[41] He added, "As long as we are all as heroic and good-willed as the Eighth Route Army, not only will everyone fight, but it will in fact be mass work and production, and we will have no need to fear any difficulty. We will be, as Meng Zi said, 'invincible in this world.'"[42]

In the period leading up to and following the War of Liberation, the three major tasks of the army were generally summed up as combat, work, and production teams. When national liberation came in 1949, the vast new districts did not require large numbers of cadres to carry out their work. Faced with this situation, the CPC Central Committee decided to convert all 2.1 million field troops into task forces. In his report at the Second Plenary Session of the Seventh General Meeting of the CPC Central Committee, Mao pointed out, "The People's Liberation Army will always be a combat team. After the national victory, in the historical period when there is no class in the country and an imperialist system continues in the world, our army will remain a combat team."[43] He went on to say, "The People's Liberation Army is another work force... As the fighting gradually decreases, its role as a work force will increase."[44] After the founding of the new China, the Party faced the arduous task of restoring the national economy. The People's Revolutionary Committee of the CPC Central Committee stated in the Instructions on the Participation of the Armed Forces in Production in 1950, that "the PLA is not only a national liberation force, but also a work and production team." This solidified the notion that it was a combat, work, and production team.

The most fundamental purpose for building the people's army was to serve the people, providing what the people needed through the army's work, and maintaining the highest standard of acting in the interests of the Chinese people to determine the tasks of the military at different periods. Without this, the army would lose its foundational premise. At the same time, the functions of the military were linked to this task. There were military, political, and economic tasks, long-term and current tasks, and basic or auxiliary tasks. The CPC's army was the most organized, conscious, and combative part of the people. Military means could be used to destroy the enemy, and military personnel could be used as propagandist and organizers of the masses. The military could also assist in agricultural sub-military and military production. All these efforts would reduce the burden on the people, support local construction, offer aid in times of natural disasters, and so forth. It was a comprehensive approach to serving the people in multiple ways. Of course, the PLA had three major tasks. As a tool for the proletarian revolution and dictatorship, its fundamental mission was that of a combat team. In different historical periods, the Party repeatedly stressed that the people's army could only accomplish other tasks if it did not put its basic task in detriment. If the fundamental task was neglected for the sake of carrying out other forms of work, it would be putting the cart before the horse, and in the end, there would be no army for the people. These special tasks, then, would have fundamentally damaged the interests of the people.

2. Upholding the Party's Absolute Leadership of the Military

a. Formulating the Notion of the Party's Absolute Leadership of the Military

The CPC attached great importance to the Party's leadership of the military even from the earliest days of its establishment of its own armed force. In October 1927, Mao led the Autumn Harvest Uprising troops to march toward Jinggangshan, where he carried out the famous "Sanwan Reorganization." It was decided then that the Party's various levels of organization were established in the army under the leadership of the CPC, understanding that "the branch is built on the company," with the squad and platoon forming a Party group, and the battalion and regiment forming a Party committee and higher level representatives. These important principles and systems laid an important organizational foundation for the realization of the Party's leadership over the military. In July 1928, when Zhou Enlai spoke of the establishment of the Red Army and the militarization of Party members in the military report of the Sixth National Congress of the CPC, he stated clearly, "The Party should play a central, leading role." The Military Work Resolution further pointed out, "All military work of the CPC should be concentrated in the Central Military Department of the CPC." In December 1929, the Red Fourth Army convened the Ninth Party Representative Congress, at which the famous resolution from the Gutian Meeting, drafted by Mao Zedong, was adopted. It clearly stated that "China's Red Army is an armed group that carries out the political tasks of the revolution," and that the Party's leading organs in the army must become "the central leadership," while stipulating that "all work will be carried out by the masses after discussion and decisions have been made by the Party," and all major issues were to be discussed at the Party Committee Meeting, and "then must be resolutely implemented." This determined a set of principles and measures for achieving the Party's leadership of the military on the political, ideological, and organizational levels and fundamentally established the distinctions between the proletarian army and all prior military forces, so that the Red Army was fully established on a Marxist basis. On this foundation, the Party's leadership of the military was further consolidated. In June 1930, the Front Line Committee of the CPC issued the Program for the Red Fourth Army at All Levels, which, alongside the Provisional Regulations on the Political Work of the Chinese Workers and Peasants Red Army (Draft) issued in the winter of 1930, formally established the Party's leadership of the military. Since then, the fundamental principle of upholding the Party's absolute leadership over the military was formally established. After that, this fundamental principle emerged in many official documents of both the Party and the military, alongside regulations on military political work that had been promulgated.

The principle of the Party's absolute leadership over the military not only gradually formed and established alongside the military's practice of building the army, but was also deeply rooted in Marxist theoretical foundations. Marxism holds that the military is a product of class struggle and a tool for certain classes and their political parties to achieve political ends. It is subordinate to a certain class and its political parties, and it serves the interests of certain levels and their political parties. There is neither an extreme class army nor an extreme political army. Rather, in modern times, the ruling class usually leads the nation through its own political parties, which have mastery over the military. Of course, the ruling class has a variety of methods for mastering the military. For example, some capitalist countries have adopted a political party that has mastery over the military, while others master the military through the rotation of two or more parties. However, regardless of which approach is adopted, it cannot change the essence of the execution of the will of the ruling class, and it cannot hide that it has the same attributes as the ruling party, the state, and the military. The rule of the bourgeoisie cannot, in any case, allow the proletariat to take charge of their regime and their army. Similarly, as the vanguard of the proletariat, the Communist Party must also hold leadership of the proletarian army firmly in its own hand, never sharing it with any other party.

In the long-term practice of revolutionary struggle, the CPC combined the basic principles of Marxism with the concrete practices of the Chinese revolution, greatly enriching and developing Marxism in many areas, including relations between classes, political parties, states, the military, and ideology. Mao once stated, "The Party is the vanguard of the proletariat and the highest form of proletarian organization. It should lead all other organizations, such as military, government, and people's organizations."[45] He likewise stated, "Work, agriculture, commerce, education, military, politics, and the Party are all under Party leadership. The CPC has absolute leadership over the military, leadership that was formed during the revolutionary war. This is an absolute condition. Without such absolute leadership from the CPC, it is impossible to even imagine that the revolutionary effort would have had such tenacity."[46] After the outbreak of the War of Resistance Against Japanese Aggression, in an effort to strengthen the Party's absolute leadership over the military, in an article entitled "Situation and Work in the Anti-Japanese War Effort After the Fall of Shanghai," Mao further emphasized the principle of adhering to independence and autonomy in the Anti-Japanese United National Front, stating, "We rejected the KMT's request to send their party members to serve as cadres in the Eighth Route Army, instead adhering to the principle of the CPC's absolute leadership of the Eighth Route Army."[47] In November 1938, at the Sixth Plenary Session of the Sixth General Meeting of the CPC Central Committee, he summarized the experiences of the Party's adherence to the principle of independence and autonomy in the united front since the anti-Japanese war. When it came to the lessons of Zhang Guotao's self-interest in the Party, he further emphasized, "Communist Party members do not fight for individual military power (which is to say that no one should follow Zhang Guotao's example). Rather, we must fight for the Party's and the people's military power," and "our principle is that the Party will command the guns. Never will we allow guns to command the Party."[48] This was Mao's most vivid summary of the principle of the Party's absolute leadership over the military. In October 1947, in the People's Liberation Army Declaration, he reiterated this, saying, "All the soldiers throughout the entire army must always remember that we are the great People's Liberation Army and are under the leadership of the great Communist Party of China. As long as we follow the Party's instructions at all times, we will certainly be victorious."[49] This was true. For decades, the most important reason the CPC's military was able to grow from small to large and from weak to strong, moving from victory to victory, was that the military was always under the absolute leadership of the Party.

b. *The Necessity of Upholding the CPC's Absolute Leadership of the Military*

Primarily, the Party's absolute leadership over the military was a guarantee of the proletarian nature of its armed forces. In the specific environment of the Chinese revolution, emphasizing the Party's absolute control over the military could effectively transform an army with peasants as its main component into a proletarian army. The nature of the Chinese revolutionary war that took place in semi-colonial, semi-feudal China was that of a peasant war led by the proletariat. The main component of the revolutionary army was inevitably the peasantry. As oppressed people, particularly a people under three colossal forms of oppression, the Chinese peasantry was very revolutionary, and they were eager to overthrow the society that had caused them to suffer. But as small-scale producers, they were often influenced by the petty bourgeoisie worldview, which was narrow-minded, lacking in foresight, free, and easily misled. To transform a peasant-dominated army into a true proletarian revolutionary army, it was necessary to transform this army's worldview to a proletarian perspective and constrain it with proletarian revolutionary discipline. All this could only be achieved under the leadership of the CPC, because only the CPC could implement the revolutionary worldview of the proletariat in the army and establish proletarian revolutionary discipline, thus effectively overcoming the various small assets brought to the army by its mainly peasant composition. The influence of the class worldview made this army one that completely and wholeheartedly fought for the interests of the people. Mao added a paragraph in the Report of the Political Department of the Left-Wing Corps in the High-Level Conference of the Northwest Bureau on the Political Work of the Army that stated, "If our army did not have the leadership of the CPC, there would be no revolutionary work and no Party-led revolution. It is impossible to imagine political work without the Party's leadership, lacking all military and political work by the army that thoroughly supports the interests of the people."[50]

Further, it was only by upholding the CPC's absolute leadership of the military that the army completed the historical mission of the revolution. This was determined by the CPC's absolute leadership over the military. The practice of the Chinese revolution demonstrated that only the proletariat and the CPC could overcome the narrow-mindedness of the peasant class, the petty bourgeoisie, and the national bourgeoisie and lead the revolution on a victorious path. The Party's leadership over the entire war determined its leadership over the military. The CPC represented the interests of the broad masses of the people and could thus broadly mobilize the masses to participate in and support their own military, allowing the war effort to gain a deep reservoir of human and material resources. The class worldview educated the army, so that the commanders and soldiers throughout the entire army had a deep understanding of the law of social development, hating all systems of exploitation and establishing the lofty ideals of communism and the idea of wholeheartedly serving the people, thus making the military highly politically aware, with excellent internal and external unity, and a thorough revolutionary, invincible, and indomitable fighting spirit. It was for this reason that it could be invincible in the revolutionary war. With its strict organizational, disciplinary, and exemplary role, the CPC made the organization at all levels unified in leadership and military work, turning the army into an unstoppable fighting group that had become a great steel wall without consideration for anyone's personal career. Taking the scientific theory of Marxism as a guide, the CPC promptly pointed out the correct political direction for the military, formulating flexible strategic approaches and tactics. The Chinese revolutionary war was long-term and complicated, and the people's army was often in a difficult position. However, because of the Party's appropriate political and military leadership, it finally grew from a weak force into a strong one and defeated all its mighty enemies, both foreign and domestic.

Finally, upholding the Party's absolute leadership of the military was a fundamental guarantee for the military's development from growth and its ability to go from victory to victory. The army was established on August 1, 1927, during the Agrarian Revolutionary War. It was known at the time as the Red Army of Workers and Peasants. During the War of Resistance Against Japanese Aggression, it was reorganized into the Eighth Route Army and the New Fourth Army. During the War of Liberation, it became the People's Liberation Army. The CPC's military grew from nothing, going from small to large and weak to strong, all as a result of the CPC's correct leadership and command. The wrong leadership of the third "leftist" error and the rightist opportunism of Zhang Guotao's opposition party depleted nine-tenths of the Red Army and the bases. The Party and Mao Zedong resolutely opposed both leftist and rightist error, insisting in the correct guidance of Marxism-Leninism in the military and adhering to the correct military approach. In particular, the Zunyi Conference established Mao's leadership in the Red Army and the CPC Central Committee, saving the Party at a critical juncture and saving the Red Army. From that time on, the correct leadership of the Party and the Red Army smashed the enemy's pursuit and maneuvers, overcoming obstacles rarely seen in the world's history, and successfully completed the Long March, a virtual miracle in human history. In the War of Resistance Against Japanese Aggression, the contrast between the enemy and the communist forces was extremely disparate, creating a difficult environment for the struggle. The Party formulated the guidelines, strategies, and tactics for carrying out an independent anti-Japanese guerrilla war. It led the army to advance into enemy territory, released the masses, carried out an enduring people's war, and finally broke the myth of Japanese invincibility. After defeating the Japanese aggressors, the Central Committee and Mao Zedong commanded the army to carry out an unprecedented war of liberation against the KMT. It took only three years to eliminate the 8 million reactionary forces in the country, achieving liberation for China. These facts eloquently proved the efficacy of the CPC's leadership of the military.

3. Adhering to the Party's Absolute Leadership of the Military through Political, Ideological, Organizational, and Institutional Means

In order to strengthen the Party's absolute leadership of the military, throughout the long-term practice of revolutionary struggle, the Party gradually formulated a set of effective systems and measures for good leadership of the army. This was a specific crystallization of the Party's experience in leading the military, and it was necessary to adhere to this approach.

Politically, the Party's absolute leadership of the military was achieved through the leadership of the Party's political program, direction, principles, and policies. The army was a tool for realizing the Party's political program and direction. Only through resolute implementation of the CPC's direction, principles, and policies was it possible to maintain the correct path for constructing the armed forces, while appropriately handling both the building of the military and the Party's central work. The relationship would enable the military to truly become an armed group that obeyed and served the Party's program, direction, and principles and better served the Party's political tasks. Therefore, the Party stipulated that the military could only publicize the Party's program, direction, principles and policies, while mobilizing and organizing the broad masses of officers and men to fight for the realization of the scene. If the military was allowed to freely publicize a variety of political ideas, it would lead to chaos in the army, possibly even resulting in a loss of direction and its adherence to the Party's leadership. In order to achieve political leadership over the military, the Party formulated a series of military principles for the armed forces, such as adhering to the principles of wholeheartedly serving the people, upholding the Party's command of the military, fully adhering to Marxism-Leninism and Mao Zedong Thought, and educating the troops regarding the Party's direction, principles, and policies. In addition, attention was given to implementation of things such the three major tasks of combat, work, and production; the Red Army's Three Rules for Discipline and Eight Points for Attention; the three aspects of political, military and economic democracy; the principles of unity among officers and men, military and civilians, and demolishing the enemy; and selecting and appointing cadres according to the principle of both ability and integrity. Emphasis was also placed on strengthening the construction of the Party organizations within the military and giving full play to the leadership role of Party committees, fighting bastions of Party branches and the exemplary role of Party members, and establishing political work systems. In the long-term revolutionary struggle, the Party insisted on building a military in accordance with this set of principles for building the army, so that the army always remained an armed group that carried out the work of the Party.

In terms of ideology, the Party's absolute leadership of the military was achieved by adhering to the leadership of Marxism-Leninism and Mao Zedong Thought, which were the guiding ideology of the Party, state, and military, and were the ideological and theoretical basis for realizing the Party's absolute leadership over the military. Because of the Party's program, direction, principles, and policies, its series of strategies for building the military were the products of the combination of Marxism-Leninism, Mao Zedong Thought, and the actual situation of the state and the military. Only through application of Marxism-Leninism and Mao Zedong Thought to the construction of the armed forces could the military develop an ideological basis with the Party, making all its actions subject to Party leadership, allowing it to improve the ability of the vast numbers of officers and men to identify and resist the erosion of various non-proletarian ideas and maintain the purity of the military's thinking. In order to achieve the ideological leadership of the military, the Party established a complete set of ideological and political work in the military and, in accordance with the development of the situation and the actual conditions of the military, to offer a variety of political education programs as befit the situation. Through such education, the Party's ideological leadership of the military was ultimately realized.

Organizationally, the Party's absolute leadership of the military would finally be realized through the centralized, unified leadership of the CPC, and the Central Military Commission, would be established at all levels in the military as the unified leadership and unity of the army would be led by the military's top echelons. Power and command would be concentrated in the CPC Central Committee and the Central Military Commission, thus achieving the Party's absolute leadership of the military. The Party's military political regulations stipulated that "the Chinese People's Liberation Army must be placed under the absolute leadership of the CPC. The highest leadership and command of the military belong to the CPC and the Central Military Commission." According to this organizational principle, in the military, only the CPC and its assisting body, the Communist Youth League, could establish Party and regiment organizations, develop Party and League members, and carry out political work. Only Party organizations could appoint leading cadres at all levels of the military. Without the approval of the corresponding political organs, members of the military could not participate in other parties or religious organizations, nor could they establish groups and organizations other than those stipulated by various regulations or participate in local people's organizations without authorization. The Party's leadership in the organization of the military was the organizational guarantee of the Party's leadership over the military. In order to realize the Party's absolute leadership over the military, the CPC adopted a series of organizational measures. Through these measures, the Party's goal of leadership through organization was achieved.

In terms of institutions, institutions were to be responsible for the division of labor under the collective leadership of the Party committee. This was a fundamental institution for upholding the Party's absolute leadership over the military. The unified leadership of the Party committee, its collective leadership, and the division of labor among the leaders were three inseparable, indispensable organic components. This sort of system of the division of labor under the collective leadership of the Party committee organically combined the collective experience and wisdom with the enthusiasm and creative spirit of individuals, which avoided one-sidedness and possible errors in individual decision-making and prevented a situation in which everything relied on the collective and no one was responsible for whatever happened. In this way, it was possible to ensure the implementation of the Party's instructions and resolutions and to ensure the completion of the tasks assigned by the Party.

4. Guiding Principles for Political Work

The CPC's idea of building a military not only emphasized the importance of political work, but also summed up the experience of the army's political work and systematically proposed the guiding principles for the political work of the military.

a. Basic Principles of the Military's Political Work

Mao Zedong stated, "The PLA has been established on the foundation of the people's war, the principles of unity between officers and men and military and civilian, and demolishing the enemy. It is on this basis that it has undertaken powerful revolutionary work."[51]

The basic idea and requirements of the Three Principles were originally introduced during the Sanwan reorganization and the Jinggangshan struggle. In September 1927, when Mao Zedong led the Revolutionary Army of Workers and Peasants to reorganize at Sanwan during the Autumn Harvest Uprising, he suggested breaking the management system and warlord style of feudal mercenary forces and implementing a democratic system. It was stipulated that the officers were not allowed to verbally abuse or beat the soldiers. Soldiers were free to speak, and a soldiers' committee was established in the upper ranks to supervise economic expenses and to supervise and criticize the cadres. This sort of democratic system was based on the complete equality of political and military personnel and had become the initial idea behind the principle of the unity between officers and men. In October 1927, Mao led the Revolutionary Army of Workers and Peasants to Jinggangshan. He proposed three major principles and gave careful attention to them. He suggested that the troops should shoulder the task of fighting and perform the work among the masses and of fundraising, while also demanding that, out of respect for the people, the army must respect the interests of the people and observe the discipline of the masses in order to achieve the goal of unity and common struggle between the military and the people, making this the first requirement in view of the principle of unity between the military and civilians. After the Revolutionary Army of Workers and Peasants had established the revolutionary base at Jinggangshan, the enemy forces of Hunan and Jiangxi organized "meetings" from time to time. When the Revolutionary Army of Workers and Peasants fought enemy forces, the CPC's military gained greater understanding of how to deal with captives, which in turn affected the views both officers and men held by the military. In February 1928, Mao stipulated three policies for the treatment of prisoners. The first was no beating, no verbal abuse, no killing, no abuse, no discrimination, no robbing, and allowing them to enjoy the same treatment as the army's own soldiers in politics and life. The second was that if they opted to volunteer to join the CPC army's ranks, they would be welcomed without any penalty. The final principle was that all wounded and sick prisoners would be treated. Those three principles became the basic premise for the military's policy toward captives. Extending courtesy to prisoners was one of the main ways the army disintegrated the enemy's forces. The basic ideas and requirements of these three principles were further confirmed in a resolution at the Gutian Meeting. The resolution required the Red Army to establish a new type of relationship between officers and men and military and civilians, and to correct its policy towards captives. It abolished the management system of the old army and its method of recruiting troops, and in this way, it gradually improved its policy of political work. On October 25, 1937, when Mao was interviewed by the British journalist James Bertram, he officially summarized the notions of unity between officers and men and between military and civilian and that of disintegrating enemy forces into the three basic principles of political work within the military.

Regarding the principle of the unity between officers and men, Mao said, "This is for the purpose of eliminating feudalism within the army, abolishing maltreatment, establishing self discipline, and practicing a life of mutual fraternity. In this way, the entire Party will be unified."[52] A solid foundation was set up for addressing any difficulty and even the most powerful enemy, adhering to the principle of enabling the military to thoroughly eliminate the remnants of feudal mercenaries and warlordism, achieving political equality, solidarity, and camaraderie among the upper and lower categories of cadres and soldiers, and working together through shared difficulties. The relationship between officers and men had a wide range of meanings, including not only the main officers and soldiers, but also between upper and lower levels and between units and departments. Because the relationship between officers and men was the most basic relationship within the military, the principle of unity between officers and men was generally representative of the basic norms for dealing with various relations within the military. In this relationship, the soldiers were the foundation and the cadres were dominant. It was necessary to educate the cadres to first care for the soldiers, treating them as brothers in a common class and giving full expression to their enthusiasm and creativity. At the same time, it was necessary to educate the soldiers to respect and care for the cadres, to consciously follow their management and command, and, motivated by fraternal love, to help correct the cadres' shortcomings and errors, promote internal unity, and form a strong, cohesive force. Mao pointed out that "The establishment of self discipline and the practice of living a life of mutual fraternity will unite the entire army."[53]

The principle of unity between officers and men went beyond good wishes and slogans. It was, in fact, a guarantee of a democratic system. This democratic system produced a powerful force. During the Jinggangshan period, the material life of the Red Army was extremely difficult and fighting was frequent, but it remained unchanged. This came about partly due to the role of the Party, and also to the implementation of a democratic system in the military. The officers did not beat the soldiers, officers and men were treated as equals, the soldiers enjoyed freedom of speech, the cumbersome etiquette system was abolished, and the economy was open. The new prisoners felt that the KMT army and the Red Army were of two completely different worlds. Though the material life of the Red Army lagged behind that of the White Army, their spirits were liberated. For this reason, a soldier who was in the White Army yesterday might have lacked courage, but he grew brave when he joined the Red Army today. Based on this observation, Mao pointed out, "China needs not only its people to be democratic, but also its military. Implementing a democratic system within the military will be an important weapon for undermining feudal forces."[54] He added that the army had been "democratized to a certain extent" for the purpose of "increasing its great fighting power, lest it fail to support the long-term war in which it is engaged."[55] During the period of the War of Liberation, the democratic system of the PLA was further developed in the political, economic, and military spheres. Political democracy aimed to enable the masses of soldiers to exercise their democratic rights in order to achieve a high degree of political unity. Economic democracy meant that soldiers were elected representatives and had the right to assist (not exceed) the company's heads to manage the support and meals of the company and improve their lives. Military democracy pointed to the training of officers and men and mutual training between soldiers. In combat, under the guidance of the heads of the company, the soldiers were mobilized to discuss the methods of warfare and exert the wisdom and intelligence of both officers and men in order to improve their technical and tactical maneuvers. The implementation of the three major democratic aspects enabled the principle of unity between officers and men to be better implemented in the PLA, which in turn effectively guaranteed victory in the war.

Regarding the principle of unity among the military and civilians, Mao said, "The relationship between cadres and soldiers should be so close that there is no division. The relationship between the army and the local people and between the local Party and government organizations should be similarly close." He added, "The army must be united with the people and, seen through the eyes of the public, it must be the people's own army. This will be an invincible force in the world."[56] In emphasizing the principle of unity between the military and civilians, it was right to expect the political work to ensure the unity of the army and government and the army and the people. Guided by this principle, the army always respected the people's government and protected the interests of the people, executing wide-scale discipline, reducing the economic burden on the people, supporting the people, abiding by local policies and decrees, respecting local cadres, strengthening the unity between the military and the people, and jointly attacking the enemy. Political work adhered to the basic principle of correctly handling military-civilian relations and could guarantee that the relationship between the army and the people was like that between fish and water. Once the military won the support of the people and the local government, it was able to win the people's war. During the early days of the army, it carried out three major tasks and three major disciplines as the specific actions for implementing unity between the military and civilians. On October 1, 1943, the CPC Central Committee issued instructions for the PLA to hold a large-scale movement for "supporting the government and loving the people" the following January. This was in line with the needs of the government and the people in the anti-Japanese base areas. A system of "supporting the army and their families" (i.e., preferential treatment of family members of anti-Japanese soldiers) was formulated following the corresponding campaign. During this movement, both the military and the civilians formulated and revised the conventions of love for the people and the local government, and thus held a Party meeting to examine and criticize their own shortcomings. This was a newly created means for implementing the principle of unity between the military and the people and fostering a close military-civilian relationship. It was a good format for handling conflicts between the military and the people, and it united the military and civilians in the anti-Japanese base areas. Even today, mass activities for supporting the people and the military are held in China before and after the Spring Festival each year.

Regarding the disintegration of the enemy and the treatment of prisoners, Mao stated, "Our victory depends not only on the combat of our military, but also on the disintegration of our enemy."[57] For this reason, the PLA "has a correct combat policy for its officers and men, and for its treatment of prisoners. For those who are sincere or are willing to participate in opposing a common enemy after laying down their weapons against our forces, they will be welcome and given proper education. For all prisoners, there will be no killing, abuse, or insults allowed."[58] This principle required the military to carry out political propaganda and organizational disintegration of the enemy's army in a political, ideological, organizational, and psychological approach as they fought, making full use of the battlefield to shout and disseminate propaganda materials, penetrating the enemy's defenses through a multi-faceted approach. They carried out political offensives, shaking the enemy's morale and weakening their combat effectiveness. In implementing the prisoner policy, they respected the humanity of enemy soldiers, particularly those who sincerely cast away their weapons, not killing or humiliating the enemy, but dealing with them leniently and welcoming their participation in communist forces, thereby weakening the hold of the enemy and strengthening its own forces. As early as the Jinggangshan days, the Red Army issued four rules for the treatment of prisoners: 1) no beating, no killing, and no abusing prisoners, 2) no searching the prisoners for money, 3) treating the injured, and 4) releasing the prisoners and allowing those who wished to stay and voluntarily join the Revolutionary Army of Workers and Peasants, where they would be treated the same as all other soldiers. In every battle, the army used a variety of propaganda methods to carry out a powerful political offensive against the enemy, while also matching their military offensive. The principle of disintegrating the enemy was thus earnestly implemented, which in turn effectively weakened the enemy's combat effectiveness. During the Red Army's period, the first to fourth "anti-encirclement" campaigns in the central revolutionary base area saw 514,000 people in the enemy army killed, and another 198,000 captured, roughly 38.5% of the total. During the War of Resistance Against Japanese Aggression, the Japanese army, which was deeply ingrained with an educational system rooted in militarism and bushido, the captured officers and men participated in the anti-aggression war, under the influence of the people's army's policy regarding the treatment of prisoners. They formed anti-aggression and revolutionary groups such as the Anti-Aggression Alliance and the Awakening Alliance, joining the Chinese people in combating the Japanese aggressors. In the War of Liberation, the army annihilated more than 8 million KMT troops. The total number of prisoners, devotees, insurgents, and the number of those reorganized was 6.36 million, accounting for 79% of the enemy's total force. These facts vividly illustrated the importance of the principle of disintegrating the enemy.

The people's army regarded the unity of officers and men and the military and civilians, alongside the disintegration of the enemy forces, as the basic principles for political work. It was also the basic purpose of the people's army from the beginning. The primary principle was that the people's army came from the people and existed for the people, having no special interests of its own. The military and the people had a political foundation based on common interests, and the officers and men came together for a common goal. For this reason, there should be great consistency between officers and men and between the military and civilians. In addition, the revolutionary war relied mainly on the masses of people and masses of soldiers for victory. Therefore, it would never allow its own army to trample the people or the soldiers. Instead, there would be consistency between the officers and men and between the military and civilians. The principles of disintegrating enemy forces and the humane treatment of prisoners were likewise inseparable from the class nature of the people's army. The people's army fought a just war against an unjust war. It was convinced that the truth would be persuasive and that the counter-revolutionary army would collapse. Most members of the enemy's reactionary fighting forces were workers and peasants who had been lured into it. For this reason, the people's army should not abuse or kill enemy soldiers who laid down their weapons. Instead, it was necessary to implement revolutionary humaneness and extend leniency, in hopes of seeing them stand up to the unjust war and, through such actions, prompt the enemy officers and soldiers to realize their error. Thus, disintegrating the enemy and the humane treatment of prisoners was not a temporary strategy for the people's army, but a basic policy for struggle against the enemy.

Mao observed that establishing proper relationships between the military and civilians and between officers and men was not a question of methodology, but a fundamental attitude (or fundamental purpose). For the three principles "to be effectively implemented, we should start from the basic attitude of respecting the soldiers, the people, and the dignity of all enemy soldiers who have laid down their weapons."⁵⁹ This democratic spirit was unique to the proletarian revolutionary army. All reactionary forces had no common interests with the people, but instead, there were numerous conflicts. For this reason, externally, there was conflict between the military and civilians, while internally there was opposition between officers and soldiers, making it impossible for soldiers or civilians to gain democratic treatment. These forces could only resort to deception or coercion, and they often slaughtered or abused enemy prisoners. All of this was inseparable from the class nature of the revolutionary forces. If they did not act in this way, they would not be able to get the most out of the officers and men, who were actually working class people, in their own anti-peoples activities, and its army would cease to be a tool of the reactionary class.

b. Three Main Democratic Aspects as Manifestations of the Mass Approach to Army-Building

From the establishment of the people's army, Mao emphasized the need to implement the mass approach and carry out democracy in the military. He pointed out that China needed not only its people to be democratic, but also its military. The democratic system within the military would be an important weapon for destroying the feudal mercenary forces. He personally established the Soldiers' Committee, implemented political and economic equality among the officers and men, and established a democratic, united relationship within the new people's army. In the resolution of the Gutian Meeting, he clearly stipulated the principle that the Red Army be "organized democratically and live under the guidance of that organization." During the War of Resistance Against Japanese Aggression, he further pointed out that democracy within the military was only one important factor in persisting in the long war of resistance. Because of the establishment of a democratic system in the military, the unanimous purpose of the officers and men was achieved and the military increased its already enormous combat effectiveness. The long-term cruel war would not have ended without their great persistence. During the War of Liberation, he further summarized the army's experience in the article "The Democratic Movement within the Army," in which he offered a profound exposition of the purpose and methods of establishing a democratic system within the military. He stated, "The internal political work policy of the military was to liberate the soldiers, the masses, the commanders, and all the staff. Through the democratic movement was under centralized leadership, we were able to achieve a high degree of political unity, improve lives, and improve military technology and tactics, which are our three main purposes."[60] Political democracy brought unity and consistency to the officers and men. Through political criticism and self-criticism, a high degree of political unity was achieved. Economic democracy meant that the representatives elected by the soldiers had the right to assist (but not exceed) the company's head to manage the company's food, implement financial disclosure, and achieve the goal of improving lives. Military democracy was the mass approach to military work. In training, the officers and men practiced mutual training. In battle, under the guidance of the company heads, the soldiers were mobilized to discuss tactical and technical issues. It was evident that the three main democratic aspects were vivid manifestations of the mass approach to the construction of the army.

To implement intra-military democracy, it was necessary to properly handle the relationship between democracy and concentration. The people's army was a highly concentrated, unified fighting group. It was essential to have both democracy and concentration. Mao pointed out that this conflict had two sides, and these two sides were simultaneously unified and in conflict. It was important not to emphasize one and negate the other. The promotion of democracy within the military and the prevention of extreme democracy and anarchism were imperative. Concentration had to be emphasized, while warlordism and authoritarianism had to be opposed. In short, the intra-military democracy to be implemented was a democracy under centralized guidance, making it fundamentally different from a bourgeois democracy.

c. *Three Major Disciplines and Eight Codes of Behavior as an Important Guarantee for the People's Army Unity in Combat*

Discipline was important on the path to execution. Strict discipline in the people's army was based on the unity and high level of political consciousness and awareness of military responsibility among all the officers and men. It was a revolutionary discipline that was subject to the fundamental interests of the people, which set it completely apart from old forms of military discipline. Mao's three main forms of discipline for the military were the basic norms for the entire army's actions, which fully embodied the essence of the people's army's conscious safeguarding of the interests of the people. When the Party formulated military discipline, its fundamental starting point was twofold. On the one hand, it was the safeguarding of the people, and on the other, it was to consolidate and improve the combat effectiveness of the troops.

As early as September 1927, after the Autumn Harvest Uprisings in Hunan and Guizhou, Mao Zedong demanded that the officers and men of the autumn harvest revolt should be treated with enthusiasm and fair trade, without humiliating, beating, and insulting. In October, Mao announced the three disciplinary principles to the troops, a response to some problems that had arisen in the implementation of discipline among the insurgents at the time. These included 1) actively listening to commands, 2) not taking anyone's sweet potatoes, and 3) handing in any objects confiscated from local tyrants. The implementation of these three disciplines effectively enhanced the unity within the military and between the military and civilians. After the troops entered Jinggangshan, there was a disruption in discipline, mainly the result of continuous marches and numerous decentralized activities. In early January 1928, when the Red Army captured the county of Luanchuan, Mao summed up the experience of conducting mass work in a timely manner. Subsequently, he proposed six additional points to notice: 1) setting door panels, 2) bundling grass, 3) gentle speech, 4) fair trade, 5) returning borrowed items, and 6) paying for damaged items. By April 1928, after the insurgents had arrived at Shatian Village in Guidong County, Hunan Province, Mao officially announced the three major disciplinary actions to all the officers and men, changing the words "not taking anyone's sweet potatoes" to "do not take anything from the peasants and workers." In 1929, when Mao led the Red Fourth Army into the southern parts of Jiangxi and western parts of Fujian, he altered the six items to eight items, adding, "When bathing, avoid women" and "do not search prisoners for money." Later, with the continued development of the situation and the practical experience gained by the troops, he changed the phrase "do not take anything from the peasants and workers" to "do not even take needle or thread from the people." He likewise altered "handing in any objects confiscated from local tyrants " to "do not beat or insult anyone" and "do no damage to the crops." He went on to alter the rule against bathing in front of women to "do not womanize" and the injunction against searching prisoners to "do not abuse prisoners." In October 1947, when the War of Liberation entered the strategic period for counter-attack, in order to strengthen discipline and gain a national victory, the Central Committee and Mao Zedong revised and unified the content of the "Three Main Disciplines and Eight Codes of Conduct," after consultation with various units. The headquarters of the PLA issued the Instructions on the Reiteration of the Three Main Disciplines and Eight Codes of Conduct, drafted by Mao, to the entire army stationed in Jia County, northern Shaanxi Province, requiring the troops to be "deeply educated" and for the Instructions to be "strictly enforced."

The importance of the three disciplines and the additional eight codes of conduct were mainly manifested in the fact that they regulated the political, military, and mass discipline of the people's army, which reflected its disciplinary characteristics.

Political discipline was the norm for military political behavior and political speech, serving as an important guarantee for adjusting the relationship between the military, the class, and its political parties, regulating which class the military and its political parties served and which class its political parties were leading. "In all actions, follow commands" was the most important part of political discipline. When Mao led the Autumn Harvest Uprising troops to reorganize in Sanwan, he set about establishing the Party's organization and its representative system in the army, establishing the principle that "the branch was built from the company." A month later, when he proposed the three disciplines, the first was to follow commands in all actions. Although the disciplines and codes were revised several times, this article was retained, and it was always listed first. It vividly reflected the nature of the people's army and its purpose of wholeheartedly serving the people, showing that the Party directed the guns, rather than allowing guns to direct the Party. In stating "in all actions, follow commands," it indicated that the army's primary concern was to obey the Party's command and leadership. The PLA was the people's army created and led by the CPC. Its heads at all levels performed their duties and accomplished their tasks under the leadership of Party organizations at each level. For this reason, there was no conflict between obeying the Party's command and obeying the command of the executive head.

The Three Major Disciplines constituted the system for discipline in the PLA. They were the norm for military personnel and military operations, and an important guarantee for the military to complete tasks such as training, duty, combat readiness, and the completion of combat missions in wartime. Consolidating and improving combat effectiveness were the starting point and foothold of all the work of the people's army. For this reason, the military had to have the strictest discipline, and it had to strengthen that discipline. "In all actions, follow commands," "submit all confiscated items," and "do not abuse prisoners" were directives that meant to resolutely enforce this discipline, and they played an important role in cultivating organizational discipline, implementing prisoner's policies, and disintegrating enemy forces. For a revolutionary soldier to be loyal to his duties and dedicate himself to national defense, he must consciously cultivate his own professional discipline, which is to say, his military discipline.

Mass discipline was the norm for adjusting behavior in military-civilian relations. The PLA was a people's army whose sole purpose was serving the people wholeheartedly. The nature and purpose of the people's army had determined that the people and the people's army would rest and live together, like fish in water, completely depending on one another. The mass discipline of not violating any of the people's interests was a sort of invincible secret weapon for the people's army. There were a total of eleven items listed in the disciplines and codes, eight of which related to mass discipline, such as "do not take even a needle and thread from the people." " gentle speech," "fair trade," "return all borrowed items," "pay for all damaged items," "do not beat or insult," "do not damage crops," and "do not womanize." All of these principles highlighted the fundamental position and attitude of the people's army toward the people, an attitude founded on love and respect for the people.

Political, military, and mass disciplines were all components of the Three Major Disciplines and Eight Codes of Conduct, and they were interconnected. Political discipline played a leading role, serving as a foundation and pointing the way, while also restricting and influencing the implementation of the other disciplines. Military discipline was the main body of the disciplines, while mass discipline was what determined the nature of the people's army.

IV

The Theory of the People's War

1. Soldiers and Civilians as the Basis of Victory

The CPC's theory of the people's war was based on the conviction that the masses of the people were the determined forces of the revolutionary war and represented the fundamental interests of the broad masses of the people. It was the product of the combination of the basic principles of dialectical materialism with the practice of the Chinese revolutionary war, and it was the fullest embodiment of the Party's mass line during the revolutionary war.

Historical materialism holds that the people's masses are the makers of world history and the decisive force in all the activity, development, and transformation of human society. All major activities of society are inseparable from the people's participation, and their final outcome is determined by the will and might of the people. Mao succinctly summarized this idea in a single sentence, saying, "The people, and only the people, are the driving force in the making of the world's history."[61] He creatively applied this idea to the field of war, laying a solid foundation for the theory of the people's war. As early as the Agrarian Revolutionary War, Mao stated, "What is the real stronghold? It is the masses, the millions of people who truly support the revolution. This is the real stronghold, and its power cannot be broken. It is completely unbreakable. The counter-revolution cannot break us. Rather, we must break the counter-revolution. By uniting the millions of people around the revolutionary government and developing our revolutionary war, we can eliminate all counter-revolutions, and we can win all of China."[62] During the War of Resistance Against Japanese Aggression, in the face of the rampant aggression of Japanese imperialism, Mao pointed with great vision to the proletarian revolutions, noting that the deepest roots and greatest power of the revolution dwelled among the people. The main reason they had dared to bully China was the unorganized state of the Chinese people. Overcoming this shortcoming, China placed the Japanese aggressors before its tens of thousands of people, who stood up, like the flame surrounding a wild bull rushing into the fire, a shocking force that would scare or even burn the bull.[63] Once the War of

Liberation began, Mao clearly pointed out that it was the people who would decide the victory or defeat of the war.

The reason the people were such a source of military might was that the war was a special process of human social activity. In the final analysis, it was inseparable from the participation of the people.

The people were the source of manpower for the war effort, and manpower was the foundation of force in the war. One of the most important factors in determining military power is the size of the military. The history of war demonstrates that when the two sides in a war are of equal quality, the side that has the larger force has a greater chance of emerging victorious. The people are the pool from which soldiers are drawn. During the Chinese revolutionary wars, the main reason the communist forces were victorious was that the people continually sent additional forces to the troops. In the Liaoshen Campaign, the Northeast turned over a great number of peasants who joined the army and participated in the war. These peasants were combined into eighty second-line corps totaling about 300,000 people, and they continued to supplement the army. In the Huaihai Campaign, the CPC mobilized 168,000 people to join the army, guaranteeing a victory in the decisive battle. Marshal Chen Yi spoke enthusiastically of the great power of the people. In the poem "Notes on the Frontiers of Huaihai," he wrote, "Hundreds of thousands of workers can't get through, their horse carts carrying food, while the army moves east and west, competing for merit on the front line." General Su Yu hailed the people as the "inexhaustible source" of the defeat of the enemy.

The people are the source of material resources for a war, and war is a contest of material power. Without certain material conditions being met, it is impossible to discuss how one might win a war, and the most powerful source of material resources is the people, who are the producers of war materials. As a special social activity of humankind, war objectively requires the people to invest a certain amount of manpower and material resources to produce combat materials for war. As the war in China progressed, the demand for materials continued to increase. In a certain sense, the side which produced more advanced weapons and equipment and stored more combat materials would be able to sustain a longer period of combat, and thus eventually win the war.

The massive demand for materials in a war cannot be separated from the production of materials for the people. The people are not only the producers of war materials, but also the supply guarantors who transport these materials to the front line. The three major battles carried out by communist forces, Liaoshen, Huaihai, and Pingjin, used more than 5 million workers, more than 100,000 stretchers, 380,000 large vehicles, 1 million head of livestock, and 9.5 billion kilograms of grain. The tools of transportation overcame various difficulties and transported a large amount of combat materials to the front line to meet the needs of the war. Mao once said, with great emotion, that the War of Liberation was mainly won by 600 million people in the north. He said, "As long as we rely on the people, we firmly believe that their creativity will be timely and reliable, and thus we trust the people. If we are one with the people, any difficulty can be overcome, and no enemy will overwhelm us. Rather, we will overwhelm all our enemies."[64]

The great strength of the war was borne in the hearts of the people. Victory in the war was inseparable from their support in the form of manpower and material resources, which was inseparable from the people's willingness to bear this burden. Whether a war is just or unjust is a question closely related to the interests of the masses. The different purposes of war determine the people's attitude toward it, which in turn determines the amount of human and material resources they are willing to invest in it. The degree of their conscious initiative in the war determines the army's ability to overcome difficulties and persist in combat, which ultimately determines the outcome of the war. Mao once asserted that the advantage Chiang Kai-shek held in terms of military strength was only a temporary factor, just as the assistance he received from American imperialists was a temporary factor. The anti-peoples nature of Chiang's war and the people's willingness to bear the burden to oppose it were enduring factors. In this respect, the PLA had an advantage. The revolutionary nature of the patriotic justice of the PLA's war required support by the people of the entire country. This was the political basis for Chiang's defeat. It was precisely because he waged a just war that Mao was able to elicit the willingness of the people to bear the burden of the war. Zhu De affirmed this point from the perspective of a summary of historical experience in his article "How the Chinese People Defeated the Chiang Kai-shek Reactionaries and the American Imperialists." He pointed out that it was no accident that Chiang Kai-shek, the running dog of American imperialists, fell so quickly and tragically. This was the inevitable ending of an adventurer against the people. This was the historical judgment Chiang had made during the 22 years of bloody reactionary rule in China and the bloody reactionary rule of the imperialists in China for more than 100 years. The reason the revolutionary war was so actively supported by the broad masses of the people was that the purpose of the revolutionary war was fundamentally in line with the interests of the broad masses of the people, and the hearts of the people were invincible.

2. The Rural Revolutionary Base Area as a Strategic Base Adhering to a Long-Term People's War

The establishment of a revolutionary base was an important part of Mao's thought on the people's war. During the Agrarian Revolutionary War, he repeatedly emphasized the importance of implementing the armed divisions of peasants and workers and criticized roving bandits. Later, in his article "Strategic Issues in the Anti-Japanese Guerrilla War," he systematically discussed the idea of establishing a base. He pointed out that the rural revolutionary base area was the strategic base for the people's war "to carry out its own strategic tasks and achieve the purpose of preserving and developing itself while destroying and expelling the enemy. Without such a strategic base, the implementation of all strategic tasks and the realization of the purpose of war will lose all support."[65] During the War of Liberation, when the army had shifted focus from a strategic defense to a strategic offense, Mao continued to instruct the army to advance into enemy-occupied territory and establish a revolutionary base to deal with the far-reaching enemy.

Why was it necessary for the people's war to establish a revolutionary base area? Primarily, fundamentally speaking, this was determined by the cruel, long-term nature of the war.

Mao stated, "The enemy of the Chinese revolution is extremely powerful. It is not only the might of imperialism, but also of feudalism, and at certain times, reactionaries from the bourgeoisie have colluded with the imperialists and feudalists and acted as enemies of the people."[66] They not only held political, economic, and military power, but also used naked violence to oppress and exploit the Chinese people and suppress the revolutionary party and the revolutionary masses. The revolutionary forces were relatively weak, and the Chinese people did not have political freedom or economic power, and it was difficult for the military forces to engage in a decisive battle with the enemy. Because the enemy was extremely powerful, the might of the Chinese revolution could not go through a long period of accumulation and exercise, and it was not capable of bringing about a final victory over the enemy. Because the enemy's suppression of the Chinese revolution was extremely cruel and the revolutionary forces were unable to undergo long-term tempering to forge their tenacity before being forced into battle, they were unable to hold their positions or seize the enemy's positions. This long-term, cruel nature of the revolutionary war was the deciding factor driving the army to focus their revolutionary struggle not on cities at the center of areas under enemy control, but on rural villages where the enemy was relatively weak. Mao observed, "If the revolutionaries are not willing to compromise with the imperialists and their lackeys, we must persist in our struggle. If revolutionaries are prepared to exercise their might to save the nation, in the absence of military strength and facing a powerful enemy, it is necessary to create forward and rear bases in undeveloped rural areas, which will lead to a great revolutionary military, political, economic, and cultural position, from which we may oppose the fierce enemy in the cities by attacking from rural bases. This will allow us to gradually strive for full victory in the long-term revolutionary fight."[67]

In addition, China's revolutionary war was essentially a peasant war under the leadership of the proletariat. To carry out a people's war, it was necessary to mobilize and rely on the peasants. Only by establishing a base in the countryside was it possible to lead the peasants to carry out an in-depth agrarian revolution, enabling the peasantry to address their own vital interests through a land struggle. This gave them a greater understanding of the CPC's leadership, engendering their trust in the revolution and establishing a solid alliance of workers and peasants. In this way, the peasants could be fully mobilized to join the people's war.

While emphasizing that China's proletariat was leading the revolution and was its most basic driving force, Mao also pointed out that the Chinese proletariat had its own inherent weaknesses. For instance, it had fewer people (relative to the peasantry) and was younger (compared to the national proletariat in capitalist countries), making it impossible for the proletariat to emerge victorious in the Chinese revolution if it fought alone. In order to fulfill its historical mission, the Chinese proletariat had to rely on its most determined ally, the peasant class.

In analyzing the dynamics of the semi-colonial, semi-feudal Chinese revolution, Mao pointed out that peasants made up 80% of China's population, making them the main force of China's national economy. More than 90% were poor or middle class peasants, of which 70% were poor farmers. They were heavily oppressed and exploited under feudalism and imperialism. In particular, poor peasants, who accounted for 70% of the total number of peasants, had either no land or insufficient land. They were a rural semi-proletarian group, the most powerful force in the Chinese revolution, the main force in the movement. As early as March 1927, Mao discussed the seriousness of the peasant issue in his Investigation Report on the Hunan Peasant Movement. In 1928, in the articles "How Can China's Red Regime Last?" and "The Struggle in Jinggangshan," he noted that the Chinese revolution had to combine armed struggle and the agrarian revolution and to establish revolutionary base areas in the countryside. In 1930, in the article "A Single Spark Can Start a Prairie Fire," he went on to discuss the establishment and development of the Red Army guerrilla forces and the Red Area as the most important form and inevitable result of the peasant struggle under the leadership of the proletariat in semi-colonial, semi-feudal China. He criticized the idea of opposing the role of the proletarian leadership and the main force of the peasant revolution. He pointed out that the revolution in semi-colonial China would only succeed if the peasant struggle secured the leadership of the proletariat and peasant leadership were not allowed to exceed proletarian leadership. Were peasant leadership to emerge, it would not be conducive to the revolution. Therefore, the armed struggle of the CPC was a peasant war under the leadership of the proletariat. This determined that the vast rural areas where the peasants were located should be the starting point and main foothold to gain victory in the Chinese revolution. The encirclement of cities with rural strongholds was the inevitable trend and result of a peasant revolutionary war.

Finally, it was necessary for the revolutionary army to defeat the enemy and avoid fighting against a powerful enemy whom it was not strong enough to defeat. It was necessary to consolidate and develop a strategic base and accumulate a revolutionary force so that, over the course of a long-term conflict, gradual accumulation of small wins would lead to a larger victory and create the conditions that would lead to ultimate victory for the revolution.

Mao said, "What is a base for guerrilla warfare? It is a base that carries out its own strategic tasks to achieve self-preservation and self-development and to destroy or expel the enemy. Without such a strategic base, the implementation and realization of all strategic tasks will lose support. An original feature of guerrilla warfare is that it occurs behind enemy lines, because it is separated from the rest of the country. However, without bases, guerrilla warfare will not survive or develop over the long-term. Such bases are also part of the guerrilla warfare behind enemy lines."[68] He observed that because of the large numbers of troops in the Red Army and the participation of the masses throughout the country, particularly in the southern provinces, roguish political thought was generated in the Red Army. Such thinking was evident in 1) an unwillingness to do hard work to establish a stronghold and establish the political power of the people, thus expanding their political influence, but preferring instead to use only mobile guerrilla methods to expand political influence, 2) expanding the Red Army but not through expanding the Red Guards and local Red forces to expanding the Red Army, opting instead to take an approach of "recruiting soldiers and buying horses" or "recruiting rebels and the captured," and 3) an impatience to struggle as one with the masses, hoping only to rush to the big city to eat and drink. The result of such roguish thinking was to hinder the Red Army in the proper execution of its tasks. For this reason, eliminating hooliganism was an important goal of ideological struggle within the Red Army. It had to be acknowledged that the history of Huang Chao and Li Zicheng's hooliganism were no longer allowed for in the current environment. Later, Mao pointed out, "The base area is very small, but it has great political power. It is quite opposed to the KMT regime. It is very difficult for the KMT to attack our army, because we have the aid of the peasants."[69] Thus, Mao pointed to the correct approach for addressing the question of the strategic base for the people's guerrilla warfare, which was to establish rural revolutionary bases.

The rural revolutionary bases were one of the main creative initiatives of the CPC during the revolutionary war. As Mao noted, "in a county covered by a White regime, there are a few small areas of Red political power. Currently, China is the only one in the world where such a thing is happening."[70] This necessity was determined by the special conditions of the Chinese revolutionary war, and it was a major development in military theory among Marxists. With the revolutionary base areas, the basic conditions were in place for self-preservation, self-development, and destroying the enemy. There was a certain human and material guarantee for long-term support of the war. The weak Red Army had a relatively stable environment for training and combat effectiveness. It was possible to choose a good battlefield on which to fight and destroy the enemy through various forms of struggle and with the cooperation of the local people.

3. System of Armed Forces in the People's War

While relying on the masses to carry out the people's war, it was necessary to work hard to organize and arm the masses, mobilizing their enthusiasm for participating in the war to the furthest extent. With its focus on armed struggle during the war years, the Party worked hard to formulate a system of armed forces that employed the three characteristic combinations of a people's war. That is, it combined the regular army with mass groups, the main forces with local armies, and armed masses with unarmed people. These three combinations not only addressed the issue of mutual cooperation in combat, but also led to cooperation between the front and rear and addressed the issue of the development and growth of the people's army and the consolidation of the revolutionary base areas.

a) *The combination of the regular army and armed mass organizations.* The term "regular army" pointed to the formal gathering of a people's army throughout various historical periods, under a unified command, system, and clothing. An "armed mass force" included armed groups such as guerrillas or militias. Guerrilla and militia troops were irregular armed groups that attacked the enemy in divergent, mobile, and offensive methods in enemy-occupied territory. They were generally characterized by a lean staff, simple organization, light equipment, and flexible mobility. The combination of the regular army and guerrilla forces was determined by the fact that the Chinese revolutionary war was a largely guerrilla war, which required the exertion of the power of the armed masses.

Mao believed that in carrying out the people's war, it was necessary to have a strong army. At the same time, it was necessary to establish extensive armed mass groups that could be combined with the regular army. He noted, "The reason for this army's power is partly due to the People's Self-Defense Force and the armed militias of the masses, which cooperate to fight with us." He added, "Without the cooperation of these armed mass forces, it would be impossible to defeat the enemy."[71] This demonstrated that the people's army and the armed mass forces were like a car and its wheels. The people's army was the backbone of the people's war, and the mass armed organizations formed its broad foundation.

It was on the basis of this understanding that in its organization and leadership in the revolutionary war, the CPC always made great efforts to create and develop the people's army on the one hand, and on the other, placed great importance on the establishment and development of armed mass organizations. During the period of the Red Army, the Red Guards were organized in various revolutionary base areas. During the Agrarian Revolutionary War, Mao emphasized the development and expansion of the masses and advocated the militarization of the countryside. He stated that it was necessary for the Red Army to help the Red Guards and the riot teams of the workers and peasants by providing weapons and to help the people be armed as much as possible without reducing the combat effectiveness of the Red Army. Before the first anti-encirclement campaign, under deployment orders from Mao, the Red Guards, Young Pioneers, pickets, security guards, and Red Army reserves were established in the base areas, and a unified commanding body of the People's Armed Forces, along with stretchers, transport crews, and modes of transport were established and carefully organized. After the victory of the first anti-encirclement campaign, in order to prepare to smash the enemy's next efforts to encircle, Mao not only corrected the wrong practice of leftist leaders at that time, but also focused on "concentrating guns in the Red Army" and local troops, while also vigorously developing the armed mass forces. Red guerrilla bases were established in white areas, and Red Guards battalions (companies) and independent battalions were established in various counties and districts along the border. The tasks, preparations, training, and tactics of these armed forces were discussed in detail, and regulations further improved their military and political quality, allowing them to effectively cooperate with the Red Army to smash the enemy's next encirclement campaign. For this reason, Mao pointed out that the guerrilla warfare of the people and the main Red Army were like two hands, right and left. He said, "Only with the guerrillas do we have the Red Army. Without the people, the Red Army would be like a one-armed general. Based on the conditions of the people and the terrain, arming the people is the appropriate form of combat. The enemy fears this tactic. That is what is most important."[72] During the War of Resistance Against Japanese Aggression, in all the anti-Japanese base areas, all eligible young adults participated in the armed mass organizations under voluntary and non-production conditions. The number of militiamen grew to 2.2 million, and the People's Self-Defense Force grew to nearly 10 million. By the time of the War of Liberation, the militia organizations in the liberated areas had grown to 5.5 million. When Zhu De discussed the great role of the mass armed forces in the people's war, he pointed out that the huge militia force in the liberated areas was like nothing ever seen before in the history of the Chinese army. The Party had learned to organize the militias. This was a matter of great significance. Once the militias were organized, they were either incorporated into the regular army or fought independently. The production movement of the people in liberated areas, the great protection of the militia, the recovery of many enemy strongholds, and the acquisition of the militias played a key role. At the same time, the militia self-defense forces also generally bore the task of production, combining military and production work with labor forces. The implementation of such tasks transformed many of the old ways in the countryside.

b) *Combining the main force and local corps*. Based on the demands of the struggle, the people's army was divided into two parts, the main force and local armies. Mao pointed out that this division was another factor contributing to the might of the people's army.

The main force was highly concentrated, possessed great organizational discipline, and had superior weapons and equipment. It was not restricted to a single fixed area, but could carry out tasks across strategic regions at any time according to the strategic needs at the national level. In cooperation with local corps and militias, it carried out large-scale battles and even strategic battles to destroy large enemy forces. The local corps were a force that operated within a certain area of the country. They cooperated with the militias to defend that place and attack the enemy in specific areas. The local corps was an important link between the main army and the armed mass groups. It was an important arm for developing the army, strengthening the people, and implementing the people's war. In terms of combat, they cooperated with the main army to take on more important tasks, while also playing a supporting role in the struggle against the enemy within a specified region. In relation to the masses, most of the commanders of these forces were born and raised in these locales, and so knew the geographical environment and the customs of the people. It was easy for them to mingle with the local people and help the war effort to root itself among the masses. For this reason, they were more able to mobilize and organize the masses to participate in and support the people's war. In expanding the military, it was easier to organize and absorb the militias and masses to join the army and, if necessary, incorporate them into the main force.

The main force and the local forces were focused on different things, but the overarching purpose of their operations was the same. Only by closely combining the two could the enemy be attacked more effectively. Mao had always attached great importance to the construction and integration of the main force and the local corps. He pointed out, "The reason this army is strong is that it divides itself into two parts, a main force and local corps. The former can carry out combat missions across locales at any time, while the latter's missions are in fixed areas and are coordinated with the militia and self-defense forces protecting that place and attacking enemy forces stationed there. This division of labor won the full support of the people. If there had been no such division, with, for instance, all attention placed on the role of the main force while ignoring the local corps, it would have been impossible to defeat the enemy given the conditions of China's liberated areas."[73]

In the period of the Agrarian Revolutionary War, some people only paid attention to the construction of the main Red Army and not to that of local forces. Mao criticized this mindset. He first affirmed the importance of building the main force of the Red Army, pointing out, "The local Red Guards alone, without the help of the official Red Army, can deal with the landlords, but not with the official White Army. Therefore, though there are good workers and peasants in such forces, if they are not formally armed with considerable strength, they will certainly not be able to create a separatist situation, nor will they be able to develop it in the long term."[74] At the same time, Mao attached great importance to the construction of local armed forces, clearly stipulating that helping develop local armed forces was a major task of the Red Army. Mao believed that there should be both the main Red Army and local armed forces, and that the two should combine and cooperate. In summing up the experience of the Jinggangshan struggle, he said, "After more than a year, we created a situation in which the struggle was an armed struggle. This was very rare, as the whole place was armed, and that was coupled with the strength of the Fourth Army and the Red Army, resulting in a force that no enemy could destroy."[75] During the anti-Japanese war, Mao further elaborated on this point of view and asked the Eighth Route Army and the New Fourth Army to help local people organize local troops and local corps led by local people's cadres. In the construction of the local corps, in an effort to adapt to the needs of the enemy's struggle, he also requested the organization of a well-trained armed task force with good military training and solid political and democratic work. After driving deeper into enemy territory, they attacked the enemy and launched the anti-Japanese struggle among the people, building effective cooperation in the anti-Japanese base areas. In order to strengthen the local armed forces, during the War of Resistance Against Japanese Aggression, the Eighth Route Army and the New Fourth Army also adopted the practice of localization of the main force in some areas. During the most difficult period of the War of Resistance, in line with the spirit of the instructions from the CPC Central Committee, the Eighth Route Army and the New Fourth Army reduced their main forces and decentralized no less than one-third of the main forces to various military divisions, independent regiments, guerrilla brigades, and so forth. The military and political qualities of the local armies consolidated their bases. In the later period of the anti-Japanese war, some local troops gathered under certain conditions and transformed into a regiment of the main force to complete large-scale regular combat missions. During the War of Liberation, the local troops were upgraded in time to make the PLA's main force rapidly expand to millions of people, due to the important conditions created by the rapid victory in the war.

c) *Combining armed and unarmed masses*. To exert the power of the people's war, it was necessary to arm the masses and create conditions for the people's direct participation in the war. But it was not enough to have only armed people, because the armed people could not be the whole of the masses of people, nor could they be the majority. Most of the people were unarmed, and it was crucial to be able to indirectly organize their forces into the war effort. Only by combining the armed and unarmed masses could the people's war of universal participation be truly formed. Thus, the combination of armed and unarmed people was a matter of the overall integration of the people's war.

It was not only a matter of establishing armed mass organizations, but also unarmed mass organizations, so that all the people could participate in certain organizations linked to the cause of the people's war. This was a key link closely connecting the two. That is to say that, on the one hand, it was necessary to establish people's forces, such as people's militias or self-defense armies. At the same time, it was important to extensively establish mass organizations such as trade unions, peasant associations, student unions, women's associations, and children's groups, and to organize all unarmed people and bring them under the leadership of the Party and the revolutionary government, so that they could exert their own strength for the sake of the victory in the people's war.

The combination of armed and unarmed people was largely evident in the combination of armed and non-armed struggle. Armed people's groups had certain military qualities, possessing weapons and fully capable of using them. For this reason, they were the basic force for carrying out the people's war. The role of the unarmed people's groups in supporting the front line and giving long-term support to the revolutionary effort likewise could not be ignored. They were an indispensable force in the revolutionary war. Most importantly, the unarmed people's groups could "help the military in all aspects of their work,"[76] which is usually referred to as supporting the front line. Primarily, support went to the regular army. For example, efforts geared at mobilizing people to join the army, transporting food for the army, offering preferential treatment to military families, and helping the troops address their material difficulties all fell under this umbrella. In addition, support was given to militias and guerrillas. This included recruiting people to join the guerrillas or militias, helping guerrilla or militia troops carry out attacks, engaging in reconnaissance of the enemy's situation on local troops' behalf, removing spies, standing guard, and transporting or protecting the wounded, all of which offered direct aid to the fighting in which these forces engaged. In the three major battles of the War of Liberation, with a slogan of "full support for the front line, all for victory," the number of workers recruited in the masses reached more than 5 million, so that the ratio of soldiers to workers reached first one to one, then one to two, then one to three. This was truly a people's war, a rarity in the history of the world. In addition, the unarmed people's groups were able to "warmly engage in the political, economic, cultural, and health construction."[77] This was referred to as the construction of the base area.

If there were no masses performing political, economic, cultural, educational, and health construction in the base areas, there would be no foundations for the people's war. During the people's war, on the one hand, the army assisted the people's various struggles in combat and, on the other, the people employed various methods of struggle (political, economic, cultural, transportation, and military) to aid the army. Without such cooperation, the revolutionary forces could not win. It is important to note here that mobilizing the masses to participate in the war was not only an organizational and military issue, but also had to have corresponding political and economic policies to ensure that the people could be masters of politics and could be practical in leading the economy. Zhu De said in his article "The Battlefields of the Liberated Areas" that the liberated areas had implemented two appropriate policies. He wrote, "The military is related to politics and economics. The basic concern of the people's war is mass war, of which politics and economics are the overriding concerns. Only when political and economic issues are being addressed can such a people's war be carried out."

In summary, the system of armed forces in the people's war was an important part of the thinking in relation to the people's war. It not only created a reliable foundation for the quality of the soldiers and self-defense forces, but also enabled the main force to garner strong cooperation from various types of armed forces in battle, forming a sort of network of people's wars. One important factor behind the army's strength was the system integrating three levels of armed forces.

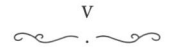

V

Strategies and Tactics in the People's War

1. Strategic Thinking Regarding Active Defense

The CPC's strategy and tactics for the people's war were born and developed through the practice of the Chinese revolutionary war. During the long period of the Chinese revolution, the enemy was strong, while revolutionary forces were weak. The enemy facing the revolutionary army, whether it was the KMT reactionary faction, Japanese imperialists, or American imperialists, had far more military and economic power than did the revolutionary forces. However, the revolutionaries held an absolutely superior position politically, as the army was led by the Communist Party of China. The war it carried out was a just war and a revolutionary war. The enemy carrying out the war was regressive, and the war unjust and reactionary. With the broad support of the people, the army's morale was high. The basic starting point of the Party's strategic and tactical thinking was to start from the actual situation of itself and the enemy and give full play to the subjective initiative on the basis of the established objective material conditions, to guide the war to greatest advantage and avoiding loss, and to defeat an enemy who possessed superior equipment. A series of military strategies were formed from this basic idea.

The Party's practice, based on an active defense policy and the practical experience gained in the Chinese revolutionary war, was to recognize active defense, oppose negative defense, implement an enduring and strategic defensive war, and implement an offensive war externally.

What are active and negative defense? This was the first issue to be addressed in the implementation of a strategic defense. Mao stated, "Active defense is also known as pre-emptive attacks or decisive defense. Negative defense is also known as pure defense. Negative defense is actually a false form of defense. Only active defense is true defense, including counter-attacks or pre-emptive action."[78] He believed that active defense was the mutual application of guided defense and offense in combat. Defending, preserving military power, and competing were means of assisting the offense or preparing to turn to offense. Negative defense did not allow for counter-attack or offensives. In combat, it only took the role of simple defense and never employed offensive means.

The strategic thinking of active defense was embodied in the strategic implementation of enduring defensive warfare in strategy, but of offensive warfare in battle. The inner line was focused on the front line, and the time for combat was determined by the long-term objectives, while pre-emptive attacks defined the form of fighting. Strategically, this was mainly determined by the situation of the enemy and the army's own relative weakness, which required the revolutionary force to take a long-lasting defensive approach, since it was in the disadvantaged position. Mao believed that, in order to fight for initiative in the war and to annihilate the enemy's vital forces, it was necessary for the revolutionaries to shift gears and engage in offensives outside of the main battle line, because the enemy would only be destroyed in large numbers by attacking them and gradually altering the gap between the revolutionary army and the enemy. Externally, the army could encircle the enemy on all sides to achieve the goal of defending against the enemy. In short, only by carrying out an offensive battle externally could the army move from a strategic passive state to an active battle, while gradually saving their living forces while smashing the enemy and preventing the enemy's constant offenses against the revolutionaries in counter-revolutionary encirclement campaigns. How could the Party transform its military from a strategic defensive warfare to an external quick-attack offensive war? The key was to adopt a policy of "inducing the enemy to go deeper." This was a planned and necessary step taken to preserve the military's reserves and attack the enemy so as to deplete its strengths. The necessity and benefits of doing this were 1) it enable the army to avoid an unfavorable decisive battle with the enemy and wait for a more favorable situation before engaging in a decisive battle, 2) it would allow the army to contract and concentrate its forces, turning its strength into weakness and the revolutionaries' weakness into strength and allowing the external battle to be an offensive, and 3) it meant the enemy would be trapped in the depth of the base areas, like a blind man riding a blind horse and finding it difficult to walk. As a result, the bloated force would grow thin, and once thinned, would be dragged to its death, greatly reducing the enemy's advantage. The revolutionary army would be like a fish in water, moving freely, which would enable it to transform its passive strategy to an offensive, seeking a favorable situation to launch a quick attack.

This strategic thinking regarding national defense was an accumulation of practical experience gained during the Chinese revolution. During the Agrarian Revolutionary War, the weak Red Army constantly faced a strong enemy attack. Its most serious task at that time was demolishing the enemy's encirclement campaigns, so the main task related to active defense was to "conserve power while assaulted, harass the stationed enemy, attack the tired enemy, and pursue the escaping enemy's force." Every encirclement would be victorious and see further development based on its success in ensuring the survival of the Red Army. The basic principle of guerrilla warfare, i.e., the "tactics of 16 characters"[79] were the initial strategic form employed for national defense, including the basic principle of allowing the enemy to approach the Party's forces then harassing the enemy, so that the enemy would tire and retreat. By the beginning of November 1930, before the first anti-encirclement campaign in the central soviet area, it clearly stated the principle of inducing the enemy to penetrate further into Red territory. In the course of the Long March, after the First and Fourth Armies of the Red Army were reunited in 1935, the strategic policy concentrating the main force to attack the north, destroying the enemy in battle, and first obtaining the southern part of Gansu to create a base area in the Sichuan-Shaanxi-Gansu area was set. During the War of Resistance Against Japanese Aggression, Mao Zedong offered in-depth clarification of the characteristics in the time of the Sino-Japanese War, analyzed the basic factors of the conflict with the enemy and the enemy's evolution throughout the course of the war, and noted that the anti-Japanese war was a protracted military effort, in which the final victory would be China's when judged objectively. He predicted that the War of Resistance would undergo three stages: strategic defense, strategic stalemate, and strategic counter-attack. The general strategic direction of the War of Resistance should be that of a protracted war. The specific strategies would include, in the first and second phases, strategic implementation of sustained defensive tactics, with combat initiatives carried out away from the main front. The third phase would be a strategic counter-attack. Mao pointed out that communist forces should see themselves as engaged in a war against an enemy, and when faced with encirclement campaigns, the main strategy employed should be an active defense to systematically break the enemy's siege and "sweeping" in an effort to continually expand the communist army's power and promote the expansion and development of the base area, gathering strength for a counter-attack. The Eighth Route Army should implement independent guerrilla warfare in the mountains. While guerrilla warfare was the basic form of efforts there, other types of maneuvers should not be relaxed, when conditions were favorable. In the early days of the War of Liberation, given the enemy's strength and the Red forces' relative weakness, the enemy's strategy was to attack the strategic defenses of the communist army, meaning an active defense to avoid the enemy front and with a cutting edge, and mobile warfare. Its main goal was to destroy the enemy's vital forces, making this the main task the communist fighters faced. Mao noted that it was possible for communist forces to defeat Chiang Kai-shek. The Party should have full confidence in this, and the main combat method employed against Chiang should be mobile warfare. For this reason, in some places, the temporary abandonment of the cities was not only inevitable, but also necessary. Temporarily abandoning a number of cities in many places was actually a great effort aimed at destroying the enemy, transforming the disparity between communist and enemy forces, and ultimately achieving a final victory. Mao proposed the strategic principle of "a primary goal of taking the enemy's vitality, without focusing on conserving our own or letting that become our primary task."[80] He likewise suggested the operational principles and methods of "concentrating superior forces and destroying the enemy."[81] After the People's Liberation Army gradually came to grasp the strategic initiative and strategic power to achieve a relative balance with the enemy, it proposed to strategically defend, strategically counter-attack, and launch strategic offensives at the right time, putting forward the well-known "Ten Major Military Principles" as the core idea for destroying the enemy. When the conditions were ripe for the decisive strategic battle, Mao accurately selected the appropriate time for that fight, stipulated the direction it would take, and formulated operational guidelines for the three major battles of Liaoshen, Huaihai, and Pingjin, combining large-scale mobile warfare with large-scale positional warfare, destroying many enemy forces. During the strategic pursuit, the principle of combining the implementation of broad encirclement and retreat was proposed, and the general policy of active defense was fully applied and developed. In short, these specific strategic directions and operational principles proposed by Mao at various stages during the revolutionary war were the specific implementation and concrete manifestation of the general policy of active defense during different periods or stages of the war. From this, we can see that there was no fixed model for how to implement the general policy of active defense. Instead, it was constantly developing according to the changing military situation.

2. Creative Use and Development of Various Forms of Combat

Mao stated that "the essence and purpose of war is to defend oneself and destroy one's enemy. However, there are three types of wars for achieving this purpose, mobile, stationary, and guerrilla warfare."[82] Adapting to the developments of a changing war situation according to the growth and decline of the enemy and the evolution of the military situation was a necessary part of self-preservation and the destruction of the enemy, and it required a military transformation that kept adaptation of military form to the current situation as its focus. One of Mao's key military achievements was his determination to employ a strategic policy that conformed to the actual, objective situation, selecting appropriate combat methods and flexibly employing multiple combat forms in a closely integrated, complementary way. Mobile, stationary, and guerrilla warfare were three different approaches to combat, the former two being models for regular warfare and the latter a form of irregular warfare. Mobile warfare was a form of offensive combat in which the regular line of a long front and large battle zone engaged in battles. Stationary warfare was a defensive form waged from a solid field or position. Guerrilla warfare was a form of decentralized combat and a form of armed mass struggle. The three forms had different characteristics and functions. The characteristics of mobile warfare were that concentrated forces or regular regiments engaged in battle. They were fluid offensive forces, and they played a major role in destroying the enemy, changing the situation of the war, and finally resolving the fate of the war. Stationary warfare was characterized by ample preparation time, good organization, and the long duration of its operations. It played an important role in defending against the attacks of a strong enemy and attacking the enemy's strongly fortified areas. The characteristics of guerrilla warfare were more active, flexible, and quicker than mobile warfare. Speed and mobility were crucial in the coordination for the survival and development of formal operations of weak forces.

In the course of leading the Chinese revolutionary war, the Party conducted in-depth research on these three types of combat methods, as well as closely integrating them, developing the theory on the forms of warfare, and creatively and flexibly applying the three forms of combat. Throughout the long-term practice of the Chinese revolutionary war over a 20-year span, the people's army flexibly applied different forms of warfare in different historical periods, depending on the historical and military conditions of the times. In the three years before the Agrarian Revolutionary War and throughout the entire anti-Japanese war, guerrilla warfare was the main form of combat. During the War of Liberation, stationary warfare became the main form, and in the later part of the War of Resistance Against US Aggression and Aid to Korea, it became the main form. The main forms of warfare employed were modified according to the changing war situation, and the three forms were closely combined, complementing each other as they were flexibly applied, so that the great might of the people's war could be put to work most effectively. As early as 1938, Mao commented, "Some people say we only advocate guerrilla warfare, and that this is a chaotic form. We have always advocated the cooperation of mobile, stationary, and guerrilla warfare." He added, "Based on the experience of the past seven months of combat, if we can use all three methods of warfare, we will make matters extremely difficult for the enemy."[83] The people's army did not reject traditional warfare on all occasions during the period it mainly relied on guerrilla warfare. Mao's policy for the Eighth Route Army during the anti-Japanese war was that "guerrilla warfare is our basic approach, but we must not neglect mobile warfare when conditions are favorable."[84] On the battlefield, there were stationary battles in the mobile warfare, and mobile battles in the stationary warfare. It was also often the case that a mobile battle could morph into a stationary battle, and vice versa. During the Chinese revolutionary war, communist forces used various forms of warfare flexibly and organically, combining them in such a way as to create one of the great military wonders of human history.

3. Formation of Combat Methods with Chinese Revolutionary Characteristics

With the main goal being the annihilation of the enemy's forces, the main operational method employed by the communist forces was to concentrate the main forces to destroy the enemy's superior force. The effect of this tactic was that it could be both thorough and quick. As a result, it became the basic principle of warfare for the communist army. The concentration of the main force and annihilation of the enemy's forces were two sides of the same coin. Only by concentrating the main force would the goal of defeating the enemy be achieved, and only by defeating the enemy could a superior force be formed, creating an advantage for communist forces.

The Chinese revolutionary war was carried out under the conditions of the local weaker, smaller force confronting a stronger, larger invader, and it relied on a strategy geared toward a long-term defensive war. For this reason, it was more difficult and more important to focus on the problem of the enemy's superior strength. To this end, during the Jinggangshan struggle, Mao consistently emphasized the use of military force in a centralized manner, an issue which he discussed thoroughly and in depth. In 1928, he observed, "In our experience, the division of soldiers has not once failed, and if the concentration of troops is less than or equal to, or occasionally slightly larger than, the enemy's troops, we often win."[85] In 1936, he summed up the communist forces' 10-year agrarian revolution, stating that during the course of the war, the issue of concentrated forces was specifically discussed, saying, "The pursuit of victory from a strategic defense basically relies on the concentration of troops."[86] Here, Mao mainly referred to the idea that the communist force was strategically weaker, but was good at consolidating its main forces, and only in this way was it able to change the disparity with the enemy, at least partially, and go from a position of weakness to strength and from a defensive to an offensive position. It also changed its strategy from fighting inside the lines to fighting outside, thus gaining local advantages and enabling various initiatives, which in turn led to the destruction of the enemy. After winning numerous skirmishes, the overall advantage shifted. This was what was meant by "relying on our own local advantages and initiatives and the enemy's partial disadvantages and passive state to win this battle and the rest. With each breakthrough, we were able to come closer to a shift in the overall situation."[87]

During the War of Liberation, Mao further discussed the idea of concentrating the main force. On behalf of the Central Military Commission, he drafted operational instructions concerning "concentrating main forces and destroying the enemy," pointing out that "this is the path to victory over Chiang Kai-shek. It is our main method of attack. If we implement this method, we will win. If we go against it, we will fail."[88] In the well-known "Ten Main Military Principles," he further stressed that "every battle concentrates the absolutely superior forces (double, triple, quadruple, and sometimes even five or six times the enemy's strength) to surround the enemy on all sides. They strive to be thorough, allowing none to get through the net."[89] He pointed out in great detail that the communist forces' military operation had to "maintain the annihilation of the enemy's forces as its main goal, not conservation or capture of a city or specific location,"[90] because it was only the annihilation of the enemy that would ultimately have the power to preserve or capture a city or certain place. In a situation in which the enemy was strong and communist forces weak, this was the only way to avoid an unfavorable decisive battle with the enemy. Mao noted, "It is not only inevitable that we will lose many places or temporarily abandon numerous cities, but is also necessary. Temporary abandonment of such places is for the purpose of achieving a final victory. Without doing so, we will not achieve ultimate victory."[91] Mao observed, "For the sake of the people, it is better to break one finger in an effort to avoid breaking ten. For the enemy, it is better to destroy ten of its divisions than to destroy just one."[92] If enemy was annihilated by the established system, it would encounter greater difficulties, and it would lose one part of its force. Such a battle of annihilation would deal a psychological blow to the enemy, frustrate its morale, and shake its military morale. For the communist troops, it would greatly inspire a military spirit. The people's hearts and morale would be lifted, and the army would be further fortified with things such as manpower, equipment, and supplies. It was difficult to achieve these goals in battle, or to gain victory through a war of attrition. Of course, this did not negate the significance of defeat in any battle under any conditions. Mao once pointed out, "Main mobile warfare is for the execution of a mission to annihilate. Positional warfare is for the execution of the task of preservation. Guerrilla warfare is for both."[93]

How could the troops be concentrated? How many needed to be concentrated in order to eliminate the enemy's advantage? Based on the experience of the communist forces, this was mainly reflected in several principles.

The first principle was to focus on the main operational direction, conserve as a secondary direction, and oppose military egalitarianism. The people's army had long been operating in a beleaguered environment. The enemies it faced were numerous and powerful. They had to concentrate on the main goal in their combat missions, not attacking or dividing their troops. Mao said, "Under these conditions, in which we face such a strong enemy, no matter how many troops there are, we must have only one direction at a time, not two."[94] The so-called concentrated main force was to focus on the dominant force and, at the decisive moment, form the main direction of the operation. In the secondary direction, only part of the force was squeezed. Only in this way could a fist be formed, creating an advantage and ensuring victory. Liu Bocheng observed, "Every offensive battle must select its main offensive direction and assemble its main force there if it is to win a decisive battle. But at the same time, in the secondary direction, the enemy must be squeezed enough to attract its attention, in order to guarantee the success of the main assault. In other words, we can use one person to defeat three enemy soldiers, so that those three will be drawn away from the main direction, opening up the way for us to gain an overall victory."[95]

In line with the experience gained and lessons learned during the PLA's many years of fighting, the Party emphasized that everything from the campaign to the tactical deployment during the War of Liberation was necessarily implemented according to the principles of concentrating the forces against each enemy and opposing military egalitarianism. Mao pointed out that in the deployment of each campaign, when the enemy used numerous brigades (or regiments) to advance on the communist army, the communist forces had to concentrate on its greatest strength at the right moment, first surrounding one brigade, then using a small force to contain the remaining brigade. In this way, the brigade under attack could not be quickly reinforced, so the communist troops could quickly annihilate it and, once that was successful, either defeat the remaining brigade as well or retreat and regroup before fighting again, depending on the situation. It was important not to look down on the enemy, dividing communist troops to face each branches of the enemy force, so this was not an approach the communist army should take. Similarly, in terms of practical deployment, when the army had concentrated on the strongest force and surrounded it on all sides, the attacking groups should not attempt to attack the other enemy brigades at the same time, or the enemy might end up surrounding the communist troops. The result would be that the communist forces' strength would be cut in half, attacking in every direction, which would only delay their inevitable defeat. By concentrating the main force, it could choose a single (never two) weaker point in the enemy's line to attack, hitting it violently, and once victory was gained, quickly expand the battle to annihilate the enemy.

The second principle was to weaken the enemy and determine the extent of the concentration of communist troops based on the scope of the annihilation. When Mao spoke of the deployment of various forces to annihilate the enemy, he required that the choice of where to attack be made first, noting that "it should be in the enemy's weaker brigades that receive less aid, or in a location or terrain that is advantageous to the people."[96] Tactically, it should "choose one weaker point (not two) based on the enemy's position."[97] In this way, the people's army would strengthen its advantage by bringing more troops to face the weaker enemy troops. This made it easier to gain an advantage by "first fighting against the weaker," so that the stronger force would grow gradually weaker.

In the Chinese revolutionary war, the Party always emphasized that the implementation of the tactical idea of "first fighting against the weaker" was closely related to the degree of concentrated forces. The basic requirement for concentrating strength was to be able to "enclose the enemy on all sides, then close all openings, letting none slip through."[98] If this could be achieved, it would form a real advantage. Mao said, "The concentrated forces we advocate are based on the principle of guaranteeing absolute or comparative advantage in battle operations. For strong enemies or critical battlefield operations, these things should be based on absolute superiority." He added, "With weaker enemies or non-critical battlefield operations, the strength of comparative advantage will be sufficient."[99] This took note of the fact that the degree of concentration of troops must be determined by the fact that they were sure to destroy the enemy. In this, not only was it important to take care of the troops, but it was also imperative that firepower be looked after. Further, it was not only about quantity, but also quality, and it was important to calculate both material and psychological factors. In addition, there were considerations of time and space. Only by considering every aspect would it be possible to avoid exaggerating the advantages of a certain aspect into a comprehensive advantage, preventing the annihilation of the enemy. For instance, in fighting a strong enemy, the level of concentration of troops was higher, while it could be lower for weaker enemies. If attacking forces had weaker combat power, they would require a higher concentration, and vice versa. In a strategic offensive and pursuit, when things moved smoothly and the geographical and social conditions were favorable, the level of concentration of troops could be lower. During a strategic defense or a difficult counter-attack, or in areas where the people or terrain were unfavorable, the requirements were higher. For a familiar enemy, it was necessary to concentrate the troops. It was easier when it was done right from the beginning. Facing an unfamiliar enemy, there was room for flexibility. In short, the strength of various forces should be flexible, and the enemy should not be able to rely too much on their own experience.

The final principle was deployment of sieges. The purpose of concentrating troops was to annihilate the enemy. For this reason, Mao pointed out, "The war of annihilation and the concentration of superior forces are the same as encircling and detouring. Without the latter, the former would not exist."[100] Without a superior force, it would be difficult to annihilate the enemy, or to escape the surrounding force through deception. Even if a particular force had an absolute advantage, it would not be able to fight. Surrounding the enemy was a tactic aimed at annihilations, putting the opposing force in a completely isolated situation without any means of escape, depending on the actual situation of the operation. There were times that a two- or three-sided siege was allowed. In tactical terms, combat operations such as detours, infiltrations, divisions, and scattering were required to separate and annihilate the enemy.

The use of the principle of concentrating strong forces to destroy the enemy also involved many aspects, such as actively creating or capturing fighters, careful organizational preparation, the use of various offensive styles, and the tenacious fighting style of the military. The important role of these things should not be ignored.

4. Strategic Offensive Thinking

Strategic offensives were one of the basic forms of combat. These were comprehensive attacks on the enemy's strategic defenses. The basic task of a strategic offensive was to annihilate the enemy in large numbers, capture strategic areas within enemy territory, and win the war. A strategic decisive battle would be the climax of a strategic offensive, the basic means of implementing a fundamental transformation of the balance of power in a war and to determine which of two enemies would emerge from the war victorious. The strategic offensive of the Chinese revolutionary war was developed from a strategic defensive. It often interfaced with strategic counter-attacks. In the early days of the Agrarian Revolutionary War and the later stages of the War of Liberation, communist forces launched two different strategic attacks that were of different sizes and forms. One came during the Agrarian Revolutionary War, when the enemy was strong and its own army weak. When the enemy's encirclement campaign was broken through, the strategic attack launched by the Red Army in the marginal areas was mainly for the purpose of opening up the revolutionary base areas. This sort of strategic offensive was small in scale, limited in purpose, regional, and decisive. The other was a national-scale strategic attack carried out during the War of Liberation. It was launched in the context of a fundamental change in the war situation. Its purpose was to destroy the enemy's heavy troops, to overthrow the reactionary rule of imperialism, feudalism, and bureaucratic capitalism, and to liberate the whole of China. When the communist army had turned to this strategic offensive, Mao noted that the Chinese people's revolutionary war had reached a turning point. This attack of the PLA repelled the reactionary troops of America's running dog, Chiang Kai-shek, and turned itself into an offensive. This was a turning point in history, ending more than a hundred years of imperialist rule in China, transforming from development to an annihilation. From the perspective of the ideological system, the theory of the strategic offensive included strategic attack, strategic decisive battles, and strategic pursuit.

a. *On Strategic Offensives*

According to the general principles of war, a strategic offensive is usually implemented when the offensive side comes to a disadvantage and the defensive side gains an advantage, or when the party which employs a strategic defense completely demolishes the enemy's offensive, pushing each party into the opposite role. The communist forces' strategic offensive during the War of Liberation broke the pattern most people usually observe or imagine. The timing of this strategic offensive was not based on the balance between the opposing forces or on the enemy's attack, nor was the enemy's offense shattered, turning it to a strategic defense. It was still a situation in which the enemy's force was large and had an advantage. It continued to implement a defensive with one force as it launched a key offensive, transferring the main offensive to its main force. The main direction of the assault of the strategic offensive was not the main group aimed straight at the enemy's key point of attack. Rather, it was the strategic depth of its gap and the central area of the enemy's ruling power that was not used to absorb a frontal attack. This allowed communist forces to implement a huge push straight into the heart of the enemy.

During the first year of the War of Liberation, communist forces implemented a policy of internal warfare, winning a great number of victories against the enemy's regular army and gaining the initiative on several battlefields, so that the war situation clearly developed in a direction favorable to the people. Of course, in the process, the communist army also paid the price in casualties and enemy occupation of large blocks of land. At that time, the KMT controlled most of the country's area and population, and it had the full support of American imperialism. Under these circumstances, it was extremely difficult to rely solely on the manpower and material resources of the liberated areas to reach the enemy's strong or weak points in the interior. What the KMT had undertaken to do was, in fact, to take the war to the liberated areas, further destroying and consuming the human and material resources there, in hopes of preventing the communists from maintaining a lasting revolutionary strategic policy. Based on the victories gained in the course of the first year, the CPC Central Committee determined that the basic task of the second year of combat was to "build a nationwide counter-attack, which means hitting the areas outside the front line with our main force, to lead the war to KMT-controlled areas and smash the enemy from the outside." To this end, the Central Military Commission formulated a plan for "attacking outward and defending the Central Plains," instructing Liu Bocheng and Deng Xiaoping to lead 120,000 people from the Field Armies of Shanxi, Hebei, Shandong, and Henan. Their first step was to attack the enemy in the Luyu District and the Yusui Soviet Area, and the second step was to attack the Central Plains. In line with this general intention, Liu and Deng's army crossed the Yellow River on the night of June 30, 1947, and successfully led the prelude to the strategic offensive. At the same time, the Central Military Commission launched a careful deployment of "cooperation between the three armies, with containment on both wings." This meant that, in addition to the implementation of the central breakthrough to the Dabie Mountain by Liu and Deng, the external troops of the Huadong Field Army Corps, led by Chen Yi and Su Yu, formed the left rear flank and advanced into the Jiangsu, Shandong, Henan, and Anhui areas. The Taiyue Corps, under the leadership of Chen Geng and others, formed the right rear flank. These three main forces aided and reinforced each other. They completed their task, then turned to the Central Plains, pushing the enemy. At the same time, communist forces in Northern Shaanxi attacked Yulin and mobilized the main force against the enemy's Hu Zongnan group. The Shandong Army launched an offensive in Jiaodong and continued to lead the Shandong enemy forces to the sea to facilitate the actions of the three armed forces. The army of Liu and Deng crossed the Longhai Line in early August 1947, then reached the Dabie Mountains in the latter part of the year. Chen Yi and Su Yu's army marched into Southwestern Shandong in early August, and Chen Geng's division crossed the Yellow River into Western Henan in late August. By the end of October, the three-pronged army had basically completed the strategic development of the Central Plains region, pushing the main battlefield of the southern line to enemy-occupied areas and cooperating with various battlefields across the country to reverse the entire military situation.

b. On Strategic Decisive Battles

A strategic decisive battle is a battle between opposing sides, using their main forces to decide the outcome of the war. Mao stated, "Only a decisive battle can answer the question of who wins or loses a war between two armies."[101] A strategic decisive battle is the climax of a strategic offensive. As Mao noted, "It is the most intensive, complex, and varied part of a whole war or battle. It is also the most difficult and challenging. In terms of command, it is the most difficult period."[102] The strategic decisive battle of the Chinese revolutionary war began after the communist army turned to a strategic offensive. One year after the army transferred to a strategic offensive, it took 4 months and 19 days from September 1948 to January 1949, to successfully struggle against the enemy through three major strategic battles in Liaoshen, Huaihai, and Pingjin. The total number of regular army divisions the enemy employed in the three battles combined was 144 regular forces (brigades) and 29 brigades or divisions of irregular forces, with a total of over 1.54 million soldiers. The victory in these three major battles eliminated Chiang Kai-shek's old civil war.

In the strategic decisive battle, the communist forces accurately grasped the timing of the final battle. Mao Zedong said that if the time for the decisive battle had not arrived, there would not be sufficient might for fighting the battle, so no battle could be waged. A battle waged at the inappropriate time would definitely not be successful. On the other hand, if it came too late, the enemy would stage a strategic retreat, and the ensuing battle might not be decisive. In March 1948, in the Circular Report on the Military Situation, Mao offered an analysis that pointed out that among the 250 enemy brigades stationed in the enemy lines from north to south, only 180 had not been annihilated by communist forces, and some of these brigades were made up of secondary forces that were still in training or formed of groups of local puppet soldiers, which meant that their combat effectiveness was very low. The average number of enemy soldiers per brigade had dropped from about 8,000 to 6,500, demonstrating the sharp drop in both the numbers and the quality of the enemy's forces. Politically, the Chiang regime had been very isolated and its economy was in a state of collapse. In terms of the communist army, both the numbers and the quality were improving, as were its weapons and equipment, and it had gained abundant combat experience. The KMT army had 550,000 people in the northeast region, and was surrounded by the three regions of Changchun, Shenyang, and Jinzhou. Communist forces had reached 700,000 people, not only surpassing enemy troops in number, but also occupying a very favorable position. It could be said that it was superior in both numbers and form. Chiang's army's supreme command was still hesitant about the enemy forces in the Northeast. All the circumstances indicated that the time had come for a decisive battle launched from the battlefield in the Northeast. If it were not launched, the enemy would be determined to withdraw its troops in the Northeast to Guangzhou or coastal areas south of the Yangtze, which would considerably increase the level of difficulty in future fighting. The victory at Liaoshen resulted in the annihilation of 470,000 enemy soldiers, which enabled the PLA to transfer its now larger numbers and liberate the entire Northeast, laying the foundation for the liberation of Pingjin, Tianjin, and Northern China, strategically consolidating liberation forces and setting up a certain industrial base in the rear. From that time on, the situation in the national war shifted dramatically, which was soon followed by victories in Huaihai and Pingjin, greatly shortening the time required to defeat Chiang Kai-shek from the initial projections of five years.

In the strategic decisive battle, communist forces settled on different guidelines for campaigns that had different aims. The operational plan of the Liaoshen campaign was to seize the enemy and shut down Chiang's northeastern forces, annihilating them. At the beginning of the campaign, Mao indicated that the main force of the Northeastern Field Army was to control the Beining Line. First, it attacked Jinzhou, a strategic location connecting Northeastern and Northern China, serving as the path to the hinterland. Mao noted that "once you've conquered Jinzhou, you've gained the initiative. It is a great victory."[103] The main target of the Liaoshen Campaign was the Beining Line, and the first step was to concentrate on Jinzhou. Once this strategic goal was achieved, it completely closed the land passage of the enemy's withdrawal from the Northeast, causing the trend of "closing the door on the dogs." In the Huaihai Campaign, the CPC Central Committee, noting that the isolation and prominence of the enemy's Huang Baitao Corps facilitated the annihilation by communist forces, promptly identified the county to be detained, cutting off contact between Xuzhou's strategic enemy group and Nanjing, and as a result, they not only quickly closed off and destroyed the enemy's Seventh Regiment, but also divided the forces of Xuzhou, Bengbu, and Mengcheng, so that Xuzhou was surrounded, creating extremely favorable conditions for communist forces to defeat the enemy. In the Battle of Pingjin, the CPC Central Committee emphasized that in the east, "the first step was to surround Tianjin, Tanggu, Lutai, and Tangshan,"[104] while in the west, "as long as Tanggu (most importantly) and the two new security guard posts are safe, they will all survive."[105] This cut off the way for hundreds of thousands of troops in the Pingjin area. In line with the different stages of development in the campaign, the CPC Central Committee adopted a policy of separating, rather than surrounding, the enemy, and of "shelving but not fighting" their forces, so as to isolate the center and prevent the enemy from regrouping or escaping.

c. On Strategic Pursuit

A strategic decisive battle basically determines the fate of the war, but in order to obtain total victory in a war, the strategic guidance should not miss the opportunity to develop an offensive penetrating to the heart of the enemy's strategy, implementing a strategic pursuit in a timely way and resolutely, clearly, and completely destroying the enemy in order to seize the entirety of the military victory. Strategic pursuit during the War of Liberation needed to focus on two issues: 1) how to expose the enemy's conspiracy to prevent the revolution from advancing through their use of hypocritical peace talks, and encourage the whole Party and army and all the people to see the war through to the end, and 2) what sort of operational policy to adopt after crossing the Yangtze River and annihilating the remaining KMT forces within the Mainland without allowing any to linger behind. The former was a political question, while the latter was a military concern. The two were closely linked. If the former was not well resolved, it would not be conducive to military victory. If the latter was not well resolved, it would be difficult to end the war. Under Mao's leadership, the Central Military Command addressed these issues wisely.

After the three major battles at Liaoshen, Huaihai, and Pingjin, the CPC Central Committee issued a great call to the entire Party and army, calling for "carrying the revolution to the end," smashing the enemy's counter-revolutionary arms with those of the revolution, and releasing the timely "command to march throughout the country," bravely continuing forward, annihilating all reactionaries in the Mainland who dared to resist, and liberating the whole of China.

Under the command of the Central Committee, the people's army exposed the enemy's false "peace talks" conspiracy in a timely manner, developing an offensive to counter the enemy's strategy, implementing a cross-river battle, and liberating large cities such as Nanjing, Shanghai, Hangzhou, and Wuhan, as well as large areas south of the Yangtze, destroying the center of the enemy's reactionary rule. After the victory of the cross-river battle, Mao admonished the entire army to "be brave enough to pursue the hard-pressed enemy and not to seek fame like the King of Xichu." As a result, the communist forces held an unprecedented strategic pursuit through the south and southeast of China, as well as the southwestern and northwestern regions. In order to seize the army, Mao instructed, "Take a major detour policy to go straight into the enemy's territory, first encircling and then hitting the enemy." In line with this tactic, the army made active, brave initiatives in South China, and many enemy troops were wiped out in the Southwest. Chiang Kai-shek's conspiracy against the Southwest and his resurgence in the mountains were completely demolished. During the strategic pursuit, some local power factions gathered Chiang's retreating troops, and they attempted to take advantage of the favorable situation. The Central Military Commission instructed the troops to hit the pursuit hard, divide the surrounding forces, and annihilate each group. For instance, the annihilation of Hu Zongnan's main force, the Northwest Field Army, quickly wiped out two local powers, Ma Bufang and Ma Hongkui, then marched into Xinjiang and liberated the Northwest. In the strategic pursuit, the communist forces fully exerted the power of the political offensive to promote the enemy's uprightness, honesty, and peaceful adaptation. Mao promptly proposed the "three ways" to disarm the enemy: the Tianjin Way, the Beiping Way, and the Suiyuan Way. The Tianjin Way involved using military means to disarm the enemy, resolutely wiping out all who resisted. The Beiping Way was to employ strong military strikes and encirclements, forcing the enemy to accept peaceful adaptation. The Suiyuan Way was to intentionally keep some of the KMT forces intact so that the communist forces could concentrate first on addressing the enemy's main force, then adapt the smaller units at the appropriate time. In the southwest and northwest regions, the Party fought for the enemy. About 800,000 surrendered and forced other enemy troops to surrender. This was a great victory for the Party's core struggle strategy.

Chapter 9

The Theory of Party-Building

I

Party-Building: A Great Project

1. The CPC's Party-Building Theory Inherited from Marxism-Leninism

Marx and Engels first proposed the theory of establishing the proletarian revolutionary party. Marx once pointed out that in the struggle of the combined power of the proletariat, the working class could only act as a class if it became an independent political party that opposed all the old parties. It was necessary that the ranks of workers become a political party to guarantee the victory of the social revolution and achieve the ultimate goal of this revolution, the elimination of classes. In order to guide the proletarian revolutionary struggle, Marx and Engels created a comprehensive, scientific communist ideology and guided the establishment of proletarian revolutionary organizations, such as the Communist Alliance and the First International, a branch of the German Social Democratic Labor Party. This created a new stage in the revolutionary struggle of the proletariat and the workers around the world. It was the great historical achievement of that movement.

However, the era in which Marx and Engels lived was an era in which the proletariat had already reached this stage of history, but the revolutionary tasks of the proletariat were not yet mature. After the failure of the revolutions in Western Europe in 1848, capitalism entered a period of peaceful development. In the 1871 Paris Commune Uprising, the proletariat conducted its first heroic attempt to seize power, but the practical struggle demonstrated that the objective conditions for seizing power were not yet sufficient. The first group of proletarian political parties in the world were established after this, and they nourished the opportunism prevalent then, due to the relatively "peaceful" nature of that period. The result was that these parties were overcome by opportunism and revisionism, allowing them to deteriorate or even collapse. For this reason, with the arrival of the 20th century, it was proposed that a new type of proletarian revolutionary party be established to adapt to the revolutionary crisis and the task of leading the revolution. It was in this historical condition that Lenin created a completely new proletarian party, the Russian Bolshevik Party, and "created a complete doctrine for building a proletarian revolutionary party."[1]

Lenin proposed the task of establishing a new type of proletarian revolutionary party, pointing out that what was needed was a new type of party with a different nature. He went on to say that one could transform an old-style party of European parliamentarism, which was actually one layer of revolutionary reformism, into a new truly revolutionary, truly communist party. He emphasized that the party must be new, meaning that it must be fundamentally different from the Second International parliamentary and reformist parties. From the beginning of their establishment, although they were also proletarian parties, these groups faced numerous challenges. After the death of Engles, partly due to the corruption of Bernstein revisionism, they deteriorated and became vassals of the bourgeois parliamentary group, thus losing their revolutionary, combative nature. They were no longer proletarian revolutionary parties, but old-style reformist parties. Lenin believed that in the early 20th century, it was necessary to establish a new type of proletarian party, and that such a party should be highly class conscious, combative, connected to the masses, and a disciplined revolutionary party. Only by establishing such a party could the demands of history in the era of imperialism be met and the revolutionary task of the proletariat be completed.

Lenin made clear that the ideological foundation of the proletarian revolutionary party must be Marxism, and it must be guided by the idea of party-building. When he founded the Bolshevik Party, Lenin wrote books such as *Where to Begin* and *How to Do It*, which resolutely opposed the economic opportunism of elevating the workers, and founded a political newspaper to promote and publicize Marxism throughout Russia. In discussing the line of thought regarding and understanding of party-building, Lenin wrote, "These are completely based on Marx's theory, because it is the first time socialism has been transformed from a dream to a scientific reality, laying a solid foundation for this science."[2] He emphasized that "only a party guided by an advanced theory can achieve the role of an advanced fighter."[3]

Lenin clearly defined the relationship between the party and the proletariat and proposed the principle that the party's ideological unity should be consolidated with the material unity of the party's organization. Lenin pointed out that the party was the advance force of the proletariat and the organized army, and it was the highest organizational form of the proletariat. The party had to be composed of the most politically conscious advanced elements of the proletariat. Party members could only make up a minority of the proletariat, never fully taking over the entire class. The party was to be organized in accordance with the principle of democratic centralism, and party members had to lead all other organizations of the proletariat. Lenin said, "In the struggle for political power, the proletariat has no other weapon besides organization. The proletariat can and will become an invincible force because it is formed according to the principles of Marxism. Unity of thought will be consolidated by the material unity of the organization."[4]

These three points were the key ideas in Lenin's theory of party-building. They pointed out the most basic direction for the construction of the proletarian revolutionary party and had universal significance. The Communist Party of China was founded and developed with Lenin's theory of party-building as a guiding principle.

However, like many universal principles of Marxism-Leninism, a Marxist-Leninist principle for a certain type of thing only reflects the most general laws of development for that sort of thing, and it is impossible for it to be complex enough to address every specific phenomenon, encompassing the full diversity of possibilities. Lenin's ideas on party-building reflect the most general law of the development of a proletarian party, but it does not and cannot include all the characteristics and development of a specific proletarian party. Because of the different historical conditions in various countries, the establishment and development of proletarian political parties in each country must have their own special rules and characteristics. For this reason, the Marxist-Leninist theory of party-building is always enriched and developed through the party-building process in each country across the world. The CPC's thoughts and experiences throughout its process of party-building under the conditions of a semi-colonial, semi-feudal China serve as a model for adhering to both the universal truth of Marxism-Leninism and the concrete practice of the Chinese revolution, which ultimately enriched and developed the Marxist-Leninist theory of party-building.

The CPC was born in the old semi-colonial, semi-feudal China. On the one hand, the seriousness and the cruelty of the exploitation and oppression of the Chinese working class was a thing rarely been seen in any country in the world. Their revolutionary thoroughness was more prominent and more combative than seen elsewhere. This feature of the Chinese working class was fundamental to the creation of the Party, providing a good class foundation for development. As once pointed out by Liu Shaoqi, the Party had a clear class consciousness from its conception, and it led the bourgeois democratic revolution in China from a proletarian standpoint, with the combination of the universal truth of Marxism-Leninism, the Chinese workers' movement, and the Chinese revolution as a foundation. It had all the fine style of an advanced proletarian political party, thus creating a new face for the Chinese revolution. On the other hand, the Party was established in an eastern country with an undeveloped economy and culture, and the peasants and petty bourgeoisie formed the majority of the population. The Party noted that it was not only surrounded by the petty bourgeoisie on the outside, but also held many members of that class within its own ranks, even accounting for a majority of the Party's membership. Further, under China's economic conditions, even the workers and proletarian Party members were easily infected with the petty bourgeoisie mindset. As a result, the ideology of the petty bourgeoisie was often reflected inside the Party in a variety of ways. This was inevitable, and not the least bit surprising. It was for this reason that the conflicts between the proletarian thinking of the Party and various non-proletarian ideologies, especially that of the petty bourgeoisie, became the main conflicts within the Party. The process of building the CPC was to constantly transform the petty bourgeoisie component within the Party and overcome the various non-proletarian ideologies with proletarian thought.

If the situation of the CPC's construction was not obvious before the 1930s because its activities were basically in the cities, then this issue was especially highlighted after the Party's work shifted to the countryside. After the failure of the Great Revolution, the Mao-led CPC began to move deeply into the countryside, following the setbacks of armed uprisings in various places. From there, a new revolutionary path more suited to China's national conditions was explored. On September 9, 1927, Mao launched the Autumn Harvest Uprising, then led the troops to Jinggangshan. During the construction of the revolutionary bases there, Mao explored a revolutionary path that focused on encircling the cities to seize political power. He pointed out that the CPC must follow this path of encircling the cities and arming the people. He believed that 90% of China's economy came from agricultural production, while only a small portion came from capitalist commodity construction, and that was concentrated in the large cities. Agricultural production, on the other hand, was scattered among small producers, maintained great independence, and could be self-sufficient. Politically, the ruling class had great power in the city, but was weak in the countryside. This imbalance in economic and political relations could enable the Party to conditionally lead the peasants in rural areas for armed struggle and to establish revolutionary base areas. In the 1930s, Mao's idea of encircling the cities in rural areas and arming the people as the revolutionary path to political power was basically formed. In fact, the Party's work shifted from urban to rural areas. As was evident in the revolutionary base areas in Jinggangshan, armed revolutionary forces were established one after another, and the agrarian revolution was carried out more intensely, opening a new situation for the revolution.

The focus of the Party's work shifted to the countryside, making the task of party-building even more arduous. This was because, as the Party's work shifted to the countryside, its organizational component changed greatly. In March 1927, the total number of Party members was 57,967, of which workers made up 53.8%, while peasants made up 18.7%. However, in 1928, during the Agrarian Revolutionary War, among the 130,194 members, workers accounted for 10.9%, while peasants accounted for 76.6%. In 1929, the percentage of workers fell to 7.5%, and by July 1930, it had fallen to 5.5%, then dropped all the way to 1.6% in September. With a majority of peasants, did this mean the CPC had become a peasant party? At that time, the Comintern's view was that it was because the cadres of the CPC were not workers that the Great Revolution failed. This was a simple emphasis on the origin of the Party's members, leading them to believe that the party organization should seek to replace non-proletarian cadres with proletarian cadres, and that the Red Army should likewise be made up primarily of workers. With the convening of the Sixth Congress of the Communist Party, the Comintern emphasized that the representation of workers should be 41 out of 75 representatives, and that when selecting Central Committee members, its composition of workers was to be at least 21 out of 36 committee members. However, most of those selected for membership in the Central Committee did not participate directly in the actual revolutionary struggle.

In discussing how to build the Party in a rural environment, the CPC proposed another idea that diverged from the path suggested by the Comintern. First, the CPC saw the seriousness of the problem. In the process of creating a revolutionary base, Mao felt that "the issue of proletarian leadership is a very important issue. In the border areas, the Party is almost entirely a peasant party. If it does not put leadership into the hands of the proletariat, its direction will be wrong."[5] In addition, Mao analyzed the causes of errors such as pure military views, extreme democratization, unorganized views, absolute egalitarianism, subjectivism, individualism, rogue ideas, and blindness, pointing out the sources of various erroneous ideas within the Party. Naturally, the largest part of the Party's organizational foundation was made up of peasant and petty bourgeoisie elements. However, the Party's leading organs lacked a consistent and determined struggle to correct these ideas, and they lacked a correct Party line for their members. Education was an important reason for the existence and development of these erroneous ideas. Finally, Mao emphasized not the simplistic approach of organizational clean-up, but a way to strengthen ideological education within the Party and improve its theoretical level. From that time on, Mao elaborated on this issue in articles such as "Against Fundamentalism," "Practical Theory," "Conflict Theory," and "The Communist Party Member," and he pointed out the problem of a peasantry that accounted for the majority of the population, but was small within the Party. The petty bourgeoisie had a strong influence on the building of a proletarian vanguard for the revolution.

2. The Practical Formation and Development of the CPC's Party-Building Theory

Throughout the prolonged period of revolutionary struggle and party-building, the Mao-led CPC enriched and developed the Marxist-Leninist theory of party-building. The formation and development of the CPC's theory of party-building was consistent with the formation and development of Mao Zedong Thought, based on the historical development of the Chinese revolution and the Party's revolutionary activity in various historical periods. It constituted a correct summary of the theoretical principles and experiences of the CPC, and was the crystallization of the collective wisdom of the Party.

From 1920 to 1927, the CPC made valuable explorations into how to establish a new type of proletarian party in China. During this period, influenced by the Russian October Revolution and China's own May 4th Movement, and with the help of the Lenin-led Comintern, the CPC had already begun to establish the nature of the Party, as well as the Party's basic program and organizational principles. The First National Congress of the CPC established the proletarian dictatorship as the goal of the Party. The Second National Congress clearly put forward the Party's anti-imperialist, anti-feudalist democratic revolutionary program. Soon after the founding of the Party, it led a vigorous revolutionary struggle. The majority of the Party members performed very well in the struggle, and party organization developed greatly as a result. It was during this period that the Party began to recognize the importance of strengthening its construction. In 1922, the Second National Congress proposed to strengthen the ideological, political, and organizational training of Party members, pointing out that the CPC must maintain its independence when uniting with bourgeois democrats. At the First Plenary Session of the Third Assembly of the Executive Committee, held in November 1923, it was proposed that Party members and the masses be educated in a dialectical materialist world view and a collective outlook on life, emphasizing an opposition to individualism. This demonstrated that in the early days of its founding, the Party had noticed the transformation of its members' ideological awareness. From that time on, at every National Congress and Expanded Meeting of the Executive Committee, corresponding resolutions were made on intra-party organizations, publicity, and education. In the Resolution on the Third Amendment to the Constitution of the Communist Party of China, passed in 1927, "party-building" was clearly laid out in a second article. However, the Party was still young at this time, and it lacked both a thorough understanding of Marxism-Leninism and theoretical preparation. The Party had just entered into mass struggle, had limited knowledge of the Chinese revolution, and lacked experience in party-building, particularly in the Marxist-Leninist theory of party-building. This combination of factors led to a lack of conscious understanding within the CPC that the Party itself had not yet formed its own strong leadership core. Party organization had not had time to consolidate this understanding, it lacked the necessary Marxist-Leninist education for Party members, and its experiences had yet to be summed up well. This made it impossible to form a more systematic theory of party-building during this period, and the theory of party-building theory was still in its infancy.

From the August 7th Meeting in 1927 to the Zunyi Meeting in 1935, the CPC began to explore how to conduct party-building within the Red Army, in armed struggle, and in the rural revolutionary base areas, and to generate many new experiences and solutions. Many major theoretical and practical problems that were not encountered or not mentioned by Marx, Engels, Lenin, or Stalin began to be formulated on the path to party-building with Chinese characteristics. The basic points on this path were:

1) *It established the principle of party-building from an ideological point of view and proposed to use the proletarian ideology to overcome various non-proletarian ideas.* In response to the massive influx of peasant revolutionaries into the Party and the bourgeois ideology of the petty bourgeoisie and the serious threat this presented to the existence of the Party, the Gutian Meeting Resolution (the Resolution), pointed out that Party members must adopt a proletarian revolutionary outlook on life. It was necessary to overcome and correct all sorts of non-proletarian ideologies within the Party, and to carry out serious criticism and self-criticism to correct such errors. Struggle within the Party was the basic way to strengthen the ideology of the proletariat and eliminate all non-proletarian ideology. These principles and methods had formed an initial ideological focus as the basic principle for party-building, laying the foundation for strengthening the Party's ideological construction in the future. Focusing on building the party from an ideological perspective became a prominent feature of the construction of the CPC.

2) *It put forward the scientific concept of the Party's organizational direction and emphasized the need to strengthen the building of Party membership and grassroots organizations.* The Resolution highlighted the scientific concept of "the Party's organizational direction" and elaborated on the issue of organizational construction under the guidance of this organizational direction. The Resolution first proposed that the Party's grassroots organizations be strengthened. Grassroots organizations mostly lived and fought among the soldiers, forming a bridge or link between

the Party and the people. To this end, the Resolution reaffirmed the need to "build a branch in each company, and a group in each class. This is one of the key principles of party organization in the military." The idea that "a branch is built in each company" was an important measure for strengthening the leadership of the Party in the military and making the branch a battle fortress for grassroots organizations.

In order to improve the combat effectiveness of the party organizations, it was necessary to strengthen party-building. This was a primary issue of organizational development. Mao Zedong set the correct direction for the development of Party members in the Red Army, emphasizing "the direction of development of for Party members, with combatants as the main target." He also proposed that in the development of Party members, the conditions and procedures for joining the Party must be strictly enforced. Only in this way was it possible to ensure the purity and combat effectiveness of Party members.

The issue of democratic life within the Party was one of the key ideas of the Party's organizational construction. Democratic centralism was the fundamental organizational principle of the CPC and the fundamental criterion for successfully establishing democratic life within the Party. The Resolution was aimed at the extreme tendency toward democratization that surfaced in the Party within the Red Army. It emphasized that in Party life, it was necessary to adhere to a democratic standard under centralized guidance. Any so-called democracy that left the Party's lines and policies and left the Party's leadership was not the authentic democracy of the proletariat, but the extreme democratization of the petty bourgeoisie, which must be opposed.

3) *Valuable theories on the Party's political construction were proposed, and emphasis was placed on the notion that the Party's construction must not be combined with the construction of Red political power*. In two articles entitles "The Struggle in Jinggangshan" and "How Can the Party Last?", Mao Zedong pointed out that the power of the CPC's organization and the correctness of its political direction were the basic conditions for the long-term existence of the Red regime, and thus it was able to be created. In the process of building Red political power, the CPC strengthened its party-building and developed its party organization, so that the CPC truly became the solid core of the Red regime. This demonstrated that although Mao had not yet completely and clearly summarized the principles of party-building around the political line, its basic ideas had already been proposed.

4) The scientific concept and basic theory of the Party's ideological direction and mass line were proposed. In the struggle against leftist dogmatism, Mao proposed the scientific concept and basic theory of the ideological line in his article "Opposing Doctrinairism." At the same time, in the resolutions from the Gutian Meeting and the article "Caring for the Life of the Masses and Giving Attention to Working Methods," the scientific concept and basic ideas of the "mass line" were proposed.

Further, during this period, the Party also gained valuable experience in correctly carrying out the struggle within the Party and establishing the Party's principle of absolute leadership over the Red Army. During this time, the Party focused on how to address issues such as the purpose of building the Party politically and ideologically, and how to ensure the nature of the Party's vanguard and to achieve strong leadership within the CPC. Although the party-building principles listed above were not yet mature or complete when they were proposed, they initiated an exploration of the basic points of and began to form a theoretical system for maintaining the Party's vanguard nature in terms of the conditions of ideological, political, and organizational conditions in the contexts of armed struggle and the rural areas. This was the result of the Mao-led CPC creatively combining Marxist-Leninist theory with the actual construction of the Party. It marked out the path for party-building with Chinese characteristics that took initial shape during this period. The Zunyi Meeting held in 1935 established Mao's leadership position in the Red Army and throughout the Party. This created the vitality of Mao's direction for party-building in the CPC's further promotion and application and its maturity and completeness in the Yan'an Rectification period, and created more ideal political conditions.

The years between the Zunyi Conference in 1935 to the Seventh National Congress of the CPC in 1945 were an important period in which the Party changed from a path of several setbacks to a series of continuous victories, and the whole process of organization saw rapid growth. It was also a period in which the Party's path for construction with Chinese characteristics was maturing. At this stage, the CPC Central Committee, headed by Mao Zedong, put forward the great task of building the masses and increasing the Marxist Bolshevik party. In the process of completing this task, Mao profoundly summed up the lessons learned in party-building since the founding of the CPC, made many reports on party-building, wrote a large number of articles on the topic, and drafted numerous important documents. He further led the whole Party to carry out the renowned Yan'an Rectification Movement, creating an effective form of party construction, exploring the issue of party-building through a combination of theory and practice, further developing and perfecting the party-building ideology through the founding of the Red Army and gradually forming the complete theoretical system of Mao Zedong's theories on party-building and the path to party-building.

At the beginning of this stage, Mao wrote two books, entitled *On Practice* and *On Contradiction*, which focused on criticizing dogmatism, systematically expounding the Party's ideological line and scientific worldview of dialectical materialism, and laying out the Party's thinking as the philosophical foundation of construction. After this, at the Sixth Plenary Session of the Sixth Central Committee of the CPC, Mao discussed the importance of studying Marxism and raising the ideological level. On October 20, 1939, the Central Committee founded *Communist* magazine at Yan'an. Mao proposed in *The Communist Party* issue that "building a nationwide, people-oriented, ideological, and political organization of a fully consolidated Bolshevik Communist Party of China is the task of party-building," and the construction of such a party was a "great project." He also summed up the party-building experience of the previous eighteen years of the CPC's existence. From 1939 to the Yan'an Rectification Movement, Mao published numerous works, including "The Chinese Revolution and the Communist Party of China," "Broad Absorption of Intellectuals," and "On Policy." During the same period, Liu Shaoqi wrote works such as "On the Cultivation of Communists," "On the Struggle Within the Party," and "Be a Good Party Member and Build a Good Party." Chen Yun's published works during the same years included "On the Cadre Policy," "How to Become a Communist Party Member," and "Several Issues Concerning the Construction of Cadres." Zhang Wentian published articles such as "Organization and Organizational Works," "On the Relationship between Party and Non-Party Masses," and "Promoting a Simple and Practical Work Style." These party-building works further enriched the theory of "great engineering" and further improved the party-building theory of the CPC.

At the same time, the initial thinking of the Party's political construction was similarly further developed. The basic points of Mao and other Party members regarding the Party's political line and political construction during this period were that 1) party-building must be in line with the Party's political direction and strategy, and 2) the Party must develop a correct political direction and strategy.

Emphasis was placed on improving the consciousness of the entire Party while implementing the political direction and developing and strengthening party organization. Party-building had to be combined with the united front and armed struggle. The construction of the Party would be a deciding factor in the success or failure of the Chinese revolution. The united front and armed struggle were the two fundamental weapons for use against the enemy, and party organization was the heroic warrior that mastered these two weapons and rushed the enemy. If party construction were done well, the Party could better grasp and use the two weapons of the united front and armed struggle to correctly lead the Chinese revolution to victory.

As Mao Zedong and other CPC members set out to address the Party's ideological and political direction, they also effectively addressed a series of problems in organizational construction. In the article "The Status of the CPC in the National War," Mao comprehensively and systematically expounded on the Party's organizational direction and construction, focusing on the criteria for selecting cadres based on "both integrity and merits" and the use of cadres "according to their competence." Emphasis was to be placed on caring for the cadres, comprehensively uniting the cadres, and proper treatment of cadres who made mistakes. At the same time, the basic principles of correctly fighting on these two fronts were put forward. In addition, in reports and other articles published by Party members such as Mao Zedong, the issues of democratic centralism and other party organization and construction were systematically expounded, thus forming a relatively complete theoretical system for party organization and construction.

After addressing the Party's ideological and political direction, beginning in 1942, the CPC launched the well-known Yan'an Rectification Movement. Through this movement, the CPC systematically summarized and continuously improved its party-building efforts, particularly the complete set of theoretical principles and policies governing its own work style.

The CPC was strengthening its party-building with the aim of realizing the Party's correct leadership over the cause of the Chinese revolution. Regarding the principle of Party leadership, in the early days of the War of Resistance Against Japanese Aggression, Mao and other Party members further discussed the historical inevitability of realizing the Party's leadership and put forward the basic conditions, principles, means, and methods for realizing the Party's leadership and formed the Party's initial theoretical system for leadership. During the rectification period in Yan'an, Mao and other Party members further discussed how to realize the principles, means, and methods of Party leadership and fleshed out its leadership principles.

During this decade, the Party became more mature ideologically and politically, and its organization was consolidated. What sort of party Mao and others were building, how to build it in an organization and style informed by ideology and politics, and how to correctly carry out the struggle between the two lines within the Party had all come together to form a complete set of theoretical principles for successfully guiding the practical construction of the Communist Party of China. At the Seventh National Congress of the CPC, Liu Shaoqi offered a high-level summary of the theoretical system of party-building and clearly put forward the scientific concept of "Mao Zedong's party-building theory," or "Mao Zedong's path to party-building." This demonstrated that Mao's theoretical system for party-building had been fully formed and the path to party-building with Chinese characteristics had matured.

From the victory of the Anti-Japanese War to the founding of the new China, the Party's organization and membership were further expanded, while the Party's principle of democratic centralism and the collective leadership system were further improved. The CPC party-building theory was especially focused on further developing the idea of organizational construction in specific ways in different periods.

1) *From the victory of the Anti-Japanese War to the National Land Conference in July 1947.* In order to adapt to a large-scale war situation, the CPC Central Committee adopted timely measures such as cadre transfers and organizational adjustment. As they focused on strengthening the leadership in local governments, they absorbed a large number of Party members and increased the Party's overall strength.

2) *From the National Land Conference to the Second Plenary Session of the Seventh General Assembly of the Central Committee in March 1949.* In order to support the PLA's strategic counterattack and strategic decisive battle, the Central Committee carried out, in conjunction with land reforms, the rectification of the Party in various liberated areas and issued a series of instructions on strengthening the Party's policy ideas, strengthening discipline, and improving the Party's democratic centralism and collective leadership system. It also decided to promptly correct the

leftist tendencies in the land reform and undertake the rectification of the Party, overcome some unorganized and undisciplined phenomena within the Party, and ensure the centralized and unified leadership of the central government and the implementation of various policies and principles to support the war.

3) *From the Second Plenary Session of the Seventh General Assembly of the CPC Central Committee to September 1949.* As the revolution neared victory in the country, the focus of the Party's work shifted from rural to urban areas. The Party's mode of activity shifted from secret to public, and the Party's status had begun to change from that of an unlawful long-term oppressed position to that of the ruling party. The CPC Central Committee formulated timely measures to prevent the erosion of the bourgeois ideology and banned inordinate praise of individual virtues and achievements, calling on the entire Party to continue to maintain a style of modesty, prudence, pride, and hard work and put forward principles for open party-building, making the necessary political and ideological arrangements for the development of the ruling party.

During this period, because of the rapid expansion of Party organization and membership, the rapid growth of revolutionary warfare, and the use of large-scale warfare and positional warfare, it was even more necessary to strengthen the coordination and unity of the Party's organizations at all levels. It emphasized the principle of centralized, unified, and collective leadership, consolidated the unity of the Party, and provided an important guarantee for gaining national victory.

3. The Basic Characteristics of Party-Building During the New Democratic Revolution

The special conditions and circumstances experienced by the CPC during the new democratic revolution were the basic starting point for building and developing the Party. The Mao-led CPC succeeded in addressing the problem of building a people-oriented Marxist proletarian party by consistently learning and mastering these basic concepts and aligning the Party with these theories and principles for building and developing the Party. The basic characteristics for building the CPC during the period of the new democratic revolution were:

1) *The CPC was established after the October Revolution, on the foundation of the Chinese workers' movement, with the Leninist Bolshevik Party as a guiding*

example and with a Marxist-Leninist revolutionary theory and style. From the beginning, the Party was not influenced ideologically or organizationally by the Social Democratic Party's Second International. China did not have a period of "peaceful" capitalist development, such as that seen in Europe, which would have allowed working class people to struggle peacefully through the parliamentary system. It likewise lacked a proletariat like that seen in Europe. As a result, the Party was founded as an armed working class revolutionary party fortified with Marxism-Leninism, but without the reformist tradition of the Social Democratic Party.

2) *The construction and development of the CPC was very closely tied to guidance from the Comintern.* From July 1922, when the Second National Congress announced its participation in the Comintern, to May 1923, when the Comintern was dissolved, the CPC was a branch under the leadership of the Comintern. On the one hand, in the long-term struggle of the Chinese revolution, the Comintern did in fact play a positive role in aiding the construction and development of the CPC. The Party's program and formulation for the united front policy, the Northern Expedition, the Agrarian Revolutionary War, the War of Resistance Against Japanese Aggression, and other important efforts during this period all received support and shows of solidarity from the Comintern and Stalin. On the other hand, the Comintern and Stalin also misdirected and interfered with various affairs, even nearly causing great trouble to the CPC and the Chinese revolution. Chen Duxiu's rightist error and Wang Ming's leftist error were all directly related to the blind leadership and wrong opinions of the Comintern and Stalin. It should be said that the building of the Party, its advances and retreats, and its victories and failures were all inseparable from the guidance of the Comintern at this time.

3) *Peasants and the petty bourgeoisie accounted for a considerable portion of the makeup of the CPC.* This was the social basis for the left-right division within the Party. Semi-colonial, semi-feudal China was a two-headed society, of which the working class, the landlord class, and the bourgeoisie only made up a small number. The most expansive classes were peasants, the urban petty bourgeoisie, and other middle classes. The Party had grown stronger through its revolutionary alliance with the peasantry and petty bourgeoisie. China did not have a strongly formed petty bourgeoisie party at the time,

making it inevitable that a large number of revolutionary elements from the petty bourgeoisie would participate in the revolutionary party of the proletariat. However, this made the percentage of peasants and petty bourgeoisie a considerable portion of the CPC. The conflict and struggle between the ideologies of the proletariat and petty bourgeoisie had become the most essential conflict the Party had experienced in a long time. This being the case, how to go about building a proletarian revolutionary party was the major issue the CPC faced during this period.

4) *The CPC was trained to embrace both struggle and unity with the bourgeoisie.* During the new democratic revolution, the CPC repeatedly established a revolutionary united front with the bourgeoisie. When this united front broke down, it also engaged in a fierce armed struggle with the upper bourgeoisie and its allies. Generally speaking, during the new democratic revolution, when the CPC formed a united front with the bourgeoisie, the likelihood of a rightist bias emerging within the Party increased. During the periods in which the Party remained generally separate from the bourgeoisie, it tended toward a leftist bias. Thus, a proper handling of the relationship between the CPC and the bourgeoisie was of great importance in party-building.

5) *The CPC was trained through long-term armed struggle.* Armed struggle was a characteristic and an advantage of China's new democratic revolution and the main form of China's revolutionary struggle. During the period of democratic revolution, the CPC carried out both a long-term domestic revolutionary war and a national war of liberation. The majority of Party members and cadres had lived a collective military life for many years and were strictly trained in ideology, organization, and daily life, and they had established a good rapport with the masses, forming a sort of life bond. This meant that party-building was closely linked to the issue of correctly handling the armed struggle. Thus, how to build the Party through armed struggle was another important issue related to party construction during this time.

6) *The CPC had grown stronger during the long-term leadership in the construction of and struggle in the revolutionary base areas.* After 1927, the Party opened up the path of encircling cities with rural strongholds in order to finally seize them. In order to conserve and better utilize their own energies, the

revolutionary team had long penetrated the countryside and transformed the rural backward areas into advanced, consolidated base areas, which resulted in military, political, economic, and cultural revolutionary positions to gradually win all revolutionary struggles. In the rural areas, in addition to focusing on resolving the building of the Party, the CPC also had to lead the people in building political power and economic and cultural construction, requiring them to learn a new set of skills for managing the country and the people. For this reason, how to build a revolutionary party with strict discipline and a centralized, unified working class and armed with Marxist-Leninist theory in a rural base area divided by the enemy, mired in a guerrilla war, and with a scattered individual economy was a major question for the CPC, one for which there were no precedents in the history of the international Communist movement.

In summary, it is evident that the conditions of the times, the social environment, and the class relations facing the CPC were very unique. This required the Party to be extremely creative when combining the principles of Marxism-Leninism with the concrete practice of the CPC. Mao's theory of party-building was precisely adapted to these historical demands and was formed and developed through the Party's leadership of the revolution and in party-building.

II

The Party's Ideological Construction

1. Focusing on the Ideological Construction of the Party as a Prominent Feature of the CPC's Party-Building Work

The need to take an ideological approach to building the Party was a prominent feature central to the CPC's theory of party-building. It was an outstanding contribution the Mao-led CPC made to Marxism-Leninism. It played a decisive role in the establishment, consolidation, and development of the CPC and in upholding the working class as the vanguard of the Party and of the Party's leadership position.

a. An Ideological Approach to Party-Building as an Important Principle of Marxist-Leninist Theories of Party-Building

From the time that Marx and Engels, the founders of the theory of a proletarian party, first established their school of thought, they placed great importance on the role of revolutionary theory and the Party's ideological construction. They advocated a combination of scientific socialist theory with the workers' movement and the use of this theory to educate the entire party. Marx pointed out in his *Critique of Hegel's Philosophy of Right*, "The weapon of criticism cannot, of course, replace the criticism of weapons. Material power can only be destroyed by material power, but once theory is mastered, it will become material power."[6] In the *Communist Manifesto*, published by Marx and Engels in 1848, further clarification was offered in the words, "In practice, Communists are the most determined element of proletarian political parties in every country, and they always push workers' movements forward. In theory, they are more advanced than the proletarian masses because of their understanding of the conditions, processes, and general results of the proletarian movement."[7] Later, in summing up the Party's experience in party-building, Engels said, "Our party has a great advantage, which is that it is a new party built on the theoretical foundation of a scientific worldview."[8] This scientific worldview was Marxist dialectical and historical materialism, and it was Communism's greatest tool for understanding and transforming the world. With the development of the proletarian movement, the expansion of the Party's ranks, and the theoretical victory of Marxism, not only did enlightened workers demand the right to participate in the Party's organization, but other people not born into the working class likewise poured into the proletarian party. In response, Marx and Engels not only emphasized the class nature of the Party, but also pointed out that it was composed of the progressive elements of the working class, and that this was the part of the Party that always promoted the movement. They further highlighted the progressive nature of the Party, pointing out the necessity of it having a scientific worldview and a theoretical foundation. They went on to discuss the specific requirements for strengthening the ideological basis for party-building, saying, "If such people from other classes participate in the proletarian movement, then it is necessary that they do not allow any remnants of the bourgeoisie or other biases to be brought in, but that they instead unconditionally embrace the worldview of the proletariat."

They further emphasized the need for "a most thorough break with traditional ownership relations" and "a most thorough break with the traditional mindset."[9] In order to maintain the progressive nature of the Party's proletariat, Marx and Engels suggested strict requirements for non-proletarian Party members, saying, "First, these people must be truly enlightened in order to benefit the proletarian movement. Second, if members of other classes participate in the proletarian movement, they must first be asked not to bring with them any remnants of the prejudices of the bourgeoisie, petty bourgeoisie, or any other class, but to unconditionally embrace the worldview of the proletariat."[10] These important ideas of Marx and Engels indicated the direction and laid the foundation for the ideological construction of a proletarian party.

Leninism was the application of Marxism in an era of imperialism and proletarian revolution. Lenin not only created a new proletarian political party in Russia, the Bolshevik Party, but also inherited, defended, and developed Marxist doctrine concerning the party. When Lenin was creating the party, he was faced with a situation in which the Second International had betrayed the role of Marxism in Russian economics, negating revolutionary theory. As a result, from the beginning, Lenin paid great attention to the significant role theory had played in building a new Russian proletarian party. Lenin particularly noted that instilling socialist thought in the working class was a basic, regular task of the party. He criticized spontaneous development of theory even in the earliest days of founding the party, insisting instead on "instilling" theory. He pointed out that "only a party guided by advanced theory can realize the role of an advanced warrior."[11] He also observed more pointedly, "Without theory, a revolutionary faction will lose its right to continue, and sooner or later, it is destined to be politically bankrupt."[12] In Lenin's view, "Whether a party is a true proletarian party depends not only of whether it is composed of workers, but also on its own identity, the content of its leadership, and its actions and political strategies. It is only the latter that determines whether it is truly a proletarian party."[13] In this, Lenin had noted that the fundamental conditions for determining the nature of a proletarian party were the sorts of ideas that occupied the dominant position within that party. He said, "If revisionist thinking is what really prevails within the party, then it is not a proletarian socialist party."[14] These important expositions of Lenin greatly enriched the Marxist theory of party-building.

From this, it was evident that without a revolutionary theory, there could be no proletarian party. The nature of the party did not depend on the origin of the party's members, but on the party's guiding ideology and political direction. This was the theoretical basis for party-building from an ideological standpoint.

b. Ideological Construction of the Party Determined by China's National Conditions

The CPC was a proletarian party established in accordance with the revolutionary theory and style of Marxism-Leninism. When Marx and Lenin discussed the conditions for party-building, they believed that only by having appropriate class and theoretical conditions and properly combining the two could the proletarian party become a reality. During the May 4th Movement, the establishment of the Communist Party of China occurred amidst China's appropriate class and theoretical conditions. At that time, the number of industrial workers had increased to 2 million, and they entered the political arena with great independence. The strikes in many central cities showed the revolutionary steadfastness, thoroughness, and great fighting power of the Chinese proletariat. It was a group with many progressive elements armed with preliminary communist power and, recognizing the power of the working class, they were determined to carry out Marxist-Leninist propaganda, education work, and organization among the working masses, thus promoting the integration of Marxism-Leninism and the Chinese workers' movement. The great anti-imperialist, anti-feudalist May 4th Movement achieved this marriage. After the May 4th Movement, the earliest urban-focused Communist Party organizations were established in Shanghai, Beijing, Changsha, Wuhan, and Shandong and among Chinese students in Japan and France. These organizations carried out extensive activities among the working masses. The Chinese workers' movement combined to produce the Communist Party of China. After the founding of the Party, it was first established and developed among the masses in the cities and among the working class, and it launched a vigorous struggle through workers' strikes.

However, the CPC's practical revolutionary struggle illustrated that the social environment, class relations, and revolutionary direction it found itself in was quite different from that facing Communist parties in Europe. As a result, in the course of its own party construction, the CPC encountered many major issues that European parties did not face at all, particularly the fact that the old China was a semi-colonial, semi-feudal society. The collusion between the imperialist and feudal forces resulted in deep national and class oppression. The feudal exploitation system occupied a clearly advantageous position in social and economic life. Although national capitalism saw some development, it was very weak, making China a two-headed, small society. The landlords, the bourgeoisie, and the working class made up only a small minority, while the peasants and other petty bourgeoisie made up the majority. This basic feature of Chinese society meant that the CPC had to be strong enough to shoulder the burden of revolutionary leadership to save the nation and the people, as it was far from possible to rely solely on the strength of the proletarian class to do so. It was important to absorb the majority of peasants and other petty bourgeoisie who were "sincere about the revolution, the belief in revolutionism, the policy of supporting the Party, and the willingness to follow its discipline and work hard," thus creating a great mass for the Party. Because the city was where the enemy was more strongly entrenched, while the countryside was where imperialism and feudal forces were weak, party organization was only undertaken with great difficulty in the city. Its vast world was the countryside, so it had to develop and expand in the countryside and lead the armed forces of workers and peasants there. After the defeat of the Great Revolution of 1927, the focus of the Party's work gradually shifted from the city to the countryside, and the Party moved away from central cities to the masses. From that time on, the Party existed and developed in the countryside. On the one hand, the Party was situated in the countryside and was surrounded by a sea of petty bourgeois peasant masses. On the other, the Party mainly absorbed its members from the petty bourgeoisie. Under this unique social condition, building a true Marxist, purely proletarian party was no doubt an extremely difficult task. As Mao pointed out, "Due to the relationships in these places, in the organization of the Party in the villages, many members of a particular branch have the same surname, making the branch meeting simply a family meeting. This being the case, a 'Bolshevik party of struggle' is extremely rare."[15] The difficulty lay in the variety of non-proletarian ideas based on a petty bourgeois ideology that infiltrated the Party from all sides, and from time to time, this petty bourgeois mentality was not addressed, leading to trouble within the Party. In such cases, it was both important and extremely difficult to maintain the proletarian nature of the Party and the purity of Communism. The CPC, represented by Mao and guided by the Marxist-Leninist theory of party-building, specifically analyzed Chinese characteristics that were different from the proletarian political parties of Europe, pointing out that "the issue of the leadership of the proletariat is an important issue. In the countryside, the Party is composed almost entirely of peasants. If it is not led by the proletariat, its direction will be wrong."[16] Emphasis was placed on the ideological construction of the party, prioritizing ideology in party-building, and thereby successfully addressing the conditions of a Chinese society where the working class was small and weak, while the peasantry and petty bourgeoisie formed the bulk of the population. The major issue, given these circumstances, was how to build the CPC into a proletarian revolutionary party.

c. Ideological Construction of the Party as the Premise and Foundation of Various Party-Building Activities

The theory of ideological construction was a central thread in party-building, running through all aspects of it and serving as both the premise and foundation for the Party's other construction efforts.

The CPC's theory of ideological construction was an important premise in its political construction. In political construction, the determination of the Party's direction, the formulation of its strategy and guidelines, and the determination of its political tasks during various historical periods all required proper scientific theoretical guidance and had to be based on an ideological line. The correctness of the ideological line directly determined whether the political line was correct. For the Party's political construction, the role of its ideological construction was manifested in several ways. First, only if the Party was correct in ideology and theory, or specifically, if there was a Marxist ideological direction, could it correctly observe and analyze the situation and propose an appropriate political mission and develop the correct political direction and its various guidelines and policies. Second, the correctness of the ideological line determined whether the Party's political direction and various guidelines and policies could be properly implemented. If the ideas within the Party were not unified, the political line would not be realized. Third, it was necessary to overcome and correct the wrong tendencies in the Party, especially overall errors. It was necessary to first clear the source of the error, then raise the level of Marxist theory within the whole Party. During the Great Revolution, Chen Duxiu mistakenly exaggerated the counter-revolutionary forces and abandoned the leadership of the proletariat. His rightist opportunism led to the defeat of the Great Revolution. The leftist errors during the Agrarian Revolutionary War included duplicating the experience of the Russian revolution, failing to study China's national conditions and the actual situation of the Chinese revolution, and violating the ideological line of seeking the truth from facts, which led to serious setbacks in the Chinese revolution. Mao Zedong adhered to the principle of seeking truth from facts, combining the basic principles of Marxism-Leninism with the concrete reality of the Chinese revolution, and discovering an appropriate revolutionary path that entailed seizing power by surrounding the cities with rural strongholds, thus putting an end to the leftist leaders at the Zunyi Conference. After this, the leadership of the Chinese revolution saw one triumph after another. The facts of history proved that the ideological line of violation or deviation from Marxism-Leninism would inevitably lead to errors in the political direction. For this reason, the success of the Party's ideological construction had direct bearing on the success or failure of its political construction.

The Party's ideological construction was the foundation for its organizational construction. In its organization, the question of whether the Party could carry out democratic centralism and safeguard the unity of the Party so that the Party could become the strong core leading the revolution and construction was a question inseparable from the Party's ideological construction. The unity of the Party was its lifeline and one of the basic requirements for its construction. This being the case, how could the Party's organization be made a unified whole? Fundamentally, only when every Party member had the same beliefs and ideals – that is, only with the consensus of the whole Party – could there be organizational consistency and political consensus. Lenin once pointed out that there was no meaning in the unity of organization if there was no unifying ideology. Such unity had never been sought before, and indeed, it would be impossible to seek it. It was because of disunity in thinking that people were divided and that organizational unity was impossible. The CPC was the strong fighting bastion that led the people's revolution, because every Party member had common beliefs and held to common ideals. In the practice of revolution, Mao always emphasized that the entire Party should seriously study Marxism-Leninism, first forming an ideological consensus, then forming political and organizational coherence throughout the Party. The CPC had always been based on ideological construction in the process of its own organizational construction.

Ideological construction was an ideological guarantee for strengthening the Party's construction of its work style. The work style was the approach Party organizations and members took to politics, ideology, organization, works, and life. It was a concrete manifestation of the nature of the proletarian vanguard. Just as the behavior of a person comes from that person's thoughts, and those thoughts determine the individual's words and deeds, maintaining and carrying forward the Party's fine traditions and style required the constant strengthening of the ideological education of Party members, strengthening each member's Party spirit, and establishing a communist outlook on and attitude toward life. In the Yan'an Rectification Movement, Mao urged the majority of Party members to earnestly study Marxism-Leninism and to rectify what was termed "the three winds," referring to the Party's style, the style of study, and the style of writing, aligning their own words and deeds to these standards. After the Yan'an Rectification Movement, not only did Marxist-Leninist theory improve, but it also formed the Party's style of excellence. People who still retained non-proletarian thinking often made the mistakes of subjectivism, sectarianism, bureaucracy, and individualism in their work, because the non-proletarian ideas were the root cause of such mistakes, and these root causes were not eliminated, inevitably leading to further error. The means and methods of eradicating the non-proletarian involved carrying out Marxist-Leninist theoretical and ideological education. The Party's style was to seek truth from facts. Everything was based in reality, and all its theories were tied to reality. The Party believed in and relied on the masses, operating "from the masses and to the masses," maintaining close contact with the masses, and taking the mass line. It was necessary to be bold in criticism and self-criticism and to uphold the truth, correct mistakes, distinguish between right and wrong, and unite the Party members. It was imperative that all Party members dare to take responsibility, not keep count of personal gains or losses, work hard, remain committed to self-denial and self-confidence, work hard and live simply, and be diligent and thrifty. One should not be arrogant or become discouraged, but should grasp the construction of the Party's work, focus on ideological education, solve ideological problems, and regularize and institutionalize the Party's ideological education. It was evident that correct ideological education for Party members was the basis for correcting their style.

2. The Main Substance of Ideological Construction

In order to strengthen the Party's ideological construction, it was necessary to clarify what constituted ideological construction. The Party's ideological construction was mainly based on the Party's proletarian worldview and methodology, armed with advanced revolutionary theory, and educating the majority of Party members to raise awareness and correct their own ideology, transform their world views, and not only earnestly join in Party organization, but also Party thinking.

a. Arming the Entire Party with Marxist Theory as a Fundamental Task of the Party's Ideological Construction

Mao believed that arming the entire Party with Marxist-Leninist theory was the CPC's fundamental task in ideological construction. Marxism-Leninism was the soul, motivation, and direction of the CPC. This was the general law of the development of the proletarian party in all countries throughout the world, and the CPC was no exception. However, the CPC had its own particularity as well, which, as mentioned earlier, grew out of its situation as a semi-colonial, semi-feudal country with an extremely large petty bourgeoisie. Because the feudalist petty bourgeoisie had a profound influence on one's thinking, and because there had been "insufficient preparation and theoretical cultivation" when the Party was founded, the conflict between proletarian and non-proletarian ideology in the Party was prominent. For this reason, it was more important to emphasize the use of Marxism-Leninism to educate the Party's own members. Mao observed, "Generally speaking, all Communist Party members with considerable research capabilities must study the theories of Marx, Engels, Lenin, and Stalin. They must study our nation's history and the current situation and trends of the movement and pass those along, educating other Party members who have lower cultural standards."[17] Liu Shaoqi stated even more clearly, "The most important issue in the construction of the Party is, first of all, the problem of ideological construction, which is to educate and transform the mindset of the proletariat with Marxism-Leninism and scientific thought and make them our Party members."[18] Mao's greatest contribution to the CPC and the Chinese people was that he accomplished the great task of integrating Marxism into Chinese society, creating the great Communist Party of China, as expressed in Mao Zedong Thought. The new Party Constitution stipulated, "The Communist Party of China has Marxism-Leninism and Mao Zedong Thought as the guiding principles for its own actions." This required the whole Party to arm its mind with Marxism-Leninism, use Mao Zedong Thought to educate its members and cadres, and use it to guide its own practice.

b. Overcoming Non-Proletarian Thought with Proletarian Thought as a Key to Ideological Construction

The key to inculcating Communist ideology throughout the entire Party, while transforming and persuading those who held various non-proletarian ideologies with a Marxist-Leninist worldview meant requiring each Party member to not only join Party organizations, but also to subscribe to the Party's thought. As early as the period of the Jinggangshan struggle, Mao was aware of the seriousness of this challenge. Because of the intensifying Agrarian Revolutionary War, the ideological education had been mentioned in increasingly urgent terms in the Party's agenda. Zhou Enlai, who served as head of the organizational department of the CPC Central Committee, pointed out, "To make the Party Bolshevik, we must first strengthen the proletarian foundation, while at the same time continuing to reform the Party's organization, particularly with the resolute opposition to petty bourgeois mindsets."[19] Within the CPC, the conflict between proletarian and non-proletarian ideologies was the main conflict, and it was an essential conflict. For this reason, this was the main problem to be addressed through ideological construction of the Party.

In 1929, at the Gutian Meeting, Mao made a clear statement regarding the manifestations, harms, root causes, and correct methods of various non-proletarian ideologies in the Party, and he laid the foundation for the CPC's theory of party-building. He believed that "the Fourth Red Army's Communist Party holds a variety of non-proletarian ideologies, and this is a great hindrance to the correct line of the Party."[20] He added, "The most pressing issue in the Red Army's Party organizations is that of education."[21] The problematic items he noted within the Red Army, including simplistic military views, extremist democratization, non-organizational ideas, absolute egalitarianism, subjectivism, individualism, rogue thoughts, and blindness, were mostly remnants from having blind attachment to a petty bourgeois mentality. The concrete manifestation of the petty bourgeoisie was mainly concentrated in three areas: a way of thinking that was characterized by making subjective, unilateral observation of a problem, taking wishes as reality when creating policies, and taking a part as the whole. Petty bourgeois intellectuals were often satisfied with book knowledge, lacked perceptual knowledge, and often expressed their thoughts in dogmatic ways. The petty bourgeoisie associated with production processes had certain perceptual knowledge, but because of the narrowness of small production, the limitations of dispersiveness, isolation, and conservatism tended to be expressed as empiricism. A large part of the petty bourgeoisie was shaken on political issues. They took little note of successes and victories, but magnified every frustration or disappointment in the revolution, sometimes even to the point of rebellion. There were numerous people among this group who worked hard and practiced for many years, yet still failed to absorb much Marxism-Leninism. They persisted in holding onto many negative thoughts and attitudes. Many of them harbored hopes for immediate success in the revolution, leading to a change in their own class status. For this reason, they lacked patience with the long-term, arduous nature of the revolution, while taking great interest in the revolutionary speech and slogans of the left. The earlier leftist error made by the Party was directly tied to these issues. For others, the temptations of the bourgeoisie were most suitable for their own tastes and were politically manifested as the right-wing and rightist views. Generally speaking, when the bourgeoise and proletariat split, leftist error tended to surface more easily within the Party, while when the bourgeoise and proletariat were united, it was more likely to produce rightist error. In organizational life, because of the limitations of the general petty bourgeois lifestyle and ways of thinking, and even more because of China's lack of development, the scattered feudal patriarchy, and the social influence of gangs, it was easy for the petty bourgeoisie to be misled on the subject of organization, sometimes resulting in them expressing wrong tendencies toward individualism and sectarianism. In the long-term guerrilla war, such erroneous tendencies were even more likely to surface. Those who espoused such wrong thinking were not dedicated to the liberation of the Party and the people. Instead, they often used the bureaucracy, patriarchal systems, punishments, individual heroism, anarchism, liberalism, sectarianism, independence, factional disputes, and even such extreme measures as hooliganism to undermine the life bond between the Party and the people and the intimate unity within the Party.

In view of the poor showing of the petty bourgeoisie, Mao emphasized that Party members should study the theories of Marx, Engels, Lenin, and Stalin, and study the history of the nation and the current situation and trends in the movement in an effort to promote the Party's scientific understanding of the world and better understand the masses individuals, collectives, and organizations within the Party. These mutual relations would improve the Party's ideological, political, and organizational direction, putting them on the correct track of Marxism-Leninism and eliminating all sorts of leftist and rightist interference. Everything then would be rooted in concrete reality, and every aspect of the Party's goal and mission would be for the benefit of the people. More dogmatic forms of Marxism-Leninism, blind duplication of foreign experience, breaking away from China's actual situation, arguing over the masses, and other unhealthy trends would be overcome, as would the ideological style and methods of subjectivism. As a result, the task of universally studying Marxism-Leninism was a major issue that needed to be addressed, and it required urgent attention.[22] It was necessary to regard the study of Marxist-Leninist theory as a regular activity of the Party. It was likewise essential to establish and improve the specialized ideological and political work institutions and combine mass self-education and transformation with specialized ideological and political work. Only in this way could the CPC continuously improve the ideological consciousness and theoretical level of all Party members and build the Party into one in which Marxism-Leninism was the guiding ideology composed of a highly conscious, disciplined, and self-sacrificing spirit, capable of representing the broad masses of people and benefiting and uniting the proletarian vanguard that would lead the masses to advance together.

c. *Actively and Correctly Carrying Out the Struggle within the Party as an Important Method for Ideological Construction*

Actively and appropriately carrying out the struggle within the Party was the basic method by which internal conflicts were to be resolved. In his "Decisions on the Boundaries of the Party," Mao wrote, "The transformation of the Party should be conducted completely according to a proletarian view… It must resolutely move past the Party's petty bourgeois mindset of freedom, independence, and idealism, fighting unhesitatingly against these." He added, "Criticism within the

Party is a weapon for strengthening party organization and enhancing combat effectiveness."[23] In an effort to use criticism as a weapon, Mao proposed that criticism be carried out during the Agrarian Revolutionary War, allowing Party members to better understand it. The purpose of this move was to enhance that Party's combat effectiveness in order to achieve victory in the class struggle. It was important that criticism not be used as a weapon to attack others. Rather, criticism had to distinguish between those inside and outside the Party. It had to pay attention to the major aspects of the revolution, prevent subjective arbitrariness and vulgarization, speak only in the basis of evidence, and always give attention to politics. In the period of the War of Resistance Against Japanese Aggression, in order to address Party members' mindset, encourage more to join the Party, improve the quality of Party members, and unite the entire Party with a proletarian outlook, Mao developed criticism and self-criticism into a rectification movement for Marxist ideological education. This gave the Marxist theory of criticism new substance and proved to be a great pioneering work in the history of party-building. In the rectification movement, Mao created a set of guidelines and policies for properly solving the conflicts between the right and wrong thinking within the Party, as well as between advanced and backward thinking, in both policy and method.

1) *Combining the study of theory with its practical application.* In the rectification movement, on the one hand, Mao called on all Party members and cadres to seriously study Marxist theory and correctly grasp its spiritual essence. On the other, he directed the entire Party to connect individual thinking with practical work, connecting theory with the history of the Chinese revolution and the Chinese situation, using Marxist-Leninist standpoints, viewpoints, and methods to learn and rectify its thinking and direction through comparison and self-reflection. In doing so, the cadres could better understand the trajectory of the Party's history from their practical experience in the present and profoundly grasp the essence of Marxism. Moreover, it would in this way more effectively overcome the subjective style of study that existed at the time, liberating many comrades from obscurantism. In order to oppose the subjectivism of theoretical and practical separation, it was necessary to carry forward the Marxist spirit of seeking the truth from facts. In the article "Reforming Our Learning," it was observed that "seeking the truth from facts" was the most effective weapon in the

hands of Party members. Through the Yan'an Rectification Movement, the spirit of linking theory with practice and seeking the truth from facts became common practices, and the learning atmosphere within the Party took on a new look.

2) *Combining criticism with self-criticism.* The fundamental purpose of carrying out the rectification movement was to "adhere to the truth and correct mistakes" and to "both clarify thoughts and unite comrades," raising the level of understanding of Marxist-Leninist theory and the level of political thought throughout the Party. Whether the rectification movement could achieve the desired results lay primarily in the study of the rectification documents and in the ability to inspire, through theoretical and practical learning, the majority of Party members to understand the truth and correct wrong mindsets. Allowing Party members to carry out criticism and self-criticism in a serious manner that was not perfunctory would promote the transformation of ideas and raise the level of understanding. Because of this, the basic approach taken by the Yan'an Rectification Movement was, from beginning to end, based on self-education and self-criticism.

In order to carry out criticism and self-criticism in a healthy manner, Mao profoundly summed up the historical experience and lessons of the struggle within the Party and pointed out the wrong policy of "continued struggle and ruthless blows" held by leftist dogmatists, stating clearly that "punishment as a warning for the purpose of healing and saving the diseased" and "healing and saving the people" were the two purposes the rectification must adhere to. In the process of guiding the Party to study rectification, the CPC Central Committee repeatedly emphasized the necessity of carrying out criticism and self-criticism as a means of seeking the truth from facts and to elevate facts and reason, persuading others and overcoming wrong ideas with correct ideas to convince the people and help every comrade to grasp the truth, discern right from wrong, and achieve true understanding. Some comrades waited for a period of time to address some problems, including their own mistakes, and allowed those errors to be repeated as they opposed the use of pressure. It was even permissible to treat internal problems as conflicts with an enemy. It was important to adopt a cautious attitude in one's treatment of others, with the goal of being neither confusing nor damaging to other comrades.

During the Yan'an Rectification Movement, leading comrades set an example through honesty and credible criticism and self-criticism, playing a leading role and dispelling the concerns of ordinary cadres as they promoted a good direction of criticism and self-criticism. This not only eliminated the unhealthy trend that existed in the Party, but also carried forward a democratic style that both clarified thinking and united Party members, making criticism and self-criticism common practice throughout the Party as the basic methods for resolving conflicts within the Party and correctly handling conflicts among the people.

3) *Combining the leadership and the masses.* The process of the Yan'an Rectification Movement fully reflected the process of combining leaders and the masses. In May 1941, the first rectification studies were carried out among senior cadres in the Central Committee, criticizing the subjectivist style and summing up the Party's historical experience. On the basis of this fundamental ideological understanding, in February 1942, a Marxist education movement was promoted throughout the entire Party, achieving an unprecedented level of unity within and throughout the Party. In October 1943, the rectification study returned to the CPC Central Committee, and the line was clearly separated from the political point of view and summed up in the Party's experiences through the Seventh Plenary Session of the Sixth General Assembly of the CPC Central Committee and the passing of its resolutions in April 1945. The Resolution on Several Historical Issues enabled the entire Party, especially its senior cadres, to achieve unity on the basis of Marxism-Leninism. The educational principle and method, moving from the leadership to the masses then back, was extended to the Party's other tasks. This working method, which combined the leadership and the masses, was summed up and promoted by Mao Zedong.

On June 1, 1943, Mao summed up the experiences since the rectification movement and drafted "Several Issues on Leadership Methods" on behalf of the Central Committee. In this document, he offered a theoretical summary of the scientific methods for realizing the Party's leadership and clearly highlighted "the principle of combining the leadership with the masses. Mao believed that in order to accomplish a task, it was necessary to give full play to the enthusiasm of the backbone of the leadership and to mobilize the enthusiasm of the masses. "In all our Party's practical work, leadership must come from the masses and flow to the masses."[24] The leadership and working methods that combined the leadership and the masses not only embodied the idea of democratic centralism, but also embodied the spirit of the mass direction and was extremely rich in substance. Of course, the formation and application of this method did not begin with the rectification movement, but the promotion and spread of this approach as an effective working method and tradition of the entire Party was one of the fruits of the rectification movement.

The rectification movement was a great pioneering work in the CPC's ideological construction. It provided experience for how to build the Party on the ideological level, setting an example and establishing several fundamental principles for carrying out ideological construction. These principles were later elevated by Mao to be the three major work styles of the Party. This work style made a clear path of the Party's ideological construction and trained a large number of outstanding cadres for the Chinese revolution.

Under the new historical conditions of the War of Liberation, a party-wide rectification movement was carried out utilizing the headings of "Three Investigations" (investigating class, ideology, and work style) and "Three Rectifications" (rectifying organization, ideology, and work style).

The CPC's historical experience proved that utilizing the rectification method to resolve conflicts within the Party, correcting its Party line, transforming its work style, strengthening its unity, consolidating its organization, and strengthening its leadership – in short, maintaining and advancing its proletarian nature – was a greatly effective weapon for building the CPC's ideology. It was an important means by which Mao could focus on building the Party from an ideological point of view, further developing his theory of Marxist construction.

3. Adhering to the Ideological Line of Seeking Truth From Facts to Strengthen the Party's Ideological Construction

In strengthening the Party's ideological line and insisting on arming the entire Party with Marxist theory, the most fundamental thing was to uphold the Party's ideological line of seeking truth from facts. The ideological line of seeking truth from facts, an approach created by the CPC, made use of dialectical materialism – that is, the underlying Marxist-Leninist worldview and epistemology – to address the practical problems of the Chinese revolution and constantly sum up the lessons learned through the struggle against and correction of various erroneous ideas. This ideological line proved through the test of the Party's long-term struggle to be completely correct, strictly scientific, and extremely combat effective. It was the lifeline of the CPC.

The ideological line of seeking truth from facts emerged during the Great Revolutionary War. In two articles entitled "An Analysis of Chinese Classes" and "Investigative Report on the Hunan Peasant Movement," Mao analyzed the various classes of Chinese society, discussed the peasant issue, and demonstrated how his views on the Chinese revolutionary path reflected the spirit of seeking truth from facts.

In formulating the ideological line of seeking truth from facts that was gradually clarified during the Agrarian Revolutionary War in 1929, Mao treated subjectivism and Marxism in opposition. He believed that subjectivism was a wrong guiding principle. He wrote, "The result of subjectivism is not opportunism, but adventurism."[25] He called on Party members to replace subjectivist methods with investigation and research. In May 1930, Mao wrote an essay entitled "Opposing Doctrinairism," in which he first used the concept of the "ideological line" and clearly put forward the principle of combining theory with practice. He noted, "The 'essence' of Marxism is to be learned, but it must be combined with the actual situation in our country. We need the 'essence,' but we must correct any doctrinairism that is out of step with the actual situation of our country."[26] To successfully combine the essence of Marxism with the actual situation in China, it was necessary to go to the masses for investigation and research, as "without investigation, one has no right to speak." During this period, though the scientific concept of seeking truth from facts had not yet arisen, Mao had already proposed it as a basic principle of the ideological line, in the form of combining theory and practice. This laid the foundation for the formation of the ideological line.

The ideological line of seeking truth from facts was officially formed during the Yan'an Rectification Movement. During this period, Mao wrote works such as "Reforming Our Learning" and "Rectifying the Party's Style," in which he clearly put forward the concept of seeking truth from facts, turning it into a scientific explanation. Beginning with the actual situation, seeking truth from facts, and linking theory with practice, he elaborated on the ideological line. The formation of this ideological line of seeking truth from facts had its basis in both theory and historical conditions.

Primarily, it was the inevitable result of the philosophical thought of the CPC as expressed in the terms "Practical Theory" and "Conflict Theory" (known collectively as "the Two Theories") that provided a philosophical argument for the Party's ideological line. First of all, the Two Theories philosophically summed up the principle of Marxism and the concrete practice of the Chinese revolution throughout its history. Based on scientific social practice, "Practical Theory" clarified the unified principle of the subjective and the objective and theoretical and practical concrete history, providing philosophical arguments for the ideological line of seeking truth from facts. Based on particular conflicts, "Conflict Theory" clarified the universality and particularity of conflict and the principle of dialectical unity, providing a philosophical argument for the ideological line of seeking truth from fact through dialectics.

In "Practical Theory," practice was viewed as the basis of cognition and the first point of view. In "Conflict Theory," the particularity of conflict was viewed as the basis for cognition, and the importance of analysis of a specific situation was to demonstrate such problems. Everything began with actual situations and sought a regular understanding of "real things." Because of the practical activities others were engaged in, it was the actual, practical things that people faced in the course of their various activities that were directly expressed as specific and unique.

In "Practical Theory," there were two leaps in the process of understanding (from practice to cognition, then back to practice). In "Conflict Theory," the basis of the process of cognition was conflict (moving from individual to general, then back to individual). Both questions were alike justified. The regularity that was sought from "real things" was a guide to action, just as a combination of guidance and practice or instruction and practice served a practical function and were tested and developed through practice.

In "Practical Theory," the general law of understanding and development came through the cycle of "practice, cognition, re-practice, re-cognition," leading to a sort of infinite wheel of thinking. In "Conflict Theory," particularity led to general understanding, then cycled back to the individual, forming another sort of infinite cycle of thought. This highlighted that the nature of seeking truth from facts was a gradual deepening of thought through a never-ending process. That is to say, even a correct understanding of the universality of conflict that was proved by practice must continue, eventually coming back to further practice, combining new thought with new concrete practice, which in turn guided more new thought. It was a continued process in which one underwent inspection and development through practical service, and this process was endless.

Another important manifestation of the Two Theories was that they provided philosophical arguments for the Party's ideological line that philosophically summarized the historical lessons drawn from the combination of the universal principles of Marxism and the concrete practices of the Chinese revolution. "Practical Theory" dug deeply into the leftist and rightist errors of the Chinese revolution, particularly leftist opportunism, while "Conflict Theory" dug deeply into the epistemological and methodological roots of Wang Ming's dogmatism. In short, for the first time, the Two Theories provided the philosophical argument for the Party's ideological line. It was on this basis that its ideological line was further developed and improved in the future.

Further, this ideological line was the product of the CPC's long-standing opposition to subjectivism. Subjectivism was a mode of thought that started when the subjective exaggerated its power to the point that it ignored objective reality. The danger of subjectivism was enormous. Throughout the history of the CPC, every flood of subjectivism caused serious setbacks and failures in the revolutionary endeavour. In particular, Wang Ming's leftist doctrine had the longest, most harmful, and worst influence on the Party, becoming the main ideological obstacle to the CPC implementing a correct line. In view of this profound historical lesson, Mao always pointed out the solution to the ideological lines and methods facing the whole Party and the struggle against subjectivism in each historical periods, particularly at the historical juncture of revolutionary transformation. In the early 1940s, Mao conducted an in-depth analysis and criticism on the basis of his earlier opposition to subjectivism, then launched the Yan'an Rectification Movement, which focused on anti-subjectivism. In 1942, Mao made an inscription of the phrase "seeking the truth from facts" for the Yan'an Central Party School. By 1945, in the report from the Seventh National Congress, the combination of theory and practice was defined as one of the Party's three main styles. The ideological line of seeking truth from facts was established within the Party. It was evident that the formation of the Party's ideological line was closely related to the ideological struggle within the Party. It was high-level summary of the Party's experience of subjectivism, especially Wang Ming's dogmatism, which embodied the struggle and enquiry of the first generation of leaders and condensed their outstanding ideological achievements.

There were three aspects to Mao's theory of seeking truth from facts:

1) *Everything starts from reality.* Mao creatively applied the materialist philosophical line to practical work, putting forward all his own views from a realistic standpoint. This so-called reality included everything that existed objectively. Mao stated, "Apart from our minds, everything is objective and practical... Only our minds (thoughts) are the subject of research."[27] Beginning from reality meant starting from the characteristics of the changing objective thing. First, it was necessary to proceed from the specific characteristics of different things. For the practical activities of proletarian parties, the most important thing was to start from the national conditions of the country. Recognizing the nature of Chinese society and China's national condition was the basis for solving all of China's revolutionary problems. The CPC recognized the semi-colonial, semi-feudal society of old China. From this basic national condition, they found a special path for the Chinese revolution. The second step was to proceed from the changing, developing, objective situation. And finally, it was necessary to engage in the sum of things in their totality.

2) *Theory is linked to reality.* Mao offered an incisive explanation of theory and practice, saying, "The CPC is only good at applying the positions, viewpoints, and methods of Marxism-Leninism, and at applying Lenin's and Stalin's theory to the Chinese revolution, removing it further from the actual historical situation. Through serious study of the actual revolutionary situation, the theoretical creation that meets the needs of China in all aspects is connecting theory and practice."[28] First, it was necessary to apply theory to practice. Mao particularly emphasized that studying Marxist theory must focus on application, saying, "For Marxist theory, it is necessary to be proficient in it and apply it. The purpose of proficiency lies in application."[29] He used the Chinese idiom "shoot the arrow at the target" as a metaphor to express the "well aimed" nature of the relationship between Marxism and the Chinese revolution, saying, "the arrow of Marxism must be aimed at the Chinese revolution,"[30] meaning that Marxist positions, viewpoints, and methods had to be put to work to solve China's problems. In addition, practice had to be guided by theory. Practice without theoretical guidance was blind practice. This was the truth of Marxism-Leninism that Mao repeatedly expounded. He pointed out that it was necessary not only to understand the conclusions of Marx,

Engels, Lenin, and Stalin regarding general laws, but to also learn their positions on and methods for observing and solving problems. Likewise, it was not only necessary to study the general theory of Marxism, but also to study the history and current situation of China. Doing so would introduce regularity and transform Marxism into a national form adapted to China.

3) *Take conscious initiative and master objective laws.* To begin with, it was necessary to conduct research and investigation, which were the premises for understanding objective laws. Investigation and research were of particular importance to the CPC. Because the Chinese revolution had no ready-made experience to learn from, it was only by conducting investigation and research that the Party could understand China's unique national conditions and find a special path for the Chinese revolution. Based on the experience of numerous investigations and studies during the Agrarian Revolutionary War, Mao summed up two studies on how to do proper investigation and research. He said, "One must keep his eyes down, not just looking at the sky. If he has no interest in or determination to look down, he will never in his life come to a real understanding of China's affairs."[31] The other criterion was to hold open investigation sessions, during which it was imperative that one not simply try to take it all in at a glance or simply listen to a few leading cadres at the grassroots level, but to crouch down and hold a variety of types of meetings among the masses. Such in-depth investigation would lead to deeper understanding. Mao emphasized his views on this sort of open investigations among the masses, saying, "Having no enthusiasm or determination to focus on the ground-level, having no desire to seek knowledge, and despising the masses like a school boy are things one absolutely must not do. It must be understood that the masses are our heroes, and that we ourselves are sometimes childish and ridiculous. Without understanding this, we will not even gain a modicum of knowledge."[32] Further, it was necessary to discover the laws of things. The emotional materials obtained through investigation were only semi-finished products, so it was necessary to put the "factory" of the mind to work to discover the internal connections between things and to form concepts and rules. Mao summarized this process of production and processing as a cycle of smoothing and refining, and thereby the ideological line of seeking the truth from facts was gradually refined in the Yan'an

Rectification Movement, becoming a theoretical weapon for unifying the entire Party's ideological understanding and promoting the unity of the Party under the banner of Mao Zedong Thought.

III

The Party's Organizational Construction

1. Democratic Centralism – the Fundamental Principle of the Proletarian Party

The organizational construction of the Party was an important part of the Marxist theory of party-building. Lenin noted, "The proletariat can and will become an invincible force because its unity of thought based on Marxist principles is consolidated by the material unity of the class organization, which unites millions of workers into one proletarian army."[33] Only through organization could the Party's correct theory, program, and line be turned into a huge material force and maximize the role of the proletarian party's combat command.

A proletarian party was the vanguard of the working class, and the core leadership and combat command of the entire class. The nature and mission of the Party determined that it must be organized through democratic centralism, because it was a political party that was the core leadership of the entire class and must have this leadership if it were to seize political power, build socialism, and achieve the ultimate goal of communism. This being the case, it was not enough to have a correct program, theory, and line. It was also necessary to rely on organization, consolidation, solidarity, and maintaining the political consensus and organizational unity of the entire party. Only by using the organizational principles of democratic centralism could the enthusiasm of all members be mobilized to the maximum extent and the will and actions of the entire party be unified and the revolutionary cause of the proletariat won.

The emergence and development of democratic centralism was a long historical process. Marx and Engels attached great importance to party organization in the struggle to create and construct a proletarian party. Their Communist Alliance

Charter and International Workers' Association Joint Charter and Organizational Regulations, approved by the General Committee in the summer of 1872, were important documents that reflected the Party's teachings and organizational principles. In these documents, Marx and Engels did not employ the concept of democratic centralism, but they always adhered to the principles of unity, democracy, and centralization. Judging from the theory and practice of Marx and Engels, the main substance of their principles for party organization were:

Organizational structure. Both the Communist Alliance and the International Workers' Association had relatively complete organizational systems that embodied the balance between centralization and democracy. At the First Congress of the Communist Alliance in June 1847, it was determined that the organization of the alliance would be composed of branches, districts, regional departments, central committees, and congresses. The alliance's constitution stipulated that the highest leading organ in the alliance was the Central Committee, which acted as the executive organ holding power. The first International Workers' Association's organizational system was more comprehensive than that of the Communist Alliance. Its highest authority was the International General Assembly. The General Council, elected by the General Assembly during the intersessional period, was to implement the resolutions of the General Assembly. There was also a core organization within the General Committee, called the Standing Committee. The Standing Committee consisted of the Chairman of the General Committee, the General Secretary, and the Communications Secretary of each country. The organization of various associations was called the Joint Commission. Below the Joint Commission were local groups, branches, and committees. It is evident that the international organizational system served as the prototype for the communist parties and workers' parties in modern nations.

A bottom-up electoral system. The draft statute adopted by the First Congress of the Communist Alliance stipulated that each branch elect its person-in-charge, that the heads of each branch form a district committee, and that the leaders be elected from the committee. The Central Committee was regularly elected by public officials from the district committees each year. If its work was unsatisfactory, committee members could be replaced at any time. The draft legislation also stipulated that every member of the International Workers' Association had the right to vote and to be elected. All elected officials were required to report their work to the electors, and they could be replaced at any time.

The party's organizational life. Communists who were members of the Communist Alliance (or the International Workers' Association) were all equal within the organization. As Engels pointed out, there was only one type of membership in the international communist community, and thus all members had equal rights and equal obligations. There were no special members. International organizational life always adhered to the principle of a minority-majority democracy. Marx was a model for abiding by this principle. For instance, at the Basel Conference, the Bakuninists asked to discuss the issue of inheritance right. Marx himself disagreed with Bakunin's view of abolishing the right to an inheritance as the starting point of a social revolution, but the General Committee, headed by Marx, agreed to discuss the issue in Congress. Marx drafted a report on behalf of the General Committee, including Bakunin's proposal, and submitted it to the meeting for discussion. The result of the discussion was that neither proposal received much support. Under these circumstances, Marx did not use the authority of the General Committee to force everyone to accept his views, instead acknowledging the status quo and letting information flow freely to the people as a part of the process of struggle.

Principles of Party activity. Marx always insisted on collective leadership in the International General Committee. Marx himself was an international leader with great prestige, but in the General Committee, it was not Marx who had final say, but a collective discussion. Any proposal, no matter who made it, was only put into effect if it was approved by the majority. When the General Committee discussed the issue, each member had a full voice and could speak freely and express his own opinions, but no one was allowed to speak for more than five minutes. According to Marx's proposal, the role of Executive Chairman of the weekly General Meeting rotated among the members.

Relationship between leaders and the masses. Marx and Engels always treated this issue according to the principles of equality and democracy, setting a shining example for the organization of all proletarian parties. Marx and Engels were recognized leaders in the international communist movement, and the activists of socialist parties in Europe and the US constantly asked them for new theories and strategies for the revolution, yet the pair always treated others as equals and only made recommendations for discussion like any ordinary member of the rank and file. They oppose others' efforts to elevate their status, and strictly prohibited self-praise. Marx once pointed out that he and Engels "both see our reputations as worthless," adding, "Because I hate all personal worship, when I travel internationally, I never make a major announcement of it. I am disgusted by such displays and never respond, or if I occasionally respond, it is only to rebuke the practice. The necessary conditions for Engels and me to continue to participate in covert groups of communists are that we must abandon everything geared to promoting superstitions forms of authority."[34]

The party's organizational discipline. The Constitution of the Communist League stipulated that all members must be politically aligned with the alliance, that their "lifestyle and activities must conform to the purpose of the alliance," that they "not participate in any anti-communist (politically or ethically) group," that they obey all resolutions of the alliance," and so on. Any who did not comply with these conditions would be considered guilty of a "crime against the league, and "depending on the circumstances, may be temporarily suspended or permanently expelled from the league." Marx believed that strict discipline was necessary to ensure the victory of the proletarian struggle. He stated, "We must absolutely maintain the party's discipline now, or we will accomplish nothing."

In the late 19th and early 20th centuries, capitalism developed into imperialism, and the revolutionary struggle of the proletariat likewise entered a special stage of seizing power. In an effort to meet the special needs of this struggle, Lenin formulated special organizational principles for the Russian Social Democratic Labor Party at precisely the right time.

From 1899 to 1904, Lenin repeatedly emphasized the need to build the party in line with the principle of centralism. In his 1899 article "Our Current Mission," he clearly laid out the principle of centralism for the first time. Lenin believed that the new proletarian party established according to the principles of centralism must have two main characteristics. First, the party's local activities should be completely free, but at the same time, a unified, and therefore centralized, party must be established. The second necessary characteristic was that the party should strive to become a revolutionary party whose main goal was striving for political freedom, while at the same time, it must resolutely avoid planning a political conspiracy. Lenin proposed three important points in connection with these two characteristics. 1) As a profound summary of the historical experience of the international communist movement, it should be opposed to and overcome group habits that existed in the early days of the establishment of the Russian Social

Democratic Labor Party. 2) He not only explicitly put forward the principle of centralism, but also regarded it as one of the main features of the new proletarian party, which was distinguished from other proletarian parties. 3) The conspiracy to oppose the minority not only clarified the centralism of the new proletarian party and the various forms of centralism that had appeared throughout history, but also made unconscious theoretical preparations for the subsequent principle of democratic centralism.

At the time, the biggest obstacle to the implementation of centralism was a school of economic thought. This group believed that the implementation of centralism violated democratic principles. In his book *What Is To Be Done?*, Lenin pointed out the necessary conditions for the implementation of democratic principles are complete openness, an electoral system, and general supervision. However, under the tsarist autocracy, the implementation of this sort of democracy was like a group of peasants carrying wooden sticks to fight the tsar's well-equipped traitors, spies, and gendarmerie troops. They often failed in the early stages, resulting in the party only being able to implement a centralized system. Beyond that, Lenin also offered an unprecedented systematic explanation of the principle of centralism, further developing specific rules for implementation and developing the centralized system into an effective, relatively complete organizational system.

At the Second Congress of the Russian Social Democratic Labor Party in 1903, the party split into Bolsheviks and Mensheviks. This system of two schools in one party lasted for nearly a decade. These two factions were constantly at loggerheads over organizational issues such as timing, scale, and scope, which went far beyond the struggle with the school of economic thought. In an effort to replace the centralized system with an autonomous system, the Mensheviks fiercely criticized the principle of centralism, claiming that it was a centralized form of "bureaucracy" and that Lenin wanted to turn the party into a "huge factory" and serve as director of its Central Committee. In the party, the "serfdom" was implemented, and party members became "cogs" and "screws." The party should be more than the sum of its various autonomous committees. The various parts of the party need not obey the whole. Some, in fact, could be autonomous from the whole. In order to fight back against the Mensheviks, Lenin published the well-known book *One Step Forward, Two Steps Back* in 1904, in which he offered an in-depth criticism of the Mensheviks' absurd point of view on organizational issues and strongly exerted the idea of centralism, expounding on its principles of organization. In the book, Lenin repeatedly emphasized that the principle of centralism was the most basic and principled aspect of the "Iskra" (spark) party-building plan. With a centralized system, the party's ideological prestige would become a power prestige. He noted that "the concentration of ideas will determine in principle the solution to all local and detailed organizational problems," and added, "It is the only principled idea." Lenin then went on to propose the principle of implementing a centralized system. He believed that if the party wanted to carry out its work correctly, it needed the minority to be subordinate to the majority, for individuals to be subordinate to organizations, subordinates to be subordinate to superiors, and local organizations to be subordinate to central organizations. It would be unthinkable to have no principles subject to the majority and the part not subordinate to the whole. Lenin suggested that the principle of centralism must be reflected in the party's constitution, because "the charter is an official expression of organization." The formulation of a good charter by the party was a fundamental organizational measure to ensure that the principle of centralism was implemented. Only when the party strictly abided by this charter could it get rid of self-interest, remove the group's arbitrary troubles, and remove its unnecessary arguments. For this reason, the principle of centralism "should run through the party's entire constitution." In this way, the idea of centralism transformed from theory into practice, into party law, and into the will of the entire party, thus transforming into a material weapon for destroying the authoritarian system of the exploiting class.

2. The CPC's Inheritance and Development of the Principles of Proletarian Organization

Democratic centralism was the fundamental organizational principle of the CPC and a basic part of Mao's party-building theory. In the long-term practice of revolutionary struggle, the Mao-led CPC continuously developed and perfected the principle of democratic centralism and greatly enriched and developed the theory of Marxist-Leninist principles of democratic centralism.

Before the founding of the CPC, Mao debated and studied with the revolutionary intellectuals who represented the rudimentary forms of Communist ideology, such as Li Dazhao, Chen Duxiu, Cai Hesen, and Zhou Enlai, considering together what sort of organizational principle was to be established. On August

13 and September 16, 1920, Cai Hesen wrote two long letters to Mao Zedong from Germany, introducing Lenin's theory of party-building and explaining the basics of his own view of party organization. In reference to party organization, Cai said that the organization of the Bolshevik Party was highly centralized, and that it had an iron discipline. It would certainly be able to develop a small number of highly conscious, highly organized elements who would adapt to the war era and undertake to effect a great transformation. Cai Hesen also proposed that the highest organ in the Party should be the Central Committee. The various parts and activities of the party, including newspaper, congress, group, or a variety of activities, must be under the command and supervision of the Central Committee. In his reply, Mao said, "Your letter is very appropriate. I do not disagree with a single word." With their advocacy, the Party was established from the beginning on the principle of democratic centralism. After the First National Congress, this principle was embodied in the constitutions of the Second, Third, and Fourth National Congresses.

In June 1927, the Politburo of the Central Committee was for the first time entrusted by the Fifth National Congress, as mentioned in the second chapter of the Third Amendment to the Constitution of the Communist Party of China (entitled "Party Construction"), with the understanding that "the guiding principle of the Party department is democratic centralism." The principle of democratic centralism was clearly put forward and affirmed in the Constitution of the Communist Party of China. The Constitution was passed by the Sixth National Congress in July 1928, offering a preliminary clarification of democratic centralism. In the resolution of the Gutian Meeting, drafted by Mao Zedong in December 1929, Mao advocated that ideological construction be closely integrated with the organization of democratic centralism, and also that it was necessary to eradicate extreme democratization and correct non-organizational views. In democratic life, the minority must obey the majority.

In 1937, China was facing the grim situation on the eve of Japanese imperialists' launch of a full-scale war of aggression against China. In order to win millions of people to enter the Anti-Japanese National United Front and jointly fight against Japanese imperialism, Mao held a meeting of communist representatives in Yan'an in May 1937. In its conclusions, not only did the congress rise to the level of providing "a guarantee against Japan," but it also stated that the Party must have power if it was to achieve the goal of defeating Japan. How could the

Party attain this power? Mao pointed out that the Party must rely on democratic centralism if it were to have the power to mobilize the enthusiasm of the entire Party. In the reactionary and civil war periods, centralism was more prominent. In the new era, centralism had to be linked to democracy. The implementation of democracy was a means to give full play to the enthusiasm of the entire Party. With the enthusiasm of the whole Party, it was possible to train a large number of cadres, eliminate the remnants of the sectarian concept, and unite the whole Party with bonds of steel."[35]

In October 1938, the War of Resistance Against Japanese Aggression was on the threshold of a strategic defensive transition phase. The Japanese aggressors turned their main forces to the enemy's back battlefields. The KMT accepted a policy of passive military resistance. Within the CPC, Wang Ming committed rightist errors and abandoned the Party's leadership. At the same time, Mao noted that "because our country is so small and with a small-production patriarchal system, and because there is still no democratic system here, this situation is reflected in our Party, which has resulted in an insufficient democratic life and hindered the full expression of enthusiasm throughout the Party."[36] In response to this situation, Mao put forward clear requirements regarding how to rely on democratic centralism to mobilize the enthusiasm of the entire Party during the Anti-Japanese War in his political report to the Sixth Plenary Session of the Sixth General Meeting of the Central Committee of the CPC, saying, "The great struggle facing the Communist Party of China requires all the Party's leading organs, members, cadres, and the entire Party to exert their enthusiasm to achieve victory. This so-called enthusiasm must be embodied in the leading organs', cadres', and Party members' creative ability, spirit of responsibility, active work, and their courage and ability to ask questions, express opinions, and criticize shortcomings, along with the supervisory role of leading cadres from a benevolent point of view. Without these, any enthusiasm is in vain. The exertion of such enthusiasm depends on the democratization of life within the Party. The democratic life of the Party cannot be achieved simply by enthusiasm, but by the forging of a large number of capable people, which is only possible through democratic life."[37]

In order to enhance the Party's combat effectiveness and make a breakthrough in the war, Mao also emphasized in his report that "expanding intra-party democracy should be seen as a necessary step toward consolidating and developing the Party and making it active in the great struggle."[38] He emphasized the importance of expanding intra-party democracy and emphasized the need to strictly abide by individual subordination to the organization, the minority's subordination to the majority, each individual subordinate to his superiors, and the entire Party subordinate to these central disciples of "Four Subordinates," so that the Party's internal relations could be kept on the right track and the Party be unified. In 1945, the War of Resistance Against Japanese Aggression was nearing victory, and it was on the basis of the Yan'an Rectification Movement that the Seventh National Congress was convened.

The Seventh National Congress recognized and demonstrated the importance of democratic centralism to the principles of organization. Liu Shaoqi pointed out in his report on the revision of the Party Constitution, "Our Party is not the sum of many simple numbers of Party members, but a unified organism organized by all Party members according to certain rules. It is the combination of the Party's members and leaders, the head of the Party, the unity of the Party's organization at all levels, and the masses of Party members in accordance with certain rules. Such rules constitute the democratic centralism of the Party."[39]

The amendments to the Constitution passed at the Seventh National Congress were an expression of democratic centralism as "centralization on the basis of democracy, and democracy under central guidance." For the first time, and in concise language, the dialectical relationship between democracy and centralization was fairly and accurately expressed. Regarding a democracy under centralized guidance, much had now been said, and some even viewed it as the theoretical basis for a centralized bureaucratic system. In fact, Liu Shaoqi explained his meaning very clearly in *On the Party*, noting that a democracy under centralized guidance occurred at all the Party's meetings, which were convened by its leading organs. Further, the Party's internal elections and resolutions had to be fully prepared and carefully considered, and it was necessary that they follow certain procedures. Finally, all Party members were necessarily bound by the Party Constitution and unified discipline, subordinating themselves to the overall situation and to the whole, and resolutely opposing extreme democratization and anarchism. All this was precisely for the purpose of promoting democracy in accordance with normal procedures and channels. In the specific work, some people understood that democracy under centralized guidance simply voted and elected according to the will of the party's leading organs, thus weakening and destroying democracy within the party. This would indeed be a serious problem deserving attention in the life of the party, but it was in fact a misunderstanding of the nature of a democracy under centralized guidance, and it did not follow that democracy should be separated from centralized guidance.

After the Seventh National Congress, Mao Zedong's theory of democratic centralism made new developments. During the War of Liberation, in September 1948, Mao summed up the experience of implementing collective leadership and drafted the decision on improving the party committee system for the central government. He pointed out that the party committee system was an important system for ensuring collective leadership and preventing individuals from organizing. At the Second Plenary Session of the Seventh General Assembly of the Central Committee in March 1949, Mao focused on the working methods of the Party Committee. Very favorable organizational preparations had been made to further enrich and develop the idea of democratic centralism, and in order to welcome the arrival of a new stage of party-building.

3. Basic Content of the Party's Organizational Construction

The Party's organizational construction was a significant part of the substance of party-building. It included the tasks of Party cadre team-building, Party member team-building, and the construction of democratic centralism. The construction of the Party's cadres was at the core of organizational construction, and the building of Party members was its foundation, while the construction of democratic centralism was an important task of the Party's organizational construction.

a. Cadre Team-Building

Party organization was made effective and powerful through Party cadre teams. Party cadres were the backbone of Party organization, the main implementers of the Party's line, principles, and policies, and the decisive force for realizing the Party's leadership.

1) *"After the political line is determined, the cadres are the deciding factor."*[40] The CPC had always believed that the issue of cadres was important, primarily because the great revolutionary struggle required a vast number of cadres to organize and lead it. Mao observed, "The CPC is a party that leads the great revolutionary struggle among a large ethnic group of tens of millions of people. Without a cadre

leadership that abounds in both virtue and talent, it is impossible for the Party to complete its historical mission."[41] Formulating a correct political line depended on correct organization, and the only way to guarantee that was to have cadres as organizers at every level of the Party and as the organizers of the revolutionary cause.

The broad masses of cadres shouldered the heavy responsibility of implementing the Party's line, principles, and policies, and of organizing and leading the masses to realize the Party's basic line at various historical stages. Only through their role as "shepherds" among the masses could the Party's general line and policies be transformed into the conscious action of hundreds of millions of people and the Party's cause be won. Mao believed that a cadre's pledge to the Party's various undertakings was not just meant for the Party's general line and overall task, but also for the specific work and tasks of a certain region and unit. For some places and units, the situation was not easily opened, the work not easily undertaken, and the people's situation not clearly evident. As Mao pointed out, "One of the basic reasons many locales and organs cannot achieve their work is that they lack a normal, sound leadership backbone to unite and connect with the masses. In a school of one hundred people, if there is no leader for the faculty, staff, and students, even if all are extremely active, decent, and astute, the school will not do well."[42]

Cadres were the bridge linking the Party to the masses. The Party was a faithful representative of the interests of hundreds of millions of people and a fighting force that wholeheartedly sought the interests of the people. The cause of the Party was the cause of the masses, and the implementation of the principles and policies formulated by the Party depended on the people's initiative. However, it was necessary for the broad masses of the people to follow the Party with sincerity and unity and to engage in various undertakings under Party leadership. An important aspect of this was the Party's reliance on the cadres to mobilize and spread propaganda among the masses and organizations. If there were not enough cadres in close connection with the masses, the Party would not survive. When the foundation was laid at Jinggangshan, Mao emphasized that the cadres should "organize, train, and send them into position for economic construction. They are the commanders on the economic front, and the masses are the combatants."[43] Later, Mao continued to consider close contact with the masses as one of the three main components of the Party's style. The Party maintained close contact with the masses through various levels of cadres, relying on them to strengthen leadership over the masses and accomplish various tasks. In this way, the Party would not be separated from the masses, and its cause would be invincible.

2) *Cadre line of meritocracy and standard of employment according to ability and political integrity.* Mao said, "In our national history, there have always been two opposing approaches in the issue of the use of cadres. One is the approach of 'meritocracy' and the other of 'nepotism.' The former is a proper approach, the other improper."[44] The selfless nature of the proletariat determined that the CPC would employ the meritocracy approach. When criticizing Guo Fan's appointment, Mao emphasized that it was necessary to "adhere to the fair, impartial style of the cadres to consolidate and unify the Party. This is an important responsibility of the Central Committee and leaders at all levels."[45] Mao insisted on "all-inclusiveness," opposing sectarianism and cliques. He once said that anyone who asked him to arrange work for them would be declined. He did not introduce, recommend, speak, or write on behalf of his friends. These were the "four nos" by which he opposed nepotism.

Adhering to the line of meritocracy in dealing with cadres meant that cadres were judged on the standards of ability and political integrity. The CPC adopted this approach from Marxism, and it borrowed the criteria for employment used by ancient Chinese politicians, creatively proposing two standards of "virtue" and "ability." This included "understanding Marxism-Leninism, having political foresight, having the ability to work, sacrificing oneself, being able to solve problems independently, remaining cool in difficult circumstances, and working loyally for the nation, class, and Party." For Mao, the standard of virtue was summarized as "resolutely implementing the Party line, following Party discipline, having close ties with the masses, having the ability to work independently and being willing to do so, and not seeking personal gain."[46]

After a cadre's standards of both ability and political integrity had been determined, the crucial issue was how to identify and select talent to leadership positions at all levels. For the investigation and identification of suitable cadres, Mao believed it was necessary to first broaden one's horizons and improve one's way of thinking. Some comrades agreed to the principle of selecting cadres with both ability and political integrity, but they found it difficult to identify talent. There were problems with thinking and method, as well as the issue of a lack of vision. During the Agrarian Revolutionary War, when he heard some people sigh and say there were no cadres, Mao retorted, "Are there really no cadres? The masses have been trained in the agrarian struggle, the economic struggle, and the revolutionary fighting, from which emerged countless cadres. How can we say that there are no cadres? They must lose their mistaken view and see the cadres standing right in front of them."[47] In addition, he proposed that the main method of identifying cadres "not only depends on the cadres' affairs, but on the whole of history and the entire cadre divisions."[48] In this way, mistakes in the use of human resources could be avoided. Mao further emphasized the need to examine and identify cadres to select and train successors in the practice of revolutionary and mass struggles. He said, "All who are truly united and connected with the masses must be formed gradually from mass struggle, and they must not depart from mass struggle."[49] He added, "The active elements generated in the struggle must be constantly promoted to replace the original deficient group or corrupt elements."[50]

3) *Cadre training and education.* The proletarian revolution required thousands of cadres. In order to ensure its revolutionary cause, the CPC paid great attention to the training and education of cadres. First, it had to "guide them." Mao believed it was necessary to push the cadres, let them work, and let them grow their talents through practice. In the process, they should be given opportunities for guidance. Leadership experience could only be gained after one had embarked on a leadership position, never before. Mao noted, "To be a capable senior commander, not fledgling and not just talking about the role on paper, requires the schoolroom of war."[51] In war, "there is often no chance to learn first, but to learn while doing and through doing." It was only in this way that one could become a mature leader, able to make a significant contribution to the cause.

It was likewise necessary to "improve them." Mao observed, "This learning opportunity will educate them so that they can theoretically improve their ability to work."[52] The most important part of improving the quality of the cadres was to raise their level of Marxist theory. Mao said, "The naked eye is not sufficient. We need telescopes and microscopes to help us see better. Marxism is a political and military microscope and telescope."[53] However, learning theory involved more than simply highlighting the memorandums and conclusions of revolutionary teachers. Mao repeatedly emphasized theoretical and practical learning methods, pointing out that "the great power of Marxism-Leninism lies in its connection with the specific revolutionary practice of each country. For the Communist Party of China, it is necessary to learn to apply Marxist-Leninist theory in the specific environment of the Chinese revolution." He went on, "Departing from China's characteristics to discuss Marxism is just abstract, empty Marxism."[54] Mao also summed up the theoretical study and research on "establishing the practical principle of studying the Chinese revolution as the center and guiding principle for Marxism-Leninism"[55] as the direction for the cadres' theoretical study.

Finally, it was important to "love and protect them." One way to love and protect the cadres was to "check their work, helping them summarize their experience, carry forward their achievements, and correct their mistakes."[56] This would allow them to make fewer, or even no, mistakes. Mao noted, "If there is no correction and no inspection except when serious mistakes are made, that is no way to love and protect the cadres."[57] The second way to love and protect the cadres was to properly treat those who had made mistakes. Mao said, "For cadres in error, generally, a method of persuasion should be adopted to help them correct their mistakes."[58] The third way to love and protect the cadres was to "take care of their difficulties." For instance, "When cadres have problems with diseases, life, and family, as much as possible, these must be addressed enthusiastically."[59] Training new cadres was of strategic importance, particularly young cadres. Some Party members were not enthusiastic about selecting new cadres, especially younger ones, because they had no concern for young cadres, and they feared the new recruits would not be able to carry their weight. But this was a case of political myopia. Mao recognized that, in order for the Chinese construction and revolutionary cause to continue, there must always be a new wave of young people to take over the work. He emphasized that "if the Party does not have a large pool of new cadres to work with the old cadres, our whole enterprise will be interrupted."[60] Thus, the entire Party was required to train a large pool of new cadres in an intentional way as part of its combat mission.

4) *Proper treatment of cadres who made mistakes.* In the practice of transforming society and the world, the broad masses of cadres would inevitably make mistakes of one kind or another. The CPC had a series of correct principles, policies, and theories regarding how such errors should be addressed.

First, it was important to focus on the reasons the mistakes were made, which is to say, "to focus on analysis of the environment at the time the mistake was made, the content of that error, its social and historical roots, and its contemporary roots."[61] Mao believed that it was inappropriate to analyze the causes of the errors in a way that "placed too much emphasis on individual responsibility." Doing so would make it impossible to unite large groups to work together, and this would not benefit the Party's cause. Further, there had to be a current policy for those who made mistakes. In response to cadres who made mistakes, the leftist opportunists such as Wang Ming resorted to "cruel struggles," "ruthless blows," and "correction to the death" policies. By contrast, Mao emphasized that "we expose mistakes and criticize shortcomings, just as a doctor treats a disease, for the purpose of saving people, not killing them." He added, "To treat ideological and political problems, we must not adopt a reckless attitude. We must adopt an approach of treating sick people in order to save them."[62] The principle of healing and saving sick people and punishment for learning from past mistakes to avoid future ones was further expounded by Mao in the principle of "unity-criticism-unity," which was based on the desire for unity and the commitment to struggle through criticism in order to resolve conflicts, thus achieving a new basis for unity. It was precisely because the CPC adhered to this sort of correct policy that the broad masses of cadres were closely united under the Party banner and achieved a great victory together. Finally, cadres who made mistakes also needed to have the mindset of correcting those mistakes. Any shortcomings and mistakes would cause harm to the Party's cause and to the people. This required the cadres at all levels of the Party to take a serious attitude in the face of those mistakes, humbly accept the criticism and help from others, and do a better job in the future. Mao had always advocated allowing others to make mistakes, and also allowing them to correct their mistakes. However, these mistakes were not only "harmful to the group, but also to the individual."

b. Democratic Centralism

Building democratic centralism was an important task of the Party's organizational construction. Only if democratic centralism were implemented could a comprehensive, rigorous party organizational system be implemented and unity of the entire Party and all its various organizations be established. It was also a necessary prerequisite for correctly handling Party leadership and the relationships between the Party's superior and subordinate organizations, members and cadres, and between various organizations, as well as for the normalization of political life within the Party and generating enthusiasm throughout the entire Party. It likewise enabled the establishment of a scientific leadership and work system, so as to formulate and implement the correct line, principles, and policies to achieve the correct leadership of the Party.

The Party understood the basic connotation of democratic centralism as that of a system based on the centralization of democracy and the unification of democracy under centralized guidance. It was the application of Marxist epistemology and the mass line in the Party's life and organization. This generalization reflected the essential features of democratic centralism and clarified the interrelationship between democracy and centralization. Democracy and centralization in the democratic centralist system were two categories of the Party's organizational principles, in a relationship that was both dialectical and unified, making them interdependent, mutually restrictive, and mutually reinforcing. Mao said, "Democratic centralism, which is both democratic and centralized, unites two seemingly conflicting things – democracy and centralism – into a certain form. There is no insurmountable chasm between democracy and centralism."[63] The dialectical unity between democracy and centralization was embodied in, on the one hand, the fact that democracy was the basis and premise of centralization. Without a broad base of democracy, correct opinions could not be centralized, and Party members and the masses would not be motivated. Such centralization would be empty and false. Only a centralization fully based on democracy would be the right, authoritative centralization. On the other hand, democracy was subject to centralization and guidance through a centralized guidance organ. Centralization was itself a requirement for democracy, because only under the central government's guidance could democracy have a proper direction and party organization, allowing the Party's enthusiasm and creativity to be put to work more fully. If there was no centralization, there would be no way to form a unified opinion, making it difficult to do anything, and thus, democracy would not be achieved. Therefore, in emphasizing the promotion of democracy, it was important for the Party to pay attention to safeguarding its unity and centralization, and when emphasizing centralization, it was necessary to give attention to democracy as the foundation, and not to emphasize either in a one-sided approach. Adherence to democratic centralism required the Party to oppose individual arbitrariness, patriarchalism, extreme democratization, and anarchism. It was necessary to overcome the problems of both insufficient democracy and insufficient centralization.

After the principles of democratic centralism were formulated and written into the Party Constitution, the CPC's understanding of this principle continued to go through a process of development. From 1927, throughout the history of party-building, the CPC made definite use of democratic centralism to guide its organizational activities. However, this brought both extremely rich experiences and extremely profound lessons. In the Party's relevant historical documents, the reports and works of Mao Zedong, Liu Shaoqi, Zhou Enlai, and Deng Xiaoping all contain theoretical summaries of these experiences and lessons, which gradually gave shape to popular ideas within the Party over time.

The first of these ideas was that democracy and centralization had to be carried out simultaneously. It was important that neither side be neglected if the Party were to persist. This was a basic view of democratic centralism. The Gutian Meeting Resolution put forward the principle of democratic living under the guidance of the organization. This united democracy and centralism organically, showing the dialectical relationship between the two. During the period of the Yan'an Rectification Movement, after a period of in-depth study of the Marxist-Leninist theory of party-building, the CPC realized that "democratic centralism is both democratic and centralized. If democracy is followed without any higher leadership, the result will be anarchy, and nothing will be done. On the other hand, if there is only higher leadership without democracy, there will be no way to expose shortcomings, and our work cannot be improved."[64] In the report of the Seventh National Congress of the Communist Party of China, Mao Zedong and Liu Shaoqi used two phrases with similar wording – "centralization on the basis of democracy, and democracy under centralized guidance" – to summarize the substance of democratic centralism and explain the dialectical relationship between democracy and centralism. At the same time, they also made it clear that, in practice, although there might be some emphasis on one or the other in certain situations, neither democracy nor centralization could be neglected. Tendencies toward both extreme democratization and bureaucratic centralism were unacceptable. From that time on, during the War of Liberation, the Party made several successive efforts to strengthen the party committee system, establish a reporting system, and improve the working methods of the party committee. All of this was done under the guidance of the basic ideas laid out above.

The second idea that took shape during this time was "the Four Subordinations," which became an important principle of democratic centralism, while at the same time providing a disciplinary principle for the Party. Generally, the Four Subordinations were an important manifestation of the Party's centralism, and "the minority is subordinate to the majority" was also a principle guiding the democratic party committee system. In October 1938, Mao summed up the historical experience in the report of the Sixth Plenary Session of the Sixth General Meeting of the Central Committee of the Communist Party of China, summarizing the Party's discipline as individuals subordinate to organizations, the minority subordinate to the majority, each individual subordinate to his superior, and the Party subordinate to the Central Committee. At the same time, the Four Subordinations were important principles of democratic centralism. The Sixth Plenary Session of the Sixth General Meeting of the Central Committee accepted these opinions presented by Mao Zedong and wrote them into a political resolution. In 1940, the Central Committee issued the Decision on Enhancing Party Spirit, in which it was noted that the Four Subordinations were an important part of Party spirit. It called on the entire Party to use it to check and effectively correct all sorts of speech and action that violated the Four Subordinations. Thus, the idea that the Four Subordinations were both a principle of democratic centralism and of party discipline was established by the entire Party. Beginning from the Seventh National Congress, the Party Constitution included clear provisions regarding this issue.

The third key idea was that it was important to pay closer attention to the building of democracy within the Party. Just as the power of the Party in 1929 was similar to the idea that "a single spark can start a prairie fire," Chen Duxiu seized on the fact that intra-party democracy was shrinking in a reasonable way to accuse and even frame the Central Committee, saying that "even the minimum democracy was fundamentally ruled out." At this time, the Central Committee correctly replied that the limits of the Party's democratization were determined according to objective and subjective conditions, and objectively speaking, the White Terror was an extremely serious matter at the time, making it impossible to demand further democratization, which was the only way to "help the Russian tsar's gendarmerie" (as Lenin put it). With the great improvement in the revolutionary situation and the fundamental change in the objective situation, Mao pointed out to the Sixth Plenary Session of the Sixth General Meeting of the Central Committee in 1938 that "expanding intra-party democracy should be seen as a necessary step to consolidating and developing the Party and making it great. The struggle is lively and active, competent and enjoyable, and is an important weapon for breaking through the difficulties of the war."[65] By 1945, the Party's view on promoting intra-party democracy on the basis of conditional permission had matured. At that time, based on the objective conditions in Yan'an and other liberated areas, Liu Shaoqi pointed out in the report on the Seventh National Congress, "Now, we must release democratic life within the Party. We must implement a high degree of intra-party democracy and implement it at a high level, under a highly centralized leadership."[66]

Based on these views, the Party emphasized the need to manage several types of relationships in the process of implementing democratic centralism.

The relationship between democracy and centralism. In democratic centralism, the relationship between democracy and centralism was a dialectical unity. They were two contradictory sides of the same unity, both contradictory and unified. Their contradiction was manifested in the fact that democracy emphasized the full of expression of individual will (before centralization), while centralization emphasized that the individual will was bound by the will of the majority, which was centralized, emphasizing the subordination of individual will. The unity between the two was manifested in the fact that democracy was a centralized method, while the foundation and processes of centralization were determined by democracy, with the result being the democratic process. It was the embodiment and condensation of the will of the majority. Correct centralization could not depart from democracy, and correct democracy could not exist without centralization. Centralization without democracy was a rootless tree, and democracy without centralization was a fruitless flower. Neither could truly realize unity of will and action.

Centralization without democracy was autocracy. Without a democratic, mass foundation, authoritarianism and arbitrariness would inevitably lead to anarchism. Democracy without centralization was extreme democratization, which led directly to anarchism. It was evident that without the centralization of democracy and democratization of centralism, both errors would lead to the same destination, anarchism.

In the process of the Party's implementation of democratic centralism, there was a tendency to separate the two, or even pit them against one another, emphasizing one at the expense of the other. Under normal circumstances, the masses, individuals, and team members emphasized democracy, while the leaders, organizations, and secretaries emphasized centralization. Both were one-sided approaches. Some engaged in pragmatism during the implementation of democratic centralism, emphasizing democracy at higher levels and centralization at lower levels. Some only gave attention to the unity of the two, separating their substance. In form they first targeted democracy, then centralization, or democracy among the masses and centralization in the leadership, or democracy among the members and centralization among the secretaries. But the will of centralization was not aligned with the will of the majority, but rather was the will of individual leaders. This form of democratic centralism was a violation of true democratic centralism and could not achieve a truly unified will.

The relationship between individuals and organizations. Party members were subject to Party organization. This was an important principle of life within the Party. Party members were the elements that made up the organization, and the organization was the sum total of the Party members, but it was not actually a matter of mere addition. Only when individual Party members were subordinate to party organization could unity in action and unity of will be achieved. Only then could the individual will of each Party member be expressed, while with its initiation, enthusiasm, and creativity, the organization could fully exert its vitality to achieve true unity in will and action. For this reason, Party members' individual subordination should be based on democracy. "Democracy in decision-making and unity in action" was an accurate summary of the relationship between Party members and Party organizations. In dealing with the relationship between individuals and organizations, there were some problems in which Party members were not subordinate to the decision of the organization, and thus did not implement the Party's resolutions. There were also cases in which some Party members failed to fully express their will, simply blindly following Party directives. In Party life, ordinary members often failed to subordinate themselves to the organization's decisions, and often adopted negative attitudes. Cadres often found it easy to take advantage of special Party members, refusing to implement organizational resolutions, or even arbitrarily changing them. This went against organizational principles and discipline.

The relationship between the minority and the majority. The idea that the minority is subordinate to the majority was the most basic principle of democratic centralism. Implementing the principle of democratic centralism required that the principles of the minority subordinating itself to the majority be carried out to the end, so as to prevent arbitrary authoritative or power-based decision-making. But because human understanding of truth is never straightforward, but always has a particular angle, truth is often first understood by a few. For this reason, the minority and the majority are able to shape one another, meaning that in implementing democratic centralism and dealing with the relationship between the majority and the minority, the correct approach is to follow the majority while respecting the minority.

In the life and leadership of the CPC, the cases of violating the principle of the minority subordinating itself to the majority frequently occurred when average Party members of a few leaders refused to abide by organizational decisions as determined by the will of the majority through the decision-making process. In the process of addressing major problems, some cadres and secretaries often chose their own path and gave the individual final say, violating the principle of subordination to the majority. In order to strictly enforce the principle of the minority being subordinate to the majority, it was important to implement a voting system based on adequate discussion of major issues.

The relationship between lower level organizations and their superiors. The notion that lower level organizations were subordinate to superior organizations was an important party organizational principle. However, this subordination was not to be followed blindly. Before the superior organization made decisions regarding subordinate organizations, it was necessary to fully hear out the opinions of those subordinate organizations and try to achieve consistency. In implementing this principle, the subordinate organization might have different opinions, but it must also listen to its superior and make adjustments in its work or its ideological and political efforts. Therefore, the correct handling of the relationship between the two required that the lower level organization be subordinate to its superior and that the superior organization respect the lower level organization, so that superior and subordinate would be coordinated. In the life and leadership work of the Party, situations in which the superior organization failed to respect its subordinate or the subordinate organization did not follow directions from its superior occurred from time to time. Some higher level organizations failed to investigate, study, or listen to the views of subordinate organizations before making decisions on major issues. Subjectivism, bureaucracy, condescension, and simply giving orders were approaches not aligned with the actual situation, and the resistance of the subordinates made it impossible to enforce any resolution. Some subordinate organizations did not understand the requirements of the overall situation, while some took a pragmatic attitude toward the higher level organization, implementing them in a favorable way. Those that offered unfavorable excuses were not aligned with the actual situation and refused to execute the directives, or sometimes changed the organizational decisions arbitrarily. These actions were not in line with the Party's organizational principles.

The relationship between the Party's various organizations and the central government. The entire Party and its organizations were subordinate to the central government. This was the most important of the basic principles of democratic centralism. In this relationship, the central government respected the innovative spirit of all party organizations and paid attention to the opinions and suggestions of various organizations. All organizations were to strictly obey the central government and creatively implement its resolutions related to the central line, principles, policies, and decisions. In the life and leadership of the Party, some organizations proceeded from local interests, refusing to implement the central line, principles, policies, and decisions of the central government. Some even operated under a banner of starting from the actual situation and creative execution to overtly disobey the directives of the central government, which clearly went against the Party's political discipline.

The relationship between collective leadership and individual responsibility. As an important system of democratic centralism, collective leadership and division of labor with individual responsibility was an important leadership system of the CPC. The two principles of collective leadership and division of labor with individual responsibility were inseparable, and neither could be neglected. The principle of collective leadership was the working system of the Party committee. In the Party's leadership work, all major issues involving the Party's line, principles, and policies, the deployment of major tasks, the appointment, removal, and handling of cadres, and major issues involving the interests of the masses had to be discussed and decided collectively by the Central Committee, a measure to prevent arbitrary decisions being made by a minority. In the implementation of these decisions and the daily work of the Party, a system of division of labor with individual responsibility had to be employed. If things were decided collectively, they had also to be responsibly implemented, with each taking responsibility for the others. They must bear responsibility, and those who failed had to be held accountable. If there was no collective leadership, scientific and authoritative decision-making could not be guaranteed. Without collective restraint, individual arbitrariness would result and private interests would interfere in the decision-making on major issues. If there were no division of labor with individual responsibility, then collective decision-making would be held up due to the unclear delineation of responsibility. In other words, if no one was responsible, no one would act. Mao presented a brilliant summary of collective leadership and the division of labor with individual responsibility, saying, "It is a case of centralized leadership on major issues with decentralized power on minor ones. Different parts act upon the Party Committee's policies and stick to principles when there is a need to make decisions, while the Party Committee has the responsibility to supervise various types of work." This was a significant guiding principle for handling the relationship between central leadership and the division of labor with individual responsibility.

In dealing with the relationship between collective leadership and individual responsibility, major issues and daily work were often confronted with great difficulties. The problems were caused by a lack of collective discussion in the process of decision-making, which weakened collective leadership, affected the level of decision-making, and led to errors in those decisions. Issues that should not have been submitted to collective decision-making were sent for collective decisions, resulting in inefficiency and ineffectiveness, both of which should have been avoided.

The collective leadership responsibilities of the Party adhered to scientific principles, including the establishment of goals, the establishment of norms, the authorization of personnel, inspection and supervision, the handling of arbitrariness, the resolution of problems, investigation and research, and establishing standards. These were to be the focus of collective leadership.

On the basis of correctly handling this relationship, the Party proposed the following basic ideas and methods for adhering to and improving democratic centralism in practice:

a) *Strengthening education on democratic centralism and enhancing awareness of its implementation within the Party.* In the course of the Party's construction of democratic centralism, some Party members and organizations had a weak concept of the Party, weak Party spirit, and weak Party organizational discipline, which led to weak implementation of democratic centralism. Therefore, in a effort to strengthen the Party's education in democratic centralism, it was important to educate Party members and cadres on the concept of the Party, Party spirit, and Party organizational discipline, while also enhancing the awareness of implementing democratic centralism.

In the education work related to the concept of the Party, Party members and cadres were taught more clearly the core leadership position and key role of the Party. In the relationship between the Party and various other organizations, the Party was in the core leadership position. The Party played a key role in the advancement and development of the revolutionary industry. The position and role of the Party determined the extreme importance of implementing democratic centralism and achieving unity in the Party's organization, will, and action. It was necessary to make clear that only Party members and cadres who knew the core leadership position and key role of the Party had the awareness necessary to implement the principle of democratic centralism.

In education related to Party spirit, it was necessary to make clear to Party members and cadres that the Party took the proletariat and the masses as its class foundation, that it represented the interests of the majority of the people, sought the benefit of the majority, and sacrificed local interests for the sake of the overall interests. These were the Party's purpose and its program. Only by clarifying this mission could Party members and cadres develop a Party spirit that would enable them to consciously achieve the Four Subordinations in organizational work and prevent them from going against these principles in favor of personal or local interests.

In education regarding organizational discipline, it was necessary to help Party members and cadres correct the relationships delineated in the Four Subordinations. Where ideological awareness and Party consciousness had not yet reached the desired levels, it was necessary to comply with the principles of organization and accept the constraints of organizational discipline.

b) *Strengthening the practical construction of a system of democratic centralism.* Institution-building was another weak link in the Party's efforts to establish democratic socialism. Because of the life and leadership work inside the Party, only the basic principles and fundamental systems of democratic centralism were in place, while specific systems had yet to be perfected and norms and procedures had not yet been established, making it difficult for Party members and cadres to follow and for operations to be organized, supervised, and inspected. Therefore, it was important to democratic centralism that a set of clear, specific, and systematic institutional norms and procedures be established and developed to provide a reliable institutional guarantee for democratic centralism. In terms of Party life, the focus was on formulating specific systems, norms, and procedures for elections, implementing and safeguarding the voting rights of Party members, and safeguarding the democratic power of Party members and the system of democratic life. The decision-making system included the collective leadership system, system of deliberation for major issues, the decision-making rules and procedures, and the voting system. The reporting system included the supervision and inspection system for major issues and for the implementation of decisions.

c) *Establish a work adjustment mechanism for the implementation of the principle of democratic centralism.* The first priority in the implementation of decisions was to prevent deformation or reshaping of the decisions, then to prevent an execution that was simply mechanical and lacking in creativity. To achieve strict, creative implementation of decisions, it was necessary to establish a work adjustment mechanism. In cases in which the work adjustment mechanism remained imperfect, some Party members, cadres, and subordinate organizations were flexible and creative, in accord with their own knowledge and standards. With great arbitrariness, it was inevitable that mastery was not always sufficiently targeted, which affected correct execution of the decision. Some organizations started from the interests of their own units or locales, then proceeded, based on the actual situation, to creatively execute the instructions of their superiors, often arbitrarily altering the decision, which resulted in a malformed execution. It was evident that the problem lay not in the implementation of the resolutions by the subordinate organizations or individuals, but rather in the arbitrary modifications in that implementation. Therefore, in an effort to organically integrate implementation and creativity in the implementation of democratic centralism, it was necessary to establish a work adjustment mechanism. If the individual's decision regarding the organization or the decision of a subordinate organization regarding its superior was deemed not conducive or unenforceable in the execution, the subordinate was to report this to the superior within a prescribed time limit, and the superior was to make a decision whether or not to change the plan. When the superior opted not to adjust the original decision, the subordinate was to resolutely obey and implement the resolution. This led to an organic unity between execution and creativity.

d) *Improve supervision and control mechanisms to strictly organize discipline.* Supervision and inspection of discipline was the ultimate guarantee mechanism for democratic centralism. Only when democratic centralism was put in place with a principle of effective supervision and a system of inspecting and prosecuting any violation of democratic centralism could the other conditions for the implementation of a system of democratic centralism play an effective role and form a guiding mechanism. Supervision and inspection were not only a guarantee for the implementation of democratic centralism, but also a strong means and guaranteeing mechanism for leadership and management. The CPC Central Committee required that every leader and manager learn to use this means of implementing leadership, managing work, and promoting the development of various undertakings.

c. Construction of Party Membership

The building of Party membership was the foundation of the CPC's organizational construction. The Party was composed of members, who were the foundation of the Party and the main body of the Party's line. Strengthening and building Party membership was of great significance for consolidating the Party's organization, maintaining its nature as the vanguard of the proletariat, keeping its relationship with the masses, and giving full play to its leadership role. Therefore, in the CPC's organizational construction, the building of Party membership was extremely important.

The years from the establishment of the CPC in 1921 to the failure of the Great Revolution in 1927 marked the initial period of the Communist Party membership and the budding of their ideology. When the First National Congress of the Communist Party of China was convened, Party membership totaled just over 50 people. With the demands of the anti-imperialist, anti-feudal revolutionary struggle, the Party grasped the link between developing Party members and establishing Party organizations, and thus continually expanded the ranks of its membership. By September 1927, there were 57,967 Party members, and the membership body had begun to take shape.

However, because the Party was still in its infancy, there was an evident immaturity in its membership construction. This was mainly reflected in a few areas. The first was the uneven development of Party membership. The distribution of Party members in April 1927 was mostly concentrated in southern provinces like Hubei, Hunan, Zhejiang, and Guangdong. Of the members, the working class accounted for a larger proportion than any other class, and of those, few were manual laborers, and there were more male than female Party members. The second area in which the immaturity of membership construction was seen was that the Party's theory of construction was limited to the development of Party members among the proletariat, ignoring the importance of developing Party members among the peasantry and soldiers. The third area was seen in Chen Duxiu's belief that "the increase in the number of Party members is the most important issue," and that if "we do not increase the number of Party members, that is a reaction to the Party, and thus is reactionary behavior." This sort of erroneous thought led to turning a blind eye to the weight and quality of the Party members developed. This was an important lesson in the construction of Party membership during this period.

With the failure of the Great Revolution in 1927, the Party had suffered a terrible defeat. A large number of Party members and revolutionary masses were massacred. The number of Party members was reduced from 57,000 to about 10,000, and the revolution was in an extremely critical situation. At the critical juncture of the Chinese revolution, the CPC convened the August 7th Meeting, corrected Chen Duxiu's rightist error, and established the general policies of agrarian revolution and armed opposition to KMT reactionaries. Later, the rural revolutionary bases were established, and the path of encircling the cities and seizing political power were launched. The focus of the Party's work was transferred from the city to the countryside. The establishment of the Party in rural areas and of the Red Army was a new problem, never before encountered in the history of Marxism. The Mao-led CPC successfully addressed the issue of constructing Party membership in both theory and practice with an extraordinary pioneering spirit. However, during this period, "part of the Party's leadership was not able to hold the correct political and organizational line," and the Party suffered from leftist error, particularly that of Wang Ming, nearly ruining the Chinese revolution. In the construction of Party membership, the main manifestations of Wang's leftist error were the development of a one-dimensional view of the ideal Party member, the levying of a Party members' index and assault, and, in Party life, the continuation of the patriarchal system and the "relentless struggle" and "ruthless struggle" as a form of overkill in Party struggle. Because of Wang's mistake, the Party suffered serious losses.

As a result, the span from the August 7th Meeting in 1921 to the Zunyi Meeting in 1935 was a period of tumultuous development of the CPC's membership and a period of basic formation of its theory. The Zunyi Meeting, held in 1935, ended the reign of Wang Ming's leftist error in the Central Committee and established correct leadership for the new Mao-led Central Committee. From that time on, the CPC's membership construction remained on the right track. The Sixth Plenary Session of the Sixth General Meeting of the CPC Central Committee in 1938 established the Party's Marxist organizational line and changes in party organization, marking the completion of the CPC's organizational work after the Zunyi Conference, particularly since the outbreak of the war. After the War of Resistance Against Japanese Aggression had entered a stage of stalemate, by 1941, the construction of the CPC's membership was carried out extensively, and the theory of membership construction was further enriched and developed.

In May 1941, the Yan'an Rectification Movement began preparations for the Seventh Plenary Session of the Sixth General Assembly of the CPC Central Committee in 1944. The construction of the Party's membership and the rectification were carried out with great care, indicating the in-depth development of the CPC's membership construction. After the success of the Seventh National Congress in April 1945, it was evident that the CPC's membership construction had been formed into a complete theoretical system.

The period from the victory of the Anti-Japanese War in August 1945 to the establishment of the People's Republic of China on October 1, 1949, was an unprecedented period of great development for CPC membership construction and a rich time for building up Party members. During this period, in an effort to win the War of Liberation, the Party made some major decisions on the issue of membership construction, which strengthened the Party's organization and improved its combat effectiveness.

There were several special features of membership construction during the period of the new democratic revolution. First, membership construction had to be carried out in a situation in which the Party functioned as the vanguard of the proletariat. In a country like China, where there was a relatively small working class and the peasantry and other petty bourgeoisie formed the vast majority of the population, building a mass proletarian party was extremely difficult.

Under Mao's leadership, the CPC proceeded from China's actual situation and proposed a party-building line that suited that situation. He said, "First, focus on ideological and political construction, then build on the organization." That is to say, party-building was not simply about giving attention to the class composition of the membership, but of transforming and overcoming various non-proletarian mindsets with proletarian views, and thus achieving the proletarianization of Party members' thought. Guided by this correct approach to party-building, during the period of the democratic revolution, the Party's ideological construction overcame the non-proletarian ideas that existed among Party members. In this way, it trained the majority of Party members to become strong pioneers for the proletariat and build the CPC into a mass, powerful proletarian party.

The second feature of membership construction during this period was seen in the work of absorbing members, where it was important to correctly handle the relationship between quantity and quality. In the work of developing Party membership, quantity and quality were two conflicting aspects, both dialectical and unified. On the one hand, there was no specified quantity regulating the development of Party membership. Because of the arduous task of the Chinese revolution, the CPC needed to have sufficient power for shouldering the heavy responsibility of leading the revolution. For this reason, the Party had to increase the flow of fresh blood into the Party, regularly and cautiously absorbing outstanding elements into the Party organization, provided they met all the conditions. On the other hand, in order to develop the work of Party members, it was necessary to pay attention to quality. Because the quality of the members directly affected the nature of the Party, it was directly related to the implementation of the Party's line, principles, and policies and the role of Party leadership. Therefore, the issue of quality was central to the development of Party members' work, and it was impossible to ignore the question of quality and focus only on quantity. During the period of the new democratic revolution, the Party's success lay in ensuring the quantity of development while also ensuring the quality of that membership. It was imperative that quantity never be pursued so single-mindedly that quality was ignored.

The third feature was the adherence to correct guidelines in the development of Party organization. During the period of the democratic revolution, there were two sorts of wrong tendencies surrounding the development of Party members. One was to lose a grip on the flow and fail to address quality, and the other was to close the door, rejecting some who wanted to join the Party but failed to meet some conditions. Both of these tendencies hindered the normal development of the Party. In the struggle to overcome these two tendencies, the Party proposed a correct policy of "daring development without letting bad elements invade," which overcame the tendency to be too closed off, allowed the Party to develop greatly, and maintained the purity of the Party.

Finally, improving the Party's combat effectiveness required Party leaders to earnestly and diligently educate Party members. Through education, a great deal could be accomplished in the membership. Ideologically, Party spirit would be strengthened and a revolutionary outlook on life firmly established. Politically, Party loyalty would be instilled, and individual members would learn to stand firm, sacrificing their personal gain, and never rebelling. Organizationally, the concept of fulfilling Party obligations would be strengthened, safeguarding the unity of the Party and strictly observing its discipline. In work, it was important to be proficient in business, work actively, and serve the people wholeheartedly. The education of Party members ran through the entire process of party-building. To subordinate all to and serve the Party's line and central work, it was important to focus attention on helping Party members establish a worldview aligned with the proletarian order and strengthen the education at this historical turning point. The principles, methods, and educational approach were to adhere to the principles of linking theory and practice, multi-level teaching, and self-direction, strictly structuring the Party's organizational life and focusing on the rectification of the Party.

The rich experience accumulated through the long-term practice of revolutionary struggle enriched and perfected the CPC's membership building theory and principles.

1) *A correct policy for the construction of Party membership was formulated.* Specifically, it was policy of "daring development, while not letting bad elements invade." It was further necessary to overcome "the tendency to close the door" and to elevate the vigilance against "even tiny molecules to elements that attempt to invade."[67] The long-term guiding principle for membership construction was indicated by Mao when he said, "The CPC should demonstrate its high degree of accumulation in national wars, and this national enthusiasm should be specifically addressed. In every respect, it should serve as a model for its pioneers in all aspects."[68] Party members were to be "models of heroic warfare, models of

command, models of discipline, models of political work, and models of unity."[69] They were likewise models of honesty, not needing private employment, but being willing to work more for less remuneration. And they were models for seeking truth from facts, as well as of models of far-sightedness and learning. Party members could only mobilize the vitality of the nation if they "played an exemplary role as pioneers, displaying strength, overcoming difficulties, defeating the enemy, and building a new China."[70]

2) *The criteria for Party membership was to be specifically and accurately presented.* In other words, they would commit their lives to struggling for communism, placing revolutionary interests above all else. They were to abide by Party discipline and strictly respect the Party's confidentiality. They would indomitably implement resolutions, serve as a model to the masses, and continually study. Chen Yun believed that one who possessed these six qualities would be a good member of the CPC and would not tarnish the reputation of the Party.

3) *The issue of Party membership had to be comprehensively and scientifically elucidated.* In the amendment to the Party Constitution passed at the Seventh National Congress, thirteen basic conditions for Party membership were listed, alongside the basic obligations, rights, development, and withdrawal of Party members. This was the first time the rights and obligations of Party members had been laid out. The obligations the Party Constitution now stipulated included a) striving to improve the one's level of consciousness and understanding of Marxism-Leninism and Mao Zedong Thought, b) strictly abiding by Party discipline, actively participating in political life within the Party and the domestic revolutionary movement, and actually implementing the Party's policies and decisions and acting in the interest of the Party in all things, c) serving the people, solidifying the relationship between the Party and the people, understanding and promptly responding to the needs of the people, and explaining the Party's policies to the people, and d) acting in a model way in abiding by the discipline of the revolutionary government and organizations, being proficient in one's own business, and playing a role in various revolutionary industries. The rights of Party members as stipulated in the Party Constitution were a) to participate in Party conferences and publications, and in practical discussions on the freedom to implement Party policy, b) to vote and be elected within the Party, c) to make recommendations to any organ of the Party, even up to the Central Committee, and d) to criticize a Party member or organization. These provisions not only

indicated that the Party had higher requirements for its members, but that Party democracy was more adequate and mature than before.

4) *The theory of the cultivation of Party members was created.* During this period, Liu Shaoqi condensed the reality of the CPC-led revolutionary struggle and offered a long-term, fruitful study and exploration in order to formulate a complete, systematic theory of the CPC's unique cultivation of its members. It was necessary to raise members' level of self-cultivation and enhance the substance of the Party-based self-cultivation and the basic ways it was practiced.

5) *It successfully addressed the issue of Party members' education.* First, the main substance of intra-Party education consisted primarily of carrying out Marxist-Leninist education, class education, and Party education within the CPC, so that Party members could understand the correct relationship between Marxism-Leninism and the Three Principles, between the national united front and class struggle, and between a national stance and class position. In addition, it meant carrying out a historical materialist education so that Party members could truly understand "the laws of the historical development of human society and the inevitable future of communist society," understand "the historical position and role of the proletariat in society," understand "the interests of the proletariat and its task of liberating the great cause of all humankind, and understand the current tasks and fundamental goals of the CPC and its members."[71] Further it was necessary to carry out education in which the interests of the revolution were placed above all else, so that Party members could "put the revolutionary Party first, and all the personal problems with the revolution and the Party's interests above all else."[72] Additionally, the CPC's discipline and education enabled Party members to "strictly abide by the individual's subordination to the organization, the minority's subordination to the majority, each person's subordination to his superior, and the entire Party's subordination to the Central Committee."[73] Finally, the education of cadres at all levels of the Party was mainly for the purpose of "actually improving the political level and working ability of the cadres."[74]

Second, Marxist ideology was the main form of education. The Central Committee believed that the rectification movement was a good form of Marxist ideological education. On the one hand, it carefully studied Marxist works, taught the documents of the Central Committee, and continuously improved the theoretical level of Party members, achieving ideological unity. On the other hand, it was connected to the actual situation and carried out serious criticism and self-criticism to overcome various non-proletarian ideas and establish a proletarian worldview. And finally, it formulated education through Party schools. The Central Committee believed that Party schools were an important vehicle for cultivating leading cadres and cadres strongly rooted in theory at all levels of the Party. The Central Committee stipulated that the basic tasks of Party schools were to "educate cadres through the theory and practice of Marxism-Leninism" and that teaching methods "should move from less to more, from shallow to deep, from China to foreign countries, and from the concrete to abstract principles in order to achieve the purpose of helping students really understand the lessons they have learned." Learning methods should be based on the principle of individual self-study under the guidance of instructors, with group study serving as a supplementary method.[75]

6) *It addressed the issue of the working attitude of Party members and cadres.* In October 1945, Mao elaborated on the correct attitude of Party members and cadres in their work on the issue of the masses of Party members and cadres in Yan'an. He pointed out that "the essence of work is struggle. Where there are difficulties or problems, we must solve them. We work and struggle to solve difficulties. The more difficult something is, the more we must address it. This is what it means to be a good comrade."[76] He urged Party members and cadres to "give to others that which you enjoy, take the responsibility to lift the burdens of others, endure hardship when you lead others, and enjoy the privilege of following others."[77] He demanded that all Party members who took the lead be mentally prepared for the task, "taking root and blossoming among the people," saying, "We must do a good job in relating to the masses, caring for them and helping them address their hardships." At the same time, "We must tell the people and our comrades that the road is arduous," and "we must prepare for the long, circuitous road." He said, "There are many difficulties before us, and we should not ignore this fact." Rather, it was necessary to "eliminate all difficulties and achieve our ultimate goal and victory."[78]

7) *It addressed the issue of the development of Party members in the base areas.* Chen Yun pointed out that it was necessary to "adopt prudent policies" in the development of Party members. He observed, "In the military, they must undergo the test of battle or fight against ravaging and be trapped. The peasants must be tested and absorbed."[79] He emphasized, "The conditions for the development of Party members are that there are three things they must dare to do: dare to claim

their land, to fight, and to take up arms. Likewise, there are three things they must not fear: leaving home, landlords, and the KMT." He added, "We must insist on positive development and individual absorption methods."[80]

8) *It addressed the issue of Party life.* Chen Yun proposed three principles: a) positively and frankly discriminating between right and wrong, b) strictly enforcing democratic centralism within the Party, and c) that each Party member had the right to express opinions and discuss issues within the Party, but must ultimately follow and actively work for whatever decision was reached. Mao proposed that "the party system is an important system for the Party to ensure collective leadership and prevent elevation of individuals in the Party."[81] He called on Party committees at all levels and Party groups in all departments to "establish a sound system of Party committee meetings" to discuss and solve major issues and implement them individually. He stated that "it must also be noted that neither collective leadership nor individual responsibility can be neglected."[82]

9) *It addressed the rectification of Party members.* The Central Committee believed that enforcing the order of the Party's style of work, separating the ideological line from the Party's line and policy, and the tendency toward selfishness and self-interest all needed to be rectified. The Central Committee's method of stipulating on behalf of the entire Party was to first convene two or three branch conferences, educate Party members, and prepare their minds. At the same time, it publicized the importance and methods of the Party to the masses and announced the list of Party members. Then, it would hold a branch meeting with people's representatives to conduct criticism and self-criticism sessions, listen to the criticisms and opinions of the people, and carry out further self-criticism and reflect on the nature of the Party. A decision would then be made regarding which Party members should receive disciplinary action, and at the same time, a decision on the amendment should be made regarding the improper handling of past affairs. Finally, democratic elections would be held and strongly supported committees and team leaders appointed, so that the branch would truly become an organization of the progressive consciousness of the group, which was the highest structural form of class organization.

10) *It addressed the need to prevent the invasion of bourgeois ideology and strengthen the Party's ideological construction.* Mao pointed out that because of the victory, the Party's pride, its feelings of self-restraint, and its desire to enjoy life without any inhibitions or the need to live a hard life would grow. He said, "Because of the

victory, the people will be grateful toward us and the bourgeoisie will come out to join us."[83] There may be some Party members who "cannot stand the attack of shells under the guise of sweets" or "are defeated by the shells under the guise of sweets." He stressed that winning the national victory was just the first step in a long journey. After victory was won in the revolution, the journey would be longer and the work more difficult. The entire Party must continue to maintain the fine style of modesty, caution, humility, and diligence.[84]

IV

Building the Party's Work Style

1. A Distinct Difference Between the CPC and Other Parties

The CPC's work style was one of its distinguishing features. Viewing the work style from the heights of the world outlook and linking it to the Party's line for the sake of analysis and resolution as part of the construction process was another feature that distinguished the CPC from other parties. This issue was organically linked to the Party's ideological and organizational construction, and it was a major development in the Marxist-Leninist theory of party-building.

What was indicated by "party style" was, in broad terms, a relatively stable style and spirit that was often expressed by a political party and its members in politics, ideology, organization, work, and life. In general discussion, the CPC party style referred specifically to its customary style of language, as well as its long-term revolutionary practice that reflected the nature, purpose, and essential characteristics of the Party. It was Mao who first proposed and systematically discussed the concept of party style. In his 1942 article "Reorganization of the Party's Style," he noted that subjectivism had to be rejected in order to enable the Party to rectify its style of study, just as sectarianism must be opposed in the rectification of the party style and the stereotyped Party jargon must be opposed in the rectification of the writing style. In his article "On the Coalition Government," he clearly proposed three main features that distinguished the CPC from other parties: that its theory was linked to the actual situation, that it was closely tied to the masses, and that it encouraged criticism and self-criticism.

Further, in the course of long-term practice, the CPC also formulated a style of modesty, prudence, humility, continual deepening of practice, investigation and research, fairness and decency, treating all with dignity on an equal basis, diligently doing business, hard work, democratic interactions, and self-sacrifice for truth and for the benefit of the people. All of these reflected the nature of the Party and the relationship between the Party's line and direction, and between the formulation and implementation of policy and the achievement of Party leadership. For this reason, the Party's work style had always been an important aspect of party-building. The formulation of the theory of building a party style enriched and developed the CPC's theory of constructing a proletarian political party.

The first contribution was seen in the fact that this was the first time the concept of building a party style was proposed in the history of the development of the theory of proletarian parties. It was a new idea that expanded the concept of party-building.

From the time the concept of a proletarian party had been conceived, it began to form a style that was distinct from other parties, effectively formulating a party style. Even so, it was important to see the actual formation and existence of a party style expressed in theoretical terms. That is to say, the formation of a systematic theory of the construction of a party style was a product of the development of party style construction reaching a certain stage. Early in the global history of the development of proletarian parties, when Marx and Engels created proletarian parties in Europe, they offered a theoretical elaboration on why they should establish an independent proletarian party, the nature of that party, its outlook on the world, and its program. Items such as approaches and strategies did not directly address the issue of party style. The practice of building a party style during this period was centered on the reasons for having an independent proletarian party at all and how to make it the vanguard of the proletariat. The style of the proletarian party previously established was ideologically and politically guaranteed. Its progressive nature was to take up the heavy responsibility of leading and promoting the workers' movements in various countries. The discourse of Marx and Engels on these topics laid the theoretical foundation for the construction of the Party's work style, particularly in connection with the communication between the leaders of workers' movements in various countries, which involved more attention to party style and its construction.

There were two aspects of this endeavor that were particularly evident. The first was that, when it came to the personal conduct of certain Party members or leaders, the concept of "style of work" arose. For instance, in 1878, Engels criticized the social reformist Gotha Program in a letter to the General German Workers' Association leader Johann Philipp Becker, saying he had attempted to "smuggle flattery style into the Party." In 1891, Engels pointed out in another letter, this time to August Bebel, that the Party's leading cadres should be generous, saying, "Don't be petty, and take a less Prussian style in your actions." In 1895, in a letter to the renowned Italian activist Filippo Turati, he severely criticized the Bakunins for pursuing a "smart style" that would harm the socialist party. Here, the concept of "style," as used by Engels, refers mainly to the quality and style of Party members and leaders. This broad sense of the concept is just one aspect of party style, but it is the initial formation of "style of work" that came to form the concept of party style. The second aspect that was evident in discussions of the theory of party-building included the proposal of some basic principles closely related to party-building. For example, it was emphasized that Party members should be "of pure quality," "voluntarily including themselves in the ranks of warriors," and "prevent the state and state organs from becoming social masters." Further statements in which the Party's style were manifested included, "I do not advocate we raise any banner of dogma," "Marx's entire worldview is not a doctrine, but a method," "criticism is the vital element of the workers' movements," and the view that "self-criticism" was an embodiment of the Party's great inner strength. In fact, it was proposed that the proletariat must cultivate the idea of being closely connected to the masses, the idea of staying rooted in actual circumstances, and the practice of criticism and self-criticism.

In the process of leading the Russian Bolshevik Revolution, Lenin practiced and developed the theories of party style construction that Marx and Engels had conceived, particularly the idea of strengthening the work style construction under the conditions in which the Party was the ruling power. After the October Revolution, Lenin repeatedly criticized the Party's tendency toward bureaucracy and procrastination, warning that one of the largest and most serious dangers for any ruling party was breaking away from the masses. If this happened, the Party would be overrun with bureaucracy and the promotion of wealth within the Party and abuse by Party members. After Lenin, Stalin further proposed a concept of "work style" and further discussed two characteristics of "Leninist style." First, it was characterized by Russian revolutionary style, and second, by the American spirit of seeking truth. The Leninist style was a combination of these two characteristics in the work of the Party and the state. Limited to their own historical conditions, Lenin and Stalin failed to explicitly put forward a scientific concept of "party style" and failed to form a systematic theory of its construction. However, they inherited and developed the relevant discussions of party style construction in the work of Marx and Engels. It was the struggle to explore the Party's work style after the Party became the ruling power and the struggle against unhealthy tendencies such as bureaucracy that undoubtedly played an important role in the later formulation of a theory of building a party style. In the historical conditions of the Chinese revolution, Mao Zedong inherited and developed the ideas of Marx, Engels, Lenin, and Stalin regarding the construction of party style, along with concepts such as "work style" and "Leninist work style." The development path summarized the fresh experience of building a party that was the vanguard of the proletariat in a semi-colonial, semi-feudal society, clearly putting forward the scientific concept of "party style" and creating the theory of its construction with the special characteristics of Chinese communism.

The formation of the concept of party style was a theoretical sublimation of the unique experience of the construction of the CPC. The special conditions in which the CPC carried out its own party-building and led the Chinese revolutionary struggle had determined the special significance the CPC would place on Marxism, on the people, on its own shortcomings and mistakes, and on the difficulties, failures, triumphs, and successes of the revolution. The most fundamental requirement for building a Marxist political party in semi-colonial, semi-feudal China was to arm the entire Party with Marxist theory. The question was the Party's attitude toward Marxist theory, whether it would seek the truth from facts or give into subjectivism. The answer to this question would determine whether the CPC could truly become the vanguard of the working class. The Party's ability to truly assume the historical responsibility of leading the Chinese revolution was linked to the rise and fall of the revolutionary cause.

The Communist Party in semi-colonial, semi-feudal China had a small number of working class members, and when the revolutionary forces began to form, it was only a single small spark, while the enemy was powerful, combining its forces with brutal imperialists, feudalists, and bureaucratic capitalists. To defeat a powerful enemy with such a small revolutionary force, the Party had to adhere to a historical materialist mindset and had to maintain a proper close connection with the masses. China's national conditions were very different from those of Western Europe and Russia. Its conflicts were very complicated, and understanding China's national conditions while formulating and implementing appropriate approaches, policies, and principles to win the revolution was a very difficult task. In the process of achieving this difficult task, it was nearly impossible to avoid mistakes, and any mistake would damage the interests of the people, to one degree or another. For this reason, criticism and self-criticism were indispensable in a party that intended to be responsible to the people. It was under these precise historical conditions that the CPC, personally led and nurtured by Mao, gradually formed an outstanding style that linked theory and practice, remained closely connected to the masses, and practiced criticism and self-criticism. The concept of party style summed up the unique experience of the CPC in its party construction and adapted to the needs of the nation to construct a suitable party for the CPC.

Mao's concept of party style was one of the ideas related to the notion of "work style" Engels had suggested, and which Lenin had employed in criticizing Party cadres and the bureaucracy and procrastination of Soviet state organs after the October Revolution. It included Stalin's proposal of demonstrating the inheritance and development of the "Leninist work style." Such development was manifested mainly in the body of behavior, including both the individual attitude and style of Party members and the overall image and style of party organization. It was further evident in the implications and extensions a party style expressed in the personal conduct and work style of Party leaders, members, and cadres in politics, ideology, organization, life, and other aspects, as well as the style of study and communication. It was a profound revelation of the inner relationship between party style, party spirit, and the Party's view of the world.

The second contribution was that Mao's concept of party style noted its importance as a guarantee that the Party's line would be implemented. In his article "Rectifying the Party's Work Style," Mao noted, "As the Communist Party, we must lead the people to defeat the enemy. Our team will be tidy, and we will move in unison. Our soldiers and weapons must be excellent. If we do not meet these conditions, we cannot overthrow the enemy."[85] It was evident that in order for the Party to lead the people to achieve the political task of defeating the enemy, it must have the proper ideological, political, organizational, and stylistic conditions. The problem at the time was that the style was not correct, with things such as subjectivism, sectarianism, and stereotyped Party communication style being pervasive within the Party. Therefore, if the Party was to attain political leadership and implement its political line, it had to rectify its work style. Under Mao's guidance, the Party overcame the three unhealthy tendencies in its midst through the Yan'an Rectification Movement, strengthening party style and ensuring that the Party would achieve leadership. Based on the great victory of rectification, at the Seventh National Congress, Mao presented a political report entitled "The Coalition Government," in which he further discussed the significance of carrying forward the Party's outstanding style of work to realize the Party's line. Since the entire Party upheld and promoted the three aspects of the party style advocated by Mao, Party organizations at all levels and the majority of Party members and cadres could, in light of the actual situation in their region or units, creatively and relentlessly implement the Party's political line and make it the direction taken for formulating and implementing policies and principles, and this line would then truly influence the actions of hundreds of millions of people. In this way, the Party's political leadership was effectively guaranteed, as was the final victory in the War of Resistance Against Japanese Aggression and victory in the War of Liberation. Historical experience proved that advancing the Party's excellent work style and strengthening the construction of that style would indeed serve as an important guarantee for implementing the Party's political line and establishing its political leadership.

  The third contribution came from Mao's discussion of the important position party style held in the CPC's own party-building work and his emphasis on the idea that strengthening the construction of party style had a positive significance for maintaining the Party's role as vanguard of the proletariat. The reason the CPC highlighted its work in party-building was that the issue of party style was closely linked to the CPC's role as vanguard of the proletariat and to the Party's worldview. Any unjust party style was a violation against the nature and worldview of the Party. Thus, it was "an enemy of the CPC, of the working class, of the people, of the nation, and of the Party's pure nature." The perfect, decent style of the Party was governed by its loyalty to Marxism and its own nature as the vanguard of the working class. Therefore, if one was to understand and address the issue of constructing party style, it was necessary to note that the Party's worldview was a feature of the CPC's own party-building efforts and an indicator of the excellence of the Party.

As early as the Agrarian Revolutionary War, Mao Zedong and Zhou Enlai noted the significance of work style to the healthy development of the Party as a whole. During the Yan'an Rectification Movement, the CPC Central Committee and Mao explicitly regarded the construction of party style as an inseparable part of party-building and adopted various effective measures to consciously correct the unhealthy style that existed within the Party, promote an outstanding party style, and strengthen construction of that excellent style. Mao once offered an in-depth discussion of the importance of upholding the excellent style of the Party, holding that the three excellent characteristics were a distinguishing mark of the CPC. This argument highlights that the question of party style was directly related to the nature of the Party. In upholding and promoting an excellent party style, it was possible to maintain the CPC's role as vanguard of the proletariat, but losing the fine traditions and style of the Party would seriously affect that role. If the Party style were completely corrupt, it could lead to a total transformation of the nature of the Party. It was precisely because the CPC attached such great importance to maintaining its role as vanguard of the proletariat that it gave such attention to strengthening its practice of party-building. This was an important factor in the Party's continued ability to maintain its status as vanguard of the proletariat, even in a country where peasants made up the bulk of the population.

That Mao discussed the issue of party style as the pinnacle of maintaining the Party's nature was not only of practical significance in guiding the CPC to intentionally strengthen the construction of party style in practice, but also in judging and identifying it in social life. The organization of the true vanguard of the proletariat had great theoretical significance. Marxists believed that any political party had its own program, theory, and style. To judge what sort of party it was, one had to examine its theory and program, and also its style. For the first time, Marx and Engels proposed a scientific argument for judging the nature of a party by its program, emphasizing that the party's program was the banner under which it was openly established, and the outside world would judge the party according to that political program. Lenin and Stalin put forward a well-known statement against the revisionist Marxist doctrine during the era of imperialism, proposing a standard by which to judge whether the nature of a party adhered to the basic principles of Marxism. They believed that all political parties that upheld the basic principles of Marxism were new proletarian revolutionary parties, while all political parties that betrayed the basic principles of Marxism were revisionist or reformist parties. According to the social and historical conditions facing the CPC, Mao further proposed the question of style as an important marker for judging the nature of a political party. This was an enrichment and development of the teachings of Marxist-Leninist parties and an important contribution of the building of the Party's style.

A fourth contribution was the discussion of the importance of strengthening the construction of party style to maintain the exalted status and prestige of the Party among the people, which emphasized that only a correct party style could succeed in harmony with the people's style and the prevailing social atmosphere. Based on the point of view of historical materialism, Mao believed that the future of the Party was determined by the hearts of the people. The people were the face of the Party. Without the support of the people, the Party had no power or vitality, and it would have no victory and no ground on which to stand. What, then, were factors that would decide the hearts of the people? For a political party, the aspect that was most direct and easily perceived by the people was the party style. Based on historical experience, it was important for the people to express their minds to the Party. It was necessary for the Party to know whether its actions were beneficial to the people, and especially to know whether the opinions of the majority of Party members and cadres were in the interests of the people and how much support the people had for the Party. For a long time, the CPC was selfless, not only suffering itself, but coming from a long line of ancestors who had endured great hardship in hopes of a better future. The CPC followed in the steps of their forefathers, bravely struggling for the masses as they maintained a close connection with the people, even spilling their own blood for the people's sake. In this way, they won the hearts of the people, along with their trust, love, and support. Historical experience indicated that the issue of party style was actually what the people noticed, as it was directly related to whether the Party could maintain its lofty status among the masses. Because of this, Mao constantly emphasized the need to uphold and push forward the Party's fine tradition and style, always playing an exemplary role as vanguard of the proletariat. On the battlefield, it was a model of heroic combat, and behind the lines, it was a model of base construction, always being brave in its work. Serving as a model was a heavy burden and required hard work, but the Party was a model of solidarity, mutual assistance, and other areas.

Mao believed that the issue of party style was not only directly related to the Party's prestige among the people, but also directly affected, or even determined, the customs of the people, to some extent. When he spoke of the importance of rectifying the Party's work style in 1942, he pointed out that the CPC was the leader of the great revolutionary cause, and that the quality of the Party's work had a great influence on the people of the country. He said, "As long as our party style is completely decent, the people of the country will learn from us. Those outside the Party who have a bad ethic will, if they are soft-hearted, learn from us and correct their mistakes, which will affect the entire country."[86] Mao explicitly linked the party style to that of the people. This not only stimulated the enthusiasm of Party members for the correct party style, but also enhanced the political responsibility of the entire Party to transform the social environment. This important concept is of guiding significance for the CPC even today in its efforts to maintain a correct party style, promote a conducive social environment, and strengthen the construction of its spiritual or moral culture.

The question of how to build and maintain a good work style remained. After much arduous exploration, the Party proposed and formulated effective methods and measures for strengthening the construction of its work style. They are:

Address the party style issue from the height of a global perspective and with a view toward party spirit. It was necessary to follow this fundamental principle in the constructing and strengthening of the Party's work style. The CPC had always believed that its work style was closely related to its worldview. The party style was the concrete manifestation of its worldview in action. The CPC's worldview was dialectical and historical materialism. Its dialectical materialist view was manifested in its unity of knowledge and action, seeking the truth from facts, and linking theory and practice. Its historical materialist view was manifested in its reliance on the masses and close contact with the masses. With its dialectical and historical materialist worldview, the CPC had to be fearless in all practical activities, even daring to criticize various unfavorable phenomena in the Party and in society, and they were bold enough to engage in self-criticism as well. In this way, the three characteristics of an excellent party were concrete manifestations of the Marxist worldview in the actions of the CPC.

Because the Party's work style was an instance of its worldview in action, then in order to carry forward the Party's outstanding work style and overcome unhealthy trends, it was necessary to focus on addressing problems from the perspective of this worldview. During the period of the Yan'an Rectification Movement, Mao's way of addressing party style was to focus on addressing issues from the perspective of a particular worldview and outlook on life. To begin with, in works such as *On Practice* and *On Contradiction*, he criticized the negative style of subjectivism and dogmatism from a higher perspective, profoundly expanding on the Party's dialectical materialist worldview and the smooth development since the Yan'an Rectification Movement, which laid the foundation for his ideological theory. Then, the CPC Central Committee and Mao also guided senior Party cadres and all Party members to begin with a study of Marxist theory and Party documents and conduct investigations and studies, while also engaging in criticism and self-criticism to further address the worldview of Party members and cadres. The so-called rectification of Party members' and cadres' worldview was mainly intended to guide them to use the basic principles of Marxism to connect their own ideological views to their practical work, consciously transforming the subjective world. There were two basic aspects in the work of transforming the subjective world: the transformation of ideology and the transformation of ideas and methods. The former was a matter of raising ideological and political consciousness, while the latter was a matter of raising cognitive ability. These two aspects were the main issues to be addressed in the transformation of the subjective world. Sine the Party had firmly grasped the fundamental problem of transforming the worldview during the rectification movement, it had effectively overcome the problem of "the three incorrect styles – which encompassed party style, study style and writing style – guaranteeing the victory of the Yan'an Rectification Movement. The Party's three characteristics of an excellent style were proposed on the basis of this great victory. This historical experience demonstrated that only by addressing the issue of party style from the higher perspective of an overarching worldview could the Party effectively overcome unhealthy trends and firmly establish a positive work style.

In the construction of party style, Mao paid special attention to party-focused education, which was the central link in addressing the issue of party style from the perspective of the CPC's worldview. He believed that party style was not a manifestation of an impure party. To completely overcome unhealthy trends, it was necessary to strengthen party spirit and the proletarian spirit of the Party. During the Yan'an Rectification Movement, with Mao's advocacy, the CPC issued a special Decision on Enhancing Party Spirit, pointing out various manifestations necessary to party spirit and proposing measures to enhance it, such as promoting the Party's excellent style and overcoming various unhealthy trends. At the same time, Liu Shaoqi also issued a Report on The Cultivation of Communist Party Members, in which he systematically discussed party spirit. The cultivation of party style meant that the Party consciously employed the excellent characteristics of the vanguard of the proletariat to conduct self-education and self-reform, so that they gradually inculcated these excellent traits. An important feature of the Party's self-cultivation was that it did not rely mainly on external forces or coercion, but on the consciousness of the Party members and on self-reform to improve ideological consciousness. Education in party organization was extremely important, and the effect of such education was to mobilize the positive factors of the Party members and rely on them to overcome their own negative traits. Mao believed that if Party members and cadres had a strong party spirit, they could give full play to their role as vanguard of the proletariat and play an exemplary role in all their work. This role as a model vanguard specifically reflected the fine style of the Party. Thus, strengthening party style was a fundamental measure for carrying forward the excellent party work style and overcoming various unhealthy trends.

Another important means of addressing the issue of party style from the perspective of its worldview was to strengthen investigation and research. Mao believed that "the plan to carry out investigation and research throughout the entire Party is the basis for transforming the Party's work style."[87] One of his well-known sayings was, "No one has a right to speak without first investigating." He had been investigating and studying this particular view for a long time, and he offered a vivid summary of his practical experience, which was a clear manifestation of his ideological line of applying Marxist dialectical materialism to the actual work of the Party. This was an important condition for establishing a proper party style.

Second, it had created a positive form of rectification for the entire Party. This was an important measure for correcting the Party's style and strengthening its work style.

In order to more effectively overcome the negative style within the Party and carry forward its style of excellence and improve the quality of the Party, the CPC created a positive overall party rectification. This overall party rectification concentrated on a comprehensive rectification of the Party's ideology, style, and organization within a certain period of time. Specifically, it was the Party's tendency to focus on the existence of the Party. It had a number of classic books, Party documents, and other works of reports by central leaders, among other materials, which offered purposeful, systematic, step-by-step guidance. The actual situation in regards to ideology, style, organization, work, criticism, and self-criticism was employed to improve the level of Marxist theory and ideological and political consciousness among the majority of Party members and cadres to overcome shortcomings and mistakes in work, achieve unity of thought and a proper style, strengthen discipline, and ensure a pure organization and greater combat effectiveness.

From the time of the War of Resistance Against Japanese Aggression to the founding of the new China, the CPC carried out three successful Party-wide rectification campaigns. The first was the Yan'an Rectification Movement in 1942. The most outstanding effect of this campaign was, in Mao's words, "to make our leading organs and numerous cadres further grasp the basic direction of the unity of the universal truth of Marxism-Leninism and the concrete practice of the Chinese revolution."[88] The second campaign was during the land reform and party consolidation of 1948. At that time, a certain degree of impurity had been exposed throughout the Party, and the campaign aimed at overcoming the tendency of some cadres in rural grassroots organizations to grow distant from the masses. The third campaign was a Party-wide rectification movement in the early days after the founding of the new China. This Party-wide rectification generally improved the ideological and political consciousness of Party members, purified the Party's ranks, strengthened the relationship between the Party and the masses, and strengthened Party leadership.

Judging from the historical experience recounted above, Party-wide rectification was indeed an effective means of strengthening the Party's work style. This was because 1) Party-wide rectification was a systematic mass-oriented Marxist ideological movement through which the theoretical level and political consciousness of the entire Party were greatly enhanced and the CPC's ideology would surely be carried forward, overcoming individualism and other non-proletarian ideas and providing a reliable ideological guarantee for a correct Party style, and 2) Party-wide rectification was a comprehensive, systematic, organized approach to the party work style and organization, which could effectively achieve "comprehensive governance," which was to say that it could effectively correct all aspects of Party life, including irregularities such as bureaucracy, subjectivism, and authoritarianism, and effectively overcome unorganized or non-disciplined phenomena such as patriarchalism, sectarianism, anarchism, liberalism, and extreme democratization. In particular, the organization and review of the Party-wide rectification would not only discipline those who had committed serious errors, but also eliminate those who harmed the Party, the opposition, and any corrupt elements to achieve the goal of a pure organization. In this way, Party-wide rectification provided a reliable organizational guarantee for proper party style. Thus, Party-wide rectification was an effective form of correcting party style and was important means for strengthening the party work style. This effort, led by Mao Zedong, was a great pioneering work in the history of the construction of proletarian parties.

2. Style of Linking Theory and Practice

The fine style of linking of theory and practice was a basic characteristic of which the CPC should have some understanding so as to transform the subjective world. To understand the basic point of this style, it was necessary to understand Marxist-Leninist theory. Only when it was combined with the concrete practice of the Chinese revolution would it truly become a weapon with which the Chinese people could win every battle.

Through the long-term practice of revolutionary struggle, the CPC adhered to and developed the scientific principles of Marxist-Leninist theory and practice, raising it to the level of one of the basic principles of Marxism.

The CPC believed that linking theory and practice was not only an important ideological principle, but also an important methodological principle. The principles of this methodology were summarized in three aspects. First, the Marxist worldview was not a doctrine, but a method. It did not provide ready-made dogma, but was the starting point for further research and the method used for that research. Second, theory had to be combined with practice. A scientific approach that achieved the unity of subjectivity and objectivity and theory and practice was an objective requirement for understanding and transforming the world. Third, theory could only be continuously enriched and developed when it was combined with practice. This was an inherent requirement for theoretical development.

Primarily, the combination of theory and practice was a methodological principle for correctly dealing with the dialectical relationship between theory and practice. When theory is divorced from practice, it is an empty theory, and practice divorced from theory is blind practice. Throughout the history of the CPC, whether it were an issue of dogmatism or empiricism, the separation of theory from practice was a major feature characterizing the subjective and objective division. Dogmatists did not understand that Marxism was not a doctrine, but a method. They separated the universal principles of Marxism-Leninism from the reality of the Chinese revolution, refused to conduct in-depth, careful investigation and research on the actual situation of the Chinese revolution, and applied Marxism-Leninism as an abstract dogma. As a result, the Chinese revolution was in crisis, one of the greatest crises in the history of the Party. Wang Ming's leftist error was even more serious. Empiricism opposed the universal principles of Marxism-Leninism and the concrete realities of the Chinese revolution, denied the guiding role of the universal principles of Marxism-Leninism in practice, and failed to understand that "without a theory of revolution, there would be no revolutionary movement." This narrow view led to the error of empiricism. Both tendencies grew out of the separation of theory and practice. Only by adhering to the combination of the theory and practice of Marxism-Leninism and linking it to the actual Chinese revolutionary situation could victory be attained in the revolution.

In addition, the combination of theory and practice was a methodological principle that would achieve the unity of subjectivity and objectivity and of understanding and objective reality. The basic problem of all philosophy is the relationship between thinking and being, which includes two aspects: 1) thinking and existence, spiritual and material, and subjective and objective, which of each pair should be the primary, and 2) whether there is consistency between thinking and existence, the spiritual and material, and the subjective and objective. The first type of question is an issue of what is there and who decides what is there. The second is a view of thinking and existence as mutually antagonistic, interdependent, and mutually transforming, which is to say, how to achieve dialectical unity. The basic problems of philosophy, reflected in real terms, are expressed as the relationship between theory and practice. Theory comes from practice, and in turn provides guidance for practice. The unity of theory and practice embodies the problem of identity and existence, subjectivity and objectivity. Discovering how to achieve unity of theory and practice and the combination of the two is what provides us with a scientific approach. Only by adhering to the method of linking theory with practice can one achieve unity of the subjective and objective and consistency between reality and understanding. At the same time, the combination of theory and practice also reflects the highest principles of Marxist philosophy. The purpose of knowing the world is to transform it. The combination of theory and practice is the scientific method by which this goal is achieved and the understanding of the world is translated into action and aimed at transforming it.

Finally, the combination of theory and practice is a methodological principle of theoretical development. Theory comes from practice, and it is also tested and developed in practice. The departure of theory from practice is the most basic epistemological source of theoretical rigidity and practical failure. Objective things are constantly moving, changing, and developing. People's understanding should likewise develop alongside the changes in the specific processes of objective things. Generally thinking, theory is relatively stable as subjective cognition, while objective changes are constantly changing and developing. This forms a process of conflict between subjectivity and objectivity, and between theory and practice, and it is the task of all people to find the historical unity between them. When specific processes of objective practice move forward, subjective knowledge should adapt to fit them. If understanding remains at its original stage, an error in which theory lags behind reality will occur. When the specific processes of objective practice have not yet been completed, it is necessary to grasp what can be done in the future and start applying it in the present, and to avoid the error of separating the subjective and the objective. The method of linking theory with practice is precisely the dialectical method of achieving a unified theory of the subjective and the objective, combining theory with concrete practice. Theory is constantly tested, revised, supplemented, enriched, and developed in the process of combining it with practice.

From the practice of the CPC during the democratic revolution, there were three areas highlighted in relation to the issue of combining practice and theory. The first was that it was necessary to be proficient in Marxism and to learn to use Marxist theory to analyze and explain China's practical problems. Marxist theory provided a scientific summary of the practical experience of the proletarian revolutionary struggle. It reflected the general conditions and universal laws of the proletarian revolution and had a universal guiding significance for proletarian revolutions in any country. However, in order to use Marxist theory to guide the proletarian revolution in all countries, it was important to use it to analyze and explain the specific situations in a country, then apply Marxist theory to that situation.

The dogmatists in the Chinese revolution failed to understand this. They "simply quoted individual utterances of Marx, Engels, Lenin, or Stalin, but did not use their positions, viewpoints, and methods to specifically study the status quo in China and Chinese history, offering focused analysis of the problems and possible solutions for the Chinese revolution."[89] Mao criticized their mistakes and pointed out their practices, saying, "One of the basic principles of Marx, Engels, Lenin, and Stalin is the unity of practice and theory." Thus, it was necessary to intentionally study Marxist-Leninist theory, then find a position, a point, or a path and apply the views of Marx, Engels, Lenin, and Stalin to solve theoretical or strategic problems in the Chinese revolution. It was important to find viewpoints and methods for studying China's actual situation and its history, and thus be "able to correctly explain the actual problems in history and in the revolution according to Marxist-Leninist prospectives, viewpoints, and methods, and to be able to conduct economic and political affairs in China. It is also important to offer explanations for economic, political, military, and cultural issues and offer a theoretical explanation for them."[90] It was also clearly noted that the scientific attitude of seeking the truth from facts "is the embodiment of party spirit, which is a Marxist-Leninist style of combining theory and practice […] It is the sort of attitude a Party member should have."[91] From this, it was evident that Mao's use of Marxist theory to analyze and explain China's actual situation was an important instance of combining theory and practice.

The second aspect was that it was necessary to base oneself on the actual situation, combining Marxist theory with Chinese revolutionary practice. Marxist theory was a powerful weapon for the proletariat to understand and transform the world. The principle of combining theory and practice gave full play to the significant role of Marxist theory in understanding and transforming the world.

In the practice of the Chinese revolution, Mao attached great importance to the combination of theory and practice, regarding this combination as an important part of his theory. In *On Practice*, he cited Stalin's idea that if theory were not rooted in practice, it would be aimless theory. Similarly, if practice were not guided by revolutionary theory, it would be blind practice. In order to stimulate the entire Party's emphasis on the combination of theory and practice, he placed this combination at the pinnacle of party spirit, saying, "Without a scientific attitude, that is, without an attitude that unifies Marxist-Leninist theory with practice, there is no party spirit, or at least an imperfect party spirit."[92]

The question remained of how to go about combining Marxist theory with Chinese revolutionary practice. On the one hand, Mao Zedong localized Marxism to the Chinese context, popularizing Marxist theory and injecting it into the practical activities of the Chinese proletariat and the broad masses of the people. He observed, "Chinese Communist Party members are international Marxists, but Marxism must be combined with the particular characteristics of our country and must be realized through certain national forms."[93] For this reason, he insisted that Marxism be made concrete in China in such a way that it possessed Chinese characteristics and a Chinese style. It would thus be mastered and applied by the vast majority of the masses in China. On the other hand, Mao insisted that Marxist theory be embodied in the Party's ideological, working, and leadership methods, combining Marxist theory with Chinese revolutionary practice. The CPC was the core leadership of the Chinese revolutionary cause, serving as its organizer and leader. In combining Marxist theory with Chinese revolutionary practice, it combined the long-term revolutionary practice with a set of scientific methods of thinking, work, and leadership that had been created by Mao. These methods were not only the embodiment of Marxist theory, but also the basic principles and methods the Party was to follow in all its work. His term "unity in contradiction" was not only an expression of the popularization and consolidation of Marxist dialectics, but also the basic method for the CPC to be effective in all its work. His idea of leadership and work methods "coming from the masses and flowing to the masses" was not only the direction and method the CPC followed in all its work, but was also the embodiment of Marxist epistemology and historical materialism. Thus, he made Marxist theory the doctrine guiding the actions of the Party, which was the original combination of Marxist theory with Chinese revolutionary practice.

The third aspect was the necessity of taking development theory as the highest aim and summing up new theories from the practice of the Chinese revolution, and in the process, enriching and developing Marxism. Marxist theory was the scientific truth derived from and proved by the practice of the proletarian revolutionary struggle. Like any truth, it did not mark the end of truth, but opened the way to truth. With actual, objective changes and the development of practice, Marxist theory had to be continuously enriched and developed. Otherwise, Marxist theory could not explain objective reality well, and it would be impossible for it to serve as an effective guide for practice, which would ultimately lead to a wide gap between theory and the actual situation. It was on this basis that the CPC attached such great importance to the enrichment and development of Marxist theory in the practice of revolution, enriching and developing Marxist theory through this combination. In the Chinese revolution, Mao regarded the enrichment and development of Marxist theory as an important part of the combination of theory and practice. He noted, "Only when the CPC has become adept at combining the theory of Lenin to the Chinese revolution, applying it through serious study to the actual situation of the Chinese revolution, can theoretical creations meet the actual needs of China in every aspect, through the combination of theory and practice."[94] Mao later pointed to the necessity of reading the works of Marx, Engels, and Lenin, saying it was a top priority. At the same time, the Communists and proletarian thinkers of any country had to create new theories, write new works, and produce new theorists in order to serve their own political situation. In any country and at any time, it was not enough to simply rely on old ideas.

These three aspects of the CPC's thought regarding the combination of theory and practice were related, yet focused on different areas. From the point of view of combining, the three aspects formed an organic whole that was so closely related as to be inseparable. Using Marxist theory to analyze and explain China's practical problems was the basis or premise for linking theory and practice. To apply Marxist theory to China's concrete reality, it was first necessary to use Marxist theory to analyze and explain China's practical problems and make Marxist theory consistent with the actual situation in China. Without analysis and explanation of China's actual situation, it was impossible to combine Marxist theory with Chinese revolutionary practice, and it was impossible to enrich and develop Marxist theory. Combining Marxist theory with Chinese revolutionary practice was the fundamental way in which theory was linked to practice. Without this combination, analysis of practical issues would lose its meaning, and Marxist theory would fail to become a great force for transforming the world and the actual situations in it. It would inevitably lead to the separation of theory and practice, and any mention of enriching and developing Marxist theory would only be empty talk.

Summarizing new theories from Chinese revolutionary practice was necessary for the enrichment and development of Marxist thought. Objective reality was rich and varied, and the development of the revolution was deepening and developing. Theory had to function as a reflection of objective reality, and any generalization of practical experience had to adapt according to actual, objective changes, growing alongside the practical developments. Failure to do so would result in theory lagging behind actual circumstances.

From the point of view of difference, the three aspects of the combination of theory and practice each had its own emphasis, thus forming three levels. Using Marxist theory to analyze and explain China's reality, focusing on specific practical understanding and a grasp of China's social, political, economic, military, and cultural situation were necessary for addressing and correctly treating and reflecting objective, practical problems. This connection between theory and practice was a low-level connection. Combining Marxist theory to transform objective reality addressed the issue of how Marxist theory could transform the world and transform reality. Because it did not stop at objective reality, but also went deep into actual, objective transformation, this theoretical and practical combination was a higher level of connection. Summarizing new theory based on Chinese revolutionary practice, enriching and developing Marxism in the process, focused on summarizing practical experience to create new theory. This addressed the need for Marxist theory to reflect reality and lead to subjective change, which would in turn guide the ongoing development of practical issues. Because it did not merely reflect objective reality, it both guided practice and enriched theory, making it the highest level of combination. Ignoring the differences between three aspects, confusing them, or even replacing high level connections with low level connections, would inevitably lead to the separation of theory and practice, unintentionally violating the principle of combining the two.

3. The Work Style of Criticism and Self-Criticism

Adhering to the work style of criticism and self-criticism was directly related to the character and style of the CPC and its proper understanding and transformation of the objective world. The basic point of this style was that transforming the old society and establishing a new society were both a new, arduous undertaking. In the process of the long-term revolution, it was inevitable that some mistakes would be made, even some serious mistakes. In order to uphold truth, it was necessary to correct those mistakes. Nurturing the revolutionary Communist Party to greater maturity was the only path to victory. Criticism and self-criticism were the driving force for correcting the Party's mistakes and continuing to move forward.

a. Criticism and Self-Criticism as Inherent Requirements for the Survival and Development of the CPC

When the revolutionary leaders created the proletarian party, they attached great importance to and repeatedly emphasized the use of criticism and self-criticism. Throughout his life, Marx always insisted on ruthless criticism of the bourgeoisie and various erroneous thoughts within the international workers' movement. Engels made it clear that criticism was the key to the life of the workers' movement. He saw mutual criticism as a means of enhancing solidarity. He said that the solidarity of democratic people did not exclude mutual criticism. Without such criticism, it was impossible to achieve unity. Without criticism, there was no possibility of mutual understanding, so there was no point speaking of achieving unity. He also emphasized that the proletarian party must have the courage to engage in criticism and self-criticism. Whether or not a party had courage to do so would determine the level of vitality it had for withstanding various tests. He proudly asked, "Where is there another party that dares to do this?"

In the process of creating and leading the proletarian party, Lenin attached great significance to the cultivation of self-criticism. He said that self-criticism was absolutely necessary for any energetic, dynamic party. He believed that a political party's attitude toward its own mistakes was a measure of whether or not the party was serious, and of whether it truly fulfilled one of the most important and reliable standards for its obligations to the proletariat. To publicly admit mistakes, expose the causes of mistakes, analyze the environment in which mistakes occurred, and carefully discuss mistakes was the mark of a serious party. It was a party's obligation to fulfill its duties, and these acts were for education and training, and for the people.

What made a proletarian party different from other parties was that it did not seek personal gain. Its purpose was to wholeheartedly serve the people, which opened up the possibility for the development of criticism and self-criticism.

b. Criticism and Self-Criticism as Precious Traditions and Political Advantages of the CPC

The CPC, guided by Marxism and established according to Lenin's party-building principles, inherited the fine traditions of criticism and self-criticism from the international socialist movement. It went on to creatively develop, through the practice of the Chinese revolution, its own characteristics of criticism and self-criticism.

In the CPC, the first generation of the central leadership group, with Mao at the center, first created a new method for Party-wide rectification, using criticism and self-criticism as the main means of achieving it. From the time of the Yan'an Rectification Movement, Mao often used the metaphors of "washing one's face every day," "sweeping the floor every day," "running water is never stale," or "a constantly-used door-hinge never gets worm-eaten" to vividly and profoundly explain the necessity for self-criticism. He pointed out that there were always conflicts between the Party and those who were less progressive, and between right and wrong. The Party's progress was based on continuous development and continuous resolution of such conflicts. Criticism and self-criticism were the main methods for resolving conflict within the Party. Mao said, "With the best interests of the overwhelming majority of the Chinese people as our starting point, the CPC believes that its cause is completely just, and we will sacrifice our personal belongings and are even prepared to give our lives to the cause. Is there any thought, opinion, or method that is not suitable for the people, and if so, are you ready to lose it? Do we welcome any political dust or germs to tarnish our clean face or erode our bodily health? Countless revolutionary martyrs have sacrificed their lives for the benefit of the people, and when each of us who are still alive remember them, we are saddened. Do we have any personal interests that we cannot sacrifice, or any errors we are not willing to abandon?"[95] It was this thoroughly materialist attitude that helped the CPC form and develop a set of actions to effectively carry out the principles and methods of criticism and self-criticism. These were to constituted the precious spiritual wealth of the Party, and they effectively guaranteed the complete victory of the new democratic revolution.

c. *Serious Criticism and Self-Criticism as an Important Test of Party Spirit*

Most fundamentally, self-criticism was the basis for conducting criticism within the Party. The CPC was the vanguard of the Chinese proletariat and a faithful representative of the interests of the people of all ethnic groups in China. This determined all its speech and action, as it had to be highly responsible to the people and could not allow the existence of any special interests, nor any shortcomings that infringed on the interests of the people. As a result, the CPC solemnly declared to the masses that it would uphold good standards in the interest of the people and correct errors for the good of the people. This was the foothold and starting point for the CPC to carry out self-criticism. It was precisely because self-criticism was based on the interests of the people that its smooth development was the basis for the development of healthy criticism within the Party.

Strengthening the cultivation of Party members through self-criticism and creating good moral conditions for criticism within the Party. Self-criticism was based on proper self-evaluation, and conducting proper self-evaluation was inseparable from cultivating morals and standards for judgment. In layman's terms, "moral judgment" referred to the rights and wrongs of a person who judged others and measured their own behavior according to their own political and moral views. This was a force of reason and heartfelt emotion, a placing of value on one's social status, degree of education, and the transformation of practical experience in the objective world. The closer this concept was to the scientific worldview, the more it could be integrated with the interests and feelings of the broad masses, and the more it could distinguish between good and evil or right and wrong, and thus the more it could consciously adhere to proper behavior and correct wrong behavior. A person's moral cultivation was a spiritual force that promoted self-criticism. A noble moral force would drive a person to adopt positive, non-conservative attitudes towards their own shortcomings and mistakes, attitudes which would make the spirit broader and moral cultivation more complete. A person who held ideal goals and pursued high morals, fulfilling his responsibilities for the benefit of the people, not allowing himself to be self-sufficient and stagnant, would undoubtedly enhance his initiative to engage in criticism and self-criticism.

Promoting the development of the spirit of intra-party democracy through self-criticism and creating a good practical foundation for criticism within the Party. It is always easy to listen to pleasant words, but difficult to listen to those we disagree with. Similarly, it is easy to criticize others, but self-criticism is difficult. This problem often cropped up among Party members and cadres. There were various causes for this problem, but fundamentally, an ambivalent democratic spirit played an important part in all those causes. There was no doubt that practice was an important principle for dealing with the relationship between Party members. In the CPC, there was a hierarchy between superiors and subordinates in their work, but they were equal in their observation of democratic centralism and various Party rules. However, some comrades, especially among the leading comrades, had a weak sense of democracy, or were selfish, rude, and authoritarian. When they criticized others, they failed to seek the truth from facts. When dealing with problems, they failed to be fair and just. The lack of proactive self-criticism was an important cause of the weak democratic awareness. The practice of party-building highlighted that, in order to diligently form a lively, relaxed environment for development within the Party, it was necessary to open the way with a democratic spirit and listen to various opinions with an open mind. When wrong, it was important not to be stubborn. When others were right, it was important to acknowledge that. Only in this way could the relationship between the Party and the people be properly maintained and a positive outlook be truly formed in the Party, promoting vigorous development of the revolutionary cause.

Promoting unity and creating a good organizational atmosphere for criticism within the Party. In order to actively carry out self-criticism, enhance the initiative and anticipation of problem-solving, and to do good job of addressing conflicts, unifying thought, and bringing the comrades together through sincere dialogue, it was necessary to always adhere to a people-oriented view and respect, understand, and care for the people. It was necessary to stay well-grounded, be patient with the people, inspire the masses through emotion, convince them, and refrain from any rude or coercive orders. Using innovative ideas, forms, and methods, the Party had to exchange views and opinions through in-depth conversation, especially on heated or difficult issues in the minds of Party members, and it had to diligently address doubts, rally the people, direct the emotions, and resolve conflicts. In short, it was important to fully understand the arduousness and complexity of party-building and development in a new situation and use high-level self-criticism to create an atmosphere of unity and development.

In addition, criticism was a political responsibility of Party members. Many comrades who had more experience of Party life felt that engaging in criticism was easier said than done. Criticism inevitably exposed conflicts and touched on sore points, so there was a widespread tendency in the Party to "plant more flowers and fewer thorns." However, the principle of party spirit made clear that this attitude toward criticism was incorrect and non-Marxist.

Everything in the world is full of conflict, and everything advances through conflict. The CPC was no exception to this rule. Without conflict in the Party and the necessary ideological struggle to resolve that conflict, the Party's life would have ceased. Very early on, Engels said that it seemed that any workers' party in a large country could only develop through internal struggle. This was in line with the general laws of dialectical development. Recognizing and facing conflicts, then correctly handling and resolving them, was the fundamental means of simultaneously transforming both the subjective and objective world through the application of Marxism. Seen from the height of this understanding, the attitude of "plant more flowers and fewer thorns" clearly abolished ideological struggle, advocating the abandonment of the principle of "harmony at all cost." That is, it replaced the priority of maintaining the Party with "not offending people," a spirit of self-interest instead of focusing on interests of the people. It was an approach that avoided criticism, resistance, struggle, and destroying all problems, large and small. These were the manifestations of a loss of party spirit. In party life, actively carrying out criticism and opposing the sort of unprincipled peace that was based on ignoring ideological struggle was the responsibility of every Party member.

Practice proved that the political responsibility for carrying out criticism within the Party was embodied in 1) the process of Party members being innovative in remedying the outdated in an effort to adapt to the needs of party-building and development, 2) the process of each Party member treating both themselves and other comrades correctly, and 3) Party members' acceptance of communist ideology and the process of education.

Finally, to carry out criticism within the Party, it was necessary to follow the correct principles and methods. It was commonly said that "if a worker wants to do something well, he must sharpen his tool." This "tool" referred not only to physical tools, but also to methods. Criticism and self-criticism were good work styles and good tools. It was necessary not only to dare to use them, but to use them well. Otherwise, they would not work, and might even be counterproductive. Only with tools and with the correct principles and methods for using them could the intended purpose of criticism and self-criticism be achieved.

First, it was essential to sum up the experience and lessons learned from conducting criticism within the Party. The CPC was a Marxist political party armed with advanced theory and organized according to the principle of democratic centralism. Thus, for a long time, it paid careful attention to the use of the tools of criticism and self-criticism to strengthen its progressive nature. The Party's successful leadership of the Chinese revolution fully proved that it was a party adept at self-criticism and self-improvement. It was capable of relying on its own strength to discover and address conflicts within the Party and correct its own mistakes and problems. Throughout this historical process, the CPC accumulated a wealth of experience. This was mainly demonstrated in the following ways:

1) *To have an appropriate purpose, it was necessary to adhere to correct policy.* Mao noted, "The goal of exposing mistakes and criticizing shortcomings is no different from a doctor treating a disease. We aim to save people, not to kill them."[96] In carrying out criticism within the Party, it was necessary to follow a policy of "imposing punishment to learn from past mistakes to avoid future ones, and to heal and save the people," starting from a desire to help and protect the comrades and from the goal of benefitting the Party and the overall cause, adopting an attitude of kindness toward others, not arbitrarily nitpicking or causing trouble, not haphazardly criticizing or amplifying errors, but speaking out of a solid knowledge of the situation, and speaking kindly without blame.

2) *It was imperative that the Party employ the proper means.* Criticism of the Party was to be "smooth and light," and offered calmly, absolutely avoiding the leftist dogmatists' tendency to "struggle to the death and striking a ruthless blow."

3) *It was necessary to be correct without straying.* It was essential to use the Party Constitution and the basic Party line, principles, and policies as the standard for determining right and wrong. Criticism had to focus on political issues and principles. It should never lead to unprincipled disputes and should not get entangled in insignificant details.

4) *It was necessary to have a realistic attitude when engaging in criticism or self-criticism.* All speech was to be based on evidence, not a mere chasing of wind or chasing shadows, and without exaggeration. It was not to be vague, and its goal was to convince, not to coerce. If it failed in a small part,

then the whole argument failed. This made it difficult to use criticism to fabricate methods for bringing others down.

Second, it was essential to seek the truth from facts. Seeking truth from facts was a fundamental line and basic style of the CPC. It was also the basic method of leadership and work in the Party. In criticism and self-criticism, it was necessary to pay attention to the implementation of the principle of seeking the truth from facts. It was important that all criticism be based on facts, supported by facts, subject to reason, not beyond limits, and not baseless.

In clarifying the facts, whatever was true was true, and whatever was not was not. There was no room for subjective speculation, chasing the wind, or entertaining hearsay. It was necessary to put a resolute stop to bad behaviors that had been trumped up or fabricated. It must always be born in mind that "speech should be based on criticism, and criticism should keep politics in mind." It was inappropriate to criticize without evidence, as such an approach would only lead to mutual suspicion among comrades, resulting in suspicion, defensiveness, and unprincipled disputes within the Party.

It was necessary to distinguish the nature and extent of the mistakes made, to neither exaggerate or understate. It was necessary that mistakes be regarded consistently and holistically, not as a cognitive or academic problem, but as a political issue, without amplifying problems and concealing the nature of the conflict. For one's own sake and the sake of others, it was important to learn to use a historical, discerning perspective to comprehensively evaluate and address errors, neither erasing merits because of mistakes nor covering up mistakes because of merit. It was important to not only see one's own strengths and advantages, but also one's shortcomings, enabling easier acceptance of criticism from others. When criticizing a comrade, even some of his correct claims could be denied. When dealing with a comrade in error, it was important that their strengths must be affirmed even as their shortcomings were pointed out, so that their achievements could be promoted and their shortcomings overcome.

It was important to allow critics to hold onto their opinions or to interpret or defend their actions, and to counter-criticize. If a critic found he was mistaken in his criticism, he must quickly correct it, being careful not to compound the original error. Once a mistake was compounded, it would hurt one's fellow comrade without reason. Only armed with an attitude of seriousness and taking responsibility for oneself, for others, and for the Party's cause, and only by earnestly adhering to the principle of seeking truth from facts could a positive environment for criticism and self-criticism be created, and only then could these sharp tools be properly used for their original purpose.

Third, it was necessary to proceed from the desire to care for and help one's comrades, not only understanding one's own mind, but also being unified with one's comrades. When engaging in criticism or self-criticism, it was necessary to keep the purpose of this tool in mind. The purpose of criticism and self-criticism was not to attack the person, but to rectify his error and prevent others from following it, helping comrades overcome their shortcomings so that all could develop and progress together to a higher standard, achieving unity within the entire Party. Mao made an elaborate statement in connection with this matter. He said, "In 1942, we summarized a democratic method of resolving conflicts among the people under the heading 'unity-criticism-unity.' Examining it in more detail, we see that criticism begins with a desire for unity, then through criticism or struggle, we resolve conflicts, thus achieving a new basis for unity." He believed that "what is most important here is that we start from a desire for unity. If there is no desire for unity, our struggles will just introduce chaos and things will quickly be out of control. Is this not simply 'cruel struggle and striking a ruthless blow'? How can that lead to party unity? From this experience, we have developed the formula 'unity-criticism-unity.' In other words, imposing punishment to learn from past mistakes and avoid future ones, and thereby healing and saving the people."[97] For this reason, when conducting criticism within the Party, it was necessary to proceed from the intention for unity and a desire to love and help one's comrades. Otherwise, it violated the essence and requirements for conducting criticism and self-criticism, and it would inevitably make the actual results run counter to the original intent.

Fourth, it was necessary to inspire Party members' inner motivation to carry out criticism and self-criticism. Party members were the cells of the Party's body and its main source of activity. The Party's ability to stimulate the inner motivation of the majority of its members was fundamentally connected to the question of whether they could carry out criticism and self-criticism actively and properly. For this reason the CPC emphasized several things that Party members must do:

Be truly aware of the necessity and importance of criticism and self-criticism. Criticism and self-criticism were sharp ideological weapons for strengthening the progressive nature of the Party. They were the fine traditions and styles that the Party had long maintained. They were also the key difference between the CPC and other parties, the distinctive marker of a communist political party. Only by making the majority of Party members aware of this could they greatly enhance their self-consciousness through criticism and self-criticism.

Truly establish correct principles of right and wrong, and consciously use these principles to evaluate their own thoughts and behaviors. It was necessary for the majority of Party members and cadres to seriously study Marxist theory and consciously arm their minds with scientific theories. On this basis, the Party had to strictly follow the standards for its members as stipulated in the Party Constitution, earnestly carrying out self-examination, identifying gaps and highlighting problems, and analyzing and reflecting through in-depth thought, then follow the truth, not relationships, stick to principles, not personal emotion, and identify and nip mistakes in the bud. It was important to acquire experience in discerning right from wrong to improve the ideological level and work ability of Party members, giving them full scope for their work while further improving the Party's work style and bringing it to a new level.

Learn to absorb political nutrients from criticism. For the CPC, criticism was like air, moisture, and sunshine. It was an indispensable element in Party life and a tool for achieving eternal youth in the political realm. In daily work, it was inevitable that defects or mistakes would occur due to inconsistencies between the subjective and the objective. People's ability to see themselves clearly has always been limited, so no matter how strict one's self-examination, it was not easy for Party members to see their own shortcomings and deficiencies. Thus, the majority of Party members and leading cadres were only able to make progress if they accepted the criticism of others and continued to absorb nutrition from it.

Enhance subjective consciousness. Members were the main active body within the Party. The Party's line, direction, and policy formation and implementation necessarily relied on the active participation of the majority of members. Its good image was likewise established and maintained by the majority of its members and its grassroots organizations. Thus, it was necessary for the majority of Party members to enhance their sense of the Party's glory and their own responsibility as one of its members. In their daily life and work, they consciously used the sharp tool of criticism and self-criticism to cleanse their minds through active ideological struggle. Where there was any impurity, they strove to correct it.

Fifth, it was necessary to engage in dialogue activities. Dialogue activities had always been an effective method in the ideological and political work of the CPC, and were an especially effective carrier for criticism and self-criticism. It happened that criticism and self-criticism often had effects that were not possible through other means. In dialogue, the Party discovered the appropriate questions that should be asked, frankly met and communicated these issues, and addressed them together. It promoted the close contact of Party cadres with the masses, harmonized the relationship between the Party and the people, and brought about unity of thought between the cadres and the masses.

4. A Work Style of Close Contact with the Masses

Close contact with the masses was a work style connected to the basic character and style that Communists should adopt in their treatment of the people. In the long-term revolutionary struggle, the CPC formed a life bond with the people. This sort of connection had withstood the test of various complicated, sinister circumstances and had become a source of strength and a potent weapon for the Party's revolution and construction in its efforts to defeat the enemy.

a. Marxist Mass Historical View as a Theoretical Basis for the Party's Close Relationship to the Masses

Marx held that a theory could only convince the masses if it was thorough. This indicated that the CPC's belief that its primary task was maintaining a close relationship with the masses was correct. The Marxist view of mass history was the theoretical basis for its close relationship with the masses. Was history created by the masses or by heroic individuals? How one answered this question was the fundamental difference between historical materialism and historical idealism. Who were the true masters of history? Before the emergence of Marxism, almost all historians and philosophers advocated the concept of heroism and believed that history was created by certain great figures or a few elites, mostly because they did not fully understood the fundamental principle that social existence determines social consciousness. Therefore, they did not understand the role of producers of material information in human society and its development. Thus, it was inevitable that the people's decisive role in history could not produce a correct understanding, and it was impossible to evaluate accurately. They all greatly exaggerated the role of a few outstanding figures, heroes, emperors, or other similar people in history. They believed these figures were the masters of history, and that the people were arbitrarily deployed as their tools. For the first time, the emergence of Marxism scientifically addressed the basic issues of this historical view from the height of philosophy. It was not that people's social consciousness determined people's social existence, but that their social existence determined social consciousness. The most fundamental aspect of this so-called social existence was the production of social material data. The production of material data was the determining force in social development. In the mode of production, productivity is the most active revolutionary factor. Therefore, productivity is the basis for human society and its development and the ultimate determining force for social development. Thus, the history of human society is primarily the history of the production of material data and is therefore the subject of the production of material data. All the material and spiritual civilizations of human society are ultimately created by the people, and the people are the decisive force promoting historical development and the true masters of history. Of course, Marxism recognized the important role played by individuals, especially outstanding figures, in human history. In the course of history, without outstanding thinkers, politicians, and strategists inspiring the consciousness of organizing the power of the masses, pointing the way forward and standing at the forefront of the revolution to guide the revolutionary struggle, it would have been impossible for the revolution to be victorious. At the same time, Marxism emphasized that the individual was only affiliated with this group as an ordinary individual. Based on the contradictory movements within the mode of production caused by the development of productive forces, as well as political and economic factors and objective conditions, great people could make a difference.

Marxism's principle that people are the creators of history scientifically addressed the relationship between the laws governing the development of social history and the practical activities of the people, offering an in-depth summary of the decisive role of the masses in the development of social history, laying a solid foundation for the mass historical view of proletarian parties and setting a correct line for party-building. From this principle of historical materialism, the revolutionary leader of the proletariat always insisted that the Party must remain in close contact with the people in their struggle to create a proletarian political party, setting it as a basic principle of party-building. The CPC emphasized that the establishment of itself as a proletarian party meant that it could never depart from the people, but must always remain a party that represented the fundamental interests of the people and sought the interests of the majority. Marx and Engels clearly stated in the *Communist Manifesto*, "Communists do not have any interests that are at odds with the interests of the entire working class."

In the practical struggle to lead the state power to create the world's first dictatorship of the proletariat, Lenin further developed the Marxist mass historical view of party-building, proposing that a new party of a different nature was needed. The party that was needed should be one truly connected to the masses and adapt to leading the people. At the same time, he believed that the might of the people would be the source of the victory. To win the revolution, it was necessary not only to obtain the sympathy and support of the vast majority of the proletariat, but the party also had to organize and lead the masses. Organizing millions of workers was the most favorable condition of the revolution and the most profound source of revolutionary victory. The Soviet Bolshevik Party followed Lenin's teachings and did very well in the work of organizing and mobilizing the masses, then leading them to victory in the October Revolution. After the victory of the October Revolution, the Party's status underwent fundamental changes, and the people truly became the masters of the country. Lenin believed that during the entire process of socialist construction, the proletarian masses were the foundation of all countries' lives and the fundamental guarantee of the Soviet Republic. The validity of the force of the masses was the basic factor for a new society. Only when the people personally participated in the construction of the country could socialism truly be built. Therefore, for the ruling party, it was important to stay in close contact with and rely on the masses, depending on them to consolidate political power and carry out socialist construction. At the same time, it was also keenly pointed out that one of the largest and most serious dangers for the vanguard of the proletariat was that it would beak away from the masses and create a bureaucracy. In order to prevent this from happening, it was important to strengthen party-building, overcome mistakes in the Party's work, keep in close contact with the people, and make practical efforts, not only emphasizing the need to respect the status of the people as history's masters, but also selecting excellent workers and laborers to participate in the management of the country and requiring Party members and non-members to supervise each other. It was precisely because of the efforts of Lenin and the Bolsheviks that the close ties between the party and the people were guaranteed, the fledgling Soviet regime was consolidated, and the rapid development of socialist construction was achieved in a short period.

b. Close Contact With the Masses as a Political Advantage

The CPC was established under the guidance of the basic theory of Marxism-Leninism, and it was educated and armed with Mao Zedong Thought. It was also a party closely connected with the people, having developed and matured in the course of fighting a common battle alongside the masses. In the long-term practice of leading the revolution and building the Party, the Mao-led CPC cultivated fine traditions and styles that were unique to it, while also creatively proposing a mass line with Chinese Communist characteristics. All of this was done for the masses, relied on the masses, and both came from and flowed to the masses.

The CPC's theory of the mass line began to form as early as the Agrarian Revolutionary War. In September 1929, the Directive from the Central Committee to the Red Army's Frontier Committee was issued, which addressed the relationship between the Red Army and the masses, emphasizing that "Party work and the work of the Red Army among the masses must go through the mass line." This was the first time the CPC had employed the concept of "the mass line." In 1933, Mao repeatedly discussed the importance of concern for the interests of the masses and improving the lives of the masses in his "Preliminary Summary of the Movement" and several articles on economic work. He emphasized that the Party and Soviet staff should face the masses, going deep among the people. During the War of Resistance Against Japanese Aggression, the CPC offered a systematic Marxist summary of its historical experience, completing a full form of the theory of the mass line. In 1942, Mao's "Several Issues on Leadership Methods" analyzed the entire process of proper leadership methods and various connections, such as "from the masses and to the masses," "centralism," and "persistence." At the same time, during this period, many ideas concerning the masses were also proposed, such as the view that the masses were the real heroes or that the interests of the masses were the starting point and destination of the CPC's revolution. Other ideas included the notion that the opinions and experiences of the masses were the basis on which the Party formulated policies, that the Party's responsibility and the people's responsibility should be consistent, that the Party learned from the people, and that the Party should wholeheartedly serve the people. In 1945, the Seventh National Congress clearly incorporated the basic spirit of the mass line into the Party's program and the Party Constitution. Liu Shaoqi pointed out in his report on the revisions to the Party Constitution that the mass line was "the fundamental political and organizational line of our Party."[98] It elaborated on four views related to the masses: *everything is for the people, all are responsible to the people, the masses are capable of liberating themselves, and it is necessary to learn from the people.*

Whoever wins the heart of the people will win the world. During the period of the democratic revolution, the CPC relied on the mass line and established a relationship with the people that was as close as that between fish and water. In doing so, it grew from small to large and weak to strong, defeating powerful rulers domestically and overseas. Heavily oppressed, it overcame three looming obstacles, achieved complete victory in the new democratic revolution, and seized national political power.

c. *The Key to Close Connection with the Masses Lay in Constructing Party Style*

In a conflict between the Party and the masses, which side had priority? The CPC pointed out that the close relationship between the Party and the people was the key to the purity of the Party's organization and work. The Party was the leader of the revolution and the embodiment of the people's interests. As long as its line, principles, and policies reflected the fundamental interests and needs of the masses, the people would support and follow the Party's leadership. On the other hand, if the Party's line, principles, and policies were not correct, or if the Party violated the interests or needs of the masses, it would be alienated from the people, creating a barrier between Party and people. It was evident, then, that in a conflict between the Party and the people, the people took priority. Beginning with improving party work and organization, the CPC pointed out a number of principles and methods for closely linking the Party and the masses, enriching the excellent style of the CPC and its close relationship with the masses, which played a huge role in guiding party-building.

It was necessary to understand the historic status and role of the people from the height of the proletarian worldview, thus rectifying the relationship between the Party and the people. Mao stated that it was "the people, and only the people, who are the driving force in the creation of the world's history."[99] This was his incisive exposition of the basic perspective of historical materialism. Zhu De likewise noted, "Only the masses are the heroes who create history."[100] It was this fundamental view based on historical materialism that formed the Party's mass line and basic views of the masses. These views were 1) all must be done for the people and the Party must wholeheartedly serve the people, 2) the Party was responsible to the people, and this responsibility must be consistently applied through all the Party's organs, and 3) the masses were capable of liberating themselves, and the Party should learn from the masses.

Only through a scientific understanding of the historic status and role of the people and by establishing these basic views of the masses would it be possible to rectify several key relationships.

1) *The relationship between the Party and the people.* This included the understanding that a proletarian party should not view the working class as its tool, but should consciously recognize that it was the organization of the people in a specific historical period to complete a specific historical mission. Confirming this concept ensured that the Party would not exceed the power of the masses, as the Party was not given power to coerce or force the people.

2) *The relationship between the individual and the masses.* If one were separated from the masses, he would never be successful. At the same time, all Party members, no matter their position, were servants of the people.

3) *The relationship between outstanding figures and the masses.* Outstanding figures could only be the representatives of the fundamental interests of the people, and they were generated from mass struggle to lead the masses and create history alongside the masses. There was no figure in the world who could be separated from the masses.

It was important to bear in mind that the Party's fundamental purpose and all its tasks were for the wholehearted service of the people. Wholeheartedly serving the people was the fundamental purpose of the Party and all its tasks. Thus, Mao repeatedly observed that the CPC "takes the best interests of the majority of the Chinese people as its starting point," and "all the CPC's actions must be upheld by the broadest masses of the people and the highest standards for the masses."[101] Party members "have to think of and for the masses, putting their interests first."[102] It was necessary to "serve the people wholeheartedly and not leave the masses even for a moment. Everything begins with the interests of the people, not from the interests of individuals or small groups."[103] There were partial interests and the overall interests of the people, just as there were immediate and long-term interests. It was important not to emphasize the local interests of the masses at the expense of overall interests, or to only give attention to immediate interests and neglect long-term interests. Rather, all had to be addressed together. If the Party "cannot represent the best interests of the overwhelming majority of the people at all times and in all circumstances, or if it cannot promptly put forward appropriate tasks, policies, and work styles, or if it cannot uphold truth and correct mistakes, then it will be separated from the people."[104] The CPC had "become an advanced force only because of its wholehearted service to the people, and it strives to help organize the people so they can fight for their own interests and will."[105]

How could the Party truly serve the people wholeheartedly? The CPC summarized a series of arguments for its long-term practice.

1) *The CPC must conscientiously resolve the issue of policy and style.* It was necessary that the interests of the people always be reflected in the Party's policies. To formulate and implement the correct policies, it was necessary to address the problem of style. Mao regarded the Party's policy as "party life," and he believed that "policy is the starting point of all practical actions of the revolutionary party, and it is manifested in the process and destination of action."[106] The formulation of the Party's correct policy had to "come from the masses and flow to the masses," and it was through its practice among the masses that its correctness or errors would be revealed. All correct polices were in line with local interests and the needs of the local people. They had to be in touch with the masses, or they were not in the interests and needs of the masses, which meant they had departed from the masses. In the process of implementing the Party's policies and accomplishing its tasks, there were sometimes acts that violated the Party's principles or disciplines, causing dissatisfaction within the Party. Zhu De pointed out that if these violations were not properly mastered, they would seriously alienate the Party from the masses.

Regarding the work style, the Party could only draw near to the people by carrying forward a correct work style and overcoming negative styles. Theory had to be closely linked to the actual situation, the Party had to remain closely linked to the masses, and it had to engage in criticism and self-criticism. These three excellent styles had been formed through the Party's long-term revolutionary practice, and they reflected the Party's dialectical and historical materialist worldview and methodology, its correct treatment of Marxist theory, and its correct treatment of the masses and their opinions. It served as a fundamental guarantee for the development of the Party and its cause. In the drive for socialist modernization, it was necessary to continue to carry forward the Party's three styles. In overcoming negative styles, CPC leaders repeatedly stressed the need to oppose dogmatism, empiricism, authoritarianism, tailism, sectarianism, bureaucracy, subjectivism, formalism, and arrogance. If any error of this sort was detected, it had to be rectified. It was necessary to correct such ills, as they would definitely harm the interests of the masses and separate the Party from the people if left unchecked.

2) It was necessary to adhere to a path of "from the masses and to the masses." It was necessary to maintain close ties between the Party and the people and address the problem of understanding the mass line, in order to enable the Party to correctly formulate and implement policies. In 1943, Mao systematically clarified the methods and work styles of the mass line, stating that Party work must move "from the masses and to the masses." He observed, "In all the practical work of the CPC, correct leadership must come from the masses and go to the masses. This means that all opinions of the masses (distributed and unsystematic opinions) are centralized (i.e., after research, they are turned into a centralized system). It is disseminated and explained to the masses, becoming the opinion of the masses, then letting the masses persist. Seeing them in action, we can then test whether these opinions are correct. From there, the correct opinions of the masses will be centralized and will continue among the masses. This infinite cycle is the most appropriate, vital, and richest expression of Marxist epistemology."[107]

The notion of "from the masses and to the masses" included several basic ideas. The first was "from the masses," which implied the process of in-depth study of the masses and of the concrete situation, conducting serious investigation in an effort to obtain rich perceptual knowledge. It was also a process of understanding the emotions, will, aspirations, and experiences generated by the masses. The people were the mainstay for understanding and transforming the world. They possessed rich practical experience. Without delving deeply into the masses and seeking to understand and investigate, it was impossible to absorb their rich experience, which would in turn make it impossible to make decisions and employ methods suited to local characteristics and the needs of local people. In actual work, many cadres wished to serve the people well, but they failed to go deeply into the masses and understand their situation or listen to their opinions. In their work, they often caused the people to suffer loss, because it was undeniable that a person who failed to go deeply into the actual situation and did not listen to the people would commit huge errors, no matter who that person may be.

The second part of this notion was to "centralize" the opinions of the masses. This meant analyzing and sorting out the perceptual knowledge of the people and forming it into a systematic, rational understanding, and from that process, the leaders would make decisions and pass laws. This so-called "centralization" was not a simple accumulation of the opinions of the mass. It was necessary to use the fundamental views and methods of Marxism to organize, analyze, discern, and generalize the scattered opinions and experiences of the masses and form them into a systematic scientific proposition. Of course, sorting, analysis, identification, and generalization could all go wrong. However, the consistent discussion with the masses and constant study of the practice of the masses could reduce errors and allow mistakes to be detected and corrected in a timely way.

The third idea was "going to the masses." This was a process of verifying whether the ideas and policies gathered were correct and attempting to rectify, enrich, or improve them through the practice of the masses. In order to "go to the masses," it was necessary to publicize the Party's policies and directives to the masses, allow the people to master them, then put them into practice. They also had to collate the experience of the masses in implementing, testing, and revising the policies. Historical experience showed that as long as the Party's policies and directives focused on the correct opinions of the masses and reflected their wishes and demands, and if the Party was adept at formulating careful, in-depth propaganda and explaining the correct policies, the people would support the Party and resolutely implement their directives and policies.

3) Party members and cadres must be strict with themselves and play a leadership role. In the revolutionary struggle, Mao always emphasized that the exemplary, pioneering role of Party members was extremely important. Zhou Enlai was strict with himself, setting "staying close to the masses, learning from them, and helping them" as a "cultivation principle" and basic requirement of a leader.[108] Chen Yun also repeatedly emphasized that "one can never separate from the masses, but must learn from them," and "the party style of the ruling party is closely related to the survival of the Party."[109] The reason for this was very clear. The entire Party was the model for the whole of society, and the leadership at all levels was the model for the whole Party. If the Party organizations put the opinions and interests of the people aside and did not care about them, then how could the masses love and trust the leadership of such a party? If the Party's leading cadres did not place strict demands of themselves, they would not comply with the Party's discipline, rulers, and regulations, but would violate them. The Party's principles had to put the interests of the people first, enduring some hardship early on so that it could later enjoy the rewards. Otherwise, it would have to deal with the aftermath of aggression, special interests, extravagance, and the loss of public interest that would occur when it separated from the masses. If the Party did not submit to the supervision of the masses, even retaliating against those who criticized them, then how could they hope to lead the masses to victory in the revolution? For this reason, the CPC always stressed that Party members and cadres should be concerned with the suffering of the masses. Listening to the opinions of the masses, Party members, especially the leading cadres, had to lead by example, be honest, and fight against various violations of rules and discipline.

From the above, it is evident that the Party put great effort into keeping close contact with the people and avoided being separated from them. This required diligent work in many areas. However, if it was able to succeed in the areas laid out above – namely, serving the people wholeheartedly, serving them well, and seeking their happiness – then the relationship between the CPC and the people would inevitably be close. The people would trust and support the Party even more, and the Party's cause would be invincible.

V

Thoughts on Party Leadership

1. The Leadership of the CPC as the Fundamental Guarantee of Victory in the Chinese Revolution

The fundamental reason the Party could lead the Chinese revolution and the construction of the new China was that it continually utilized scientific theory as an ideological tool to explore and gradually master the laws governing the historical development of modern Chinese society and represent the fundamental interests of the Chinese people of all ethnic groups. It also lay in the use of Marxist political teachings to continually summarize the leadership work experience and gradually form its own leadership theory.

The CPC's leadership theory was based on a scientific outlook and methodology led by the proletariat. It was a highly creative theoretical system, of a distinctly practical and class nature, rich in content, and logically complete.

The Chinese people's War of Resistance was extremely heroic. In the history of modern China, the Chinese people carried out a number of indomitable struggles to save the nation from unprecedented national and social crisis, and countless benevolent people painstakingly pioneered on the path to saving the nation and the people. Each struggle and pioneering effort had an impact on the advancement of Chinese society, but the direct outcome of each one was a failure. Facts had proven that the self-improving movement and reformism that did not address the foundation of feudalism, the old-style peasant wars, the democratic revolution led by the bourgeois revolutionaries, and various other schemes that sought to duplicate Western capitalism could not complete the national mission of saving the country and the historical mission of opposing imperialism and feudalism. China was looking to new social forces to find progressive theories to open a new revolutionary path.

The tasks of leading the anti-imperialist, anti-feudalist revolutionary struggle, striving for national independence and the liberation of the people, and achieving the great mission of revitalizing China all fell to the Communist Party of China. After the CPC, the vanguard of the proletariat, had ascended to the pinnacle of the Chinese political arena, the Chinese revolution entered a new democratic revolutionary phase. Throughout the practice of long-term revolutionary struggle, the CPC exerted its political and organizational superiority to unite the Chinese people, who had before been like "loose sand," into an invincible force that moved in unison. After twenty-eight years of hard-fought struggle through the Northern Expedition, the Agrarian Revolutionary War, the War of Resistance Against Japanese Aggression, and the National War of Liberation, the reactionary rule of imperialism, feudalism, and bureaucratic capitalism was finally overthrown and the great victory of the new democratic revolution finally achieved. The Chinese people's long-cherished desire to establish an independent, free, democratic, unified, prosperous, and powerful new China was at last a reality. China finally made the great transformation from a country in a tragic situation to one with a bright future, all because of the leadership of the CPC. The oft-repeated phrase, "Without the Communist Party, there would be no new China," was the most fundamental and most significant conclusion drawn by the Chinese people based on their modern historical experience. It was a great truth that the Chinese people confirmed through their own personal experience.

The CPC's leadership position could not have been achieved simply by someone's personal wishes or will, no matter who the person may be. After the Revolution of 1911 successfully overthrew the feudal monarchy, throughout the first half of the 20th century, China had several options for what type of country it would establish, and various forces fought fiercely to decide this issue. One faction, represented first by the Northern Warlords and later by the Kuomintang, was carried out by the rule of the big landlords and upper bourgeoisie. Their chosen path would see China continue as a semi-colonial, semi-feudal nation. Another option was championed by some moderate factions or intermediaries. Their dream was to establish a bourgeois republic, leading Chinese society down a path toward the independent development of capitalism. The third option, represented by the CPC, was a people's republic based on the alliance of workers and peasants under the leadership of the proletariat, following a path through new democracy to socialism. These three paths or schemes were repeatedly tested through the development of Chinese social history. The result of these tests was that the first option was abandoned by the Chinese people, and the reactionary ruling power championing this program was overthrown, while the second option was not endorsed by the Chinese people, with even the majority of its representatives admitting that it was not realistic to hope this dream could be achieved in China. Only the third option ultimately won the support of a large majority of the Chinese people, including the national bourgeoisie and its political representatives. It was a solemn historical choice for the Chinese people to accept the leadership of the Communist Party of China and accept the path of transition from new democracy to socialism.

The Chinese people's acceptance of the CPC's leadership was ultimately determined by the progressive nature of the Party. After its establishment, the CPC took up the mantle placed on them by the will of the people as representative of China's advanced productive forces. The Party's new democratic revolution aimed to oppose the imperialist plundering of China, eradicate the exploitation and oppression of the landlord class and the bureaucratic bourgeoisie, change the production relations of feudalism, and transform the existing decay by introducing a new economic foundation. It would build a new political superstructure that would establish a people's democratic dictatorship at its core, fundamentally liberating the bound productive forces. From the very beginning, the CPC took Marxism-Leninism as the most advanced, most scientific ideological weapon, using it as a guide and combining it with the actual situation of the Chinese revolution to propose and develop advanced theories and cultures that could greatly mobilize, inspire, and guide the Chinese people. As China's most advanced political class, the CPC not only represented the interests of the proletariat, but also of all the Chinese people and the entire nation. Throughout the new democratic revolution, all the struggles carried out by the Party were, in the final analysis, in the basic interest of the overwhelming majority of the people. The Party not only proposed a democratic revolutionary program against imperialism and feudalism, but also put forward clear goals and political slogans at every stage of revolutionary development, laying a political foundation for uniting the people throughout the country. The Party called on all its members not to be afraid of sacrifice, but to fight heroically for victory in the revolution. The majority of Party members engaged in countless heroic achievements, displaying infinite loyalty and self-sacrifice for the people, establishing a warm bond between the Party and the people through the Party's wholehearted dedication to serving the people. Through such model behavior, the Party won the support and trust of the Chinese people. The Party's theories, program, line, principles, policies, and work during the new democratic revolution all demonstrated that the CPC was worthy of standing at the forefront at all times, representing the demands of China's advanced productive forces, moving toward an advanced culture, and representing the fundamental interest of the overwhelming majority of the Chinese people. As a party that had worked tirelessly for the great rejuvenation of the Chinese nation and made great sacrifices to achieve it, it was precisely because of the advanced nature demonstrated by the CPC that the Chinese people came to the profound realization that it was a faithful representative of their interests and will, and thus voluntarily chose and accepted Party leadership and taking a new place under the leadership of the CPC in the struggle for the victory of the democratic revolution. From this, it is evident that the CPC had a deep foundation in the core leadership role and position in the Chinese people's revolutionary cause, which could not be shaken or changed by any force.

The path the CPC took in leading the Chinese revolution was extremely torturous and difficult. The Chinese people had paid a huge price for winning the revolutionary victory and the social progress that came with it. Through this process, the CPC had accumulated a wealth of experience. In summing up the historical experience of the new democratic revolution, Mao noted, "The three main weapons we used to defeat the enemy were a disciplined Marxist-Leninist theory armed with self-criticism and a party that connects with the masses, an army led by such a party, and a united front of revolutionary factions of the revolutionary classes under the leadership of such a party."[110]

As the guiding ideology for the Communist Party of China, Marxism-Leninism is a scientific theory and method that correctly interprets objective reality and has a theoretical character that advances with the times. Its vitality lies in its close integration with social practice, which could point people in the direction of truth and open the way forward. In the long-term, complex revolutionary struggle, the CPC, mainly under Mao's leadership, overcame the erroneous tendencies of merely duplicating Marxist-Leninist books or other countries' experiences. Through arduous exploration, it summed up extremely rich, original practical revolutionary experience, achieving the first historical leap of the basic principles of Marxism-Leninism combined with the actual situation of the Chinese revolution, and thus producing Mao Zedong Thought. This theoretical achievement not only reflected the basic principles of Marxism-Leninism, but also contained the Chinese people's outstanding ideas based on their experience and the CPC's practical revolutionary experience. The Party closely combined the tasks of the national revolution with those of the democratic revolution, creating the theory and direction of the new democratic revolution, creating a revolutionary path with Chinese characteristic based on surrounding the cities and seizing political control. The formation and development of Mao Zedong Thought were deeply rooted Marxism-Leninism in Chinese soil. Once this Chinese Marxism-Leninism was accepted and mastered by the Chinese people, it was transformed into a great material force for revolutionizing Chinese society, thus allowing the CPC to lead the Chinese revolution to victory. It was precisely because it adhered to the correct direction of combining the basic principles of Marxism-Leninism with the reality of the Chinese revolution that it was so adept at grasping the changes in the objective situation, summing up the practical experience of the people, and persisting in emancipating the mind through a line of thought that sought truth from facts and unswervingly followed its own path. This was the most basic experience to be drawn from the Party's history.

The CPC was a faithful representative of the fundamental interests of the overwhelming majority of the Chinese people. Adhering to the fundamental purpose of serving the people wholeheartedly at all times and maintaining a life bond with the people were the fundamental conditions for the CPC to overcome all sorts of difficulties and win the victory in the new democratic revolution. In the struggle for national independence and the liberation of the people, the Party had always relied on the masses and sincerely pursued the interests of the people. In all its activities, the Party shared the same fate with the people, always regarded the will and interests of the people as both the starting point and the destination of all its work, and always drew from the wisdom and strength of the people to advance the revolutionary cause. The Party did its utmost to gradually form a set of mass lines regarding believing in, relying on, coming from, and going to the masses. The Party used the leadership and work methods of the mass line to enable the formation and implementation of the masses to the greatest extent, to receive the support of the masses, and to enable the revolutionary enthusiasm and creativity of the masses, constantly growing and improving. This was an important guarantee for the Party's continued victory.

It was imperative that the CPC play the role of vanguard of the proletariat and lead the people to gain the victory in the Chinese revolution. It also had to closely focus on its own political line, strengthen its construction, and continuously enhance its creativity, cohesiveness, and combat effectiveness. The CPC was the product of the combination of Marxism-Leninism and the Chinese workers' movement. The growth and maturation of the working class was a fundamental condition for party-building. However, under China's social conditions, the vast majority of Party members came from the peasantry and manual laborer class, with many intellectuals and revolutionaries from non-labor classes. At the same time, the Party had long been in the environment of the rural revolutionary base areas. Based on these characteristics, the Party saw its own construction as a great project and attached much importance to its ideological, organizational, and work style construction, successfully addressing the fundamental issue of maintaining its nature as the vanguard of the proletariat and building a Marxist-Leninist party. Through frequent Marxist-Leninist ideological education, criticism and self-criticism, and summing up the experiences of and rectifying the Party, the CPC was able to overcome subjectivism, sectarianism, and both rightist and leftist political errors, learning from various mistakes and failures to progress and gradually mature. Through long-term struggle, the Party cultivated and formed an excellent style of linking theory and practice, closely connecting with the people, and engaging in criticism and self-criticism. It took these three styles as markers differentiating it from other political parties, emphasizing persistence, promotion of the Party's excellence, and the role of party style in fulfilling the CPC's political mission. After a long period of revolutionary trials, party organization had continued to grow and develop. The CPC had begun with just fifty members, but had by September 1949 become a nationwide Marxist-Leninist political party of the masses with more than 4.8 million members. The CPC was the most advanced, powerful leadership force guaranteeing the victory of the Chinese revolution.

2. The Basic Conditions for the Realization of Party Leadership

Liu Shaoqi observed that it was the Party's mass line that enabled the CPC to establish correct relations with the people, enabling it to lead the masses with the correct attitude and in the correct way, which was through its own leading organs and leaders. The CPC's leadership of the people was a proper relationship. This notion was an indication of the brilliance of Marxist leadership theory. Marxists believed that it was only the people who are real heroes, and only the people who could liberate themselves. The responsibility and role of the leader can only be to understand the needs of the masses, to consolidate the wisdom of the masses, to propose slogans and programs that reflect the fundamental interests of the masses, and to inspire the consciousness of the masses, enabling them to recognize their own interests, offering guidance to organize the masses to struggle for their own interests, and summing up the experiences of mass struggle to lead the peoples' enthusiasm to a higher stage. In this process, the main body and basic force are the masses. The leadership role is both that of scholar and student. Moreover, if the students of the masses do not first remain consistently focused, then they are not qualified to serve the people.

Proletarian leaders never regard the people as tools for their own purposes, but rather consciously identify themselves as the people's tools for achieving a specific historical task. The reason the CPC could lead the masses lay in its wholehearted service to the people. In a broad sense, it served the masses. In a more direct sense, it served as their leaders. The idea of leadership as service was the fundamental position of the proletarian party for correctly understanding and handling the relationship between the leaders and masses. It was from this standpoint that Mao repeatedly stressed that it was necessary to closely link the care of the masses with the political tasks of the Party, taking the visible material interests of the masses, or at least not damaging their interests, as one of the fundamental conditions for achieving leadership and adhering to the best interests of the overwhelming majority of the people and the support of the broadest masses as the highest standard for the entire Party's speech and actions.

For this reason, the question of whether or not the Party could get the support of the masses and become qualified to serve as their leader depended on its ability to address ideological concepts. Only by firmly standing for the masses could the Party produce policies, methods, and approaches that fundamentally represented the interests of the people. If it instead adopted the perspective of individuals or small groups, using the masses as a tool to achieve the interests of those individuals or groups, it would eventually stand in opposition to the masses, with its policies, methods, and approaches inevitably determined from the perspective of how to drive and control the masses. Such an approach was antithetical to Marxist leadership theories, and the CPC repeatedly emphasized that such leaders would certainly end up abandoning the masses.

Leadership is based on the premise of mastering certain powers. In the practice of leading the people in the revolutionary struggle, the CPC pointed out that it was very important to theoretically, and particularly ideologically, discover exactly where power originates. The ruler of an exploiting class is treated as either sacred or as "a great individual," and thus always regards his position as a privilege that is solely attributable to his superior status in relation to the masses. Guided by this sort of concept of power, the most open-minded political thinkers could only advocate a position as "lord of the people," a system in which the master is still oneself, not the people. In opposition to this view of power, the CPC believed that only the people were the true masters of society, while the leaders were merely public servants who carried out their duties in accordance with the will of the people. The power they held was given by the people. It was not the leader who was master of the people, but the people who were masters of themselves. The masses' obedience to power was subject to their collective will. If the leader violated the will of the people in his exercise of power, the people could withdraw that power and replace him at any time. Guided by two very different views of power, the exercise of power would not only produce diametrically opposite results in regards to the interests of the masses, but would also create leaders with different positions, talents, characters, and styles.

Who creates history? Whom does it serve? Who holds power? In short, these are the broad questions that are the subject of history. The broad masses of the people are the forces that represent the advanced production forces and the historical trajectory of society. Thus, it is only the masses that are the main body of history. With a deep understanding of the true meaning of this social history, leaders will continuously put themselves in the position of public servants and conscientiously perform their duties in that capacity.

3. The Basic Rules of the Party's Leadership Activities

Based on the mass perspective of Marxism, the CPC summed up its experience of the Party's leadership of the revolutionary struggle. From the height of epistemology, it analyzed the great significance of implementing correct leadership and emphasized the need to adhere to the ideas of "from the masses and to the masses" and "consolidation and persistence," avoiding the tendency to lose touch with the actual situation or to lose touch with the masses. It further sought to overcome subjectivism, bureaucracy, and authoritarianism and fully utilize and mobilize the people's consciousness, enthusiasm, and creativity, while ensuring that leaders made correct decisions and implemented them smoothly. The ideological basis of this leadership approach was to seek truth from facts, providing organizational guarantees through democratic centralism. The close combination of seeking truth from facts, the mass line, and democratic centralism revealed the essential characteristics of various proletarian leadership methods in activities geared at understanding and transforming the world and embodied the most basic rules of leadership.

Seeking truth from facts was the only correct line of thought guiding leaders in making scientific decisions and correcting mistakes. The CPC emphasized that all work be accomplished through seeking truth from facts and the mass line, allowing the two to complement one another. Seeking truth from facts was the prerequisite for adhering to the mass line. When Mao addressed the issue of leadership methods, he first began by solving the leaders' thoughts and methods and purifying the ideal spirit. He first proposed that "the victory of the Chinese revolution depends on Chinese comrades understanding China's situation" and that "there is no right to speak without investigation," or "anyone who does not conduct proper investigation has no right to speak," then fully elaborated on these political slogans regarding leadership methods, thus making seeking truth from facts, investigation, and research the ideological norms of all Party cadres. The first element for achieving proper leadership was seeking truth from facts, which had to be based on the mass line, and the most basic channel for understanding the actual situation was to investigate the masses. All truth could only come from the people who directly engaged in each specific practical activity. If leaders did not humbly learn from the masses or did not conduct thorough investigations among the people, they would be doomed to make mistakes in their decisions, opinions, and solutions to various problems, because the connection to the actual situation and to the people was so important. Thus, in order to implement the scientific leadership, it was important to get started with the practice of understanding the masses. In 1930, Mao observed that leaving the masses to practice or live from books would not only lead one to fall into opportunism or blindness, but would also put one in danger of starting down a counter-revolutionary road.

The mass line was the fundamental guarantee for achieving the goal of leadership. Correct decision-making from the perspective of the masses could only be achieved by a persistent close connection to the people. Without a close bond between the enthusiasm of the Party and that of the people, it would be impossible to achieve anything of significance. Thus, believing in the masses and believing in the Party were the two inseparable fundamental principles that the

CPC long adhered to in relation to the people and were the foundation for the fine leadership work conducted by the Party. The more work done, the more frustrations would naturally abound, and the more pressures, frustrations, and difficulties that arose, the more necessary it became to emphasize these two principles. In the practice of revolution, there were people who believed that foreign powers were more trustworthy than their own Party or people, or who were opposed to the Party and the people. As a result, there were major problems. Therefore, the CPC emphasized that leading cadres at all levels must go deeply into the grassroots and deeply into the masses, working in a down-to-earth manner to implement the Party's line, principles, and policies. This was the correct way to follow the rules of leadership, improve leadership efforts, and raise the level of leadership.

Democratic centralism was the Party's fundamental organizational principle and state policy, the vitality of the Party's mass line, and the manifestation of the country's political life. The basic principles and system of democratic centralism, such a collective leadership and the minority's subordination to the majority, were based on trust and relied on the wisdom and strength of the mass. If the leader believed that he had surpassed the follower, it would result in individualistic arbitrariness. If he believed a small number of people around him instead of the masses, it would lead to sectarianism. Either of these would undermine democratic centralism and combat the enthusiasm of the masses. Democratic centralism was also the organizational guarantee for adhering to the leadership of the mass line. Coming from the masses meant gathering the opinion of the masses, and it could only focus on majority opinions, according to the principles and procedures of democratic centralism. Going to the masses and seeing them in action required some authority, and this authority could only be based on democratic centralism. In the report of the Seventh National Congress of the CPC, Liu Shaoqi pointed out that democratic centralism was the Party's organizational rule, and the correct organizational line was the mass line. This offered great clarification of the principle that adhering to democratic centralism was an objective requirement of the rules of leadership.

4. Basic Methods of the Party's Leadership Work

In the process of leading the people to fight for national liberation, the CPC conducted in-depth exploration of the rules of leadership and formed an initial set of effective leadership methods. The first of these was that leadership must seize the center and show concern for others. The CPC played different roles in central work in different periods of historical development, and all Party work had to be carried out around this central work. Thus, the leadership of a region or unit had to put its work in an appropriate position and conduct it in an orderly, rhythmic manner, like playing a piano. First of all, it was necessary to distinguish between central work and regular work. Central work was often related to and often different from regular work. Regular work was the foundation, and central work could lead regular work, or it might oversee regular work while focusing on the main task. If one forgot the long-term nature of work or failed to be in touch with actual situations, he would be a short-term politician. If one failed to work regularly with the Party's central work, he would become a blind businessman. Only by becoming skilled at linking regular work to the Party's central work and struggle goals at a certain period of time could one become a politically brilliant revolutionary, and only then would the Party's leadership be fruitful. In addition, it was necessary to correctly handle the relationship between the universal and the local, and the work should achieve consistency between the two. Leaders needed to be skilled at distinguishing tasks from urgencies, primary work from secondary work, and central from regular work. They had to ensure focus and concern for others, and to strive to align the universal with the local.

The second method was that the core issue of leadership style was to properly handle relationships between superiors and subordinates. The CPC pointed out that upper and lower levels had to trust one another, on the basis of safeguarding the interests of the Party and the people. This was an important condition for performing well in maintaining good relations between superiors and subordinates. The key to achieving mutual trust and respect was that the superior should humbly learn from the subordinate, absorbing and summarizing the experiences of the subordinate, while enthusiastically helping the subordinate, giving full play to the enthusiasm and creativity of the lower level, strengthening the subordinate's professionalism and sense of responsibility, and improving their policy level and work ability. Mao once noted that the responsibility of leaders came down to two main things: the idea and the use of cadres. Chen Yun similarly noted that the leading organs set a plan, but that the subsequent implementation and inspection must be consistent with each other. Only in-depth practical investigation and research, listening to subordinates' experience and opinions, and finally forming a resolution or task would be aligned with the actual situation and stand the test of practice. At the same time, the superior should help the subordinate correctly implement the resolution or task and check the results of the execution. Specific analysis and treatment of new problems arising in the course of the practical work should lead to the formulation of new policies or flexible application of existing ones, allowing the lower levels to be dispatched according to the actual conditions. After clarifying work tasks, it was necessary to propose corresponding measures and offer specific guidance to subordinates to ensure the smooth, healthy completion of tasks. In the process of achieving and practicing leadership, the CPC emphasized that superiors had to be bold enough for self-criticism and dare to take responsibility. This was an effective way to address conflicts between the upper and lower levels and improve relations between superiors and subordinates.

The third method was to carry out all work to fully mobilize the masses. The masses were the basis for the Party's existence, the impetus for its consolidation and development, and the only source of its strength. At the same time, the Party was also a tool for the masses to wage their war of liberation. Therefore, the CPC pointed out that the Party's work must begin with the problems that the masses urgently wanted to see addressed. This was the key to effective leadership. Concern for the lives of the people and careful attention to their vital interests was an important part of fully mobilizing the masses and realizing the effective leadership of the Party. It was important that the Party be adept at linking its slogans, opinions, and policies to the vital interests of the masses.

The fourth idea was that it was necessary to flexibly apply various working methods according to the specific situation. To conscientiously implement the Party's line, principles, policies, and directives from higher authorities, it was important to pay careful attention to the art of leadership and adopt flexible, diverse working methods according to specific situations and locales. Chen Yun pointed out that all working methods must be decided according to the specific situation in each place. The general principles and methods could refer to various central resolutions, but at the same time, they had to be carefully combined to the local situation to propose appropriate slogans and flexibly apply various working methods. Determining the work policy according to the actual situation was the most basic approach to thinking and working methods that all Party members had to bear in mind. The implementation of the Party's line, principles, and policies and the spirit of the instructions from higher authorities had to be combined with the actual situation. It was important to study new situations, solve new problems, sum up new experiences, open up new situations, formulate new plans, and implement them creatively in practical work. As the cause of revolution and construction pushed forward, there were two types of wrong tendencies that needed to be opposed. One was the excuse that special circumstances prevented execution, and the other was blind implementation regardless of the actual situation on the ground. If one blindly followed the directives or instructions of his superiors and failed to adapt them to the local situation, this was not a good working method, but contrary to the superior's instructions. Mao pointed out in his article "Opposing Doctrinairism" that blindly executing instructions from a superior without any objection was not really an indication that the instructions had been followed. Rather, sometimes objection was the best way to complete those instructions.

5. Correct Style of Party Leadership

Leadership style was intrinsically linked to the nature of leadership, and it was the leader's position and external manifestation in the world. When Mao spoke of the CPC's three key styles at the Seventh National Congress, he pointed out that the CPC's work style, armed with Marxist-Leninist Theory, was the mark distinguishing the CPC from other political parties. The CPC emphasized that in order to implement the correct style of leadership, it was necessary to first give attention to the difference between its own and other leadership styles. It must be noted that it based its understanding on its progressive theory and its closeness to the people. On this basis, the Party pointed out that the way to deal with the masses was first of all an issue of position, purpose, and emotion for the leader of the proletariat. Sincerely treating oneself as an ordinary member of the masses, beginning from the goal of respecting and loving the people, and wholeheartedly serving the people were the three pillars that would consciously formulate and maintain an excellent leadership style. If the fundamental transformation of a worldview and one's feelings regarding his position were not realized, it would be impossible for him to maintain a close relationship with the masses. Even more, once the official sensed that he was superior to the masses, misconceptions of the masses would surely arise and grow. The image of the leader would no longer be that of public servant, but of official and master, resulting in a loss of leadership or difficulty establishing effective leadership.

The connection between theory and practice was the main manifestation of a leader overcoming subjectivism and adhering to the spirit of the proletarian party. It required leaders to have a solid foundation in theory, to have a real understanding of the actual situation, and to practice specific analysis of specific situations. It was both realistic and demanding, striving to combine Marxism-Leninism, Mao Zedong Thought, and the spirit of instructions from the superior in conjunction with the specific local conditions to solve problems creatively. It was necessary to dare to do this and to take the path no predecessor had walked before. And it was important to be firm and make timely examination of whether one's own opinions in fact conformed to the objective laws and could withstand the test of practice. The CPC had always emphasized the necessity of carrying forward this tradition if correct leadership was to be achieved.

Maintaining the closest of connections with the broadest masses was the source of the wisdom and strength of the leaders of the proletariat, and also a fundamental guarantee for maintaining the Party's nature as the "people's public servants." It required leaders to constantly understand the wishes of the people, feel the pulse of the masses, caring for their suffering and learning from their experience. Ideologically, the Party had to stand taller, look further, and promptly propose tasks that were needed by the masses. In action, it had to persist in advancing with the majority of the people. When most people were conscious, the Party must promptly and decisively organize mass action. When most people were not yet conscious, the Party must wait patiently and be a source of inspiration, practicing modesty, caution, and patience. Party life must be arduous but simple, not special or privileged. In short, the Party could not separate from the people, and it must not be above the masses.

Party members had to have the courage to carry out criticism and self-criticism, carry out active ideological struggle, uphold truth, and correct errors. This was the manifestation of its solemn responsibility to the people. The CPC believed that Party members had to begin with meeting the needs of the overwhelming majority of the people, its leaders working for the people, avoiding arrogance, speaking the truth, and addressing its own shortcomings and mistakes in leadership work. Regardless of whether hearing criticism or making self-criticism, one had to listen and correct mistakes. If one was proud or arrogant, the matter might be overstated, or the blame for failure pushed to the leader or to the masses who lagged behind. This would inevitably result in a loss of trust from the masses and alienate the leader.

CHAPTER 10

The Establishment of Mao Zedong Thought as the Guideline for the Party

I

The Party's Recognition and Acceptance of Mao Zedong Thought

1. The Conception of "Mao Zedong Thought"

Since its birth, the CPC had taken Marxism as its guideline, integrating it steadily with China's revolution, giving rise to Marxism with Chinese characteristics. Party members called the theoretical innovation with Chinese traits "Mao Zedong Thought," as a tribute to Mao's role as one of the primary pioneers in the localization of Marxism and one of the major founders of Marxist theory with Chinese traits. Mao Zedong Thought "came into maturity when it was systematically summarized and practiced in multiple ways during later part of the Agrarian Revolution and the Anti-Japanese War."[1] The conceptualization of Mao Zedong Thought served as a recognition of and theoretical conclusion to the historical fact.

Mao Zedong Thought underwent a long period of exploration from its birth to maturity. By the same token, the conception of Mao Zedong Thought went through quite a long process from its conception to its proposal and ultimately to the common understanding of the entire Party.

The CPC grew more competent in addressing the issues concerning China's revolution after it decided on Mao Zedong's leadership in the Party at the Zunyi Meeting in 1935. About the time of the beginning of the Anti-Japanese War, the Party succeeded in transforming the civil war into the Anti-Japanese War, and Mao's leadership within the Party was consolidated and recognized by the Comintern. In September 1938, at the Politburo Meeting and the Sixth Plenary Meeting of the Sixth Central Committee, Wang Jiaxiang, who came back from Moscow, communicated the Comintern's and Dimitrov's affirmation of the CPC's direction and Mao Zedong's leadership. The Comintern pointed out that since the Anti-Japanese War, "the Communist Party has adopted the right political line and applied Marxism-Leninism in a true sense under the complicated and challenging circumstances."[2] It also suggested that the issues concerning leading authorities "should be resolved under the leadership of Mao Zedong to build an environment for close collaboration."[3] All this contributed greatly to the Party in carrying forward an innovative spirit to resolve, under the guidance of Marxism and Leninism, issues occurring during China's revolution. It also encouraged the entire Party to pay attention to and study Mao Zedong's theoretical contributions.

Soon after the publication of "On New Democracy," the notion of "Comrade Mao Zedong's theory" came into shape. Early in May 1940, at the opening ceremony of the "Zedong School for Young Cadres" in Yan'an, Wang Ming, the then Secretary of the Central Secretariat, was invited to deliver a speech entitled "Studying Mao Zedong,"[4] applauding Mao as "a great statesman and strategist of China's revolution" and "a great theorist," and calling for "the study of Comrade Mao Zedong's life and theories." He further explained Mao's "innovative spirit," represented in "building up Soviet political power," "building a Chinese army of workers and farmers," "designing military strategy and tactics for the revolution," "building a united national front," and "building new democratic political power," which served as the initial summary of Mao's theoretical contribution. In particular, Wang Ming mentioned "On New Democracy," stating that it was a new contribution to Marxism-Leninism on the issue of the state. While his accolades for Mao and Mao's theoretical contribution might not be heartfelt, judging from what he said and did later, this speech was quite influential, given his status and overseas educational background.

Those who worked on theories concerning the Party played a key role in facilitating studies on Mao's theoretical contributions. In February 1940, Ai Siqi published an essay, specifically pointing out that on the basis of practices, China "has developed some theories on furthering Marxism, hence its own Marxism."[5] This statement played an introductory role in proposing "localized Marxism" and "Mao Zedong Thought." From March 1941 to February 1942, Zhang Ruxin offered, in different essays, a range of key notions and diagnoses, using such phrases as "Comrade Mao's thought," "the system of Mao Zedong's theory and tactics," and "Maoism." He stated that Mao's speeches and works were "the best representation of localized Marxism-Leninism," that "Mao's theory is the Chinese version of Marxism-Leninism," and that "we need to study how Mao applied the fundamental principles to the circumstances in China and how he pushed forward innovative Marxism."

In his innovation and development of Marxism, Mao categorized it from different perspectives into either three or four aspects, then elaborated on them, namely the class relationship in Chinese society and the traits of China's national democratic revolution, the national united front, the regime of China's national democratic revolution, the construction of the revolutionary army, the foundation of the base area, and the strategy and tactics for revolution. Further, he developed the Party's ideological guidelines and methodology, political guidelines and science, and military guidelines and science. In his editorial on July 1, 1942, "The Party Learning Mao Zedong Thought to Commemorate July 1," Deng Tuo stated that "the Communist Party has nationalized and localized Marxism-Leninism in its twenty-one years of struggle," and that "Mao Zedong Thought is in a sense Marxism-Leninism with Chinese characteristics. Every single Chinese Marxist-Leninist must actually and only be Maoist." Like Zhang Ruxin's article, this one classifies Mao Zedong's theoretical contribution into the scientific thought, political scientific theory, military scientific theory, and tactics for elaboration, and stresses that "the very core of Mao Zedong's thought lies in the policy of specifying, nationalizing, and localizing Marxism." Later Deng Tuo turned to the term "Comrade Mao Zedong's theory." In their works, Hu Qiaomu, Chen Boda, Tao Zhu, Lu Dingyi, Hua Gang, and others analyzed and approached problems utilizing Mao's fundamental theories and research methods, which indicated the academic community's recognition of Mao Zedong's contribution.

With the intensification of the Yan'an Rectification Movement, the Party went further in its recognition of Mao Zedong's contribution to the localization of Marxism in China, which was evident in many top-level leaders' publication of articles to air their views.

On July 1, 1942, Zhu De turned to the concept of "localized Marxism-Leninism" in the article "In Commemoration of the 21st Anniversary of the Founding of the Party," stating that "now the Party has acquired plenty of experience through various struggles, become well-acquainted with Marxist-Leninist theories, and created the localized Marxist-Leninist theories guiding China's revolutionary practice."[6]

On the same day, Chen Yi pointed out at the meeting commemorating the 21st anniversary of the founding of CPC that[7] Mao Zedong "proposes to address the issue of localizing Marxism-Leninism in China with scientific methods and ways of thinking" and hence created "the proper ideological system." Chen summarized Mao's theories concerning China's revolution in five aspects. First was the nature of Chinese society, the motivation for and prospect of revolution, and the corresponding strategy and tactics. This was followed by the issues of organizing and leading the revolution, then by the theory and construction of the Soviet power. Next was the building of the Party. Finally, he addressed proper thinking, handling new academic findings of Western Europe and Chinese national traditions, the reform of Chinese academic thought, and other issues.

In June, 1943, Ren Bishi wrote an article pointing out that Mao Zedong was able to "concretize and localize Marxism-Leninism" basically because of "his keen awareness of the masses and his inclination to learn from the public," which constituted "the most distinctive feature of Mao's way of thinking and working." To study Marxism and Leninism, it was important to particularly study the localized version of Marxism in China.[8]

On July 6, 1943, Liu Shaoqi used the two concepts of "Comrade Mao Zedong's thought" and the "Comrade Mao Zedong's thought system" in his article "Liquidating Menshevist thought within the Party."[9]

On July 8, 1943, Wang Jiaxiang published the article "The Path of the CPC and Chinese National Liberation," using for the first time the concept "Mao Zedong Thought," which subsequently remained in use. He also elaborated on the process of the "budding, bursting, and maturing" of Mao Zedong Thought, pointing out that "Mao Zedong Thought is the Chinese version of Marxism-Leninism. It is Chinese Bolshevism and Communism." It was an innovation and expansion of Marxism-Leninism in China.[10]

On August 2, 1943, Zhou Enlai delivered a speech at the reception held for him by the General Office of the CPC, stating that the twenty-two years of history of the CPC had proven that "Comrade Mao Zedong's views permeate throughout Party history, turning into a route of localizing Marxism-Leninism, i.e. of Chinese Communism." Communism, having been applied and developed by Mao Zedong, had been rooted in China land.[11]

On November 10, 1943, Deng Xiaoping pointed out in his speech delivered at the mobilization meeting for Yan'an Rectification Movement at the Bureau Party School in the north that since Zunyi meeting, the party cause had been carried forward under the guidance of localized Marxism-Leninism, or Mao Zedong Thought.[12]

The above situation demonstrated that, with the continuous accumulation of revolutionary experience, the publication of a series of important works by Mao Zedong, the development of the Party-wide rectification movement, and especially the discussion of historical issues by the Party's senior leading cadres, the Party not only developed Marxism-Leninism through Mao Zedong Thought, but also came to a consensus, developing an overview that included the fruitful achievements made by China's brand of Marxism – namely the scientific expression of Chinese Marxism known as "Mao Zedong Thought" and a preliminary summary of its basic content. In the mean time, there were numerous references to "the theory of Comrade Mao Zedong," "the doctrine of Comrade Mao Zedong," and "Mao Zedong Thought." After the election, the CPC Central Committee passed the Resolution on Several Historical Issues, which was ratified by the time of the Seventh National Congress.

On April 20, 1945, having been adopted by the Seventh National Congress, the Resolution on Several Historical Issues (or, "the Resolution") was the theoretical result of the discussion of the Party's historical issues by senior leaders in the rectification movement. It fully affirmed Mao's historical status and established Mao Zedong Thought as the Party's guiding ideology.

The Resolution summarized the Party's historical experience, beginning from the founding of the CPC, and summarized several major historical issues. It emphasized the Party's erroneous tendency toward Marxist dogmatism and toward elevating the directives of the Comintern and the Soviet experience during the Agrarian Revolutionary War, then went on to reveal the leftist error in various political, military, organizational, and ideological areas, along with their social and ideological roots. At the same time, it spoke highly of Mao Zedong's outstanding contributions to the use of Marxism-Leninism throughout the Chinese revolution and affirmed its great significance in establishing Mao's leadership position in the Party. According to the draft resolution adopted by the Seventh Plenary Session of the Sixth General Meeting of the Central Committee of the CPC, "The Party produced its own leader over the past twenty-five years, Comrade Mao Zedong, and formulated a correct line of thought, while also rectifying any wrong line of thought."[13] This was the first official use of the concept of Mao Zedong Thought in Party documents. The Resolution discussed the basic content of Mao Zedong Thought from political, military, organizational, and ideological perspectives, expounding on the ways in which Mao used Marxists positions, viewpoints, and methods to produce a set of theories directions, guidelines, and frameworks that were in line with the needs of the Chinese revolution. The Resolution emphasized that the future task of the entire Party was "to unite all the Party's comrades like a harmonious family on the basis of consensus with Marxism-Leninism, in order to win complete victory in the War of Resistance Against Japanese Aggression and the struggle for the complete liberation of the Chinese people."[14]

The convening of the Sixth Plenary Session of the Seventh General Meeting of the CPC Central Committee and its adoption of the Resolution marked the success of the rectification movement, strengthening the unity of the entire Party on the basis of Mao Zedong Thought and putting the groundwork for ideological developments and the guiding role of Mao Zedong Thought into the Party Constitution ahead of the Seventh National Congress.

2. Establishing the Guiding Position of Mao Zedong Thought

Held from April 23 to June 11, 1945, the Seventh National Congress of the CPC occupied a particularly important position in the historical process of the development of Chinese Marxism. On the one hand, it pushed the Party's theory of revolutionary nation-building. At the same time, it systematically summed up the achievements of Chinese Marxism and clearly stipulated the guiding position Mao Zedong Thought held within it.

Mao's written report, oral report, and published conclusions under the title "The United Government" further enriched the ideas of the new democratic revolution. First, it offered a full explanation of the general trend of the new democratic revolution, noting that it was "an anti-imperialist, anti-feudalist mass revolution led by the proletariat." Mao observed, "Our line and program can be summed up in a single sentence: the new democratic revolution is the anti-imperialist, anti-feudalist revolution of the masses under proletarian leadership. Within this line is the issue of our forces and the enemy's, as well as a question of who leads or commands our force." He particularly emphasized the importance of the peasantry in the Chinese revolution, pointing out that the peasants were "the most important part of the masses" and "the main force of the Chinese revolution." He added, "If you overlook the peasantry, there will be no democratic revolution in China. Without the democratic revolution, there will be no Chinese socialist revolution, nor any type of revolution at all," and "the proletariat must provide the main leadership for the peasantry."

In addition, in an effort to further solidify and expand the new democratic political, economic, and cultural programs, Mao not only distinguished the Party's highest from its lowest programs, but also for the first time drew a distinction between its general and specific programs at the stage of democratic revolution. The general program was meant to advocate "the establishment of a national system of democratic alliances based on a united front rooted in an absolute majority within the country," namely "the new democratic national system."[15] Under this national system, new democratic systems of politics, economics, and culture were established. Among these, Mao especially addressed the issue of "the widespread development of capitalism," explaining that "this report is different from *New Democracy* in that it prioritizes the need for broad development of capitalism and anti-authoritarianism."[16] This raised the question of why Communists did not fear capitalism and advocated its development. This was because "grasping the development of capitalism to replace the oppression of foreign imperialism and domestic feudalism is not only a step forward, but also an inevitable process that benefits not only the bourgeoisie, but also the proletariat. Currently, China is in greater danger from foreign imperialism and domestic feudalism than from an excess of domestic capitalism. In fact, quite to the contrary, we have too little capitalism."[17] Of course, what is indicated here as "the broad development" of capitalism is one that "cannot manipulate the livelihood of the people," or simply, "new democratic capitalism."[18] Mao pointed out that such a proposal was aligned with "populism." He listed 40 articles in this program, including eliminating the Japanese aggressors and refusing to compromise with centrists, abolishing the KMT's single-party dictatorship and establishing a democratic coalition government, implementing land reforms and liberating the peasants, developing industry and fighting to industrialize and modernize Chinese agriculture, and uniting and educating intellectuals to develop cultural and educational efforts. In order to develop industry, Mao noted that, as long as it obeyed Chinese laws and promoted the Chinese economy, foreign investment was welcome.

Finally, it proposed a viewpoint for judging the historical role of political parties by productivity standards. Mao observed, "Whether the principles and practices of all political parties in China are good, bad, big, or small should be measured according to the people. In the final analysis, is it helpful to the development and growth of the Chinese people's productivity, and does it bind productivity or liberate productive forces?"[19] The CPC's programs were aimed at liberating and developing China's social productive forces and binding China into an independent, free, democratic, unified, and prosperous country, something eagerly welcomed by the Chinese people.

Further, in the above-mentioned report by Mao Zedong, Zhu De's military report entitled "On the Battlefield in Liberated Areas," Liu Shaoqi's "Report on Amending the Party Constitution," and Zhou Enlai's "On the United Front," the Party's military approach consisting of strategic tactics for the People's Army, the people's war, and the people's guidelines for war focused primarily on ideological and political construction, while continuing to focus on the party-building line, the mass line, an excellent work style, and democratic centralism in its organization. The lessons learned since the Great Revolution regarding issues such as the united front were fully elaborated. The Seventh National Congress added a good deal of new material to Chinese Marxism.

The Seventh National Congress offered a systematic summary of the fruitful achievements of Chinese Marxism and officially established the guiding position of Mao Zedong Thought. This was an important part of the efforts made by the Seventh National Congress to promote the cause of Chinese Marxism, a contribution mainly reflected in Liu Shaoqi's "Report on Amending the Party Constitution" and the new amendment to the Constitution passed by the General Meeting.

Liu Shaoqi's collated report was a great achievement for the entire Party's understanding. He offered a systematic, comprehensive summary and interpretation of the first historical leap of Chinese Marxism as it was embodied in Mao Zedong Thought. The report began with explanation of the arduousness of the task of developing Chinese Marxism and a recounting of the reasons Marxism could be successfully localized into the Chinese context. Liu Shaoqi pointed out that the uniqueness of China's social and historical development and the fact that Chinese science remained largely underdeveloped made it necessary for Marxism to be systematically adapted from its European form into a style more suited to China, which was what became Chinese Marxism. The principles and methods of Marxist teaching were applied to address various issues in the Chinese revolution, including many questions that Marxists in other countries had never raised or addressed. This was a unique, and very difficult, undertaking. It was not merely about successfully reading, memorizing, or citing Marxist works, but also required that these be combined with a high degree of scientific and revolutionary thought. It was a task that required a wealth of historical and social knowledge, revolutionary experience, and a spirit of fighting for the people's cause. The CPC excelled at applying Marxist methods to engage in scientific analysis of objective situations and at combining experience with the will and thinking of the people. Through this process, it was possible to combine China's actual situation with the outstanding achievements of Marxism and express this in a distinctly Chinese form, turning it into a tool to guide the struggle of the Chinese people. Liu noted that "it is only our comrade, Mao Zedong, who has successfully carried out this unique, difficult task of integrating Marxism into China." Why was this? It was because Mao was "not only the greatest revolutionary and politician in China's history," daring to serve as a leader for the entire Party and all the people in the course of numerous earth-shaking battles, "but he is also the greatest theorist and scientist in Chinese history" with "the highest level of theoretical cultivation and greatest theoretical courage." He boldly proposed theoretical innovations, "abandoning some outdated individual principles and conclusions of Marxist theory that were not suited to China's specific environment and replaced them with new principles and conclusions suitable for China's historical situation." That is to say, Mao grasped the inherent conditions necessary for all aspects of theoretical innovation, which allowed him to successfully carry out all the difficult tasks involved in integrating Marxism into China.[20]

In addition, the report defined Mao Zedong Thought from multiple angles, revealing its rich implications and essential characteristics. The first was its definition of Mao Zedong Thought from the perspectives of its internal relationships, which noted that "Mao Zedong Thought is the combination of Marxism-Leninism with the practice of the Chinese revolution, which is to say, it is Chinese Communism and Chinese Marxism." Further, "it is something Chinese, and also something thoroughly Marxist." The second angle for defining Chinese Marxism was that it was an application of Marxism to a specific time and place. The report noted, "Mao Zedong Thought is the continued development of Marxism in the democratic revolution of colonial, semi-colonial, and semi-feudal countries in the present era, and it is an excellent example of localizing Marxism to suit the needs of each nationality." The third angle defined the function of the Chinese revolution. It pointed out that Mao Zedong Thought was "the special, comprehensive theory of the Chinese people's revolutionary nation-building," and "it is the application of correct theory and policy by the Chinese proletariat and all its laborers to liberate themselves." The fourth angle defined Mao Zedong Thought through the intra-party struggle to establish a correct party line, noting that Mao Zedong Thought was not only applied to the struggle against domestic and foreign enemies, but also within the Party. The various erroneous opportunist ideas further grew and developed the principle of struggle, generating "the correct guiding principle of the Party and a correct party line." Liu observed, "There have been countless historical facts in the past. Now, if the revolution is not guided by Comrade Mao Zedong and his thought, it will fail and retreat."[21] Liu's arguments were in line with the objective laws of the formation and development of Mao Zedong Thought, correctly explaining the relationship of individuality and universality, and of learning, application and innovation between Mao Zedong Thought and Marxism, as well as the relationship between Mao Zedong Thought and the progress and retreat, and the success and failure of the Chinese revolutionary struggle, which demonstrated the inevitability and necessity of establishing the guiding role of Mao Zedong Thought.

Further, the report summarized the main content of Mao Zedong Thought. Liu Shaoqi noted that, as the complete revolutionary theory upon which the Chinese revolution was built, Mao Zedong Thought, "expressed in Comrade Mao's various works and numerous Party documents, is Mao's analysis of the situation in the modern world and of China's national situation. It addresses theory and policy on new democracy, on the liberation of the peasantry, on the united front, on armed struggle, on the revolutionary base areas, on building a new democratic republic, on party-building, on culture, and on other related subjects." These theories and policies were "the highest expression of the Chinese nation and the greatest generalization of theory."[22] The nine aspects of Mao Zedong Thought summarized in the report constituted a new democratic theoretical system with Chinese characteristics, addressing questions such as what sort of revolution China aimed to carry out, how it intended to do so, and what sort of country it would be after the revolution. This was the most important result of the first historic leap in the integration of Marxism into China.

Finally, the report called for "a movement to learn Mao Zedong Thought throughout the Party" and to welcome "the pinnacle of Marxist culture." This was a call to further advance the cause of integrating Marxism into China.

Liu's scientific discourse on Mao Zedong Thought was an important milestone in the development of the CPC's theoretical understanding of Mao Zedong Thought. If the creation of Mao Zedong Thought was the pinnacle of Chinese Marxism at that time, then Liu's scientific elucidation of it was the highest level of understanding of Mao Zedong Thought attained during that period. Although some of his expressions, references, or even analysis were not entirely appropriate, their profound look at and logical argument for Mao Zedong Thought established it as the guiding thought for the entire Party and promoted the Party's understanding and grasp of this theoretical system, making it a unique, irreplaceable contribution to its development.

The General Outline of the Constitution of the Communist Party of China, which was adopted by the Seventh National Congress, clearly stated, "Armed with the theory of Marxism-Leninism combined with the practice of the Chinese revolution, the CPC adopts Mao Zedong Thought as a guide for all its work and opposes any dogmatism's empirical biases."[23] This historic decision was the most authoritative confirmation of the great achievements of the first historic leap of Marxism in China.

It should be noted that the understanding of the Party's guiding ideology in Mao's name was closely related to the understanding of the relationship between "Mao Zedong Thought" and "the thoughts of Comrade Mao Zedong." At that time, there was no distinction between the two, including in Liu's report, which is to say, attention was not given to the relationship between individual creation and collective wisdom, which resulted in equating one with the other. However, it should be noted that Mao himself did not consider Mao Zedong Thought his personal creation, an understanding he expressed in clear terms at the Seventh Plenary Session of the Sixth General Meeting of the Central Committee and the Seventh Preparatory Meeting. At the Seventh Plenary Session, he noted his explanation of the draft resolution, saying, "The resolution gives me credit for many good things. I don't object to that, but it does not negate the fact that I have flaws. It simply means that I considered the Party's positions, not that I authored them."[24] At the Party's Seventh Preparatory Meeting, he said in his speech on the working principle of the conference, "The resolution credits me with many good things, so I want to make a point. I am simply the representative who wrote these ideas down, but that is good. If I had written them on my own, we would not be a Party."[25] Not only this, but Mao also did not agree with putting his name alongside the founders of Marxism-Leninism. In the process of formulating Mao Zedong Thought, Mao said in a letter to He Kaifeng, Acting Minister of the Propaganda Department of the CPC Central Committee, "My theory (of Marxism-Leninism) is not yet mature, so it is still time for continued study, not for advocating the idea. Some pieces are to be advocated (such as the articles on rectification), but we should not promote the entire system of thought, as the ideas are not yet fully mature."[26] In August 1948, Wu Yuzhang, President of North China University, stated in a telegram that he wanted to propose to "mainly study Maoism" and to "change Mao Zedong Thought into Maoism" at the school's opening ceremony. Mao replied, "It's very inappropriate to say that. There is no Maoism now, so we should not speak of Maoism. We should not 'mainly study Maoism,' but encourage the students to study Marxist theory and the practical experience of the Chinese revolution. The 'practical experience of the Chinese revolution' I'm referring to here includes certain pamphlets written by Chinese Communists (including myself) in line with Marxist theory and the documents and policies of the CPC. In addition, my name should not stand alongside Marx's in the publication, and it is wrong to say 'Marx, Engels, Lenin, Stalin, and Mao.' Your statement is not in line with this idea. In fact, it is quite harmful and really must be resolutely opposed."[27] At the Second Plenary Session of the Seventh General Meeting of the Central Committee in March 1949, Mao once again emphasized that "Chinese Communists should not be mentioned alongside

Marx, Engels, Lenin, and Stalin."[28] All of these statements provide an indication of Mao's understanding of "Mao Zedong Thought."

Before and after the Seventh National Congress, in an effort to meet the entire Party's need to study Mao Zedong Thought, some in the anti-Japanese base areas and in the liberated areas published multiple versions of the *Selected Works of Mao Zedong*. In 1927 to 1943, Mao's works had already appeared in a variety of monographs, special anthologies, and essay collections, and some works had been compiled into two collections of Party documents, such as *After the Sixth National Congress*, *Before the Sixth National Congress*, and *Two Paths*, which created the conditions for editing *A Mao Zedong Anthology*. The first of such anthologies was edited and published by the *Jinchaji Daily* in 1994. Divided into five volumes, it totaled roughly 400,000 words in 29 different works by Mao, mainly drawn from the period of the War of Resistance Against Japanese Aggression. The *Jinchaji Daily* released a news article stating that the purpose of publishing the book was to "implement Mao Zedong Thought throughout the entire Party in the border region." It noted that only through the guidance of Mao Zedong Thought could victory be won in the Chinese revolution, so no matter which part of the Party one was in, it was necessary to engage in in-depth study of Mao Zedong Thought.[29] Using this collection as a foundation, the Dalian Public Bookstore issued another volume, with some minor omissions and additions. In 1946, a five volume set of the *Selected Works of Mao Zedong* were published. In 1947, the Jinchaji Central Bureau updated and published the six volumes of the *Selected Works of Mao Zedong*, along with some additional material. After that, the Northeast Bureau of the CPC Central Committee published its six-volume *Selected Works of Mao Zedong* in 1948, under the imprint of the Northeastern Bookstore (a six-volume hardcover set). This was another influential collection of Mao's works, which included 50 of his articles written between March 1927 and December 1947, and totaled about 800,000 words. In addition to the above works, on the eve of the victory of the Anti-Japanese War in 1945, the Suzhong Publishing House issued a single-volume *Selected Works of Mao Zedong*. One of its striking features was its early compilation of works by 18 writers, including Zhu De, Zhou Enlai, and Liu Shaoqi, who spoke of Mao's work and used the term "Mao Zedong Thought." These were compiled as prefaces to the book. In 1948, the Jinjiluyu Central Bureau of the CPC Central Committee edited and published the *Selected Works of Mao*

Zedong as an "intra-Party document," collecting sixty-one of Mao's articles in two volumes arranged in three sections, labeled "The Great Revolution Period," "The Civil War Period," and "After the Anti-Japanese War." It contained a total of about 900,000 words, making it the most voluminous and varied edition of the *Selected Works of Mao Zedong* published before the founding of the new China. The publication of these editions provided textbooks for the entire Party to study Mao Zedong Thought, playing a positive role in promoting Mao Zedong Thought in various revolutionary base and liberated areas.

II

The Strategy of Transferring from Rural to Urban Areas

1. Historical Conditions for the Strategy of Transferring From Rural to Urban Areas

China's social and historical conditions dictated that the new democratic revolution had to follow a strategy of encircling cities with rural strongholds. The timely transformation from a rural to an urban focus provided a fundamental guarantee for the end of the revolution and the capture and consolidation of national victory.

In the second half of 1947, the Chinese People's War of Liberation reached a turning point. The People's Liberation Army turned to a nationwide attack and undermined Chiang Kai-shek's counter-revolutionary plan to continue to lead the war to the liberated areas in an attempt to completely destroy them. Mao noted that this was a turning point in history, marking the move of Chiang's twenty-year counter-revolutionary rule toward extinction. This was the turning point that completely eradicated a century of imperialist rule in China. It was truly a great event. In October 1947, Mao solemnly issued the great call to "Overthrow Chiang Kai-shek and liberate the whole of China" in his Declaration to the Chinese People's Liberation Army, stating, "We are now shouldering the most important, most glorious task in the history of the Chinese revolution. We should work hard to complete this task." It was in this historical situation that the Central Committee promptly raised the issue of placing great importance on and strengthening urban work, launching a transformation in political strategy. Urban work had become an important agenda of the Central Committee. In February 1948, the Central Committee demanded that "the Party's attention should not be focused on war and rural work, but should begin to give attention to urban work."[30] In September, the Expanded Meeting of the Politburo clearly stated that it was necessary to "strengthen the management of urban and industrial work so that the Party's focus may be gradually transferred from the countryside to the city."[31] From the end of 1948 to the beginning of 1949, the CPC Central Committee issued a number of instructions regarding control of the military, organization of representatives from all walks of life in the cities, management of urban policy issues such as real estate, employee wages, prices, resumption of factory work, and the receipt of cultural and educational institutions, a clear indication that the Party's focus had shifted to urban areas. In March 1949, the Second Plenary Session of the Seventh General Meeting of the CPC Central Committee stated more clearly, "From 1927 to the present, our work has focused on the countryside, consolidating strength and surrounding the cities there, then taking the cities. The time for such work methods has ended. Now is the time for work to begin moving from the city to the countryside… The Party's work must be focused on the city. It must put great effort into learning to manage and build the cities."[32]

Faced with this great historical task, the CPC once again promoted and developed new democratic theory and practice with bold ideology and an unbridled revolutionary spirit, forming and developing the strategic idea of transferring its focus from rural to urban areas.

2. The Need to Establish Urban Work as the Party's Central Task in a Timely Manner

Since the cities had always been the focus of China's imperialist and reactionary rule, an enemy who hoped to avoid failure must inevitably fight in a variety of ways. Mao Zedong specifically pointed out that upon entering the city, it was imperative that the Party wage political, economic, and cultural struggles against the imperialists, the KMT, and the bourgeoisie there, as well as diplomatic struggles against the imperialists. In these urban struggles, it was important to rely wholeheartedly on the working class, unite with laborers, fight for intellectuals, and strive for as many elements and representatives of the national bourgeoisie as were willing to cooperate, or at least keep them neutral, if the CPC was to make systematic progress against its enemies. At the same time, Mao emphasized that great effort had to be exerted in learning to manage and build the cities. From the first day the Party took the cities, it had to keep an eye on the recovery and development of productive forces. All other work in the cities was centered around production. Similarly, in the old liberated areas, the Party's task was "to mobilize all forces to restore and develop production, which is the focus of all work."[33]

Guided by these strategies and guidelines, the CPC elaborated several aspects of its strategic thinking regarding urban work.

a. Learning to Manage the City while Taking the City

Liu Shaoqi noted that it was necessary to have a perspective of integrating the urban and rural areas. In the past, the Party had only focused on the countryside, now it was adding the city, which meant adding new problems, such as big industry, state-owned enterprises (of a socialist nature), state capitalism, and urban-rural relations. If the Party hoped to shift its entire focus to center on urban work, it had to consider and address such problems. The "one-on-one" approach had to change, or the CPC would commit various errors. Liu believed that there were two key issues to be settled in the course of taking over the cities. The first was the recovery of private enterprises, and the other was that these enterprises had to be quickly organized and then handed over to the proper authorities for the resumption of normal production. The problem of urban management after receiving the enterprises had not yet been resolved. After the Second General Meeting of the CPC Central Committee, everyone needed to work hard to resolve this issue. It was not enough to receive the enterprises; they also had to be transformed and managed well. Some old things had to be removed, but this could not be done to too great an extent. At the same time, new things had to grow. Building and developing the city was not only a matter of management, but also a means of drawing the workers closer to the peasants.[34]

b. The Power of Urban Work is Dependent on the Working Class

Liu Shaoqi emphasized that Mao had raised the question of whom to rely on and what to do in the management of the city. Mao's suggestion was to rely on workers to develop production. This was a good general rule, as Marxism held that the proletariat was the most reliable class. In the specifics, however, there were still problems, so it was necessary that the Party put great effort into ensuring that the working class was completely reliable. If it neglected to rely on the working class without doing its own work diligently, then the working class would not be reliable. The CPC had once had a good relationship with the working class, but then it had been forced to transfer its attention to the countryside. The KMT had continued its activity among the workers for many years, spreading its influence, so there was much inner conflict among the proletariat. For this reason, the CPC had to diligently study and always give attention to Chairman Mao's directives concerning relying on and strengthening the workers, and in the process, making them completely reliable. There were three main methods for doing so. The first was to ensure that the workers' living standards were not too low, the second to educate the workers, and the third to organize the workers.[35] Deng Zihui pointed out that some mistakes in the early stages of entering the city indicated that in the future, the center of Party work would be transferred to the city. After entering the city, relying on the working class and paying close attention to restoring and developing production, it was very necessary for Chairman Mao to make these two issues clear and confirmed. Beyond addressing who to rely on after going into the city, the plans were vague. As a result, Zhengzhou and Kaifeng first attracted poor, hardworking laborers, neglecting industrial workers. This was a common phenomenon, and the idea of relying on the proletariat was unclear. The core of urban work was to resume production. Without any prior understanding of this, many thought it was necessary to mobilize the workers before starting production. But without resolving the issue of the workers' livelihood, how could the Party engage in a workers' movement?

c. Promoting the Industrialization of China as the Most Essential Requirement for Urban Work

Ren Bishi believed that moving the focus of the Party's work from rural to urban areas was a "historical issue." The basic concept of the urban focus was built around reliance on the working class, recovery and development of industrial production – including light industry, heavy industry, and transportation – and organizing trade. All other urban work, such as municipal construction, public activities, finance, culture, education, and party-building, was to be subordinate to industrial development. In short, this was the beginning of industrialization, which was the most essential issue in urban work.[36] He laid out the importance of industrialization from three perspectives.

1) *The need to implement independent policy.* Having achieved political and military independence, these were no longer issues, but it was only in achieving economic independence that the Party could truly be fully independent. In other words, aside from anything not available from its own pool of resources, it was important that China solve its own problems. To have a strong machine manufacturing industry, it was necessary to have a military manufacturing industry capable of manufacturing items such as aircraft, tanks, and ships, which would help create an independent defensive force.

2) *The need to transform the revolutionary cause into socialism.* If only military and political concerns were addressed, without considering economic matters or the development of production, it was impossible to turn to socialism. This was the leftist error that had been made in the past. In the old Chinese national economy, industry only accounted for about 10% of the economy. Ren Bishi believed the new China should gradually shift toward socialism, and industry should make up at least 30% of its national economy. Thus, after the victory of the national revolution, it was still necessary to have two or three five-year plans in place to guide the move to socialism.

3) *The need to consolidate the alliance of peasants and workers.* Both at this point in time and in previous years, the union of workers and peasants was mainly manifested in the granting of land to the peasants, liberating them from the feudal system, and helping to unify them. From this point on, agriculture needed to be developed and peasants' lives needed to be improved by supplying them with affordable industrial products. At the same time, the peasants would supply the cities with their agricultural products, allowing industrial development and the lives of the workers to be improved. This would strengthen the alliance between workers and peasants. It would further advance the continued development of industry, and tractors and combine harvesters would provide the needed assistance to allow for the collectivization of agriculture. Agriculture would produce large amounts of food and raw materials to balance the surplus agricultural products, labor, and support industries, developing foreign trade and balancing imports and exports. It was important to understand this mutually reinforcing relationship between industry and agriculture.[37]

d. Training a Large Number of Urban Working Class Cadres

There was at this time a prominent issue to be addressed in the transition from rural to urban areas, the question of where a mass of urban working class cadres would come from. Mao Zedong had always attached great importance to the cadres. Since the beginning of 1948, he had repeatedly suggested that attention be given to intellectual cadres and to recruiting intellectuals, particularly engineers and technicians with both knowledge and experience, inviting them to join the revolutionary ranks. In the report from the September meeting, he proposed that it was important to not only rely on cadres from the old liberated areas, but to also give attention to absorbing cadres from the big cities previously under KMT rule, allowing many workers and intellectuals to join the CPC. At the Second Plenary Session of the Seventh General Meeting of the Central Committee, he further stated that "preparation must be made for the full conversion of our 2.1 million field troops into a task force... The army of 2.1 million soldiers must be regarded as a huge cadre school."[38] Zhu De likewise emphasized that in the past, the transition from urban to rural areas had been a big change, and now a similar change was to be made in the reverse direction. The Party's work needed to adapt to this huge shift. It would be a big transition for the army as well, gradually transforming it from a combat team to a task force. The CPC was a school for training people to do certain things, one of which was the future management and building of production.

3. Proposing the Task of the "Three Imperatives"

Faced with the transition from countryside to city and with the test of holding national political power, the CPC put forward a series of guidelines and policies for strengthening its own construction.

a. Strengthening Discipline and Improving the System of Democratic Living Within the Party

The Communist Party of China was founded on the basis of Marxism-Leninism's revolutionary theory and democratic centralism. From its inception, it was characterized by strict organizational discipline. Because the CPC and the

People's Liberation Army under its leadership had been in an environment of division by the enemy and guerrilla warfare for so long, they had allowed local Party organizations and military bodies to maintain a high degree of autonomy. The autonomy of these Party organizations and armed forces led to a great deal of initiative and enthusiasm on their part, and it was a contributing factor enabling them to pull through a lengthy, arduous situation. At the same time, however, certain undisciplined, anarchic states, localism, and guerrillaism had emerged, and these errors had developed even further during the War of Resistance Against Japanese Aggression, doing damage to the revolutionary cause. The situation as it stood simply could not meet the demands of full political power. To this end, the meeting held in September 1948 brought in-depth clarification of the importance of strengthening party-building under the new historical conditions.

The September Meeting concluded that, in order to meet the needs of the current state of revolutionary development and ensure the complete unification of the various policies implemented throughout the entire Party and military and to see the full implementation of the military plan through, the entire Party had to expend its utmost efforts to overcome these erroneous tendencies and make it possible to reach all of its goals. It was further necessary to see that power was concentrated in the hands of the Central Committee and its representative organs. In his speech at the meeting, Deng Xiaoping noted that of the three guidelines of "moving the army forward, growing production, and strengthening discipline," the most important was strengthening discipline, as it was a critical safeguard for the victory of the revolution. Strengthening discipline was connected to developing intra-Party democracy, and the key to addressing this issue lay in the higher level organizations, the District Party Committees, and the Party's senior cadres. Bo Yibo said that strengthening discipline was a strategic issue, and the entire Party must fully understand its far-reaching significance. Mao suggested that the comrades of the Central Committee should do this with all their might. In the third year of the war, the Party and the army would overcome these negative tendencies, unite the people throughout the country, quickly expel American imperial aggressor forces from China, and defeat the reactionary rule of the KMT. The meeting also pointed out that, due to a combination of the war environment and its own underground nature, normal democratic life had only seen stunted development within the CPC up to this point. The Party Constitution adopted at the Seventh National Congress noted that even after the convening of Party congresses and representative conferences, the situation had not changed. At the same time, in order to adapt to the special circumstances and the demands of the struggle, normal democratic life within the Party could not be restricted. Some serious bureaucratic elements had arisen within the Party organizations and government agencies resulting in the Party withdrawing from the people, to an extent. In addition, some erroneous ideas, unjust sectarian styles, and undisciplined states had covertly spread through the Party, causing many losses among the people. The meeting held that the revolution would soon achieve national victory. The situation, demands, and conditions had changed, and it was necessary to address the insufficient level of intra-party democracy in order to improve the political quality of the Party and enhance its combat effectiveness.

In his report, Mao pointed out that the implementation of intra-party democracy was a system of implementing congresses and representative meetings. The advantages of the cadre meeting were that it was quick, convenient, and easy to convene. It was not too complicated to hold such a representative meeting to preserve the benefits of the cadre meetings. It must be recognized that the Party's ideological level was low and needed to be improved. Such a large party needed to be strongly rooted in theory, and numerous theoretical issues had to be consolidated. For instance, the class makeup of the CPC demonstrated its low level of theory. There were many new intellectuals and cadres from the working class and peasantry in the Party, and they did not have a grasp of many basic ideas or issues. There were millions of students, professors, and acting groups in the country. Anyone who could not present reasonable thoughts to such people would have no choice but to listen to their views instead. It was important for the Party to improve and spread its theory. The members of the Central Committee and the Politburo needed to take up these roles as their political tasks. Otherwise, they would have to accept the errors of their comrades.

Ren Bishi said that during the war, particularly in the areas involved in direct combat, it was important to centralize. He was correct in his emphasis on leadership, saying, "The liberated areas of Northern China are now relatively peaceful. Those both inside and outside the Party should focus on democracy and establishing a democratic system. A democratic system must be established."[39] He observed, "There is still a tendency within the Party to suppress the people. This is a result of the condition of the Chinese Party and it is used under the army's guidance within the Party."[40]

In view of the fact that existing Party members had complaints about their direct leaders but dared not to bypass and report the hierarchy, and the tendency toward "underground broadcasting" among the masses, Ren Bishi noted, "The main issue is that there is still a lack of criticism and self-criticism, and if that is true, there will not even be limited broadcasting." He held that representative meetings, elections, and the like were forms of promoting democracy, and it was essential to include criticism and self-criticism. He said, "If there is only a representative meeting and underground broadcasting does not allow these things to be said at the meeting, then it is merely the form of democracy, but lacking the essence."[41] The implementation of democracy depended on long-term training. Ren added, "Only when there is democracy in the Party can the people's democracy truly be established."[42]

Ren Bishi emphasized that strengthening discipline was an objective requirement for the development of production after the regulation of troops, the centralization of operations, and the reunification of the region. More importantly, "as we move from the countryside to the city and focus more on unity and discipline, we need to avoid problems such as those encountered with Zhang Guotao. The more progress and victories we enjoy, the more likely we are to encounter these negative tendencies." Ren added, "If we are not careful, we will not be able to defeat the influence of the international and domestic bourgeoisie."[43] He pointed out clearly that the implementation of discipline was unconditional, but the development of discipline was conditional. He said, "There are two conditions for strengthening discipline. The first is that the Party must have at least 500 cadres who understand Marxism. Once these cadres have mastered Marxism-Leninism, the unified implementation of policy is guaranteed, and many issues will be decided in advance. The resolutions of the Sixth National Congress have been issued, but not yet implemented. If every county had someone mastering these policies, the situation would be very different. The five books of Marxism must be read, not merely explained in haste, lest our haste squeeze the life out of them." And "the second condition is that we must establish a system and formulate decrees, such as regulations for deserters, for the people's courts, and so forth." In addition, we must have major laws and minor regulations, with the minor regulations subordinate to the major laws. Some people can negotiate through conventions, but the law must be unified. There must be a system for the army and party organizations, and that system must be observed." Would observing discipline and emphasizing centralization and unity weaken local enthusiasm and creativity? Ren's answer to this was, "Strengthening discipline by no means weakens local enthusiasm. Rather, it removes the blindness from enthusiasm and carries forward the enthusiasm more systematically."[44]

To this end, the meeting also specifically discussed adopting the "System for Reporting to the Central Committee by the Central Politburo, Branch Office, Military Region, and Military Commission Branch" and the "CPC Central Committee Resolution on Convening Congresses and Representative Meetings at various levels of the Party." After the meeting, Mao Zedong drafted the Policy for Perfecting the Party Committee System on behalf of the Central Committee.

b. Clinging to the "Two Imperatives" in the Face of Great Victory

At the Politburo meeting the following January, Mao suggested, "Don't allow victory to go to our heads."[45] He said that it was possible for this to happen at that time, and that it would be even truer in the future. The greater the victory won, the greater the burden, as it was always easier to be unified through difficult times. This issue required vigilance. In the Party's efforts to educate the cadres, it was first necessary for senior cadres to understand that once the war was over, the real work would begin, so they should not be lulled into idleness when times were easier.

At the Second Plenary Session of the Seventh General Meeting of the Central Committee, Mao once again warned the entire Party that its victory could easily lead to pride in the Party, along with a lack of self-restraint, a tendency to halt progress, or reluctance to continue living a hard life. Because of the victory, the people would feel gratitude toward the Party, and the bourgeoisie would seek to join its ranks. It had been proven that the CPC could not be conquered by the enemy's force, but it was possible that the support of the bourgeoisie might conquer the weak will of some Party members. There were some members who could not be conquered by the guns wielded by enemy hands and had proven worthy heroes when faced with such enemies, yet they were unable to withstand a sugar-coated bullet. The sweet words wielded as weapons by the enemy now would surely fell them, and it was the Party's responsibility to prevent this.

Mao went on to point out, "This is the first step in the long march toward winning the national victory. If this step is one worthy of our pride, it is still only a small step, with many more to come after it. Witnessing what China will become a few decades after the victory of the people's democratic revolution will make us aware that this moment is just a short prelude to a long drama. The drama must begin from the prelude, but the prelude is not to be mistaken for the climax. The Chinese revolution is great, but the journey after the revolution will be longer and more difficult, and it will require more work. This must now be explained to the entire Party. It is imperative that our comrades continue to be modest, cautious, humble, and unyielding. It is imperative that we continue the arduous struggle."[46]

At the conclusion of the meeting, Mao made it clear that it was forbidden to commemorate the birthdays of leaders or to use their name for places, streets, or enterprises. It was necessary to put a halt to the tendency to over-praise or exalt the merits of the leaders.

c. The Task of Strengthening the Construction of the Ruling Party

In his speech at the Second Plenary Session of the Seventh General Assembly of the Central Committee, Ren Bishi suggested that with the shift of focus in the Party's work, party-building should likewise be adapted to fit the new focus. He held that after the failure of the Great Revolution, the CPC had long struggled in rural areas. By this time, 85% to 90% of the Party's members were peasants. "This is natural," Ren observed, "but it is also a weakness, in that it tends toward distraction and a lack of discipline." After entering the city, "if we don't have a Party foundation among the workers and can't establish close ties with the proletariat, we cannot speak of true independence for the working class."[47] For this reason, the development of the Party in the cities was mainly to be among industrial workers, followed by handicraftsmen and clerks. If the development was too slow, the work would suffer setbacks. How then could the quality of members be ensured? Ren proposed that first, they must be strictly censored, and that a ceremony should be held for new members, the purpose of which was to "educate Party members." Second, it was necessary to strengthen education and improve organizational life. And finally, it was important to constantly check the work of Party members, engage in criticism and self-criticism, and strictly enforce discipline.

Ren then warned Party leaders and organizations at all levels that strong cadres must always pay attention to party work, including the construction of branches, the mode of leading the Party, work style, and the ideological dynamics of Party members. He said, "If we are busy in various affairs related to economic construction and administration, but lax in our party-building efforts, it will be very dangerous." This would be "particularly important when we become the national ruling party."[48]

4. Developing Production and Unifying Financial Work

Regarding economic work, the September Meeting highlighted the issues of developing production and financial integration. The formulation of "increasing production" was discussed at the Expanded Meeting of the CPC Central Committee, then re-introduced at the September meeting.

The meeting held that the restoration and development of industrial and agricultural production in the liberated areas was an important link in support of the war and the defeat of the KMT reactionaries. On the one hand, the PLA had to successfully attack KMT-held regions, and the human and material resources needed for the war would largely be taken from the KMT and the areas it held. On the other hand, all effort had to be made to restore and develop the old liberated areas. Industrial and agricultural production had to increase compared to current levels. Only when these two tasks were completed could defeat of the KMT's reactionary rule be achieved. Without completing these tasks, victory would be impossible.

Mao observed, "If the army moves forward, production must increase by an inch. If it fails to do so, there will be no food to eat."[49] This idea often shortened to the phrase "increasing production."

Ren Bishi said, "The economic burden of the people in the old liberated areas is now very heavy. When the burden of servitude is added, the people's load is even heavier, particularly along the Pingchuan Road. According to financial research, it is best not to allow the burden to exceed 20% (not including the indirect burden), or it will be difficult to achieve increasing production."[50]

In order to ensure that the army was progressing, Ren suggested that the old liberated areas "should work harder and excel at production without imposing any extra burden on the people."[51] He added, "The Central Plains region should mobilize the masses and generally reduce rents and interest rates. In the fourth or fifth year of the war, they will be the supporting forces behind the troops that march to Jiangnan."[52]

The meeting held that the recovery and development of production required better organizational work, strong leadership of the markets within the liberated areas and skillful control of foreign trade, and addressing the issue of the lack of certain machines and raw materials. The first issue to be addressed was the problem of transportation and the repair of the railways, highways, and waterways. It was necessary to oppose waste and promote conservation, to pay attention to the seizure of public interests, to protect the Party's own livelihood, to protect its weapons, to save ammunition, and to protect prisoners. It was likewise important to reduce the expenditure of state agencies behind the line, reduce the mobilization of unnecessary human or animal power, and reduce the time spent in meetings. It was necessary to pay attention to agricultural seasons, avoid violating agricultural cycles, save costs in industrial production, increase labor productivity, mobilize the entire Party to learn to manage industrial production, agricultural production, and commerce, and properly organize the economy of the liberated areas to overcome market risks, as much as possible.

In his report, Mao raised the issue of financial and economic unification. He said, "The Financial Committee of the North China People's Government unifies possible and necessary construction and administrative work in the economic, financial, trade, commercial, transportation, and military industries in the three regions of North China, East China, and Northwest China. Not everything is unified, but it is sometimes both possible and necessary to unify, and at other times both impossible and unnecessary. Where it is necessary but impossible, a temporary lack of coordination will result. For instance, this is currently true in areas like agriculture and small handicrafts, where financial work and the issuance of currency must first be unified. The unification of the north is to be managed by the North China Finance Committee. The Party, government, and military of these three regions must guarantee the implementation of the unified orders of the North China Finance Committee."[53]

III

Efforts to Adhere to the Concept of a New Democratic Society

1. Elucidation of the New Democratic Social Ideology

From the time the CPC put forward the idea of a new democratic society, with the development of its victory in the democratic revolution, and the CPC's continuous deepening of its understanding of this issue, the new democratic theory was further developed and enriched throughout the late 1940s and early 1950s. This theory and the new democratic revolutionary theory together constituted the complete system of the new democratic theory.

In 1925, the resolutions of the Fourth National Congress had pointed out that "the victory of the national revolutions can be followed by the proletarian revolution. Whether it must pass through the bourgeois democratic system and to what extent the revolution of the proletariat can operate in the national revolution will be determined by the objective social conditions of that time."[54] In 1926, Stalin gave a brief account of this issue in his speech at the Comintern Committee Meeting. He held that China's future revolutionary regime was "a democratic regime of the dictatorship of the proletariat and peasantry," adding, "This will be a stage in China's development toward a non-capitalist state, or more precisely, its transitional regime to socialism. This is the direction the Chinese revolution must take."[55] Here, Stalin made it clear that the transformation of the Chinese revolution from a democratic revolution to socialism required a transitional regime, but he did not indicate how the regime would achieve this transition. Two years earlier, Cai Hesen had written an article emphasizing that "Soviet power of a peasant dictatorship" was an important factor in the future revolutionary transformation. He called the workers and peasants regime a "transforming crane," saying that after the victory of the democratic revolution, the soviet government of workers and peasant should "confiscate all major foreign enterprises, then confiscate all the capital of the higher level capitalists, then use this to organize and direct the economic life of the country" and to "quickly prepare for the transition to the conditions of a socialist revolution – that is, to eliminate the capitalist market economy and replace it with an organized collective economy under the industrialized rate of organized state-owned cities." When history developed to this stage, it would be "early-stage socialism."[56] From Cai's discussion, it is evident that the process of transforming the democratic revolution to socialism was not merely a process of eliminating the capitalist economy, but also a process of forming the rural collective economy under state-owned industrial command. In this discussion, Cai put the main tasks it involved in very clear terms, but he was more interested in elucidating Marxist theory, and his understanding of the actual future process of transforming the Chinese revolution was not yet sufficiently clear. Because the CPC was then in its infancy, its understanding of many problems came from the guidance of the Comintern. Moreover, the new democratic revolution was just beginning, and the CPC lacked revolutionary practice and experience. As a result, its understanding of how to make this transition could not possibly be very complete.

After the failure of the Great Revolution, the CPC started to shift focus to the countryside, further integrating China's revolution with its national conditions. In the process, the concept of transformation was made clear. In the 1930s, with the intensifying Chinese revolution, a Soviet government of workers and peasants was established in many revolutionary base areas, with an economy mainly composed of "state-owned undertakings, cooperative businesses, and private undertakings." The principle underlying economic policy at that time was "concentrate economic power to supply the war effort, while at the same time trying to improve the lives of the people, consolidate economic power and the economic union of workers and peasants, ensure the proletarian leadership of the peasantry, and strive for the leadership of the state-owned economy, leading to the development of socialism in the future."[57] In December 1935, Mao Zedong's report at the Wayaobao Meeting proposed that the Republic of Workers and Farmers be transformed into the People's Republic, in an effort to unite the majority of the people. He noted, "The government of the People's Republic is mainly composed of workers and peasants, while also accommodating other anti-imperialist, anti-feudal classes."[58] It went on to specially propose to protect the development of national capital industry and commerce. These ideas that arose through the practice of the Chinese revolution became an important basis for the concept of a future new democratic society. In May 1939, in his article "The May 4th Movement," Mao said, "The democratic revolution intends to establish a social system that has not existed at any point in Chinese history, a democratic social system. The predecessor of such a society is a feudal society (or a semi-colonial, semi-feudal society, over the past century), and what comes after is a socialist society. If you ask a Communist how to struggle from a bourgeois democratic system to socialism, he will reply that the only way to do so is to go through history."[59] With that, Mao clearly pointed out that there was a transitional society in the process of moving from a semi-colonial, semi-feudal society to a socialist society, though he did not in this passage call it a new democracy. Even so, it was clear that this was what he meant. After further theoretical exploration, in January 1940, in *New Democracy*, Mao made his first explicit proposal of the concept of a "new democratic society." He pointed out that the first step and first stage of the Chinese revolution was "to establish a new democratic society under the joint government of China's various revolutionary classes, under the leadership of the proletariat [...] And then, to develop it to the second stage of building a socialist society in China." He held that the policies to be adopted in the new democratic society were that it would be an alliance of workers and peasants under the political leadership of the proletariat, with all anti-imperialist, anti-feudal people uniting with the rule of the democratic republic, which would hold political power. The form of government would be a people's congress system, which implemented democratic centralism. Economically, large banks, large industries, and large enterprises would be owned by the state, allowing the existence of small or medium-sized capitalist industry and commerce, while the landlords' land would be confiscated and distributed to the peasants, implementing a system in which "the cultivators own the fields." Culturally, it advocated a popular stand among the people against imperialism and feudalism. In Mao's own words, "the whole result of the Chinese revolution is, on the one hand, the development of capitalist factors, and on the other, the development of socialist factors." Mao discussed the political, economic, and cultural forms of the new democratic society, saying that it was through the combination of these forces that a new democratic society would be formed.

In April 1945, Mao further elaborated in his report to the Seventh National Congress on the historical necessity of establishing new democracy before establishing socialism. He said, that the CPC would push China to be a socialist and communist society, but "it is only through democracy that we can reach socialism, which is the ultimate intent of Marxism." In China, the timeframe for the political, economic, and cultural struggles for the new democracy was the long-term. Otherwise, "it is a complete fantasy that we could build socialism on the ruins of our semi-colonial, semi-feudal society." This was for no other reason than that "our capitalism is lacking." Thus, in a new democratic society, aside from the country's own economy, the individual economy of the working people, and the cooperative economy, private capitalism was necessarily "not only an improvement, but also an inevitable process" for manipulating development within the scope of manipulating the national economy and the people's livelihood.

At the Second Plenary Session of the Seventh General Meeting of the CPC Central Committee held in March 1949, although the development direction that moved through a new democratic society to a socialist society was mentioned, it was only proposed as a future development rather than as a current pressing need. At this meeting, it was still said that a new democratic state would be formed after the victory of the revolution, and the policy proposed after the meeting analyzing the state of China's economic composition at the time was still a new democratic policy. Mao stated at the meeting, "For a long period of time after the victory of the revolution, it will be necessary to make full use of the enthusiasm of urban and rural capitalism in order to take advantage of the progress of the national economy. During this period, everything not harmful to the national economy, such as components of urban and rural capitalism that are favorable to the national economy, should be allowed to continue and develop. This is not only inevitable, but also economically necessary." In all aspects, it was only necessary to "adopt appropriately restrictive policies."[60] Further, it was both inevitable and necessary that in such a new democratic country, there would be a main economic component such as a state-run economy that was socialist in nature, a private capitalist economy, an individual economy, and a state capitalist economy that would cooperate with the state and private sectors. These economic components constituted the new democratic economic form. That June, Mao re-emphasized in his article "On the People's Democratic Dictatorship," that all urban and rural capitalist factors favorable to the national economy should be employed. He noted, "Our current policy is to control capitalism, not to eliminate it."[61]

Before and after the founding of the new China, Liu Shaoqi had numerous discussions on this topic. On May 29, 1949, he said at a cadre meeting in Beijing that the Chinese economy was underdeveloped mainly because there was too little capitalism. After the victory of the democratic revolution, it was inevitable that capitalism would be developed, but it must be restricted and developed gradually. The transformation to socialism was something that would take decades. It was difficult to talk about specifics, but it would definitely be a long-term process, not a short-term one. On the eve of the founding of the new China, when discussing the "Draft Common Program of the Chinese People's Political Consultative Conference," some democrats proposed to write into it the future of socialism in China. On behalf of the Central Committee, Liu replied, "We do not think this is yet appropriate. Because it is necessary that we go through stages to reach socialism in China, it is still quite far in the future. If this goal is written into the common program, it could easily confuse or disrupt the practical steps we are taking today."[62] Zhou Enlai's report on the drafting of the common program and its characteristics similarly explained the reasons for not writing the socialist future into it.

On June 23, 1950, Mao Zedong said in the closing speech to the Second Session of the General Committee of the Chinese People's Political Consultative Conference that the implementation of private enterprise nationalization and agricultural socialization was "still in the distant future." He added, "Our country is steadily advancing in this direction. After the war, after the new democratic reforms, after the future national economic and cultural undertakings have prospered and various conditions been met, all the people of the nation can consider bringing these things to maturity. After everyone agrees, we will be able to walk properly and with ease into the new era of socialism."[63] How far in "the distant future" this lay was not specified by the Central Committee.

At the Politburo meeting in September 1948, Mao predicted that after the national victory – perhaps fifteen years later – the democratic revolution could begin to press the entire socialist agenda.[64] In his speech at the Second Plenary Session of the Seventh General Meeting of the Central Committee, he said, "After the victory of the national revolution, we still require two or three five-year plans before we can move to socialism."[65] In 1949, Liu Shaoqi visited the Soviet Union. In a letter, he wrote that it would take fifteen years to implement socialism. During the CPPCC meeting in September of that year, people outside the Party asked when socialism would be implemented. Mao replied that it would take two or three decades.[66] In April 1950, Zhou Enlai told Party members and leading cadres at the United Front Work Conference that it would take about fifteen years.[67] It is evident from this that the new democratic society established after the victory of the new democratic revolution would not simply be a transitional social stage lasting for a few years in China. Rather, it was a period of long-term preparation for socialism. This was the consensus of the entire Party. Liu Shaoqi referred to it as "the stage of new democratic construction."[68]

On March 28, 1951, Liu Shaoqi delivered a report to the First National Organizational Work Conference of the CPC, in which he clearly stated, "The ultimate goal of the CPC is to establish a communist system in China. It is currently establishing a new democratic system. In the future, the struggle will be to fight for the transformation to a socialist system and to ultimately establish a communist system."[69] On September 9 of that year, the First National Organizational Work Conference adopted the Basic Program for the Rectification of the Party, laying out in its second paragraph the standards for Party membership (i.e., the "Eight Conditions for Members of the Communist Party of China"). It stated, "The ultimate goal of the CPC is to achieve a communist system in China. It is now struggling to consolidate the new democratic system. In the future, it will be nationalized in industry and collectivized in agriculture. In other words, we will fight to transform it into a socialist system."

The scientific concept embraced by the CPC was that it would establish a new democratic society after the victory of the new democratic revolution, which would include a stage of constructing the new democratic society and a transition period. After the new democratic construction had achieved its goal, which was to make the various material and spiritual conditions for the transition to socialism fully available, it would enter a transitional period, which would mark the beginning of the socialist revolution. Upon entering the transition period, it would still be a new democratic society that would continue to coexist with multiple economic components. However, the capitalist economy would have shifted at this point from "allowing development" to "accepting transformation." The capitalist economic policy would no longer be centered around usage and restriction, but around transformation and elimination. The peasantry and handicraft industries would be guided toward collectivization. When these tasks were complete, a socialist society would be born.

The theory of the new democratic society was a crystallization of the experience of the CPC and the Chinese people. It was the great creation of the leaders of the CPC, including Mao Zedong. Paired with the new democratic revolutionary theory, this theory constituted the complete system of new democratic thought.

2. Construction of the Theory of the People's Democratic Dictatorship

A political program generally includes the state system and the form of political organization, that is, the state and political body. In political science, "state body" refers to the class nature of the state, noting that social class is the core issue in a country. "Government" refers to the organizational form of state power, that is, the choice of ruling class and the form of organization imposed on political organs and the implementation of their rule and management. The state body determines the political system, is manifest in it, and adapts to it. The dictatorship of different classes forms different national bodies. The historical conditions and traditions of each country are different, and its politics are different. Even countries with a similar state body can adopt different political forms.

A new democratic political form mainly includes the social foundation of the regime of the new democratic state and the politics of the new democratic state.

Regarding the social foundation of the new democratic state regime, Mao pointed out in *New Democracy* that the Chinese proletariat, intellectuals, and other petty bourgeoisie were the basic forces that would determine the destiny of the country. These classes, whether already enlightened or still being enlightened, had to form a basic part of the makeup of the Chinese Democratic Republic, with the proletariat holding leadership power. The Chinese Democratic Republic to be established at this point in time could only be a democratic republic that gathered all the anti-imperialist, anti-feudalist people under the leadership of the proletariat. This was a new democratic republic. It was distinguished on the one hand from an old-style European-American capitalist republic under bourgeois dictatorship, which was an old democratic republic, a form that was already outdated. On the other hand, it was different from a soviet style socialist republic under the dictatorship of the proletariat, the sort of socialist republic that had been prospered in the Soviet Union and was to be established in various capitalist countries, and which would undoubtedly become the national composition of all advanced industrial countries and the form of rule that would be built in such countries. However, such a republic did not apply to colonial and semi-colonial countries in a certain historical period. Therefore, the national form adopted by all colonial and semi-colonial countries in a certain historical period could only be a third form, what was called a new democratic republic. This was a form suited to a certain historical period, a transitional form, but also a necessary form that could not be neglected. Mao pointed out that in the various national systems seen in the world, based on the class nature of their political power, could basically be divided into just three groups: republics under a bourgeois dictatorship, republics under a proletarian dictatorship, or united republics under a dictatorship of all revolutionary classes. The first sort was characteristic of old democratic countries. At that point, after the outbreak of the second imperialist war, many capitalist countries had lost their democratic atmosphere and changed into or were in the process of changing into a bloody military dictatorship of the capitalist class. Some countries where land owners and the bourgeoisie formed a dictatorship could be grouped into this category. The second category was brewing in various capitalists countries besides the more obvious example of the Soviet Union. In the future, this would form a type of global rule for a certain period of time. The third type was a transitional state form adopted by the revolutions of colonial and semi-colonial countries. The revolutions of these various countries would inevitably have different characteristics, but this was only a small difference amidst much greater similarities. As long as there was a colonial or semi-colonial revolution, the makeup of the country and its regime would be basically similar, that is, there would be several new democratic countries in which the classes that opposed imperialism would form a united dictatorship. In China at that time, this form of new democratic state was seen in the Anti-Japanese National United Front. It was against Japan and all imperialism, and it was also a united front of several revolutionary classes.

In order to further clarify the implications of new democratic politics, Mao discussed the issue of what was called the "state body." He observed that the national body had not been clarified since the end of the Qing Dynasty, but only the issue of the status of all social classes had been examined. The bourgeoisie always concealed class status, using the term "national" to achieve its own single-class dictatorship. Such concealment held no sway with revolutionary people and should be clearly identified. The term "national" could be used, but nationalists did not include counter-revolutionaries and traitors. All revolutionary classes would rule counter-revolutionary traitors, which was the goal to be achieved at this point in time. As Mao noted, "The so-called civil rights system in the world's nations is often proprietary to the bourgeoisie and a suitable tool for oppressing civilians. If the KMT's civil rights were shared by the general public, they would no longer be the private possession of a minority."[70] There was also what was called the question of government, which was what form the regime would take in terms of the particular social class that would organize the regime to oppose the enemy and protect itself. Without a proper form of political authority, it could not represent the country. China could now adopt the system of the National People's Congress, Provincial People's Congress, County People's Congress, District People's Congress, and Township People's Congress, and the government would be elected by these various Congresses. However, it was necessary to implement a truly universal, equal electoral system without differences based on gender, faith, property ownership, education, or other criteria, making it suitable for the status of revolutionary classes throughout the country, to act in expressing public opinion and directing revolutionary struggles, and to be suitable for the spirit of new democracy. Such a system was a centralized system of democracy. Only a democratic, centralized government could fully exert the will of all revolutionary people and become the most powerful force to oppose the enemies of the revolution. The spirit of "non-minority and non-privatization (of public property)" should be manifested in the composition of the government and the military. Without a real democratic system, this could not be achieved. It was a case of the political system and state body being incompatible. Mao clearly pointed out that the state referred to the united dictatorship of all revolutionary classes, while the state body referred to democratic centralism. This was new democratic politics, the new democratic republic, the republic of the Anti-Japanese National United Front, and the republic of the new three principles of democracy with the three major policies. It was truly a "republic of China." At this point, there was still no such thing as a "republic of China." It was, rather, still a work in progress. It was the internal political relationship that revolutionary China and anti-Japanese China must establish. It was the only correct direction for "nation-building" at that time.

In 1945, at the Seventh National Congress, Mao further elaborated on new democratic politics, saying that the CPC advocated the establishment of a national system of democratic alliances based on a united front under the leadership of the proletariat, that is, a new democratic national system, after thoroughly defeating the Japanese aggressors. The new democratic political organizations were to adopt a democratic centralized system, and the people's congresses at all levels were to decide on major policies and elect the government. This was a national system that was truly suitable for the most demanding requirements of the

Chinese population. In China, there were still conflicts between various classes, and each had its own different requirements, such as the noteworthy instance of the contradiction between labor and capital. However, such conflicts and their various demands could be adjusted, and they should not be developed beyond the common requirements during the new democratic stage.

In December 1947, Mao explicitly proposed a new democratic political platform. He said, "The combined workers, peasants, and soldiers of various oppressed classes, people's organizations, democratic parties, ethnic minorities, overseas Chinese, and other patriotic elements formed a national united front, defeated Chiang Kai-shek's authoritarian government, and established a democratic coalition government. It was the most basic political program of the CPC and the People's Liberation Army."[71]

In September 1948, Mao clearly stated in his report to the meeting of the Politburo that he would "establish a people's democratic dictatorship based on an alliance of workers and peasants under proletarian leadership," and added, "The class nature of our regime is that the alliance of workers and peasants under the proletariat is not limited to workers and peasants, but is a people's democratic dictatorship that allows the participation of bourgeois democrats."[72] Shortly after this, he issued a call to carry out the revolution to the end, clearly clarifying the victory of the revolution and "establishing a nationwide republic of the people's democratic dictatorship of the workers and peasants under the dictatorship of all the people of the nation."[73] On June 30, 1949, Mao published an article entitled "On the People's Democratic Dictatorship," which laid out the historical inevitability of establishing a people's democratic dictatorship in China, clarified the basic tasks of the people's democratic dictatorship, the relationship between democracy and dictatorship, and the various classes in the people's democratic dictatorship. The status and other issues thus completed the formulation of the theory of the people's democratic dictatorship.

a. *Mao's In-Depth Clarification of the Historical Inevitability of Establishing a People's Democratic Dictatorship in China*

The article offered an in-depth summary of the positive and negative aspects of China's historical experience over the previous century. It depicted the path that Chinese progressives had experienced toward better understanding of revolutionary truth since the Opium War, demonstrating that Marxism-Leninism was the guiding light of the Chinese revolution. It noted that it was only by implementing the people's democratic dictatorship that the Chinese people would overthrow the three major obstacles and progress toward socialism. Mao criticized the plan for a bourgeois democratic republic advocated by various representatives of the bourgeoisie, observing, "The bourgeois republic that has worked in foreign countries will not work in China, since we are a nation oppressed by imperialism," and "summarizing our experience and focusing on a single point, the people's democratic dictatorship led by the working class (via the CPC), based on an alliance of workers and peasants. This dictatorship must be united with international revolutionary forces. This is our formula, our main experience, and our main program."[74]

b. Clarifying the Nature of the New China and the Status and Interrelationship of Various Classes in State Power

Mao pointed out that the People's Republic of China, which was soon to be born, would be a country under the leadership of the proletariat and the people's democratic dictatorship based on the alliance of workers and peasants. In China at that stage, the people included the ranks of the proletariat, the peasantry, the urban petty bourgeoisie, and the national bourgeoisie. The proletariat was the leading force of the people's democratic dictatorship, because the working class was the most far-sighted, most selfless, and most revolutionary class. History had proven that without the leadership of the proletariat, the revolution would fail. With the leadership of the ranks of the proletariat, the revolution would be victorious. The basis of the people's democratic dictatorship was the alliance of the working class, the peasantry, and the urban petty bourgeoisie, but mainly the workers and peasants. Because these two classes accounted for 80-90% of the Chinese population, overthrowing the imperialist and KMT reactionaries and beginning the journey toward socialism had to rely mainly on the might of an alliance between these two classes. In addition, the people's democratic dictatorship also included a special alliance between the proletariat and the national bourgeoisie. Mao pointed out that "in order to counter the oppression of imperialism and improve its own underdeveloped economic status, China must use all the advantages of the national economy and the people's livelihood, not harmful urban and rural capitalist factors, to unite the national bourgeoisie and work together. Our current policy is to control capitalism, not to eliminate it."[75] However, the national bourgeoisie could not serve as the leader of the revolution and should not occupy a dominant position in state power.

c. Explaining the Concept of the People's Democratic Dictatorship and the Relationship Between Democracy and Dictatorship

Mao pointed out that "the combination of the democratic aspect of the people and the dictatorship of the reactionaries is a people's democratic dictatorship."[76] This directly and accurately noted the two aspects of the people's democratic dictatorship.

Implementing a people's democracy ensured that the working people were masters of the country and that they fully enjoyed all freedoms and democratic rights. It was particularly important to ensure that laborers managed the country and its various enterprises, culture, and education, acting in line with democratic principles among the people and implementing democratic centralism. Conflicts among the people could only be solved by democratic methods, through self-education and self-transformation. Only in this way could the Party fully reflect the will, interests, and needs of the people, so that the broad masses could enhance their sense of responsibility and ensure the smooth progress of the Party's cause.

The enemy's rule dictated hostile elements, oppressed the people, and restricted their behavior, preventing them from speaking of uprising. The moment anyone mentioned uprising, he was immediately censored or subject to sanctions. Mao observed, "If this continues, the revolution will fail, the people will suffer, and the country will perish."[77] Of course, the rule of the enemy was not entirely suppressed or physically eliminated after their regime was overthrown. Provided they did not rebel, loot, rise up, or confiscate land or work, they would be allowed to transform themselves through labor and become new people.

Mao pointed out that the relationship between democracy and dictatorship was mutually integrated, interactive, and indivisible. Historical experience proved that without the people's democracy, there could be no dictatorship opposing the enemy, while leaving the enemy's dictatorship in place would not guarantee a people's democracy.

d. Proposing the Basic Tasks of the People's Democratic Dictatorship

The first thing that had to be done was to strengthen the state apparatus, which meant strengthening the people's army, people's police, and the people's courts to consolidate national defense and protect the interests of the people, resist the internal reactionary class, and resist the external aggression and subversion of imperialism. The second task was to systematically implement a solution to the problem of national industrialization, learning to carry out economic work and undertake the serious task of economic construction. The third was to reform the non-socialist economy and educate and transform the national bourgeoisie so that private enterprise could be nationalized in the future, to educate and transform small-scale production despite "the serious obstacle of educating the peasants," and to use careful, long-term work to implement the socialization of agriculture so that China could steadily move from being an agricultural nation to an industrial nation. The fourth task was to fight in the arena of political ideology against old ideas, using democratic methods for self-education and self-transformation, eliminating bad habits and negative ideas that had been learned in the old society and moving toward socialism and communism.

The people's democratic dictatorship was a new form of rule for the CPC, based on Marxist state doctrine infused with Chinese characteristics suited to China's national conditions. It had both similarities to and differences from the dictatorship of the proletariat. The main similarity was that both were led by the proletariat and its political parties. In addition, they were based on an alliance of workers and peasants, and they both provided political guarantees for the development of socialism. The differences lay in the scope of the people's democracy. Under proletarianism, the people did not include the bourgeoisie, while the people's democratic dictatorship included not only the working class, peasantry, and petty bourgeoisie, but also the national bourgeoisie. Further, the objects of these types of dictatorships were different. Under the dictatorship of the proletariat, the bourgeoisie was the object of the dictatorship, while under the people's democratic dictatorship, the object was not the national bourgeoisie, but only reactionaries or enemies. By 1956, the socialist transformation was basically completed, the bourgeoisie and capitalist exploitation system no longer existed, the socialist system was fully established, and the people's democratic dictatorship in China was essentially a dictatorship of the proletariat.

The theory of the people's democratic dictatorship was a product of the Marxist-Leninist proletarian revolution, combining the theory of proletarianism with China's concrete situation. It was the great creation of the CPC leading the people through the practice of long-term revolution and construction and the highest stage of development in the new democratic political theory and program. China's people's democratic dictatorship had gone through three stages of development. In the first, during the democratic revolution, the people's democratic dictatorship established in the revolutionary base areas was a partial rather than a national political power under the leadership of the proletariat, the CPC, and the dictatorship of the united revolutionary classes, and its task was to overthrow the reactionary rule of imperialism, feudalism, and bureaucratic capitalism and to engage in the work of the democratic revolution. In the second stage, beginning with the founding of the People's Republic of China, the people's democratic dictatorship had gone through two stages of development, a transitional period from new democracy to socialism and the socialist period. Mao and the CPC had repeatedly pointed out that the people's democratic dictatorship during these two stages was essentially a dictatorship of the proletariat. Therefore, over the course of a long period of time in China, the two ideas of the people's democratic dictatorship and the dictatorship of the proletariat coexisted and were seen as being one and the same. This occurred because the two were political parties led by the proletariat, while state power resided in an alliance of workers and peasants. The basic aspects of destroying class and realizing the historical mission of communism were no different from the state functions of the new type of democracy and new type of dictatorship. Lenin said, "All nations will go to socialism. This is inevitable. But the movements of each nation will not be exactly the same as that of others, through one form of democracy or another, or through the dictatorship of the proletariat. In choosing which type, and in the socialism or the speed of socialist transformation, each nation will have its own characteristics."[78] China's people's democratic dictatorship was the type of proletarianism that suited China's national conditions and revolutionary tradition.

In connection with these characteristics of the theory of the people's democratic dictatorship, the new democratic society transformed the theory of socialist society, further enriching and perfecting the Party's new democratic political theory, making this theory a relatively complete system.

The Party's theory of revolutionary transformation included several aspects. The first was that, after the victory of the democratic revolution, China must immediately turn to socialist revolution. Mao pointed out, "The Chinese revolution is a revolution that includes both the nature of a democratic revolution characterized by the bourgeoisie and a socialist revolution characterized by the proletariat" as two stages of the revolution. The former was a necessary stage of preparation for the latter, and the latter was a result of the development of the previous stage, as "the socialist revolution is the necessary end of the new democratic revolution." When the new democratic revolution was completed, it must immediately be transformed to a socialist revolution. This was the law of development for the Chinese revolution. Mao also held that in new democratic countries, there were already favorable factors for the future development of socialism. Specifically, in the new democratic society, the leadership of the CPC and the proletariat were already established, and the people's democratic dictatorship was based on an alliance of workers and peasants that included all democratic classes and had a state-run economy with a socialist nature. The semi-socialist cooperative economy and the formation of a socialist country's favorable international environment made the final result of the Chinese bourgeois democratic revolution inevitably one of avoiding capitalism and realizing a socialist future. A revolutionary change of mind was a instance of the Marxist theory of "continuing revolution," making people not only the defined objects of the current revolutionary struggle, but also effectively laying the groundwork for the socialist future.

The second aspect was that the transition from a semi-colonial, semi-feudal society to a socialist society could not be carried out directly in China. In between, it must pass through a transitional period, that of a new democratic society. The nation had to establish a new democratic state. Mao noted that China's new democratic revolutionary stage was "a stage of transition between the colonial, semi-colonial, semi-feudal society and the establishment of a socialist society."[79] Only by establishing this transitional phase could China become a new democratic republic. This new democratic republic was a transitional state form adopted by the revolutions of colonial and semi-colonial countries. As long as such a nation engaged in revolution, the state established after the revolution could only adopt the form of a new democratic republic. The new democratic republic was only a form for a particular historical period, but it was a "necessary, immutable form" that would lead to the transformation to a socialist society. Mao similarly pointed out that the transition period would be quite long. He set no regulations for how long it might take, but we can see from his relevant comments that it would not be a short time. He said that in the Chinese revolution, "the first step is a new democracy" and that "this first step will take quite long. It cannot be achieved overnight."[80] Thus, in the political transitional period, it would take a long time for the new state to form and to form various democratic alliances between classes. Economically, for some time after the victory of the revolution, it would be necessary to make full use of the enthusiasm of urban and rural private capitalism to facilitate the advancement of the national economy. Liu Shaoqi likewise noted that "this transition will take much longer than that among the democratic people of Central and Eastern Europe."[81] Based on the long-term understanding of the transition period, Mao emphasized the arduous nature of the work of consolidating the new democratic state.

The third aspect was that the new democratic state had a very important position and role in the process of revolutionary transformation. Mao publicly stated that after the task of "completing China's bourgeois democratic revolution," the CPC was prepared to "transform it to a stage of socialism once all the necessary conditions are in place." What were these conditions? Mao believed that the new democratic state would play an important role in the transformation. He said that in China, "if there is no new democratic unity of the country, no development of the new democratic state economy, no development of the private capitalist and cooperative economies, no national science, mass culture, or new democracy, then the development of the culture will lack the liberation and development of the individuality of countless people. In a word, without the CPC-led bourgeois democratic revolution, building a socialist society on the ruins of the past semi-colonial, semi-feudalist society would be a complete pipe dream."[82] Here, Mao proposed the conditions for achieving revolutionary transformation: 1) there is a new democratic state power that includes all classes under the leadership of the proletariat, 2) the new democratic economy is fully developed, 3) the new democratic cultural cause is fully developed, and 4) other necessary material preparations have been made. These conditions could only be gradually formed through new democratic countries, demonstrating their important role in the transition to a socialist society.

The new democratic theory laid the political foundation for the People's Republic of China. At the First Plenary Session of the Chinese People's Political Consultative Conference, held in September 1949, under the guidance of the new democratic political teaching, the delegates formulated the Common Program that acted as an interim constitution. The Common Program stipulated that the nature of the People's Republic of China was "a new democratic country, which is a people's democracy." It was "under the leadership of the proletariat, based on an alliance of workers and peasants, and unites all democratic classes and the people's democracy of all nationalities." It also stipulated the form of political organization compatible with its nature as a people's democratic dictatorship, that is, the system of people's congresses and democratic centralism. It stated, "The state power of the People's Republic of China belongs to the people. The organs of the people's exercise of state power are the people's congresses and the People's government at all levels, and the state's political organs at all levels implement democratic centralism." It also stipulated the form of ownership allowed in the new democratic state, saying, "The People's Republic of China must eliminate all the privileges of imperialist countries in China, confiscate the bureaucratic capital owned for the people's government, and systematically transfer feudal and semi-feudal land ownership to the peasantry, protecting state and public property and protecting the economic interests of workers, peasants, the petty bourgeoisie, and the national bourgeoisie, and developing a new democratic people's economy on the path to a steady transformation of the agricultural state into an industrial state." In addition, it regulated all military and diplomatic aspects, reflecting all the provisions for every part of the country in the new democratic political theory.

3. The Understanding and Application of the New Democratic Economic Theory

During the period of the new democratic revolution, the CPC combined Marxist economics with the practice of the Chinese revolution, revealing the historical characteristics of China's semi-colonial, semi-feudal socio-economic system and proposed the development of China's economic requirements through the new democratic form, making the basic program of new democracy with Chinese characteristics a relatively complete theoretical form.

After 1840, China was gradually reduced to a semi-feudal, semi-colonial society from a completely independent feudal society. Mao determined that the result of imperial aggression against China "in one aspect prompted the disintegration of Chinese feudal society, leading China to develop capitalist factors, turning the feudal society into a semi-feudal society. On the other hand, the imperialists ruled China cruelly, turning an independent China into a colonial or semi-colonial China."[83] Here, Mao correctly pointed out that China's semi-feudal, semi-colonial economic form had undergone great changes. On the one hand, in the vast rural areas, the landlord still maintained the feudal economic form of most of the land, but throughout the whole of China, the natural economy had disintegrated. To turn a feudal society into a semi-feudal society meant that there was another side to the semi-feudal society, specifically, the emergence of a capitalist production relationship. By the 1920s, capitalist relations of production developed into an economic relationship that dominated the national economy. This was the economic foundation of the neo-democratic revolution led by the proletariat, but it had the nature of a bourgeois democratic revolution. On the other hand, what was called semi-colonialism indicated that foreign aggressors had forced the Chinese government to cut its land as a form of indemnity through acts of war, causing China to lose part of its political sovereignty. Most importantly, economically, it forced the Chinese government to borrow funds and incur foreign debts, using tariffs, salt taxes, and liquefied gold as collateral, which resulted in China losing autonomy in tariffs and thus opening the way for various projects such as mines, railways, factories, and banks on Chinese soil, giving foreign powers control of China's economic lifeline and relegating China to a semi-colonial economic status.

Faced with this social form, based on its own in-depth practical exploration and theoretical exposition, the CPC believed that China's semi-feudal, semi-colonial characteristics were manifested in several areas. In production relations, the natural economic foundation of self-sufficiency in the feudal area had been destroyed, but the roots of feudal exploitation, the exploitation of the peasants by land owners, remained, and in fact it was not only maintained, but was combined with the exploitation of comprador and usury capital. Together, these had a clear advantage in the social and economic life of old China. Capitalism had developed and now played a significant role in China's political and cultural life, but it was weak. The imperialists manipulated China's fiscal and economic lifeline. Under the dual oppression of imperialism and feudalism, the Chinese people, especially Chinese peasants, became increasingly impoverished, even going bankrupt in droves. They lived a life of hunger and want, without any political freedom.

From the perspective of productivity level and distribution characteristics, old Chinese society was very backward in productivity and multi-level in structure. The output value of modern industry only accounted for about 10% of the total output value of the national economy. Among these, state monopoly capital (known as bureaucratic capital) accounted for about 80% of the fixed assets of the national industrial and transportation industry, and private capital industry was the second leading modern industry, making it a force that could not be ignored. Industrial workers accounted for only about 0.6% of the population, or roughly 3 million people, and about 90% of those were distributed among the individual agricultural and handicraft industries, underdeveloped sectors that did not show any major difference from the overall economy. Mao said that such productivity was "the result of the imperialist and feudal systems oppressing China, which were the sort of economic performance seen in China's old semi-colonial, semi-feudal society."[84] The basic characteristics of industrial distribution were concentrated in the six northeastern and coastal provinces. In these two regions, the land area accounted for 18% of the country, while the population accounted for 42% and the industrial output value for about 80% of the national total. The industrial output of Shanghai alone was more than 25% of the national total. Mao observed, "China's industry used to be concentrated in the coastal area… All of China's light and heavy industry have a distribution of about 70% in coastal areas and 30% in the interior. This is an unreasonable situation."[85] Economic development was extremely unbalanced, and "the weak capitalist economy and severe semi-feudal economy coexist. Some modern industrial and commercial cities and stagnant rural areas likewise coexist. Millions of industrial workers and tens of millions of peasants and handicraft workers under the old system coexist… There are a number of railway lines and single-vehicle roads, paths only accessible on foot, and others hardly accessible at all."[86]

The CPC's analysis of China's semi-feudal, semi-colonial economic form led to the conclusion that the new democracy was the foundation for forming the economy. The practice of a new democratic economy first began during the Agrarian Revolutionary War.

The struggle had been fully elaborated and practiced since the Agrarian

Revolutionary War. During the War of Resistance Against Japanese Aggression, the Party began to more fully recognize the extreme importance of economic construction, and thus undertook to implement it in the anti-Japanese revolutionary base areas, putting economic efforts to work in service of the revolutionary war. Economic work could not be separated from the war effort, with the Party focusing only on economic issues. Rather, ensuring the needs of the war and an adequate supply of military resources was inseparable from economic construction. To this end, the CPC began to form a series of distinctive economic policies and principles.

The CPC pointed out that the national economy was then composed of military enterprises, cooperative enterprises, and private enterprises. Currently state-owned economic undertakings were limited to areas that were both possible and necessary. State-run industries and commerce were likewise beginning to develop. Though they currently only counted for a small proportion, they enjoyed tremendous potential for future development. For the private economy, as long as it was not outside the scope of government law, it should not be stopped, but should instead be promoted and rewarded, because the development of the private economy was necessary for national interests, even though such enterprises were currently dominant and would continue to be for a long period into the future. To this end, the CPC laid out the principles underlying its economic policy, which were to carry out all possible and necessary economic construction, concentrate on supplying the war effort, and at the same time striving to improve people's lives, consolidate the economic alliance between workers and peasants, and ensure proletarian leadership of the peasantry and the state-owned economy's leadership of the private economy, leading to the future development of socialism. This was in line with the changes in the level of production and the shifting production relations at various stages. In 1935, the international and domestic situation changed. In order to win more people to participate in the united front of the democratic revolution, Mao further demanded that the Party clarify the economic policy of capitalism. In his article "On the Strategy for Opposing Japanese Imperialism," he observed "The republic in the era of the bourgeois democratic revolution failed to abolish imperialist, non-feudal private property and to confiscate national bourgeois industry and commerce. In fact, it encouraged the development of these industries." He added, "In the democratic revolution, the labor and capital struggle was limited."[87] The labor law of the Republican period protected the interests of workers, but it did not oppose the capitalization of national interests, and it did not oppose the development of national industry and commerce, because such a development would not be conducive to the imperialists, but to the Chinese people. The implementation of such economic policies could have brought about political changes, expanded the united front, and better accomplished political tasks.

Guided by these principles for its economic policy, the Party pointed out that the central tasks for economic development in the base areas were to develop agricultural production, industrial production, trade, and development cooperatives. With this foundation, the Party proposed specific measures for economic construction.

In order to develop agricultural production, it was first necessary to address the land issue, dismantling the solid foundation of the feudal exploitation system and production relations, establishing the land ownership of the peasantry, and encouraging the agricultural production policy. The enthusiasm of the peasants could be heightened, and on this basis, assistance could be given to peasant organizations, such as labor mutual aid societies, arable land teams, and plow animal cooperatives, to address problems such as limited labor or livestock resources. Mao emphasized that, under current conditions, agricultural production was the first priority in China's economic construction work. At the same time, he criticized the earlier land policy of complete confiscation and redistribution as a "leftist" error, believing that this was a blow to the middle classes in rural areas that was not conducive to the CPC's struggle in the countryside. For the development of industrial production, Mao emphasized the planned development of handicraft and some industries, one for self-sufficiency and the other for export. It was necessary to make efforts to develop foreign trade and open up the market inside and outside the Red areas to adjust surplus. The Party also attached great importance to the development of the cooperative economy. It believed that the cooperative economy was the best economic form at the time for increasing productivity. It cooperated with the state-run economy, and after some long-term development, it would become a huge force in the economy, eventually coming to dominate it and gain leadership status.

Of course, during this period, the Party's investigation into various economic perspectives was still preliminary and not yet sufficiently mature in the theories it developed, having not yet made use of the scientific concept of the new democratic economy. It had yet to clarify both the national economy and new democracy, which was the inherent logical connection at this particular historical stage.

The leap in understanding of the new democratic economy came after the beginning of the War of Resistance Against Japanese Aggression. During the Anti-Japanese War, Mao elaborated on the theory of the new democratic economy in several works, such as "The Chinese Revolution and the Communist Party of China," *New Democracy*, "Economic and Financial Issues in the Anti-Japanese Period," and "On the Coalition Government," which marked the beginning of the Party's new democratic theory.

First, the concept of the new democratic economy was proposed. After systematic analysis of the characteristics of China's semi-feudal, semi-colonial society, the Party reaffirmed that the nature of the Chinese revolution at this stage was still that of a bourgeois democratic revolution, but it was no longer an old-style bourgeois democratic revolution. It was instead a new-style special democratic revolution, a "new democratic revolution." This sort of revolution required the establishment of a new democratic politics, economy, and culture. Mao pointed out that the CPC had struggled for many years for China's political, economic, and cultural revolution, and the purpose of this struggle had been to build a new Chinese society and nation. He said, "To establish such a republic in China, it must be politically and economically new democratic,"[88] because economic issues were expressed in political and cultural issues. But what constituted a new democratic revolution? It was "focused on the big capital and big enterprise of imperialists and reactionary traitors, subjecting big industry to state management and distributing the land of the landlord class to the peasantry, while preserving the general private capitalist enterprise and not abolishing the wealthy peasant economy."[89] On the one hand, a revolution of this sort cleared the way for capitalism, while on the other, it laid the material groundwork for socialism.

In addition, the construction of a new democratic economy had to follow a path of "restraining capital" and "equalizing land rights." It was necessary for the new democratic economic construction to formulate and implement policies based on China's historical characteristics and economic conditions while exploring the proper development path. China should neither duplicate the model of the Soviet Union's economic development nor the economic form of European and American capitalism, but should rather establish a new type of economic relationship. After emphasizing that big banks, big industries, and big businesses were owned by the new democratic state, Mao recounted the relevant aspects of the KMT's grand declaration that "any foreign enterprise may have an exclusive nature or be too large. For the sake of private power, sectors such as banking, railways, and transportation are to be managed by the state, so that the private capital system cannot manipulate the livelihood of the people. This is the key to controlling capital."[90] This was the correct policy for the economic structure of a new democratic republic. Regarding the capitalists' economic policy, Mao clearly indicated that after the victory of the new democratic revolution, because the obstacles to the development of capitalism had been cleared away, the capitalist economy would have a considerable degree of development in Chinese society. This should not be surprising, since the Chinese economy was still very underdeveloped. Therefore, the criteria for the confiscation of capital was to see if the Party could manipulate the national economy and the people's livelihood. At the same time, it was necessary to encourage the development of the state-owned and cooperative economies, gradually increasing their size in relation to the overall economy, and providing economic guarantees for avoiding capitalism's development prospects. The confiscated land of rural land owners would be divided among those peasants who owned no land, allowing for the implementation of the principle of "the cultivators owning the fields" to eliminate feudal relations in rural areas while allowing for the existence of wealthy peasants in the economy. This was the principle of "equalizing land rights." In the new democratic revolution period, socialist factors were not generally seen in the establishment of a socialist agriculture, but in the various cooperative economies developed on the basis of the peasants owning their own fields. The new production relationship established by the principles of restraining capital and equalizing land rights was suitable for the development level of the social productive forces at that time. This was also the concentrated expression of Sun Yat-sen's Three People's Principles and the CPC's new democratic program.

Finally, the basic principles and correct path to developing a new economy was that it be composed of the national economy, the private economy, and the collective economy. Without the coordinated development of these three economies, it was impossible for the Chinese people to build the socialist economy on a semi-feudal, semi-colonial foundation. To this end, the Party had formulated some specific policies for economic development. In terms of labor policies, the dual policy was implemented to appropriately improve the life of workers without hindering the legitimate development of the capitalist economy so as to improve the labor-capital relation and drive the overall economy. In the land policy, it was necessary to constantly adapt to the changes in the Party's central task in different periods, from the approach of "confiscating all land" during the ten year period of the civil war to the dual policy of requiring landlords to reduce rents and interest rates and peasants to pay rents and interests during the Anti-Japanese War, playing a positive role in uniting landlords and wealthy peasants to the anti-Japanese cause. In dealing with private capitalist policies, Mao pointed out that the state-run economy and cooperative economy should be developed, but currently, in the rural base areas, the main economic component was not state-owned but private, and the most revolutionary policy at that point was to let the liberal capitalist economy develop so that it could be used in the fight against Japanese imperialism and semi-feudalism.[91]

Publicly affirming the view of the CPC's distinctive economic revolution, Mao noted, "Some people do not understand why the communists are not afraid of capitalism, but instead advocate its development under certain conditions. The answer is a simple one. If there is some development instead of the oppression of foreign imperialism and domestic feudalism, this is not only an improvement, but also an inevitable process. It not only benefits the bourgeoisie, but also the proletariat, and is in fact even more conducive to the proletariat. We would prefer domestic capitalism to foreign imperialism and domestic feudalism. In fact, we have too little capitalism."[92] Under the special historical conditions of China and other new democratic countries, this system was not one of abolishing private property, but of generally protecting private property, while opposing capitalism within the Party and certain socio-economic aspects of capitalism. After 1940, the anti-Japanese base areas and the Shaanxi-Gansu-Ningxia border area entered their most difficult period. In order to overcome these difficulties, Mao Zedong listed the development economy as the first place for construction of the border areas and base areas. He held that the Anti-Japanese War was not only a political and military contest, but more importantly, an economic contest. He also suggested, "Developing the economy and guaranteeing supply is the goal of our general policy of economic and financial work."[93] In carrying out the military-civilian production movement, a policy of self-employment and self-sufficiency was implemented. The correct way to develop the economy was to overcome the individual decentralized management and gradually collectivize, and the only way to achieve collectivization was through cooperative organization, with emphasis on the need to develop both heavy and light industry and create conditions for the transformation of agricultural counties into industrial counties. In particular, social productivity standards were introduced. Seeing the theoretical depth and superior wisdom of such moves, Mao said, "The policies and practices of all political parties in China should be decided based on an analysis of China's situation and it should be determined whether they are helpful to the development of the people's productivity and whether they contain or liberate productivity."[94]

With the smooth progress of the War of Liberation, the victory of the Chinese democratic revolution was only a matter of time. At this time, the CPC engaged in deeper, more systematic thought concerning the development of the new democratic economy after the victory of the revolution and offered a comprehensive explanation of the new democratic economic program.

After testing through the long-term revolutionary struggle and the continuous summarization of lessons learned through that struggle, in 1947, Mao proposed the three major economic programs of the new democracy in his article "The Current Situation and Our Mission." Specifically, he stated, "The land confiscated from the feudal class is owned by the peasants. The confiscation of monopoly capital headed by Chiang Kai-shek, T.V. Soong, H.H. Kung, and Chen Lifu is owned by the new democratic state and protects national industry and commerce."[95]

The first major economic principle was that the land confiscated from the feudal classes was owned by the peasants. This was one of the central ideas of the new democratic revolution and the basic new democratic program. The peasant issue was central to the Chinese revolution and central to achieving the leadership of the proletariat. The peasant problem was first and foremost a land issue. In semi-colonial, semi-feudal China, the landlord class used its feudal land system of occupying the land to cruelly exploit the peasants, which seriously hindered the development of rural productivity and was one of the root causes of poverty and backwardness in China. Thus, it was a major task of the new democratic revolution to launch a land reform among poor peasants, eliminate the land system of feudal exploitation, and implement a policy by which "the cultivators own the fields."

At the dawn of this new historical stage, the Party highly affirmed the realistic path and method for land allocation formulated during the Agrarian Revolutionary War, that of relying on poor farmers, uniting middle class peasants, restricting wealthy peasants, protecting small and medium sized industrial and commercial workers, and eradicating the landlord class. The feudal land ownership system was transformed to one of peasant land ownership. With the township as the unit, the land was distributed equally according to the population, and on the basis of the original cultivated land, adjustments were made upward or downward and taken from those who had much and given to those who have little. During the War of Resistance Against Japanese Aggression, in order to meet the demands of uniting and resisting Japan, the CPC changed its policy of confiscating the land of feudal landlords for redistribution among the peasantry, while also ensuring that the policy of reducing rent and interest rates conformed to the actual state of development.

On the basis of accumulating a wealth of experience and theory through these two historical stages, on May 4, 1946, the Central Committee issued its Instructions on Land Issues and the May 4th Directive, which changed the policy of rent and interest reduction during the Anti-Japanese War and the policy of confiscation of land from the landlord class for distribution among the peasantry and implemented land reform in the liberated areas. In 1947, the National Land Conference formulated the first relatively complete new democratic land program in the history of the CPC, the Outline of Chinese Land Law, which clearly stipulated "The abolition of feudal and semi-feudal exploitation of the land system and the implementation of the policy of the cultivator owning the field." At the Party meeting that December, Mao summarized the experience of the land reform and pointed out that the principle of land reform was to "rely on poor peasants, consolidate and unify middle class peasants, and eliminate the feudal and semi-feudal exploitation systems of the landlord class and the old wealthy peasantry."[96] At the same time, in response to the issue of land reform, two basic principles were emphasized. "First, we must meet the needs of poor peasants and farmers. This is the most basic task of the land reform. Second, we must resolutely unite the peasants and not harm their interests."[97]

In January 1948, in a speech at an expanded meeting of the former Northwest Field Army, Mao asked local democratic governments to pay attention to the fact that, in land reform, the landlord class should be eliminated, but individuals should be protected, saying, "abolishing the private ownership of the landlord class doesn't mean we want nothing to do even with the individual person. The landlords and old-style wealthy peasants account for ten percent of the rural population. There are 36 million of such individuals in the country. This is the labor force of our society, and thus a form of wealth. Give him the chance to participate in production. He can lift a stretcher, produce food, and hand over public grain, which is all for the good of the country."[98] Mao also pointed out that the fight against Chiang Kai-shek and the eradication of the landlord class were "aimed at economically destroying the feudal comprador's production relations and liberating bound production forces. In the countryside, it is to liberate the peasants, break feudal land ownership, and implement a thorough redistribution of the land, granting land ownership to the peasants so that they can be assured of bold production and improvement in farming methods."[99] In April that year, in his speech at Jinsui Cadres Meeting, Mao clearly stipulated the Party's overarching land reform policy and guideline, i.e., "relying on the poor peasants, uniting the middle-class peasants, and systematically and discriminately eradicating the feudal system to develop agriculture."[100] These lines, policies and guidelines maximized unity and won over all the forces that could be united in the countryside. They represented the interests of the vast majority of the people in rural China, guaranteeing the smooth progress of the land reform, liberating and developing rural productivity, and consolidated the union of workers and peasants, laying the foundation and establishing the conditions for the victory of the Chinese revolution and the achievement of national industrialization.

The second major economic principle was that the monopoly capital confiscated belonged to the new democratic state. This was another key element of the new democratic economic program. The bureaucratic capital represented by the four families, Chiang, Song, Kong, and Chen, was formed in the later period of the Agrarian Revolutionary War and reached its peak during the War of Resistance. The KMT's bureaucratic capital consisted of two parts. The first was state monopoly capital, which was the capital of the big landlords represented by the four families and the capital of the upper bourgeois state. The second was the private capital owned by the four families and other bureaucrats and warlords. These two parts of the capital monopoly were the national economic lifeline, and they represented reactionary production relations, which was a serious obstacle to China's economic and social development. Confiscation of bureaucratic capital entailed the construction of these two types of capital.

The confiscation of bureaucratic capital had a two-tiered revolutionary nature. On the one hand, bureaucratic capital was a feudal, comprador state monopoly capitalism, the economic basis of KMT rule, and opposition to bureaucratic capital was opposition to feudal comprador capital, which was in essence a new democratic revolution. On the other hand, opposition to bureaucratic capital was opposition to the upper bourgeoisie, and it concentrated this enormous power and put control of the economic lifeline of the country in the hands of the new democratic state, making it the main source of the socialist-style state owned economy and creating conditions for socialist transformation. Therefore, when bureaucratic capital was confiscated, it was also in essence a socialist revolution.

During the War of Liberation, the CPC began to confiscate bureaucratic capital from the already liberated cities in the northeastern region. After the three main campaigns, it had basically confiscated the bureaucratic enterprises north of the Yangtze River. By the end of 1949, the bureaucratic capital of all regions except Taiwan had been taken over and were owned by the people's government. The completion of the revolutionary task of confiscation of bureaucratic capital was of great significance for several reasons. Primarily, with the confiscation of the monopoly of bureaucratic capital, the new democratic state had mastery of the state's economic lifeline, and the state-owned economy was in a leading position in the overall national economy. In addition, the proletariat could utilize the economic power transferred from bureaucratic capital to consolidate the new people's republic. Finally, it laid the foundation for the establishment of a new democratic society and the corresponding economic system, laying the foundation for the transition toward socialism.

The third major economic principle was that the protection of national industry and commerce was a distinctive feature of the new democratic economic program. As mentioned earlier, the CPC divided Chinese capitalism into two parts, bureaucratic capitalism and national capitalism, and it adopted completely different policies for the two. For national capitalism, it implemented a protection policy. That is, under new democratic conditions, there was development of a capitalist economy that did not manipulate the national economy or the livelihood of the people.

Because the transformation from a new democracy to socialism had been completed prematurely in the Party's actual work, the transformation of national capitalism and criticism of capitalism was also undertaken prematurely in the 1960s. The end result was a series of leftist mistakes, leading many to believe that Mao had always been "populist" or "utopian." However, in the process of the new democratic revolution, especially in the disputes surrounding the founding of the country in 1949, after the War of Resistance Against Japanese Aggression, only the Mao-led CPC repeatedly declared that they were in the new democratic stage. In social aspects, not only did it not fear capitalism, it actually promoted the development of certain types of capitalism. No type of bourgeois party dared to propose the idea of developing capitalism. Only the CPC protected national industry and commerce, holding that the development of capitalism was beneficial to the national economy and the livelihood of the people. In terms of its own economic program, the CPC profoundly analyzed and criticized the populist ideas within the Party in both theory and practice.

Mao pointed out that first, socialism must take socialized large-scale production as a solid material foundation, and its decision whether or not to proceed on this basis was "where Marxism is different from populism." Second, the type of agricultural socialism that advocated the destruction of industry and commerce and advocated absolute egalitarianism – that is, the so-called socialism advocated by populists on the basis of small rural production – was a type of thinking that was "reactionary, retrogressive, and backward-looking in nature. We must criticize such thinking." Third, such socialism not only protected underdeveloped small production, but would also certainly maintain feudalism and alienate socialism, turning it to a sort of authoritarianism that suppressed individual liberation. Mao noted that "if the bound individual is not liberated, there will be no democracy, nor will there be socialism." In short, the socialism advocated by the populists went against the rules of social development and was an idealistic, reactionary idea.

Why was it necessary to protect national industry and commerce and allow a capitalist economy that did not manipulate the national economy and the people's livelihood to develop? Mao pointed out that first of all, "taking some sort of capitalist development to replace the oppression of foreign imperialism and domestic feudalism is not only an improvement, but is also an inevitable process." Second, the conditional development of capitalism would "not only benefit the bourgeoisie, but also the proletariat. In fact, it will be even more beneficial to the proletariat. Currently, there is much foreign imperialism and domestic feudalism in China, but there is not too much domestic capitalism. In fact, there is too little." In short, the development of capitalism was beneficial under the new democratic regime. Thus, the CPC advocated "new democratic capitalism, which has a vital, revolutionary nature." In fact, "in aiding socialism, it is both revolutionary and useful, and it is conducive to the development of socialism."

The conception of the new democratic economic structure was the core of the new democratic economic theory and an important part of the Party's new democratic social thinking. With the triumph of the new democratic revolution and the implementation of the three major economic principles, the concept of a new democratic economic structure had gradually taken shape. Mao's *New Democracy* referred to the economic structure of a new democratic society, pointing out that "big banks, big industries, and big businesses are all owned by the new democratic state… under the leadership of the proletariat, making the state-run economy of the new democratic republic socialist in nature and the leading force of the entire national economy." Further, "it does not confiscate private property or other capital and does not prohibit the development of capitalist production that does not manipulate the national economy or the people's livelihood. This is for the sake of the still underdeveloped Chinese economy." And "the confiscation of the landlords' land… is to make it the property of the peasants," because "at this stage, it is not yet time for the general establishment of the socialist economy, but the laying of a foundation in the principle of 'the cultivator owning the field,' leading to the various cooperative economies having socialist features." And finally, "the rural wealthy peasant economy must be allowed to exist."[101] From this, it is not difficult to see that Mao's new democratic structure contained five economic components at the time. These were the state-run economy, the cooperative economy, the private capitalist economy, the individual economy, and the rich peasant economy. This concept was further improved over the following several years. In December 1947, Mao further clarified the new democratic economic structure in his article "The Current Situation and Our Mission," in which he noted that "1) The state-owned economy is the formation into which leadership is divided, 2) the agricultural economy is gradually developed from the individual toward the collective, and 3) the economy of independent small business people and the small and medium private capital economy are all part of the national economy in a new democratic economy."[102] This division referred to the individual economy and wealthy peasant economy as the agricultural economy. Although this was a more concise and scientific definition than that found in *New Democracy*, it only included the state economy, the private capitalist economy, and the agricultural economy. The economic component, which was obviously incomplete, required further development of this theory. It was Zhang Wentian who completed the development.

In July 1948, at the joint meeting of the ministers and propaganda ministers of the county Party committees held in the Northeast Bureau of the CPC Central Committee, Zhang summed up the findings of his research over the previous several years and proposed six components of the coming new democratic economy, suggesting that it would include: 1) the state-run (or public) economy, 2) the state capitalist economy, 3) the private capitalist economy, 4) the small commodity economy (mainly the peasant economy), 5) the cooperative economy, and 6) the nomadic economy. Although this formulation was not perfect and its explanation was not in-depth enough, it established a complete framework for the ultimate proposal of the new democratic economy. Two months later, on the basis of his own report on the work of the Northeast Bureau, Zhang wrote a report to the Central Committee, the Outline of the Northeast Economic Composition and Construction, which clearly laid out the new democratic economy. The five components were "the state-owned economy, the cooperative economy, the state capitalist economy, the private capitalist economy, and the small commodity economy (and there is still a small part of the natural economy, though rationally, it is of only very minor significance)." This was the earliest and most complete exposition of the scientific generalization of the new democratic economy. Zhang also fully elaborated on the nature, status, development direction, and mutual relationships of these five economies. 1) The state-run economy was a socialist economy and the leader in the national economy. 2) The cooperative economy was an economically viable economy with varying degrees of socialism and was the most reliable assistant to the state-owned economy. Only through the cooperative economy could agricultural collectivization be realized and farmers move through new democracy toward socialism. 3) The state capitalist economy, that is, the capitalism of "management and supervision" by the new democratic state, was a form of private capitalist economy that was most conducive to the development of the new democratic economy. Thus, it was important to consciously promote and organize the category of state capitalism. 4) The private capitalist economy was a capitalist economy. Because of the lack of development in China's national economy, the development of private capitalism was inevitable and necessary, within certain limits. However, it could not be allowed to develop freely, but must, to a degree, be managed, supervised, and restricted. 5) The commodity economy was an economy that stood at the crossroads between capitalism and socialism. After a long period of education and struggle, under a new democratic state led by the proletariat, it would develop into socialism, but it would "be different from the process seen in various Eastern European countries." Zhang held that "correctly understanding the nature, status, development direction, and mutual relationship of these five economies is the starting point and basis for correctly determining the economic policy of the Northeast, and only from this point on can we grasp the correct line on the economic front and realize the correct leadership of the proletariat for social and economic construction." This scientific discourse of Zhang Wentian marked the true maturity of this concept, opening the way for its ultimate maturation a year later. The full expression of the idea was found in two important documents written by Mao, the Report on the Second Plenary Session of the Seventh General Meeting of the CPC Central Committee and the Common Program of the Chinese People's Political Consultative Committee (referred to below as "Common Program"), which discussed the provisions for the new democratic economic structure.

Mao first discussed the extreme importance of making the state-owned economy the leader of the overall economy, saying, "China's private capitalist industry… is a force that must not be ignored… In this period, everything that is not harmful to the national economy but is a component of urban or rural capitalism and is beneficial to the national economy should be allowed to exist and develop. This is not only inevitable, but is economically necessary."[103] For the scattered individual economy, Mao believed that "it is possible for it to develop in the direction of modernization and collectivization, and this must be managed cautiously and gradually, with active guidance. The idea of letting it flow naturally would be wrong."[104] Mao also recognized the importance of the cooperative economy. He said, "With a state-run economy that lacks a cooperative economy, it would be impossible to lead the individualized economy of the working class to gradually collectivize, which would make it impossible to develop from a new democratic society to a socialist society and to consolidate the leadership of the proletariat into a state power."[105] Finally, he summed up, "The state-run economy is socialist, while the cooperative economy is semi-socialist. These, together with the private capitalist economy and the individual economy, are the main components of a people's republic. Together, they constitute the new democratic economic form."[106]

Because the Common Program served the role of an interim constitution, the economic structure of the new democracy determined by it was undoubtedly authoritative and effective. The provisions it laid out for the structure of the new democratic economy were the model of development for this concept for decades, determining its course. The Common Program's discussion of the nature, role, status, and future direction of the five economic components allowed in the new democratic society basically followed Mao's formulation, clearly defining the fundamental principle of the economic construction of the People's Republic of China as the goal of developing productive forces and prospering the economy by adopting a policy of public-private considerations, labor management and mutual benefit, urban-rural mutual assistance, and internal and external exchanges. The state was to adjust the individual economy of the state-run economy, cooperative economy, peasant and handicrafts economy, private capitalist economy, and state capitalist economy in terms of business scope, raw material supply, sales market, labor conditions, technical equipment, fiscal policy, and financial policies. Under the leadership of the state-run economy, various social and economic components, division of labor, and cooperation, each had a role in the promotion of the development of the overall social economy. This policy conformed to the actual social situation brought about by China's history and its revolution, and it allowed space for the advantages of various economic components and promoting the rapid development of the social economy.

4. Building a New National Scientific People's Culture

During the War of Resistance Against Japanese Aggression, Mao published several works in succession, including *New Democracy*, "Reforming Our Learning," "Speech at the Yan'an Forum on Literature and Arts," "Uniting Handicraft Workers with Workers, Peasants, and Soldiers," "Cultural Work," and "The United Front and the United Government." These works expressed the CPC's understanding of cultural issues, systematically constructing the concept of a new democratic culture and formulating a new democratic cultural platform. The CPC revealed the historical inevitability of the new democratic culture from the perspective of studying the changes in social and cultural structure after the Opium War. Mao believed that after the Opium War in 1840, China had gradually grown from a fully feudal society into a semi-colonial, semi-feudal society. Changes in social and political structure inevitably led to changes in culture and cultural structure. Before the Opium War, Chinese culture was a single feudal culture. After the Opium War, in addition to this feudal culture, there was the oppressive culture of imperialism and the emerging democratic culture of the national bourgeoisie. That is to say, after the Opium War, the social and cultural nature of China was changed from a single monolithic form to a multiplicity of forms. At this time, on the one hand, the old culture of feudalism continued to be entrenched and controlled the spiritual life of the Chinese people. On the other hand, the feudal culture, the oppressed culture, and the democratic culture coexisted in continuous conflict. The particularity of China's modern social development and the complexity of the ideological and cultural change determined the multiplicity of its modern social and cultural nature. In the contradictory evolution of China's modern pluralistic culture, the bourgeois democratic culture was a new force on China's cultural front. The evolution in China's feudal culture directly served the purposes of the Chinese revolution and represented the direction of the evolution of Chinese society. During the Hundred Days Reform Movement and the Revolution of 1911, Chinese progressives actively studied and promoted Western democratic literature, attempting to imitate Western democratic culture and establish a democratic culture in China. They used the bourgeois democratic culture as a weapon to fight feudal culture and tried to awaken the people's transformation and promote their prosperity. Since the Chinese bourgeois democratic culture was not born from the soil of the domestic feudal culture but had been transplanted from the West, its class foundation was weak. China's feudal culture had a long history and had grown from feudalism. The system had formed a solid psychological structure for the national culture. The oppressed culture fostered by imperialism had colluded with it and formed a cultural alliance to confront bourgeois democratic culture. Therefore, in the struggle between these opposing sides, the bourgeois democratic culture would only be able to fight a few rounds, before it was ultimately defeated by this reactionary alliance. Mao observed, "In the era of imperialism, the old bourgeois democratic culture had been corrupted and become powerless. Its failure is inevitable."[107] The new democratic culture was born in this historical situation. That is to say, the bankruptcy of the old democratic culture in the era of imperialism and the emergence of a new democratic culture were the inevitable result of the development of modern history. After the May 4th Movement in 1919, the advanced proletariat stepped onto the stage of Chinese history, with its uncompromising anti-imperialist, anti-feudal ethos, showing itself to be a new, powerful political force, adding a new dimension to modern Chinese society. After the May 4th Movement, the New Cultural Movement quickly developed into a Marxist ideological movement. In this way, a new cultural item had been injected into modern China's already pluralistic culture, bringing about a historic turning point in modern culture. On the one hand, this was because China's old-style democratic culture had been riddled by the culture of imperialist and feudalist oppression, and it had been defeated repeatedly, but it had still not lost its progressiveness. On the other hand, China's old-style democratic culture was indeed powerless to defeat oppressive feudal and imperialist culture. Only an advanced proletarian new democratic culture guided by Marxism could defeat feudal culture and oppressive imperialist culture. The proletarian-led new democratic culture had gradually grown into the main force of China's modern cultural revolution. The CPC pointed out that the new democratic culture was the anti-imperialist, anti-feudalist people's culture led by the proletariat. This was the most distinctive historical feature of new democratic culture. Mao pointed out that China's cultural and ideological fronts formed two different historical parts before and after the May 4th Movement. Before the May 4th Movement, the struggle on the cultural front was between the new culture of the bourgeoisie and the old culture of the feudal class. Before the May 4th Movement, the disputes between school and imperial exam, between new school and old school, between Western and Chinese education were all of this nature. The so-called school, new studies, and Western studies at that time were basically the natural sciences and the socio-political sciences of the bourgeoisie (and basically, there were many Chinese feudal positions in between). He believed that the so-called new studies thinking played a revolutionary role in the struggle against Chinese feudal ideology and served the Chinese bourgeois democratic revolution in the old era. However, because of the powerlessness of the Chinese bourgeoisie, and because the entire world had entered a period of imperialism, this bourgeois ideology could only fight a few rounds before it would ultimately be defeated by the reactionary ideology of foreign imperialism and Chinese feudalism. Retired by such an allied reactionary force before it could even mount a small counter-attack, the so-called new studies would be suffocated, losing body and soul. For this reason, he concluded that the old bourgeois democratic culture, which had been completely corrupted in the imperialist era, was already powerless, and its failure was inevitable.

After the May 4th Movement, China produced a completely new cultural force, that of the Communist cultural ideology led by the CPC, specifically through its communist cosmology and social revolution. Since the period was situated in the aftermath of World War I and the October Revolution, a time when the national question and the colonial revolutionary movement was changing the face of the world, the Chinese revolution was closely connected with the world revolution. Because the Chinese political force – the Chinese proletariat and the CPC – had entered China's political arena, this cultural force had opened up its own battle with new garments and new weapons, uniting all possible allies in a heroic attack against imperialist and feudalist culture. This new force was seen in the fields of social science, literature, and art (drama, film, music, carving, and painting), and it saw great development. The sharpness of this new cultural army, in both thought and form (text or otherwise), was a great, invincible revolutionary force. Its might was both vast and violent. Its broad mobilization surpassed any before seen in China. Thus, Mao emphasized that before the May 4th Movement, China's new culture was a culture of the old democratic nature and part of the capitalist cultural revolution of the bourgeoisie worldwide. After the May 4th Movement, China's new culture was a culture of a new democratic nature and part of the socialist cultural revolution of the proletariat worldwide. Before the May 4th Movement, China's cultural movement and its cultural revolution were led by the bourgeoisie. After the May 4th Movement, the cultural thoughts of this class lagged behind politically, and they lost leadership of the movement. At most, they could still continue as members at this political point. Leadership qualifications, however, were only seen in proletarian cultural thought. This was an undeniable, ironclad fact. Based on this understanding, Mao came to the conclusion that the so-called culture of the new democracy was the culture of the people's anti-imperialist, anti-feudalist movement. At that time, it was embodied in the culture of the Anti-Japanese National United Front. This sort of culture could only be led by the cultural thoughts of the proletariat, which was communist ideology. The cultural thoughts of any other class could not lead. What was called new democratic culture could be summed up in a single phrase: the people's anti-imperialist, anti-feudal culture under the leadership of the proletariat.

The new democratic culture was the new democratic people's anti-imperialist, anti-feudal socialist thought and culture led by the proletariat. These were the fundamental attributes of the new democratic culture. Mao first criticized the bourgeois diehard culture that prevailed at the time. He pointed out that bourgeois die-hards were completely mistaken in regards to cultural issues and their political rights. They did not know the historical characteristics of China's new era, and they did not recognize the culture of the people's new democracy. Their starting point was bourgeois despotism, which led to bourgeois cultural despotism. Some of the so-called European and American culturalists had actually sponsored the KMT government's culture and now seemed to be backing "limiting" and "instigating" policies. They did not want the workers and peasants to rise up politically, nor did they want them to rise up culturally. The road to this cultural authoritarianism of the bourgeois die-hards was unworkable. Similar to the issue of political power, the international and domestic conditions to support such a system simply were not in place, leading cultural authoritarianism to "retreat."

He went on to criticize the idea that because the leadership of the new democratic revolution belonged to the proletariat, the new democratic culture was necessarily socialist in nature. As a guideline for national culture, the guiding role was the ideology of communism, and the CPC should strive to promote socialism and communism among the working class, using socialism in appropriate ways to educate the peasants and the rest of the people. However, that did not mean the entire culture was yet socialist. The politics, economy, and culture of the new democracy had socialist factors because they were led by the proletariat, and these were not ordinary factors, but decisive factors. However, the overall political situation was not socialism, but a new democracy. Because the basic task at this stage of the revolution was mainly to oppose foreign imperialism and domestic feudalism, it was a bourgeois democratic revolution, not a socialist revolution aimed at overthrowing capitalism. As far as national culture was concerned, it was wrong to assume that the entire national culture was or should be a socialist national culture. This was to regard the propaganda of the communist ideology as the practice of the current program of action, using the positions and methods of communism to observe problems, acquire knowledge, handle work, and train cadres for every stage of the entire Chinese democratic revolution. Armed with socialism, the policy of natural education and culture must reflect the political and economic aspects of socialism. There were socialist political and economic factors, reflecting the socialist cultural factors, but as far as the whole society was concerned, China had not yet formed this overall socialist politics and economy, so there still could be no such overall national socialist culture. Because the current Chinese revolution was part of the worldwide proletarian socialist revolution, the current new Chinese culture was also part of the world's new proletarian culture and was part of its great allied army. Yet, though this part contained major features of socialist culture, it was not yet qualified to participate in socialist culture for the entire national culture. It was based on the qualifications of the people's anti-imperialist, anti-feudalist new democratic culture. Since the current Chinese revolution could not depart from the leadership of the proletariat, that meant the current Chinese new culture could not depart from the leadership of Chinese proletarian cultural thought, which was to say, it could not depart from the leadership of communist ideology. However, at this stage, the thought that was leading the people's anti-imperialist, anti-feudal fight in a political and cultural revolution was new democratic, not socialist. At the time, there was no doubt that communist ideological propaganda needed to be expanded and Marxist-Leninist education enhanced. Without such propaganda and education, it would be impossible to guide the Chinese revolution to a future state of socialism, nor was it possible to guide the current democratic revolution to victory. However, it was important to distinguish communist propaganda from socialist institutions and the practices of the new democratic action program, and to distinguish the communist theories and methods of observing problems, researching to gain knowledge, handling work, and training cadres from the new democratic principles that served the overall national culture. To confuse them was undoubtedly inappropriate.

On the basis of this analysis, Mao pointed out that the idea of China's new national culture at this stage was neither that of the cultural authoritarianism of the bourgeoisie nor the simple socialism of the proletariat, but the cultural thought of the proletarian-led anti-imperialist, anti-feudalist people's new democracy.

Based on the current state of China's social politics and economic development, and with the goal of establishing a new democratic society, Mao proposed the basic framework for building a new democratic culture. He pointed out that the new democratic culture was first of all national. He said, "It opposes the oppression of imperialism and advocates the dignity and independence of the Chinese nation. It is of our nation and carries our national characteristics."[108] Mao always emphasized that Chinese culture must have its national form, since it "is of our nation." He advocated that Chinese culture should have a national form but be new democratic in nature. However, he did not simply "like the new because he was tired of the old," but emphasized that Chinese culture should have a historical inheritance, specifically, traditional Chinese culture, since that was the source and root of the national characteristics he admired. Emphasis on the independence of the Chinese nation's cultural development was rooted in the themes of imperialism and the proletarian revolution, as well as the full affirmation of the significance of the political and cultural struggle against imperialism in modern China. At the same time, Mao believed that in the sense of the worldwide revolution, the national identity that emphasized cultural development was not meant to establish a closed culture of narrow nationalism. On the contrary, the construction of a new culture for the Chinese nation should be open and in sync with the world. The socialist and new democratic culture of other ethnic groups was united to China's own, and a relationship of mutual absorption and development was established to form a new worldwide culture, a revolutionary national culture.

Mao linked national culture with the development of worldwide culture. This height of ideology had a strong foundation and future for the development of China's new democratic culture. In his "The Position of the CPC in the National War," Mao criticized the "separation of the substance and the national form of internationalism, as is the practice of people who do not understand internationalism at all."[109] He believed that Chinese culture should "unify the socialist culture and new democratic culture of an ethnic group, establishing a relationship of mutual absorption and development and jointly forming a new worldwide culture."[110] He advocated "absorbing more new things from other countries, not only their program, but also their fresh ideas," absorbing the necessary ingredients from foreign languages.[111] Mao pointed out, "China should absorb a great deal of foreign progressive culture as raw material for its own cultural sustenance. Such work has not been done nearly enough in the past."[112] Mao held that not only the current socialist and new democratic culture, but also useful parts of the ancient and modern cultures of foreign countries, such as the culture of Enlightenment era in capitalist states, should be absorbed by the present culture. Regarding the new democratic culture as the result of the absorption of the spiritual wealth of China and even the whole of humankind, Mao maintained the dialectical and overall cultural stand of the early Chinese Marxists, making the new Chinese culture truly distinct from Li Dazhao and Chen Duxiu. The exploration of these development issues completed an important part of the historical cultural development of China.

Here, Mao proposed a well-known principle: "Like food, all foreign things must go through the digestive process of chewing and gastrointestinal movements, with the necessary juices released to break it down to its essence, then the waste can be eliminated, while the nutrients are absorbed and nourish the body. But nothing should be absorbed without criticism."[113] This was not only a historical summary of the Chinese revolutionary experience, but also the correct understanding of the direction for development of the new cultural movement after the May 4th Movement. In his article "Opposition to Stereotyped Writing," Mao criticized the formalism of the May 4th Movement, pointing out that many of its leaders did not have an understanding of the critical essence of Marxism, so that the approach they used was generally a formalist, bourgeois approach. "They opposed the old stereotyped writing and the old dogma, and they advocated science and democracy. This was quite right. But they lacked the critical spirit of historical materialism for the status quo, for history, and for foreign things. The so-called bad was an absolute bad, bad through and through, while the so-called good was an absolute good, good through and through. This formalistic approach to problems affected the later development of the movement."[114] Dogmatism and "Westernization" were the right and left extremes of this formalism. Mao specifically mentioned the negative influence of formalism on the Chinese communist movement and the spread of Marxism. He pointed out that the basic principles of Marxism had to be completely and properly unified with the concrete practice of the Chinese revolution. That was to say, "the combination of characteristics, following a certain national form, is useful, but must not be applied subjectively."[115] "Formal Marxism" was undoubtedly a subjective dogmatic form of Marxism, taking "orthodoxy" and "doctrinairism" as its starting point and emerging with a very "leftist" face that caused huge losses to the Chinese revolution. Mao pointed out that the Chinese revolution should oppose "formal Marxism." Similarly, Chinese culture should have its own form, a national form, and "this national form, containing the new democracy, is our new culture today."[116]

In addition, the new democratic culture was scientific. Mao noted, "it is against all feudal and superstitious thoughts, advocating seeking truth from facts, objective truth, and the coherence of theory and practice."[117]

Inheriting the spirit of advocating scientific nationality from the May 4th Movement, Mao pointed out that in the cause opposing imperialist and feudal superstition, the scientific thinking of the Chinese proletariat could have a progressive bourgeois materialist nature in China. Scientists had established a united front to complete the Enlightenment agenda after the May 4th Movement. Here, Mao proposed principles of scientific methodologies to examine historical and cultural heritage. First, he made this judgment on the nature of Chinese history and culture, saying, "In China's long-term feudal society, a splendid culture was created." Thus, when tidying up ancient cultural heritage, it was necessary to "remove its feudalism" and absorb its democratic essence, which was a necessary condition for the development of the new culture of the Chinese nation to enhance its self-confidence. Second, such cleanup work could not be uncritically eclectic. It was necessary to distinguish all the rotting things of the ancient feudal ruling class from the excellent people's culture. In other words, it was necessary to locate what was democratic and revolutionary. Third, history should not be cut, because the new culture in China was developed from the old culture, so it was important to respect one's own history. However, Mao noted, "this sort of respect is to give history a scientific position and respect the development of its dialectics, not to attempt to be both ancient and modern, and not to praise feudal poison."[118] Using Marxist positions, viewpoints, and methods, Mao argued that the May 4th Movement transcended "ancient, modern, Chinese, and Western" culture, successfully addressing the principle and methodology of inheriting cultural traditions. Undoubtedly, this principle was not only the inevitable result of the development of the dialectical and comprehensive cultural stand held by Li Dazhao and other early Chinese Marxists, but also a regular summary of the historical movement of Chinese culture.

Mao believed that creating a new culture could only begin by insisting on starting from practice. In his article "Strategic Issues in the Chinese Revolutionary War," published in December 1936, he stated, "Reading is learning, and practice is also learning, and it is the more important part of learning."[119] This demonstrated his learning methodology. In "Rectifying the Party Style," he issued a call to the whole Party to "learn to apply Marxist-Leninist positions, viewpoints, and methods, seriously study Chinese history, and study China's economy, politics, military, and culture,"[120] because "in mastering Marxist theory, the goal of proficiency is application."[121]

Always a proponent of the advanced nature of the new culture, Mao believed that the progressiveness of its cultural effects was reflected in the fact that culture should represent the direction of social development, represent the interests of the advanced classes, and play a role in promoting social development and progress. In *New Democracy*, he clearly stated, "To turn a China ruled by the old culture, and thus ignorant and backward, into a China that is ruled by the new culture and thus advanced in civilization […] requires that we build a new culture of the Chinese nation. This is our purpose in the cultural field."[122] Because of this, he fully affirmed the great significance of the anti-imperialism and anti-feudalism of the May 4th New Culture Movement, which was completely uncompromising, because it was related to the anti-imperialist, anti-feudal democratic revolutionary task of modern China, a prelude to China's new democratic revolution.

Finally, the new democratic culture was a culture of the masses. Mao pointed out that it should serve more than 90% of the workers and peasants throughout the nation and gradually become their culture. It was necessary to distinguish the educational knowledge of the revolutionary cadres and of the revolutionary masses in terms of degree, helping them connect and enhance one another. This was another vivid manifestation of the Party's ideological line of "seeking truth from facts." On the one hand, cultural construction must serve the fundamental purpose of the revolution. On the other, cultural construction had laid the ideological and cultural foundation for the revolution.

Concerning the direction of cultural construction, the Party emphasized that it was necessary to link democracy with cultural construction, thus reversing the one-sidedness of the cultural movement, making it penetrate deeply into society, particularly among the workers and peasants, and allowing it to become a bottom-up social and cultural revolution. To this end, the Party pointed out that a mass and democratic culture did not mean that all objects were not differentiated, and cultural education was carried out with the same model, method, and content. Mao believed that two differences and connections that should be taken note of were that the educational knowledge of the revolutionary cadres and that of the revolutionary masses should be both distinguished from and connected to one another, and improvement and popularization should be both distinguished from and connected to each other. Mao's thinking on these points was stated clearly in his speech at the Yan'an Forum on Literature and Arts. He held that the premise and foundation of popularization and improvement should be the workers and peasants, because "our literature and art, being basically for the workers, peasants, and soldiers, is for the so-called universal population, that is the popularization among workers, peasants, and soldiers, and for improvement from them."[123] He observed that popularization was the foundation and improved development. He said, "Improvement should be emphasized, but it would be wrong to do so in a one-sided way, or to emphasize it to an inappropriate degree."[124] The mistake would be to ignore the actual ideological and cultural conditions of the Chinese workers and peasants, failing to recognize the task of popularization and improvement. Because "popular things are relatively simple, it is easier for the masses to accept them quickly [...] so under the current conditions, the task of popularizing is more urgent."[125] Mao emphasized that, even though the task of popularization was the more urgent one, it did not mean the work of improvement could be neglected. It was his belief that the two could not be separated. Because popularity needed to be developed, the general culture would continue to improve the ideology and culture of the workers and peasants, and thus it would not be satisfied with simplistic popularization and improvement. Because of this, "the work of popularization is not only a hindrance to improvement, but also a basis for improving the current limited scope of the work, and is also a necessary condition for preparing for a broader range of future work."[126] Mao divided improvement into two types. One was the improvement of the masses, and the other was the improvement of the cadres. The connection between the two types of improvement lay in the people and their degree of education. Therefore, he proposed that literature and art should be "developed from the primary literature and art for the higher levels, so that high-level art will be required for the people's cadres, while inferior art and literature that are guided by such higher level skills will be what is most often needed by the masses now."[127]

The new democratic culture of the masses should also be a powerful weapon for the people's revolution. The Party pointed out that revolutionary culture was the revolutionary ideological preparation before the actual revolution. In the revolution, it was a necessary part of the overall battle line. Revolutionary cultural workers were the commanders at all levels on this cultural front. "Without revolutionary theory, there would be no revolutionary movement." It is evident how important the revolutionary cultural movement was to the practical revolution. Such a cultural and practical movement was of the masses. Thus, all progressive cultural workers needed to have their own cultural army in the War of Resistance Against Japanese Aggression, and this army was the people. If the revolutionary cultural worker did not approach the people, that is, if he were "a commander without soldiers," his firepower would be sufficient to defeat the enemy. In order to achieve this goal, the text must be reformed under certain conditions, so that the words could draw near to the people. The people had to be the infinitely rich source of revolutionary culture.

The establishment of the new democratic cultural program marked the completion of an important theoretical link in the historical process of integrating Marxism into China. It had discovered the basic direction of Chinese cultural development in the clues of the Chinese cultural revolution in modern times, opposing national nihilism. It was also distinguished from narrow nationalism and opposed both the leftist and rightist errors in thought, laying a theoretical foundation for the development of Chinese culture.

NOTES

Chapter 1

1. Liang Qichao. "Travels in Europe." *Collected Works of Yibingshi*. 23rd edition. Zhonghua Book Co., 1989. p. 11–12.
2. Zheng Zhenduo. "Reform Activities in Modern Society." *New Society*. Issue 12. February 11, 1920.
3. "A Red Blush on the Sea." *Min Xing*. Volume 2, Issue 8. January 26, 1920.
4. Zhang Dongsun. "Why We Must Speak of Socialism." *Liberation and Revolution*. Volume 1, Issue 7. December 1919.
5. "Power Struggles and the Beginnings of Struggle." *Min Xing*. Volume 1, Issue 3. December 25, 1919.
6. "A Memo." *The Communist Party*. Issue 1. November 7, 1920.
7. *Marxist Studies* lists the publication date as May 1919, though research indicates that September 1919 is more accurate. See *The Complete Works of Li Dazhao, Volume 3*. People's Publishing House, 2006. p. 353. "*My View of Marxism* textual analysis," *My View of Marxism* Parts 1–7, first published in *New Youth*, Volume 6, Issue 5; Parts 8–11 first published in Volume 6, Issue 6. The publication date of Issue 6 is marked as November 1, 1919.
8. *New Youth*. Volume 7, Issue 6. May 1, 1920.
9. *New Youth*. Volume 8, Issue 1. September 1, 1920.
10. Li Dazhao. "The Value of Material History in Modern History Studies." *New Youth*. Volume 8, Issue 4. December, 1920.
11. Li Dazhao. "Further Thoughts on Issues and Ideology." *Weekly Review*. Issue 35. August 17, 1919.
12. Li Da. "On Socialism and Liang Ren." *New Youth*. Volume 9, Issue 1. May 1, 1921.
13. Li Dazhao. "Chinese Socialism and Global Capitalism." *Critical Theory*. Volume 1, Issue 2. March 20, 1921.
14. Chen Duxiu. "On Socialist Theory." *New Youth*. Volume 8, Issue 4. December 1, 1920.

15. Chen Duxiu. "Socialist Criticism: A Speech at the Guangzhou Public Law School." Published in the *Guangdong Group Newspaper*. January 19, 1921.
16. Cai Hesen. *The History of the Development of the Communist Party of China (Outline)*. See *The Evolution of the First National Congress of the CPC, Volume 3*. People's Publishing House, 1984. p. 61.
17. Compiled by the China Li Dazhao Research Association. *The Complete Works of Li Dazhao, Volume 3*. People's Publishing House, 2006. p. 271.
18. *The Complete Works of Cai Hesen*. People's Publishing House, 1980. p. 51.
19. Müller, Richard. *The Revolutionary Fire*. (Russian edition.) Irkutsk, 1957. p. 144–145.
20. The First Research Department of the CPC Central Party History Research Office. *Communist International, Union (cloth bound) and Chinese Revolutionary Archive Series, Volume 1*. Beijing Book Publishing House, 1997. p. 40.
21. Shevely, K. B. "History of the Communist Party of China." See *The Evolution of the First National Congress of the CPC, Volume 3*. People's Publishing House, 1984. p. 167–168.
22. *China Youth*. Volume 2, Issue 9. March 15, 1921.

Chapter 2

1. Cai Hesen. "The Chinese Revolutionary Movement and International Relations." May 2, 1923.
2. Document Research Center of the CPC Central Committee. *Mao Zedong Chronicles, Volume 1*. Central Leadership Publishing House, 2002. p. 151.
3. Qu Qiubai. *Chinese Communism and Dai Jitao Thought*. August 1925. See the China Archives for the original.
4. Ibid.
5. Ibid.
6. *The Collected Works of Mao Zedong, Volume 1*. People's Publishing House, 1991. p. 4.
7. Ibid, p. 9.
8. "The Current Political Situation in China and the Resolutions of the Communist Party of China." October 1925.
9. Li Dazhao. *Collected Writings of Li Dazhao, Volume 2*. People's Publishing House, 1984. p. 834.
10. Resolution on the Position of the Peasants Movement Within the National Revolution. May 1926.
11. *The Collected Works of Liu Shaoqi, Volume 1*. People's Publishing House, 1981. p. 1.
12. Deng Zhongxia. "Several Important Issues in the Renaissance of the Labor Movement." May 1925.
13. *Workers' Road, Special Issue*. Issue 37, 1925.
14. *Resolution on the Relationship between the Communist Party of China and the Kuomintang*. July 1926.

15. National Revolutionary Army Command. *Political Work Notes*. 1926.
16. Qu Qiubai "The Question of Armed Struggle in the Chinese Revolution. *New Youth*. Issue 4. May 25, 1926.
17. Central Bureau letter to Hubei District. September 26, 1926.
18. Chen Duxiu. "Why are We Fighting Now?" *Guide*. September 23, 1926.
19. *Selected Documents of the CPC Central Committee, Volume 2*. CPC Central Party School Press, 1989. p. 455.
20. *Political Report*. December 13, 1926.
21. Report of the Central Committee of the Communist Party of China to the Entire Membership. August 7, 1927.
22. Compiled by the Document Research Center for the Central Committee of the CPC. *The Chronicles of Mao Zedong, Volume 1*. Central Literature Publishing House, 2002. P. 208.
23. Cai Hesen, "Unification, Lending, and the Kuomintang." *Selected Documents of the CPC Central Committee, Volume 1*. CPC Central Party School Press, 1982. p. 88.
24. Resolution on Land Issues. *Selected Documents of the CPC Central Committee, Volume 4*. CPC Central Party School Press, 1983. p. 196.
25. Circular No. 28 of the Central Committee: A Strategy for Peasant Movements. *Selected Documents of the CPC Central Committee, Volume 5*. CPC Central Party School Press, 1983. p. 13.
26. Su Hua, "The Development of the Chinese Capitalist Economy." *The Chinese Economy*, Volume 1, Issue 6. September 1933.
27. Zhang Wentian. "The Socio-Economic Basis for the Chinese Revolution." The CPC History Press, 1990, p. 479.
28. Compiled by the CPC Central Committee Secretariat. *Before the Sixth National Congress*. People's Publishing House, 1980. p. 902.
29. "Political Resolution of the Sixth National Congress of the Communist Party of China." July 9, 1928.
30. Bo Gu. "On the Current Stage of the Soviet Union's Economic Policy." *Struggle*. Issue 8, April 15, 1933.
31. Qu Qiubai. "A New Path for the Chinese Revolution after the Death of the KMT." *Bolshevik*. Issue 1, January 24, 1927.
32. Qu Qiubai. "A New Strategy for the Proletariat in the Chinese Revolution." *Bolshevik*. Issue 7, December 5, 1927.
33. Cai Hesen. "The Nature of the Chinese Revolution and its Future." *Bolshevik*. Volume 2, Issue 1, November 1, 1928.
34. Ibid.
35. Qu Qiubai. "Marxism or the People's Livelihood?" (Part 2) *Bolshevik*. Issue 14, 1928.
36. Cai Hesen. "The Nature and the Future of the Chinese Revolution." *Bolshevik*. Issue 2, November 1, 1928.

37. Hua Gang. "The Future and Tasks of the Transformation of China's Revolution." *Bolsheviks*. Volume 4, Issue 5, September 10, 1931.
38. Political Resolution of the Sixth National Congress of the Communist Party of China. July 9, 1928.
39. Hua Gang. "The Future and Tasks of the Transformation of China's Revolution." *Bolshevik*. Volume 4, Issue 5, September 10, 1931.
40. The Current Situation in China and the Resolutions of the Communist Party. November 1927.
41. Qu Qiubai. "What Kind of Revolution is the Chinese Revolution?" *Bolshevik*. Issue 5, 1927.
42. "Communist International Resolution on China." *Bolshevik*. Issue 24, July 25, 1928.
43. Cai Hesen. "The Nature and Future of the Chinese Revolution." *Bolshevik*. Volume 2, Issue 1, November 1, 1928.
44. Communique of the CPC Central Committee Politburo on the Communist International Resolutions. April 30, 1928.
45. Editorial: "China's Soviet Power and Socialism." *Bolshevik*. Issue 14, 1928.
46. "Resolution on the Current Situation in China and the Party's Task." November 9, 1927.
47. Letter from the Central Committee to Hubei Province. September 24, 1928.
48. Letter from the CPC Central Committee to the Northeastern Bureau. August 10, 1929.

Chapter 3

1. *Selected Works of Mao Zedong, Volume 2*. People's Publishing House, 1991. p. 533.
2. Ibid.
3. Ibid.
4. *Selected Works of Mao Zedong, Volume 2*. People's Publishing House, 1991. p. 534.
5. *Selected Works of the Central Committee of the CPC, Volume 10*. CPC Central Party School Press, 1989. p. 702.
6. Ye Qing. "On Political Parties." *Mopping-up Operation*. January 22, 1938.
7. Chiang Kai-shek. "The System of the Three People's Principles and its Procedures." May 7, 1939.
8. *Selected Works of Mao Zedong, Volume 2*. People's Publishing House, 1991. p. 558.
9. Ibid, p. 559.
10. Ibid, p. 563.
11. Ibid, p. 563.
12. *Selected Works of Mao Zedong, Volume 2*. People's Publishing House, 1991. p. 647.
13. Ibid.
14. Ibid.
15. *Selected Works of Mao Zedong, Volume 2*. People's Publishing House, 1991. p. 663.
16. Ibid, p. 707.

17. Ibid, p. 686.
18. *Selected Works of Mao Zedong, Volume 2*. People's Publishing House, 1991. p. 686.
19. Ibid, p. 613.
20. Ibid, p. 605–606.
21. *Selected Works of Mao Zedong, Volume 2*. People's Publishing House, 1991. p. 762.
22. Ibid, p. 763.
23. *Selected Works of Mao Zedong, Volume 2*. People's Publishing House, 1991. p. 764.
24. Ibid, p. 769.
25. Central Literature Research Office, ed. *Mao Zedong's Writings Since the Founding of the People's Republic of China, Volume 10*. Central Literature Publishing House, 1996. p. 29.
26. *Selected Works of Mao Zedong, Volume 2*. People's Publishing House, 1991. p. 636.
27. *Selected Works of Mao Zedong, Volume 4*. People's Publishing House, 1991. p. 1245.
28. Ibid, p. 1244.
29. *Selected Works of Mao Zedong, Volume 4*, People's Publishing House, 1991. p. 1472.
30. *Selected Works of Mao Zedong, Volume 4*. People's Publishing House, 1991. p. 1480.

Chapter 4

1. *Selected Works of Mao Zedong, Volume 2*. People's Publishing House, 1991. p. 633.
2. *Selected Works of Mao Zedong, Volume 2*. People's Publishing House, 1991. p. 665.
3. Ibid, p. 630.
4. Ibid, p. 626.
5. *Selected Works of Mao Zedong, Volume 1*. People's Publishing House, 1991. p. 188.
6. *Selected Works of Mao Zedong, Volume 2*. People's Publishing House, 1991. p. 630.
7. *Selected Works of Mao Zedong, Volume 2*. People's Publishing House, 1991. p. 666.
8. *Selected Works of the Central Committee of the CPC, Volume 1*. CPC Central Party School Press, 1989. p. 115
9. Ibid.
10. Ibid.
11. *Selected Works of the Central Committee of the CPC, Volume 1*. Central Party School Press. 1989. p. 333.
12. Ibid, p. 337.
13. *Selected Works of The Central Committee of The CPC, Volume 2*. Central Party School Press, 1989. p. 671–672.
14. Ibid, p. 672.
15. *Selected Works of The Central Committee of the CPC, Volume 3*. Central Party School Press, 1989. p. 19–20.
16. Ibid, p. 21.
17. Ibid, p. 21–22.
18. *Selected Works of Mao Zedong, Volume 1*. People's Publishing House, 1991. p. 77.

19. Ibid, p. 130.
20. *Selected Works of Mao Zedong, Volume 2*. People's Publishing House, 1991. p. 668.
21. *Selected Works of Stalin, Volume 1*. People's Publishing House, 1979. p. 126.
22. Ibid, p. 673.
23. Ibid, p. 673–674.
24. *Selected Works of Mao Zedong, Volume 2*. People's Publishing House, 1991. p. 674.
25. Ibid, p. 672–673.
26. Ibid, p. 674.
27. *Selected Works of Mao Zedong, Volume 1*. People's Publishing House, 1991. p. 276.
28. Ibid.

Chapter 5

1. Translator's note: i.e. Before starting another proletariat revolution, a bourgeois dictatorship and a period of capitalist economic growth were needed after the victory of the national revolution.
2. *Selected Works of Mao Zedong, Volume 2*. People's Publishing House, 1991. p. 647.
3. *Selected Works of Mao Zedong, Volume 4*. People's Publishing House, 1991. p. 1313.
4. *Selected Works of Mao Zedong, Volume 2*. Central Literature Publishing House, 2002. p. 502.
5. *Selected Works of Mao Zedong, Volume 3*. People's Publishing House, 1991. p. 1079.
6. *Selected Works of Mao Zedong, Volume 2*. People's Publishing House, 1991. p. 645.
7. Ibid.
8. *Selected Works of Mao Zedong, Volume 2*. People's Publishing House, 1991. p. 641.
9. Ibid, p. 147.
10. *Selected Works of Mao Zedong, Volume 2*. People's Publishing House, 1991. p. 106.

Chapter 6

1. *Selected Works of Mao Zedong, Volume 2*. People's Publishing House, 1991. p. 635.
2. Letter from the Hunan Provincial Party Committee. August 30, 1927.
3. Letter from the Central Committee of the CPC to the Guangdong Provincial Party Committee. December 18, 1927.
4. *Selected Works of the Central Committee of the CPC, Volume 4*. CPC Central Party School Press, 1989. p. 757–763.
5. Directive from the Central Committee to the Northeast Special Commission. July 14, 1928.
6. Directive from the Central Committee to the Shaanxi Provincial Party Committee. October 10, 1929.

NOTES 557

7. *Selected Works of the Central Committee of the CPC, Volume 6*. CPC Central Party School Press, 1983. p. 17 and 21.
8. Resolution on the Current Political Mission. Adopted by the Politburo Meeting on June 11, 1930.
9. Directive of the Central Party for the Red Army in Soviet Areas. June 16, 1931.
10. Telegram from the Central Committee of the CPC to the Communist International Reporting its Win Over a Province as a Moral Victory and Regarding the Misunderstanding of Four Aspects of Military Power. November 8, 1935.
11. *Selected Works of Mao Zedong, Volume 1*. People's Publishing House, 1991. p. 152.
12. *Selected Works of the Central Committee of the CPC, Volume 3*. Central Party School Press, 1989. p. 439.
13. "The Significance of and Lessons from the Guangzhou Riot." January 3, 1928.
14. Letter from the Central Committee of the CPC to the Hunan Provincial Party Committee. Early January 1928.
15. Letter from the Central Committee of the CPC to the Hunan Provincial Party Committee. February 18, 1928.
16. Letter from the Central Committee of the CPC to the Fujian Provincial Party Committee. May 7, 1928.
17. *Chronicle of Mao Zedong, Volume 1*. Central Literature Publishing House, 2002. p. 204.
18. Ibid, p. 205.
19. *Chronicle of Mao Zedong, Volume 1*. Central Literature Publishing House, 2002. p. 208.
20. Ibid, p. 209.
21. Ibid.
22. *Chronicle of Mao Zedong, Volume 1*. Central Literature Publishing House, 2002. p. 210.
23. The Report to Hunan Provincial Committee from CPC Special Committee for Hunan-Jiangxi border and Fourth Red Army Military Committee, July 4, 1928.
24. *Selected Works of Mao Zedong, Volume 1*. People's Publishing House, 1991. p. 48–49.
25. *Selected Works of Mao Zedong, Volume 1*. People's Publishing House, 1991. p. 49.
26. Ibid, p. 50.
27. Ibid.
28. *Selected Works of Mao Zedong, Volume 1*. People's Publishing House, 1991. p. 97.
29. Ibid, p. 97–98.
30. *Selected Works of Mao Zedong, Volume 1*. People's Publishing House, 1991. p. 98–99.
31. *Selected Works of Mao Zedong, Volume 1*. People's Publishing House, 1991. p. 115.
32. Ibid, p. 109.
33. *Selected Works of Mao Zedong, Volume 1*. People's Publishing House, 1991. p. 189.
34. *Selected Works of Mao Zedong, Volume 2*. People's Publishing House, 1991. p. 635.
35. Ibid, p. 635–636.
36. See *Selected Works of Mao Zedong, Volume 2*. People's Publishing House, 1991. p. 542–543.
37. *Basic Issues in Mao Zedong Thought*. CPC Central Party School Press, 2001. p. 46–47.
38. *Selected Works of Mao Zedong, Volume 1*. People's Publishing House, 1991. p. 71–72.

39. Ibid, p. 72.
40. *Selected Works of Mao Zedong, Volume 1*. People's Publishing House, 1991. p. 73.
41. *Selected Works of Mao Zedong, Volume 1*. People's Publishing House, 1991. p. 139.
42. Ibid, p. 140.
43. *Selected Works of Mao Zedong, Volume 1*. People's Publishing House, 1991. p. 53.
44. Ibid, p. 119.
45. *Selected Works of Mao Zedong, Volume 1*. People's Publishing House, 1991. p. 123.
46. Ibid, p. 140.
47. *Selected Works of Mao Zedong, Volume 1*. People's Publishing House, 1991. p. 131.
48. Ibid, p. 134.
49. People's Education Publishing House, ed. *Comrade Mao Zedong's Education Work*. People's Education Press, 2000. p. 7.
50. Jiangxi Provincial Archives and Party School of the Jiangxi Provincial Committee of the CPC. *Selected Works of The Central Revolutionary Bases, Volume 2*. Jiangxi People's Publishing House, 1982. p. 331.
51. *Selected Works of Mao Zedong, Volume 2*. People's Publishing House, 1991. p. 742.
52. Ibid, p. 750–751.
53. *Selected Works of Mao Zedong, Volume 3*. People's Publishing House, 1991. P. 809.
54. Ibid.
55. *Selected Works of Deng Xiaoping, Volume 1*. People's Publishing House, 1994. p. 9.
56. United Front Work Department of the Yan'an Land Committee and the Yan'an Revolutionary Memorial Hall. *Selected Materials of Li Dingming*. Shaanxi People's Publishing House, 1980. p. 124.
57. *Selected Works of Mao Zedong, Volume 3*. People's Publishing House, 1991. p. 895.
58. *Selected Works of Mao Zedong, Volume 3*. People's Publishing House, 1991. p. 891.
59. Mao Zedong. *Economic and Financial Issues*. Liberation Society, 1944.
60. Mao Zedong. "On the New Stage of the Anti-Japanese National War and the Anti-Japanese United Front." Report to the Sixth Plenary Session of the Expanded Meeting of the CPC, October 12–14, 1938. *Liberation Society*, 1942.
61. *Selected Works of Mao Zedong, Volume 2*. People's Publishing House, 1991. p. 618.
62. Ibid, p. 768.
63. *Selected Works of Mao Zedong, Volume 2*. People's Publishing House, 1991. p. 708.
64. Central Archives. *Selected Works of the Central Committee of the Communist Party of China, Volume 11*. CPC Central Party School Press, 1989. p. 488.

Chapter 7

1. Chen Duxiu. "Revolution and Counter-Revolution." *Guide*. Issue 16.
2. Qu Quibai. "The Controversy of the Chinese Revolution." *Before the Sixth National Congress*. People's Publishing House, 1980. p. 674.

3. Peng Shuzhi. "The Fundamental Problem of the Chinese Revolution." *Before the Sixth National Congress*. People's Publishing House, 1980. p. 770.
4. Ibid.
5. "The CPC's First Proposal for the Current Situation." *Before the Sixth National Congress*. People's Publishing House, 1980.
6. Cai Hesen. "Unification, Debt, and the Kuomintang." *Guide*. Issue 1.
7. Cai Hesen. "Grounds on which Sun and Wu Can Unite." *Guide*. Issue 4.
8. Qu Qiubai. "The National Convention and the May 4th Movement." *New Youth*. Issue 3.
9. Qu Qiubai. "The Controversy of the Chinese Revolution." *Before the Sixth National Congress*. People's Publishing House, 1980. p. 675.
10. Translator's note: pen name of Hendricus Sneevliet.
11. Chen Duxiu. "Chinese National Revolution and Social Classes." *Forward*. Issue 2.
12. Chen Duxiu. "The KMT and the Labor Movement." *Guide*. Issue 71.
13. Deng Zhongxia. "Our Strength." *The Chinese Worker*. Issue 2.
14. Peng Shuzhi. "Who is the Leader of the National Revolution?" *New Youth*. Issue 4.
15. *Communist International Literature on the Chinese Revolution, Volume 1*. China Social Sciences Press, 1981. p. 327.
16. Ibid, p. 283.
17. *Communist International Literature on the Chinese Revolution, Volume 1*. Chinese Social Sciences Press, 1981. p. 186.
18. Ibid, p. 328.
19. *Selected Works of the Central Committee of the CPC, Volume 10*. Central Party School Press, 1989. p. 604.
20. Ibid, p. 606.
21. *Selected Works of Mao Zedong, Volume 2*. People's Publishing House, 1991. p. 157.
22. Central United Front Work Department and Central Committee Archives. *Selected Works of the Central Committee Regarding the Anti-Japanese National United Front, Volume 2*. Archive Press, 1985. p. 130.
23. Central United Front Work Department and Central Committee Archives. *Selected Works of the Central Committee Regarding the Anti-Japanese National United Front, Volume 2*. Archive Press, 1985. p. 251–252.
24. *Selected Works of Mao Zedong, Volume 1*. People's Publishing House, 1991. p. 262.
25. Ibid, p. 262–263.
26. Ibid, p. 246.
27. *Selected Works of Mao Zedong, Volume 2*. People's Publishing House, 1991. p. 378–379.
28. Ibid, p. 394.
29. *Selected Works of Mao Zedong, Volume 2*. People's Publishing House, 1991. p. 540.
30. Ibid, p. 151.
31. *Selected Works of Mao Zedong, Volume 1*. People's Publishing House, 1991. p. 253.
32. *Selected Works of Mao Zedong, Volume 2*. People's Publishing House, 1991. p. 539.
33. Ibid, p. 640.

34. Ibid, p. 639.
35. *Selected Works of Mao Zedong, Volume 2*. People's Publishing House, 1991. p. 765.
36. *Chronicle of Mao Zedong, Volume 2*. Central Literature Publishing House, 2002. p. 127.
37. *Selected Works of Mao Zedong, Volume 2*. People's Publishing House, 1991. p. 745.
38. *Chronicle of Mao Zedong, Volume 2*. Central Literature Publishing House, 2002. p. 198.
39. *Selected Works of Mao Zedong, Volume 2*. People's Publishing House, 1991. p. 749.
40. *Selected Works of Mao Zedong, Volume 2*. People's Publishing House, 1991. p. 745.
41. Ibid, p. 746.
42. Ibid, p. 783.
43. Ibid, p. 748.
44. *Selected Works of Mao Zedong, Volume 1*. People's Publishing House, 1991. p. 148.
45. *Selected Works of Mao Zedong, Volume 2*. People's Publishing House, 1991. p. 763.
46. *Selected Works of Mao Zedong, Volume 5*. People's Publishing House, 1977. p. 308–309.
47. *Selected Works of Mao Zedong, Volume 4*. People's Publishing House, 1991. p. 1231.
48. Ibid, p. 1257.
49. *Selected Works of Mao Zedong, Volume 4*. People's Publishing House, 1991. p. 1256.
50. Ibid, p. 1253.
51. *Selected Works of Mao Zedong, Volume 4*. People's Publishing House, 1991. p. 1254.
52. Ibid.
53. *Selected Works of Mao Zedong, Volume 2*. People's Publishing House, 1991. p. 639.
54. *Selected Works of Mao Zedong, Volume 2*. People's Publishing House, 1991. p. 1226.
55. *Selected Works of Mao Zedong, Volume 4*. People's Publishing House, 1991. p. 1316–1317.
56. *Selected Works of Mao Zedong, Volume 1*. People's Publishing House, 1991. p. 148.
57. *Selected Works of Mao Zedong, Volume 4*. People's Publishing House, 1991. p. 1188.
58. Ibid, p. 1174–1175.
59. *Selected Works of Zhou Enlai, Volume 1*. People's Publishing House, 1990. p. 286.
60. *Chronicle of Mao Zedong, Volume 3*. Central Literature Publishing House, 2002. p. 78.
61. Ibid.
62. *Selected Works of Liu Shaoqi, Volume 1*. People's Publishing House, 1981. p. 378.
63. Resolution of the Central Committee of the Communist Party of China on the Promulgation of the Outline of the Chinese Land Law. October 10, 1947.
64. The Outline of The Chinese Land Law. Adopted by The Communist Party of China National Land Conference, September 13, 1947.
65. *Selected Works of Mao Zedong, Volume 4*. People's Publishing House, 1991. p. 1250–1251.
66. Ibid, p. 1252.
67. *Selected Works of Zhou Enlai, Volume 1*. People's Publishing House, 1980. p. 286.
68. *Selected Works of Mao Zedong, Volume 4*. People's Publishing House, 1991. p. 1289.
69. Ibid, p. 1288.
70. *Selected Works of Mao Zedong, Volume 4*. People's Publishing House, 1991. p. 1326.
71. *Selected Works of Mao Zedong, Volume 4*. People's Publishing House, 1991. p. 1326.
72. Ibid, p. 1314.

73. *Selected Works of Mao Zedong, Volume 4*. People's Publishing House, 1991. p. 1326.
74. Ibid, p. 1211.
75. *Selected Works of Zhou Enlai, Volume 1*. People's Publishing House, 1980. p. 269.
76. Ibid, p. 270.
77. *Selected Works of Zhou Enlai, Volume 1*. People's Publishing House, 1989. p. 271.
78. *Selected Works of Mao Zedong, Volume 4*. People's Publishing House, 1991. p. 1225.
79. Ibid, p. 1224–1225.
80. "Seven Documents of the CPC Central Committee on the May 20th Patriotic and Democratic Movement." *Literature and Research*, Issue 2, 1985.
81. *Selected Works of Zhou Enlai, Volume 1*. People's Publishing House, 1980. p. 270.
82. Ibid.
83. "Seven Documents of the CPC Central Committee on the May 20th Patriotic and Democratic Movement." *Literature and Research*, Issue 2, 1985.
84. Central United Front Work Department and Central Archives. *Selected Works of the United Front of the CPC Central Committee During the War of Liberation*. Archive Press, 1988. p. 195.
85. Selections from the Birth of the Chinese People's Consultative Conference. *Five Stars on the Red Flag Rising*. Literature and History Information Publishing House, 1984. p. 151.
86. CPC Central Party School History, Teaching and Research Division. *Selected Works from the Chinese Democratic Party History*. (New Democratic Revolutionary Period.) p. 89–90.
87. Central Literature Research office of the CPC. *Chronicle of Mao Zedong, Volume 3*. People's Publishing House, 2002. p. 575.
88. *Selected Works of Mao Zedong, Volume 4*. People's Publishing House, 1991. p. 1273.
89. Ibid.
90. Ibid.
91. *Selected Works of Mao Zedong, Volume 4*. People's Publishing House, 1991. p. 1254.
92. Ibid, p. 1254–1255.
93. Ibid, p. 1289.
94. *Selected Works of Mao Zedong, Volume 4*. People's Publishing House, 1991. p. 1285.

Chapter 8

1. *Selected Works of Mao Zedong, Volume 2*. People's Publishing House, 1991. p. 544.
2. Zhou Enlai. "Evaluating Hu Shih's Efforts." *Youth*, Issue 6. December 15, 1922.
3. Central Literature Research Office of the CPC and PLA Academy of Military Sciences. *Selected Military Works of Zhou Enlai, Volume 1*. People's Publishing House, 1997. p. 7.
4. *Selected Works of Mao Zedong, Volume 2*. People's Publishing House, 1991. p. 542.
5. Ibid.
6. Ibid, p. 541.
7. Ibid, p. 543.

8. Ibid, p. 544.
9. *Selected Works of Mao Zedong, Volume 1*. People's Publishing House, 1991. p. 98.
10. *Selected Works of Mao Zedong, Volume 2*. People's Publishing House, 1991. p. 637.
11. *Selected Work of Mao Zedong, Volume 4*. People's Publishing House, 1991. p. 1185.
12. Ibid, p. 1161.
13. *Selected Works of Mao Zedong, Volume 2*. People's Publishing House, 1991. p. 543.
14. *Selected Works of Stalin, Volume 1*. People's Publishing House, 1979. p. 487.
15. *Selected Works of Mao Zedong, Volume 2*. People's Publishing House, 1991. p. 604.
16. Ibid, p. 544.
17. *Selected Works of Mao Zedong, Volume 2*. People's Publishing House, 1991. p. 610.
18. Ibid, p. 547.
19. Ibid, p. 612.
20. *Selected Works of Mao Zedong, Volume 2*. People's Publishing House, 1991. p. 609–610.
21. *Selected Works of Mao Zedong, Volume 2*. People's Publishing House, 1991. p. 636.
22. Zhu De. "The People's Liberation Army's People's War." *People's Daily*. August 1, 1958.
23. *Selected Works of Mao Zedong, Volume 2*. People's Publishing House, 1991. p. 625.
24. "Statement of Support for the Righteous Struggle of American Blacks Against American Imperialist Racial Discrimination." (August 8, 1963). *The People of the World Unite to Defeat the American Aggressors and All their Running Dogs*. People's Publishing House, 1964. p. 4.
25. *Selected Works of Mao Zedong, Volume 2*. People's Publishing House, 1991. p. 474.
26. *Selected Works of Mao Zedong, Volume 2*. People's Publishing House, 1991. p. 171.
27. *Selected Works of Lenin, Volume 3*. People's Publishing House, 1995. p. 672.
28. *Selected Works of Mao Zedong, Volume 2*. People's Publishing House, 1991. p. 547.
29. *Selected Works of Mao Zedong, Volume 3*. People's Publishing House, 1991. p. 1024.
30. *Selected Works of Mao Zedong, Volume 1*. People's Publishing House, 1991. p. 119–120.
31. Mao Zedong. "On the Tenth National Congress." *People's Daily*. December 26, 1976.
32. *Selected Works of Mao Zedong, Volume 1*. People's Publishing House, 1991. p. 178.
33. *Selected Works of Mao Zedong, Volume 1*. People's Publishing House, 1991. p. 182.
34. *Selected Works of Mao Zedong, Volume 1*. People's Publishing House, 1991. p. 179.
35. *Selected Works of Mao Zedong, Volume 3*. People's Publishing House, 1991. p. 1039.
36. *Selected Works of Mao Zedong, Volume 2*. People's Publishing House, 1991. p. 668.
37. *Selected Works of Mao Zedong, Volume 1*. People's Publishing House, 1991. p. 86.
38. Ibid.
39. *Selected Works of Mao Zedong, Volume 3*. People's Publishing House, 1991. p. 1039.
40. Ibid, p. 1106.
41. Ibid, p. 1107.
42. *Selected Works of Mao Zedong, Volume 3*. People's Publishing House, 1991. p. 929.
43. *Selected Works of Mao Zedong, Volume 4*. People's Publishing House, 1991. p. 1426.
44. Ibid.

NOTES 563

45. CPC Central Literature Research Office. *Chronicle of Mao Zedong, Volume 2*. Central Literature Publishing House, 2002. p. 402.
46. *Selected Works of Mao Zedong, Volume 1*. People's Publishing House, 1991. p. 184.
47. *Selected Works of Mao Zedong, Volume 2*. People's Publishing House, 1991. p. 393.
48. Ibid, p. 547.
49. *Selected Works of Mao Zedong, Volume 4*. People's Publishing House, 1991. p. 1239.
50. CPC Central Literature Research Center. *Chronicle of Mao Zedong, Volume 2*. Central Literature Publishing House, 2002. p. 506–507.
51. *Selected Works of Mao Zedong, Volume 4*. People's Publishing House, 1991. p. 1248.
52. *Selected Works of Mao Zedong, Volume 1*. People's Publishing House, 1991. p. 379.
53. *Selected Works of Mao Zedong, Volume 1*. People's Publishing House, 1991. p. 379.
54. Ibid, p. 65.
55. *Selected Works of Mao Zedong, Volume 2*. People's Publishing House, 1991. p. 511.
56. *Selected Works of Mao Zedong, Volume 2*. People's Publishing House, 1991. p. 512.
57. Ibid, p. 379.
58. *Selected Works of Mao Zedong, Volume 3*. People's Publishing House, 1991. p. 1039.
59. *Selected Works of Mao Zedong, Volume 2*. People's Publishing House, 1991. p. 501.
60. *Selected Works of Mao Zedong, Volume 4*. People's Publishing House, 1991. p. 1275.
61. *Selected Works of Mao Zedong, Volume 3*. People's Publishing House, 1991. p. 1031.
62. *Selected Works of Mao Zedong, Volume 1*. People's Publishing House, 1991. p. 139.
63. *Selected Works of Mao Zedong, Volume 2*. People's Publishing House, 1991. p. 511–512.
64. *Selected Works of Mao Zedong, Volume 3*. People's Publishing House, 1991. p. 1096.
65. *Selected Works of Mao Zedong, Volume 2*. People's Publishing House, 1991. p. 481.
66. *Selected Works of Mao Zedong, Volume 2*. People's Publishing House, 1991. p. 634.
67. Ibid, p. 635.
68. *Selected Works of Mao Zedong, Volume 2*. People's Publishing House, 1991. p. 418.
69. *Selected Works of Mao Zedong, Volume 1*. People's Publishing House, 1991. p. 190.
70. Ibid, p. 57.
71. *Selected Works of Mao Zedong, Volume 3*. People's Publishing House, 1991. p. 1040.
72. *Selected Works of Mao Zedong, Volume 1*. People's Publishing House, 1991. p. 227.
73. *Selected Works of Mao Zedong, Volume 3*. People's Publishing House, 1991. p. 1040.
74. *Selected Works of Mao Zedong, Volume 1*. People's Publishing House, 1991. p. 50.
75. Ibid, p. 79.
76. *Selected Works of Mao Zedong, Volume 3*. People's Publishing House, 1991. p. 1041.
77. Ibid.
78. *Selected Works of Mao Zedong, Volume 1*. People's Publishing House, 1991. p. 198.
79. Translator's note: In Chinese, the slogans used to advocate these principles were sixteen characters long.
80. *Selected Works of Mao Zedong, Volume 4*. People's Publishing House, 1991. p. 1199.
81. Ibid, p. 1197.
82. *Selected Works of Mao Zedong, Volume 2*. People's Publishing House, 1991. p. 501.

83. Interview with Wang Gongda, reporter with Tonghe Publishing. February, 1938. *Liberation*, Issue 32.
84. *Selected Works of Mao Zedong, Volume 3*. People's Publishing House, 1991. p. 984.
85. *Selected Works of Mao Zedong, Volume 1*. People's Publishing House, 1991. p. 67.
86. Ibid, p. 224.
87. Ibid, p. 491.
88. *Selected Works of Mao Zedong, Volume 4*. People's Publishing House, 1991. p. 1198–1199.
89. Ibid, p. 1247.
90. Ibid.
91. *Selected Works of Mao Zedong, Volume 4*. People's Publishing House, 1991. p. 1187.
92. *Selected Works of Mao Zedong, Volume 1*. People's Publishing House, 1991. p. 237.
93. *Selected Works of Mao Zedong, Volume 2*. People's Publishing House, 1991. p. 501.
94. *Selected Works of Mao Zedong, Volume 1*. People's Publishing House, 1991. p. 225.
95. Military Academy of the Chinese People's Liberation Army. *Liu Bocheng's Selected Military Works*. People's Liberation Army Press, 1992. p. 61.
96. *Selected Works of Mao Zedong, Volume 4*. People's Publishing House, 1991. p. 1197.
97. Ibid, p. 1198.
98. Ibid, p. 1247.
99. *Selected Works of Mao Zedong, Volume 1*. People's Publishing House, 1991. p. 227.
100. *Selected Works of Mao Zedong, Volume 1*. People's Publishing House, 1991. p. 237.
101. *Selected Works of Mao Zedong, Volume 1*. People's Publishing House, 1991. p. 214.
102. Ibid, p. 215.
103. *Selected Works of Mao Zedong, Volume 4*. People's Publishing House, 1991. p. 1337.
104. Ibid, p. 1364.
105. Ibid, p. 1365.

Chapter 9

1. *Selected Works of Liu Shaoqi, Volume 1*. People's Publishing House, 1981. p. 182.
2. *Selected Works of Lenin, Volume 1*. People's Publishing House, 1995. p. 237.
3. Ibid, p. 312.
4. *Selected Works of Lenin, Volume 1*. People's Publishing House, 1995. p. 510.
5. *Selected Works of Mao Zedong, Volume 1*. People's Publishing House, 1991. p. 77.
6. *Selected Works of Karl Marx, Volume 1*. People's Publishing House, 1995. p. 9.
7. Ibid, p. 246.
8. *Selected Works of Marx and Engels, Volume 2*. People's Publishing House, 1995. p. 118.
9. *Selected Works of Marx and Engels, Volume 1*. People's Publishing House, 1995. p. 293.
10. *The Complete Works of Marx and Engels, Volume 19*. People's Publishing House, 1982. p. 189.
11. *Selected Works of Lenin, Volume 1*. People's Publishing House, 1995. p. 312.
12. *The Complete Works of Lenin, Volume 6*. People's Publishing House, 1984. p. 367.

13. *The Complete Works of Lenin, Volume 39*. People's Publishing House, 1985. p. 246.
14. *The Complete Works of Lenin, Volume 13*. People's Publishing House, 1985. p. 443.
15. *Selected Works of Mao Zedong, Volume 1*. People's Publishing House, 1991. p. 74.
16. Ibid, p. 77.
17. *Selected Works of Mao Zedong, Volume 2*. People's Publishing House, 1991. p. 532–533.
18. *Selected Works of Liu Shaoqi, Volume 1*. People's Publishing House, 1981. p. 327.
19. *Selected Works of Zhou Enlai, Volume 1*. People's Publishing House, 1980. p. 8–9.
20. *Selected Works of Mao Zedong, Volume 1*. People's Publishing House, 1991. p. 85.
21. *Chronicle of Mao Zedong, Volume 1*. People's Publishing House, 1993. p. 94.
22. *Selected Works of Mao Zedong, Volume 2*. People's Publishing House, 1991. p. 533.
23. *Selected Works of Mao Zedong, Volume 1*. People's Publishing House, 1991. p. 90.
24. *Selected Works of Mao Zedong, Volume 3*. People's Publishing House, 1991. p. 899.
25. *Selected Works of Mao Zedong, Volume 1*. People's Publishing House, 1991. p. 112.
26. Ibid, p. 111–112.
27. *Selected Works of Mao Zedong, Volume 1*. People's Publishing House, 1991. p. 182.
28. *Selected Works of Mao Zedong, Volume 3*. People's Publishing House, 1991. p. 820.
29. Ibid, p. 815.
30. Ibid, p. 820.
31. Ibid, p. 789–790.
32. *Selected Works of Mao Zedong, Volume 3*. People's Publishing House, 1991. p. 790.
33. *The Complete Works of Lenin, Volume 8*. People's Publishing House, 1986. p. 415.
34. *Selected Works of Karl Marx, Volume 4*. People's Publishing House, 1995. p. 628.
35. *Selected Works of Mao Zedong, Volume 1*. People's Publishing House, 1991. p. 278.
36. *Selected Works of Mao Zedong, Volume 2*. People's Publishing House, 1991. p. 529.
37. *Selected Works of Mao Zedong, Volume 2*. People's Publishing House, 1991. p. 528–529.
38. Ibid, p. 529.
39. *Selected Works of Liu Shaoqi, Volume 1*. People's Publishing House, 1981. p. 358.
40. *Selected Works of Mao Zedong, Volume 2*. People's Publishing House, 1991. p. 536.
41. Ibid, p. 526.
42. *Selected Works of Mao Zedong, Volume 2*. People's Publishing House, 1991. p. 898–899.
43. *Selected Works of Mao Zedong, Volume 1*. People's Publishing House, 1991. p. 125.
44. *Selected Works of Mao Zedong, Volume 2*. People's Publishing House, 1991. p. 527.
45. Ibid.
46. Ibid.
47. *Selected Works of Mao Zedong, Volume 1*. People's Publishing House, 1991. p. 125.
48. *Selected Works of Mao Zedong, Volume 2*. People's Publishing House, 1991. p. 527.
49. *Selected Works of Mao Zedong, Volume 3*. People's Publishing House, 1991. p. 898.
50. Ibid.
51. *Selected Works of Mao Zedong, Volume 1*. People's Publishing House, 1991. p. 181.
52. *Selected Works of Mao Zedong, Volume 2*. People's Publishing House, 1991. p. 527.
53. *Selected Works of Mao Zedong, Volume 1*. People's Publishing House, 1991. p. 212.

54. *Selected Works of Mao Zedong, Volume 2*. People's Publishing House, 1991. p. 534.
55. *Selected Works of Mao Zedong, Volume 3*. People's Publishing House, 1991. p. 802.
56. *Selected Works of Mao Zedong, Volume 2*. People's Publishing House, 1991. p. 527.
57. Ibid.
58. Ibid, p. 527–528.
59. Ibid, p. 528.
60. *Selected Works of Mao Zedong, Volume 3*. People's Publishing House, 1991. p. 824.
61. Ibid, p. 938.
62. Ibid, p. 828.
63. *Selected Works of Mao Zedong, Volume 2*. People's Publishing House, 1991. p. 383.
64. *Selected Works of the Central Committee of the CPC, Volume 12*. CPC Central Party School Press, 1989. p. 73.
65. *Selected Works of Mao Zedong, Volume 2*. People's Publishing House, 1991. p. 529.
66. *Selected Works of Liu Shaoqi, Volume 1*. People's Publishing House, 1981. p. 361.
67. *Selected Works of Mao Zedong, Volume 2*. People's Publishing House, 1991. p. 524.
68. Ibid, p. 521.
69. Ibid, p. 522.
70. Ibid, p. 523.
71. Editorial Board of the CPC Central Committee. *Selected Works of Chen Yunwen (1926–1999)*. People's Publishing House, 1989. p. 72.
72. Ibid, p. 73.
73. Editorial Board of the CPC Central Committee, *After the Sixth National Congress (Volume 2)*. People's Publishing House, 1981. p. 242.
74. Ibid, p. 214.
75. CPC Central Committee. "Instructions on Managing Party Schools." February 15, 1940.
76. *Selected Works of Mao Zedong, Volume 4*. People's Publishing House, 1991. p. 1161.
77. Ibid, p. 1162.
78. Ibid, p. 1163.
79. Editorial Board of the CPC Central Committee. *Selected Works of Chen Yun (1926–1999)*. People's Publishing House, 1989. p. 227.
80. Ibid, p. 239.
81. Ibid, p. 242–243.
82. *Selected Works of Mao Zedong, Volume 4*. People's Publishing House, 1991. p. 1341.
83. *Selected Works of Mao Zedong, Volume 4*. People's Publishing House, 1991. p. 1438.
84. Ibid.
85. *Selected Works of Mao Zedong, Volume 3*. People's Publishing House, 1991. p. 811.
86. *Selected Works of Mao Zedong, Volume 3*. People's Publishing House, 1991. p. 811.
87. *Selected Works of Mao Zedong, Volume 3*. People's Publishing House, 1991. p. 802.
88. *Selected Works of Mao Zedong, Volume 4*. People's Publishing House, 1991. p. 1252.
89. *Selected Works of Mao Zedong, Volume 3*. People's Publishing House, 1991. p. 797.
90. Ibid, p. 814.

91. Ibid, p. 801.
92. *Selected Works of Mao Zedong, Volume 3*. People's Publishing House, 1991. p. 800.
93. *Selected Works of Mao Zedong, Volume 2*. People's Publishing House, 1991. p. 534.
94. *Selected Works of Mao Zedong, Volume 3*. People's Publishing House, 1991. p. 820.
95. *Selected Works of Mao Zedong, Volume 3*. People's Publishing House, 1991. p. 1096.
96. *Selected Works of Mao Zedong, Volume 3*. People's Publishing House, 1991. p. 828.
97. Mao Zedong. "On the Correct Handling of Conflict Among the People." February 27, 1957.
98. Editorial Board of the CPC Central Committee. *Selected Works of Liu Shaoqi, Volume 1*. People's Publishing House, 1981. p. 342.
99. *Selected Works of Mao Zedong, Volume 3*. People's Publishing House, 1991. p. 1031.
100. *Selected Works of Zhu De*. People's Publishing House, 1983. p. 284.
101. *Selected Works of Mao Zedong, Volume 3*. People's Publishing House, 1991. p. 1096.
102. Mao Zedong. "On Cooperatives" (1943). *The Masses*. Volume 9, Number 3, Issue 4.
103. *Selected Works of Mao Zedong, Volume 3*. People's Publishing House, 1991. p. 1094–1095.
104. Editorial Board of the CPC Central Committee. *Selected Works of Liu Shaoqi, Volume 1*. People's Publishing House 1981. p. 344.
105. *Selected Works of Deng Xiaoping, Volume 1*. People's Publishing House, 1994. p. 217–218.
106. *Selected Works of Mao Zedong, Volume 4*. People's Publishing House, 1991. p. 1286.
107. *Selected Works of Mao Zedong, Volume 3*. People's Publishing House, 1991. p. 899.
108. *Selected Works of Zhou Enlai, Volume 1*. People's Publishing House, 1997. p. 125.
109. Editorial Board of the CPC Central Committee. *Selected Works of Chen Yun (1956–1985)*. People's Publishing House, 1986. p. 245.
110. *Selected Works of Mao Zedong, Volume 4*. People's Publishing House, 1991. p. 1480.

Chapter 10

1. *Collection of Important Literature Since the Third Plenary Session, Volume 2*. People's Publishing House, 1982. p. 826.
2. *Selected Works of Wang Jiaxiang*. People's Publishing House, 1989. p. 138.
3. Ibid, p. 141.
4. Speech by Wang Ming. First published in *New China*, reprinted in *Chinese Youth*, Issue 9, Number 2.
5. *Chinese Culture*. Issue 1, February 15, 1940.
6. Zhu De, "In Commemoration of the 21st Anniversary of the Founding of the Party." *Liberation Daily*. July 1, 1942.
7. Chen Yi, "The Great 21 Years – Remarks in Commemoration of the 21st Anniversary of the Founding of the Party." *Yanfu Newspaper*. See *The Mission of CPC Members*. Sunan Xinhua Bookstore, 1949. p. 30–32.
8. *Selected Works of Ren Biao*. People's Publishing House, 1987. p. 304–305.

9. *Liberation Daily.* July 6, 1943.
10. *Liberation Daily.* July 8, 1943.
11. *Liberation Daily.* August 6, 1943.
12. *Selected Works of Deng Xiaoping, Volume 1.* People's Publishing House, 1994. p. 88.
13. This statement was changed in the full resolution adopted by the First Plenary Session of the Seventh General Meeting of the CPC Central Committee to read, "The Party has produced its own leader, Comrade Mao Zedong, through the process of struggle, forming a Chinese Marxist thought system, called Mao Zedong Thought." See *Hu Qiaomu's Reflections on Mao Zedong.* People's Publishing House, 1994. p. 325. After the founding of the People's Republic of China, as an appendix, the Resolution of Several Historical Issues cited in the *Selected Works of Mao Zedong, Volume 3,* omitted the phrase "forming a Chinese Marxist thought system, called Mao Zedong Thought." Other places where "Mao Zedong Thought" was mentioned were likewise omitted, some replacing it with "the Marxist-Leninist line." In this way, the term "Mao Zedong Thought" was entirely excluded from the work.
14. *Selected Works of Mao Zedong, Volume 3.* People's Publishing House, 1991. p. 955.
15. *Selected Works of Mao Zedong.* Northeastern Bookstore, 1948. p. 312. In the *Selected Works of Mao Zedong* published after the founding of the new China, the words "under the leadership of the proletariat" were added.
16. *A Mao Zedong Anthology.* People's Publishing House, 1996. p. 275.
17. *Selected Works of Mao Zedong.* Northeastern Bookstore, 1948. p. 316.
18. *A Mao Zedong Anthology, Volume 3.* People's Publishing House, 1996. p. 322, 384.
19. *Selected Works of Mao Zedong.* Northeastern Bookstore, 1948. p. 333.
20. *Selected Works of Liu Shaoqi, Volume 1.* People's Publishing House, 1981. p. 335–337.
21. *Selected Works of Liu Shaoqi, Volume 1.* People's Publishing House, 1981. p. 334.
22. Ibid, p. 335.
23. *Selected Works of the CPC Central Committee, Volume 15.* CPC Central Party School Press, 1991. p. 115.
24. *A Mao Zedong Anthology, Volume 3.* People's Publishing House, 1996. p. 284.
25. Ibid, p. 297.
26. Ibid, p. 15.
27. *A Mao Zedong Anthology, Volume 5.* People's Publishing House, 1996. p. 123.
28. Ibid, p. 260.
29. *Jinchaji Daily.* July 1, 1944, and September 26, 1944.
30. "Central Committee Directive on Attention to Summary of Experience in Urban Work," February 25, 1948.
31. *Selected Works of Mao Zedong, Volume 4.* People's Publishing House, 1991. p. 1347.
32. Resolution of the Second Plenary Session of the Seventh General Meeting of the CPC Central Committee. March 13, 1949.
33. *Selected Works of Mao Zedong, Volume 4.* People's Publishing House, 1991. p. 1429.
34. *Chronicle of Liu Shaoqi, Volume 2.* Central Literature Publishing House, 1996. p. 185.

35. Ibid, p. 185–186.
36. Editorial Board of the CPC Central Committee. *Selected Works of Ren Bishi*. People's Publishing House, 1987. p. 464.
37. Ibid, p. 464–465.
38. *A Mao Zedong Anthology, Volume 4*. People's Publishing House, 1991. p. 1426.
39. Editorial Board of the CPC Central Committee. *Selected Works of Ren Bishi*. People's Publishing House, 1987. p. 460.
40. Ibid.
41. Editorial Board of the CPC Central Committee. *Selected Works of Ren Bishi*. People's Publishing House, 1987. p. 460.
42. Ibid, p. 461.
43. Ibid, p. 459.
44. Ibid, p. 459–460.
45. *Chronicle of Mao Zedong, Volume 2/3*. Central Literature Publishing House, 2002. p. 430.
46. *Selected Works of Mao Zedong, Volume 4*. People's Publishing House, 1991. p. 1438–1439.
47. CPC Central Committee Editorial Board. *Selected Works of Ren Bishi*. People's Publishing House, 1987. p. 471.
48. Ibid, p. 472–473.
49. Mao Zedong. "Report and Conclusions of the CPC Central Committee Politburo." September 8, 1948.
50. Editorial Board of the CPC Central Central Committee. *Selected Works of Ren Bishi*. People's Publishing House, 1987. p. 457–458.
51. Ibid, p. 458.
52. Ren Bishi. Speech at the Politburo Meeting, September 13, 1948.
53. Mao Zedong. Report and Conclusions of the Meeting of the CPC Central Committee Politburo. September 8, 1948.
54. *Selected Works of the CPC Central Committee, Volume 1*. Central Party School Press, 1989. p. 337.
55. *Communist International Literature on the Chinese Revolution (1919–1928)*. China Social Sciences Press, 1981. p. 269.
56. *Selected Works of Cai Hesen*. People's Publishing House, 1980. p. 205.
57. *Selected Works of Mao Zedong, Volume 1*. People's Publishing House, 1991. p. 130.
58. Ibid, p. 159.
59. Ibid, p. 559.
60. *Selected Works of Mao Zedong, Volume 4*. People's Publishing House, 1991. p. 1431.
61. Ibid, p. 1479.
62. *Selected Works of Liu Shaoqi, Volume 1*. People's Publishing House, 1981. p. 435.
63. *Manuscripts of Mao Zedong Since the Founding of the People's Republic of China, Volume 1*. Central Literature Publishing House, 1988. p. 416.
64. *Manuscripts of Mao Zedong Since the Founding of the People's Republic of China, Volume 2*. Central Literature Publishing House, 1988. p. 664.

65. Ibid.
66. Ibid, p. 665.
67. Ibid.
68. *Manuscripts of Mao Zedong Since the Founding of the People's Republic of China, Volume 2.* Central Literature Publishing House, 1988. p. 664.
69. CPC Central Literature Research Office. *Chronicle of Liu Shaoqi, Volume 2.* Central Literature Publishing House, 1996. p. 274.
70. *Selected Works of Mao Zedong, Volume 2.* People's Publishing House, 1991. p. 676.
71. *Selected Works of Mao Zedong, Volume 4.* People's Publishing House, 1991. p. 1256.
72. See "Mao Zedong's Report to the Politburo Meeting." September 8, 1948.
73. *Selected Works of Mao Zedong, Volume 4.* People's Publishing House, 1991. p. 1375.
74. *Selected Works of Mao Zedong, Volume 4.* People's Publishing House, 1991. p. 1480.
75. Ibid, p. 1479.
76. Ibid, p. 1475.
77. *Selected Works of Mao Zedong, Volume 4.* People's Publishing House, 1991. p. 1475.
78. *Complete Works of Lenin, Volume 28.* People's Publishing House, 1991. p. 163.
79. *Selected Works of Mao Zedong, Volume 2.* People's Publishing House, 1991. p. 647.
80. Ibid, p. 684.
81. Editorial Board of the CPC Central Committee. *Selected Works of Liu Shaoqi, Volume 1.* People's Publishing House, 1981. p. 427.
82. *Selected Works of Mao Zedong, Volume 3.* People's Publishing House, 1991. p. 1060.
83. *Selected Works of Mao Zedong, Volume 2.* People's Publishing House, 1991. p. 630.
84. *Selected Works of Mao Zedong, Volume 4.* People's Publishing House, 1991. p. 1430.
85. *Selected Works of Mao Zedong, Volume 5.* People's Publishing House, 1991. p. 269–270.
86. *Selected Works of Mao Zedong, Volume 1.* People's Publishing House, 1991. p. 188.
87. *Selected Works of Mao Zedong, Volume 1.* People's Publishing House, 1991. p. 159.
88. *Selected Works of Mao Zedong, Volume 2.* People's Publishing House, 1991. p. 678.
89. *Selected Works of Mao Zedong, Volume 2.* People's Publishing House, 1991. p. 647.
90. Modern History Board of the Chinese Academy of Social Sciences. *The Complete Works of Sun Yat-Sen, Volume 9.* Zhonghua Book Company, 1986. p. 120.
91. *Selected Works of Mao Zedong, Volume 3.* People's Publishing House, 1991. p. 793.
92. Ibid, p. 1060.
93. Ibid, p. 891.
94. Ibid, p. 1079.
95. *Selected Works of Mao Zedong, Volume 4.* People's Publishing House, 1991. p. 1253.
96. Ibid, p. 1250.
97. *Selected Works of Mao Zedong, Volume 4.* People's Publishing House, 1991. p. 1251.
98. *Selected Works of Mao Zedong, Volume 5.* People's Publishing House, 1991. p. 23–24.
99. Ibid, p. 23.
100. *Selected Works of Mao Zedong, Volume 4.* People's Publishing House, 1991. p. 1315.
101. *Selected Works of Mao Zedong, Volume 2.* People's Publishing House, 1991. p. 678.

102. *Selected Works of Mao Zedong, Volume 4*. People's Publishing House, 1991. p. 1255–1256.
103. *Selected Works of Mao Zedong, Volume 4*. People's Publishing House, 1991. p. 1431.
104. Ibid, p. 1432.
105. Ibid.
106. Ibid, p. 1433.
107. *Selected Works of Mao Zedong, Volume 2*. People Publishing House, 1991. p. 697.
108. *Selected Works of Mao Zedong, Volume 2*. People's Publishing House, 1991. p. 706.
109. *Selected Works of Mao Zedong, Volume 2*. People's Publishing House, 1991. p. 534.
110. Ibid, p. 706.
111. *Selected Works of Mao Zedong, Volume 3*. People's Publishing House, 1991. p. 837.
112. *Selected Works of Mao Zedong, Volume 2*. People's Publishing House, 1991. p. 706–707.
113. Ibid, p. 707.
114. *Selected Works of Mao Zedong, Volume 3*. People's Publishing House, 1991. p. 832.
115. *Selected Works of Mao Zedong, Volume 2*. People's Publishing House, 1991. p. 707.
116. Ibid.
117. Ibid.
118. *Selected Works of Mao Zedong, Volume 2*. People's Publishing House, 1991. p. 708.
119. *Selected Works of Mao Zedong, Volume 1*. People's Publishing House, 1991. p. 181.
120. *Selected Works of Mao Zedong, Volume 3*. People's Publishing House, 1991. p. 814.
121. Ibid, p. 815.
122. *Selected Works of Mao Zedong, Volume 2*. People's Publishing House, 1991. p. 663.
123. *Selected Works of Mao Zedong, Volume 3*. People's Publishing House, 1991. p. 859.
124. Ibid.
125. Ibid, p. 862.
126. Ibid, p. 863.
127. Ibid.

INDEX

A
A Mao Zedong Anthology **Vol. 1**: 493
"A Single Spark Can Start a Prairie Fire" **Vol. 1**: 179, 181, 331, 411
AB League **Vol. 3**: 102
Abe Awang Jinmei **Vol. 3**: 119
Abolition Party **Vol. 3**: 102
"Absorbing a Large Number of Intellectuals" **Vol. 1**: 210
Accelerating the Training and Education of Young Cadres **Vol. 3**: 457, 459
Accelerating the Progress of Science and Technology **Vol. 3**: 398
Active Military Officers Law **Vol. 3**: 436
advanced socialist culture with Chinese characteristics **Vol. 3**: 386, 387, 388, 389, 391, 394, 466, 474, 476, 487, 514, 525, 546
African Union **Vol. 3**: 216
agrarian revolution (Agrarian Revolutionary War) **Vol. 1**: 43, 65, 80, 95, 105, 110, 130, 136, 137, 143, 144, 151, 163, 165, 167, 168, 172, 174, 175, 176, 179, 182, 183, 188, 254, 277, 279, 284, 288, 296, 298, 311, 326, 329, 331, 334, 336, 341, 344, 350, 361, 371, 379, 382, 385, 389, 393, 405, 420, 434, 459, 467, 481, 486, 525, 531, 533; **Vol. 2**: 49
Agreement on Trade in Goods Vol 3: 518
Agriculture, Sixty Articles of **Vol. 2**: 235, 236, 238, 254, 255
agricultural cooperatives **Vol. 2**: 71, 73, 75, 76, 108, 113, 118, 122, 123, 124, 125, 126, 182, 188, 192, 193, 194, 236

Air Force Engineering University Vol 3: 434
Ali Hassan Mwinyi **Vol. 3**: 264, 265
All-China Federation of Industry and Commerce Vol 3: 242
All-China Federation of Trade Unions **Vol. 1**: 126; **Vol. 2**: 40
All-China Women's Federation Vol 3: 312
Allied Army of the World Socialist Revolutionary Front **Vol. 1**: 110, 112, 118
Allied League **Vol. 1**: 62
American Association in Taiwan Vol 3: 213
An Overview of Social Issues **Vol. 1**: 9
An Ziwen **Vol. 2**: 67; **Vol. 3**: 72
Anguo County **Vol. 2**: 204
Anhui Province **Vol. 1**: 79, 171, 352; **Vol. 2**: 328; **Vol. 3**: 102, 103, 106, 155, 318, 384
Anti-Encirclement **Vol. 1**: 82, 157, 158, 159, 183, 194, 319, 334, 341
anti-Japan base (anti-Japanese base area) **Vol. 1**: 66, 73, 108, 198, 199, 200, 201, 202, 203, 210, 231, 241, 262, 318, 334, 336, 493, 530; **Vol. 2**: 32, 46, 269, 308
Anti-Japanese Guerrilla War **Vol. 1**: 184, 198, 298, 311, 329
Anti-Japanese National United Front **Vol. 1**: 66, 68, 69, 79, 80, 81, 108, 200, 201, 204, 228, 229, 230, 232, 233, 234, 235, 236, 237, 238, 239, 240, 241, 243, 249, 280, 289, 300, 400, 514, 515, 542; **Vol. 3**: 106
Anti-Japanese Salvation **Vol. 1**: 199
anti-landlord class **Vol. 1**: 50

anti-Leftism movement **Vol. 2**: 203, 220
anti-Marxist **Vol. 1**: 164; **Vol. 2**: 177, 290, 294, 327
anti-Party **Vol. 2**: 280, 294, 315; **Vol. 3**: 23, 76, 91, 100, 101, 102, 323
anti-rash advance (anti-rash progress) **Vol. 2**: 188, 189, 190, 207, 246, 255
Anti-Revolt Campaign **Vol. 3**: 102, 103
anti-revolutionary group **Vol. 1**: 49, 52, 283; **Vol. 2**: 320; **Vol. 3**: 100, 103, 105, 170
Anti-Rightist Movement **Vol. 1**: 58; **Vol. 2**: 152, 173, 174, 178, 180, 182, 183, 184, 186, 188, 190, 191, 192, 207, 220, 222, 230, 231, 239, 241, 242, 245, 246, 251, 253, 254, 255, 257, 258, 274; **Vol. 3**: 83, 84, 85, 88, 90, 93
anti-Socialist Vol 2: 294; **Vol. 3**: 91, 323
anti-war movement **Vol. 1**: 260, 274; **Vol. 2**: 263
April 5th Movement (*see* Tiananmen Incident) **Vol. 2**: 309, 316; **Vol. 3**: 9, 10, 11, 12, 15, 53, 54
Arkhipov, Ivan **Vol. 3**: 219
Armed Division of Workers and Peasants **Vol. 1**: 164, 166, 169, 170, 172, 173, 174, 175, 176, 178, 180, 188
armed revolution **Vol. 1**: 143, 283, 284, 361
armed struggle (theory or doctrine) **Vol. 1**: 36, 37, 43, 45, 55, 78, 83, 91, 102, 149, 171, 173, 174, 175, 176, 184, 187, 273, 274, 275, 276, 277, 278, 279, 282, 283, 284, 285, 286, 287, 331, 333, 336, 337, 361, 364, 366, 368, 372, 491; **Vol. 2**: 135, 292; **Vol. 3**: 72, 106
arming the masses **Vol. 1**: 210, 305
ASEAN and Chinese Leaders' Meeting **Vol. 3**: 518
Asia-Africa Summit **Vol. 3**: 517–518
Asian Cooperation Dialogue **Vol. 3**: 518
Association for Cross-Strait Relations **Vol. 3**: 414
Association for Relations Across the Taiwan Straits (ARATS) **Vol. 3**: 414
Audio-Visual Products Management Regulations **Vol. 3**: 394
Audit Office **Vol. 3**: 278
August defeat **Vol. 1**: 170, 173
August 7th Meeting **Vol. 1**: 43, 44, 46, 47, 48, 51, 53, 55, 57, 151, 154, 166, 167, 169, 277, 364, 420, 421
Autumn Harvest Riots **Vol. 1**: 151, 154, 167, 168, 174, 189, 306, 315, 323, 324, 361

B
Basic Law of the Hong Kong Special Administration Region **Vol. 3**: 236, 266
bad elements **Vol. 1**: 423; **Vol. 2**: 167; **Vol. 3**: 113, 126, 145, 146, 147, 309
Bai Chongxi **Vol. 1**: 234
Baiwan Village **Vol. 3**: 199
Bakunin, Mikhail **Vol. 1**: 6, 396
Bakuninists **Vol. 1**: 396, 430
balanced development **Vol. 1**: 62; **Vol. 3**: 285, 301, 302, 303, 305, 306, 307, 309, 310, 362, 486
Bao'an County **Vol. 3**: 277
Bao Huiceng **Vol. 1**: 19
Baoding **Vol. 2**: 204; **Vol. 3**: 313
Basel Conference **Vol. 1**: 396
Basic Program for the Rectification of the Party **Vol. 1**: 512
Basic Views and Policies on Religious Issues in the Socialist Period of China **Vol. 3**: 116, 127
Battle of Guangzhou **Vol. 1**: 36
Battle of Pingjin **Vol. 1**: 354
Bebel, August **Vol. 1**: 430
Becker, Johann Philipp **Vol. 1**: 430
Beidaihe **Vol. 2**: 191
Beidaihe Working Conference (Beidaihe Work Conference) **Vol. 2**: 195, 196, 212, 256, 257
Beijing **Vol. 1**: 3, 14–19, 61, 92, 162, 214, 256, 267, 275, 376, 510; **Vol. 2**: 61, 78, 205, 233, 243, 318, 319, 324, 326, 336; **Vol. 3**: 11, 12, 23, 24, 30, 31, 35, 43, 52, 53, 59, 72, 75–79, 99, 112, 123, 138, 139, 142, 143, 147, 173, 178–180, 199, 200, 210, 218, 219, 221, 227, 234, 236, 237, 263, 280, 305, 317, 318, 322, 323, 325, 372, 408, 414, 416, 417, 450, 455, 458, 462, 470, 472, 482, 513, 524, 536, 542
Beijing Coup **Vol. 1**: 92, 214
Beijing Communist Party Organization **Vol. 1**: 18

Beijing Daily **Vol. 3**: 11
Beijing Military Region **Vol. 3**: 76, 77
Beijing Normal University **Vol. 1**: 18; **Vol. 3**: 317
Beijing-Qinhuangdao Railway **Vol. 3**: 210
Beijing Treaty **Vol. 3**: 234, 416
Beijing University (*see* Peking University)
Beiping Way **Vol. 1**: 356
Beiyang government **Vol. 1**: 267
Beiyang Warlords (*see also* Northern Warlords) **Vol. 1**: 136
Bengbu **Vol. 1**: 354
Bertram, James **Vol. 1**: 231, 316
Big Bang Theory **Vol. 2**: 285
Big Character Poster **Vol. 2**: 182, 300; **Vol. 3**: 78, 79
Blowe, Mitchell **Vol. 2**: 18
Bo Yibo **Vol. 1**: 500; **Vol. 2**: 42, 238; **Vol. 3**: 53, 74, 81, 189, 283
Bo Yibo Group **Vol. 3**: 54
Bohai Sea **Vol. 3**: 210
Bolshevik **Vol. 1**: 59, 358
Bolshevik Party **Vol. 1**: 38, 358, 366, 367, 370, 375, 377, 382, 398, 400, 430, 458, 459; **Vol. 2**: 54, 118, 122, 137, 209, 210, 213, 217
Borodin, Mikhail **Vol. 1**: 40
bourgeois law **Vol. 2**: 268
bourgeoisie (bourgeois) **Vol. 1**: 5, 7, 9, 13, 25–32, 34, 35, 37, 41, 44, 46–47, 51–57, 60, 62, 63, 70–76, 80–81, 87, 92–94, 96–98, 100–118, 120–129, 131, 134, 138–146, 150, 172, 181, 185–186, 195, 199–200, 210, 213–219, 221–226, 230, 233–234, 237–244, 246, 253, 258, 261–263, 269–272, 277–278, 283, 292–293, 295, 298–299, 301, 308–310, 322, 329, 358, 360, 362–365, 370–375, 377–378, 381–384, 421, 427–428, 447, 466–468, 487, 495, 502–503, 507, 509, 513, 514, 516–519, 521–524, 526, 528, 530, 533–535, 540–544, 546; **Vol. 2**: 4, 10, 17, 26–29, 31–34, 36–37, 39, 41–43, 45–47, 49–50, 59–64, 69–70, 79–80, 83, 91–95, 103–105, 109, 116, 125–129, 136, 170, 181, 183–186, 191, 197, 201–202, 212, 241, 251, 257, 259, 265, 268–271, 273, 275, 279–291, 293–297, 307, 315, 328; **Vol. 3**: 22–24, 27, 54, 81, 88, 113, 160, 247, 255, 304, 315–316, 318, 323
bourgeois civil rights revolution **Vol. 1**: 51, 52, 53, 54, 103, 105
bourgeois republic **Vol. 1**: 71, 106, 467, 517
bourgeois revolution **Vol. 1**: 5, 28, 52, 107, 118, 121, 122, 123, 134, 301, 466
Branch Office **Vol. 1**: 503; **Vol. 3**: 143
Brezhnev, Leonid **Vol. 2**: 264, 287, 289; **Vol. 3**: 217
bribery **Vol. 2**: 104; **Vol. 3**: 294, 298, 299, 304, 309, 321
British colonial rule (Hong Kong) **Vol. 3**: 234, 416
Buddhist temples (in Han areas) **Vol. 3**: 127
Bukharin, Nikola Ivanovic **Vol. 1**: 153; **Vol. 2**: 164
Bureau of Religious Affairs (Religious Affairs Bureau) **Vol. 3**: 127
bureaucracy **Vol. 1**: 136, 203, 380, 383, 414, 430, 431, 432, 440, 458, 473; **Vol. 2**: 104, 138, 153, 160–161, 163, 167, 175–182, 297; **Vol. 3**: 47, 57, 146, 271, 281, 284, 372
bureaucratic capitalism **Vol. 1**: 88, 130–131, 133, 138, 245–247, 253, 262–263, 265, 268, 283, 287, 350, 467, 520, 525–534; **Vol. 2**: 26, 37, 87; **Vol. 3**: 148, 252
Bush, George H. W. **Vol. 3**: 215
Bush, George W. **Vol. 3**: 519
Business Group of the United Front Work Conference **Vol. 2**: 92
Business Performance Management Regulations **Vol. 3**: 394

C

Cadre Censorship Bureau **Vol. 3**: 17
Cadre Education **Vol. 3**: 449
cadre retirement system **Vol. 3**: 288
Cadre Route **Vol. 3**: 13
cadre system **Vol. 3**: 185, 286–287, 291, 458, 460
Cai Chang **Vol. 3**: 288
Cai Hesen **Vol. 1**: 16, 17, 29, 30, 49, 52, 53, 92, 102, 167, 219, 399, 400, 507
Cai Tingkai **Vol. 1**: 233, 264
Cai Xitao **Vol. 3**: 30

576 INDEX

Cai Yuanpei **Vol. 1**: 14, 233
Cao Diqiu **Vol. 3**: 75
Cao Juren **Vol. 3**: 227
Caolanzi Prison **Vol. 3**: 74
capitalism **Vol. 1**: 3, 5, 6, 7, 8, 10, 12, 13, 20, 26,
    30, 31, 39, 53, 54, 76, 88, 94–98, 102–105, 107,
    108, 109, 111, 112, 113, 116, 117, 118, 130, 131, 133,
    138, 139, 140, 145, 146, 161, 186, 216, 245, 246,
    247, 253, 262, 263, 265, 268, 277, 283, 285, 287,
    350, 358, 377, 397, 466, 467, 487, 488, 496, 510,
    518, 520, 522, 524, 526, 528, 529, 530, 533–538,
    543; **Vol. 2**: 4–6, 14, 17–19, 26, 28–35, 37, 39,
    41, 43–47, 51–52, 58–59, 61–62, 67, 70, 74, 83,
    91, 94–95, 103, 107–108, 111, 113–116, 118, 120,
    124–128, 131, 135–137, 151–152, 185, 201, 203,
    214, 218–219, 234, 257–259, 267, 272–275, 277–
    281, 283, 286–288, 290–292, 294, 304–305, 331;
    Vol. 3: 21–22, 27, 46, 56, 93, 146, 148, 233, 235,
    241, 246–247, 249, 252, 268, 304, 309, 316, 328,
    333, 345–348, 382, 487
capitulationism **Vol. 1**: 232, 240, 280
Carter, Jimmy **Vol. 3**: 145, 213–214
cat theory (Deng Xiaoping) **Vol. 2**: 249, 255
Caudine Forks of capitalism **Vol. 2**: 135
Central Action Committee **Vol. 1**: 61
Central Advisory Committee **Vol. 3**: 67, 180,
    186, 188–189, 242, 244–245, 269, 290, 311, 410,
    450, 453, 464
Central Bureau **Vol. 1**: 20; Vol 2: 64, 73, 77, 233,
    234; **Vol. 3**: 67
Central Bureau of the Shaanxi-Gansu-Ningxia
    Border Region **Vol. 1**: 199
Central Committee Vol 1: 20, 25, 36, 38, 39, 40,
    43–46, 48, 50, 51, 55–59, 63, 66, 67, 71, 75, 79,
    83, 86, 87, 88, 92, 94, 103, 104, 105, 150–161,
    163–169, 176, 178, 181, 183, 189, 199, 203, 204,
    205, 207, 210, 211, 222, 226–238, 240, 244, 245,
    248, 249, 250, 251–254, 257, 259, 260, 261, 263,
    264, 265, 271, 275, 276, 279, 283, 299, 304, 305,
    306, 309, 311, 313, 318, 324, 337, 351, 354, 355,
    362, 366, 367, 369, 370, 382, 386, 387, 395, 398,
    400, 401, 403, 405, 411, 415, 419, 421, 424, 425,
    426, 427, 434, 437, 459, 482, 485, 486, 492–496,
    499, 500, 501, 503, 504, 505, 510, 511, 532, 537,
    538; **Vol. 2**: 3, 5, 9, 11, 16, 22, 29, 32–33, 35–40,
    42, 44–45, 49–52, 56–65, 71–79, 81–87, 89,
    91–93, 95, 97–99, 101, 103–105, 107, 109–110,
    113–114, 116–119, 122–123, 132, 142, 144–145,
    148–152, 154–158, 161, 168, 174–181, 183–185,
    188–189, 192–193, 195, 199–200, 202–203,
    205–207, 209–210, 214–215, 222, 226, 231–238,
    240–241, 243–245, 247–252, 254, 256–258,
    260, 272, 277, 290, 299–302, 313, 315, 318, 323,
    329–332, 334–338; **Vol. 3**: 3, 6, 9–13, 16–17,
    34, 37–38, 40, 46, 48, 51–55, 57, 59–83, 85,
    87–99, 101–117, 119–129, 131, 135–139, 141–142,
    144–145, 147–163, 165–168, 170–171, 173–180,
    182–183, 186, 188–189, 192–193, 196, 198–203,
    205, 207, 217, 219, 221, 225–227, 232, 234–235,
    240–242, 244–249, 252–255, 257–260, 263,
    265–266, 268–270, 273–274, 279–281, 283,
    286–295, 297–299, 302, 305–327, 334–335,
    337–338, 343, 345–348, 350, 352–355, 357–358,
    363–364, 368–370, 373–374, 376–377, 379–384,
    386, 390–391, 393–394, 397–405, 407–413, 416,
    419, 421, 427, 429, 432, 440, 443, 446–450,
    452–470, 479, 481–483, 488, 491, 493–497,
    499–502, 506–517, 519–521, 523–526, 531–532,
    536, 538, 542, 544–545, 550–551
Central Committee for Ethnic Affairs Vol 2:
    250
Central Disciplinary Inspection Commission
    (Central Commission for Discipline
    Inspection) **Vol. 3**: 60, 62, 77, 80, 93, 180,
    186, 188–189, 242, 244–245, 294, 296, 311,
    320–321, 410, 450, 453, 462–465, 467, 483, 524
Central Economic Work Conference **Vol. 3**:
    512
Central Leading Group **Vol. 2**: 199; **Vol. 3**: 352,
    387, 398, 446
Central Military Commission **Vol. 1**: 59, 61,
    238, 239, 313, 314, 346, 351, 355; Vol 2: 326,
    331; **Vol. 3**: 10, 42, 73, 75, 189, 203, 282, 307,
    429–432, 434, 437–439, 516–517
Central Organizational Department **Vol. 2**:
    67; **Vol. 3**: 14–17, 54, 66–68, 70–72, 77, 79, 81,
    84–86, 89–90, 93–99, 101, 103–104, 106–108,
    111, 114–117, 245, 278–279, 296, 311, 373, 410,
    450–454, 460, 464, 471
Central Party School **Vol. 1**: 391; **Vol. 2**: 30,

322; **Vol. 3**: 14, 35–36, 90, 154, 269, 348, 358, 449–450, 472, 502
Central People's Government **Vol. 1**: 268; **Vol. 2**: 77–78, 80; **Vol. 3**: 103, 273
Central Plains **Vol. 1**: 59, 351, 352, 505; **Vol. 3**: 107–108
Central Political Report **Vol. 1**: 39
Central Political System Reform Seminar Group **Vol. 3**: 269–270
Central Project Group **Vol. 3**: 71
Central Provisional Politburo Vol 1: 48, 167
Central Secretariat **Vol. 1**: 238, 482; **Vol. 2**: 154, 251; **Vol. 3**: 99, 115, 117, 218, 235, 269, 273, 311–312
Central Soviet Area **Vol. 1**: 157, 341; **Vol. 3**: 15, 102
Central Soviet Government **Vol. 1**: 61
Central Special Task Force **Vol. 3**: 54, 70, 100
Central Steering Committee for Party Consolidation **Vol. 3**: 281–283
Central Task Force **Vol. 3**: 72, 81
Central United Front Department (Ministry) **Vol. 2**: 80; **Vol. 3**: 89–90, 111, 113, 126
Central Working Conference **Vol. 2**: 103, 237–238, 240, 243, 257, 259, 336; **Vol. 3**: 11–12, 48, 52, 54, 59–61, 73, 93, 100, 123, 135, 138, 259, 286, 305
centralism **Vol. 1**: 190, 359, 365, 368, 369, 379, 387, 394, 395, 397–403, 408–419, 427, 450, 452, 474, 475, 488, 499, 509, 515, 518, 523; **Vol. 2**: 26, 48–49, 159–160, 169, 190, 221–222, 243–244, 246; **Vol. 3**: 57–58, 62, 136, 150, 161, 163, 172, 176–177, 184–185, 190, 281, 370
Chairman of the General Committee **Vol. 1**: 395
Chaling County **Vol. 1**: 189
Changchun **Vol. 1**: 353; **Vol. 3**: 115
Changsha **Vol. 1**: 16, 19, 25, 58, 61, 151, 152, 168, 174, 376; **Vol. 2**: 233
Changxindian Railway Vol 1: 14
Chen Boda Vol 1: 483; **Vol. 2**: 194, 204, 278; **Vol. 3**: 73–75, 77, 79
Chen Chi **Vol. 3**: 30, 74
Chen Duxiu **Vol. 1**: 4, 7, 8, 12, 14, 15, 17–20, 29, 33–34, 38–41, 44, 46–47, 92–93, 101–102, 121–122, 125, 218–219, 227–228, 230, 277, 371, 378, 399, 411, 420, 545
Chen Geng **Vol. 1**: 352
Chen Gongbo **Vol. 1**: 19
Chen Gongpei Vol 1: 19
Chen Jingrun **Vol. 3**: 30
Chen Jiongming **Vol. 1**: 24, 274
Chen Jitang **Vol. 1**: 234
Chen Lifu **Vol. 1**: 246, 531
Chen Mingshu **Vol. 1**: 233
Chen Muhua **Vol. 3**: 189
Chen Pixian **Vol. 3**: 189
Chen Qiyou **Vol. 1**: 264
Chen Shaomin **Vol. 3**: 107–108
Chen Shui-bian **Vol. 3**: 419
Chen Tanqiu **Vol. 1**: 19
Chen Wangdao **Vol. 1**: 18
Chen Yeping **Vol. 3**: 71
Chen Yi **Vol. 1**: 172, 327, 351, 352, 484; **Vol. 2**: 156, 251, 300; **Vol. 3**: 73
Chen Yun Vol 1: 195, 424, 426, 427, 464, 476, 477; **Vol. 2**: 62, 150, 188, 246–249, 304, 324; **Vol. 3**: 11, 14–15, 33–34, 49, 53, 56, 62, 167, 179, 186–189, 193, 200, 245–246, 285, 289, 344
Chen Zaidao **Vol. 3**: 62, 72
Chendai Town **Vol. 3**: 320
Chiang Ching-kuo **Vol. 1**: 271; **Vol. 3**: 413
Chiang Kai-shek **Vol. 1**: 38, 42, 66, 69–70, 85–88, 93–94, 131, 163, 217–218, 221–222, 226, 234, 236, 245–248, 250, 253, 256, 258, 263, 269, 271, 276, 281, 284, 290, 292, 328, 346, 350, 353, 494, 531, 533; **Vol. 3**: 145, 225–228, 252
China Agenda for the 21st Century **Vol. 3**: 250, 424
China Buddhist College **Vol. 3**: 127
China Catholic Theological and Philosophical College **Vol. 3**: 127
China Christian Nanjing Jinling Union Theological College **Vol. 3**: 127
China Democratic League **Vol. 1**: 264
China Human Rights Alliance (China Human Rights League) **Vol. 3**: 142
China Human Rights League (*see* China Human Rights Alliance) **Vol. 3**: 143
China Islamic Economics College **Vol. 3**: 127

China News **Vol. 1**: 10
China Petrochemical Group Corporation **Vol. 3**: 405
China Petroleum and Natural Gas Corporation **Vol. 3**: 405
China Taoist College **Vol. 3**: 127
China Tibetan Language Department Senior Buddhist College **Vol. 3**: 127
China-Africa Cooperation Forum **Vol. 3**: 518
China-ASEAN Comprehensive Economic Cooperation Framework Agreement **Vol. 3**: 518
China-ASEAN Strategic Partnership for Peace and Prosperity Action Plan **Vol. 3**: 518
China-ASEAN Summit **Vol. 3**: 425
China-Russia border **Vol. 3**: 519
China-Russia Joint Declaration on International Order in the 21st Century **Vol. 3**: 517
China-Russia Summit **Vol. 3**: 517
China-Russia Tokk Exchange **Vol. 3**: 519
Chinese Academy of Sciences **Vol. 2**: 156, 215; **Vol. 3**: 23
Chinese Academy of Social Sciences **Vol. 3**: 26, 41, 43, 193, 195, 311, 438
Chinese Association of Science and Technology **Vol. 3**: 43
Chinese Buddhist Association **Vol. 3**: 127
Chinese Catholic Patriotic Congress **Vol. 3**: 127
Chinese Christian Three-Self Patriotic Movement Committee **Vol. 3**: 127
Chinese Culture **Vol. 1**: 21, 76, 209, 540, 544–547, 550; **Vol. 2**: 254; **Vol. 3**: 415, 471, 511
Chinese Customs Commission **Vol. 3**: 200, 288, 290
Chinese Federation of Trade Unions **Vol. 1**: 15
Chinese Foreign Ministry **Vol. 3**: 215, 218
Chinese Industry Association **Vol. 1**: 15
Chinese KMT Democratic Promotion Meeting **Vol. 1**: 264
Chinese Land Law **Vol. 1**: 250–251, 255, 532
Chinese Marxism **Vol. 1**: 485–486, 488–491; **Vol. 2**: 261, 267, 273, 299, 304–305, 309–310, 338; **Vol. 3**: 7, 359, 546

Chinese Marxist Workers' Movement **Vol. 1**: 15
Chinese Muslim pilgrimage group **Vol. 3**: 128
Chinese National Liberation Action Committee **Vol. 1**: 233
Chinese National Salvation Congress **Vol. 1**: 264
Chinese Peasants **Vol. 1**: 33, 102, 287, 525
Chinese People's Political Consultative Conference **Vol. 1**: 87, 244, 511, 523; **Vol. 2**: 4, 25, 48, 50
Chinese Red Army **Vol. 1**: 153; **Vol. 3**: 15
Chinese Revolution **Vol. 1**: 23, 25, 27, 29–32, 36–37, 43–45, 47, 49–56, 58–60, 62–63, 65–66, 69, 72–79, 81–84, 86, 91, 93–97, 99–107, 109–110, 112–118, 128–131, 133–134, 136–137, 139–147, 150–153, 157, 159, 161, 163–164, 166, 172–173, 176, 178–182, 184–186, 188, 213, 222, 230, 237, 244, 246, 257, 263, 273, 275–276, 278–287, 292, 299, 308–310, 329–331, 339, 341, 360, 363, 367–368, 371, 379, 385, 388, 390–393, 407, 420, 422, 431, 439–441, 443–445, 448, 452, 466, 468–471, 474, 486–487, 489–494, 504, 507–509, 517, 521–523, 528, 531, 533, 540, 542, 544, 546; **Vol. 2**: 24, 27–29, 32, 35, 38–40, 52, 90, 98, 114, 143–144, 210, 326; **Vol. 3**: 40, 132, 150, 162, 164, 169, 248, 317
Chinese Soviet **Vol. 1**: 160, 191, 194; **Vol. 3**: 105
Chinese Taoist Association **Vol. 3**: 127
Chinese Workers' and Peasants' Red Army **Vol. 1**: 178, 470
Chinese Workers' Movement **Vol. 1**: 16–17, 360, 370, 376, 470; **Vol. 2**: 330
Chinese Youth **Vol. 3**: 11
Chinese Zhi Gong Party **Vol. 1**: 264
Chongqing **Vol. 1**: 152, 167, 281
City-centered Theory **Vol. 1**: 149–151, 153–154, 157, 159–161, 163–164, 166
Civil Morality Construction **Vol. 3**: 391
Civil Servants Law **Vol. 3**: 460, 541
class analysis **Vol. 1**: 33, 80, 103, 121–123, 125
class struggle **Vol. 1**: 8, 10–11, 20, 24, 27–28, 32, 100, 129, 198, 218–219, 236–237, 277, 288–290, 293, 308, 385, 425; **Vol. 2**: 8, 10, 13–14, 47, 65, 103, 136, 138, 167–168, 170, 173–174, 178, 180, 182–187, 189, 207, 219, 221, 224, 226, 245,

256–259, 265, 270–278, 281, 285–286, 292–298, 312, 316, 325, 335; **Vol. 3**: 4, 51, 55, 60, 66, 93, 130, 135, 140–141, 161, 170, 173, 191, 254, 283, 332, 525, 531

class war **Vol. 1**: 59, 159

Classical Marxist Writers **Vol. 2**: 19, 69, 113, 121, 134, 165, 200, 254, 273, 317; **Vol. 3**: 34

Clausewitz, Carl **Vol. 1**: 289

clearing up historical problems **Vol. 3**: 66

clique **Vol. 1**: 235, 242, 248, 271–272, 281; **Vol. 2**: 289–290; **Vol. 3**: 73, 124

Cold War **Vol. 2**: 101, 120, 131, 225; **Vol. 3**: 426–427, 429, 437

collectivization **Vol. 1**: 498, 512, 531, 537–538; **Vol. 2**: 31, 71, 73, 75–76, 85, 99, 115, 120–125, 138, 193, 195, 209

college entrance examination **Vol. 3**: 9, 17–20

Combating Serious Criminal Activities in the Economic Field **Vol. 3**: 306, 319–320

Comintern (*see also* Communist International) **Vol. 1**: 18–20, 25, 38, 40, 42–44, 47, 49, 51–56, 58, 62–63, 65–66, 68, 92, 94, 103–104, 106, 150, 152–154, 157, 164, 169, 178, 214–215, 217–219, 221–228, 232, 362–363, 371, 482, 486, 507–508

Commerce, Forty Articles of **Vol. 2**: 237

Commission for Economic Reform (*see also* State Economic Reform Office) **Vol. 3**: 194

commodity economy **Vol. 1**: 96, 162, 537–538; **Vol. 2**: 6, 8–10, 15, 20, 35–36, 44, 120–121, 137–138, 218, 224, 226, 267–268, 271, 291, 294, 307; **Vol. 3**: 21–22, 192–196, 198–201, 241, 243–244, 249–251, 283, 294, 302, 323, 335–337, 345, 365, 447

Common Program **Vol. 1**: 87, 268, 511, 523, 538–539; **Vol. 2**: 4–5, 25–26, 48, 50–58, 60, 62, 72, 78, 80–82, 89, 99, 103–104, 114, 116, 141

Communications Secretary **Vol. 1**: 395

Communist Alliance **Vol. 1**: 357, 394–396

Communist International (*see also* Comintern) **Vol. 1**: 17, 25, 121

Communist International East Asia Secretariat **Vol. 1**: 17

Communist League **Vol. 1**: 397

Communist Manifesto **Vol. 1**: 79, 97, 374, 458

Communist morality **Vol. 2**: 160

Communist Organization **Vol. 1**: 18

Communist Party of Beijing **Vol. 1**: 18, 406

Communist Party of China (*see also* CPC) **Vol. 1**: 13–14, 18–20, 23–30, 33, 35, 49, 57, 64–65, 73, 75, 78, 89, 93, 97, 103, 107, 114, 123, 129–130, 132, 139, 141–142, 146, 149, 153–154, 215, 224, 229–230, 232, 235, 237, 256, 284, 309, 339, 359, 363, 367, 369, 376, 382, 400–401, 410–411, 419, 466, 468–469, 491, 499, 512, 528; **Vol. 2**: 3, 5, 7, 13, 16, 21, 25, 27, 32, 41, 45, 52–53, 56, 61, 66, 73–74, 84, 86, 89, 97–99, 109, 118, 123, 140, 142, 148, 158, 166, 168, 170, 183, 186, 194–195, 210, 217, 229, 231, 233, 237, 249, 266, 274, 292, 311, 316, 319, 330, 336; **Vol. 3**: 3, 6, 12, 33, 37, 44, 45, 53, 59–61, 63, 65–66, 73, 75, 77–79, 89, 91, 94–95, 99, 102–106, 109–110, 112, 115–117, 119–125, 127–133, 138, 146, 148, 151, 154, 158–159, 161–163, 169, 172–174, 176, 179–182, 186, 194–196, 198, 200, 203, 207, 216, 221, 225–228, 230–231, 239–240, 242, 247–249, 251–255, 258, 260, 262, 265–266, 273, 279–281, 287–289, 291–295, 297–299, 303, 306, 311–316, 318, 320–322, 324–327, 334–338, 340, 343, 345–346, 350, 353, 355, 357, 359–361, 363–364, 366–368, 370–373, 375, 377, 379, 382–384, 388–389, 391, 393–394, 398, 400–401, 411, 413, 415–416, 419, 422, 427–429, 434, 440, 444, 446–447, 450, 457, 459, 461, 466–467, 470, 474–476, 480, 482–483, 490, 521, 523–527, 531–533, 536, 542, 544, 546, 550

Communist Party Political Consultative Conference (*see also* CPPCC) **Vol. 1**: 266, 406

Communist Surge **Vol. 2**: 236

Communist Youth League **Vol. 1**: 40, 61, 314

Comrades Union of the Three People's Principles (Nationalism, Democracy, the People's Livelihood) **Vol. 1**: 264

"Conflict Theory" **Vol. 1**: 389–391

Conference on Educational Work **Vol. 3**: 82, 102

Confucianism **Vol. 1**: 4, 16

Congress of Chinese Literature and Arts Workers **Vol. 3**: 198

Constitution of the People's Republic of China **Vol. 2**: 117; **Vol. 3**: 122, 231, 287, 377, 475

Construction of Socialist Spiritual Civilization **Vol. 2**: 116; **Vol. 3**: 249, 308, 313–314, 368, 383–384

construction of the People's Army **Vol. 1**: 82, 299; **Vol. 2**: 116; **Vol. 3**: 308

contracted production **Vol. 2**: 202, 248, 328

contradiction **Vol. 1**: 118, 367, 412, 437, 516; **Vol. 2**: 14–15, 33, 36, 39–40, 45, 84, 91–92, 94, 102–103, 105–106, 111, 124, 128–129, 139, 146–147, 157, 164–170, 174, 178, 185–186, 218–219, 226, 236, 245, 256, 258–259, 319; **Vol. 3**: 27, 85, 130, 171, 191, 199, 251, 259, 292, 328–329, 344, 346, 362, 430, 433, 491, 494

Contradictions **Vol. 1**: 66, 68, 118, 228; **Vol. 2**: 165

corruption **Vol. 1**: 197, 358; **Vol. 2**: 104, 309; **Vol. 3**: 293–295, 297, 299, 307–309, 319, 323, 325, 331, 447–448, 454, 460–462, 464–467, 474, 531, 536, 546, 549

counter-revolutionaries **Vol. 1**: 124, 143, 193, 284, 514; **Vol. 2**: 57, 167, 252; **Vol. 3**: 104–105, 113, 115

counter-revolutionary **Vol. 1**: 31, 43, 74, 85–87, 112, 122, 127, 160, 181, 192, 214, 250, 268, 272, 275–276, 279, 284, 291, 298, 320, 340, 355, 378, 474, 494, 514; **Vol. 2**: 111, 136, 284–285, 294, 298, 314, 316; **Vol. 3**: 72, 77, 86, 161, 163, 285

countryside Vol 1: 56, 83, 115, 128, 136, 140, 144, 150–151, 154–155, 157, 160–162, 164, 166, 169, 171, 174–175, 178–180, 182, 184–185, 187, 189, 330–331, 334–335, 360–361, 373, 377–378, 420, 495–497, 499, 502, 508, 527, 533; **Vol. 2**: 30, 32, 38, 41, 65–66, 69, 72, 87, 102, 111, 124, 175, 189, 193–194, 196, 206, 248, 259, 301; **Vol. 3**: 4–6, 148, 250, 282–283, 378, 450, 509, 528, 542–545

County People's Congress **Vol. 1**: 515

CPC **Vol. 1**: 20–21, 24–28, 32–45, 47, 49–58, 61, 63, 66–72, 75, 77–79, 82–87, 89, 91–95, 99–101, 103–106, 108–110, 115–116, 118–121, 123, 125–126, 129–134, 139, 141–143, 145–146, 149–158, 160–161, 163–167, 169, 172, 174, 177–178, 183–184, 186–189, 191–192, 198–203, 208–211, 213–245, 247–273, 275, 277–279, 281–282, 284–285, 287–288, 291–294, 299, 301, 304–311, 313–314, 316, 318, 324, 327, 331–333, 337, 351, 354–355, 360–373, 376–379, 381–382, 384, 386–389, 391–393, 399, 401, 403, 405–408, 410, 414–415, 419–425, 428–429, 431–442, 444–456, 458–463, 465–479, 481–482, 484–486, 489, 491–493, 495–497, 499–501, 503–505, 507–510, 512, 515–517, 519–524, 526, 528, 531–532, 534–539, 541–543, 545; **Vol. 2**: 11, 16, 20–22, 26, 28, 30, 32, 40, 48–49, 52–54, 57, 62, 64, 78–81, 90, 99, 105, 109, 117, 130, 133, 135, 140–143, 145, 152–153, 155, 157–162, 170, 173, 176, 202, 210, 220, 222, 249, 264, 267, 274–277, 279, 291–292, 295, 299, 302, 320, 329, 338; **Vol. 3**: 3–7, 10–13, 15, 46, 52, 59, 63, 70, 74, 76–78, 80–84, 86, 91–93, 98, 100, 103, 105–106, 109, 113–114, 126, 128, 132–133, 136, 139, 141, 146–147, 150, 157, 161–163, 168, 174, 177–178, 180, 189, 191, 199, 225–226, 232, 234, 239–240, 242, 247–248, 253, 255, 257, 275, 280, 290, 298–299, 301, 305, 307, 324, 329, 334, 341, 348, 350, 352, 360, 363, 365, 370, 372–373, 375, 381, 390, 394, 397, 415, 417, 419–421, 432, 438, 443–444, 446–447, 449–450, 454, 457, 459, 461, 465–466, 474, 479–484, 486, 488, 494, 509–510, 513, 515, 517–518, 520–521, 526, 528, 550

CPPCC (*see also* Communist Party Political Consultative Conference) **Vol. 1**: 266–268, 272, 511; **Vol. 2**: 48, 55–56, 62, 64, 111, 117, 154, 249, 319; **Vol. 3**: 129, 133, 136, 269, 374, 450, 454

criterion of truth **Vol. 2**: 11, 23, 321, 324, 327–329, 332, 334, 336, 338–339; **Vol. 3**: 32, 35, 37, 40–41, 43–45, 58, 135, 140, 152–154, 157–158, 162

criticism **Vol. 1**: 5, 13, 41, 61, 79, 102, 154, 160, 265, 322, 364, 374, 380, 385–387, 391, 398, 408, 425, 427–428, 430, 432, 437, 439, 446–456, 463, 471, 479–480, 502, 504, 534, 546; **Vol. 2**: 10–11, 23, 62, 73, 76, 139, 141, 143, 156–157, 162–163, 167, 176–177, 179, 182, 184, 202, 207, 219, 225, 242, 244, 246, 255–256, 259, 268–269, 272, 275, 283–287, 291, 295, 299, 301–304, 307, 314–316, 326, 334, 338; **Vol. 3**: 27, 33, 101, 144, 194–196, 280–281, 284, 455–456

Critique of the Gotha Program **Vol. 2**: 90

INDEX 581

Crook, Isabel **Vol. 3**: 117
cross-century development **Vol. 3**: 5, 384, 397, 403, 412
cultural construction **Vol. 1**: 82–83, 135, 189, 197, 208–211, 373, 548; **Vol. 2**: 158, 295; **Vol. 3**: 120, 123, 191, 364, 366, 387–388, 393, 395, 503–504, 511, 528, 534
Cultural Revolution **Vol. 1**: 76, 528, 541–544, 548, 550; **Vol. 2**: 10–11, 14, 23, 155, 174, 187, 191, 221, 230, 236, 252, 260–262, 267, 269–270, 272, 274–280, 282–285, 287, 291–293, 295–303, 305–317, 319–322, 325, 329–330, 335, 337–338; **Vol. 3**: 9–10, 12, 14–16, 18–20, 29–33, 35, 37, 42, 44–45, 53–54, 56, 61–63, 69–70, 73–74, 76–88, 92–93, 96, 98, 100–101, 105, 108–110, 114, 117–118, 122–123, 126, 128, 132, 136, 140–142, 159–160, 162–163, 166–168, 170–171, 187, 203, 228, 253, 283–285, 525, 530
Cultural System **Vol. 2**: 156; **Vol. 3**: 251, 389, 393, 511

D

Dabie Mountains **Vol. 1**: 352
Dachen Island **Vol. 3**: 226
Dadan Island **Vol. 3**: 228
Dalai Lama **Vol. 3**: 123–124
Dalian **Vol. 1**: 493; **Vol. 3**: 112, 410
Daqing **Vol. 2**: 269; **Vol. 3**: 21–22
Daqing Oilfield **Vol. 2**: 269
Das Kapital **Vol. 1**: 10; **Vol. 3**: 353
Dazhai **Vol. 3**: 21–22
decentralization **Vol. 2**: 102, 125, 149–150; **Vol. 3**: 271, 352, 356, 445
Decision on the China Issue **Vol. 1**: 152
Declaration of the Second National Congress of the CPC **Vol. 1**: 120, 215
democracy **Vol. 1**: 4–5, 8, 29, 65, 67, 69, 71, 73, 75–79, 81, 83, 85, 87, 89, 99, 101, 106–112, 114, 117, 131, 146, 190, 192, 199–200, 209, 216, 224, 232, 237, 241–242, 244–245, 258, 264, 266, 268, 272, 281, 298, 312, 317, 321–322, 365, 395–396, 398, 401–403, 409–413, 425, 449–450, 467–468, 482, 487, 491, 500–502, 509, 513, 515–516, 518–520, 522–523, 525, 528, 531, 534–537, 539, 542–544, 546, 548; **Vol. 2**: 4, 8, 10, 13, 25–34, 37, 40–42, 45, 47–49, 51–53, 56–59, 62–63, 65, 69–70, 72, 76–79, 81–83, 86–91, 95, 98–99, 104–105, 111–112, 114, 116–117, 119, 121, 130, 136, 141, 152–154, 159, 163, 169, 176, 179, 183, 185–186, 207–209, 221–222, 226, 232, 241, 245–246, 250, 274, 291, 298, 312, 320, 325, 339; **Vol. 3**: 31, 48, 56–58, 62, 129, 136–138, 140–147, 150, 152, 155, 161, 177, 182, 184, 191, 241, 252, 257–258, 269, 272, 305, 314, 316, 318, 364, 367, 369–372, 376–381, 385, 449, 452–453, 458, 460, 484–485, 509–510, 528, 532, 534, 545
Democratic Alliance **Vol. 1**: 224, 527, 535; **Vol. 2**: 30, 49
democratic centralism **Vol. 1**: 190, 359, 365, 368–369, 379, 387, 394–395, 398–403, 408–419, 427, 450, 452, 474–475, 488, 499, 509, 515, 518, 523, 527, 535; **Vol. 2**: 26, 48–49, 159–160, 190, 221–222, 243–244, 246; **Vol. 3**: 57–58, 62, 150, 161, 163, 172, 176–177, 184–185, 190, 281, 370
Democratic Management in Rural Areas **Vol. 1**: 527, 535; **Vol. 3**: 377
democratic parties (other) **Vol. 1**: 87, 120, 224, 256, 262–269, 271–272, 516, 527, 535; **Vol. 2**: 49, 53, 61, 79–81, 127, 129, 152–153, 170, 179, 249–250, 319–320; **Vol. 3**: 128–133, 168, 180, 242, 245, 372–375, 454
Democratic Republic Vol 1: 27, 72, 76, 100, 109–110, 117, 236, 491, 509, 513, 515, 517, 521, 527, 529, 535–536; **Vol. 2**: 28–29, 49
democratic system within the Party **Vol. 1**: 527, 535; **Vol. 3**: 452
Democratic United Front **Vol. 1**: 29, 87–88, 213, 244–245, 254, 256, 259, 261–262, 264, 268–269, 271, 527, 535; **Vol. 2**: 53, 79–80, 87, 153, 170, 320
Deng Enming **Vol. 1**: 19
Deng Liqun **Vol. 3**: 25, 125, 189, 193, 195, 199–200
Deng Xiaoping **Vol. 1**: 158, 200, 351, 352, 410, 485, 500; **Vol. 2**: 9, 11, 18, 21, 23, 142, 153, 160–163, 166, 197, 233, 237–238, 240, 245, 248–249, 251, 254–255, 299, 302–305, 307, 309–310, 312, 316–321, 324–328, 330–332, 334–339; **Vol. 3**: 4–5, 7, 9–11, 14–15, 18, 20, 24–26, 28, 34, 39–40, 45–47, 49–51, 57–60,

62–63, 74, 88, 90, 94, 110, 123, 125, 129, 132–133, 136–138, 140, 144–152, 157, 159, 162–163, 165–168, 178–181, 186, 188–189, 193, 195, 199–200, 202, 205–208, 210–211, 213, 215, 217–219, 221, 225, 229, 231–233, 235–237, 240–242, 245–246, 255, 258–266, 268–269, 286–291, 301, 304–311, 315–319, 323–338, 340, 344–349, 351, 354, 357–364, 366, 368–372, 380, 382, 385, 390, 392–393, 398–401, 406, 415, 427, 430, 440, 446–449, 468, 472–476, 479, 481, 483–484, 492, 500, 502, 504, 514, 524–526, 533, 550–551

Deng Xiaoping Chronology **Vol. 3**: 137

Deng Xiaoping Theory **Vol. 3**: 5, 7, 63, 301, 326, 357–360, 368, 448, 468, 472–476, 483–484, 500, 504, 514, 524–526, 533, 550–551

Deng Xiaoping's Selected Works **Vol. 3**: 372, 448–449

Deng Yingchao **Vol. 3**: 62, 179, 188–189, 288

Deng Zhongxia **Vol. 1**: 14–15, 17, 29, 35, 102, 123–127, 139, 274

Deng Zihui **Vol. 1**: 497; **Vol. 2**: 166, 248

Deng's Six Articles **Vol. 3**: 232

Department of Theory of the Ministry of Publicity and Propaganda **Vol. 2**: 104

Developing Civilized and Courteous Activities **Vol. 3**: 367

Diaoyu Islands **Vol. 3**: 212

dialectical materialism **Vol. 1**: 64, 83, 294–295, 302, 326, 367, 388, 438; **Vol. 2**: 164, 232; **Vol. 3**: 41, 154, 156, 158, 168, 505

dictatorship of the proletariat **Vol. 1**: 13, 27–28, 34, 53–54, 60, 78, 89, 100, 103, 108, 190–191, 194, 227, 458, 507, 513, 519–520; **Vol. 2**: 49–50, 92, 135, 219, 262, 277–282, 290, 294, 296, 299–300, 306, 315, 318–319; **Vol. 3**: 21, 23, 49, 51, 140–142, 145, 147, 149–150, 283, 329

Ding Guangen **Vol. 3**: 245

Ding Guangxun **Vol. 3**: 127

Dingxi County **Vol. 3**: 277

diplomatic guidelines **Vol. 3**: 203

Discipline Commission (provincial or municipal) **Vol. 3**: 164, 200, 288, 294, 298–299, 318, 321–322, 460, 464–465, 467

Dispute Settlement Mechanism Agreement **Vol. 3**: 518

distribution **Vol. 1**: 13, 174, 199, 251, 420, 525, 532; **Vol. 2**: 4, 8, 107, 126, 128, 135, 141, 201, 205, 219, 236, 238, 268, 270, 280, 287, 294, 297, 301, 328, 334; **Vol. 3**: 14, 21–28, 37, 150, 194–195, 201, 249, 292, 329, 337, 349, 351, 355, 365–367, 394, 401, 473–474, 480, 489, 492, 496, 507, 510, 529, 531, 533, 541, 543, 548

District People's Congress **Vol. 1**: 515

doctrinairism **Vol. 1**: 366, 389

dogmatism (dogmatist) **Vol. 1**: 61, 65, 68, 157, 183, 188, 366–367, 391, 437, 441, 463, 485, 491, 546; **Vol. 2**: 8, 11, 13, 15, 17–18, 20, 23, 50, 120, 134, 139–143, 145, 156, 176–177, 184, 197, 204, 209–213, 220, 225, 273–274, 309–310, 312–313, 315–317, 319, 321, 323, 325, 328, 332, 338–339; **Vol. 3**: 332

Dong Biwu **Vol. 1**: 19, 38, 257; **Vol. 2**: 153

Dong Fureng **Vol. 3**: 199

Dong Yingbin **Vol. 1**: 234

Dong Zhentang **Vol. 3**: 104

Dong Zhiyong **Vol. 3**: 299

Double Hundred policy **Vol. 3**: 390

Draft Law of the People's Republic of China **Vol. 3**: 275

Duanjin **Vol. 1**: 191

E

East China Bureau **Vol. 2**: 249

Eastern Europe **Vol. 1**: 522; **Vol. 2**: 15, 40, 46, 50, 133; **Vol. 3**: 247, 323, 326

Economic and Technical Cooperation Agreement for the Construction and Reconstruction of Industrial Projects in China **Vol. 3**: 219

Economic Center of the State Council **Vol. 3**: 194

economic construction **Vol. 1**: 105, 193–197, 204–205, 292–294, 404, 505, 519, 526–528, 538–539; **Vol. 2**: 5–8, 26, 35, 38, 44, 46, 51, 78, 82, 84, 91, 94, 98–99, 101, 118, 120, 122, 131–132, 136, 138, 147–148, 174, 181, 186–188, 190, 192, 197, 202, 205, 211, 245, 268, 270, 306, 335; **Vol. 3**: 4, 21,

45, 47, 61, 148, 150, 161, 170–172, 174, 181–182, 191, 202–203, 207, 225, 243, 251–252, 254–256, 261, 266, 280, 293, 301, 309–310, 314, 318, 328, 334, 336, 339, 364, 386, 399, 408, 412, 433, 435, 484, 501, 503, 525, 531, 535, 545, 547
Economic Research **Vol. 3**: 24, 26, 192
economic system reform **Vol. 3**: 193, 198, 201–202, 241, 268, 313, 334–335, 344–346, 348–352, 354, 367, 378, 428, 488–489
Economic, Trade, and Science and Technology Commission **Vol. 3**: 219
Editorial Department of Philosophical Research **Vol. 3**: 43
egoism **Vol. 2**: 282–284
Eight-Character Principle **Vol. 3**: 132
Eight Conditions for the Standard of Communist Party Members **Vol. 2**: 86
Eight Major Routes **Vol. 2**: 74, 181, 185
Eight-Grade Wage System **Vol. 2**: 294
Eight-Nation Alliance **Vol. 1**: 3
Eighth Five-Year Plan **Vol. 3**: 212, 337, 364, 481
Eighth National Congress of the Communist Party of China **Vol. 2**: 7, 13, 183, 194; **Vol. 3**: 253
Eighth Political Report **Vol. 2**: 183
Eighth Route Army **Vol. 1**: 69, 202, 231, 241, 285–286, 305, 308–309, 311, 336–337, 342, 344
Eleventh Five-Year Plan **Vol. 3**: 177, 503, 508, 530, 550
Eleventh National Congress of the Communist Party of China **Vol. 3**: 3, 177, 530
emancipating the mind **Vol. 1**: 470; **Vol. 2**: 8, 21, 140, 209, 211, 226, 325, 328–329, 332, 334, 339; **Vol. 3**: 35, 57, 60, 68–69, 90, 153–155, 158, 173, 243, 333, 336, 343, 359, 472, 525, 549
Engels, Friedrich **Vol. 1**: 7, 97, 163, 188, 224, 357, 364, 374–375, 381, 384, 393–397, 429–432, 434, 443, 445, 447, 451, 458, 492–493; **Vol. 2**: 12, 53, 113, 125, 135–137, 164, 209, 211–212, 215, 280, 299; **Vol. 3**: 41, 481
Enlightenment Society **Vol. 3**: 143
Enlightenment (Western Enlightenment) **Vol. 1**: 5, 545, 547; **Vol. 3**: 143

equalitarianism **Vol. 2**: 77, 201, 235, 238; **Vol. 3**: 365
Erdan Island **Vol. 3**: 228
ethnic groups (ethnic minorities) **Vol. 1**: 201–202, 228, 258, 266, 268, 289, 298, 449, 466, 516, 545; **Vol. 2**: 22, 53–55, 81–82, 135, 152, 157–158, 250, 298, 332; **Vol. 3**: 119–123, 126, 130, 131, 133, 137, 177, 179, 229, 231, 240, 242, 358, 367, 372, 482, 527, 530, 550
ethnic policy **Vol. 2**: 55; **Vol. 3**: 116, 118–122, 125
ethnic relations **Vol. 2**: 55, 157; **Vol. 3**: 120–122, 125, 130
etiquette system **Vol. 1**: 317
European Capitalist Society **Vol. 1**: 161
European proletarian revolution **Vol. 1**: 161
Exchange and Payment Agreement **Vol. 3**: 219
Executive Committee **Vol. 1**: 33, 35, 38–39, 51, 54, 103–104, 152–153, 190–191, 215–217, 221, 226–227, 232, 275, 363; **Vol. 3**: 105, 537
extremism **Vol. 2**: 305

F
fake party **Vol. 3**: 79
fall of Shanghai **Vol. 1**: 308
Fallaci, Oriana **Vol. 3**: 163, 289
Fan Hongjie **Vol. 1**: 17
Fang Fang **Vol. 1**: 257
Fang Jisheng **Vol. 3**: 32
Fang Lingxuan **Vol. 3**: 32
Fang Lizhi **Vol. 3**: 316, 318
Fang Yi **Vol. 3**: 42, 189
Fang Zhenwu **Vol. 1**: 233
Fang Zhimin **Vol. 1**: 175, 178
February Countercurrent **Vol. 3**: 54, 76
February 7th Movement **Vol. 1**: 36
February Revolution **Vol. 1**: 28, 89
Federal Republic of China **Vol. 2**: 54
Federation of China **Vol. 2**: 54
Federation of Industry and Commerce **Vol. 2**: 127, 319; **Vol. 3**: 242
Feng faction: **Vol. 1**: 215
Feng Wenbin **Vol. 3**: 154
Feng Yuxiang **Vol. 1**: 214, 234, 248
Fenghua **Vol. 3**: 227

Fengtian warlords **Vol. 1**: 214
feudalism **Vol. 1**: 28, 37, 45, 52, 60, 62, 72–74, 88, 92, 94, 96, 98–100, 107, 114, 119–120, 130–131, 133–137, 140, 145, 246–247, 263, 268, 278, 280, 283, 285, 287, 316, 329, 331, 350, 466–468, 487, 509, 520, 525, 530, 535, 540–541, 543; **Vol. 2**: 26, 31, 37, 53, 83, 91, 93, 111, 116, 286; **Vol. 3**: 57, 148, 252, 309
Fifth Anti-Encirclement Campaign **Vol. 1**: 82, 158–159, 194
Fifteenth National Congress of the Communist Party of China **Vol. 3**: 359, 361, 363, 368, 371, 388, 400, 408, 419, 434
Fighting, Criticizing, and Reforming **Vol. 1**: 296
Fighting Egoism and Repudiating Revisionism **Vol. 2**: 283
Figueiredo, João **Vol. 3**: 264
Finance and Economic Commission **Vol. 2**: 37
Financial and Trade Economy **Vol. 3**: 193
First Congress of the Chinese Socialist Youth League **Vol. 1**: 25
First Five-Year Plan **Vol. 2**: 98, 101–102, 106, 131–132, 148–149, 188, 190; **Vol. 3**: 160, 482
First International **Vol. 1**: 357, 395
First National Congress of the Communist Party of China **Vol. 1**: 19, 29, 419
First National Labor Conference **Vol. 1**: 25
First Resolution of the Communist Party of China **Vol. 1**: 20
First World War (*see also* World War I) **Vol. 1**: 4; **Vol. 2**: 54
Five Always **Vol. 3**: 468
Five Coordinations **Vol. 3**: 495, 505
Five Determinations **Vol. 2**: 238
Five Emphases and Four Beauties **Vol. 3**: 312
Five Emphases, Four Beauties, and Three Loves **Vol. 3**: 313
Five Guarantees **Vol. 2**: 238
Five Oppositions Campaign **Vol. 2**: 94, 103–105, 109, 259, 292; **Vol. 3**: 93
Five Principles of Peaceful Co-existence **Vol. 3**: 206–208, 221, 426–427
Five Surges **Vol. 2**: 230, 232

Five-Year Plan **Vol. 1**: 498, 511; **Vol. 2**: 98, 101–102, 106, 114, 117–119, 124, 131–132, 147–149, 183, 188–190, 209, 260–261; **Vol. 3**: 160, 183, 212, 254, 261–262, 265, 286, 313, 337, 364, 381, 384, 399, 401–402, 481–482, 503, 508, 550–551
focus of work **Vol. 1**: 155; **Vol. 2**: 136, 145, 185, 330, 332; **Vol. 3**: 49, 51–55, 60–61, 254
Foreign Experts **Vol. 3**: 116–118
Foreign Language Bureau **Vol. 3**: 117
Foreign Language Institute **Vol. 3**: 117
Foreign Liaison Department **Vol. 3**: 82
Former Businessmen **Vol. 3**: 113–114
Four Adherences **Vol. 3**: 155
Four Basic Principles **Vol. 3**: 4, 136, 144, 148–152, 154–155, 162, 241, 243, 252, 254–256, 259, 281, 305, 310, 314, 318, 323–324, 336, 339, 525, 546–547
Four Cardinal Principles **Vol. 3**: 135, 484
Four Clean-ups **Vol. 2**: 259, 269; **Vol. 3**: 93–96
Four Clean-ups Movement **Vol. 2**: 269; **Vol. 3**: 93–96
Four Clearance Movement **Vol. 2**: 221
Four Little Dragons **Vol. 3**: 331
Four Modernizations **Vol. 2**: 03, 309, 327, 333–335, 339; **Vol. 3**: 28, 47, 49, 51, 53, 58, 64, 70, 115, 129–130, 136–137, 140, 145, 147–149, 154, 158, 175, 229, 258–261, 263, 267, 286–287, 290–292, 307, 309, 311, 319, 398, 458
Four Nevers **Vol. 3**: 520
Four Obediences **Vol. 3**: 453
Four Purifications Movement **Vol. 3**: 83, 85, 92
Four Subordinations **Vol. 1**: 410–411, 417
Fourth Army **Vol. 1**: 69, 202, 241, 285–286, 299, 307, 311, 323, 336–337; **Vol. 3**: 106–107
Fourth National Congress of the Communist Party of China **Vol. 1**: 30–34, 101–102, 125–126, 128, 139, 218, 220, 225–226, 400, 507; **Vol. 2**: 277, 302
Fourteen Articles for Scientific Research **Vol. 2**: 285
Fourteen Articles of Science **Vol. 2**: 240, 254
free market **Vol. 2**: 151, 287
French Revolution **Vol. 1**: 105, 165
Front Line Committee **Vol. 1**: 307

Fu Chongbi **Vol. 3**: 75–76
Fu Zuoyi **Vol. 1**: 234
Fujian Front Force **Vol. 3**: 228
Fujian Province **Vol. 1**: 299; **Vol. 3**: 96, 298, 313, 320–321
Further Development of the Western Region **Vol. 1**: 263; **Vol. 3**: 337, 508

G

Gang of Four **Vol. 2**: 303, 309–310, 313–317, 319, 321, 323–324, 326, 334–335, 337; **Vol. 3**: 9–14, 17, 20–23, 28–29, 32–34, 36, 40, 47, 49–52, 54, 60, 65, 72–73, 75–77, 79, 81, 83, 85, 88, 92–93, 100–101, 110, 118, 121, 126, 128, 130, 147–151, 154, 156, 159, 161, 163–164, 170, 175, 187
Gansu Province **Vol. 3**: 277
Gao Gang **Vol. 3**: 101
Gao Shanquan **Vol. 3**: 199
Gao Shuxun **Vol. 1**: 248
Gaozhou City **Vol. 3**: 456
General Administration of Civil Aviation of China **Vol. 3**: 539–540
General Administration of Customs **Vol. 3**: 278
General Administration of Radio and Television **Vol. 3**: 455
General Assembly **Vol. 1**: 19–20, 153, 202, 221, 232, 369–370, 387, 395, 403, 421, 504; **Vol. 2**: 148, 160, 212, 243, 245, 304, 319; **Vol. 3**: 139–141, 179–180, 182, 185–188, 190, 220, 224, 240, 244, 360, 473, 521, 524, 551
General German Workers' Association **Vol. 1**: 430
general line of the new democratic revolution **Vol. 1**: 143
General Political Department (PLA) **Vol. 3**: 82, 106, 156, 306, 432
General Secretary **Vol. 1**: 395; **Vol. 3**: 6, 78, 123, 189, 207, 211, 219, 221, 245, 324, 497, 516, 526, 545
Geng Biao **Vol. 2**: 317
German Democrats **Vol. 1**: 224
German Social Democratic Labor Party **Vol. 1**: 357
"going global" **Vol. 3**: 402

Gong Yuzhi **Vol. 2**: 3; **Vol. 3**: 199
Gorbachev, Mikhail **Vol. 3**: 219–221
Gotha Program **Vol. 1**: 430; **Vol. 2**: 90
governance **Vol. 1**: 119, 208, 439; **Vol. 2**: 292; **Vol. 3**: 4–5, 234, 241, 301–302, 325, 366, 440, 449, 465, 503, 511–513, 516, 534, 546
Government of the Ningkang County Workers, Peasants, and Soldiers **Vol. 1**: 136, 189, 202, 255
Government of the Workers and Peasants of Chaling County **Vol. 1**: 136, 189, 202
Government of the Workers, Peasants, and Soldiers of Suichuan County **Vol. 1**: 136, 189, 202, 255
Government of the Yongxin and Lianhua County Workers, Peasants, and Soldiers **Vol. 1**: 136, 189, 202, 255
Government Work Report **Vol. 1**: 136, 202; **Vol. 3**: 254, 262
Gramsci, Antonio **Vol. 2**: 18
Grasping Revolution and Promoting Production
grasping with both hands ("two handed grasp") **Vol. 3**: 302, 304, 309, 331, 364, 382
grassroots autonomy **Vol. 1**: 36 **Vol. 3**: 376
Great Hall of the People **Vol. 3**: 148, 239, 242
Great Harmony World **Vol. 3**: 533
Great Ideological Liberation Movement **Vol. 2**: 311
Great Leap Forward **Vol. 2**: 8–9, 130, 185, 187–193, 197, 199–200, 203–204, 206, 208–209, 211–216, 218–222, 226, 230–232, 234, 237–244, 246, 250, 253–254, 267–268, 270, 273, 276, 293, 325; **Vol. 3**: 332
Great Proletarian Cultural Revolution (*see* Cultural Revolution)
Great Revolution **Vol. 1**: 29, 42–47, 52, 58, 65, 79, 82, 112, 137, 145, 149–150, 152, 154, 163, 167, 172, 176, 180–181, 185, 189, 217, 222, 228, 234, 249, 278, 284, 361, 377–378, 419–420, 488, 494, 504, 508; **Vol. 2**: 170, 332–333; **Vol. 3**: 49, 51, 359, 546
Gu Bai **Vol. 1**: 158
Gu Mu **Vol. 2**: 331; **Vol. 3**: 46, 189

Gu Zhenfu **Vol. 3**: 414, 419
Gu Zhun **Vol. 2**: 307–309
Guangdong Province **Vol. 1**: 33; **Vol. 3**: 277, 322, 331, 456, 468, 500
Guangdong Province Second Peasant Congress **Vol. 1**: 33
Guangdong Provincial Committee **Vol. 3**: 322
Guangming Daily **Vol. 2**: 322; **Vol. 3**: 12, 24, 35–36, 53
Guangxi Province **Vol. 1**: 234; **Vol. 3**: 80, 96, 106, 125, 284, 455
Guangxi Student Army **Vol. 3**: 106
Guangzhou **Vol. 1**: 16, 18–19, 24, 36, 51, 61, 151, 165, 214, 353; **Vol. 2**: 235, 251, 254; **Vol. 3**: 143, 468–469
Guangzhou Conference **Vol. 2**: 254
Guangzhou National Government **Vol. 1**: 214
Guangzhou Uprising **Vol. 1**: 151, 165
guerrilla forces **Vol. 1**: 331, 333
guerrilla war **Vol. 1**: 83, 152, 169, 184, 198, 231, 298, 311, 329, 333, 373, 383
Gui Shifu **Vol. 3**: 199
guiding ideology **Vol. 1**: 3, 5, 7, 9, 11, 13, 15, 17, 19, 21, 23, 25, 27, 29, 31, 33, 35, 37, 39, 41, 43, 45–47, 49, 51, 53, 55, 57–59, 61, 63, 84, 157, 199, 205, 313, 370, 376, 384, 469, 485, 491; **Vol. 2**: 82, 125, 144, 157, 161, 171, 179–180, 203, 209, 229, 246, 255, 260, 277, 293, 314, 317–318; **Vol. 3**: 3, 6–7, 20, 51–53, 55, 59, 61, 63, 67, 95, 118, 141, 152, 158, 163, 169, 171–172, 174, 181, 283, 313, 334, 360, 365, 384–385, 387, 389, 443, 465, 468, 473–476, 492, 501, 512, 514, 526, 533, 550
Guidong County **Vol. 1**: 323
Guiyang City **Vol. 3**: 94
Guizhou Province **Vol. 1**: 323; **Vol. 3**: 78–79, 94–96
Guo Fan **Vol. 1**: 405
Guo Hongtao **Vol. 3**: 105
Guo Junyu **Vol. 1**: 17
Guo Moruo **Vol. 1**: 264
Gutian Congress **Vol. 1**: 178
Gutian Meeting **Vol. 1**: 289, 304, 307, 316, 321, 364, 366, 382, 400, 410

H

Ha'erbin (Harbin) **Vol. 1**: 16: **Vol. 3**: 277–278
Hai Rui **Vol. 2**: 222
Hainan Island **Vol. 3**: 226, 320–321
Han **Vol. 1**: 201; **Vol. 2**: 55, 81, 157; **Vol. 3**: 11, 62, 120–121, 124–125, 127, 189
Han Tianshi **Vol. 3**: 189
Han Zhixiong **Vol. 3**: 11
Handan **Vol. 2**: 204
Handicrafts, Thirty-five Articles of **Vol. 2**: 236
handicraft workers **Vol. 1**: 128, 292, 525, 539; **Vol. 2**: 62, 125
Handling Cases before the Cultural Revolution **Vol. 2**: 152; **Vol. 3**: 87
Hangzhou **Vol. 1**: 260, 355
Hankou **Vol. 1**: 18, 34, 40, 42–43, 166–167, 222
Hankou Special Meeting **Vol. 1**: 222
Hao Jianxiu **Vol. 3**: 189
Harmonious Socialist Society **Vol. 3**: 466, 514, 523, 525, 530–535
harmonious world **Vol. 3**: 516–518, 548
Hartling, Paul **Vol. 2**: 280; **Vol. 3**: 22
He Changgong **Vol. 3**: 288
He Kaifeng **Vol. 1**: 492
He Long **Vol. 1**: 178; **Vol. 3**: 81
He Mengxiong **Vol. 1**: 17
He Shuheng **Vol. 1**: 19
He Xiangning **Vol. 1**: 264
He Zhigui **Vol. 3**: 299
Heath, Edward **Vol. 3**: 139, 235
Hebei Province **Vol. 3**: 277
Hegel, Georg Wilhelm Friedrich **Vol. 1**: 374
hegemony **Vol. 2**: 263, 305; **Vol. 3**: 160, 181–182, 184, 203–207, 327, 421, 426, 437
Heilongjiang Province **Vol. 3**: 122, 299
Henan Province **Vol. 2**: 204; **Vol. 3**: 90, 277
Higher Education, Sixty Articles of **Vol. 2**: 240, 254
historical idealism **Vol. 1**: 92, 456
historical materialism **Vol. 1**: 7–11, 92, 302, 326, 374, 435–436, 444, 456–457, 461, 546; **Vol. 2**: 135, 164, 327; **Vol. 3**: 50, 84, 168, 329, 332–333, 506
History and Class Consciousness **Vol. 2**: 17

History of the Communist Party of China **Vol. 2**: 118
Hong Kong **Vol. 1**: 25, 34, 36, 228; **Vol. 2**: 42; **Vol. 3**: 56, 132, 134, 182, 216, 227, 231–237, 260, 266, 416–417, 420, 519–520
Hong Kong Business Group **Vol. 3**: 233
Hope Project **Vol. 3**: 383–384
"How Can the Party Last?" (article) **Vol. 1**: 193, 365
Howe, Jeffrey **Vol. 3**: 263
Hu Fuming **Vol. 3**: 35
Hu Jintao **Vol. 3**: 6, 439, 455, 458–459, 465, 499–503, 510, 512, 515–521, 523–524, 526, 532, 545
Hu Jiwei **Vol. 3**: 12, 42, 139
Hu Qiaomu **Vol. 1**: 483; **Vol. 3**: 22, 25, 28, 48, 62–63, 72, 139, 145, 165, 178, 185, 189
Hu Qili **Vol. 3**: 189, 245
Hu Sheng **Vol. 2**: 40, 229; **Vol. 3**: 139
Hu Shih **Vol. 1**: 10–11, 14, 24
Hu Yaobang **Vol. 2**: 322, 326; **Vol. 3**: 12–17, 33, 35, 38, 62–63, 67, 71, 96, 107, 111, 123–125, 133, 136–140, 145, 165, 177–179, 182, 186, 189, 199–200, 206–207, 211, 218, 245, 317, 323
Hu Zhaopei **Vol. 3**: 193
Hu Zongnan **Vol. 1**: 352
Hua County **Vol. 3**: 277
Hua Gang **Vol. 1**: 483
Hua Guofeng **Vol. 2**: 317, 324, 331, 333; **Vol. 3**: 10–12, 22, 40, 52, 54, 57, 59, 63, 136, 138, 171, 179, 203, 289
Hua Luogeng **Vol. 3**: 30
Huadong Field Army Corps **Vol. 1**: 351
Huaibei Base **Vol. 3**: 106
Huaihai **Vol. 1**: 327–328, 342, 352–355
Huainan Base **Vol. 3**: 106
Huairen Hall **Vol. 3**: 380
Huang Baitao Corps **Vol. 1**: 354
Huang Chao **Vol. 1**: 332
Huang Hua **Vol. 3**: 217
Huang Huoqing **Vol. 3**: 62
Huang Kecheng **Vol. 3**: 62, 81, 91, 164, 189, 288
Huang Lingshuang **Vol. 1**: 12
Huang Rikui **Vol. 1**: 17
Huang Zhen **Vol. 3**: 104, 139
Huang Zhongyue **Vol. 3**: 104–105
Huangpu Student Army **Vol. 1**: 274
Hubei Province **Vol. 1**: 43; **Vol. 2**: 109; **Vol. 3**: 85
Hubei Provincial Party Committee **Vol. 3**: 72–73, 108
Hume, David **Vol. 3**: 41
Hunan Peasant Movement **Vol. 1**: 331, 389
Hunan Province **Vol. 1**: 38, 169, 323; **Vol. 2**: 233
Hunan Provincial Party Committee **Vol. 1**: 151, 169, 174
Hunan-Guangdong-Guangxi Border War **Vol. 1**: 59
Hundred Days Reform Movement **Vol. 1**: 540
Hungarian Incident **Vol. 2**: 181
Huxi **Vol. 3**: 84, 105–106

I

ideological and cultural education **Vol. 2**: 82
ideological construction **Vol. 1**: 364, 373–376, 378–382, 384, 388, 400, 422, 427; **Vol. 3**: 432, 448
ideological emancipation **Vol. 2**: 11–12, 142, 186, 222, 312–313, 320–321, 325, 327, 329–330, 332, 334, 338–339; **Vol. 3**: 24, 32, 44–45, 69, 118, 136, 154–155
Ideological Liberation Movement **Vol. 2**: 311, 339
ideological line **Vol. 1**: 63–64, 66, 366–367, 378–379, 388–391, 393, 427, 438, 548; **Vol. 2**: 5, 11, 203, 232–235, 313, 316, 324, 327, 329, 338; **Vol. 3**: 34, 55, 58, 60, 69, 135, 153–158, 254, 472
imperialism **Vol. 1**: 3–4, 13, 24–27, 30–31, 34, 37, 44, 51–54, 56, 60–62, 66, 72–74, 87–88, 92–95, 98–100, 105, 107–108, 111–115, 119–123, 125–127, 130–131, 133–137, 140, 145, 160, 173, 187, 238, 243, 245–247, 253, 263, 268, 272, 275, 280, 283, 285, 287, 289, 292, 326, 329, 331, 350–351, 358, 375, 377, 397, 400, 434, 466–468, 487, 509, 514, 517, 519–520, 525–526, 530, 535, 540–541, 543–545; **Vol. 2**: 16, 18, 26, 31, 33, 37, 40–41, 53, 55, 60–61, 83, 91, 116, 136, 262–266, 274, 285, 288; **Vol. 3**: 145, 148, 172, 182, 226, 234, 252, 332, 416

Indies Social Democratic Alliance **Vol. 1**: 224
industrialization **Vol. 1**: 251, 497–498, 519, 533; **Vol. 2**: 5–6, 31, 64–65, 73, 76–78, 85–86, 88, 100–102, 104–105, 107–110, 112–115, 117–120, 122, 130–131, 137–138, 141, 146–150, 183, 187, 209–210, 218, 223, 225; **Vol. 3**: 253, 485, 490, 499, 529, 543
Industry, Seventy Articles of **Vol. 2**: 238–239, 254
Information Engineering College **Vol. 3**: 434
Information Work Office **Vol. 3**: 539
informationization **Vol. 3**: 437, 439
initial stage of capitalism **Vol. 1**: 475
Inner Mongolia **Vol. 1**: 202; **Vol. 3**: 15, 116, 122, 125, 277, 455
Institute of Philosophy **Vol. 3**: 43
institution building **Vol. 3**: 279
institutional reform program **Vol. 3**: 276, 538
Instructions on Land Issues (May 4th Instructions) **Vol. 1**: 249, 532
integrating Marxism into China **Vol. 1**: 77, 489, 491, 550; **Vol. 2**: 27, 273, 299, 303, 306, 310; **Vol. 3**: 550
intellectuals **Vol. 1**: 5, 7, 11–12, 14–16, 20, 46, 57, 72, 76, 113–114, 117, 128, 144, 198, 210, 215, 241, 253–254, 262–263, 288, 293, 367, 383, 399, 471, 488, 495, 499, 501, 513; **Vol. 2**: 61–62, 80–81, 130, 154–155, 157, 177, 179, 239, 241–243, 250–251, 254, 259, 263–264, 270, 288, 291, 301, 309–310, 320; **Vol. 3**: 18, 20, 30, 88, 110–112, 129–131, 145, 185, 242, 308, 317, 339, 372
International Law Commission **Vol. 3**: 224
International Monetary Fund **Vol. 3**: 224
International General Committee **Vol. 1**: 396
International Labor Day Commemorative Event **Vol. 1**: 15
International Workers' Association **Vol. 1**: 395–396
intra-Party struggle **Vol. 1**: 490; **Vol. 3**: 141
Iskra **Vol. 1**: 399
Islamic Union **Vol. 1**: 224

J
James Soong **Vol. 3**: 521

Jameson, Friedrich **Vol. 2**: 18–19
January Revolution **Vol. 3**: 66, 75
Japan **Vol. 1**: 9, 18–19, 30, 73, 75, 81, 229–230, 233–240, 242–243, 290, 297, 376, 400, 514, 532; **Vol. 2**: 263–264, 330; **Vol. 3**: 46, 106, 210–212, 228–229, 241, 347, 419, 423–425
Japanese imperialism **Vol. 1**: 61, 66, 73, 80, 98–99, 160, 238, 243, 289, 326, 400, 526, 530
Ji Dengkui **Vol. 3**: 70, 104
Ji Pengfei **Vol. 3**: 104
Jia Shuang **Vol. 3**: 299
Jiang Qing **Vol. 2**: 292, 294, 300, 304, 310, 313, 320; **Vol. 3**: 75–77, 79, 86, 170, 187, 285
Jiang Qing Anti-Revolutionary Group **Vol. 3**: 170
Jiang Zemin **Vol. 2**: 21; **Vol. 3**: 6, 245, 324–326, 338, 348–349, 351–352, 358–360, 364–365, 368–371, 375, 378–380, 383, 387–388, 390–392, 397, 401–402, 408, 410, 415, 417, 419, 421, 423–424, 426–427, 429–431, 433–435, 438, 444, 446–447, 454, 456, 458–459, 462, 468–472, 484, 526
Jiangshan Island **Vol. 3**: 226
Jiangsu Province **Vol. 1**: 352; **Vol. 3**: 53, 87, 105, 141, 263
Jiangxi Province **Vol. 1**: 38, 41, 178, 299; **Vol. 3**: 91
Jiangxi Provincial Political Committee **Vol. 1**: 38
Jiao Ren **Vol. 3**: 414
Jicheng County **Vol. 3**: 277
Jilin Province **Vol. 3**: 39, 122
Jin-Cha-Ji Territorial Doctrine **Vol. 3**: 76–77
Jinan **Vol. 1**: 19; **Vol. 3**: 38
Jinchaji **Vol. 1**: 202, 211, 493
Jinchaji Daily **Vol. 1**: 493
Jinggangshan (Jinggangshan Revolutionary Base) **Vol. 1**: 105, 168–170, 173–174, 189, 191, 306, 315, 317, 319, 323, 331, 336, 345, 361, 365, 382, 404
Jingxi Hotel **Vol. 2**: 300
Jinjiang Region **Vol. 3**: 298, 320–321
Jinjiluyu Central Bureau **Vol. 1**: 493
Jinmen Islands **Vol. 3**: 228

Jinsui Cadres Meeting **Vol. 1**: 533
Jinzhai County **Vol. 3**: 384
Jinzhou **Vol. 1**: 353–354
Joint Commission **Vol. 1**: 395
Joint Statement of the People's Republic of China and the Government of Portugal on Macao **Vol. 3**: 237
joint-stock enterprises **Vol. 3**: 406
July 1st Speech (Jiang Zemin) **Vol. 3**: 115, 471

K

Kang Sheng **Vol. 2**: 279; **Vol. 3**: 54, 73, 77, 79, 100–101
Kant, Immanuel **Vol. 3**: 41
Khrushchev **Vol. 2**: 143, 256, 264, 289; **Vol. 3**: 163, 247
KMT Legislative Body **Vol. 1**: 258, 260
KMT Revolutionary Committee **Vol. 1**: 258, 264
KMT ruling clique **Vol. 1**: 258, 271, 281
Kong Xiangxi (H H Kung) **Vol. 1**: 246
Korean War **Vol. 2**: 84–85, 99; **Vol. 3**: 226
Kosygin **Vol. 2**: 287, 289
Kowloon **Vol. 3**: 234, 416
Kropotkin, Peter **Vol. 1**: 6
Kung, H H (*see* Kong Xiangxi)
Kuomintang (*see also* Nationalist Party) **Vol. 1**: 24, 26, 29, 32–33, 35, 41, 48–49, 66, 69, 85, 102, 115, 123, 126, 136, 153, 192, 197, 215, 223, 235, 239, 248, 254, 257, 261, 467; **Vol. 2**: 37, 43, 49–50, 57, 60–61, 91–93, 116; **Vol. 3**: 79, 104, 107, 130–131, 226–228, 230, 232, 413, 419, 521
Kuomintang New Army **Vol. 1**: 33, 136
Kuybyshev, Valerian **Vol. 2**: 118

L

labor market **Vol. 3**: 354
labor-based distribution **Vol. 3**: 21, 23–27, 37
Lakeside Prefectural Committee **Vol. 3**: 105
Lan Gongwu **Vol. 1**: 11
land ownership **Vol. 1**: 51–52, 136–137, 143, 162, 523, 527, 532–533; **Vol. 2**: 26, 63–65, 123
Land Reform **Vol. 1**: 87, 250–256, 263, 271, 370, 439, 531–533; **Vol. 2**: 39, 57, 61, 63–67, 69, 71, 73–77, 87, 92, 94, 98, 102, 107, 111, 116; **Vol. 3**: 166
landlord class **Vol. 1**: 37, 52–54, 56, 75, 87, 93, 98, 129, 131, 135–138, 171, 185, 200, 246, 249–252, 271, 280, 288, 293, 371, 468, 528, 531–533; **Vol. 2**: 61, 64, 105, 286
landlords **Vol. 1**: 33, 46, 74–75, 80–81, 122, 129, 136–138, 143–145, 201, 237–238, 240, 249–255, 271, 278, 336, 377, 427, 467, 530, 532–533; **Vol. 2**: 64, 136, 257; **Vol. 3**: 112–113
Law of the Unity of Opposites **Vol. 2**: 168, 281; **Vol. 3**: 236
leadership of the CPC **Vol. 1**: 42, 87, 108, 115, 142, 172, 174, 178, 186, 198, 200, 229, 262, 264–265, 267, 272, 307, 310, 313, 368, 414, 466–467, 469, 521; **Vol. 2**: 152–153; **Vol. 3**: 257, 270, 483, 486
leadership system **Vol. 1**: 368–369, 415, 418; **Vol. 2**: 161, 186, 223, 230; **Vol. 3**: 3, 188, 241, 244, 268, 270, 337, 371, 449, 454, 513–514
League membership **Vol. 3**: 92
Lee Teng-hui **Vol. 3**: 418–419
Left-Wing Corps **Vol. 1**: 310
leftism **Vol. 2**: 138, 175, 200, 202–204, 206–208, 213, 216, 230–231, 234, 247, 252–253, 262, 302–303, 312; **Vol. 3**: 155
Leftist bias **Vol. 1**: 252, 254, 372; **Vol. 2**: 64
Leftist errors (*see also* Leftist mistakes) **Vol. 1**: 47, 58, 63, 251, 285, 378; **Vol. 2**: 10, 42, 95, 250, 258, 260, 277, 298, 319, 321; **Vol. 3**: 28, 31, 62–63, 66, 98, 126, 131, 135, 159, 162, 164, 171
Leftist mistakes (*see also* Leftist errors) **Vol. 1**: 55, 534; **Vol. 2**: 8, 10, 59, 175, 239, 246, 336; **Vol. 3**: 92, 174, 185, 250, 252, 334
Leftist tendencies **Vol. 1**: 105, 370; **Vol. 2**: 62, 74; **Vol. 3**: 283
Legislative Adjustment Bill **Vol. 3**: 213
Legislative Law Lecture **Vol. 3**: 380
Lenin, Vladimir **Vol. 1**: 6, 25, 149–150, 163, 188, 289, 291, 358–359, 364, 375–376, 379, 381, 384, 393–394, 397–399, 411, 430–432, 434, 443, 445, 447, 458–459, 492–493, 520; **Vol. 2**: 16, 18–19, 45, 54, 66, 118–119, 121, 126–127, 136–137, 140, 164, 181, 209, 211–212, 215, 266, 274, 280, 299;

Vol. 3: 28, 39, 147, 246, 332, 512
let a hundred flowers bloom and a hundred schools of thought contend **Vol. 2**: 156–157, 178, 183, 241; **Vol. 3**: 365, 390
Letter to Taiwan **Vol. 3**: 228
"letting in" and "reaching out" **Vol. 3**: 402–403
Li Chang **Vol. 3**: 189, 311
Li Da **Vol 1**: 9, 12, 18–20; **Vol. 3**: 104
Li Dazhao **Vol. 1**: 7–8, 10–12, 14, 16–19, 21, 29, 33, 102, 127, 399, 545, 547
Li Dingming **Vol. 1**: 202
Li Fuchun **Vol. 1**: 38; **Vol. 2**: 101, 156, 238; **Vol. 3**: 73
Li Hanjun **Vol. 1**: 9–10, 18–20
Li Honglin **Vol. 3**: 139
Li Jiantong **Vol. 3**: 100
Li Jingquan **Vol. 3**: 94, 288
Li Jishen **Vol. 1**: 248, 264
Li Jun **Vol. 1**: 17
Li Kenong **Vol. 1**: 234
Li Lisan **Vol. 1**: 52, 58–62, 105, 157, 285; **Vol. 2**: 40, 166; **Vol. 3**: 72
Li Peng **Vol. 3**: 221, 245, 275
Li Ruihuan **Vol. 3**: 245
Li Shangyin (Tang Dynasty poet) **Vol. 3**: 187
Li Siguang **Vol. 3**: 30
Li Tieying **Vol. 3**: 245
Li Weihan **Vol. 1**: 95; **Vol. 3**: 189
Li Xiannian **Vol. 2**: 300, 324, 326, 328, 333; **Vol. 3**: 11, 40, 48–49, 73, 179, 188–189, 200, 215, 246, 289
Li Ximing **Vol. 3**: 245
Li Zhangda **Vol. 1**: 264
Li Zicheng **Vol. 1**: 332
Li Zongren **Vol. 1**: 234
Liang Qichao **Vol. 1**: 5, 7
Liaoning Province **Vol. 3**: 122, 141
Liao Chengzhi **Vol. 3**: 189
Liao Jili **Vol. 3**: 198
Liao Zhongkai **Vol. 1**: 7
Liaoshen **Vol. 1**: 327–328, 342, 352–355
Liberation **Vol. 1**: 27–28, 37, 53, 76, 85–88, 105, 111, 113, 130, 132, 135–137, 142, 188, 203, 210, 224, 233, 244–245, 247–248, 255, 258, 261–263, 265, 267, 269–271, 278, 281, 284–286, 300, 305–306, 309, 311–313, 317, 320–321, 324, 327–329, 334, 337–338, 342, 344, 346–347, 350–351, 353, 355, 372, 383, 388, 403, 410, 421, 433, 466–467, 470, 475, 477, 484, 486, 491, 494, 500, 516, 522, 531, 534–535; **Vol. 2**: 32, 41–42, 49, 53–54, 99, 141, 252, 263, 272, 278–280, 295, 311, 327, 339; **Vol. 3**: 23, 29, 41, 65, 82, 97, 106, 109, 114, 137, 148, 153, 162, 169, 178, 225–229, 240, 244, 309, 327, 358, 433, 435, 487, 496, 517
Liberation Army Daily **Vol. 2**: 278–279; **Vol. 3**: 41, 137
Lien Chan **Vol. 3**: 521
Lihuang Municipal Committee **Vol. 3**: 106
Lin Biao **Vol. 1**: 179; **Vol. 2**: 269, 280, 300–301, 303, 310, 316, 320–321, 324, 326; **Vol. 3**: 40, 60, 72–77, 79, 83, 85–86, 93, 100–101, 121, 126, 130, 147–148, 150, 154, 156, 159, 161, 163–164, 170, 175, 187, 285
Lin Feng **Vol. 3**: 72
Lin Jianqing **Vol. 3**: 139, 199
Lin Zuhan **Vol. 1**: 38
lingering historical issues (post Cultural Revolution) **Vol. 3**: 53, 55, 82–88, 103
linking theory and practice **Vol. 1**: 423, 436, 440, 445, 471
Lisan Road **Vol. 1**: 157
literature and art **Vol. 1**: 198, 210, 300, 549; **Vol. 2**: 240, 242, 254, 259; **Vol. 3**: 32, 304–305, 315, 393
Literature and Art, Ten Articles of **Vol. 2**: 240
Literature and Art, Eight Articles of **Vol. 2**: 240, 254
Liu Binyan **Vol. 3**: 316, 318
Liu Bocheng **Vol. 1**: 347, 351; **Vol. 2**: 249; **Vol. 3**: 288
Liu Changsheng **Vol. 1**: 257
Liu Demin **Vol. 3**: 299
Liu Guoguang **Vol. 3**: 195
Liu Jingfan **Vol. 3**: 100
Liu Lantao **Vol. 3**: 72
Liu Renjing **Vol. 1**: 17, 19, 21
Liu Shaoqi **Vol. 1**: 34, 102, 249, 360, 367, 369, 381, 402, 410, 412, 425, 438, 460, 471, 475,

484, 489–490, 493, 496, 510–512, 522; **Vol. 2**: 33–34, 36, 42–44, 46–48, 50, 59, 64, 67–69, 72–74, 76, 78, 82–83, 85–86, 89, 91, 99–100, 109, 116–117, 129, 142, 147, 151, 153, 158–159, 165, 178, 188, 193–194, 212, 216, 219, 222, 233, 243, 247–248, 254, 257, 295, 299–300; **Vol. 3**: 15, 66, 77–78, 81
Liu Shaoqi Memorial Conference **Vol. 3**: 78
Liu Wenhui **Vol. 1**: 234
Liu Xiang **Vol. 1**: 234
Liu Xiao **Vol. 1**: 257, 259
Liu Xinwu **Vol. 3**: 30
Liu Zhidan **Vol. 3**: 66, 100–101
local nationalism **Vol. 2**: 149, 157; **Vol. 3**: 121
local religious organizations **Vol. 2**: 149; **Vol. 3**: 126
localization of Marxism **Vol. 1**: 481, 484; **Vol. 2**: 3–5, 8, 10–11, 13, 16–17, 20–25, 27–28, 41, 54, 57, 89–90, 95, 120, 125–126, 132–134, 145–146, 158, 163–164, 168, 170–171, 173–174, 182, 186, 191–192, 197, 200, 203, 206–208, 220–223, 225–227, 230–232, 234, 238, 245, 252–254, 258, 260–261, 299, 310–313, 315, 319, 321, 328–330, 332, 335–339; **Vol. 3**: 3, 6–7, 169, 335, 341, 376, 395, 417, 443, 461, 525, 527, 546, 550
localized Marxism **Vol. 1**: 444; **Vol. 2**: 170
Lominadze, Vissarion **Vol. 1**: 43, 56–58
Long March **Vol. 1**: 159–160, 286, 311, 341, 504; **Vol. 3**: 37, 104, 140, 154, 513
Long Yun **Vol. 1**: 234
Longhai Line **Vol. 1**: 352
Lu Dingyi **Vol. 1**: 483; **Vol. 2**: 193; **Vol. 3**: 72, 81
Lu Ping **Vol. 3**: 78–79
Luanchuan **Vol. 1**: 323
Lukács, György **Vol. 2**: 18
Luo Ronghuan **Vol. 3**: 105
Luo Ruiqing **Vol. 2**: 326; **Vol. 3**: 42, 76, 81
Luo Yinong **Vol. 1**: 276
Luo Yunguang **Vol. 3**: 299
Luo Zhanglong **Vol. 1**: 17
Luojing Mountains (Luojing Mountain Rage) **Vol. 1**: 169, 171
Lushan Conference **Vol. 2**: 175, 186, 191, 208, 216–217, 219–222, 226–227, 229–231, 255; **Vol. 3**: 91, 164
Lushan Preparatory Conference **Vol. 2**: 200
Lutai **Vol. 1**: 354
Luxemburg, Rosa **Vol. 2**: 18
Luyu District **Vol. 1**: 351

M

Ma Bufang **Vol. 1**: 356
Ma Guorui **Vol. 3**: 189
Ma Hong **Vol. 3**: 28
Ma Hongkui **Vol. 1**: 356
Ma Mingfang **Vol. 3**: 15
Ma Mingshan **Vol. 3**: 299
Ma Wanqi **Vol. 3**: 237
Ma Xulun **Vol. 1**: 264
Macao **Vol. 3**: 132, 134, 182, 231–234, 237, 416–417, 420
MacLehose, Barry **Vol. 3**: 234
macro-control (of the economy) **Vol. 3**: 302, 347, 349–351, 354–356, 365–366, 480, 491–492, 495–496, 505, 507, 538–539, 541
mandatory planning **Vol. 3**: 191
Malenkov, Georgy **Vol. 2**: 118
Malthusian theory **Vol. 1**: 8
Malyn, **Vol. 1**: 19
Manabendra Nath Roy **Vol. 1**: 222
Manchu **Vol. 1**: 201
Mao Zedong **Vol. 1**: 16, 19, 29–31, 33, 46, 51–53, 57, 66–79, 81–86, 89, 91–92, 95, 99, 102, 105–117, 127, 129–133, 139–141, 143, 146–147, 150, 158–161, 164, 166–176, 178–199, 203–210, 216, 228–249, 252–258, 262, 264, 266, 269–271, 273, 276–286, 288–292, 294–302, 304–308, 310–313, 315–324, 326–350, 353–356, 361–363, 365–369, 377, 379–382, 384–389, 391–401, 403–411, 416, 423–424, 426–428, 431–438, 440, 443–445, 448, 452–454, 459, 461–464, 469–470, 472, 474, 476, 478–479, 481–497, 499–501, 503–549; **Vol. 2**: 5–8, 11, 13–14, 16, 18, 20, 22–24, 27–32, 34, 37–41, 43, 47, 49, 51–53, 55, 59–65, 74–77, 79–82, 84–85, 88, 91–93, 97, 99–101, 103–105, 109–111, 114–117, 119–120, 122–123, 126–127, 130, 132, 134, 141, 143–144, 146–157, 161, 163, 166–170, 174–181,

184–191, 193–194, 196–197, 199–217, 220–222, 227, 231–235, 238, 244–245, 254, 256–259, 262, 265–267, 269–280, 282–283, 286, 291–292, 294–296, 299, 301–305, 307–308, 311, 313–319, 321–327, 329, 334, 336–339; **Vol. 3**: 10, 22–23, 33–40, 42, 58, 60, 62–63, 66, 73, 79, 93, 104, 126, 128, 132, 135–136, 140, 142–151, 154, 157, 161–170, 173, 180, 184, 204, 226–227, 234, 247–248, 252, 259, 280, 285, 315, 325, 327, 332, 337, 340, 358–360, 364–365, 385, 393, 416, 444, 472–476, 483, 500, 504, 513–514, 525–527, 533

Mao Zedong Thought **Vol. 1**: 81, 83–85, 183, 188, 279, 312–313, 363, 382, 394, 424, 459, 469–470, 479, 481–495, 497, 499, 501, 503, 505, 507, 509, 511, 513, 515, 517, 519, 521, 523, 525, 527, 529, 531, 533, 535, 537, 539, 541, 543, 545, 547, 549; **Vol. 2**: 13, 22, 82, 88, 143, 161, 170, 262, 272–273, 278, 282–283, 286, 303, 307, 313, 315–319, 321–324, 326–327, 329, 336–338; **Vol. 3**: 33–37, 39–40, 42, 58, 60, 62–63, 126, 128, 140, 142–145, 147, 149–151, 154, 157, 161–169, 173, 180, 184, 280, 325, 337, 340, 359–360, 365, 385, 393, 472–476, 483, 500, 504, 514, 525–527, 533

Maoism/Maoist **Vol. 1**: 483, 492; **Vol. 2**: 264, 303
Maoming City **Vol. 3**: 468
Mari Incident **Vol. 1**: 166
Marin (Jakob Rudnick, Comintern leader) **Vol. 1**: 215, 224
market economy **Vol. 1**: 54, 507; **Vol. 2**: 4, 13, 15, 23, 152, 196, 222, 225–226, 291; **Vol. 3**: 6, 195, 200, 328–329, 344–354, 357, 362, 366, 371, 379–382, 385–386, 391, 393, 404–405, 410, 432, 436, 444–447, 454, 461, 467, 480, 488–489, 492–497, 507, 513–514, 525, 540, 543, 545, 547
market regulation **Vol. 2**: 14, 288; **Vol. 3**: 191–197, 199, 344–348, 350, 365, 488
Marx, Karl **Vol. 1**: 7–8, 97, 163, 188, 224, 357, 364, 374–376, 381, 384, 392, 394–397, 429–431, 434, 443, 445, 447, 456, 458, 493; **Vol. 2**: 12, 19, 53, 90, 113, 119, 125, 127, 135–137, 144, 164, 209–212, 215, 266, 280, 299; **Vol. 3**: 39, 332
Marxism **Vol. 1**: 3, 5–19, 21, 23, 27, 29, 37, 63, 65, 67–71, 77, 79, 81, 92, 102, 134, 141, 149–151, 163–164, 302, 308, 311, 358–359, 367, 374–375, 381, 385, 389–393, 405–407, 420, 431, 433–435, 437, 440–442, 444, 446, 448, 451, 456–457, 464, 473, 481–486, 488–491, 496, 502, 509, 535, 541, 546, 550; **Vol. 2**: 3–28, 30, 39, 41, 47, 50, 54, 56–57, 66, 73, 77, 82, 87–90, 94–95, 104, 113, 120, 125–126, 130–134, 136, 139–140, 142–146, 148, 156–158, 163–164, 168, 170–171, 173–174, 177, 182, 186–188, 191–192, 195, 197, 200, 202–204, 206–210, 215–216, 219–227, 230–232, 234, 238, 245, 252–254, 258, 260–262, 264–268, 271–274, 276–278, 282, 284, 290–291, 294, 298–306, 309–316, 319, 321–325, 327–330, 332, 335–339 **Vol. 3**: 3, 6–7, 28, 36–37, 39, 41, 63, 110, 169, 181, 185, 191–192, 202, 233, 243, 250–251, 315–317, 329, 332–335, 338, 340–341, 346, 357, 359–360, 368, 376, 388–389, 395, 397, 403, 417, 443, 461, 468, 475–477, 487, 495, 497, 504–505, 514, 525, 527, 530, 535, 546, 549–550

Marxism with Chinese characteristics **Vol. 1**: 6, 481; **Vol. 3**: 334
Marxism-Leninism (*see also* Marxist-Leninist Thought) **Vol. 1**: 26, 63, 65, 67–68, 79, 82–84, 89, 99, 106, 116, 128, 130, 144, 150, 164, 188, 218, 276, 311–313, 357, 359–360, 363, 371, 373, 376, 379–384, 387, 392, 405–406, 424–425, 439, 441, 459, 468–470, 479, 482–486, 490–492, 502, 517; **Vol. 2**: 8, 14, 21, 28, 54, 82–83, 128, 143–144, 162, 210, 233, 244, 283, 286, 322–324, 326–327, 329–330, 336–337; **Vol. 3**: 33–35, 37, 39–40, 58, 60, 62, 126, 128, 140, 143, 145–147, 149–151, 154, 157, 169, 184, 280, 325, 340, 359–360, 365, 385, 393, 472–474, 476, 500, 504, 514, 526–527, 533

Marxist Economic Theory **Vol. 1**: 7, 9; **Vol. 3**: 20, 488, 493
Marxist epistemology **Vol. 1**: 409, 444, 463; **Vol. 3**: 41, 137, 452
Marxist line **Vol. 2**: 321; **Vol. 3**: 241
Marxist line of thought **Vol. 2**: 321
Marxist-Leninist Thought (*see also* Marxism-Leninism) **Vol. 1**: 24, 65; **Vol. 2**: 262, 265, 272, 277–279, 281, 298; **Vol. 3**: 483, 504
Marxist Research Society of Peking University **Vol. 1**: 17
Marxist Studies **Vol. 1**: 7, 20

Masayoshi Ōhira **Vol. 3**: 210, 260
mass historical view **Vol. 1**: 41, 456–458
mass line **Vol. 1**: 41, 326, 366, 380, 409, 459–461, 463, 470–471, 474–475, 488; **Vol. 2**: 161, 219, 243, 246, 319; **Vol. 3**: 16, 72, 155, 163, 169, 177, 296, 452, 457–458
mass movement **Vol. 1**: 39, 41–42, 220, 228, 231, 259, 285; **Vol. 2**: 190, 193, 299; **Vol. 3**: 12, 50, 52, 60, 93
masses (peasant masses) **Vol. 1**: 9, 13–15, 24, 33, 35, 37–38, 42–44, 48, 52–53, 58–59, 73, 75, 85–86, 95, 108–109, 124, 130–131, 133, 143, 150, 156, 168, 171, 173–177, 179–181, 183–185, 187, 190–194, 198, 200–201, 207, 209–212, 218, 226, 237, 241–242, 247, 249, 251–252, 254–256, 258–261, 267, 270, 277–278, 284–287, 293, 300–307, 310–312, 315, 317, 320–321, 326, 328–329, 332–335, 337–338, 358, 363, 366–367, 372, 374, 376–377, 380, 384, 387, 389, 393, 396, 402, 404–409, 412–413, 415, 417, 419–420, 424, 426–428, 430, 432, 435–436, 439, 444, 449–450, 456–465, 469–475, 477–480, 484, 487, 502, 506, 518, 548–549; **Vol. 2**: 9, 65, 67, 78, 80, 84, 104, 124, 129, 159–163, 175–176, 179, 181, 188, 190–192, 206, 218–219, 224, 234–236, 241, 244–245, 249, 252, 261, 269, 276, 286, 292, 295, 297–298, 301, 303, 305–306, 309, 311–312, 314, 316–318, 323, 327, 339; **Vol. 3**: 10, 12–13, 15, 19, 38, 53–54, 58, 69, 72–75, 77, 81, 83, 85, 102, 106, 109, 113–114, 121–122, 126, 142–143, 146–147, 150, 157–158, 161, 177, 184–185, 202, 252–253, 257, 271–272, 281–282, 284–285, 291, 308–309, 323, 338–339, 362, 367, 377–378, 380, 382, 386, 388, 393, 418, 445, 447, 451, 453, 456–459, 471, 476, 531, 547
material stimulus **Vol. 2**: 31 **Vol. 3**: 183
May Day **Vol. 1**: 16
May 7 Instructions **Vol. 2**: 269–272
May 16 Notice **Vol. 2**: 270
May Instructions **Vol. 1**: 223
May 4th Movement (May Fourth Movement) **Vol. 1**: 5, 7, 12, 14, 19, 36, 72, 81, 110, 114–116, 139, 259, 267, 363, 376, 508, 541–542, 546–547; **Vol. 3**: 31
May 19th Movement **Vol. 1**: 108

May 30th Movement **Vol. 1**: 29–34, 36, 274
May 4th Instructions **Vol. 1**: 250–251, 254
Mazu **Vol. 3**: 228
McNamara, Robert **Vol. 3**: 205
means of production **Vol. 1**: 6, 12, 162; **Vol. 2**: 6, 65, 112, 115, 118–119, 122, 124–128, 133, 135–136, 138, 141, 147, 165, 181, 185, 196, 216, 218, 223, 281; **Vol. 3**: 149, 193–195, 250, 355, 365
Meeting of Theoretical Work **Vol. 1**: 215, 265; **Vol. 3**: 137–139, 141
Meng Zi **Vol. 1**: 305
Mengcheng **Vol. 1**: 354
Mensheviks **Vol. 1**: 398; **Vol. 2**: 54
militant communism **Vol. 2**: 268, 271
Military and Civilian Congress of the Jinchaji Border Region **Vol. 1**: 211
Military Commission Symposium **Vol. 2**: 335
Military Committee **Vol. 1**: 172
Military Dialectics **Vol. 1**: 288
military drills (Taiwan) **Vol. 3**: 418
Military Facilities Protection Law **Vol. 3**: 436
Military Movement Resolution **Vol. 1**: 275
military reform **Vol. 3**: 429, 431, 438–439, 516
Military Region **Vol. 1**: 503 **Vol. 3**: 43, 50, 73, 76–77
military revolution with Chinese characteristics **Vol. 3**: 429
Military Service Law **Vol. 3**: 436
Min Xing **Vol. 1**: 6
Ming Pao Daily **Vol. 3**: 233
Ministry of Central Organizations **Vol. 3**: 97, 99
Ministry of Civil Affairs **Vol. 3**: 89–90, 103, 378
Ministry of Communications Vol 3: 539–540
Ministry of Construction Vol 3: 539–540
Ministry of Culture **Vol. 3**: 39, 82, 312
Ministry of Culture (Japan) **Vol. 3**: 212
Ministry of Economy and Trade **Vol. 3**: 322
Ministry of Education **Vol. 2**: 240; **Vol. 3**: 18–19, 67, 312, 455
Ministry of Environmental Protection **Vol. 3**: 540
Ministry of Finance **Vol. 3**: 455, 538–539
Ministry of Foreign Affairs **Vol. 3**: 217
Ministry of Health **Vol. 3**: 312, 540

Ministry of Housing and Urban-Rural Construction **Vol. 3**: 540
Ministry of Human Resources and Social Security **Vol. 3**: 540
Ministry of Information Industry **Vol. 3**: 539
Ministry of Land and Resources **Vol. 3**: 455
Ministry of National Defense **Vol. 3**: 91
Ministry of Organizations and Personnel of the Central Committee **Vol. 3**: 279
Ministry of Personnel **Vol. 3**: 277, 279, 540
Ministry of Propaganda **Vol. 2**: 104, 156, 240; **Vol. 3**: 37–38, 312, 384, 471
Ministry of Public Security **Vol. 2**: 104, 215; **Vol. 3**: 67, 89–90, 117, 312
Ministry of Publicity **Vol. 3**: 138, 312
Ministry of Railways **Vol. 3**: 87, 298–299, 539
Ministry of the Machinery Industry **Vol. 3**: 47
Ministry of Transportation **Vol. 3**: 539
minority ethnic groups **Vol. 2**: 157; **Vol. 3**: 121
moderately well-off society (moderately prosperous society) **Vol. 3**: 4, 260, 263, 266, 347, 479–488, 491, 495, 497, 501, 506–507, 523–524, 527–531, 533–534, 542, 545, 551
modern enterprise system **Vol. 1**: 24; **Vol. 3**: 351–353, 404–406, 410–412, 451, 494
modernization **Vol. 1**: 35–137, 463, 538; **Vol. 2**: 12, 15–17, 19–20, 23, 71, 76, 113, 130, 139–140, 181–182, 197, 210, 213, 216–217, 220–221, 225, 227, 253, 260–263, 267–268, 271–272, 284, 298, 302, 316, 325, 329–330, 332, 336–338; **Vol. 3**: 3–5, 7, 46–47, 49–52, 55, 57–63, 118, 130, 133, 136–137, 148–149, 151, 171–175, 177, 179–182, 185–186, 190, 192, 202, 205, 207, 210, 223, 225, 239–240, 243–245, 251, 254–260, 262–263, 266–268, 270, 279–280, 286–287, 290, 299, 303, 305, 307, 309–312, 314–315, 318–319, 322, 324, 326, 333–334, 336–337, 339–341, 343, 345, 348, 350, 357–360, 362–364, 366, 369, 373, 383–384, 387, 390, 392, 397–401, 403, 423, 434, 436–437, 441, 443, 446, 473, 475–476, 479, 482–488, 494, 498–500, 502, 505, 508–509, 516, 523–526, 531, 535–536, 543–544, 547, 549–550
modernization of Marxism **Vol. 2**: 12, 15–17, 19–20, 23, 113, 139–140, 182, 210, 216, 220–221, 227, 253, 267–268, 316, 325, 332, 338

Molotov, Vyacheslav **Vol. 2**: 118
Mongolia **Vol. 1**: 61, 202; **Vol. 3**: 15, 116, 122, 125, 201, 218–220, 222, 277, 455
Montargis Conference **Vol. 1**: 17
Mopping-Up Operation **Vol. 1**: 69
Moral Education **Vol. 3**: 383, 466
Moscow Conference **Vol. 2**: 189
multi-ethnic **Vol. 2**: 54–55; **Vol. 3**: 97, 172
multi-party **Vol. 1**: 209, 262, 264–265, 268; **Vol. 2**: 7, 52–54, 79, 152–153; **Vol. 3**: 272, 316, 365, 367, 372–373, 375–376, 510
Mutual Aid Organizations **Vol. 1**: 206; **Vol. 2**: 73, 76
Mutual Assistance Groups **Vol. 2**: 123
My View of Marxism (Li Dazhao article) **Vol. 1**: 7

N

Nakasone Yasuhiro **Vol. 3**: 211, 263
Nanchang **Vol. 1**: 57, 61, 168, 176
Nanchang Uprising **Vol. 1**: 57, 168
Nanjing **Vol. 1**: 18, 34, 61, 93, 156, 231, 235, 249, 256, 260, 354–355; **Vol. 3**: 35, 127, 234, 414, 416
Nanjing Peace Talks **Vol. 1**: 256
Nanjing Treaty **Vol. 3**: 234, 416
Nanning Conference **Vol. 2**: 185
National Army **Vol. 1**: 40, 214–215
national bourgeoisie **Vol. 1**: 27, 31–32, 37, 51–52, 56, 70, 74, 80, 87, 106, 114–115, 127, 138, 143, 145, 213, 216–218, 233–234, 237–238, 240, 242, 244, 253, 258, 261–263, 270–271, 283, 310, 468, 495, 517–519, 523, 540; **Vol. 2**: 4, 26–27, 41–44, 46, 49–50, 59–61, 63–64, 69, 80, 92–93, 103–105, 116, 126–129, 170, 202
national capitalism **Vol. 1**: 98, 138–139, 377, 534
National Civil Service Bureau **Vol. 3**: 540
National Civilization and Politeness Month **Vol. 3**: 312
national conditions **Vol. 1**: 25, 27–28, 66, 81, 91, 94, 130, 133, 140, 150, 161, 163–164, 175, 179–180, 186, 224, 298, 361, 376, 379, 392–393, 432, 508, 519–520; **Vol. 2**: 6–7, 11, 13, 19, 27, 39–40, 46–47, 54, 59, 66, 69, 87, 89, 93, 116, 129–130, 139–140, 144–146, 154, 166, 173, 187, 204, 206–207, 213, 234, 238, 246, 260, 264,

266–267, 296; **Vol. 3**: 170–171, 174, 241, 243, 246–248, 252, 257, 259, 266, 336, 351, 361, 369, 371, 397–399, 421, 488, 525–527, 544
National Conference on Education **Vol. 3**: 37
National Conference on Scientific and Technological Work **Vol. 3**: 264
National Congress of Workers, Peasants, and Soldiers **Vol. 1**: 191, 255; **Vol. 3**: 112
National Cultural System Reform Work Conference **Vol. 3**: 511
National Defense Law **Vol. 3**: 436
National Development and Reform Commission **Vol. 3**: 538–539
National Economic Plan **Vol. 3**: 61
National Energy Leading Group **Vol. 3**: 539
National Ethnic Work Conference **Vol. 2**: 250
National Ethnic Work Plan **Vol. 2**: 158
National Federation of Literature and Arts **Vol. 2**: 240
National Federation of Trade Unions **Vol. 3**: 311, 450
National General Assembly **Vol. 1**: 19
national independence **Vol. 1**: 173, 466, 470
National People's Congress **Vol. 1**: 268, 515; **Vol. 2**: 26, 48, 53, 153, 249, 251, 260, 277, 302; **Vol. 3**: 24, 56–57, 118–119, 123, 198, 217, 224, 226, 228, 230–232, 236, 254, 261–262, 269, 271, 274–275, 287, 299, 319–320, 349–350, 373, 376–377, 380–381, 384, 399, 402, 413, 436, 439, 475, 482, 500, 503, 509, 517, 536, 551
National Planning Conference **Vol. 2**: 333–334; **Vol. 3**: 48
national religious groups **Vol. 3**: 126
national reunification **Vol. 3**: 413, 438
National Revolutionary Groups of the Far East **Vol. 1**: 92
National Riot Plan **Vol. 1**: 61
national salvation **Vol. 1**: 13, 233, 264, 282
National Salvation Times **Vol. 1**: 233
National Science and Technology Commission **Vol. 2**: 240; **Vol. 3**: 42
National Science Congress **Vol. 2**: 332; **Vol. 3**: 20, 45, 110
National Security Bureau **Vol. 3**: 104
National Socialist Party **Vol. 1**: 69

National Statistical Bureau **Vol. 3**: 278
National Symposium on Ethnic Work **Vol. 2**: 250
National United Front Conference **Vol. 2**: 59, 250
National United Front Work Conference **Vol. 2**: 79, 250; **Vol. 3**: 129–131, 133, 375
national unity **Vol. 2**: 157, 250; **Vol. 3**: 119–122, 124, 126, 336, 401
National University of Defense Science and Technology **Vol. 3**: 434
National Workers, Peasants, and Soldiers Congress **Vol. 1**: 105, 191, 255; **Vol. 3**: 112
Nationalism, Democracy, the People's Livelihood **Vol. 1**: 264, 518
Nationalist Party (*see also* Kuomintang) **Vol. 1**: 41, 93, 109, 266
nationalities (*see also* ethnic groups) **Vol. 1**: 523; **Vol. 2**: 26, 157, 249; **Vol. 3**: 314
nationalization of industry **Vol. 2**: 72, 85
nationalization of Marxism **Vol. 2**: 225
Naval Engineering University **Vol. 3**: 434
Navy **Vol. 3**: 156–157, 226
new capitalism **Vol. 2**: 45, 335; **Vol. 3**: 394, 508
New China **Vol. 1**: 72–73, 76, 79, 81, 85–86, 132, 210, 263, 265, 306, 369, 424, 439, 466–467, 494, 498, 510–511, 517; **Vol. 2**: 4, 11–12, 16, 20, 22, 24, 26, 32, 39, 41, 44–45, 48, 52–53, 55–56, 58–59, 61–63, 65–66, 70, 80, 82–83, 87–95, 97–101, 103, 108–111, 114–116, 119, 122, 126, 129, 132, 140, 146, 148, 155–156, 165, 180, 187, 203, 226, 231, 238, 253, 261, 284–285, 293, 296, 298, 308, 312, 315, 320, 325, 333, 335, 337; **Vol. 3**: 6, 15–16, 18, 47, 60, 80, 84, 92, 96, 98, 102–103, 109, 114–115, 119, 126, 128, 130, 141, 145–146, 148, 155, 158–162, 164–168, 170–171, 174, 203, 208, 225, 234, 240, 248, 252, 256, 270, 274, 316, 358, 363, 373, 387, 394, 404, 416, 427, 484, 498, 508, 512–513, 530, 545
New Citizen Study Society **Vol. 1**: 17; **Vol. 2**: 45, 335; **Vol. 3**: 394, 508
New Constitutional Referendum **Vol. 2**: 45, 335; **Vol. 3**: 394, 508, 521
New Cultural Movement **Vol. 1**: 4–5, 8, 10, 541, 546, 548

New Democracy **Vol. 1**: 65, 67, 69, 71, 73, 75–79, 81, 83, 85, 87, 89, 99, 106–108, 110, 112, 117, 131, 146, 199, 209, 268, 467–468, 482, 487, 491, 509, 513, 515, 520, 522–523, 525, 528, 531, 534, 536–537, 539, 542–544, 546, 548; **Vol. 2**: 4, 13, 25, 27–34, 37, 40–42, 47, 49, 51–52, 56–59, 62–63, 65, 69–70, 72, 76–78, 81–83, 86–91, 95, 98–99, 104–105, 111–112, 114, 116–117, 119, 121, 141, 208–209, 274; **Vol. 3**: 252, 364

New Democracy National Founding Program **Vol. 2**: 95

New Democracy Program **Vol. 2**: 4, 57, 63, 69, 81, 87, 117

New Democratic Outline for the Founding of the People's Republic **Vol. 1**: 527, 535; **Vol. 2**: 4

New Democratic Revolution **Vol. 1**: 23, 25, 27, 29, 31, 33, 35, 37, 39, 41, 43, 45, 47, 49, 51, 53, 55, 57, 59, 61, 63, 71–73, 75, 78, 84–85, 89, 91, 93, 95, 97, 99, 101, 103, 105, 107–111, 113, 115–119, 121, 123, 125–127, 129–133, 135, 137–141, 143–147, 188, 199, 245–247, 263, 266, 268, 301, 370, 372, 421–422, 448, 460, 467–470, 487, 494, 508, 511–512, 521, 523, 527–529, 531, 534–536, 543, 548; **Vol. 2**: 3–4, 11, 27–29, 38–39, 41, 48, 53, 56, 63, 69, 72, 87, 89, 94, 98–99, 110, 114, 117, 126, 129, 143–144; **Vol. 3**: 180, 247, 252, 358

New Democratic Revolutionary Theory **Vol. 1**: 130, 507, 512, 527, 535; **Vol. 2**: 25, 32

New Democratic Socialization Theory **Vol. 1**: 527, 535; **Vol. 2**: 25

New Democratic Sociology **Vol. 1**: 527, 535; **Vol. 2**: 27, 41

New Democratic Theory **Vol. 1**: 73, 81–82, 85, 89, 107, 109, 130, 198, 495, 507, 523, 527–528, 535; **Vol. 2**: 4, 70, 93, 105, 117

new deployment of rural reform **Vol. 3**: 536

New Fourth Army **Vol. 1**: 69, 202, 241, 285–286, 311, 336–337; **Vol. 3**: 106–107

New Great Project **Vol. 3**: 443–444, 447–448, 474, 476, 484

New Historical Period **Vol. 3**: 18, 120, 130–131, 170, 182, 191, 254, 311, 457, 525

New Long March **Vol. 3**: 37, 140, 154

New Right (KMT) **Vol. 1**: 41, 93, 216, 221, 226

New Territories (Hong Kong) **Vol. 3**: 234, 416

New Youth (Youth Magazine) **Vol. 1**: 4, 7–8, 12, 16

Ni Zhengyu **Vol. 3**: 224

Ni Zhifu **Vol. 3**: 189

Nie Rongzhen **Vol. 2**: 156, 240, 300; **Vol. 3**: 33, 73, 76, 179, 188–189, 288

Nie Yuanzi **Vol. 2**: 300; **Vol. 3**: 78

Nikolsky, Vladimir **Vol. 1**: 19

Ningdu Uprising **Vol. 3**: 104

Ningxia Province **Vol. 1**: 76, 160, 199, 201, 203–204, 206–209, 211, 530; **Vol. 2**: 30, 323; **Vol. 3**: 122, 125, 455

Ningxiang County **Vol. 2**: 233

Ninth Five-Year Plan **Vol. 3**: 380, 384, 399, 401, 481

Ninth National Congress of the Communist Party of China **Vol. 3**: 179, 380

non-Party democrats **Vol. 2**: 81, 179, 249 **Vol. 3**: 133

non-public enterprises **Vol. 3**: 452

Nong'an County Committee **Vol. 3**: 115

North China Bureau **Vol. 2**: 71–72, 74, 76

North China Finance and Economic Commission **Vol. 2**: 37

North China University **Vol. 1**: 492

North China Territorial Doctrine **Vol. 3**: 76–77

North Korean Denuclearization Target Document **Vol. 3**: 519

Northeast Army **Vol. 1**: 234

Northeast Group **Vol. 3**: 53

Northeast Military Work Committee **Vol. 1**: 234

Northern Expedition **Vol. 1**: 24, 37–38, 40, 110, 150, 171, 221, 226–227, 267, 273, 275, 277, 279, 283–284, 371, 467; **Vol. 3**: 227

Northern War **Vol. 3**: 71

Northern Warlords (*see also* Beiyang Warlords) **Vol. 1**: 137, 150, 226, 467

Northwest Bureau **Vol. 1**: 310; **Vol. 3**: 101–102

Northwest Field Army **Vol. 1**: 356, 532

Northwest United University **Vol. 3**: 97

Northwestern High-level Conference **Vol. 1**:

205
Nuclear Power Management of the National Defense Science, Technology, and Industry Commission **Vol. 2**: 304; **Vol. 3**: 176, 211, 539
Nyers, Rezsō **Vol. 3**: 197

O

October Revolution **Vol. 1**: 6–7, 28, 30, 60, 89, 92, 108, 110–113, 150, 154, 162, 164–165, 182, 188, 227, 274, 276, 363, 370, 430, 432, 458, 542; **Vol. 2**: 14, 121, 126, 136, 142, 278; **Vol. 3**: 146
Office of Institutional Reform **Vol. 3**: 277
old cadres **Vol. 3**: 187, 286, 290
Ombudsman **Vol. 3**: 407
On Contradiction **Vol. 1**: 367, 437; **Vol. 2**: 80, 188; **Vol. 3**: 5, 206, 226, 282, 514
"On Investigation" (*see also* "Opposing Doctrines") **Vol. 2**: 233
On New Democracy **Vol. 1**: 491; **Vol. 2**: 27–30, 37, 45, 49, 86, 141
On Practice **Vol. 1**: 367, 437, 443; **Vol. 2**: 136, 174, 211, 233, 313; **Vol. 3**: 332
On Ten Relations **Vol. 2**: 7, 148, 150, 210
On the Correct Handling of Contradictions Among the People **Vol. 1**: 178; **Vol. 2**: 7, 168
On the Party **Vol. 1**: 117, 178, 249, 391, 402; **Vol. 2**: 144, 161, 180, 221, 295; **Vol. 3**: 34, 52, 88
On the People's Democratic Dictatorship **Vol. 1**: 89, 178, 249; **Vol. 2**: 116, 144
"On the People's Democratic Dictatorship" (article) **Vol. 2**: 49
On the Ten Relations **Vol. 1**: 178, 249
"On the United Government" **Vol. 2**: 30, 37, 45
one center, two basic points **Vol. 1**: 349; **Vol. 3**: 227
one country, two systems **Vol. 1**: 349; **Vol. 3**: 227
Open Rural Affairs **Vol. 3**: 377
Opium War **Vol. 1**: 3, 50, 96, 110, 114, 133, 517, 540; **Vol. 3**: 234, 416
opportunism **Vol. 1**: 44, 57, 120, 122, 145, 277, 296, 311, 358, 378, 389, 391, 474; **Vol. 2**: 38, 177, 235, 256; **Vol. 3**: 92, 160
"Opposing Doctrines" ("On Investigation") **Vol. 2**: 233

"Opposing Doctrinairism" (article) **Vol. 1**: 478
Organic Law of the CPPCC **Vol. 1**: 267–268
organization **Vol. 1**: 8, 12–13, 17–20, 45, 56, 68, 78, 80, 88, 140, 142, 144, 184, 187, 190, 208, 210–211, 219–220, 222, 225–226, 228, 233, 241, 255, 258–259, 261, 265–268, 271, 282–283, 285, 290, 304, 307–308, 310, 314, 321, 324, 333, 336, 343, 359, 361, 363–370, 372, 374, 376–377, 379–383, 385, 388, 394–396, 399–400, 402–404, 409–410, 413–415, 417–419, 421–422, 424–425, 427–428, 432, 434, 438–440, 460–461, 471, 488, 495, 513, 523, 531; **Vol. 2**: 49, 78, 116, 159–160, 192–193, 195–196, 223, 288, 292, 295, 298, 302, 322, 338; **Vol. 3**: 15, 17, 71, 79, 91, 93–94, 104, 106, 109, 112, 114, 181–182, 186, 271, 280–282, 296–297, 307, 354, 357, 377, 406, 414, 424, 427–429, 433, 448, 450–452, 465, 532
Organization Newsletter **Vol. 3**: 17, 94
Organizational Communications **Vol. 3**: 90, 447
organizational construction **Vol. 1**: 364–365, 368–369, 379, 394, 403, 408, 419, 428; **Vol. 3**: 280, 447–448, 450, 452
Organizational Work Conference **Vol. 1**: 512; **Vol. 2**: 86; **Vol. 3**: 447
orthodoxy **Vol. 1**: 164; **Vol. 2**: 23, 138
Outline of Vision for 2010 **Vol. 3**: 384
overseas Chinese **Vol. 1**: 228, 258, 261, 266, 268, 516; **Vol. 2**: 53, 250; **Vol. 3**: 67, 132, 134, 182
Overseas Chinese Daily **Vol. 3**: 233
Overseas Chinese Office **Vol. 3**: 67
Overseas Economic Cooperation Fund **Vol. 3**: 210

P

Palace of Hell **Vol. 3**: 82
Pan Hannian **Vol. 3**: 80–81, 98
Pan Keming **Vol. 3**: 299
Paris Commune Uprising **Vol. 1**: 358
Paris Coordination Commission **Vol. 3**: 217
Party Charter **Vol. 1**: 8, 362, 406; **Vol. 2**: 292; **Vol. 3**: 281
Party Committee System **Vol. 1**: 403, 410–411, 503
Party constitution **Vol. 1**: 84, 382, 402, 410–411,

424, 452, 455, 460, 486, 488, 500; **Vol. 2**: 159–162, 244, 314; **Vol. 3**: 151, 177–178, 181, 184–186, 188, 190, 287, 340, 360, 453, 467, 474–475, 526

Party construction **Vol. 1**: 75, 285, 367–368, 372, 376, 432; **Vol. 3**: 451–452

Party discipline **Vol. 1**: 405–406, 411, 424; **Vol. 2**: 160; **Vol. 3**: 62, 280, 298, 320–322, 464–465

Party Group **Vol. 1**: 307; **Vol. 2**: 240; **Vol. 3**: 43, 66, 87, 99, 108, 117, 121, 299, 321

Party leadership **Vol. 1**: 43, 88, 165, 230, 243, 275, 308, 313, 368–369, 404, 408, 422, 429, 439, 466, 469, 471, 478; **Vol. 2**: 180, 276, 288, 300–301, 309; **Vol. 3**: 47, 360, 514

Party Life **Vol. 1**: 200, 365, 413, 418, 420, 427, 440, 450–451, 455, 479

Party membership **Vol. 1**: 57, 364, 419–420, 422–424, 512; **Vol. 2**: 69; **Vol. 3**: 85, 97, 105–108, 188, 287

party organization **Vol. 1**: 18–20, 68, 78, 220, 228, 258, 361–365, 368, 370, 377, 381, 385, 394–395, 400, 403, 409, 413, 421–422, 432, 438, 471; **Vol. 2**: 223, 288, 292, 298; **Vol. 3**: 79

Party spirit **Vol. 1**: 70, 380, 411, 416–417, 423, 432, 436–438, 443–444, 449, 451

party-building **Vol. 1**: 46, 284–285, 357, 359–379, 381, 383, 385, 387, 389, 391, 393–395, 397, 399–401, 403, 405, 407, 409–411, 413, 415, 417, 419, 421–423, 425, 427–429, 431, 433–435, 437, 439, 441, 443, 445, 447–451, 453, 455, 457–461, 463, 465, 467, 469, 471, 473, 475, 477, 479, 488, 491, 497, 500, 504–505; **Vol. 2**: 162–163

Party's absolute leadership of the military **Vol. 1**: 306, 311–313

Party's basic line **Vol. 1**: 404; **Vol. 3**: 4, 152, 174, 239, 243–244, 253–257, 303, 325, 328, 332, 358, 361, 363, 366, 368, 385, 398, 432, 447, 453, 458, 514, 533

Pastoral Work, Forty Articles of **Vol. 2**: 250

Patriotic Education **Vol. 3**: 383

peaceful evolution **Vol. 3**: 323, 332, 447

peaceful reunification **Vol. 3**: 225, 228–230, 232, 340, 414–415, 420, 438, 516, 520–521, 546

peasant class (*see also* peasantry) **Vol. 1**: 33, 72, 109, 113, 127, 129, 141, 143, 185, 253, 283, 288, 310, 330; **Vol. 2**: 41, 49, 80, 83

peasant movements **Vol. 1**: 50, 171

peasant party **Vol. 1**: 153, 361–362; **Vol. 2**: 67, 69–70

peasant revolution **Vol. 1**: 33, 44–45, 47, 49–50, 52, 54, 58, 62, 143, 152, 287, 331

peasant self-defense force **Vol. 1**: 153

peasantry (*see also* peasant class) **Vol. 1**: 33–34, 50, 53–54, 63, 120–123, 125, 127–129, 140–141, 143–144, 163, 168, 191, 194, 196–197, 219, 227, 241, 246, 252–253, 279–280, 282, 309, 330, 362, 371, 378, 420–421, 471, 487, 491, 501, 507–508, 512, 517, 519, 523, 526–528, 532

peasants' allied force **Vol. 1**: 164

Peking Girl's High School **Vol. 1**: 8

Peking People's Art Theatre **Vol. 3**: 32

Peking University (Beijing University) **Vol. 1**: 8, 10, 14–15, 17, 258; **Vol. 3**: 23, 78–79, 434

Peking University Civilians Lecture Group **Vol. 1**: 14

Peng Dehuai **Vol. 2**: 217, 275; **Vol. 3**: 15, 53–54, 81, 91, 93, 101–102

Peng Gongda **Vol. 1**: 57

Peng Peiyun **Vol. 3**: 78–79

Peng Shuzhi **Vol. 1**: 124–125

Peng Zemin **Vol. 1**: 264

Peng Zhen **Vol. 3**: 72, 81, 179, 188–189, 211

Peng, Gao, and Xi Anti-Party Group **Vol. 3**: 101–102

Penghu **Vol. 3**: 228

People's Bank of China **Vol. 3**: 354, 538–539

People's Commune Movement **Vol. 2**: 9, 130, 192, 195–197, 199–200, 204, 206, 211–213, 218, 221–222, 231, 239, 246, 267, 270, 273, 325

People's Congress **Vol. 1**: 190, 192, 268, 509, 515; **Vol. 2**: 7, 26, 48, 50, 53, 77–78, 141, 153, 221, 243, 246–247, 249–254, 256–257, 260, 277, 302; **Vol. 3**: 24, 56–57, 118–119, 123, 198, 217, 224, 226, 228, 230–232, 236, 254, 261–262, 269, 271–272, 274–275, 287, 299, 319–320, 349–350, 365, 367, 373, 376–377, 380–381, 384, 402, 413, 436, 439, 454, 475, 482, 500, 503, 509–510, 517, 536, 551

People's Court (provincial or municipal) **Vol. 3**: 321
People's Daily **Vol. 1**: 7; **Vol. 2**: 117, 143, 166, 179, 188–189, 272, 278–280, 296, 314, 322–323, 328; **Vol. 3**: 12–13, 17, 19, 21, 24, 26, 28, 30, 32, 35–38, 40–42, 53, 79, 137, 153, 165, 195, 217, 318, 373, 394
people's democratic dictatorship **Vol. 1**: 85, 89, 146, 261, 268, 282, 468, 510, 513, 516–521, 523; **Vol. 2**: 7, 25, 32, 41, 48–51, 79–80, 87, 92, 116, 153; **Vol. 3**: 250, 316, 318, 337, 365, 367, 440
People's Democratic United Front **Vol. 1**: 87–88, 244–245, 254, 256, 261–262, 264, 268–269, 271; **Vol. 2**: 53, 79–80, 87, 153, 170, 320
People's Liberation Army (PLA) **Vol. 1**: 86, 188, 247, 258, 261, 281, 286, 305, 309, 311, 313, 342, 494, 500, 516; **Vol. 2**: 53–54, 272, 295; **Vol. 3**: 41, 82, 137, 153, 169, 178, 225–226, 228–229, 433, 435, 517
People's Liberation War **Vol. 1**: 86, 188
People's Literature **Vol. 3**: 30
People's Republic **Vol. 1**: 88, 268, 284–285, 421, 467, 508, 517, 520, 523, 534, 539; **Vol. 2**: 4–5, 25–26, 39, 48, 51–55, 57, 63, 69, 76–77, 79, 82, 86–87, 89–90, 110–111, 117–118, 165, 183, 209, 233, 240, 304; **Vol. 3**: 4, 44, 77, 87, 97, 108, 111, 119, 122, 131, 140, 144, 158–159, 161–163, 165, 167–169, 172, 213–215, 224, 228–229, 233–237, 248, 252–253, 263, 275, 287, 310–311, 333, 335, 345, 376–378, 402, 413, 416–417, 460, 475, 498, 519, 541, 551
People's Republic of China **Vol. 1**: 88, 268, 284–285, 421, 517, 520, 523, 539; **Vol. 2**: 25–26, 39, 48, 51–53, 55, 57, 63, 77, 79, 86, 89–90, 110–111, 118, 165, 183, 233, 240, 304; **Vol. 3**: 4, 44, 77, 87, 97, 108, 111, 119, 122, 140, 144, 158–159, 162–163, 165, 169, 172, 213–215, 224, 228–229, 233–237, 248, 252–253, 263, 275, 287, 310, 345, 376–378, 402, 413, 416–417, 460, 475, 498, 519, 541, 551
People's Self-Defense Force **Vol. 1**: 333–334
personnel system **Vol. 3**: 269, 271, 277, 279, 295, 460
Petőfi Club **Vol. 2**: 259

Pingjiang **Vol. 1**: 61
Pingjin **Vol. 1**: 328, 342, 352–355
Pioneer **Vol. 1**: 13, 16; **Vol. 2**: 338
PLA (*see also* People's Liberation Army) **Vol. 1**: 86–89, 188, 248, 254, 256, 265–266, 268, 280, 285, 290, 298, 306, 315, 317–319, 324–325, 328, 350, 353, 505; **Vol. 2**: 314, 326; **Vol. 3**: 36, 42, 73, 156, 158, 176, 228, 281, 306, 429, 433–434, 436, 438–440
planned economy **Vol. 1**: 202; **Vol. 2**: 13–15, 17, 20, 36, 105–106, 108, 119, 130, 132, 151–152, 174, 186, 223–226, 287–288; **Vol. 3**: 21, 191–192, 194–196, 199–201, 328–329, 335, 344–348, 352, 357, 365, 461, 480, 540, 545
police **Vol. 1**: 260–261, 519; **Vol. 3**: 435, 464
Policies for Foreign Experts and Allies **Vol. 2**: 113; **Vol. 3**: 117
Policy of Intelligence Workers **Vol. 1**: 195
Politburo **Vol. 1**: 42, 45, 48, 51, 55–59, 79, 103–104, 154, 167, 199, 222, 229, 231–232, 240, 400, 482, 495, 501, 503, 511, 516; **Vol. 2**: 32, 51, 60, 63, 85, 105, 110, 143, 156, 166, 188, 191, 214, 240, 247, 257, 300; **Vol. 3**: 10, 12, 16, 38, 52, 54, 59, 62, 71, 73, 91, 138, 165, 168, 175–179, 189, 200, 218, 232, 245–246, 259, 268–270, 273, 286, 306, 309, 319, 323–325, 331, 380, 409, 455–456, 465, 509, 513, 515
political boundary issues **Vol. 3**: 518
political consultation **Vol. 1**: 87, 264; **Vol. 2**: 7, 52–54, 79, 152; **Vol. 3**: 272, 365, 367, 372–373, 375, 510
political line **Vol. 1**: 63–64, 285, 365, 367, 378, 403–404, 433, 470, 482; **Vol. 2**: 306; **Vol. 3**: 4, 13, 28, 53, 157–158, 285, 331, 457
political strike **Vol. 1**: 153
political struggle (*see also* struggle) **Vol. 1**: 35, 115, 122, 259–260, 263, 290; **Vol. 2**: 138, 190, 242, 281
political system reform **Vol. 3**: 244, 255, 268–270, 273, 275, 316–317, 369–372, 376, 380, 547
Political Weekly **Vol. 1**: 103
Polytechnic University **Vol. 3**: 434
populism **Vol. 1**: 55–56, 535; **Vol. 2**: 30, 39
popularization of Marxism **Vol. 3**: 7

Practical Theory **Vol. 1**: 66, 68, 183, 389–391
practice is the sole criterion for testing truth **Vol. 3**: 157
pre-Qin scholars **Vol. 3**: 31
primary stage of socialism **Vol. 2**: 133; **Vol. 3**: 152, 239, 241, 243, 245, 249–252, 254–258, 266, 268, 270, 303, 325, 335, 338, 354, 358, 360–363, 366–368, 493–494, 526, 544
Printing Industry Management Regulations **Vol. 3**: 394
private sector **Vol. 3**: 451
production **Vol. 1**: 4–6, 8, 12, 29, 44, 53, 123, 127, 131–132, 162, 174, 184, 192–193, 196–197, 203–208, 246–247, 255, 270–271, 282, 293–294, 302, 304–306, 312, 328, 335, 361, 383, 393, 457, 468, 473, 496–500, 502, 505–506, 519, 524, 526–527, 529–530, 533, 535–536; **Vol. 2**: 4, 6, 9, 15, 26, 28, 30–31, 33–35, 39–40, 42–44, 51, 57–58, 60, 62, 64–69, 72, 74–76, 84, 87–88, 91, 94, 100, 102–103, 105–108, 112–115, 118–119, 121–128, 131–133, 135–139, 141, 146–148, 150–151, 154–155, 164–165, 168–169, 181, 183, 185, 187, 189–190, 192–193, 195–197, 200–203, 205, 207, 214, 216–219, 222–223, 235–239, 243, 247–250, 253–257, 260–261, 267, 269–271, 281, 284, 286–288, 293–294, 297, 299–300, 302–304, 310, 320, 327–328, 333–334; **Vol. 3**: 3, 10, 21–22, 25–27, 48–51, 55, 61, 64, 72, 75, 142, 149, 171, 183, 192–195, 197–198, 200–201, 209, 250–251, 253, 256, 260, 262, 275, 304, 309, 325, 329, 344, 349, 352–353, 355–356, 365, 394, 406–407, 433, 435, 480, 489, 493, 498, 503, 507, 509, 511, 531–532, 542–544
program of action **Vol. 1**: 246, 543; **Vol. 2**: 48; **Vol. 3**: 244, 343
proletarian (*see also* proletariat) **Vol. 1**: 12, 17, 21, 28, 30, 35, 37, 39, 53, 63, 75, 100, 102, 104, 107–108, 110–114, 116–118, 123, 126–128, 140–142, 149, 153–154, 161, 163–164, 178, 185–186, 188, 194, 213, 217–220, 225, 229, 271, 275–277, 284–285, 288, 299, 301, 306–310, 321, 326, 331, 357–364, 370, 372, 374–378, 380–382, 384–385, 388, 392, 394, 396–399, 406, 421–423, 426, 429, 434, 437, 440, 442–445, 447, 457–458, 461, 472, 474, 479, 487, 507–508, 514, 516, 520, 526, 541–542, 544–545; **Vol. 2**: 18, 20, 27, 33–34, 36, 50–51, 118, 135–136, 139, 143, 152, 166, 208, 262, 274–276, 278–279, 282, 295, 301–302, 315; **Vol. 3**: 77–78, 101, 119, 137, 146, 160–161, 169, 240, 242, 245–246, 316
proletarian dictatorship **Vol. 1**: 12, 363, 514; **Vol. 2**: 34, 50–51, 118, 136, 143, 152, 166; **Vol. 3**: 137, 146
proletarian organization **Vol. 1**: 308, 399
proletariat (*see also* proletarian) **Vol. 1**: 4, 13, 19–20, 26–30, 32, 34–35, 50, 53–54, 57, 60, 63, 72–78, 89, 92, 94, 100–106, 108–118, 122–125, 127–131, 138–146, 149–150, 152, 154, 162–163, 171, 173, 175–176, 180, 190–191, 194, 196–197, 199, 213–215, 217–218, 220–222, 224–225, 227, 230–231, 241, 243, 252, 255, 263, 267, 269, 276–279, 282–284, 286–287, 298, 301, 308–310, 330–331, 357–359, 362, 364–365, 371–372, 374–378, 381, 383, 394, 397, 405, 417, 419–422, 425, 429–431, 433–435, 438, 443–444, 447, 449, 457–458, 466–468, 470–471, 478–479, 487, 490, 497, 504, 507, 509, 513, 515–517, 519–524, 530–531, 534–536, 538, 541–544, 547; **Vol. 2**: 25, 27–28, 31–37, 43–47, 49–51, 53–54, 91–92, 103, 125–126, 135–136, 184–185, 219, 257, 262, 272–273, 275, 277–283, 288, 290, 294–296, 299–300, 306–307, 315, 318–319, 335; **Vol. 3**: 21, 23, 49, 51, 58, 140–142, 145, 147, 149–150, 161, 252, 283, 329
propaganda **Vol. 1**: 7–8, 25, 36, 40, 48, 69, 75, 128, 144, 163, 191, 210–211, 220, 222, 248, 286, 319, 376, 404, 464, 492, 537, 543–544; **Vol. 2**: 6, 56, 72, 82, 85, 104, 110, 115, 117, 135, 156–157, 176–177, 179, 184, 240, 289, 315, 317, 323; **Vol. 3**: 37–39, 55, 63, 68, 82, 89–90, 121–122, 138, 140–142, 144, 154, 158, 312, 316, 325, 373, 383–384, 393, 470–471
Propaganda Outline **Vol. 2**: 6, 110, 115
Protection of Taiwanese Compatriots' Investment **Vol. 3**: 413
Protection of the Rights of Party Members **Vol. 3**: 453, 466
Proudhon, Pierre-Joseph **Vol. 1**: 6

Provincial Civil Affairs Department **Vol. 3**: 108
Provincial Military Control Council **Vol. 3**: 96
Provincial People's Congress **Vol. 1**: 515
Provincial Reform Commission **Vol. 3**: 96
Provincial Reform Committee **Vol. 3**: 72–73
public ownership **Vol. 2**: 6, 8, 14, 103, 106, 108, 114, 118, 120, 124, 130, 141, 165, 193, 195–196, 200–202, 205, 213–214, 219, 223, 237, 297–298; **Vol. 3**: 21, 146, 150, 193–195, 200–202, 249–251, 279, 329, 335, 337, 345, 349–350, 352, 365–366, 410, 473, 489, 491, 493–494, 496, 507, 511
Public Welfare Culture Reform **Vol. 3**: 511
Publicity (Propaganda) Committee **Vol. 1**: 20, 131
Publishing Management Regulations **Vol. 3**: 394
Pudong **Vol. 3**: 4, 354
Pudong District **Vol. 3**: 4

Q
Qi Qi **Vol. 3**: 192
Qian Qichen **Vol. 3**: 220
Qian Ying **Vol. 1**: 257; **Vol. 3**: 72
Qiao Shi **Vol. 3**: 189, 245
Qiliying **Vol. 2**: 204
Qin Jiwei **Vol. 3**: 189, 245
Qing Dynasty (Qing court) **Vol. 1**: 133, 135, 267, 514
Qingdao **Vol. 1**: 34; **Vol. 3**: 277, 410
Qinghai Province **Vol. 3**: 125, 502
Qingming Festival (see Tomb-Sweeping Day)
Qinhuangdao Port **Vol. 3**: 210
Qionglai County **Vol. 3**: 277
Qu Qiubai **Vol. 1**: 29–30, 34, 36, 43, 52–53, 55–56, 58, 102, 105, 126–127, 139, 167, 274; **Vol. 3**: 81
Quanzhou City **Vol. 3**: 320

R
radicalism **Vol. 2**: 262, 264
Radio and Television Management Regulations **Vol. 3**: 394
re-education **Vol. 3**: 121–122
re-employment of laid-off workers **Vol. 3**: 408

reactionary **Vol. 1**: 24, 26, 37, 41, 44, 56, 60, 62, 77, 85–89, 127, 135–136, 138, 149, 163, 172, 181, 197, 216, 242, 245–250, 258, 260, 265, 268–270, 272, 274, 276, 280–282, 288, 291–293, 301, 312, 320–321, 329, 339, 350, 355, 401, 420, 467, 495, 500, 505, 519–520, 528, 533, 535, 540–541; **Vol. 2**: 49, 104, 257, 264, 275, 283, 286, 289–291, 295–297; Vol 3: 22, 151, 226, 228, 304
Reagan, Ronald **Vol. 3**: 215–216
rectification **Vol. 1**: 54, 83–84, 210, 282, 366–370, 380, 385–389, 391, 394, 402, 410, 421, 423, 425, 427–428, 433–434, 437–440, 448, 484–486, 492, 512; **Vol. 2**: 167, 175–182, 184–185, 188–189, 192, 199, 203, 207–209, 211, 213, 215, 220–221, 226–227, 230, 235, 237, 246, 297, 299, 302–303, 309, 312–313, 320, 324, 329, 335–336, 339; **Vol. 3**: 4–5, 10, 19, 65–66, 78, 81, 84, 88, 90, 93–94, 100, 118, 139, 152, 155, 158–159, 175, 183, 186, 280, 282–284, 301–302, 325, 334, 454–457, 515
Rectification Movement **Vol. 1**: 83–84, 210, 282, 367–368, 380, 385–389, 391, 394, 402, 410, 421, 425, 433–434, 437, 439, 448, 484–486; **Vol. 2**: 175–182, 184–185, 189; **Vol. 3**: 155, 457
Red Army **Vol. 1**: 59–62, 66, 153, 156–161, 164, 168–172, 174–176, 178–181, 183, 185, 193, 229–231, 233–236, 279, 285–286, 288, 296, 299–300, 304–305, 307, 311, 316–317, 319, 321, 323, 331–332, 334, 336, 341, 350, 361, 364–367, 382, 420, 459; **Vol. 3**: 15, 104–105, 432
Red Army University **Vol. 1**: 288
Red Flag **Vol. 1**: 59, 170, 176, 279; **Vol. 2**: 190, 194, 278–279, 314, 323; **Vol. 3**: 33, 38, 40, 55, 79–80, 137
Red Flag Party **Vol. 3**: 79–80
Red Guards **Vol. 1**: 175, 332, 334, 336
Red regime **Vol. 1**: 53, 170–173, 179–180, 182, 292, 331, 365
redeployment **Vol. 3**: 124
Reform and Opening Up **Vol. 2**: 22–23, 249, 304, 310, 313, 329–330, 332, 334–338; **Vol. 3**: 3–5, 7, 9, 18, 32, 44–45, 48–49, 51–52, 56, 61, 123, 129, 132–133, 181, 192, 225, 241–243, 251–252, 254–256, 279, 292, 297, 301–306, 310,

313, 318, 323–324, 326–328, 330–337, 341, 343, 348, 350, 352–353, 355, 357–359, 364, 369, 379, 381, 384, 387, 391, 397, 402, 408, 416, 422, 427, 435, 437, 444, 446–447, 454, 461, 475, 480, 482, 484, 488, 497–498, 501–502, 506, 513, 524–526, 531, 534, 536, 541, 545–547, 549–551

Reform Group of the Financial and Economic Committee **Vol. 3**: 193
Reform Movement of 1888 **Vol. 1**: 140
Reform Movement of 1898 **Vol. 1**: 110
reform of the cultural system **Vol. 2**: 20; **Vol. 3**: 389, 393, 511
rejuvenating the nation **Vol. 3**: 398
Religious Affairs Bureau (*see also* Bureau of Religious Affairs) **Vol. 3**: 126, 128
Religious Policy **Vol. 3**: 116, 122, 126, 128
Removing Chaos **Vol. 2**: 327
Ren Bishi **Vol. 1**: 254, 484, 497–498, 501–502, 504–505; **Vol. 2**: 40
Ren Wanding **Vol. 3**: 142
Ren Zhuoxuan (*see* Ye Qing) **Vol. 1**: 70
Republic of China **Vol. 1**: 4, 24, 88, 114, 268, 284–285, 421, 517, 520, 523, 539; **Vol. 2**: 25–26, 39, 48, 51–53, 55, 57, 63, 77, 79, 86, 89–90, 110–111, 118, 165, 183, 233, 240, 304; **Vol. 3**: 4, 44, 77, 87, 97, 108, 111, 119, 122, 140, 144, 158–159, 162–163, 165, 169, 172, 213–215, 224, 228–229, 231, 233–237, 248, 252–253, 263, 275, 287, 310, 345, 376–378, 402, 413, 416–417, 460, 475, 498, 519, 541, 551
Republic of China in Taiwan **Vol. 3**: 233
Republic of Workers and Farmers **Vol. 1**: 508
Resolution of the Central Committee of the Communist Party of China on Some Historical Issues of the Party Since the Founding of the People's Republic of China **Vol. 3**: 3
Resolution on Land Issues **Vol. 1**: 49
Resolution on Relations between the KMT and the CPC **Vol. 1**: 215
Resolution on Several Historical Issues **Vol. 1**: 387, 485; **Vol. 3**: 102, 131, 163, 165, 168, 311, 335
Resolution on the Party's Organizational Issues **Vol. 1**: 45

Resolution on the Relationship between the Communist Party of China and the Kuomintang **Vol. 1**: 35
Resolution on the United Workers and Peasants **Vol. 1**: 32
Restructuring Party **Vol. 3**: 102
revisionism **Vol. 1**: 358; **Vol. 2**: 14, 184, 219, 253, 256, 259, 265–266, 268, 273, 279–280, 282–283, 287–291, 294–295; **Vol. 3**: 27, 161
Revolutionary Army of Workers and Peasants **Vol. 1**: 140, 315
Revolutionary Base Area **Vol. 1**: 36, 82, 140, 174, 176, 189, 329
revolutionary bourgeoisie **Vol. 1**: 101, 121, 140
revolutionary path (se also revolutionary road) **Vol. 1**: 37, 49, 140, 149, 151, 153, 155, 157, 159–161, 163, 165–167, 169, 171, 173, 175, 177–179, 181–183, 185, 187, 189, 191, 193, 195, 197, 199, 201, 203, 205, 207, 209, 211, 361, 379, 389, 466, 470
revolutionary practice **Vol. 1**: 23, 25, 29, 37, 81–82, 140–141, 151, 163, 169, 188, 273, 406, 428, 443–446, 463, 484, 508; **Vol. 2**: 262; **Vol. 3**: 37, 41–42
revolutionary road (*see also* revolutionary path) **Vol. 1**: 140, 149, 163, 176, 178; **Vol. 2**: 5
revolutionary struggle **Vol. 1**: 23, 25, 29, 37, 45, 47, 50–51, 54, 56, 62, 78, 92, 130, 140, 142, 149, 151, 155, 157, 161, 176, 182, 186, 190, 192, 198, 271, 277, 283, 285–286, 300, 308, 312–313, 330, 357, 362–363, 372, 376, 397, 399, 403, 419, 423, 425, 431, 440, 442, 444, 456–457, 464, 466–467, 469, 472–473, 490, 521, 531; **Vol. 2**: 53, 136, 268; **Vol. 3**: 62, 101, 115
Revolutionary United Front **Vol. 1**: 29, 93, 140–141, 218, 227, 235, 244, 268, 372
rich peasant (*see also* wealthy peasant) **Vol. 1**: 536; **Vol. 2**: 63, 65–66, 68–69, 125; **Vol. 3**: 113
right opportunists **Vol. 3**: 66, 87
Right-Wing Correction Office **Vol. 3**: 90
rightism **Vol. 2**: 183, 230, 312
Rightist deviation **Vol. 3**: 91, 93
Rightist errors **Vol. 1**: 46, 58, 232, 391, 401, 550; **Vol. 3**: 252

rightist labels **Vol. 3**: 87
Rightist tendencies **Vol. 3**: 241
riot **Vol. 1**: 48, 61, 151, 156, 165, 167–169, 179, 237, 276, 334
Rogachev, Igor **Vol. 3**: 219
Ruan Ming **Vol. 3**: 139
rule of law **Vol. 2**: 163, 269, 298; **Vol. 3**: 58, 137, 146, 379–381, 436, 499, 510, 514, 520, 532–534
ruling party **Vol. 1**: 285, 308, 370, 430, 458, 465, 504–505; **Vol. 2**: 158–159, 161–163, 183, 185, 190, 296–297; **Vol. 3**: 241, 243, 280, 336, 446, 472, 512–514
Rural People's Commune Work Regulations **Vol. 2**: 9, 235; **Vol. 3**: 52, 60, 112
Rural People's Commune Work Regulations (60 Agricultural Articles) **Vol. 2**: 9
rural policy **Vol. 2**: 63, 235, 328
rural reform **Vol. 3**: 61, 262, 335, 509–510, 523, 536, 542–545
rural revolutionary base **Vol. 1**: 82–83, 157–158, 164, 174–176, 195, 329, 364, 471
Rural Socialist Education Movement **Vol. 3**: 93
rural system **Vol. 3**: 544
rural to urban (transfer) **Vol. 1**: 370, 494–495, 497, 499
rural work **Vol. 1**: 83, 155, 255, 495; **Vol. 2**: 189, 328; **Vol. 3**: 543–544
Russell, Bertrand **Vol. 1**: 18
Russian Bolshevik Party **Vol. 1**: 358
Russian Revolution **Vol. 1**: 56, 113, 149, 152, 379; **Vol. 2**: 54, 137
Russian Social Democratic Labor Party **Vol. 1**: 397–398

S

SACO **Vol. 3**: 109
Saneatsu Mushakoji **Vol. 1**: 6
Sanming City **Vol. 3**: 313
Sanwan Reorganization **Vol. 1**: 315
SARS **Vol. 3**: 500–502
scar literature **Vol. 3**: 31
School of Marxism **Vol. 2**: 73
science education **Vol. 3**: 29
Science, Fourteen Articles of **Vol. 2**: 240, 254

scientific evaluation **Vol. 3**: 135, 159
Scientific View of Development **Vol. 3**: 479, 494, 497, 500–507, 512, 514, 523, 533, 550–551
Second Civil Revolutionary War **Vol. 2**: 46
second combination **Vol. 2**: 7, 14, 143, 145
Second Expanded Plenary Session of the Central Executive Committee **Vol. 1**: 39
Second Leap **Vol. 2**: 3, 9, 11–13, 16–17, 20–23, 133–134, 182, 222, 225–226, 310–313, 329, 332, 335–336, 338; **Vol. 3**: 359, 490
Second National Conference of Workers and Peasants **Vol. 1**: 195
Second National Congress of the Chinese Soviet Workers, Peasants, and Soldiers **Vol. 1**: 191, 255; **Vol. 3**: 112
Second National Congress of the Communist Party of China **Vol. 1**: 26–28
Second National Labor Conference **Vol. 1**: 32, 126
Second National Workers, Peasants, and Soldiers Congress **Vol. 1**: 105, 255; **Vol. 3**: 112
Second Revolutionary Civil War **Vol. 1**: 296; **Vol. 3**: 103
Second World War (*see also* World War II) **Vol. 1**: 113; **Vol. 2**: 19, 46, 138, 187, 263–264, 269; **Vol. 3**: 46
Secondary Education, Fifty Articles of **Vol. 2**: 240
Secretariat in Irkutsk **Vol. 1**: 19
seeking truth from facts **Vol. 1**: 294, 379, 388–391, 424, 453–454, 463, 474, 546; **Vol. 2**: 5, 11, 21, 203, 233–234, 243, 245–246, 313, 316, 319, 321, 324–325, 328–329, 336–337; **Vol. 3**: 20, 33–35, 39, 51, 55, 57–58, 60–61, 63, 67, 69, 74, 83–84, 86, 89, 97, 108, 135, 150, 155, 165, 169, 173, 243, 332–333, 336, 338, 344, 359, 393, 472, 525, 549
Selected Works of Mao Zedong **Vol. 1**: 73, 79, 493–494; **Vol. 2**: 29, 315
self-criticism **Vol. 1**: 322, 364, 385–387, 426–428, 430, 432, 436–437, 446–456, 463, 469, 471, 477, 502, 504; **Vol. 2**: 162, 167, 176, 179, 244–246, 249, 283; **Vol. 3**: 55, 57, 280–281, 284, 455–456
semi-colonial, semi-feudal society **Vol. 1**: 3, 50,

72, 91, 96, 99, 110, 115, 133, 173, 376, 392, 431, 509–510, 521, 525, 540
semi-socialist economy **Vol. 2**: 26, 33, 51
separation of Party and government **Vol. 1**: 191; **Vol. 3**: 269–270, 273, 275
September 13 Incident **Vol. 2**: 122, 306
September Letter **Vol. 1**: 178; **Vol. 2**: 122
serving the people wholeheartedly **Vol. 1**: 299–300, 302, 325, 465, 470; **Vol. 3**: 281, 308, 447–448, 459
Seven Thousand People's Congress (*see also* 7,000 People's Congress) **Vol. 2**: 221
Seventh National Congress of the Communist Party of China **Vol. 1**: 410
Seventh Plenum of the Executive Committee of the Comintern **Vol. 1**: 38
Seventh Regiment **Vol. 1**: 354
Seventeenth National Congress of the Communist Party of China **Vol. 3**: 524, 527, 546
Seventh Five-Year Plan **Vol. 3**: 183, 261, 265, 313
Shaanxi Province **Vol. 1**: 324; **Vol. 3**: 101–102
Shaanxi-Gansu-Ningxia Border Region **Vol. 1**: 76, 199, 201, 203–204, 206–209, 211; **Vol. 2**: 30
Shandong Province **Vol. 3**: 38, 84, 88, 450
Shanghai **Vol. 1**: 4, 6, 11, 15–19, 24–26, 34, 56, 58, 61, 155–157, 162, 167, 223, 256, 259–261, 276, 308, 355, 376, 525; **Vol. 2**: 43, 77, 151, 178, 200, 202, 204, 206, 300; **Vol. 3**: 4, 11, 31–32, 49, 66, 74–75, 141, 143, 147, 263, 318, 324, 327, 347, 354, 405–406, 414, 428
Shanghai Association **Vol. 3**: 414
Shanghai Baoshan Iron and Steel Works **Vol. 3**: 49
Shanghai Bureau **Vol. 1**: 259–261
Shanghai Commune **Vol. 2**: 300
Shanghai Communist Party **Vol. 1**: 18
Shanghai Conference **Vol. 2**: 200, 202, 206
Shanghai General League Strike **Vol. 1**: 61
Shanghai Municipal Committee **Vol. 3**: 75
Shanghai Party Organization **Vol. 1**: 18
Shanghai People's Commune **Vol. 3**: 74–75
Shanghai Stock Exchange **Vol. 3**: 406

Shanghai Xinbao Steel Group Company **Vol. 3**: 405
Shangyu County **Vol. 3**: 277
Shanxi Province **Vol. 1**: 160, 202, 234, 249, 251; **Vol. 2**: 71–76, 85, 108, 122; **Vol. 3**: 277
Shanxi Provincial Party Committee **Vol. 2**: 72–73, 76
Shao Lizi **Vol. 1**: 18
Shao Piaoping **Vol. 1**: 10
Shapiro, Sidney **Vol. 3**: 117
Shatian Village **Vol. 1**: 323
Shen Chong **Vol. 1**: 258
Shen Chong Incident **Vol. 1**: 258
Shen Junru **Vol. 1**: 233, 264
Shen Xuanlu **Vol. 1**: 18
Shen Yanbing **Vol. 1**: 18
Shenyang **Vol. 1**: 353; **Vol. 3**: 50
Shenzhen **Vol. 3**: 277–278, 327–328, 349, 354, 406, 468
Shenzhen Stock Exchange **Vol. 3**: 406
Shi Cuntong **Vol. 1**: 18–19
Shi Yousan **Vol. 1**: 239
Shijiazhuang **Vol. 2**: 204
Shijiusuo Port **Vol. 3**: 210
Shu Tong **Vol. 3**: 14
Shuai Mengqi **Vol. 3**: 72
Sichuan Province **Vol. 1**: 234; **Vol. 2**: 233, 249, 328; **Vol. 3**: 66, 79, 103, 109, 154, 277
Sinicization of Marxism (*see also* integrating Marxism into China) **Vol. 2**: 17
Sino-American Civil Aviation Agreement **Vol. 3**: 213
Sino-American Cooperative Organization (SACO) Prison **Vol. 3**: 109
Sino-American Maritime Transport Agreement **Vol. 3**: 213
Sino-American Textile Agreement **Vol. 3**: 213
Sino-British Joint Statement **Vol. 3**: 236
Sino-foreign joint ventures **Vol. 3**: 293
Sino-French War **Vol. 1**: 110
Sino-Japan relations **Vol. 2**: 304
Sino-Japanese Joint Declaration **Vol. 3**: 424
Sino-Japanese Joint Statement **Vol. 3**: 211
Sino-Japanese relations **Vol. 3**: 210–212, 424–425

Sino-Japanese Treaty of Peace and Friendship **Vol. 3**: 211
Sino-Japanese War **Vol. 1**: 4, 110
Sino-Soviet relations **Vol. 2**: 265; **Vol. 3**: 203, 206, 217–218, 221
Sino-Soviet Treaty of Friendship, Alliance, and Mutual Assistance **Vol. 3**: 217
Sino-US Joint Communiqué **Vol. 2**: 304
Sino-US relations **Vol. 2**: 304–305; **Vol. 3**: 206–207, 213, 215, 217, 423
Sixth Anti-Encirclement Campaign **Vol. 1**: 157
Sixteen-Character Principle **Vol. 3**: 133, 465
Sixteenth National Congress of Communist Party of China **Vol. 3**: 498
Sixth Five-Year Plan **Vol. 3**: 183, 261–262
social class **Vol. 1**: 119, 397, 513, 515; **Vol. 3**: 130, 141, 308, 504
Social Democratic Party **Vol. 1**: 111, 371, 397; **Vol. 3**: 102, 308, 504
Socialism **Vol. 1**: 6–10, 12–13, 16, 18, 24–25, 27, 30–31, 50, 54–56, 70, 75–76, 85, 89, 103–108, 111–114, 116–118, 144, 146, 196, 221, 301, 359, 394, 417, 458, 467–468, 498, 507–512, 517, 519–522, 526, 528, 534–538, 543–544; **Vol. 2**: 4–6, 9, 13–15, 17–20, 22, 27–30, 33, 37, 39–41, 43, 45–47, 50, 52, 56, 58–59, 61–62, 70, 72–73, 76, 80, 83, 85–86, 88–91, 94–95, 97–99, 101–103, 105–121, 123–126, 128–139, 142–145, 151–152, 154–155, 158, 164, 169–170, 173–174, 176, 180–182, 184–185, 187–188, 190, 192–193, 195–197, 199–200, 202, 205, 211–214, 216–219, 223, 226, 229–231, 234–236, 242, 245, 253–255, 257–259, 261–262, 264, 266–272, 274–275, 280–281, 284–285, 291, 294, 296–298, 304–306, 308, 311, 320, 325, 327, 329, 332, 334, 336–338; **Vol. 3**: 4–7, 27–28, 36, 58, 91, 93, 110, 115, 129–135, 141–143, 146–147, 150–152, 159, 170–171, 173–174, 181, 184–185, 189, 191–192, 195, 202, 233, 235, 239, 241, 243–258, 266–268, 270, 283, 286, 301, 303, 309, 312, 314–315, 318, 325–340, 343–348, 350–351, 354, 357–369, 371, 380, 382–383, 385–391, 393, 397, 400, 440, 447–448, 458–459, 468, 472–473, 475–476, 482–484, 486–487, 493–494, 504, 511, 513, 523–527, 530–531, 533–535, 540, 544–547, 549–551
socialism with Chinese characteristics **Vol. 1**: 509; **Vol. 2**: 13, 130, 329, 336–338; **Vol. 3**: 4–7, 134, 142, 152, 173–174, 181, 185, 189, 243–244, 246, 255, 257, 268, 286, 301, 303, 314, 318, 325–327, 331, 333–338, 340, 350–351, 357–360, 362, 364–366, 368–369, 371, 380, 382–383, 385–391, 393, 397, 400, 447–448, 459, 468, 472, 475–476, 483–484, 486, 504, 513, 523–527, 531, 533–535, 545–547, 549–551
socialist commodity economy **Vol. 2**: 9; **Vol. 3**: 22, 77, 192, 201, 241, 249, 302, 335
socialist commodity production **Vol. 2**: 15; **Vol. 3**: 21–22
socialist construction **Vol. 1**: 145, 458–459; **Vol. 2**: 5, 7–8, 13, 15, 22–23, 110, 116, 118–120, 128, 134, 136–138, 141, 145–148, 154–155, 158–159, 165–166, 170, 173, 185, 187–188, 190, 192, 195, 197, 201, 209–210, 212, 214, 217, 221, 225, 244, 268, 270–271, 273, 291–292, 308, 325, 328–330, 337; **Vol. 3**: 20, 27, 61, 63, 77, 123, 126, 142, 159, 171–172, 180–181, 184, 188–189, 191, 218, 253, 335–336, 339, 360, 443, 476, 505, 530, 534–535
Socialist Education Movement (*see also* Four Clean-ups) **Vol. 2**: 258, 269, 275, 292; **Vol. 3**: 93
socialist market economic system **Vol. 3**: 5–6, 63, 77, 202, 334, 343, 348–353, 355–357, 366, 370, 379, 384, 409–411, 447, 465–466, 474, 480–481, 484–486, 488–489, 491–496, 499, 501, 507–508, 528, 534
socialist model **Vol. 2**: 12–13, 21, 23, 87, 121, 139–141, 170, 195, 215, 253, 255–256, 271
Socialist Reform **Vol. 2**: 10–11, 13–15, 23, 138–140, 145, 174, 181, 186, 221, 255, 268; **Vol. 3**: 5, 334, 358
Socialist Youth League **Vol. 1**: 25, 214
Some Historical Issues **Vol. 2**: 6; **Vol. 3**: 4, 158–159, 165, 172, 248, 345
Song Baoqi **Vol. 3**: 30
Song Jiaoren **Vol. 1**: 7
Song of the Heart **Vol. 3**: 32
Song Ping **Vol. 3**: 245

Song Qingling **Vol. 1**: 233
Song Renqiong **Vol. 3**: 62, 68, 81, 189
Song Shuo **Vol. 3**: 78–79
Song Zheyuan **Vol. 1**: 234
Song Ziwen (TV Soong) **Vol. 1**: 246
Songjiang County **Vol. 2**: 77
Soong, TV (*see* Song Ziwen)
South Beijing Riot **Vol. 1**: 61
South China Sea **Vol. 3**: 425
Southern Anhui Incident **Vol. 1**: 79
Southern Expedition **Vol. 3**: 71
Southern Talks (Deng Xiaoping) **Vol. 3**: 327–328, 333, 338, 347, 362, 366
sovereignty (Hong Kong) **Vol. 1**: 524; **Vol. 3**: 203, 212, 231, 235–237, 416–417, 421, 426, 519
soviet **Vol. 1**: 7, 43, 48, 51, 53–54, 59, 61, 63, 66, 79, 84, 109, 113, 149–150, 153, 155, 157–160, 164–165, 180, 189, 191–192, 194–197, 224, 227, 230, 232, 304, 341, 351, 432, 458–459, 482, 484, 486, 507–508, 511, 513–514, 528; **Vol. 2**: 5–8, 12–15, 18–21, 23, 27, 40, 44–46, 50, 54–55, 59, 66, 76, 87, 89, 91, 94–95, 97, 102, 105–106, 108–109, 113, 116–122, 124–125, 129–134, 136–145, 147–153, 156, 159–160, 163, 165–166, 173, 187–189, 191–192, 200, 209–211, 213–220, 231, 238, 252–253, 255, 258, 262, 264–268, 271, 274, 287–291, 298, 305, 308, 325; **Vol. 3**: 15, 38, 47, 84, 102–105, 163, 193, 203–206, 208–209, 213, 217–221, 246–247, 326, 347, 423, 437, 512
Soviet Communist Party **Vol. 1**: 51; **Vol. 2**: 12, 44, 50, 109, 124, 139, 141, 143, 163, 166, 184, 209–210, 213, 288–290; **Vol. 3**: 221, 247, 512
Soviet Government of the Workers, Peasants, and Soldiers **Vol. 1**: 189, 255; **Vol. 3**: 112
Soviet Revisionist Group **Vol. 2**: 288–291
Soviet Union **Vol. 1**: 7, 53–54, 66, 84, 109, 113, 149, 180, 232, 511, 513–514; **Vol. 2**: 5–8, 12–15, 20, 23, 40, 45–46, 50, 54, 59, 66, 89, 91, 102, 106, 108, 113, 116–120, 122, 124, 130–134, 137–144, 148–153, 156, 159–160, 165–166, 173, 191–192, 200, 209–211, 213–214, 216–218, 220, 252–253, 255, 265, 287–290, 305, 308, 325; **Vol. 3**: 47, 104, 193, 203–204, 206, 208–209, 213, 217–221, 246–247, 326, 347, 423, 437

Special Article on the Development of Hong Kong Border Sites **Vol. 3**: 234, 416
Special Case Office **Vol. 3**: 71
Special Committee **Vol. 1**: 172, 174; **Vol. 3**: 373
Speech at Chun Qu Zhai (Liu Shaoqi) **Vol. 3**: 10
Speech at the Yan'an Forum on Literature and Art **Vol. 1**: 300; **Vol. 3**: 10
Stalin, Joseph **Vol. 1**: 51, 94, 113, 227, 283, 364, 371, 381, 384, 393, 430–431, 434, 443, 492–493, 507; **Vol. 2**: 6, 18, 91, 109, 118–119, 121–122, 137, 139, 141, 143, 164–165, 209–212, 214–215, 218, 265, 290; **Vol. 3**: 21, 247
Standing Committee **Vol. 1**: 43, 167, 276, 395; **Vol. 2**: 111, 115, 153, 247, 257; **Vol. 3**: 11–12, 38–39, 50, 53–54, 56–57, 62, 75, 119, 137–138, 156–157, 160, 178–180, 189, 217, 226, 228, 230, 245, 269, 273–274, 298–299, 309, 319–321, 324, 331, 373, 376–377, 381, 413, 431, 455–456, 509, 515
State Bureau of Defense Science, Technology, and Industry **Vol. 2**: 304; **Vol. 3**: 176, 211, 539
State Bureau of Foreign Experts **Vol. 3**: 117
State Civil Aviation Administration **Vol. 3**: 539
State Commission for Reform of Sports and Physical Education **Vol. 3**: 450
State Construction Commission **Vol. 3**: 127
State Council **Vol. 2**: 80, 82–83, 152, 156, 188, 245, 249, 301–302, 314, 331, 333; **Vol. 3**: 10, 21–22, 24–25, 28, 40, 46–48, 51–52, 56, 67, 71, 74, 103, 121–122, 125, 127–128, 160, 193–194, 196, 198, 215, 221, 259, 269, 271, 273–274, 276–278, 289–290, 293–294, 297–299, 306, 313, 318–319, 322, 344, 350, 353–355, 373–374, 377, 380–381, 398–399, 406–410, 413, 419, 436, 461–463, 465, 467, 482, 506, 508–509, 511, 519, 536, 538–539
State Economic Commission **Vol. 3**: 322
State Economic Reform Office (Commission for Economic Reform) **Vol. 3**: 194
State Environmental Protection Administration **Vol. 3**: 540
State Environmental Protection Bureau **Vol. 3**: 278

State Food and Drug Administration **Vol. 3**: 540

State General Administration of Labor **Vol. 3**: 23–24

State Personnel Department **Vol. 3**: 278

State Planning Commission **Vol. 2**: 237; **Vol. 3**: 23–24, 196–197, 262, 346

state power **Vol. 1**: 13, 131, 138, 188, 246, 458, 513, 517–518, 520, 522–523, 538; **Vol. 2**: 26, 34, 41, 48–50, 121–122, 196, 223, 292–293, 298

State Tax Administration **Vol. 3**: 278

state-owned enterprises **Vol. 1**: 195, 496; **Vol. 2**: 238–239; **Vol. 3**: 196–197, 349, 351–353, 378, 402–412, 450–451, 460, 464, 489–490, 494, 496

Stirner, Max **Vol. 1**: 6

Straits Exchange Foundation (SEF) **Vol. 3**: 414–415, 419

Strategic military policy in a high-tech environment **Vol. 1**: 182, 341–342; **Vol. 3**: 429

"Strategy for Opposing Japanese Imperialism" **Vol. 1**: 229

strike **Vol. 1**: 25, 36, 47, 58, 61–62, 124, 153, 156, 185, 187, 192, 243, 258, 261, 278, 280; **Vol. 2**: 175; **Vol. 3**: 127, 142, 304

struggle **Vol. 1**: 8, 10–11, 13–15, 20–21, 23–25, 27–37, 41–43, 45–48, 50–52, 54–56, 58–60, 62, 66–68, 70, 78, 80, 82–83, 86, 88–89, 91–92, 100–103, 105–106, 109, 112–113, 115, 119, 122, 125, 129–130, 133–135, 139, 141–142, 144, 146, 149–151, 155, 157–159, 161, 164–166, 169–171, 173–177, 180, 182, 184–187, 189–190, 192, 198, 210, 212, 218–219, 221, 223–224, 230, 232, 234, 236–245, 247–249, 252–254, 257–261, 263, 265, 269, 271, 273–279, 281–291, 293–295, 297, 299–305, 307–309, 311–313, 315, 317, 319–321, 323, 325, 327, 329–333, 335–339, 341, 343, 345, 347, 349, 351–353, 355–359, 361–369, 371–372, 376, 382, 384–386, 388, 391, 394, 396–399, 401, 403, 406, 408, 412, 419, 421, 423, 425–426, 431, 440, 442, 444, 451, 454–458, 461, 464, 466–467, 469–473, 476, 479, 483, 486, 489–491, 501, 504, 509, 512, 521, 525–528, 531, 538, 540–541, 545; **Vol. 2**: 6, 8, 10, 13–14, 20, 28, 33–34, 36–37, 42–43, 45, 47, 49, 53, 59–61, 65, 91–93, 99, 103, 105, 116, 128–129, 135–136, 138, 153, 161–163, 167–168, 170, 173–174, 178–180, 182–187, 189–191, 207, 219, 221, 224, 226, 230–231, 234, 241–242, 244–247, 251–252, 254–259, 265, 268–279, 281, 285–286, 292–299, 301, 303, 307, 309, 312, 314, 316, 321, 325, 333, 335, 338; **Vol. 3**: 4, 11, 17, 32–33, 40, 48, 51, 55, 60, 62–63, 66, 72–73, 80, 85, 88–93, 96, 99, 101, 106, 115, 120–121, 130, 135, 140–141, 143, 152, 160–161, 170, 173, 191, 205, 207, 228, 253–254, 257–258, 261, 264, 283, 299, 307, 311, 319, 323, 332, 362, 368, 390, 415, 418, 429, 431–432, 437–440, 454, 460–461, 464–465, 483, 516, 520, 525, 527, 530–531, 548

Struggle, Criticism, and Reform Campaign **Vol. 1**: 425, 450; **Vol. 2**: 272

Stuart, John Leighton **Vol. 1**: 281

Su Hua **Vol. 1**: 50

Su Jin **Vol. 3**: 104

Su Shuyang **Vol. 3**: 32

Su Yu **Vol. 1**: 327, 351

Su Zhaozheng **Vol. 1**: 39

Sun Yat-sen **Vol. 1**: 3, 7, 24, 93, 111, 126, 224–225; **Vol. 3**: 358

Sun Yifang **Vol. 2**: 9, 307, 309

Sunzi **Vol. 1**: 296

superstructure **Vol. 1**: 131, 137, 468; **Vol. 2**: 4, 70, 81, 113–114, 164, 167–169, 189, 239, 245, 253, 281–283, 293–294, 302, 327, 333, 335; **Vol. 3**: 27, 49–50, 57, 64, 191, 250, 256, 329–330, 498, 503, 543, 547

Supreme State Conference **Vol. 2**: 179, 249

sustainable development **Vol. 3**: 372, 398–400, 485, 490, 496, 501, 503, 505, 542

Suzhou **Vol. 1**: 260

Symposium of the Secretary of Culture and Education **Vol. 3**: 37

Symposium on Implementing the Cadre Policy **Vol. 3**: 84

T

Taiping Heavenly Kingdom **Vol. 1**: 133

Taiping Rebellion **Vol. 1**: 110

Taiwan **Vol. 1**: 228, 534; **Vol. 2**: 55, 61; **Vol. 3**: 56, 132, 181, 206–207, 213–217, 225–234, 413–416, 418–420, 520–522
Taiwan Relations Act **Vol. 3**: 206, 214–215
Taiwan Strait **Vol. 3**: 225–226, 229–230, 413–415, 420
Taiwan Strait Exchange foundation **Vol. 3**: 414
Taiwan's Legal Independence **Vol. 3**: 521
Taiwanese independence **Vol. 3**: 438
Taiyue Corps **Vol. 1**: 352
Taking and managing the cities **Vol. 1**: 453
Tan Pingshan **Vol. 1**: 19, 38–39, 57, 226, 264
Tan Zhenlin **Vol. 1**: 189; **Vol. 2**: 300, 326; **Vol. 3**: 40, 72–73, 81, 189
Tang Aoqing **Vol. 3**: 30
Tang Sheng-chih **Vol. 1**: 38
Tang Shubei **Vol. 3**: 414
Tanggu **Vol. 1**: 354
Tangshan **Vol. 1**: 16, 354; **Vol. 3**: 50
Tangxian County **Vol. 2**: 204
Tao Xingzhi **Vol. 1**: 233
Tao Xisheng **Vol. 1**: 94–95
Tao Zhu **Vol. 1**: 483; **Vol. 3**: 15, 53–54, 72, 81
Taoist temples (in Han areas) **Vol. 3**: 127
Ten Combinations **Vol. 3**: 546, 549
Ten Military Principles **Vol. 1**: 86
Ten-Year Summary (Mao Zedong) **Vol. 2**: 130
Tenth Five-Year Plan **Vol. 3**: 401–402, 482, 508
testing truth **Vol. 2**: 21, 233, 322–323, 326; **Vol. 3**: 20, 35–36, 38–42, 44, 58, 60, 137–138, 153–157, 243, 336, 338
Thatcher, Margaret **Vol. 3**: 231, 235
Thaw Society **Vol. 3**: 143
The Chinese Peasant **Vol. 1**: 33
The Chinese Revolution and the Communist Party of China **Vol. 1**: 7, 20, 34, 37, 50–51, 63, 71, 73–75, 79, 97, 100–101, 103, 107, 114, 122–123, 125, 133, 142, 146, 155, 159, 176, 178, 185, 204, 237, 247, 251, 264, 269, 307, 313, 321, 334, 352, 369, 372, 375–376, 384–385, 387, 400, 410, 412, 427, 436, 442, 444, 454, 474, 483, 499, 508, 514–515, 532, 534, 545; **Vol. 2**: 10, 14, 17, 20, 27, 32, 49, 53, 55, 65, 74, 89–90, 142, 144, 147, 155, 160, 165, 169, 201, 214, 224, 237, 246, 268, 294, 314–315, 327; **Vol. 3**: 4, 11–12, 18, 21, 32, 62–63, 73, 75, 88, 99, 127–128, 139, 149, 168, 170, 195, 200, 208, 213–214, 224, 236, 247, 252–253, 259, 265–266, 270, 278, 283, 317, 327, 330, 355, 371, 375, 411, 427, 431, 433, 448, 466, 499–500, 502, 515, 517
The Communist Manifesto **Vol. 1**: 79, 97, 374, 458; **Vol. 3**: 527
The First Program of the Communist Party of China **Vol. 1**: 20
The History of the Communist Party of the Soviet Union (Bolshevik) **Vol. 2**: 118, 122
the masses **Vol. 1**: 7, 9, 14–15, 20, 24, 34–35, 37, 42, 44, 48, 50–53, 58–59, 63, 71, 73–75, 79, 85–86, 95, 100–101, 108–109, 114, 122, 125, 130–131, 133, 142, 150, 155–156, 159, 168, 171, 173–179, 181, 183, 185, 187, 190–194, 198, 200–201, 204, 207, 210–212, 218, 226, 237, 241–242, 247, 251, 254–255, 258–261, 264, 269–270, 277, 286, 293, 301–307, 310–311, 313, 315, 317, 320–321, 326, 328, 332–335, 337–338, 352, 358, 363, 366, 369, 372, 375–377, 380, 384–385, 387, 389, 393, 396, 400, 402, 404–406, 409–410, 412–413, 415, 417, 419, 424, 426–428, 430, 432, 435–436, 439, 442, 444, 449–450, 454, 456–465, 469–475, 477–480, 483–484, 487, 499, 502, 506, 508, 514–515, 532, 534, 545, 548–549; **Vol. 2**: 9–10, 14, 17, 20, 32, 49, 53, 55, 65, 67, 74, 78, 84, 89–90, 104, 142, 144, 147, 155, 159–163, 165, 169, 175–176, 179, 181, 191, 201, 206, 214, 218–219, 224, 234–237, 241, 244–246, 249, 252, 261, 268–269, 276, 286, 292, 294–295, 297, 301, 303, 305–306, 309, 311–312, 314–318, 327; **Vol. 3**: 4, 10–13, 15, 18–19, 21, 32, 53–54, 58, 62–63, 69, 72–73, 75, 77, 81, 83, 85, 88, 99, 106, 109, 113–114, 121–122, 127–128, 139, 142–143, 146–147, 149–150, 158, 161, 168, 170, 177, 184–185, 195, 200, 202, 208, 213–214, 224, 236, 247, 252–253, 259, 265–266, 270, 272, 278, 281, 283–285, 291, 308–309, 317, 323, 327, 330, 338, 355, 367, 371, 375, 377–378, 393, 411, 427, 431, 433, 447–448, 451, 453, 456–459, 466, 476, 499–500, 502, 515, 517, 531, 547
"The Scars" **Vol. 3**: 31

The Socialist Economic Problems of the Soviet Union **Vol. 2**: 139, 165, 209–211, 213–214, 216, 218
"The United Government" (article) **Vol. 1**: 487
The Weekly Review **Vol. 1**: 18
Theoretical Dynamics **Vol. 2**: 322; **Vol. 3**: 36, 340
Theoretical Education of Cadres **Vol. 2**: 118; **Vol. 3**: 340
theoretical work **Vol. 1**: 37, 72, 78; **Vol. 3**: 137–145, 149, 152, 159, 310, 340
Theory of Continuing Revolution (permanent revolution) **Vol. 1**: 359, 362; **Vol. 2**: 277–279, 281–283, 291, 293–294, 296, 298, 310, 319, 322; **Vol. 3**: 170, 493
theory of descent **Vol. 1**: 359, 362; **Vol. 3**: 493
Third Beijing People's Congress **Vol. 2**: 78
Third Five-Year Plan **Vol. 3**: 254
Third Party **Vol. 1**: 233; **Vol. 3**: 102
Third World **Vol. 2**: 263–264, 305; **Vol. 3**: 128, 206, 260, 268, 426
Thirteenth National Congress of the Communist Party of China **Vol. 2**: 3; **Vol. 3**: 112, 151, 239, 241–242, 249, 266, 273, 289, 303, 327, 335–336, 361, 372, 455
Three Advocates **Vol. 3**: 454–457, 468
Three Great Transformations **Vol. 2**: 266
Three Guarantees **Vol. 3**: 490
Three Major Disciplines and Eight Codes of Behavior **Vol. 1**: 322
Three Major Tasks **Vol. 1**: 245, 298, 304–306, 312, 318; **Vol. 2**: 125; **Vol. 3**: 181, 207
Three Orientations **Vol. 3**: 390
Three People's Principles **Vol. 1**: 69–71, 77, 106, 109, 264, 529; **Vol. 3**: 227
Three Principles **Vol. 1**: 8, 223, 243, 280, 315–316, 320, 425, 427, 515; **Vol. 3**: 211, 427
Three Represents **Vol. 3**: 6–7, 388, 432, 443, 468–477, 479, 483–484, 487, 462, 500, 502, 504, 514–515, 524–526, 533, 551
Three Rules for Discipline and Eight Points for Attention (*see* Three Major Disciplines and Eight Codes of Behavior) **Vol. 1**: 312
Tian Jiaying **Vol. 2**: 204, 231
Tian Jiyun **Vol. 3**: 245

Tian Zengpei **Vol. 3**: 219
Tiananmen Incident (April 5th Movement) **Vol. 2**: 316; **Vol. 3**: 9–12, 15, 53–54
Tiananmen Poetry **Vol. 3**: 11
Tiananmen Square **Vol. 3**: 11–12, 142, 323
Tianjin **Vol. 1**: 18, 34, 256, 353–354, 356; **Vol. 2**: 42–44, 59, 70, 204–205; **Vol. 3**: 50, 143, 157, 451
Tianjin speech (Liu Shaoqi) **Vol. 2**: 43–44, 59, 70
Tianjin Way **Vol. 1**: 356
Tibet **Vol. 2**: 55, 61, 201; **Vol. 3**: 116, 123–125, 127, 226
Tomb-Sweeping Day **Vol. 2**: 316; **Vol. 3**: 11, 54
Tong Dalin **Vol. 3**: 139, 199
Tong Dizhou **Vol. 3**: 30
Top Documents **Vol. 3**: 338
Torui Huko **Vol. 3**: 241
Touring Europe (Liang Qichao article) **Vol. 1**: 5
Township People's Congress **Vol. 1**: 515
Trade Union **Vol. 1**: 219; **Vol. 3**: 49
Training and Selection of Excellent Young Cadres **Vol. 3**: 459
transition to socialism **Vol. 1**: 105, 512; **Vol. 2**: 5, 30, 37, 56, 59, 70, 76, 85–86, 89–90, 95, 97–99, 102–103, 105–113, 115–117, 120–121, 124–125, 136
tribalism **Vol. 2**: 157
Trotsky Doctrine Incident **Vol. 3**: 105–106
Trotskyists **Vol. 1**: 95, 116; **Vol. 3**: 84, 105–106
Tsinghua University **Vol. 3**: 317, 434
Turati, Filippo **Vol. 1**: 430
Twelfth Five-Year Plan **Vol. 3**: 550–551
Twelfth National Congress of the Communist Party of China **Vol. 3**: 133, 174, 180, 182, 194–195, 248, 254, 262, 280, 287, 312, 345
Two Directions **Vol. 1**: 61
"Two Step" System **Vol. 1**: 103
Two Theories **Vol. 1**: 389, 391; **Vol. 2**: 25
Two Whatevers **Vol. 2**: 317, 319, 336–337; **Vol. 3**: 55, 173

U
Ulanhu **Vol. 3**: 189

ultra-Leftist **Vol. 2**: 10, 314–315; **Vol. 3**: 30, 79, 92, 150, 156, 175
UN Human Rights Commission **Vol. 3**: 426
Underground Party Organizations **Vol. 3**: 80, 97
UNFPA **Vol. 3**: 225
UNICEF **Vol. 3**: 225
United Front **Vol. 1**: 27, 29, 33, 40–41, 43, 49–51, 66, 71, 74–75, 78–83, 87–88, 93, 108–109, 123, 137, 141–142, 198–201, 204, 210, 213–221, 223, 225, 227–241, 243–247, 249, 251–269, 271, 280, 283, 289, 300, 309, 368, 371–372, 400, 425, 469, 483, 487–488, 491, 511, 514–516, 526–527, 539, 542, 547; **Vol. 2**: 30, 49, 53–54, 59, 62, 64, 79–81, 87, 92, 129–130, 153–154, 157–158, 170, 239, 249–250, 302, 305, 320; **Vol. 3**: 67, 80, 82, 89–90, 106, 111, 113, 118–122, 126, 128–134, 204, 339, 360, 373, 375, 469
United Front Ministry **Vol. 2**: 80, 249; **Vol. 3**: 126
United Front Work Conference **Vol. 1**: 511; **Vol. 2**: 79, 92, 250; **Vol. 3**: 129–131, 133, 217, 375, 469
United Nations **Vol. 2**: 304; **Vol. 3**: 220–221, 224–225, 426–427, 518–519, 521
United States Navy **Vol. 3**: 226
university enrollment **Vol. 3**: 17
Unjust and False Cases **Vol. 3**: 12–17, 61, 66, 68–70, 82–85, 92, 95, 100, 110, 114, 118, 175
Unjust, False, and Wrong Charges **Vol. 3**: 66, 85
urban center **Vol. 1**: 60, 158, 161
Urban Residents' Committee **Vol. 1**: 60
urban work **Vol. 1**: 60, 83, 154, 156, 158, 165–166, 186–187, 494–498; **Vol. 2**: 42, 58–59; **Vol. 3**: 451
US-Taiwan Joint Defense Treaty **Vol. 3**: 214
utopian **Vol. 2**: 69, 73, 76, 193, 196, 212, 284, 298; **Vol. 3**: 329, 533

V
vanguard of the proletariat **Vol. 1**: 308, 419, 421, 429, 431, 433–435, 438, 458, 466, 470–471; **Vol. 2**: 295

Vietnam War **Vol. 2**: 263; **Vol. 3**: 203
Villagers' Committee **Vol. 3**: 377
Voitinsky, Grigori **Vol. 1**: 17–18, 40

W
Wall of Democracy **Vol. 1**: 310; **Vol. 3**: 142–143, 145, 147
Wallace, Mike **Vol. 3**: 288
Wan Li **Vol. 3**: 124–125, 189, 245, 320
Wang Bingnan **Vol. 1**: 234
Wang Congwu **Vol. 3**: 189, 288
Wang Daohan **Vol. 3**: 414, 419
Wang Dongxing **Vol. 3**: 10–11, 23, 26, 37–38, 63, 70
Wang Feng **Vol. 1**: 234
Wang Guangmei **Vol. 3**: 72
Wang Heshou **Vol. 3**: 62, 189
Wang Hongwen **Vol. 2**: 313
Wang Jiaxiang **Vol. 1**: 238, 482, 484; **Vol. 2**: 252
Wang Jingwei **Vol. 1**: 38, 115, 217–218, 222, 239
Wang Jinmei **Vol. 1**: 19
Wang Ming **Vol. 1**: 65–67, 105, 157, 159, 195, 232, 280, 285, 401, 408, 420, 482
Wang Minglu **Vol. 1**: 62
Wang Ninzhi **Vol. 3**: 199
Wang Renzhong **Vol. 3**: 15, 62, 72, 81, 289
Wang Ruowang **Vol. 3**: 316, 318
Wang Shao'ao **Vol. 1**: 264
Wang Xuewen **Vol. 3**: 192
Wang Xuren **Vol. 3**: 105
Wang Yitang **Vol. 1**: 239
Wang Youping **Vol. 3**: 104
Wang Zhen **Vol. 3**: 11, 49, 62, 189, 289
Wang Zhuo **Vol. 3**: 197–198
Wang-Gu Talks **Vol. 3**: 414, 418
War Against Japanese Aggression **Vol. 1**: 130, 297–298, 549
war of aggression **Vol. 1**: 135, 290, 297–298, 400, 549; **Vol. 3**: 204
War of Liberation **Vol. 1**: 85, 87–88, 130, 136–137, 188, 244–245, 248, 255, 262–263, 265, 267, 269, 271, 284–285, 297–298, 305, 311, 317, 320–321, 324, 328–329, 334, 337–338, 342, 344, 346–347, 350–351, 355, 372, 388, 403, 410, 421, 433, 467,

477, 494, 531, 534, 549; **Vol. 2**: 32, 41, 49; **Vol. 3**: 240

War of Resistance Against Japanese Aggression **Vol. 1**: 66–67, 69–70, 72, 79–85, 106, 108, 110, 115, 130–131, 135, 137, 183–184, 186, 198, 200, 202, 204–206, 209–211, 228–229, 231, 240–242, 244, 246–247, 249, 253, 261–262, 267, 279–282, 284–285, 289–290, 297–298, 300, 305, 308, 311, 319, 321, 326, 334, 337, 341, 344, 368, 371, 385, 401–402, 421, 433, 439, 459, 466–467, 486, 493, 500, 526, 528, 532–533, 535, 539, 549; **Vol. 2**: 29, 38, 49, 97, 99, 271; **Vol. 3**: 227, 247, 286

War of Resistance Against US Aggression and Aid to North Korea (*see* Korean War) **Vol. 2**: 99

warlord bureaucrats **Vol. 1**: 26, 98, 135

warlords **Vol. 1**: 4–5, 23–27, 30–32, 34, 36, 40, 56, 92, 100, 105, 120–122, 124–125, 127, 134–137, 150, 171, 173, 185, 214, 216, 226, 274–275, 278, 292–293, 467, 533

Wayaobao Meeting **Vol. 1**: 160, 508

wealthy peasant (*see also* rich peasant) **Vol. 1**: 54, 62, 129, 138, 144, 201, 250–255, 270, 529–532; **Vol. 3**: 112

Wei Guofan **Vol. 3**: 299

Wei Guoqing **Vol. 3**: 137, 189

Wei Jingsheng **Vol. 3**: 143

Wen Jiabao **Vol. 3**: 245, 502, 518

Wenhui Newspaper **Vol. 3**: 31

West Lake Conference **Vol. 1**: 224

Western Enlightenment **Vol. 1**: 5

Western Marxism **Vol. 2**: 18

Westernization **Vol. 3**: 241, 249, 365

Whampoa Military Academy **Vol. 1**: 40

White Area **Vol. 1**: 82–83, 89, 257

White regime **Vol. 1**: 170–171, 173, 332

White Terror **Vol. 1**: 47, 411; **Vol. 3**: 97

wholeheartedly serve the people **Vol. 1**: 447, 460–461

Work and Mutual Aid Group **Vol. 1**: 14

Work of Mixed and Diaspora Ethnic Minorities **Vol. 3**: 121

work style (Party style) **Vol. 1**: 367–368, 380, 388, 428–434, 436–440, 446, 455–456, 462, 471, 478, 488, 505; **Vol. 2**: 180; **Vol. 3**: 111, 444, 461

Workers and Peasants League (Workers' and Peasants' Alliance) **Vol. 1**: 33, 195, 249, 470, 548

Workers and Peasants' Revolutionary Army **Vol. 1**: 548

Workers' Picket Corps **Vol. 1**: 36, 470

working class (*see also* proletariat) Vol 1: 9, 15, 17, 20, 32–34, 36, 45, 53, 72, 74, 87–89, 100, 115, 117, 120–125, 127, 131, 139, 141, 149, 154, 162, 185, 195, 219, 263, 268–269, 271, 276, 300, 321, 357, 360, 371, 373–378, 394, 420–421, 431, 433, 458, 461, 471, 495–497, 499, 501, 504, 517, 519, 538, 543; **Vol. 2**: 17, 30, 39, 41–43, 48–50, 53, 58, 83–84, 87, 91–92, 94, 105, 113, 119, 121, 126–127, 129, 136, 155, 159, 165, 170, 177, 183; **Vol. 3**: 20, 110, 129–130, 185, 337, 365, 367, 412, 440, 451, 468, 474

World Bank **Vol. 3**: 205, 224

World Federation of Taiwan Fellow Citizens **Vol. 3**: 419

World Multi-polarization and the Establishment of a New International Order **Vol. 3**: 424

World Trade Organization (WTO) **Vol. 3**: 357, 427

World War I (*see also* First World War) **Vol. 1**: 4–6, 108, 542

World War II (*see also* Second World War) **Vol. 1**: 117; **Vol. 2**: 113, 274; **Vol. 3**: 438

Worldwide Proletarian Socialist Revolution **Vol. 1**: 113, 544

Wu Bangguo **Vol. 3**: 409

Wu Guozhen **Vol. 1**: 260

Wu Jiang **Vol. 3**: 139

Wu Jichang **Vol. 3**: 30

Wu Lengxi **Vol. 2**: 204; **Vol. 3**: 139

Wu Peifu **Vol. 1**: 214

Wu Yuzhang **Vol. 1**: 257, 492

Wu Zhonghua **Vol. 3**: 30

Wuchang **Vol. 2**: 199, 205–206, 215; **Vol. 3**: 327

Wuchang Conference **Vol. 2**: 199, 206, 215

Wuhan **Vol. 1**: 19, 58, 60–61, 69, 155–156, 223,

355, 376; **Vol. 2**: 214; **Vol. 3**: 72–73, 112, 143, 277, 410
Wuhan Kuomintang government **Vol. 1**: 223
Wuhan-Changsha Railway **Vol. 1**: 61
Wuhan Military Region Party Committee **Vol. 3**: 73

X

Xi Maozhao **Vol. 3**: 109
Xi Zhongxun **Vol. 3**: 62, 72, 81, 100–102, 189
Xi'an **Vol. 1**: 235–236, 282; **Vol. 3**: 101–102, 401, 410
Xi'an Incident **Vol. 1**: 235–236, 282
Xiamen University **Vol. 3**: 193
Xiao Chunu **Vol. 1**: 102
Xiao Jinguang **Vol. 3**: 288
Xibaipo **Vol. 2**: 32
Xidan Wall of Democracy **Vol. 3**: 142–143
Xie Fuzhi **Vol. 3**: 54
Xie Huimin **Vol. 3**: 30
Xie Minggan **Vol. 3**: 199
Xie Weijun **Vol. 1**: 158
Xie Xide **Vol. 3**: 30
Xikou **Vol. 3**: 227
Xin Douyin **Vol. 1**: 276
Xinhai Revolution **Vol. 1**: 3–4
Xinhua Gate **Vol. 3**: 143
Xinhua News Agency **Vol. 2**: 323; **Vol. 3**: 12, 36, 38, 53, 109, 113, 117, 276
Xinjiang **Vol. 1**: 356; **Vol. 2**: 55; **Vol. 3**: 15, 116, 122, 125
Xinmin Congbao **Vol. 1**: 7
Xinxiang **Vol. 2**: 204
Xishan Conference **Vol. 1**: 225
Xiuwu **Vol. 2**: 204
Xu Chi **Vol. 3**: 29
Xu Jun **Vol. 3**: 299
Xu Kexiang **Vol. 1**: 276
Xu Qian **Vol. 3**: 179, 288
Xu Qianfu **Vol. 3**: 189
Xu Qianqian **Vol. 3**: 33, 73, 76, 188–189
Xu Shiyou **Vol. 3**: 189
Xu Xiangqian **Vol. 2**: 300
Xue Muqiao **Vol. 3**: 193, 195

Xushui County **Vol. 2**: 204
Xuzhou **Vol. 1**: 354

Y

Yagodin, Gennadiy **Vol. 2**: 290
Yan Xishan **Vol. 1**: 234
Yan'an **Vol. 1**: 71–73, 76, 106, 116, 199, 210, 230, 232, 240, 281, 300, 366–369, 380, 386–387, 389, 391, 393, 400, 402, 410, 412, 421, 426, 433–434, 437, 439, 448, 482, 484–485, 539, 548; **Vol. 2**: 176–177; **Vol. 3**: 79–80, 104, 155, 457
Yan'an Cadre Conference **Vol. 1**: 281
Yan'an Cadre Trial Campaign **Vol. 3**: 79
Yan'an Rectification Movement **Vol. 1**: 367–368, 380, 386–387, 389, 391, 402, 410, 421, 433–434, 437, 439, 448, 484–485; **Vol. 2**: 176; **Vol. 3**: 155, 457
Yan'an Senior Cadre Conference **Vol. 1**: 199
Yang Anan **Vol. 1**: 9
Yang Dezhi **Vol. 3**: 189
Yang Hucheng **Vol. 1**: 234; **Vol. 3**: 79
Yang Jingren **Vol. 3**: 119
Yang Liyu **Vol. 3**: 232
Yang Mingzhai **Vol. 1**: 18
Yang Qixian **Vol. 3**: 193, 199, 201
Yang Rudai **Vol. 3**: 245
Yang Shangkun **Vol. 3**: 54, 81, 189, 221, 245
Yang Xiguang **Vol. 3**: 12, 35
Yang Yong **Vol. 3**: 189
Yang Zhong **Vol. 3**: 299
Yang, Yu, and Fu **Vol. 3**: 66
Yangtze River **Vol. 1**: 51, 221, 249, 355, 534; **Vol. 2**: 63; **Vol. 3**: 263
Yanshi Railway **Vol. 3**: 210
Yantai **Vol. 3**: 88
Yao Wenyuan **Vol. 2**: 278, 280; **Vol. 3**: 23, 74–75, 100
Yao Yilin **Vol. 3**: 49, 63, 189, 245
Yasukuni Shrine **Vol. 3**: 212
Ye Jianying **Vol. 1**: 231; **Vol. 2**: 300, 317, 324; **Vol. 3**: 11, 14, 57, 73, 104, 137–138, 158, 160–161, 165, 179, 186, 188–189, 230–231, 248, 288, 310, 363, 415
Ye Qing **Vol. 1**: 70, 77

Yellow River **Vol. 1**: 351–352
Yeltsin, Boris **Vol. 3**: 424
Yichang **Vol. 3**: 85
Yokohama Ohira **Vol. 3**: 212
Yongcheng County **Vol. 3**: 90
young and middle-aged cadres **Vol. 3**: 187, 286–287, 290–291
Young Pioneers **Vol. 1**: 334
Youth Magazine (New Youth) **Vol. 1**: 4
Yu Guangyuan **Vol. 3**: 24–25, 28, 139, 199
Yu Lijin **Vol. 3**: 75–76
Yu Muming **Vol. 3**: 521
Yu Qiuli **Vol. 3**: 189
Yu Xiusong **Vol. 1**: 18
Yuan Mu **Vol. 3**: 199
Yuan Shikai **Vol. 1**: 4, 134
Yuan Xuezu **Vol. 3**: 104
Yuanping County **Vol. 3**: 277
Yugoslavian nationalists **Vol. 1**: 113
Yulin **Vol. 1**: 352
Yun Daiying **Vol. 1**: 21, 29, 102, 274, 464
Yunnan Province **Vol. 1**: 160, 176–177, 234; **Vol. 3**: 79, 96–97, 116, 125
Yuquan Mountain **Vol. 3**: 199
Yusui Soviet Area **Vol. 1**: 351

Z

Zedong School for Young Cadres **Vol. 1**: 279; **Vol. 2**: 336
Zeng Qinghong **Vol. 3**: 502
Zeng Tao **Vol. 3**: 12
Zeng Zhi **Vol. 1**: 79
Zenko Suzuki **Vol. 3**: 210
Zhang Bojun **Vol. 1**: 233, 264
Zhang Chunqiao **Vol. 2**: 280, 294, 313; **Vol. 3**: 23, 74–75
Zhang Dongsun **Vol. 1**: 11–12
Zhang Guangdou **Vol. 3**: 30
Zhang Guotao **Vol. 1**: 14, 17–20, 502; **Vol. 3**: 33
Zhang Jieqing **Vol. 3**: 72
Zhang Luping **Vol. 3**: 109
Zhang Naiqi **Vol. 1**: 233
Zhang Pinghua **Vol. 3**: 39
Zhang Ruxin **Vol. 1**: 483

Zhang Shenfu **Vol. 1**: 18–19
Zhang Shizhao **Vol. 3**: 227
Zhang Tingfa **Vol. 3**: 189
Zhang Wentian **Vol. 1**: 50, 68, 71, 95, 195, 230–231, 367, 537–538; **Vol. 2**: 9, 35–36, 306–307, 309; **Vol. 3**: 81, 91
Zhang Xueliang **Vol. 1**: 234
Zhang Zhen **Vol. 3**: 431
Zhang Zhiyi **Vol. 3**: 107
Zhang Zhizhong **Vol. 1**: 249
Zhang Zuolin **Vol. 1**: 214
Zhangqiu **Vol. 3**: 450
Zhao Bosheng **Vol. 3**: 104
Zhao Cangbi **Vol. 3**: 71
Zhao Puchu **Vol. 3**: 127
Zhao Shiyan **Vol. 1**: 19, 276
Zhao Yimin **Vol. 3**: 72
Zhao Ziyang **Vol. 3**: 179, 189, 199–200, 210–211, 215, 221, 224, 240, 242, 245, 324
Zhejiang Province **Vol. 1**: 177–178, 420; **Vol. 2**: 204, 233; **Vol. 3**: 53, 79, 263, 277, 455
Zheng Bijian **Vol. 3**: 199
Zheng Boke **Vol. 3**: 96
Zheng Shaowen **Vol. 3**: 107
Zheng Weisan **Vol. 3**: 107–108
Zheng Zhenduo **Vol. 1**: 5
Zhengding County **Vol. 2**: 204
Zhengzhou Conference **Vol. 2**: 199–202, 204–206, 213–214, 226, 230–231, 236
Zhengzhou Railway Administration **Vol. 3**: 298
Zhongnanhai **Vol. 3**: 143, 196, 199, 380
Zhongshan Warship Incident **Vol. 1**: 221, 226–227
Zhou Enlai **Vol. 1**: 19, 29, 35–36, 57, 71, 102, 178, 181, 231, 234, 257, 259–260, 262, 274, 276, 307, 382, 399, 410, 434, 464, 485, 493, 511; **Vol. 2**: 11, 53, 55–56, 59, 79–80, 82, 86, 92, 111, 115, 142, 147–151, 153–154, 156, 188, 193, 207, 212, 216, 233–234, 237, 245, 249, 251, 254, 260, 299–302, 304–305, 309–310; **Vol. 3**: 11, 32, 74, 226–227, 254
Zhou Fuhai **Vol. 1**: 19
Zhou Hui **Vol. 3**: 62
Zhou Yang **Vol. 3**: 139

Zhu De **Vol. 1**: 175, 231, 234, 238, 288, 299, 304, 328, 334, 338, 461–462, 484, 493, 499; **Vol. 2**: 233, 246; **Vol. 3**: 74
Zhu Muzhi **Vol. 3**: 139
Zhu Wushan **Vol. 1**: 17
Zhu Xuefan **Vol. 1**: 245
Zhu Zhixin **Vol. 1**: 7
Zhuang Autonomous Region **Vol. 3**: 284
Zhuhai **Vol. 3**: 327
Zhuo Jiong **Vol. 3**: 193
Zhuozi Mountain **Vol. 3**: 277
Zong Fu **Vol. 3**: 11
Zong Fuxian **Vol. 3**: 32
Zou Taofen **Vol. 1**: 233
Zunyi Conference (Zunyi Meeting) **Vol. 1**: 63, 84, 159, 182, 285, 311, 364, 366, 379, 421, 482, 485; **Vol. 3**: 285

Numbers

17th Route Army **Vol. 1**: 234
1911 Revolution **Vol. 1**: 25, 33, 92, 134; **Vol. 3**: 234, 358, 416
26th Route Army **Vol. 3**: 104
3-3 System **Vol. 1**: 199–200, 262
57th Army **Vol. 1**: 234
61 traitors (61 People's Case) **Vol. 3**: 74
7/20 Incident **Vol. 3**: 72–73
7,000 People's Congress (*see* Seven Thousand People's Congress) **Vol. 2**: 243, 246–247, 249–254, 256–257

ABOUT THE AUTHOR

HUANG YIBING was born in November 1968 in Anhui Province. He earned his Ph.D. in Law from Renmin University of China, where he serves as a researcher, one of the "four batches" of talents in the national publicity and cultural system, and the first batch of leaders in Philosophy and Social Sciences in the National Ten-thousand Talents Plan. He is a key member of the Marxist theoretical research and construction project team, and an expert entitled to the special government allowances granted by the State Council. He is currently the Director of the No. 1 Research Department of the Central Party History and Documentation Research Institute, and a representative of the Nineteenth National Congress of the Party. His major research interests are the theory and practice of the localization of Marxism, and the history of the Reform and Opening Up policy.

ABOUT THE TRANSLATORS

SHELLY BRYANT divides her year between Shanghai and Singapore, working as a poet, writer, and translator. She is the author of nine volumes of poetry (Alban Lake and Math Paper Press), a pair of travel guides for the cities of Suzhou and Shanghai (Urbanatomy), a book on classical Chinese gardens (Hong Kong University Press), and a short story collection (Epigram Books). She has translated work from the Chinese for Penguin Books, Epigram Publishing, the National Library Board in Singapore, Giramondo Publishing, HSRC, and Rinchen Books, and edited poetry anthologies for Alban Lake and Celestial Books. Shelly's poetry has appeared in journals, magazines, and websites around the world, as well as in several art exhibitions. Her translation of Sheng Keyi's *Northern Girls* was long-listed for the Man Asian Literary Prize in 2012, and her translation of You Jin's *In Time, Out of Place* was shortlisted for the Singapore Literature Prize in 2016. Shelly received a Distinguished Alumna Award from Oklahoma Christian University of Science and Arts in 2017.

SUN LI is a professor of English Literature, Language, and Translation at Shanghai International Studies University, where she has taught since 1992. Her work includes translation, editing, and teaching. She has been involved in numerous translations of academic and literary writing, and has been a part of the editorial team for the The Cambridge History of American Literature and The New Century Multifunctional English-Chinese Dictionary. Her most recent translation projects include translation of *A New Way Forward for Tibet* (National University of Singapore Press) and editing the Chinese translation of *Journey to the Beginning of the World* (Rapscallion Press).